**FAITH BY EXPERIENCE**

The Royal Bank has always believed in the worth of Canada's basic resources and in sound industrial enterprise as an essential of national development. It is a belief which experience has justified and which varying conditions have not altered.

**THE**

# ROYAL BANK
### OF CANADA

...STONE ...COMMUNITY

THE Bank is indispensable to modern civilization. Its activities are bound up with the welfare of the community, to which it both gives and owes its life daily. It must be conservative, yet it must move to meet the times. It must fill worthily a position of honour, responsibility and trust.

*You will like banking at the Royal*

# The Royal Bank of Canada

## Holiday Money

THE extent of your holiday will be governed by the amount of money you have saved toward it.

Small sums saved regularly throughout the year will enable you to realize your dreams, whether of pleasure or more serious things.

*When travelling, protect your money by carrying Travellers' Cheques.*

G 530

# The Royal Bank of Canada

## The Trend of Business

YOU will find our monthly review of business conditions an authority on matters affecting agriculture, trade and finance.

Particular attention is given to conditions in Canada, the West Indies and South America.

*We shall be glad to place your name on our mailing list.*

# The Royal Bank of Canada

**THE LONG VIEW PAYS**

Experience proves that it pays to look ahead and make provision for unknown future needs when one is able. Regular deposits in a Savings Account soon accumulate. The money is always ready for use, and it never depreciates in value.

**THE**

# ROYAL BANK
### OF CANADA

## Progress

SOUND business principles and a policy of gradual expansion have marked the steady growth of this Bank for over fifty years.

Today, one of the largest and strongest banks in the world, it serves every phase of business and private life at home, and is taking a leading part in the expansion of trade in foreign markets.

G 528

# The Royal Bank of Canada

# Quick to the Frontier

# Quick to the Frontier

## *Canada's Royal Bank*

Duncan McDowall

M&S

**Canadian Cataloguing in Publication Data**

McDowall, Duncan, 1949-
  Quick to the frontier

Includes bibliographical references and index.
ISBN 0-7710-5504-8

1. Royal Bank of Canada – History.    I. Title.

HG2708.R6M3  1993      332.1'22'0971      C93-094838-6

———◆◆◆◆◆———

*for*
*H. Blair Neatby*
*RBC Wawota, Liberty & Windthorst,*
*Saskatchewan*
*1941-42*

———◆◆◆◆◆———

*Page Design and Composition:* Joseph Gisini, Andrew Smith Graphics, Inc.

Printed and bound in Canada on acid-free paper.

McClelland & Stewart Inc.
*The Canadian Publishers*
481 University Avenue
Toronto, Ontario
M5G 2E9

# TABLE OF CONTENTS

# Preface

BANK HISTORIES ARE SUPPOSED TO BE ABOUT MEN IN DARK SUITS AND buildings with pillars. They are also supposed to present their subjects as the embodiment of unshakeable probity and stability. In 1994, Royal Bank celebrates 125 years of doing business as a chartered bank. Indeed, its roots reached back even before its incorporation in 1869, to 1864, when it began as a private merchants' bank. Its history is one of probity and stability – these are the abiding virtues of Canadian banking in general. And, yes, it has frequently been a bank of dark-suited gentlemen. In 1908, it even built a Montreal head office fronted with four massive pillars.

For many at Royal Bank, however, there has been a sense that there is more to their corporate culture than sober wardrobes and neo-classical façades. This is not just because Royal Bank is Canada's largest bank or its most internationally diverse. From the time it stepped onto the national stage at the turn of the century, there was always the sense – in the words of one early-century junior – that this bank was an "up-and-coming" institution.

Despite this, the bank had not given much systematic or sustained thought to its history. To some degree, this has been the product of self-effacement; other banks, notably the Bank of Montreal, were perceived as Canada's "national" banks. To a larger degree, there was overt scepticism about the prospect of the snooping inquiries of an historian. When a senior manager in the 1950s mooted the idea of hiring Merrill Denison, a seasoned business journalist, to celebrate the Royal's evolution in book form, James Muir, the bank's autocratic president, killed the scheme with a flat "Drop it!" "History and all that goes with it was made by people long since dead and gone," Muir wrote a friend in London, "and the past is theirs." The bank's hundredth anniversary in the 1960s slipped quietly past with only the publication of a competent, but internally published, chronology, Clifford Ince's *The Royal Bank of Canada: A Chronology, 1864-1969.*

In 1989, with the bank's 125th anniversary looming, the Royal was finally prompted to action. Allan Taylor, the bank's chairman and chief executive officer, took a proposal to the Public Policy Committee of the bank's board. Should the bank celebrate its upcoming anniversary by producing a history that would not only reliably chronicle its long road from Halifax but would also explore its uniqueness? The idea was given form by Edward Neufeld, the bank's chief economist and a former academic, who had himself written extensively on Canadian financial and business history. Taylor and Neufeld were in agreement that a history of the bank was not only long overdue, but that it had potential not simply as an instrument of public relations but as something of lasting value. Good history could provide illumination and confidence for those who serve and are served in the bank today.

The Public Policy Committee and the board as a whole agreed. They also agreed that, if a history was worth doing, it was worth doing thoroughly. From the outset, therefore, they agreed to give the research and writing of this book sufficient time and freedom to maximize its chances of success. In June 1990, I left my teaching duties at Ottawa's Carleton University and for two years immersed myself in the life and times of Canada's largest bank. Wherever I turned, there were helping hands. Ed Neufeld set the main timbers of the project in place. Deputy Chief Economist Bob Baguley provided operational overview. Gordon Rabchuk, the bank's archivist, put his superbly organized collection of documents at my disposal. Archivists Diane Brazeau and Beth Kirkwood guided me through the bank's magnificent photo collection and trained me in the efficiencies of computer-assisted research. It was a huge task, made manageable by the constant help of two marvellous research assistants, David Boucher and Kathy Minorgan. Kathy opened my eyes to the richness of bank popular culture – seventy years of the bank's fine magazine packed into an efficient database. David Boucher's research and analytical skills made my journey through the rooms of primary documents immensely easier and more enjoyable.

Archives elsewhere helped to fill out the picture, as did numerous interviews with former bank employees. Perhaps the most memorable of these interviews came on a hot, August afternoon in Brampton, Ontario, when 101-year-old Alex Kearney, the bank's oldest pensioner, told me of his 41 years with the bank. "I decided I was going to bank," he said of his 1909 decision to join the Royal, "and I never regretted it." In my own way, I believe I can now say the same thing.

I returned to Ottawa in June 1991 to write this book. For thirteen months, I enjoyed the use of a fine little office in the bank's Ottawa Towne Centre branch. It was a splendid place to work. Not only did its manager, Claude Lauzon, and his wonderful staff accommodate my every need, but I was privileged to live the life of a modern branch for a year. I saw loans made and mutual funds purchased. I saw the automatic banking machines replenished. The annual RRSP campaign came and went. Above all else, I saw the constant ebb and flow of clients that is the lifeblood of any branch. Vivid also is my memory of the masked man, who, on a February night last year in the Ottawa branch of a competitor, gave me some first-hand exposure to the unrewarding art of bank robbery.

This, then, is the story of Canada's largest bank and its relation to the nation it serves. Royal Bank found its origins on the waterfront of Halifax in the 1860s. By 1900, it had become a national institution with branches from coast to coast. By 1925, it had established a significant international presence in the Caribbean, South America, and Europe. Since then, it has expanded and diversified its services within Canada, maintained its international prowess, and, most recently, moved into the world of integrated global banking.

The book thus concludes with a brief, narrative Epilogue on the dramatic changes of the 1980s: global banking and financial deregulation. Historians are generally ill at ease dealing with the near past – the dust, as they say, has hardly settled. Yet, the events of the 1980s are of such magnitude that it is impossible to resist the temptation of making some initial observations on them and the bankers who moulded and reacted to them.

I should make one final comment about nomenclature throughout the book. In 1990, The Royal Bank of Canada changed its legal name to Royal Bank of Canada. The former name had been in use since 1901, when it replaced the name Merchants' Bank of Halifax, which had, in turn, been in use since 1869. From 1864 to 1869, the bank was simply called the Merchants Bank. The convention adopted for use in this text has been to represent the bank in authentic title according to the foregoing chronology. Thus, the bank in 1875 was the Merchants' Bank of Halifax, in 1925 The Royal Bank of Canada, and since 1990 Royal Bank of Canada.

DUNCAN McDOWALL
OTTAWA, 1993

# "Always Moving, Alive, and Active"

FREDERICK T. WALKER WAS A YOUNG BANKER WITH A MISSION ON THE WEST Coast. Like so many of his fellow employees, he was a Maritime "boy," Moncton born and bred, caught up in the floodtide of Canadian bank expansion at the turn of the century. In 1890, at age fifteen, he had joined the Merchants' Bank of Halifax, an upstart Maritime bank just entering its third decade of operation, as a clerk for the paltry salary of $75 a year. Within a decade he found himself in Vancouver, where the Merchants' was eagerly attempting to tap into the mineral, forest, and fishery wealth of the burgeoning British Columbia economy. By 1904, Walker was earning $2,000 a year as assistant manager in Vancouver and, three years later, he was manager, earning $3,000. Walker's growing stature reflected that of his bank; in 1901 it had shed its original Maritime title and had adopted a more cosmopolitan identity as The Royal Bank of Canada. In 1907, form followed style as the Royal moved its head office from Halifax to Montreal's bustling St. James Street, Canada's undisputed financial capital.

In the summer of 1907, Montreal had a special assignment for its man in Vancouver. Success in Canadian banking came to those who anticipated national growth and were there to meet it. The Royal's initial plunge into British Columbia in the late 1890s had conformed to this pattern of frontier-mindedness; branches were frantically established in mining boom towns such as Rossland and Atlin. So great had been the haste in the gold-rush town of Bennett Lake that the bank had made the mid-winter purchase of a lot, only to discover in the warmth of spring that their prize location was in fact a piece of frozen lake. Despite such folly, aggressive expansion paid handsomely. By 1907, the Royal had a profitable network of twenty branches throughout the province. Elsewhere in Canada, sixty-four branches bore the Royal name, companions to a small chain of foreign branches in Cuba, New York, Puerto Rico, and Newfoundland.

1

The key to frontier banking was to beat the competition to these outposts of development; careful scouting and decisive commitment were essential. Such was the case in August 1907, when the directors in Montreal approved plans to open in the as-yet-unincorporated timber town of Alberni on the Pacific coast of Vancouver Island.[1] Caught in the grip of real-estate fever, Alberni beckoned to eastern bankers. To this date, its banking needs had been provided at distance from Victoria and Nanaimo. The task of seizing the opportunity fell to Walker. Stealth would be the key to the operation.

Walker was instructed to "proceed to Alberni in the most secret manner and engage premises." So as not to attract suspicion, Walker brought his wife along on the expedition; tourists, not bankers, travelled with their wives. In Victoria, the couple boarded the CPR coastal steamer *Tees* and sailed north. As the ship lurched through the heavy Pacific swells, Walker succumbed to seasickness. He spent the entire journey "reclining on a pile of lumber and hoping the ship would sink."[2] Only once the *Tees* had gained the more tranquil waters of the Alberni Canal could Walker turn his thoughts to the task at hand. Docking at midnight, he took a room in the local hotel, only to be roused early the next morning by the arrival of a coded cable from his supervisor in Vancouver. Rumours had reached the Vancouver branch that a rival bank, probably the Commerce, was launching its own bid for Alberni's business. Time was now of the essence.

Armed with "a very moderate sum in cash," Walker set to work. Within two hours of the telegram's arrival, he secured rented space in a dilapidated building on the main street, bought a selection of pens, ink, and paper suitable for passbooks, and prevailed on the local undertaker to prepare a cloth banner announcing the "Temporary Office – Royal Bank of Canada." At ten o'clock sharp, the branch opened for business. Almost immediately, a customer – the publisher of the Alberni *Pioneer News* – appeared, deposited "nearly $2,000," and was issued a makeshift passbook. Throughout the day, Walker stuck to his job and "did almost every form of banking business, including even the sale of drafts." At day's end, lacking a safe, he locked up his deposits in the local dry-goods store and retired to the hotel, where he bought a round of drinks for all and sundry.

The next morning's overland stage from Nanaimo brought representatives of the competition, who, upon seeing the Royal well established in Alberni, abandoned their plans and retreated on the afternoon stage. A day later, reinforcements arrived from Vancouver in the form of a regular manager, a clerk, and a crate of banking supplies. Thus The Royal Bank of Canada came to Alberni.

Frederick Walker's expedition up the Pacific coast is remarkable

*Alberni branch, c.1910.*
*This was a typical frontier branch, with upstairs living quarters for the manager.*

in two respects. In the first place, the Royal's arrival in Alberni, like the arrival of its rival banks in numerous other frontier towns, vividly demonstrated that, by the turn of the twentieth century, Canada had coast-to-coast banking, a *national* financial system that was able not only to keep pace with but also to facilitate national development. In the first four decades of Confederation, Canadians had displayed particular genius in devising a banking system that was not inextricably tied to the regional components of the national economy. It was a system that had borrowed the best characteristics of Scottish branch banking and American bank methods and had applied them to the exigencies of a young, sprawling nation, thinly populated and dynamically expanding.

Despite periodic bank failures, it was a system that bred growth and stability through trust in its integrity. What could speak louder to this fact than the willingness of an Alberni citizen to entrust $2,000 to a "bank" that lacked a safe and operated under a flimsy cloth banner? By the advent of what Laurier christened Canada's century, Canadians had learned to put their financial trust in a collection of emerging national banks, all of which boasted metropolitan affiliations with cities like Halifax, Montreal, Toronto, Winnipeg, and Vancouver. By 1925, this process would have further condensed – by means of aggressive amalgamation and isolated failure – into a banking system that radiated

3

from Montreal and Toronto almost exclusively. Walker's hurried mission to Alberni was but one brief episode in this evolution, an evolution which would coincidentally see the Royal emerge by the mid-1920s as Canada's largest bank – a status it has never relinquished.

F. T. Walker's progression from Moncton to Alberni is illustrative of a second crucial aspect of Canadian banking at the turn of the century: banking institutions were *national* employers at a time when the vast majority of Canadians spent their entire working life tied to unending local employment or, if they were transient, a succession of small employers. For innumerable young men from small-town Canada, banking was a step up into the urban, professional, middle class. It furnished stable-yet-mobile employment. Pay was often poor and working conditions arduous, but for the determined young banker, a career with a bank opened up professional vistas largely unknown in the nineteenth century.

Walker was a superb example of a "bank boy" on the move. Vancouver was not his ultimate resting place. In 1912, he became manager in Montreal, at the Royal's flagship branch. Five years later, he was appointed agent in the bank's pivotal New York office. After the First World War, he busied himself cruising the coast of South America, seeking banking opportunities in Latin American trade. Just as he had in Alberni, Walker supervised the Royal's establishment in

*F. T. Walker near retirement in the 1930s, at the end of a remarkable career. Bankers seldom relaxed for portraits: a tie and a countenance of steadfastness and foresight were standard trademarks.*

Rio de Janeiro, Buenos Aires, and innumerable Caribbean islands. His yearly salary on retirement in 1937 was well in excess of $20,000. He had grown with the bank. When Walker had become a lowly clerk in 1890, the Merchants' employed fewer than 200 men. By 1907, he was one of 629, and by his retirement there were 6,877 Royal Bankers spread throughout Canada, the United States, Europe, the Caribbean, and Latin America.

The history of Canadian banking is thus the history of a *national* institution, both in the broad sense of material development and in the human sense of those who worked in banking. This is hardly a new observation. Since the original seed of the system was sown in the 1870 Bank Act, Canadian banking has been laboriously honed through a process of ten-year reviews of the same act. Foreigners are often struck by the seeming oddity of Canada's "big banks" being obliged to renew their charters every decade. "I say that there is no class of company in the world," Tory finance critic R. B. Hanson noted at the 1944 Bank Act revision hearings, "that is so cabined, cribbed and confined as the commercial banks of Canada."[3] Within this framework, Canadian banking has cautiously evolved, pushing up against the boundaries of prescribed practice every decade or so, broadening its horizons in a new Bank Act, and again moving ahead.

There is something quintessentially Canadian in the success of our banks. The values held up as being at the heart of Canadian banking – prudence, conservatism, evolutionary change, "character," and stability – are the same broad values Canadians tend to embrace. One of our leading novelists, Robertson Davies, has remarked that at the heart of English Canada's identity is the instinct "to present itself to the world as a Scotch banker."[4] Americans, fed on a diet of persistent bank failure and instability, induced by overreliance on regional banks, have been quick to cast envious glances across the border. As early as 1910, Joseph Johnson, Dean of New York University's School of Commerce, praised Canadian banking as "a product of evolution... grown up gradually under the fostering care of experienced bankers, no changes having been made until experience proved them necessary or advisable."[5] It is not too much to argue that, by the turn of the century, the success of banking in the country had become a mainstay of Canadian nationalism; banking was something Canadians did right. As the first historian of Canadian banking, the American academic R. M. Breckenridge, noted in 1894: the system was "unique" and "productive of the highest possible advantage."[6]

Indeed, Canadian banking can best be described in oxymoronic terms. To borrow a uniquely Canadian phrase from our political lexicon, it is a "progressive conservative" system. When in 1893 the

Canadian Bankers' Association began offering an annual prize to the best essay on banking practice, one of the first winners extolled the virtue of "cautionary boldness" in the young teller.[7] Similarly, Canada's leading financial journal, the *Monetary Times*, in 1918 upheld the success of "careful and efficient and daring banking" in Canada.[8]

If the Royal Bank of Canada has prospered in the years since its creation in the Halifax of the 1860s, it is because it has always been quick to test the outer limits of the Canadian banking consensus; it has tended more to "boldness," while never losing sight of the necessity for "caution." As early as 1875, the Halifax *Chronicle* saw the bank as "always moving, alive and active."[9] The pattern persisted, leading the Royal not only to Alberni, but also as far afield as Havana, Paris, and even revolutionary Russia. The Royal usually has found itself on the leading edge of Canadian banking procedure, technology, and "corporate culture." It remains the only domestic chartered bank listed in the *Financial Post*'s one hundred "best companies" to work for in Canada.[10]

Although the Royal has displayed corporate reticence about any public declaration of its place in Canadian history, individual Royal Bankers have acquitted themselves more boldly. Since coming to national prominence in the 1910s, the Royal has taken a highly visible role in the moulding of Canadian banking. Edson Pease, the bank's chief executive until 1922, was the first public proponent of a central bank for Canada. In 1934, when the Bank of Canada was finally created, it was Graham Towers, a Royal assistant general manager, whom the government appointed as governor. In the grim days of the Depression, another assistant general manager, S. R. Noble, championed, as John Maynard Keynes had, the idea of monetary expansion as a solution to the nation's ills.[11] Throughout, the Royal maintained intimate links with influential Canadian academic economists, notably Stephen Leacock at McGill and Frank Knox and Clifford Curtis at Queen's.

Other Royal Bankers have acted as prominent theoreticians of the Canadian banking system. A succession of seminal works on Canadian banking have come from Royal Bank pens, notably those of A. B. Jamieson, D. B. Marsh, J. A. Galbraith, and E. P. Neufeld.[12] Thus, we have come to understand the fundamental underpinnings of Canadian banking without any clear appreciation of one of its central structures, the Royal Bank.

How does one write the history of a bank? There are abundant examples of what might be called "traditional" bank histories. They are generally impressive tomes, handsomely illustrated, regally paced,

*A quiet, spring-thaw day at Bennett Lake branch in March 1900.*
*James W. Fulton, the manager, seated on the left, would enjoy the kind of mobile career*
*that banks expected of their employees in the late-nineteenth century.*
*After joining Montreal branch as a clerk in 1890, Fulton served in Halifax, Vancouver,*
*Skagway, Nanaimo, Bennett Lake, Montreal, Santiago (Cuba),*
*and various Ontario mining towns like Cobalt and ended his career back in Montreal*
*where, by the mid-1920s, he was known as "the dean of our Montreal branch managers."*

and, in the final analysis, rather lifeless. In the Canadian context, these volumes do usually succeed in conveying a solid sense of the structural development – the nuts and bolts of the Bank Act – of our banks. They tend to be Whiggish and "top down" history, a celebration of "great" bank presidents marching onward and upward. Lastly, they contain little sense of the broad social and economic context of banking. In short, one is often left wondering: where are the people?

As early as 1910, the *Journal of the Canadian Bankers' Association* warned that "books on banking and financial matters are voted dry reading" by the young bank employee and that "some definite incentive" is needed to induce readership.[13] The same is perhaps true today. There is undeniably no escaping the central role of the men at the top of the Royal and the strategic direction they have imparted to the organization. Similarly, the Bank Act *is* important. None the less, the "definite incentive" this volume seeks to present to its readers is an investigation of what has come in recent years to be labelled "corporate culture," the core values, beliefs, and traditions that propel a business. What made a Maritime lad like Fred Walker stick with a bank that initially paid him poorly and exposed him to seasickness in strange places? How has a huge, unwieldy organization like the Royal handled the transition from the exclusively male culture – a world of "bank boys" – that dominated its first half century to one that must now acknowledge the fact that 74 per cent of its members are female?

Special challenges confront the historian of the Royal, especially if the history produced is to engage Canadians at large. How has the bank interacted with the society it serves? Most prominent among its "stakeholders" are its employees. Given its size (57,000 employees in 1991), the Royal has had an immense reach in Canadian society. Again, Mr. Walker in Vancouver provides us with a telling example. As Vancouver manager, Walker secured the services of Charles Hibbard Tupper, son of a Tory prime minister and a former Maritime politician resident on the West Coast, as bank legal counsel. At the same time, he employed William Woodward, son of a prominent local dry-goods merchant, as a bank clerk and shipped him off to service in Havana. The pattern continues. Employment in the Royal has in more recent times touched the lives of Canadians as varied as Gordon Lightfoot, Peter Jennings, and Gerald Bouey. At one time all these extraordinary Canadians were "ordinary" Royal Bank employees. This history will endeavour to measure the culture they inhabited. How has technology affected the bank workplace? Why are bankers such avid golfers?

What of the Royal's other stakeholders? Some attention must be paid to the marketplace, to the bank's customers and their needs. From travellers' cheques to electronic banking, the Royal has responded to societal changes and, to some degree, moulded them. Customer relations have at times been fractious; given the cyclical nature of Canadian agriculture, bankers and farmers have seldom seen eye to eye. Similarly, bankers have been obliged to frequent the corridors of power in Ottawa. Despite the success of collective action through the Canadian Bankers' Association, individual banks have had individual axes to grind with politicians and bureaucrats. The Royal has been no exception.

No Canadian bank history would be complete without acknowledging the multi-ethnic composition of this country and Royal Bank of Canada today. For much of its history the Royal staff was fundamentally Anglo-Canadian. Its customers have frequently been otherwise. How has the bank responded to this tension? In the first decade of the century, Walker's East End Vancouver branch at Hastings and

Main opened a Chinese Department, staffed with Chinese-Canadians.

In the East, the bank has always grappled uneasily with the French fact in Canada. Not until the social tumult and "Quiet Revolution" of the 1960s did the Royal fully recognize Canada's multicultural make-up and its implications for employment and customer service. While James Muir in the 1950s may have believed that the past was "long since dead," the bank historian quickly learns that the past informs the present and that attitudes formed concerning customers, ethnicity, and products can powerfully stimulate or impede an institution's growth. Once formed, corporate cultures in banks are tough and resilient.

One last challenge awaits the bank historian. In the absence of a published history, a pervasive mythology has grown up around some aspects of the Royal's evolution. Probably the hoariest notion about the bank is the belief that the Royal was the creature of Sir Herbert Holt, its secretive president from 1908 to 1934 and chairman until his death in 1941. Holt, it is said, "made" the Royal. It is an inviting belief. As Canada's most prominent, and most reviled, monopoly capitalist, Holt has become a shibboleth of capitalist wrongdoing. Those expecting substantiation of this view in these pages will come away disappointed. Whatever his other business activities, Holt's role in the Royal's affairs was titular and transitory. Professional bankers, particularly Edson Pease from 1899 to 1930 and Morris Wilson up to 1946, in fact "made" the Royal. Pease invited Holt to join the bank; Holt did not barge his way through the doors on St. James Street in 1905. Only once, in the early Depression, did Holt's personal business adventures intrude, admittedly in disastrous proportion, on the Royal's stability. If there are to be heroes in this history, they are the men – and today women – in dark suits who put in long hours and mastered the art of "cautionary boldness."

Similarly, there is the persistent notion that the Royal consciously forsook its Maritime roots, that it, together with other Halifax banks, somehow conspired to deny the region its legitimate economic destiny. In fact, the Royal never left the Maritimes. The bank's longest-serving president, Haligonian businessman Thomas Kenny, was part of an influential coterie of Nova Scotians who turned their business and political talents in the 1870s and 1880s to ensuring that the marriage of the Maritimes and Upper Canada succeeded. Himself a Tory MP, Kenny repeatedly assured John A. Macdonald, Charles Tupper, and John Thompson – all prime ministers – that it was his "desire to do anything I can to help the development of this end of Canada."[14] The same was true of the Merchants'. Commerce and industry in the Maritimes have always received a sympathetic hearing in the bank's boardroom. The Royal has, however, also pursued the dictates of the Canadian marketplace, responding to the pattern of Canadian resource endowment and the financial requirements it threw up.

The historian's ability to unravel the realities and myths of the Royal's past is contingent upon the quality of the documentary record put at his disposal. It is to the everlasting credit of bygone managers at the Royal that behind the glass-and-aluminium façade of Place Ville Marie in Montreal lies one of Canada's finest corporate archives. It is in this huge collection that the real contribution of Sir Herbert or loan practices in late-nineteenth-century Halifax come to life in correspondence, minute books, and reminiscences. To these pages we now turn our attention in order to enter the cozy, but precarious, business world of Halifax in the 1860s.

# "The *Little* Bank in the *Big* Building"

E VERY SPRING THE ARRIVAL OF THE TRADE SHIPS FROM EUROPE BROUGHT the harbour to life. It was a magnificent harbour, ice-free, sheltered, and unrivalled on the Atlantic seaboard north of Boston. Along its narrow neck, the merchants' wharves protruded like stubby fingers into the tide of commerce. They bore the names of the merchants – Cunard, Collins, Kinnear, and Tobin – and of the trade routes – such as Bermudian – which had made Halifax in the early 1860s a port of colonial prominence. Of these, no name was better known than Cunard: since the War of 1812 Samuel Cunard had thrived on the timber and West Indian trades, leaping the Atlantic in the 1840s to establish himself as a steamship operator in Liverpool. Just beyond the wharves lay the merchants' warehouses, crowded along Upper and Lower Water streets and north along Bedford Row, Hollis, and Granville. Through the doors of buildings like T. & E. Kenny & Co.'s "magnificent granite warehouse," dominating eighty feet of Granville Street, ebbed and flowed the wholesale trade of the colony.

The rhythms of the trade were easily discernible. Spring brought the inflow of European goods ordered the previous winter in the showrooms of London, Manchester, and the Continent. Most Haligonians could readily identify the silhouettes of familiar barques and steamers as they slipped into port. Ships of the Cunard, Allan, Anchor, Boston and Colonial, and Quebec and Gulf Ports lines all frequented Halifax's docks. To alert consignees of the impending arrival of their cargo, the ships displayed jaunty little pennants on their masts. T. C. Kinnear & Company boasted a red star on white, bordered in red; T. & E. Kenny & Co. a proud blue "K," bordered in red. The seasoned observer could quickly put cargoes and merchants together: the Glasgow ships generally bore goods for William Stairs Son & Morrow, while Manchester and Liverpool vessels serviced the Kenny dry-goods firm.[1]

Thus, after months of winter slackness, the port of Halifax hummed with the frantic business of unloading and warehousing goods ranging from basic cottons to exotic teas. Having safely stored their goods, the merchants looked inland to their network of retail buyers scattered along the coast and through the hinterland. Small merchants from Pictou, Yarmouth, or Truro "were as sure to turn up when the ice was clear as the swallows that came in the spring."[2] "Our *stock* of Foreign and Domestic *Dry Goods* is now complete," T. & E. Kenny advised its regular buyers by postcard. "A stock of *Good Teas* always on hand. Inspection invited."[3] Other goods were repacked and dispatched up the Gulf of St. Lawrence to retailers in Lower and Upper Canada.

In the fall the pattern reversed, as Halifax became the commercial centre through which passed Nova Scotia's exports of timber and fish and the by-products of the port's West Indian trade in sugar, rum, and molasses. Again there was specialization. Thomas Kinnear's ships frequented the West Indies and Brazil. As early as the 1810s, Samuel Cunard had sent schooners into the Caribbean, before tapping into the East Indian tea trade and eventually branching out into transatlantic shipping. Shipbuilding and shipping provided a natural parallel to trade for the Halifax commercial elite. Constructed not only in Halifax but also in the sheltered bays of counties like Hants, Nova Scotian sailing ships allowed Halifax business to diversify and capture the profits of the carrying trade. Merchants became ready partners in syndicates formed to build and sail these vessels. The Kennys of Halifax were quick to form such alliances. With the Dickie family of Upper Stewiacke, they built the barque *Harold* in 1872 and with the Frieze family, general merchants in Maitland, they sent forth the romantically named *Snow Queen* in the early 1880s.[4] In the 1860s, sensing that the heyday of wood and wind was waning, they shrewdly anticipated the future, building the 1,715 ton, iron-hulled *Eskasoni* in England in 1866. With Confederation, Nova Scotia became the young nation's leading shipbuilder, producing 36 per cent of the ships built in 1872 and 47 per cent of the tonnage.[5] Canada's richest man was rumoured to be Nova Scotia shipowner Enos Collins.

The early 1860s brought added vitality to the Halifax waterfront. Civil war in the United States not only stimulated British military activity in the port, but also opened up the prospect of capturing Southern trade, now barred from the ports of the Union. A Confederate agent was posted to the city, and Haligonians openly sympathized with the cause of the South. "I hear of such warm feelings being manifested on our behalf in Halifax," wrote Eugenia Johnston from beleaguered Savannah to her cousin Maggie, the wife of merchant A. G. Jones, in 1864.[6] Like many Haligonian merchants Jones's firm was active in the profitable business of smuggling goods to the rebels. When Sherman's

*A William Notman view of Halifax from the Citadel, 1877.*
*Then, it was a city dominated by ships' masts and church spires;*
*today, bank towers predominate.*

army smashed its way into Georgia later in the year, gloom pervaded Halifax. The city's traditional rivals in commerce, New York and Boston, were apparently on the verge of victory.

Halifax's twenty-five thousand citizens in the early 1860s were bound together, and to a degree held apart, by a rich institutional life. The city was carefully structured around a series of sometimes rigidly demarcated, sometimes overlapping, social circles. Religion and politics separated Haligonians into distinct camps; Tory, Reformer, Catholic, and Protestant were badges worn with ardour. Since emigrating from Ireland in the mid-1820s, dry-goods merchant Edward Kenny had, for instance, championed the Irish-Catholic cause in Halifax, becoming a close friend of Archbishop Connolly and serving as president of the Charitable Irish Society. Kenny staunchly backed Reformer Joseph Howe in his 1840s campaign to bring responsible government to Nova Scotia, but broke ranks and joined the Tories in the 1850s when Howe assailed religion in politics.[7] Politics was thus alive with sectarian and ethnic jealousies. In 1875, Kenny's friend John Dickie, the Truro merchant, achieved notoriety in becoming the first and only Speaker in Canadian parliamentary history to be impeached; his crime was his inability to rule over the notoriously unruly Nova Scotia Assembly.[8]

If Haligonians were divided in faith and on the hustings, they found ample scope for common purpose in their social and commercial lives. Marriage provided one bond. By the 1860s the Cunard and Duffus families were related, as were the Tobins and Dwyers. Others built marital bridges elsewhere. In 1855, Edward Kenny's son Thomas married Margaret Burke of New York, thereby providing an entrée into the flourishing commercial class of that city, notably the well-connected Roosevelt family. Marriage was but one aspect of an elaborate social fabric. In 1862, over a hundred of Halifax's leading citizens banded together to form the Halifax Club and housed it in a splendid building on Granville. At the other end of the city, the élite sailed together on the North West Arm. Along South Park Street and surrounding the Arm, the merchant princes built their grand homes. A. G. Jones's "Bloomingdale" was but a stone's throw from the Kennys' "Thornvale" beside the Arm.

However, it was in defence of the city's commerce that the merchants found true unity of purpose. As early as 1804, they had joined together in the Halifax Committee of Trade to protect and expand the city's stake in the British colonial system of trade. In true mercantilist spirit, they sought to monopolize the trade of the American seaboard and the West Indies. Over the next half century, they were largely frustrated in this ambition. Britain's adoption of free trade in the 1840s left Halifax desperately trying to shore up its trading position. In the 1850s, Halifax's merchants began to advocate the advantages of railways, combined with free access to the American market, as a means of holding and extending its rocky hinterland. This period of prolonged economic insecurity first suggested to the colony that its economic destiny might lie in the direction of "British American integration" with its sister colonies in the interior.[9] When politicians from the central and maritime colonies met in 1864 to discuss such a union at Charlottetown and Quebec, Halifax merchants were hardly disinterested spectators.

Confederation, like other political issues, split the Halifax mercantile élite. Grits, following the lead of Joseph Howe, saw danger in the scheme, an abandonment of the colony's oceanic heritage. Merchants like A. G. Jones, Jeremiah Northup, William J. Stairs, and T. C. Kinnear eagerly affixed their signatures to anti-union petitions that were sent to London.[10] Other merchants saw promise in the union; Edward Kenny and John Tobin joined with their bishop, Connolly, to champion the proposal. In the spring of 1867, John A. Macdonald invited Kenny to join the first federal cabinet. Elevated to the Senate, Kenny would serve as receiver general. On July 1, 1867, Kenny's friend, Halifax doctor Charles Tupper told the crowds in the Halifax Parade Square that Kenny's "high social, commercial and legislative position" eminently qualified him "to represent the interests of Nova Scotia in the General Government."[11] A few months later, Kenny's close friend but political foe A. G. Jones would be elected to go to Ottawa as a Grit on an anti-Confederation platform. Tupper would be the only Macdonald Tory elected in the province.

Thus behind the majestic display of sail in the harbour, the Halifax business community of the 1860s was a curiously unified and disunified group living in a world in which their economic and political power was gradually but fundamentally shifting. Behind the façade, a sense of precariousness pervaded their lives. The danger could be physical. In 1859, fire had swept down Granville Street through the business district. In 1866, the s.s. *England* brought cholera to the

*Jeremiah Northup*

mouth of the harbour. Four years later, a group of Halifax merchants, including Kenny's son Edward, left Halifax on their annual winter buying trip to England on the Inman Line's *City of Boston*. The ship and its passengers vanished without a trace.

It was the less-tangible dangers involved in mid-nineteenth-century business, however, that induced the deepest-seated anxiety, and often brought on ruination. The Nova Scotian economy was an economy on the margin of a vast imperial trading system. As such it had scant control over the factors that determined its livelihood. The price of the commodities it traded onto European markets was set in distant and unpredictable marketplaces. Demand for fish or lumber was notoriously fickle. Competitors – Baltic timber merchants, for instance – might flood into the English market, pushing prices down and leaving the Canadian producer with no option but to dump his season's cut onto a glutted market. Canadian commodity production was by its very nature a seasonal affair: timber cutters and fishermen sought credit in the spring for crops that would not reach market until late in the fall, and for which there was precious little guarantee of price. What made the process all the more agonizing in the early post-Confederation decades was the arrival of a persistent global recession, which depressed commodity markets throughout the 1870s and 1880s. In this atmosphere, commercial failure became rampant. When two prominent Halifax firms failed in 1872, the *Monetary Times* reported that the news had provoked the "circulation of rumours of the most absurd kind…so that a stranger in Halifax…would be inclined to think the whole commercial fabric about to crumble."[12]

Much of Halifax's commercial edifice rested on a foundation of precarious partnerships, which were anchored in law in only the flimsiest way. There were no joint-stock companies to spread risk and draw in broader capitalization; until 1869 there was not even a semblance of an insolvency law, and that which followed placed few burdens on the debtor.[13] Partnerships thus formed and broke apart with great regularity. Fortunes were made and lost and then remade. The historian is afforded a privileged glimpse into this shifting business world through the confidential reports of the R. G. Dun & Company agent in Halifax. The Dun agency, which had spread across the continent from its New York base in the 1850s, was responding to a chronic lack of commercial information in the marketplace; parties engaged in trade had little knowledge of the worth or credit-worthiness of those with whom they sought to trade. Dun's responded by appointing agents in prominent commercial centres and selling the resultant intelligence. The Dun credit-rating books for Halifax in these years thus furnish an intimate insight into a nervous business community.

*Thomas C. Kinnear (left) and John Tobin (right)*

The business fortunes of Thomas C. Kinnear, prominent in the West Indies and Brazil trade, provide one portrait of the precarious nature of business success in Halifax. In 1864, Dun's agent reported that the Kinnear firm was "A1 in every respect...the credit of the concern is beyond question."[14] The young A. G. Jones had clerked in Kinnear's firm, and in the 1860s Kinnear had taken a leading role in the Halifax City Railroad and the Nova Scotia Telegraph. In spite of this, in 1874 Kinnear was obliged to auction off his personal effects at his South Street home to make good his business losses,[15] but he quickly recovered. When he died in 1880, he left a personal estate of about a half-million dollars, although he had recently "met with a number of heavy losses" as an investor.[16]

This seesaw of success could also induce mental imbalance. Since emigrating from Kilkenny as a lad, John Tobin had found self-made success as a trader and railway promoter. By 1860, the Dun agent could describe him as "first class rich" with "unquestionable credit for all transactions." John A. Macdonald later enlisted Tobin in the campaign for Confederation. Perhaps because Nova Scotians failed to embrace Canada with the same enthusiasm, or perhaps because of the build-up of business pressures, Tobin slipped into despondency and, on the morning of June 9, 1869, retired to his garden with a rifle and shot himself. His friend Bishop Connolly quietly arranged for Tobin to be buried in consecrated ground in the prestigious Holy Cross Cemetery.[17]

Given the mercurial nature of Halifax's oceanic economy, its merchants came to place great stock in the "character" of those with whom they did business. With few legal guarantees and little accurate commercial intelligence to rely on, traders had no option but to proceed on the basis that a man's word was his bond. Dun's agent paid particular attention to character assessment: "rather free spoken and lacking in ballast," "suffers from mental depression and is now absent in the U.S.," "lives expensively," and "some family quarrel and dissolved the partnership."[18]

One consistently stable Halifax house was that of the Kenny family. Dun's 1853 entry encapsulated the family's success: "do a large business, import largely from Great Britain. Been here 25-30 years. Came from Ireland poor. Capable businessmen...Irishmen, wealthy, good." By 1876, the report was "no change, undoubted." Born in County Kerry, Thomas and Edward Kenny had come to Halifax as clerks of a Cork firm that traded across the Atlantic. In 1828, they established T. & E. Kenny & Co. as a dry-goods wholesaler and retailer. Edward was the more dynamic of the two, serving, for instance, as Halifax mayor in 1842. As Bishop Connolly later told Prime Minister Macdonald, he was "no talker but he is what is boundlessly better a doer. He is in American terminology a whole team."[19] When bachelor Thomas died in 1868, he left over £100,000 and control of the firm to his brother. The death at sea of son Edward junior in 1870 meant that, after this date, day-to-day oversight of the firm would devolve on Edward's younger son, Thomas E., born in 1833. In 1876, the senior Kenny would retire completely, the succession secure. Dun's agent valued the business at over a million dollars.

The Kennys prospered on the Halifax waterfront because they learned to minimize their exposure to risk. In 1850, they withdrew from volatile retailing to concentrate on wholesaling. They diversified into shipping and began to take positions in fledgling new financial and industrial enterprises in the city. Clearly, the Kennys sensed that breadth of enterprise was the best guarantee of survival in an economy buffeted by oceanic insecurity. They saw the same potential security in the prospect of confederation with the Upper Canadas in 1867. As Thomas E. asserted his leadership in the family in the 1870s, he also assumed his father's mantle as chief spokesman of Irish-Catholic Halifax. Together with such Halifax professional friends as Charles Tupper and John Thompson, Kenny soon learned to speak out for Canada. In 1878, Macdonald sought to enlist Kenny as a federal Tory candidate. "My father and brother retired from our firm about a year ago," Kenny respectfully replied. "I have no partner in my business. I am consequently a very busy man, and it is impossible for me to take

*Sir Edward Kenny*

any prominent part in politics."[20] Macdonald would write again.

Just as the Kenny business sought to insulate itself from risk, so too did the mercantile community as a whole. The entire trading economy was linked together by a fragile chain of credit that, in the case of a company like T. & E. Kenny, stretched from the showrooms of Manchester, where goods were purchased on credit in mid-winter, to the dry-goods stores of rural Nova Scotia, where the goods were eventually sold – again often on credit to local farmers or fishermen. Halifax controlled only the centre link in the chain. The process was made all the more confused by the welter of currencies in circulation in the British North American colonies. Although "Halifax currency," rated at five shillings to the Spanish silver dollar, had prevailed since the 1760s as the "official" colonial currency, there was in reality no uniform measure of exchange in the colony. Frequently there was simply not enough "specie" – best defined as "visible money," a varied assortment of gold and silver coins – in circulation to service the fledgling economy. For longer-term financial transactions, merchants relied on an intricate system of bills of exchange and promissory notes, which were subject to all sorts of uncertainty, not the least of which was the ever-fluctuating rate of exchange. For those in a position to broker this system by selling foreign exchange or discounting bills of exchange,* there were handsome profits to be made.

Throughout the first half of the nineteenth century, Halifax merchants wrestled to bring this process more within their control, to diminish the financial dominance of London and New York over their precious trade. Nova Scotians did not pioneer banking in British North America:[21] Montreal merchants had organized a crude bank, the Canada Banking Company, as early as 1792; by 1822 they had created a fully-fledged chartered bank in the Bank of Montreal.[†] In true mercantilist form, Halifax merchants in 1801 subscribed £50,000 in the hope of obtaining a monopoly over the colony's banking needs, but the Nova Scotia Assembly balked at the request. The lack of circulating currency and inadequate credit again roused the Halifax Committee of Trade to agitate for a charter in 1811. Rejecting this, the government responded by circulating Treasury Bills as a surrogate for currency. The merchants were unappeased and, after a third rebuff in 1822, organized a private bank in 1825. The Halifax Banking

---

* Bills of Exchange are crucial to any understanding of the workings of the early Canadian economy. Thomson's *Dictionary of Banking* (London, 1911) cites the 1882 British Bills of Exchange Act to define a bill of exchange as "an unconditional order in writing, addressed by one person to another, signed by the person giving it, requiring the person to whom it is addressed to pay on demand or at a fixed or determinable future time a certain sum in money to or to the order of a specified person, or to bearer." If the holder of a bill does not wish to hold it to maturity, he may seek to surrender it to his bank or an intermediary and receive full payment minus a discount commission. Thus, a Truro merchant in the 1860s might issue a bill agreeing to pay "on demand ninety days hence to John Smith [a Halifax wholesaler]...the sum of one hundred dollars for value received." A postage stamp affixed to the bill gave it legal standing.

† The Bank of Montreal was organized in 1817, but did not formally receive its charter until 1822.

Company had no charter and operated as the closely held instrument of a tight circle of merchants dominated by Enos Collins. Collins had grown wealthy on the proceeds of privateering in the War of 1812, and then engaging in post-war shipping. "Collins' Bank," as it was nicknamed, was located in a stone building nestled behind the wharves on Water Street. Having won a *de facto* monopoly, the Halifax Banking Company prospered on foreign-exchange dealings with New York and Boston and on the circulation of its own notes among local merchants.[22]

Success bred jealousy. Collins's grip on commercial finance provoked rival merchants to seek a charter for a bank more accessible to the broader mercantile community. A bitter political fight ensued, as Collins and his cronies tried to stave off would-be competition. They lost. The charter granted the Bank of Nova Scotia by the colony's Assembly in 1832 has been described as "the most advanced of its day."[23] In an early example of Canadian banking pragmatism, the charter stipulated the bank's capital base and its note-circulating privilege, and, most importantly, dictated various sureties for its shareholders and clients. The bank was forbidden from lending into the notoriously volatile real-estate market, nor was it to make loans secured by its own stock. Annual meetings were mandatory, as was the presentation of an annual statement to the government. Shareholders were liable up to the sum of twice the value of the stock they owned.

The Bank of Nova Scotia prospered. Its notes quickly found their way into circulation and its Bedford Row office became a ready source of commercial credit. It had "unlimited resources," Dun's agent reported in 1855, and rated it "good as it is possible to be" in 1864. Branches were opened in 1837 in Windsor and Saint John. Coteries of other Halifax merchants soon picked up the pattern. In 1856, William Stairs spearheaded a subscription drive for the Union Bank of Halifax. The next decade saw similar charters for banks in Yarmouth and Windsor and for the People's Bank of Halifax. All were essentially merchants' banks, offering to discount bills, to handle foreign exchange, and to take deposits at 3 per cent per annum. It is worthwhile noting that, in these same years, Halifax merchants were also active in creating other financial-service agencies. In 1862, seven merchants, including such well-known names as Tobin, Duffus, and Jones, banded together to form the Acadia Insurance Company.[24] No Nova Scotia bank failed in the years before Confederation. "The banking system as originally worked out," Breckenridge concluded, "caused so few difficulties and promoted so much the convenience and prosperity of the colonies, that they felt very little temptation to change it" with the advent of the new nation.[25]

Given this proliferation of banks, it was hardly surprising that the Civil War-induced prosperity of the early 1860s should have spawned yet another Halifax bank. At first there were only rumours of its creation. It was later reported that the "capitalists" behind the rumours "had kept their own counsel so well that few persons in the community were aware of the movement."[26] Rumour became truth on February 4, 1864, when, "after transaction of routine business" at the board meeting of the Union Bank, two directors, John Duffus and Thomas Kinnear, informed President Stairs that they were resigning, "having associated themselves with other gentlemen in the formation of a new Banking Institution."[27] The "other gentlemen" were all familiar faces on the waterfront. James Merkel, who would soon become president of the new bank, was a retired commission merchant and auctioneer. From what little we know of Merkel, he was "quiet and unoffensive" and "deservedly esteemed for uprightness and integrity."[28] Of the other seven promoters, William Cunard was undoubtedly the best known. Son of the redoubtable Samuel Cunard, William was extensively involved in shipping, ship repair, and the development of Cape Breton coal. The Dun credit book rated him "A1" in "pecuniary strength" and "A1" in "general credit." The remaining six merchants were all solidly established in trade: Thomas Kinnear, Edward Kenny, Sr., Jeremiah Northup, John Tobin, George Mitchell, and John Duffus.

*James W. Merkel (left) and William Cunard (right)*

*Market day on Bedford Row, in an undated Notman photo from the mid-1880s.
This short waterfront street was the seedbed of several Halifax banks.
The Merchants Bank first opened its doors in 1864 at 86-8 Bedford Row,
a building on the upper left side of the street in this photo.*

The eight merchants opted for the Halifax Banking Company pattern of an unchartered, private bank, unconstrained by any public requirements. In late April, they placed advertisements in the local press announcing their intention "to discount promissory notes and acceptances, make advances on approved securities, purchase and sell bills of exchange, receive money on deposit and transact all other business matters connected with a Banking Establishment."[29] The capital was $200,000, of which $160,000 was said to be paid up. The old Bank of Nova Scotia offices at 86-88 Bedford Row were rented, and on May 2 the Merchants Bank opened for business.

The Merchants Bank left only a scant documentary record of its

*The Merchants Bank building on Bedford Row*

earliest years. As a co-partnership, it had no public shareholders nor any obligation to explain itself to the mercantile community it served. "It is recently established," Dun's agent noted in 1865, "but in good repute, as a competent though not very wealthy institution, as compared with older ones, some of the wealthiest men here are share-holders."[30] In most of its ways, it moved mysteriously. We do know that its directors met every day but Sunday at midday (Bedford Row being only a short stroll from the wharves) to approve discounts and credits placed before them by Cashier George Maclean, the bank's senior salaried official. They met upstairs above the bank's rather dingy office, gathering around a small oval table, which now adorns the bank's Montreal boardroom. The meetings seldom took more than a few minutes; the bank's clients were well known to the directors. To facilitate trade, the bank acted as an agent of the Imperial Bank in London and of three colonial banks, the Union in Newfoundland, the Union in Prince Edward Island, and the New Brunswick Bank. For all the directors, the bank was an activity on the periphery of their principal commercial interests. None the less, their time was well rewarded; between 1864 and 1869, the Merchants paid an annual return of 9 per cent on capital invested.

By April 1869, the bank's notes in circulation, its deposits, and its current accounts totalled $500,000. This was secured by "specie" of $335,000. All initial expenses had been paid off; low overheads and a small annual tax paid to the city were the bank's only expenses. There were initially only three employees: the cashier, thirty-year-old George Maclean,* the teller, Henry Romans, and a messenger, William Hood, who was required to live on the premises. A clerk, Cyril Francklyn, was hired by 1869.[31] The Merchants was thus the smallest cog in the Halifax banking world in the 1860s.

Confederation found the merchants of Halifax in a mood of self-satisfaction as far as their banking interests were concerned. In 1869, they drew the attention of the finance minister of the new Dominion to the fact that "the banking system in existence in Nova Scotia has been in successful operation for more than thirty years, and has been largely instrumental in aiding the development of the resources of the province and building up its trade and commerce....That the public are satisfied with the system, and neither ask nor desire any change."[32] Such was not the case in Upper Canada. The relatively smooth evolution of Canada's nine Maritime banks contrasted with the more volatile history of the eighteen central-Canadian banks in existence in 1867. The vigorous growth of the central-Canadian economy in the 1850s and 1860s had produced a *pot-pourri* of banks of varying pedigrees. Most conspicuous were those banks holding colonial charters. Dominating these was the Bank of Montreal, with its assets of $6 million and a privileged relationship with the provincial government as its banker and fiscal agent. If Halifax banks, led by the Bank of Nova Scotia with assets of only $560,000, had an anxiety in 1867, it was that Montreal's St. James Street would turn a hungry eye on their territory – a fear that was soon borne out. Central Canada also possessed private, joint-stock banks and a lone Royal Charter bank, the Bank of British North America. There was also a handful of "free" banks, the result of an 1850s experiment that sought to duplicate the New York State pattern of small, locally rooted banks operating under a code of general banking principles.[33]

Variety was not in itself the vital problem of central-Canadian banking. What plagued the system was its overheated growth. At the

* Maclean may well have been the brother of John S. Maclean, a Halifax merchant and president of the Bank of Nova Scotia from 1874 to 1889. The documentary evidence is inconclusive.

In the late 1860s, William Notman, Montreal's pre-eminent photo portraitist,
established a studio on George Street in Halifax. The city's social and commercial élite
hurried to be captured by Notman's lens. The early directors of the Merchants' Bank were
no exception. Notman's portraits project them as men of solidity, earnestness,
and substance, worthy attributes in bankers. As the bank expanded, staff members
began to frequent the Notman Studio; Cashier David Duncan (above) and
Accountant Edson Pease (with his family, below right) both sat in the mid-1880s.

same time, vulnerability to sharp commercial "crashes," notably in 1857, and a penchant for overextending itself in real-estate loans made for instability. In 1866, the Bank of Upper Canada failed, followed a year later by the Commercial Bank. Like the Atlantic colonies, central Canada also suffered from a chronic shortage of specie; in 1866, the Upper Canadian government made a clumsy attempt to introduce a government-based currency.[34]

But despite the flux in central-Canadian banking, there was no doubt in the minds of Canadians that the scattered banks of their new Dominion were the predominant engine of financial growth in their nascent economy. "They accounted for three-quarters of financial intermediary assets," economist E. P. Neufeld has noted, "they handled the foreign exchange business; and their stock was by far the most important security traded on the embryonic stock exchanges."[35] Canadians trusted their notes. Thus, implicit in the Confederation pact was the expectation that some norm of national banking would be established.

Whereas the Americans had placed their national trust in a system of "unit" banks, each constrained by the limits of an existing local capital base, Canadians embraced the model of Scottish branch, or satellite, banking. The cellular growth of branch banking would allow capital to be moved expeditiously between areas of surplus and need. Much like Canada's new-found political structure, each bank would be a federation of a strong head office and its scattered branches. The British North America Act consequently gave exclusive authority in all matters pertaining to currency and banking to the federal government. Initially, the task of integrating the various colonial banking regimes was shunted aside by the demands of political nation-building. In 1867, "An Act respecting Banks" was rushed through Parliament, basically preserving the *status quo* until the end of 1869. Provincial banks were empowered to expand nationally, a right the Bank of Montreal exercised in Halifax. Otherwise, banking reform was postponed. In 1868, the provincial notes that were put in circulation in 1866 were made Dominion notes.

Confederation had a distinctly mixed impact in the boardroom of the Merchants Bank. It cleanly divided into two diametrically opposed political camps. One remarkable facet of the Halifax mercantile elite was its ability to coexist in commerce, while battling tooth and nail in politics. Between 1867 and 1870, the copartners of the Merchants fought out Nova Scotia's political destiny in microcosm; by the early 1870s the pro-Confederationists would win the day and turn the bank into an institution prepared to make its destiny within the young confederation. However, in 1867, this was by no means preordained.

Partners Jeremiah Northup and Thomas Kinnear joined Joseph Howe in railing against Confederation as a reckless gamble. Northup won election to the provincial Assembly as an "anti-Confederate" Grit, drawing support from the prominent Stairs and Jones families. On the other side of the directors' table, John Tobin and Edward Kenny rallied to the Confederation cause, Tobin going down to defeat as a pro-Confederationist in the federal election of 1867 and Edward Kenny, Sr., entering Macdonald's cabinet through the back door of the Senate.

A generous application of John A.'s "soft soap" and patronage soon swayed Nova Scotian sensibilities. By 1869, Ottawa's man in Halifax, Charles Tupper, had negotiated a series of "better terms" with Howe, and opposition to the new nation waned. By 1870, Macdonald had shrewdly called Northup to the Senate and had ingratiated himself with such erstwhile anti-Confederationists as John F. Stairs, William's son. Nova Scotia's allegiance to Ottawa secured, the senior Kenny returned to Halifax with a knighthood (Howe having joined the federal cabinet) and went into semi-retirement. Son Thomas was left to nurture the new-found affection for the federal cause felt by both his father's bank and city.[36]

The spring of 1869 found President Merkel and the directors of the Merchants in an uneasy mood. As lucrative as their copartnership had been, it was clear that they would soon have to conform to some pattern of national banking. The temporary banking legislation of 1867 was slated to expire at the end of the year and, regardless of what followed, it seemed that a federal charter would be the minimum price of admission into the new world of Canadian banking. Similarly, the federal government's intention of introducing some form of national currency would also hinge on the working out of an accommodation with the chartered banks. Consequently, in April 1869, the board declared its intention of obtaining a federal charter: "The anticipated changes in both the Banking and Currency laws of this Province have induced us to obtain a charter enabling us to convert the present copartnership, known as the Merchants Bank, into a Joint Stock institution."[37] Without a federal charter, provincial banks could not expand nationally. The new federal bank would be known as the Merchants' Bank of Halifax, thereby differentiating it from the Merchants Bank of Canada, which was already active in central Canada. Modelling their charter on that of the Union Bank of Halifax, the directors announced a capital base of $1 million, of which they would retain half and the other half would be sold gradually to the public in $100 shares; the bank would have an initial capitalization of $300,000.

The winning of Royal Assent for the new charter on June 22, 1869,[38] did not entirely remove the anxiety from the Merchants'

An 1879 Merchants' Bank of Halifax $4 note. As was the case with the bank's corporate
seal, the motif was oceanic. The centrepiece and left-hand vignette sailing ship
sketches were done by one of the bank's clerks. President Kenny and Cashier Maclean
actually signed each bill issued; the directors oversaw the destruction of old bills
in a furnace in the head-office basement. Like other Canadian banks,
the Merchants'/ Royal continued to issue its own notes until the early 1940s.

boardroom. Director John Tobin had taken his own life just ten days
earlier. On a corporate level, there was deep concern over the shape of
Ottawa's proposed bank act. For his finance minister, Macdonald had
turned to John Rose, a Montreal corporate lawyer. Rose in turn looked
to the fiscal agent of the new federal government, the Bank of
Montreal, for guidance on the direction of federal banking legislation.
Powerfully influenced by E. H. King, that bank's general manager,
Rose opted for a national banking and currency scheme that would
have stripped the existing banks of the right to issue their own notes
against the security of their general credit. Instead, the government
would issue its own notes, releasing them to the banks only in return
for deposits of Dominion bonds. One or two "greater banks" –
undoubtedly, in King's mind, the Bank of Montreal – would thus be
left to handle the financing of national trade, while the rest would be
relegated to the status of local currency-dispensers. Whatever the
merit of a uniform national currency, Rose's plan appeared to pull
Canadian banking in the direction of an unstable structure of local, or
"unit," banks. Canadian bankers acted in virtual unanimity to
condemn the proposal. It threatened to strike at their ability to generate profits on note circulation and, more importantly, cut into their
ability to finance the annual ebb and flow of trade. Monies needed to
buy Dominion securities for deposit in Ottawa would be unavailable
for trade financing. Branches would have to be closed as banks
retreated to single-office operations.

This striking early example of collective defensive action by Canadian bankers forced Rose to abandon his scheme – and later his job – by mid-June. Halifax bankers met in April to draw up a petition advising Ottawa that its plan was too "radical." Their notes had always been convertible into gold, and Rose's plan was nothing more than a "compulsory loan" to the government that would starve Canadian trade of credit. To get their message to Ottawa, they despatched Peter Jack of the Union Bank to the capital to represent "all the Halifax banks." Ontario and Quebec bankers, with the conspicuous exception of King in Montreal, joined in the chorus.[39] In an unrehearsed manner, bankers in Toronto, Montreal, and Halifax had thus come together to make common cause – to act as a national industry. Few finance ministers after John Rose ever found themselves at such loggerheads with the nation's bankers. The fracas of 1869 set a precedent. After that bankers and politicians consulted more and any change was introduced gradually in the interests of national stability.

The Bank Acts of 1870 and 1871 provided proof of this new spirit of accommodation. Rose's replacement, former railway promoter, banker, and politician Sir Francis Hincks, methodically canvassed the banks and then introduced a bank act that respected the banks' note-issuing privilege. Ottawa would issue only one- and two-dollar notes, leaving all large-denomination bills above $4 to the banks. The banks would be obliged to secure their circulation with a cash reserve that was at least one-third constituted Dominion banknotes. The act was refined in 1871 with the inclusion of regulations governing the mechanics of banking. New charters required a minimum capital of $500,000, at least 20 per cent of which must be paid up before operations might commence. To curb recklessness in banking, monthly statistical reports were to be made to the government, and shareholders were subject to double liability in the event of bank failure. Any bank suspending specie payment for more than ninety days automatically lost its charter. Much of pre-Confederation bank legislation was maintained through the 1870-71 acts, including the crucial provision allowing credit to be secured by traders' bills of lading. To keep the system vital and open to shifts in economic opportunity, all Canadian bank charters were to be reviewed every ten years, a distinctly Canadian provision that found its origins in pre-Confederation colonial banking legislation. Implicit in the entire reform was an acknowledgement that private-sector banking could and should grow with the young nation; government would facilitate and to a degree regulate this growth, but the onus was on the banks to meet the challenge.

The bank act was still very much in gestation when fifty-one shareholders of the newly chartered Merchants' Bank assembled in the

*James B. Duffus*

Halifax YMCA for a "general shareholders' meeting" on October 18, 1869. Much of the meeting was taken up by the process of fulfilling the conditions of the charter: oaths were administered, quorums specified, and by-laws approved. Seven directors were then elected out of nineteen candidates. William Cunard topped the poll. Thomas Kenny replaced his father in the boardroom. President Merkel being in "infirm health," the directors elected T. C. Kinnear to the presidency. To his keeping, almost like a badge of office, were entrusted the keys to the money chest and vault. Once every three months, the president and at least one director were to inspect the vault and laboriously count the bank's cash. That cash, at the first counting in November 1869, amounted to $441,003, of which $224,000 was in gold and the rest in notes. Paid-up capital in the Merchants' was $300,000, and liabilities totalled $729,163, secured by a rather unsubstantial reserve of $20,000.[40]

The 134 names on the shareholders' list testified to the fact that the Merchants' was a *merchants'* bank. The mercantile elite of Halifax had invested in the bank's future; the Almon, Boak, Black, Blackadar, DeBlois, Duffus, Dwyer, Esson, Jones, Stairs, and Wier families all held stock. The motif of the bank's corporate seal was an ocean paddle-wheeler, purportedly a Cunard liner, though in fact, the obligations of oceanic trade wreaked havoc on the board's early operation. In

*Thomas E. Kenny*

December, when Kinnear left on a four-month buying trip to England, James Duffus, brother of copartner John, served as *pro tem* president. When Duffus himself left for England, the directors approached T. E. Kenny. Kenny protested that "his private business occupied a great portion of his time," and that if the bank were ever to prosper, it "ought to have at its head a gentleman who could be in attendance during banking hours."[41] Kenny, none the less, relented and began what was eventually to become a thirty-eight-year presidency, the longest in the bank's history. Within weeks, he was already lobbying Finance Minister Hincks in Ottawa on the Bank Act.[42] Although he frequently asserted in public that his role in the bank was "simply advisory,"[43] Kenny was continually an active ingredient in the Merchants' evolution. Over time, his longevity and involvement in bank affairs would be a decisive element in moving the Merchants' from its regional base in Halifax to a national standing. With the exception of the Bank of Nova Scotia, the other Halifax banks suffered from somnolent leadership and eventually paid the price.

Kenny's first achievement was in turning the board into an active promoter of business for the bank. Halifax was an intensely parochial city, and to succeed the bank would have to tap into a series of religious, political, and familial communities. Kenny consciously structured the Merchants' directorate so as to draw in this business. As one veteran of the Halifax years later recalled, there was "a sort of understanding that the Board should be equally divided, both in religious affairs and in politics – three Conservatives and three Liberals, three Roman Catholics and three Protestants."[44] Such quintessential Canadian pragmatism did not always work. In March 1870, Kenny boldly put forward the name of A. G. Jones, a Liberal and, until shortly before, an anti-Confederationist, for election to the board. The shareholders duly obliged the directors, but Jones, sensing the awkwardness of openly allying himself in commerce with those he opposed on the hustings, declined the offer. Jones preferred to stay a quiet friend, and shareholder, of the bank, meeting Kenny over lunch at the Halifax Club or strolling beside the Arm.[45] What Jones declined, another former supporter of Joseph Howe, Senator Northup, took up with alacrity. Northup remained on the Merchants' board and, in 1872, in response to a provision in the new Bank Act, became the bank's first vice-president.

Under Kenny's direction, the Merchants' adopted a twofold strategy for growth in the 1870s. Using its intimate ties with Halifax merchants, it would build up a foundation of mercantile accounts in the city and then strike out into the hinterland, pursuing business along the arteries of trade that bound innumerable Nova Scotian towns to their

*"The little bank in the big building." The bank's first purposely designed head office, opened in 1879, at the corner of George and Hollis in Halifax.*

metropolis. Given the breadth of the board, business in Halifax came relatively easily. In line with the city's other banks, the Merchants' offered to discount bills of exchange for between 6 and 8 per cent. Moving the rate up or down a per cent afforded the bank a crude measure of control over the demand for money. Depositors were offered 3 per cent, sometimes 4 per cent if capital was required for loaning. Under this regime, the bank expanded its credit handsomely throughout the 1870s. In 1869, only $266,970 in bills was discounted; by 1879, this had swollen to $2,206,500.[46] The spread between money loaned and money taken in gave the bank the bulk of its profits. The Merchants' quickly established a dividend of 8 per cent a year and maintained it.

Additional business was found on the Halifax waterfront in the steady flow of foreign exchange that accompanied trade. Correspondence arrangements were established with London and New York to facilitate international transactions. After William Cunard moved to London in the early 1870s, he acted as the bank's *de facto* representative in that city, arranging, for instance, to purchase colonial debentures through Williams Deacon's Bank in Liverpool (the city through

*"Thornvale," the Kenny home on the North West Arm, in a Royal Engineers' photo, c.1890.*

which so much of the Kenny trade moved). At the heart of the bank's business were the big commercial accounts brought by the directors and their trade allies. By 1875, for instance, T. & E. Kenny & Co. had a liability of $182,580 with the Merchants'.[47] Similarly, the Merchants' won the account of S. Cunard & Co., which brought with it a lucrative connection with Cape Breton's nascent coal industry. Kenny assiduously reinforced these mainstays by drawing new names to the board: Thomas A. Ritchie, a leading local lawyer; James Butler, a prominent Grit merchant on Lower Water Street; and Joseph Wier, another influential merchant, all joined in the first decade.

As a traditional Halifax bank, the Merchants' enjoyed "steady and satisfactory" progress in its first years, as Kenny told the shareholders in 1875.[48] Business soon stretched the shabby Bedford Row premises to the limit and, in 1876, the board called in New York architect T. R. Jackson and gave him a $62,000 commission for a four-storey head office on the corner of Granville and George. A year later Senator Northup laid the cornerstone of what the Halifax *Reporter* predicted would soon be "an ornament to the city." The same evening President Kenny entertained the directors "in elegant style" at "Thornvale" on the Arm.[49] Two years later the annual general meeting was held in the new building, symbolizing a kind of coming of age for the bank. Some years later Kenny wrote to his neighbour A. G. Jones, who had by then found prominence in federal politics, and urged him to avail himself of the Merchants' as a means of remitting the proceeds of a provincial railway loan from London: "then remember me – or rather, the *little* bank in the *big* building at the corner of George and Granville," he urged his friend.[50]

What distinguished the Merchants' from its Halifax counterparts in these early years was its aggressive expansion into the city's hinterland. Between 1870 and 1886, the Merchants' opened twenty-five agencies and sub-agencies in Nova Scotia, New Brunswick, and Prince Edward Island. By way of comparison, the older Union Bank of Halifax opened just a single branch in these same years. Only the larger Bank of Nova Scotia approached the Merchants', opening fifteen branches in the years down to 1883. While not all the Merchants' agencies in the hinterland proved profitable, the board's eagerness to establish them spoke volumes of the Merchants' determination to broaden its base. It was almost as if Kenny and his board sensed that complacency on the shores of Halifax harbour would condemn the bank to an existence on the margin. Kenny habitually prowled the hinterland. In 1884, for instance, news that the Caraquet Railway was under development in New Brunswick confirmed the intuition that, in 1882, led to the opening of agencies in Bathurst, Dorchester, and other New Brunswick outposts. Eventually, this same intuition would lead Kenny and the bank out of the Maritimes, deeper into the continent, to tap into other cities' hinterlands.

The Merchants' earliest "agencies" were only distant cousins of the modern bank branch; they more closely resembled franchises, which bore the corporate identity of the Halifax head office but tended to set their own operational course. Hours were irregular, and clients were issued with temporary receipts for their deposits. Permanent receipts were issued only from head office in Halifax. Similar agencies were established along the arteries of Maritime trade, in the bays and valleys where fish were landed or timber assembled. Their business was highly seasonal, reflecting the rhythms of economic life in communities that fished, chopped, or planted. Credit was, for instance, needed to finance the annual campaign in the woods and to underwrite the importing of every-day necessities. These transactions had traditionally been serviced in an *ad hoc* manner by banks in Halifax and Saint John; the opportunity was always there to capture – and monopolize – such business *in situ*. In many instances, local merchants raised petitions inviting Halifax banks to consider "the great desirability of

# MERCHANTS' BANK OF HALIFAX:
## BRANCH EXPANSION 1869-1887

Quebec

Montreal
1887

1885

1882

1883

New Brunswick

Prince Edward Island

1882

1872

1881

1882

1886

1882

1874

1873

1877

1870

1871

1882

1887

1882

1882

1871

1882

1871

St. Pierre & Miquelon
1886

1887

Halifax
1869

1873

1871

1871

1871

Nova Scotia

Bermuda
1882

| | | |
|---|---|---|
| 1869 Halifax (head office) | 1873 Charlottetown | 1882 Bathurst |
| 1870 Pictou | 1874 Summerside | 1882 Kingston |
| 1871 Bridgewater | 1877 Souris (sub.) | 1882 Dorchester |
| 1871 Truro | 1881 Port Hawkesbury | 1883 Newcastle |
| 1871 Weymouth | 1882 Londonderry | 1885 Paspebiac |
| 1871 Antigonish | 1882 Baddeck | 1886 Moncton |
| 1871 Lunenburg | 1882 Guysborough | 1887 Fredericton |
| 1872 Sydney | 1882 Sackville | 1887 Woodstock |
| 1873 Maitland | 1882 Richibucto | 1887 Montreal |

having a bank agency" locate in their area.[51] For the directors of the Merchants', the advantage lay in the grafting of their fledgling bank onto their well-established network of trade relationships with Halifax's hinterland. Easier access to credit would enhance their own trade with outlying merchants and serve to broaden the bank's lending and note circulation.

The earliest agencies were thus formalizations of old trading relationships. In July 1870, the board voted to establish an agency in

Early agencies: Bridgewater (opposite page), opened 1871, and Guysborough (above), opened 1882. In branch portraits, the staff was invariably arrayed on the doorstep like a ship's company.

Pictou, where William Ives, a local dealer in hardware and ship chandlery, was already well known to them. In return for an annual stipend, Ives opened the agency in a back room of his store. The service offered by an agency was very rudimentary: the agent accepted deposits and issued drafts only on a temporary basis. Once Halifax had verified the transaction, a regular deposit receipt or draft on New York was despatched to the agent and forwarded to the client. Such service was furnished as a sideline to the agent's regular business.[52] In 1871, another agency was opened in Truro, where Kenny's old ally in shipping syndicates John Dickie was made agent. Dickie installed the agency in the back of his store and employed his son, Martin, as an unpaid clerk. For this Halifax paid him $1,000 a year. A year later, director Joseph Wier enlisted Sydney merchant John Burchell as an agent in that town. When Burchell later complained that he was "altogether without experience in banking," the bank sent an accountant in his store to apprentice under Ives in Pictou.[53] In 1873, Kenny capitalized on his friendship with Maitland shipowner David Frieze to establish an agency in that town. Frieze cemented the association by holding bank shares.[54] The pattern established in Pictou, Truro, Sydney, and Maitland persisted and carried the Merchants' into New Brunswick, Prince Edward Island, and finally to the timber town of Paspébiac, Quebec, by 1885. Only the Bank of Nova Scotia offered any competition to the Merchants' in this expansion and, where the two came into conflict, quiet deals were struck with Thomas Fyshe, Scotia's cashier, for a division of territory.[55]

While Kenny may have assured the 1871 annual meeting that the early agencies were operating "very satisfactorily," it quickly became apparent that the agency network was to be plagued by the same kind of instability that haunted Halifax's economy. The agencies were only loosely affiliated with head office and subject to the whims of agents whose principal business loyalties lay elsewhere. As early as 1875, the board learned to its dismay that David Duncan, the head-office accountant, had found the books in Pictou "in a very unsatisfactory condition." The directors threatened to send a clerk from head office "to take charge."[56] Maitland also succumbed to slipshod methods. "I have nothing further to add about the M.O. [money order] account," Cashier George Maclean barked at David Frieze, "the matter is so plain, that I am astonished you cannot understand the working of it."[57] John Dickie's announcement in 1874 that he would contest the Colchester County seat in the Assembly caused consternation among the directors in Halifax. They hastily resolved that "the interests of so important an agency as that of Truro should be kept free from all the many incidents connected with a contested election."[58] Elsewhere, drink and fraud debilitated agents' performance. In the absence of any form of regular inspection and systematized banking procedures, the agencies were capable of the most mercurial behaviour. They gave the bank a hinterland, but at the same time accentuated the risk.

The bank's ability to make good in the hinterland was also limited by the faltering Maritime economy. The 1870s and 1880s saw several sharp checks administered to the Maritimes by periodic downturns in the price of its mainstay commodities. Timber, particularly on the New Brunswick North Shore where the Merchants' was fast expanding, was particularly hard hit. Beyond these swoons was the continuing structural deterioration of the region's wood, wind, and water economy.[59] At the 1876 annual meeting, President Kenny decried the "universal depression" and its effect in diminishing the bank's profit. He would later admit that, in the early 1870s, he had felt "bitter disappointment" over the failure of Confederation to reverse the region's economic woes.[60] "I need not tell you of the very depressed state of the times, and seemingly no early change for the better," Vice-President Northup wrote to Frieze in Maitland in 1877. "The Bank met with losses last year and luckily enough [was able] to pay an 8% dividend and a little more. Consequently, the directors feel unable to increase salaries."[61]

The Merchants' ability to pay its dividend without interruption throughout the years 1869 to 1887 suggests that, despite the uneasiness induced by its steady expansion, growth brought an element of protection from the economic woes of the region. Other Maritime banks were not so fortunate. In 1873, the narrowly based Bank of Liverpool and Bank of Acadia both collapsed. Merchants' cashier Maclean hurried to Liverpool and learned that "the affairs of the [Liverpool] Bank had been conducted in so reckless a manner, as to entail very serious loss to the shareholders."[62] A year later, the Bank of Summerside was in difficulties, the result Kenny reported of "two or three directors monopolizing the bank's loans."[63] In 1881, the Bank of Prince Edward Island suspended payment in the wake of a bout of poorly secured lending.[64] When the Maritime Bank in Saint John encountered difficulties in 1883, Kenny briefly toyed with the idea of an amalgamation with the troubled bank as a means of penetrating New Brunswick. Knowledge of the extent of the Maritime Bank's losses stymied the deal.[65] As the *Monetary Times* concluded the next year, the smaller banks were "sadly given to carrying 'too much sail' and keeping too little money in reserve."[66]

The breadth of the Merchants' network of agencies thus tended to minimize the impact of bad loans or cyclical downturns in any one pocket of the Maritimes on the overall stability of the bank. By the 1880s, the board was consciously structuring its loans portfolio to spread the bank's risk as widely as possible. The North Shore timber industry was usually given the widest berth. It was clear, however, by the late 1870s that by tying itself solely to the arteries of traditional Maritime trade, the bank was playing a risky game. An untimely conjuncture of bad loans or a deep region-wide slump might pull the bank under. Consequently, the board began to look for new sectors of the economy in which to place funds, and once again, the directors' personal business instincts pointed the way. Thomas Kenny began to assume a leading role in promoting local industry – particularly sugar refining and cotton production – in the 1870s. The Dickie family in Truro similarly introduced the bank to the Truro Condensed Milk and Canning Company. Nearer head office, Kenny's friend and banking rival William J. Stairs brought the Merchants' into financial contact with the Starr Manufacturing Company in Dartmouth, world-famous makers of Acme skates. In 1881, the Cunard connection delivered the account of the Halifax Company, with its coal holdings around Stellarton. Loans to these nascent industrial concerns offered financial exposure to promising new areas of the regional economy, areas

*The Nova Scotia Sugar Refinery under construction in the early 1880s;
"infant" industry arrives in Halifax.*

less subject to the twists and turns of offshore commodity demand.

Development of home-market manufacturing received a tremendous fillip in 1879 when Sir Leonard Tilley, Macdonald's finance minister from New Brunswick, unveiled the National Policy, an avowedly protectionist attempt to build up in Canada just the kind of "infant industries" Kenny and his Halifax associates had been eying with interest. The young Canadian economy would be swaddled in tariffs in an attempt to displace imports with home-manufactured goods. Implicit in the National Policy was the necessity of the Maritimes reorienting, or at least diversifying, its economy away from the sea and inland to the continental interior. The completion of the Intercolonial Railway from Halifax to Quebec in 1876 had given the first hint of this shift. Now Macdonald's protectionism created the prospect of a new Maritime economy.

What most excited the directors of the Merchants' in the early 1880s was the thought of sugar and steel production within their hinterland. Sugar refining was a natural outgrowth of the region's traditional trade in West Indian sugar and molasses. Iron and steel seemed a logical extension of Canada's railway mania and an inducement for innumerable small towns to begin home production of stoves, ploughs, and other implements of progress. With the Intercolonial tapping into the interior, Maritime sugar and steel might find their way to central Canadian markets. In the minds of men like Thomas Kenny, the National Policy held the promise of "nationalizing" Halifax.

Within months of Tilley's budget, Halifax merchants were agitating for the establishment of a sugar refinery.[67] By the next spring, a nine-storey "sugar house" was under construction beside the harbour. Not only were Merchants' directors such as Kenny and Michael Dwyer prominent promoters of the Nova Scotia Sugar Refining Company, but their bank was instrumental in financing the young enterprise. By 1882, the refinery owed the bank $460,000, a loan secured by bills of lading on stored sugar and a mortgage on the premises.[68]

Steel followed sugar into the boardroom. In December 1882, Kenny met with the promoters of the Steel Company of Canada, a small iron-and-steel concern which had been struggling to establish itself in Londonderry, in central Nova Scotia, since the mid-1870s. The company was seeking an advance of $200,000.[69] It was a tantalizing prospect. The following April the Merchants' approved an $80,000 overdraft. "It was stated," the minutes read, "that the demand for the product of the Company's works was so great that there was actual difficulty in executing orders from customers."[70] Kenny also took a prominent role in the establishment of the Nova Scotia Cotton Manufacturing Company and, as the decade wore on, contributed his time to other, more-public ventures intended to enhance Halifax's new economic orientation. Membership in a federal royal commission on railways and a founding role in the reinvigorated Halifax Board of Trade were typical of his energetic promotion.

Besides diversifying the bank's lending practices, the board worked to tighten bank procedures and recruit more competent staff. The early 1880s saw a conscious effort to systematize the relationship between head office and the agencies. The original free-wheeling agents were displaced by regular staffers who owed their loyalty to head office alone. John Dickie in Truro was obliged to resign and hand over his agency to his son, Martin, who became a full-time bank employee. In 1883, it became "the settled policy" of the Merchants' that agents could not maintain a business of their own.[71] Political involvement was similarly discouraged, as were family entanglements. A year later, the board decreed that "no officer in the service should marry unless his salary was $1,000 or over, except he received the special sanction of the Board."[72] The object in all these reforms was to groom a disciplined and mobile corps of employees, available for posting throughout the growing agency network and free from local

*Head Office staff, Halifax, c.1880. Well into the twentieth century, such photographs visually demonstrated the hierarchy. Junior staff were lined along the left, mounting in seniority to the manager in the centre. The bank messenger, usually an older, ex-military man, was placed alone on the far right; the messenger was not considered a career banker. When women began joining the bank as stenographers in the early twentieth century, they were invariably placed with the messenger. In this photo, Cashier George Maclean reigns outside his office door and David Duncan, accountant, attends him to the left. Note the spittoon in the lower left corner.*

temptation. The term "the service" began to creep into bank correspondence. To consolidate all these procedures, a slim booklet entitled *Rules and Regulations* was published in 1885, and the cashier in Halifax began despatching crude circular letters laying down bank policy to the agencies.[73] To instil respect for these standards, inspectors began to arrive unannounced at the agencies, demanding access to the books. To ensure standardization in paperwork, a stationery department was established. The opening of a telephone line from head office to Bridgewater in 1883 represented the bank's first attempt to conquer distance with technology.

Telephones and circulars alone did not make a modern bank. The nerve-shattering defalcation and dismissal of Cashier Maclean in 1882 (see vignette) prompted the directors to pay more attention to the quality of their staff. Most new recruits were hired away from other banks; most had exposure to Scottish or central-Canadian banking. Maclean's replacement, David H. Duncan, was a dour Scot who had first come to the Merchants' in 1872 from the Bank of British North America. As cashier, Duncan fast became a stickler for detail and routine. If Duncan anchored the bank in Scottish bank procedure, other recruits brought bolder skills. In January 1883, the board hired a young, Quebec-born accountant, Edson Loy Pease, away from the Commerce.

As histrionic as it may sound, Pease's acquisition would prove to be the most providential the bank ever made. He was by birth and training a central Canadian; although a Halifax resident from 1883 to 1887, he never bought a home there, choosing instead to board on South Park Street. Pease arrived with an inbred restlessness that soon infected the bank's directorate, which almost immediately began to employ him as a troubleshooter, negotiator, and promoter. Reading the bank's minute books for these years, one gains the sense of Pease in perpetual motion, breaking out of the inhibiting confines of Halifax. He served as a vigilant agency inspector, descending, for instance, on Baddeck in 1886, finding it in "deplorable condition," suspending the accountant there, and eventually closing the operation.[74] When the Maritime Bank in Saint John faltered in 1883, the Merchants' sent Pease to discuss a possible bail-out and amalgamation.[75] Like Kenny, Pease was also soon convinced that the Merchants' would have to break out of the Maritimes. The natural inclination of a bank dominated by Haligonian merchants was to follow the city's trade routes south to Britain's warmer colonies or to other centres in the Atlantic fishery; in 1882, David Duncan had negotiated the bank's entry into Bermuda. In 1886 Pease travelled to St. Pierre and

*(continued on p. 48)*

# DEFALCATION
## The Banker's Secret Shame

IT WAS THE MOST SINISTER WORD IN THE lexicon of nineteenth-century banking, bringing a shudder to bank director and client alike. Despite its Dickensian aura, defalcation could be reduced to a simple dictionary definition: "a fraudulent deficiency of money owing to breach of trust, in short, embezzlement." In any banking system, but particularly an immature one, confidence in the integrity of the institution is the fundamental prerequisite of growth. A lack of trust brought a lack of stability, and a well-publicized defalcation by a bank employee was the surest route to both.

In 1870, just a year after the Merchants' obtained its charter, the Halifax banking world was rocked by the disclosure that Cashier James Forman of the Bank of Nova Scotia had defrauded his bank of $315,000 over twenty-five years. The ensuing scandal revealed that the cashier as a bank's senior employee was in a virtually unchecked position to "cook" the books. Twelve years later, the same lightning struck the Merchants'. "It having come to the knowledge of the board," the minutes of November 17, 1882, read, "that Mr. Maclean, cashier, was a defaulter to the Bank to the extent of $10,729.18...he was discharged." David Duncan's first discovery as the bank's new cashier was that Maclean had also pilfered $2,188 in cash. After 1882, the bank's cash was entrusted to the joint custody of the cashier and the accountant. Disgraced, Maclean found work as an insurance salesman in Truro, eventually regaining a junior position in the Union Bank. When the Royal took over the Union in 1910, Maclean was immediately pensioned off.

Why did men steal from their employers? While some pointed to the temptation brought on by low salaries, most adopted a moralistic line. "Character" was seen as being at the heart of banking: "There is no mercantile profession," a Bankers' Association essay-winner, D. M. Stewart, wrote in 1894, "in which character plays so prominent a part as banking." Well-trained bankers did not steal. The *Rules and Regulations* spelled out the procedures that instilled character. For instance, ledger entries were to be made in ink, not erasable pencil. Bank fraud was almost always discovered when the perpetrator broke routine – for a holiday or transfer. In 1885, an Officers' Guarantee Fund was created, whereby bank employees were required to post bonds. Defalcation insurance was also purchased. In response to demands for government inspection, bankers pointed to the vigilance of their inspection staff. None the less, reforms crept into the system: in 1913, the Bank Act stipulated an independent shareholders' audit, and in 1923 the Office of Inspector General of Banks was created in Ottawa.

When confronted with evidence of defalcation, directors had several options. Some were prosecuted, but legal costs were high and juries often sympathetic to young clerks. In the

*An entry in the directors' minute book, April 8, 1899*

United States, however, the short-story writer O. Henry, a bank teller by occupation, was none the less jailed for defalcation. In other cases, the bank, fearing adverse publicity, quietly settled out of court. Families of the wrongdoer often made good the loss. Large defalcations invariably resulted in a chase into the United States, with Pinkerton agents hired by the bank tracking down wayward employees.

As the Canadian banking system matured in the early twentieth century, the incidence of defalcation diminished. Even the word slipped out of common usage. Yet, no system is completely immune to the effect of temptation. Particularly in times of recession or rampant speculation, men succumbed to the thought of quick gain. Such was the fate of a young Chatham, Ontario, clerk who in 1929 filched $26,000 to play the stock market. He was later arrested driving his new Pontiac along Sunset Boulevard in Los Angeles. The bank paid the local police chief $200 as a gratuity.

Miquelon to open an agency to serve the French fishery.[76] The phrase "on the recommendation of Mr. Pease" began regularly to punctuate the reporting of directors' decisions. Pease would soon harken to a less-familiar and less-oceanic call: the continental interior and its potential for financial expansion.

The expansionistic intuitions of Kenny and Pease were borne out in electrifying fashion when the bank's high hopes for Nova Scotia's fledgling sugar and steel industries proved ill-founded. From the outset of production in 1881, the Nova Scotia Sugar Refinery was in trouble. The company overspent its initial capital of $300,000 and by 1885 owed $680,000 to the bank.[77] Various culprits were fingered. According to the *Monetary Times*, Montreal sugar producers had an "unfair" advantage in transportation costs and better tariff protection was needed to enable Halifax sugar to enter foreign markets.[78] Whatever the cause, the company quickly became a huge liability to the bank. Kenny and Allison Smith, the refinery president and a bank director since 1876, struggled to refinance the refinery. At the annual meeting in 1886, Kenny reluctantly informed the shareholders that such a course involved "substantial losses" for the bank. A month later, the refinery was sold to, and refinanced by, a new company. The Merchants' surrendered its $350,000 mortgage on the mill, taking back $200,000 mortgage bonds and $50,000 cash, thus writing off $100,000.[79] The refinery soon found both markets and profits and in 1893 merged with two other mills to become the Acadia Sugar Company. Kenny remained a director and large shareholder throughout. As bank president, however, Kenny extracted from the sugar episode the lesson that Maritime industry, with its resources and markets unintegrated into the continental economy, was a precarious vehicle for bank growth.

The steel industry retaught the same lesson. Despite the roseate expectations that had accompanied the giving of an $80,000 line of credit to the Steel Company in Londonderry (where the bank opened an agency in 1882), the "infant" industry was soon in trouble. In September 1883, the directors "expressed surprise" in learning that the steel company was already deeply in debt to another creditor. Surprise turned to shock three months later when the other creditor forced the steel company into liquidation.[80] The bank immediately lodged a claim against the assets of the company, and while Thomas Ritchie, the bank's Halifax counsel, remained sanguine about the outcome, the matter soon sank into a legal quagmire. Like the sugar company, the steel company was eventually refinanced under the auspices of a group of Montreal and English capitalists.[81]

However, unlike the sugar setback, in which the loss was simply made up out of earnings, the steel loss had to be covered by the transfer of $80,000 from the bank's reserve. This procedure struck at the heart of the bank's existence. The reserve, or "rest," was a bank's ultimate contingency fund, monies set aside out of profits in good years to cover bad debts in leaner times. The ambition of young banks was to build up their reserve fund to levels approximating their paid-in capital. Since 1869, the Merchants' had laboriously built up its rest from a meagre $20,000 to a comfortable $200,000 in 1884. Now it had been publicly chopped by $80,000, accompanied by the bank's first annual loss, $45,109. Repeated losses and an unsubstantial rest account were a recipe for banking disaster, an epitaph written on the tombstone of many a small bank. Kenny knew it. As he told his shareholders in 1886, the directors resorted to the rest account because they "felt it was their duty to do this in order that they might emphatically state that *all* bad and doubtful debts had been provided for."[82]

By the fall of 1886, the Merchants' Bank of Halifax had arrived at a watershed. It could remain a bank bound to the imperatives of the Halifax hinterland. There were undoubted profits here; the bank would carry many of its original mercantile accounts from Water Street deep into the twentieth century. Yet with such specialization came the vicissitudes of a cloistered economy, too great a dependence on the boom and bust of commodities. Similarly, the agonies of sugar and steel promotion seemed to indicate that the Maritimes were drawing on an increasingly limited pool of capital. Banks without access to ample capital soon withered. On the other hand, the National Policy pointed the way to "nationalization" of the bank's operations. If the sugar and steel accounts had initially inflicted painful losses, the lesson was perhaps that such accounts would pay only when fledgling Maritime industries were truly integrated into the continental Canadian market and the capital access it afforded. The same was therefore true for the banks. In the wake of the steel fiasco, Kenny found himself thinking along continental lines. Many in Halifax were drawing contrary conclusions; G. P. Mitchell & Sons, an original bank shareholder and client, would describe the National Policy as a "curse to us" in a letter to the *Monetary Times*.[83] Kenny thought otherwise and in January 1887 allowed his Tory friends to draft him as their federal candidate for the County of Halifax. Not to have done so, he told Sir John in Ottawa "would injure party in county and province." Kenny reserved the right to quit politics if the demands of his business life so dictated.[84]

One of the peculiarities of nineteenth-century Canadian politics was that county seats in the Commons, such as Halifax, carried double representation. Kenny was therefore joined on the Tory ticket by John Stairs, his close friend and promoter of Halifax industry. The

Stairs family business, William Stairs Son & Morrow, was a client of
the bank, and Stairs's father was a linchpin in the Union Bank of
Halifax. The opposing ticket featured A. G. Jones and local hardware
merchant H. H. Fuller. Both were well known to the Merchants';
Fuller would join the board in 1890. The Halifax mercantile community thus split its political allegiance and, on February 22, 1887, so did
the Halifax electorate. In a very tight contest, Kenny and Jones took
the honours. As soon as the House convened in the spring, Kenny
began making his mark as a Maritime champion of the National
Policy. In May, he sponsored the incorporation bill of the Londonderry
Iron Company. It was, he said, an important *national* industry.
Similarly, he urged the improvement of Halifax harbour as a matter of
"national" importance.[85]

Kenny now became a regular commuter on the Intercolonial, hurrying to Ottawa to tend to his political duties and then home again to
oversee his commercial and banking concerns. He did not travel long
unaccompanied. The Merchants' too was hearing the call of the interior. In July 1885, the board had received a loan request to finance
logging operations in Manitoba.[86] In 1886, an agency was opened in
Moncton, the crucial Intercolonial junction for trains heading inland.
Later that year, Edson Pease went to Montreal to sell surplus foreign
exchange. Both Kenny and Pease could see that Montreal, with its
growing industrial base and transcontinental rail links, was the
crucible of Canadian finance. If the Merchants' was ever to broaden its
lending and put its notes into wider circulation, the magnetism of
Montreal could not be resisted.

The board was clearly divided on the wisdom of establishing a presence in Montreal. For many, the Merchants' was a *Halifax* bank.
Neither Kenny nor Pease denied this. Montreal simply provided an
avenue to future growth, an assurance that the bank would not join
the already long list of extinct Maritime banks. It took two full days of
board discussion to decide the issue. After this "full discussion," "it
was decided to open there under the charge of Mr. Pease."[87] The next
day, August 5, 1887, after a final interview with the directors, Pease
took a sleeping compartment on the Intercolonial's "Quebec Express"
and, at 6:00 p.m., left Halifax for Montreal. An inveterate traveller,
Pease would take many trips in his life. This was the most important.

# 1887-1908

# Going National

*"Our Progressive Ideas"*

T O A MARITIMER, STEPPING OFF THE TRAIN, MONTREAL IN 1887 WAS A CITY of expanding wealth and possibilities. It was Canada's largest city: its population, just cresting 200,000 in 1887, dwarfed Halifax's, which had not even reached 40,000. From Montreal's stations, one could board the newly completed Canadian Pacific Railway and be in Vancouver in five days or – as Edson Pease and Tom Kenny would so often do – ride the Grand Trunk to Rivière-du-Loup and there connect with the Intercolonial for all points east. To varying degrees, Ottawa, Toronto, and the emerging cities of the West all seemed caught in Montreal's web. The iron tube of the Victoria Bridge, a marvel of Victorian engineering, had conquered the St. Lawrence and given the city access to its bustling American rivals to the south, Philadelphia, Boston, and New York. In their nineteenth-century passion for anatomical metaphors, economic commentators portrayed the St. Lawrence as the pulsing commercial aorta of Canadian commerce, with Montreal as its throbbing heart. If Halifax was struggling to maintain its frail hinterland, Montreal tapped its hinterland with relative ease and profit.

Nowhere was the power of Montreal more tangibly displayed than on St. James Street, the bastion of the Anglo-Scottish entrepreneurship that had for over a century propelled the city forward. The narrowness of the street as it ran through the area just to the north of the port accentuated the seeming omnipotence of its looming commercial buildings. The grandeur and solidity of the Merchants Bank of Canada, Molsons Bank, or the Montreal City and District Savings Bank were clearly evident. Only when St. James broadened out into Place d'Armes was an ampler perspective afforded. On the south side of the square stood Notre-Dame Basilica, a Gothic Revival monument to Quebec's Catholicism. Across the square stood the equally impressive head office

*Montreal's Place d'Armes, 1890. The massive pillars of the Bank of Montreal dominate the north side of the square. The original wooden dome, a victim of rot in 1859, would be replaced in 1903, giving the building a basilica-like look.*

of the Bank of Montreal, a columned study in Roman Revival architecture built in the mid-1840s. Even after the rigorous Montreal winter had necessitated the removal of its wooden dome in the 1850s, the Bank of Montreal building continued to project the reassuring image of Canada's first chartered bank, an institution unlikely to be swept away by financial panic or scandal. The great banking hall inside, remodelled and expanded in 1886, reinforced the impression with its magnificent coffered ceiling and marble pillars. A half-century later, Stephen Leacock would note that visitors to the city sometimes mistakenly wandered into this temple of commerce intent on prayer. "The Bank permits it, in fact is glad," he quipped. "A thing like that is a splendid Ad."[1]

The Bank of Montreal was without dispute Canada's leading bank; many would have argued that it was *Canada's* bank. In 1880, it commanded 22.4 per cent of Canadian bank assets, as compared to the Merchants' meagre 1.5 per cent. Of the forty-five other banks in Canada, only the Bank of Commerce in Toronto in any way rivalled the Bank of Montreal. By 1890, it could claim 8.9 per cent of Canadian bank assets, less than half the Montreal bank's 18.9 per cent.[2] The Bank of Montreal enjoyed more than simple statistical pre-eminence. It acted as the federal government's fiscal agent, and its general managers had served as virtual *ex officio* finance ministers since Confederation. In a credit squeeze or when the government looked to the London bond market, it was always to the offices overlooking Place d'Armes that the finance minister directed his confidential missives. As early as 1855, the Bank of Montreal had opened an agency in New York and was soon well placed on London's Lombard Street to capture Canada's crucial overseas financial business. Its Canadian branches spread through Quebec and Ontario. With Confederation, it moved majestically into the Maritimes. No other bank could move capital about the country with the ease of the Bank of Montreal. Nowhere was this more evident than in the construction of the Canadian Pacific; the railway was by 1887 inseparably bonded to its banker in the kind of corporate account that other Canadian banks could only dream about. In 1887, Donald Smith, one of the original CPR promoters, assumed the bank's presidency, following in the footsteps of another CPR promoter, George Stephen, who had been president from 1876 to 1881.[3]

From the day Edson Pease arrived in Montreal, the Merchants' Bank of Halifax was to have an ambivalent relationship with Canada's leading bank, a relationship that mingled envy and ambition. The Bank of Montreal occupied ground that Pease quickly determined to trespass upon. If the gamble to locate a branch in Montreal was to succeed, the Merchants' would have to make substantial progress in several directions. First it would have to ensure a wider circulation for its notes; the velocity and breadth of circulation dictated a large measure of any bank's profits and commercial reputation. With its bustling trade, Montreal also offered lucrative foreign-exchange opportunities, the bank's second goal. Note circulation and exchange would both stimulate an expansion of the Merchants' network of agencies; just as it had in Halifax, agencies could be profitably grafted onto the city's trade arteries. Finally, Montreal held the prospect of a broadened loan portfolio, a chance to finance Canada's emerging industrial heartland. Surplus capital from Maritime operations might be applied to Montreal business, and new deposits won in the city could be recycled into corporate loans. Even in a growing economy, all of these goals entailed taking market share from the banks already established in the city. From the outset, Pease determined to manage his Montreal branch aggressively.

Passivity in the Montreal banking world would relegate a small Halifax bank to perpetual secondary status in the ranks of national banking. None the less, a modicum of cooperation had to be maintained with other banks; banks accepted each others' notes and drafts, and interest rates were generally set as the result of a loose consensus between the banks. Given this environment, the Bank of Montreal cast a long shadow over Pease's ambitions. As veteran employee F. T. Walker later remembered, relations with the Bank of Montreal were always "rather intricate."[4] Almost immediately, Pease found himself not on speaking terms with Vincent Meredith, accountant at the rival bank's head office. When Meredith later ascended to the presidency of the Bank of Montreal in the 1910s, it would mark the beginning of a decade of particularly icy relations with Pease's bank, which was by then challenging it for dominance. In other instances, the Halifax bank worked harmoniously, though not without a good deal of envy, with its senior rival in Montreal. After Pease's colleague William Torrance attended an Ottawa meeting of Canadian bankers hosted by the Montrealers, he grudgingly reported to Pease that: "The Bank of Montreal certainly do things up well, fancy cooking and servants from Montreal."[5]

Pease not only had the Montreal competition on his mind. He was also acutely aware that his position was tenuous in the eyes of many of the bank's Halifax directors. Kenny was behind him, but others thought Montreal a costly and dangerous departure from familiar Maritime turf. In 1891, for instance, Pease and Kenny urged the board to buy mortgage bonds of the new Montreal Board of Trade building, on the grounds that "it would be advisable to identify ourselves with the undertaking." The board minutes uncharacteristically recorded that the directors were "not quite unanimous" in supporting the initiative.[6] To counter this scepticism, Pease immediately began to agitate for a measure of independence from head office in Halifax. Montreal was deliberately styled a branch, not an agency. Soon he exercised autonomy over foreign exchange and credit approvals up to $10,000 (he had asked for $15,000), and he grew increasingly annoyed by the frequent necessity of returning to Halifax to coax the directors into supporting his central-Canadian initiatives. He shrewdly fell into the practice of waylaying President Kenny as he changed trains in Montreal on his journeys between the House of Commons and his constituency. Kenny was usually a quick convert. Less winnable was the bank's cashier, David Duncan. While Duncan saw the possibilities of Montreal, he was unwavering in reminding the directors of the importance of building up the bank's reserves and of exacting credit reviews. "I have to request," he lectured Pease in 1888, "that you will continue your cautious policy and not be anxious to do too much."[7] His advice more and more fell on deaf ears. A dynamic tension thus ran through the bank's affairs in the years down to the turn of the century, the creative conflict between the Montreal manager's eager ambitions and the caution of head office. In the end, Pease usually won out; the bank's president increasingly endorsed his agressive ways. Sydney Dobson, a young clerk in Cape Breton who would rise to the bank's presidency in the 1940s, later captured the essence of the relationship: "Mr. Pease had the vision and Mr. Kenny was the balance wheel. The two made a wonderful team."[8]

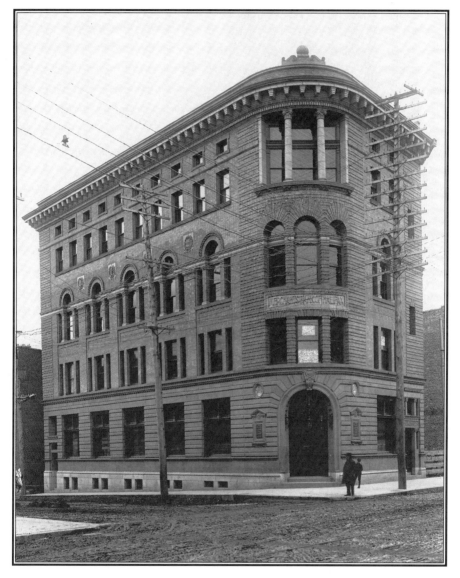

*The des Seigneurs branch, opened in 1890, was the bank's first attempt to "reach out" into the Montreal market, to tap the potential of the city's industrial district. The building pictured here was built in 1894 at a cost of $58,000, and represented the bank's first real-estate investment in Montreal.*

*The Bell Telephone Building on Notre Dame Street West. From 1895 to 1908, the Merchants' Bank of Halifax rented space on the ground floor of this prestigious building.*

In banking, location is everything and, in Montreal, Place d'Armes was *the* location. Pease initially secured rented premises for the Merchants' at 55 St. François-Xavier Street, just off the square. He installed electric light, a wire to the telegraph office, and a modern vault. For Pease, however, there was always a better location, and within a year he was angling for a spot on Place d'Armes. In 1889, he found it when the Banque d'Hochelaga vacated its premises at the corner of François-Xavier and Notre Dame. Having just visited the airy offices of several New York banks, Pease determined to make the new office "distinctly original": "I noticed in New York bank fittings in oak and plate glass, which certainly looked very striking."[9] The Merchants' would try to diminish the Stygian gloom of most bank interiors; the accountant's desk would be open to public view. To draw customers into the branch, safety-deposit boxes were offered, and, in a move that hinted at the growing importance of urban retail banking, a savings department was begun. Five years later, Pease was complaining that the office was "becoming too small" and convinced the board to rent the ground floor of the prestigious Bell Telephone Building on Notre Dame.

Pease was alive to the banking possibilities inherent in Montreal's urban growth. Noticing that the Bank of Montreal had opened a branch near the industrial plants of the Lachine Canal, Pease told the directors in Halifax they must do the same.[10] For the first time outside the Maritimes, the Merchants' bought a lot and built its own premises. The West End branch would principally collect deposits from companies and their workers; to ensure this, Pease hired the bank's first French-Canadian employee, François-Xavier Leduc, as teller. A francophone, he told Halifax, was "absolutely necessary." In 1894, Pease drew the board's attention to Côte St. Antoine, "a progressive suburb of Montreal," where members of the affluent Anglo middle class were building homes. When the Montreal manager reported that he had secured the municipal account for the district, a sub-branch was opened in what was soon to become the Town of Westmount.

Branches planted the flag; accounts made the profits. To put Merchants' notes into Montreal circulation, Pease negotiated agreements with the Merchants Bank of Canada and Molsons Bank for the reciprocal acceptance of each other's notes at par. Without such agreements, other banks would charge a commission on all "sundry" notes presented to them, and customers would consequently spurn such notes. In 1889, a similar deal was struck with the Bank of British Columbia, providing an early intimation of Pease's continental aspirations. Parallel to these arrangements, Pease moved to invigorate the Merchants' offshore reciprocal agreements. He negotiated a comprehensive pact with the Chase National Bank in New York and entrusted the bank's affairs in London to the redoubtable Bank of Scotland. To ensure that the Merchants' new-found respectability was broadly appreciated, Pease began cultivating the press. Tombstone advertisements were placed in the *Monetary Times* and the *Journal of Commerce*, and Pease sought out personal interviews with their editors. Not by coincidence did the Merchants' quickly acquire the account of Hugh Graham, the aggressive proprietor of the mass-circulation Montreal *Star*, whom Pease had assiduously cultivated. All this struck Halifax head office as unbankerly; the press were scoundrels, and it was unseemly for banks to advertise. "The board are anxious to know," Duncan wrote tongue-in-cheek, after one Montreal paper disparaged the young Halifax bank, "if when you interviewed the Editor, a revolver was within reach and open to his view."[11] Pease persisted.

At the fulcrum of Pease's assault on Montreal was his concerted attempt to win corporate clients. Since the 1840s, Montreal had been the seat of Canada's "industrial revolution." Ease of transportation and British North America's most concentrated market had fostered industrial growth along the banks of the Lachine Canal, growth now accelerating under the impetus of the protectionist National Policy. Within weeks of arriving in the city, Pease had subscribed to the Bradstreet credit-rating service and was soon knocking on business doors. He could not hope to dominate any one company's financial needs, but he could aim for a portion. Two early conquests were Lyman Sons & Co., a wholesale chemical and drug producer, and the Pillow Hersey Manufacturing Co., a metal-working enterprise. On August 22, 1887, for instance, the board approved a $25,000 loan at $5\frac{1}{2}$ per cent to cover part of Pillow Hersey's payroll. Other accounts followed: St. Lawrence Sugar Refining, Montreal Blanket, Frothingham & Workman, Drummond McCall, Dominion Cotton, Bell Telephone, and Belding Paul & Co. Pease was seldom content to let an account sleep. By 1895, for instance, he had convinced Pillow Hersey, a long-time Commerce client, to bring its entire account to the Merchants' in return for a $225,000 line of credit. Operating loans to industry led naturally to industrial promotion, and Pease was soon providing call loans to such prominent Montreal stockbrokers as L. J. Forget and the Hanson Brothers, both principally interested in utilities investment. As if to

*The bustle of St. James Street, 1896. Again, the columns of the Bank of Montreal dominate the view. If Canada had a bankers' row, this was it. In 1908, the Royal would situate its new Montreal Head Office at 147 St. James (just to the left of the streetcar).*

complement these, Pease arranged the listing of Merchants' shares on the Montreal Stock Exchange in 1893. Pease found another urban lending frontier in the retail industry, making loans to the proprietors of emerging department stores such as Henry Morgan & Co. and Robert Simpson & Co.

Pease could not do it all alone. Such heated expansion required experienced bankers. Cashier Duncan in Halifax was competent but unadventurous; Pease valued his friendship, but realized new blood was needed to sustain his Montreal effort. Just as he poached accounts from other banks, Pease recruited "his" men from competitors. Over the years, more than any other bank, the Toronto-based Commerce was to lend men and ideas to the Merchants'. It had trained Pease himself, and from it emerged William Torrance in 1887 as Pease's replacement as accountant in Halifax. In the same year, the Merchants' also snapped up William Botsford, an accountant from the bankrupt Maritime Bank, and A. E. Brock from the Eastern Townships Bank. Appointed accountant in Montreal, Brock quickly became Pease's trusted lieutenant. Pease also invigorated the all-important inspectors' position, hiring W. F. Brock and an aggressive, young Bankers' Association prize-winner, D. M. Stewart, away from the Commerce in the 1890s to head the Merchants' inspectorate. With such talent at his disposal, Pease revamped bank procedures along systematic lines. For instance, a standardized credit-approval letter – later dubbed Form 199 – was developed to hasten the granting of loans.[12] Pumped through the bank by a growing tide of circular letters, standardized methods meant that the bank was now dispensing the same standard of service in its Sydney branch as it was in West End Montreal. The level of managerial discretion might be lifted or lowered, but the net effect was that the bank was building a system in which both methods and men were interchangeable.

Beyond its own reforms, the Merchants' participated in the general advance of Canadian banking towards increased commonality. One of the aggravations of mid-nineteenth-century banking was the slowness with which settlement was made between banks. Money drafts, commercial cheques, and bills had to be laboriously sorted and delivered to designated banks for payment. This "peddling" of drafts, usually delegated to a junior, slowed the financial pulse of all the businesses and banks involved. In 1887, Halifax bankers discussed establishing a "clearing" house "for the purpose of effecting a more perfect and satisfactory settlement of daily balances between them."[13] In operation early in 1888, the Halifax clearing house was little more than a room full of wickets, at which clerks deposited and received notes and bills in their own bank's name at a daily clearing. Within a year, the idea had spread to Montreal, where Pease joined six other Montreal banks in establishing a clearing house that opened in January 1889.[14] As Canadian banking spread across the nation, the clearing-house system spread with it, opening in key regional centres such as Winnipeg and Vancouver, ultimately permitting Canadians to become a nation of cheque-writers.

The clearing houses were indicative of the relatively smooth evolution of Canadian banking in general in these years. The generous structure of the original 1870-71 Bank Act proved ample to accommodate the pressures of national financial growth. The Bank Act revisions of 1880, 1890, and 1900 can best be described as mere tinkering. The capital stock obligations of would-be banks were, for instance, stiffened in 1880; the use of bills of lading and warehouse receipts as a surety for loans was broadened in 1890 to encompass new, growing areas of the economy.[15] Pragmatic reform of the legislative constraints on Canadian banking was from the outset the product of the informal, consensual relationship of Canadian bankers and politicians. At the first revision in 1880, Finance Minister Sir Leonard Tilley urged the bankers to form a common front and to present him with "some plan mutually advantageous to the Government and the Banks."[16] So workable was this consensus that, in 1891, the bankers formed a voluntary association to embody it, the Canadian Bankers' Association. Chartered in 1900, the Association was empowered to provide educational services, to operate the clearing houses, and, if a bank went into liquidation, to appoint a curator to administer its affairs. The Merchants' was a willing participant in these developments, joining the CBA in early 1892 for a fee of $120 a year.

Only one issue jeopardized the ability of bankers and politicians to regulate the banking industry: public trust in the integrity of the system. As the disquieting news of widespread bank failures in America and Australia in the early 1890s mixed with Canadian memories of isolated failures in the 1880s, Canadians began to demand more stringent inspection of their banks. In 1900, banks were obliged to pay 5 per cent of their circulation into a government-administered Bank Circulation Redemption Fund. If a bank failed, its notes would be redeemed out of the Fund. Several spectacular Canadian bank "smashes" in the first decade of the new century would revive the agitation for government inspection. The Merchants', which was not immune to improprieties in these years, felt this pressure to the point that, by 1910, Edson Pease, who emphatically shared the industry's aversion to government intrusion into its affairs, was prepared to countenance an audit of bank affairs by shareholder-appointed accountants.[17] Moved by much the same desire to court public confidence, the directors had worked almost compulsively to build up the bank's rest account as a measure of insurance against any reoccurrence of such embarrassments as the steel and sugar troubles of the 1880s. By the turn of the century, the *Monetary Times* noted that the bank's annual report afforded evidence – another $100,000 transferred from earnings to reserves – that ought "to prove satisfactory to shareholders."[18] In 1905, the bank's reserve for the first time exceeded its paid-up capital.

The *Monetary Times* was not alone in noticing the Merchants' ascendancy on the Canadian financial scene. Pease's aggressive management of the Montreal branch brought the bank widespread recognition. A young clerk, Robert McCormick, stationed in Montreal by the Ontario Bank in 1900, recalled that he had grown bored by his assignment and, hearing that the Merchants' was "an up-and-coming" bank, successfully sought employment there. McCormick sensed that Pease's bank offered a more dynamic future; it did indeed, as young McCormick was soon despatched to pioneer the bank's presence in the Ottawa Valley.[19] The Ontario Bank collapsed in 1906.

Clerks were not the only competing bankers to notice the Merchants' in Montreal. In his determination to make a market for his bank in the city, Pease quickly came into conflict with the established banking community. In many eyes, he appeared a bumptious upstart intent on poaching customers and cutting corners. The first bone of contention was the note-exchange agreement with the Merchants Bank of Canada. Almost immediately, Pease felt constrained by the agreement, believing that it would condemn his bank to a perpetual secondary status in Montreal banking. A constant theme in Pease's letters to George Hague, general manager of the Merchants Bank of Canada was that the Merchants' of Halifax would not "belittle ourselves."[20] Pease wanted equal status in note exchange. For his part, Hague and his Montreal manager Charles Meredith began to suspect that Pease was luring their customers away by offering "low and absurd" borrowing rates.[21] Sensing that this in fact was Pease's intent, David Duncan in Halifax characteristically counselled caution: "better have one friend among the large Banks. There is a large field, try the customers of the other Banks if you want to fight. No doubt the names [of clients] you mention are very desirable, but this only tends to increase Meredith's anger against you."[22] Montreal soon proved a lucrative hunting ground for Pease. As early as January 1888 he reported winning the dry-goods account of Hodgson, Summer & Co. As Pease happily reported: "The Bank of Commerce looked upon this account as the best one they had and greatly regretted the loss of it."[23]

Pease thus acquired a deserved reputation as a wily operator in the otherwise gentlemanly world of Montreal banking. He once said of his

*William Notman's Montreal studio proved just as popular with Royal Bankers as had his Halifax studio. Given that many of those associated with the Royal Bank in its early Montreal years were newcomers to the city's business and society, a Notman portrait was one small way of establishing one's prestige. Seen here is a pensive Edson Pease in 1909.*

tactics against the competition, "I think it better to go quietly along, and hit them a dig when they least expect it."[24] This reputation was doubtless reinforced by the fact that Charles Meredith was the brother of Vincent Meredith of the Bank of Montreal, "who has some grounds to complain and doubtless they talk me over."[25] Whatever the gossip, the Halifax bank that had asserted itself onto the Montreal banking stage in the 1890s acquired a spirit of aggressive self-confidence that would soon carry it into the Canadian West and south into the Caribbean. "I hear that we are the subject of comment among the Bankers West, who all predict that we will suffer yet from our progressive ideas," Superintendent of Branches Torrance wrote to Pease in Vancouver in 1900. "I think we can show them that we are able to take care of ourselves."[26]

Pease's impatience with the established rules of banking was further reflected in his perception of French-Canadian bankers. Institutions such as the Banque d'Hochelaga and the Banque Jacques-Cartier had displayed considerable enterprise in serving francophone clients, but were beginning to face the limitations of a growth predicated on one ethnic group rooted in one region.[27] In Pease's opinion, they, like Maritime banks, had to broaden their affairs in order to survive. When the French banks refused this course, choosing instead to cater exclusively to francophone clients, Pease grew exasperated. He often remarked on their "peculiar character" and his belief that they were "incompetently managed."[28] Not surprisingly, it was an ailing branch of the Jacques-Cartier in Ottawa that Pease bought in 1899 to give the Merchants' its beachhead in Ontario. From the outset, therefore, the Merchants' conceived of its culture and its clientele in Anglo-Canadian terms. It had come to Montreal to tap into Anglo commerce; it was pleased to have the patronage of the city's francophone working class and capitalists like Louis Forget, but it resigned any ambition of moving into the Quebec hinterland. A few sporadic attempts all met with failure. A branch was briefly operated in the English farming town of Ormstown in the 1890s, but branches were not opened in Quebec City and Joliette until 1909. A branch in the tobacco district of L'Epiphanie was unsuccessfully attempted just before the Great War.

Given Pease's thrusting ambitions, it was clear by the late 1890s that his "vision" of the bank's future was beginning to overwhelm President Kenny's "balance wheel." Despite the tension, the relationship of president and Montreal manager proved remarkably productive; each left a lasting stamp on the ethos of the bank. Kenny was universally remembered by Merchants' employees for his avuncular concern for the welfare of the bank's employees. He made a practice of regularly visiting each of the bank's branches, moving behind the counter and chatting with young clerks. In the tight social world of the Maritimes, Kenny could put names, families, and towns together *and* remember them. "This made quite an impression on my mind," a junior from Guysborough remembered of a 1905 Kenny visit, "he was a hearty, genial man with nothing the least 'high hat' about him, and I liked his friendly and informal gesture. It was perhaps my first lesson on the development of *esprit de corps*."[29] Similarly, the assistant manager in Halifax in 1903 remembered Kenny as "a suave old Irishman," who "when he spotted a new face he would come to me for biographical information, and then welcome the newcomer to Halifax as though the future of the branch was now assured."[30] However paternalistic it may now seem, Kenny's insistence on the bank as a "family" of Maritime "boys" outlasted his tenure as president. Loyalty to the organization and a *noblesse oblige* on the part of senior management stayed with the Merchants' long after it spread out from the Maritimes.

Beyond the bank, Thomas Kenny played out his Maritime role as Conservative MP for Halifax, where he continued to be a champion of Macdonald's vision of Canada. He repeatedly sought federal assistance for Haligonian ambitions: steamship subsidies, patronage appointments, and railway grants. In 1891, he fought the Liberal heresy of free trade with the United States. He became by 1896 "the old war horse of Halifax."[31] Political life did not, however, sit well with Kenny. Politics, he told Sir John, were a "luxury" which an "ordinary businessman" could not afford.[32] After Macdonald's death, Kenny became embroiled in the disintegration of federal Conservatism. In December of 1892, his close friend John Thompson won the premiership, only to succumb to a heart attack; another friend, Charles Tupper, fought valiantly but in vain to stem the tide of Laurier Liberalism in 1896. Kenny, it was rumoured, turned down a cabinet post in the midst of this imbroglio. His stature in the eyes of Haligonians throughout these years diminished; for some, he had done too little to arrest local economic decline, and for others, particularly Protestants, his defence of the education rights of Manitoba Catholics made him no longer acceptable. In the election of 1896, the loss of his seat was at least tempered by the knowledge that Robert Borden, a Halifax Tory lawyer, had won. Borden had done legal work for the bank and held some of its shares.

For all his geniality, Kenny increasingly represented a beleaguered Maritime vision. With the advent of the Laurier boom in the late 1890s, the Maritime economy began shrinking in relation to the national economy as a whole. This was no sudden collapse; the Merchants' continued to hold a strong portfolio of Maritime accounts:

companies like the Rhodes, Curry engineering works in Amherst, Dominion Iron and Steel of Cape Breton, and the People's Heat and Light of Halifax commanded generous lines of credit. The appearance of Montreal and Toronto and even foreign names in the promotional lists of these concerns indicated, however, that Atlantic capital and entrepreneurship was becoming stretched. Companies lacking access to national markets and capital were condemned to live according to the whims of the regional economy. In 1904, this was rudely brought to Haligonians' attention by the failure of the venerable Kenny family firm. Although Tom had handed the firm over to a son in 1893, the blow was still sharp. It was the result, the *Monetary Times* concluded, not of any failure of business skill, but of "a number of losses and disappointments" unexpectedly dealt by the local economy.[33]

The shores of the St. Lawrence, not the Halifax waterfront, shaped Edson Pease's world view. The Pease family home at Coteau Landing, just west of Montreal, was a stone's throw from the river. Here Edson had been born in 1856, the son of a successful dry-goods merchant whose business had flourished since his coming to Canada in 1823 from Massachusetts. Pease's Wharf became the commercial focal point of the town. Donald Creighton, the first, great historian of the "commercial empire" of the St. Lawrence, eloquently argued that the great river seduced those who saw its shores; it drew them inland into transcontinental endeavours. Creighton saw this in Macdonald of Kingston; the bank historian can see it in Pease of Coteau Landing. As the twelfth of fourteen children, Edson could have entertained no hope of taking over the family business; his brother Charles was already assuming the reins. Pease would find his career up the St. Lawrence.

Pease found a model for his ambitions in his childhood friend Charles Rudolph Hosmer. Five years Pease's senior, "Charley" was the son of Coteau Landing's carriage-maker, who had left the town for a career, not on the river, but beside it, working as a telegrapher for the railway. Business historian Alfred Chandler has argued that the railways were America's "first modern business," requiring engineering and managerial precision to build and operate. Their promotion was predicated on broad strategic vision, since they transcended regions, reshaping markets and building economic interdependence. Whole sections of the industrial economy – notably iron and steel – became organized for and by the railways. The telegraph was the natural concomitant of the railway; precision and velocity in railway management demanded fast, timely information.[34] Together, trains and telegraphs opened commercial vistas as no other technology had done before and, in Canada's case, made political union a practicality. C. R. Hosmer's career and subsequent wealth graphically proved the case.

*Charles R. Hosmer
in 1897, also photographed
in the Montreal
Notman studio.*

"Charley" Hosmer first put his finger to a telegraph key at age fourteen. He followed the wires out of Coteau, joined the Grand Trunk Railway, and was, within six years, managing the Kingston office of the Dominion Telegraph Company. A stint in Buffalo brought further promotion and a return to Montreal in 1881 as the president of the Canadian Mutual Telegraph Company. The builders of the Canadian Pacific, realizing the crucial importance of telegraphy to the efficient movement of freight, sought out Hosmer in 1886 to head their telegraph system. There Hosmer remained until 1899, growing influential and rich. His influence stemmed from his friendship with railway moguls William Van Horne and Thomas Shaughnessy, who in turn opened for him the doors of Montreal commerce, not the least of which were those of the Bank of Montreal. Hosmer's wealth flowed from a generous salary and his ability to capitalize on the business opportunities at the other end of the telegraph wire. Those erecting a telegraph system usually had the first whiff of potential on the frontier. Hosmer's Montreal central telegraph office, "that bee-hive of industry,"[35] stood at the crossroads of Canadian commercial intelligence. When the CPR pushed a branch line into the British Columbia interior in the 1890s,[36] Hosmer was quick to draw the attention of Montreal financiers to the area's mineral bounty.*

---

* A small B.C. town on the CPR line bears Hosmer's name.

A brilliant manager and a prescient promoter, Hosmer was also a debonair member of Montreal society. Witty, affluent, and well-travelled, he was a model of self-made prosperity. He represented a new type of Montreal wealth, generated not by the old staple trades but by new technologies and new hinterlands. He seemed to possess a Midas touch. Dinner invitations to the Hosmer home were enviously regarded. Away from home, Hosmer found himself much courted. Edward, Prince of Wales, soon learned to share his epicurean instincts with the Canadian telegrapher. When, in the fall of 1887, Edson Pease began making his presence known in Montreal as the manager of an obscure Halifax bank, it was not long before he found himself at the dinner table of his old boyhood friend and inspiration, Charley Hosmer.[37] There, over chitchat and boasting of transcontinental enterprise, Pease was soon socializing with the likes of Van Horne and Shaughnessy, and, through them, with a young railway contractor by the name of Herbert Holt.

Like his mentor, Pease had been carried out of Coteau Landing by the telegraph. Leaving school at fourteen, he had worked as a telegraph operator in Ogdensburg, New York, before joining the Bank of Commerce in Montreal as a junior in April 1875.[38] Canada's evolving branch-banking system shared telegraphy's sense of national vista, and Pease bridged the two.[39] When the directors of the Merchants' hired Pease as an accountant in 1883, they undoubtedly saw in him the talents of a trained, Upper Canadian banker who would help to preclude any repetition of the Maclean scandal. What they probably did not detect was Pease's continental vision, bred by exposure to the St. Lawrence and the telegraph, an impatience to get to the centre of the continent. The oceanic perspective bred in the Halifax directors was by no means irrelevant to Pease; the Maritimes were a foundation for growth, which had historically turned towards international expansion into the Caribbean and Europe. But Pease was initially a continentalist. As early as 1890, Charley Hosmer was supplying his friend with passes to ride the CPR to the West.[40] "A good many of our banks are opening up in the growing towns of Manitoba and the NWT," the Montreal manager reported to President Kenny. "From what I can learn Banking operations have been very satisfactory in these smaller places. Certainly they offer a good field for circulation."[41] The problem was choosing *which* "smaller places."

Throughout the late 1880s and early 1890s, Pease and the often-sceptical board agonized over what Halifax accountant Torrance described as "the burning question of going West."[42] There was much to cloud the strategic vision of the executive. Canada was still locked in economic recession; immigration to the West was still a trickle, and low commodity prices stunted Prairie agriculture. Even the mighty CPR had to labour to meet the expectations of its backers. Where could the Merchants' safely plant its flag? Ontario with its growing industrial strength clearly beckoned, but there, competition with well-established banks would be stiff. Perhaps the American mid-West provided a better future? Just as the Montreal railways tried to siphon off American trade, so too would Montreal-based banks seek out trade financing in Chicago. The competition had also to be considered. The Merchants' had, in the words of Thomas Fyshe, the cashier of the Bank of Nova Scotia, "stolen a march" on its Halifax rival by opening in Montreal, although Fyshe hastily opened a Montreal agency in 1888.[43] The Scotia had, however, leapfrogged over the competition by opening in Minneapolis in 1884 and would position itself to capitalize on the Chicago World Exposition by opening there in 1892. Finding virgin, but promising, territory would be difficult.

In the fall of 1888, David Duncan toured the American mid-West and reported good prospects for loans. Money was subsequently lent in Minneapolis, but no agency was established. Pease, somewhat uncharacteristically, preached caution. Any increase in the bank's note circulation in these regions meant an expansion of its capital base and a possible crimping of funds available for the all-important Montreal market. "I believe rather," he told Kenny, "in paying moderate dividends and increasing our reserve fund. It is a dangerous time when money is plentiful as at present – speculation is rife."[44] Pease did, however, shrewdly recognize that good money *was* to be made in the United States by investing the bank's reserves in American railway bonds. Throughout the 1890s, bond accounts were maintained at the Chase National and Bank of Scotland so that, by 1899, the bank's holding in bonds such as the Montana Central and the Chesapeake and Ohio totalled well over a million dollars.[45] None the less, the bankers were aware that any attempt to establish an actual presence in the United States would encounter a thicket of state bank regulations. When a New York agency was eventually established in 1899, it was intended to service the Merchants' sortie into Cuba, not its continental ambitions.

Thus, the building up of Montreal business as a platform for further growth dominated the bank's energies in the early 1890s. Elsewhere, a stand-pat policy was pursued. Few new branches were opened. Kenny lectured the shareholders each year about "the continuous commercial depression." A keen eye was kept on Toronto, but no choice location presented itself. Elsewhere, opportunity presented by the spectacular collapse of the Commercial Bank of Newfoundland and the Union Bank of Newfoundland diverted the bank's attention temporarily eastwards. With the commerce of the colony in financial paralysis, the Merchants' joined with the Bank of Nova Scotia and the Bank of Montreal in a rescue mission which saw the Merchants' open in St. John's in early 1895, where it quickly acquired the account of a prominent St. John's trader, Bowring Brothers. Not until the summer of 1897 did Pease finally make his move in the West and, not surprisingly, he made it in the company of Charley Hosmer.

The election of the Laurier Liberals in 1896 coincided with the first inkling of an economic upturn in the Canadian economy: "1897 showed a marked improvement in the business of the western portion of the Dominion," Kenny told the shareholders early in 1898, "due to good crops and good prices in the Province of Ontario and Manitoba and the North West Territories, also to the development of the mineral wealth of British Columbia."[46] The breadth of the upturn prompted Pease to declare his strategy: instead of trying to occupy the middle ground of the Prairies, the Merchants' would vault to the Pacific coast and establish itself in British Columbia's booming mineral economy. From Hosmer, Pease learned of feverish mining activity in the B.C. interior, where mines with bullish names such as War Eagle and Silver King tapped the copper, gold, silver, and lead veins below boom towns like Rossland and Nelson. In July 1897, Pease "strongly recommended the Board to open in British Columbia, especially in Rossland, Nelson and Vancouver." Ever cautious, the directors instructed Pease to revisit the land of his enthusiasm and to open branches only if he remained convinced of its potential.

Picking up Martin Dickie from Truro branch and Hosmer in Montreal, Pease hurried west. In staccato fashion, branches were opened in Rossland, Nelson, Vancouver, Victoria, and Nanaimo. Staff was rapidly deployed westward; young clerks and tellers were offered handsome increases – $300 on a $600 teller's salary – to accept marching orders to towns many of them had never heard of. The bank's senior inspector, William Botsford, was pressed into service as Vancouver manager. A young Fredericton lad, Charlie Neill, was shipped out to act as accountant. A lot was bought in Rossland, and premises were rented on Hastings Street in Vancouver. Throughout 1898, Pease kept up the pace; new frontier branches were opened at Atlin, Grand Forks, Bennett Lake, and Ymir. In anticipation of the spring rush to the mines, branches were hastily thrown open in midwinter. To establish in Atlin in the northern interior, a four-and-a-half-ton safe was hauled by horse and pulleys through the mountain pass from Skagway.[47] In 1899, a branch was established in Republic, Washington, where Montreal mining interests had investments and where the Merchants' saw an opportunity to profit from foreign

*Vancouver branch staff portrait, 1904. The woman in this branch portrait may be*
*Jennie Moore, who was probably the first woman employed by the bank.*
*Hired in 1902 to replace a male stenographer, Moore was typical of the bank's*
*early female employees; until the First World War women were assigned*
*to behind-the-scenes roles such as stenographers or clerks.*

exchange. When the Vancouver East End branch opened in 1898, the Merchants' became the only bank to have two branches in the same city west of Toronto. The surge into British Columbia was not without setbacks: Ymir and Atlin were both closed in 1900, Republic in 1904. None the less, by 1908 the bank had twenty-one branches in British Columbia. It soon became a tradition for two or three of the Halifax directors to troop westward each summer, hosted by the aging Kenny, to inspect the little empire that Pease had made for them on the Pacific. The high point of such tours was a trip in the "tub" down to the three-hundred-foot level of the War Eagle mine. Many Merchants' directors and officers bought shares in such mines, often regretting their investment as these speculative stocks fluctuated wildly in value.[48]

Pease sensed that the key to successful expansion lay in growth balanced between areas which saved and areas which borrowed. Surplus capital from savings on which the bank paid 3 per cent could be transferred to regions hungry for capital and lent for 6 to 7 per cent, not only enhancing profits but, more importantly, building up

*Opened in 1909, the Gowganda, Ontario, branch was typical of banking on the frontier.
Hastily established, often poorly equipped, and staffed by recruits
hurriedly trained in Montreal, these branches gave the Royal a presence
in communities with growth potential.*

clientele. This arithmetic underlay the commonly expressed theory of Canadian branch banking: "this involves," CBA president Byron Walker of the Commerce had noted, "the savings of one slow growing community being applied to another community where the enterprise is out of proportion to the money at command in the locality."[49] Given the consolidated manner in which the bank reported its financial operations to shareholders, it is difficult to dissect exactly how this formula was applied. It is clear, however, that in these turn-of-the-century years of expansion the Maritimes and British Columbia were supplying capital to the bank's Montreal operations. A detailed profit-and-loss statement that survives from the first six months of 1902 shows the two Montreal branches dominating the bank's loans with advances of $4,596,594. Montreal loans, it should be noted, were often applied to "national" purposes and were not strictly regional. Halifax and Truro only distantly rivalled Montreal in advances. Both the Maritime and British Columbia branches contributed surplus savings to the Montreal operations. "Montreal Branch seems to gobble up all we can lay our hands on," Torrance boasted in 1900.[50] The spread between Montreal's $6.2 million in advances – lent at 6 per cent – and $3.2 million in deposits – taken in at 3 per cent – was made up by a $3-million injection of head-office funds. Not surprisingly, the bank's most profitable branches were: Montreal, contributing $73,179 of the bank's six-month profit of $164,876; Halifax, producing $22,247; and Truro with profits of $13,706. New York agency reported profits, but derived them from different activities. Most rural branches in the Maritimes and British Columbia ran small operational deficits.[51]

The success of cross-subsidization within the bank's now quasi-national branch system made a move across the Ontario border increasingly attractive and imperative. The ailing branch of the Banque Jacques-Cartier in Ottawa was bought in 1899, but the real sally into Ontario came in February 1903, when a Toronto branch was opened in leased premises at Yonge and Wellington streets. Pease then turned his attention to building up a rural, small-town presence in the province. Here the competition was stiff and often ugly. The bank's aggressive reputation usually preceded it. A branch opened in Arthur, outside Toronto, in 1906 ran headlong into determined opposition from the established Traders Bank branch. Hostilities broke out when a Traders teller began defacing the newcomer's notes, while his manager invited wavering customers into a local hotel and "after partaking of refreshments advanced the following arguments, we two go to the same church, we are hail fellows well met, and a long harangue of that kind." Pease's complaint about such tactics brought an apology from the Traders head office in Toronto for such "boyish nonsense."[52] However, in reality, there was only enough business in such small towns for one bank. Three years later, Pease would take over the Traders and close its Arthur branch. Similarly, branches were thrown open along Ontario's mining frontier. In 1906, W. A. Wheaton was despatched to the silver-boom town of Cobalt, where he nailed a board across two stumps and did business with cash stuffed in one pocket and a revolver in the other.[53] By 1908, the bank had twenty-five Ontario branches.

The Prairies represented the last frontier of Canadian banking. With the creation of the provinces of Alberta and Saskatchewan in 1905 and a growing tide of immigrants, eastern bankers from Montreal and Toronto flooded onto the western plains. The construction of two new transcontinental railways largely dictated banking's advance, with branches sprouting up at the "end of steel." From the outset, the West created special demands on banking. Unlike British Columbia with its instant mineral wealth, the Prairies would be capital-dependent from the outset. A bank loan was as necessary for start-up farming as was seed. Like fishing in the east, farming also exerted peculiar seasonal pressures on the financial system. Loan demand peaked in the spring, and demand for currency to buy and move the crop peaked in the fall.

# ROYAL BANK OF CANADA:
## BRANCHES, 1909

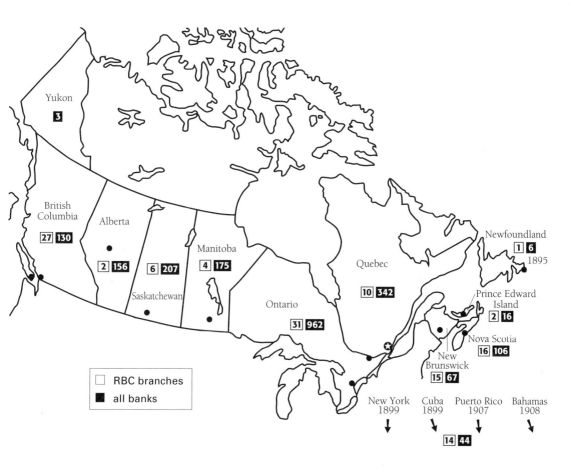

Yukon
**3**

British Columbia
**27** **130**

Alberta
**2** **156**

Saskatchewan
**6** **207**

Manitoba
**4** **175**

Quebec
**10** **342**

Ontario
**31** **962**

Newfoundland
**1** **6**
1895

Prince Edward Island
**2** **16**

Nova Scotia
**16** **106**

New Brunswick
**15** **67**

☐ RBC branches
■ all banks

New York
1899

Cuba
1899

Puerto Rico
1907

Bahamas
1908

**14** **44**

| Figures for end of 1909 | | |
|---|---|---|
| | **RBC** | **All Canadian banks** |
| Canada | 113 | 2,164 |
| Newfoundland | 1 | 6 |
| New York | 1 | 44 |
| Caribbean | 13 | |
| **Total** | **128** | **2,214** |

To accommodate the autumn surge in circulation, the Bank Act was amended in 1908 – after consultation with the CBA – to allow banks to increase note circulation in "crop-moving" season to 115 per cent of their capital base. Once again, the Canadian banking system had shown its malleability. Western towns clamoured for the opening of a bank branch on their main street and farmers bet their fledgling homesteads on the ability of rising grain prices to service their debts.[54] Pease did not join the headlong rush onto the Prairies; he lacked the manpower and capital resources to plunge westwards. Branches were none the less opened at strategic points such as Winnipeg in 1906 and Regina and Calgary in 1907. By 1908, the bank had a branch in every provincial capital.

Turn-of-the-century expansion had attenuated the Merchants' Bank in both style and management. By 1908, it had 93 branches and a staff of over 800. Although there was a distinct Maritime flavour to its corporate culture – Nova Scotia "lads" pervaded the branch system – Halifax was becoming less pivotal to the system's functioning. Pease was the dynamic force in the bank and he resided in Montreal. His letters in the late 1890s betray an increasing annoyance with the bothersome trips up the Intercolonial to inform and cajole the Halifax directors. David Duncan, who as cashier was nominally "in charge" of the bank, was aging and in poor health. Kenny had retreated from Ottawa politics; he lost by twelve votes in a bid for re-election in the 1900 federal election. Impatient with the *status quo*, Pease agitated for and got a change. Shareholders were informed at the annual meeting in February 1899 that the head office was to be "reorganized." Duncan and Pease were to become joint general managers of the bank; the quaint Scottish title of cashier was retired. Duncan would oversee the business of head office and the Maritime branches; Pease would have sway over the western and Montreal branches, as well as the growing Cuban business. William Torrance, a Pease man, would become superintendent of branches. Duncan's reduced grip on control was frail; he was to retire at the end of the year – on a $4,000 pension – after which Pease would reign supreme as general manager.

To consolidate his gain, Pease immediately "suggested" to the board that the addition of three or four Montreal directors be considered to act as an advisory committee. Pease was empowered to consult Hosmer on the matter. To bolster his forces in Montreal, Pease then won approval to hire D. M. Stewart away from the Commerce to serve as Montreal inspector.[55] Attesting to this new authority, rumours swirled through the financial press through the summer that Pease was being wooed by an American syndicate to head a new bank in London, the American Bank of London. Pease even boldly took the proposition to the Merchants' board. Nothing came of the proposal except that it enhanced Pease's image as a forceful, "progressive" banker.[56] His power now assured, Pease moved from structure to style. It is clear that Pease and the Montreal staff found the bank's name with its distinct regional affiliation a burden. With branches now as widespread as Victoria and Havana, the bank's apparent regional identity clashed with its growing national and international aspirations. Pease knew that, with a board dominated by Halifax "nationalists" and a shareholders' list heavy with old Nova Scotia names, any consideration of a name change would have to be broached with the utmost delicacy. In this decisive moment, T. E. Kenny did not desert either the national perspective he had adopted in the 1870s nor the man he had hired in 1883 as bank accountant; the bank's name would change. It was, Pease would later recall, "a question with him of dividends versus sentiment."[57]

Two days before the end of the century, the board decided to instruct its solicitor "to take the necessary steps to change the name

*The Royal-Union Bank of Canada Hockey Team, 1901. The Bank Hockey League in Montreal provided semi-professional hockey which was avidly watched by large crowds.*
*As two smaller "out-of-town" banks, the Royal and Union combined their athletic juniors in a single team. In March 1901 – just two months after changing its name to Royal – the bank's team won the league championship, defeating the Bank of Montreal, 3-2.*

*D.M. Stewart in 1906, photographed by the Notman studio in Montreal.*

of the Bank to The Royal Bank of Canada." Newspaper notices announced the board's intention of altering the act of incorporation, which caused a "great deal of adverse criticism in the Maritime Provinces."[58] At the annual meeting on February 14, 1900, it fell to Kenny, long practised in the art of persuasive speechmaking, to convince the shareholders of the wisdom of the name change. With forty-two branches scattered across the continent, the bank's "changed circumstances" demanded "a title distinctive and comprehensive." There was also the practical issue of avoiding confusion with the Merchants Bank of Canada. To clinch the matter, the resolution to change the by-law was placed before the meeting by director Michael Dwyer, a stalwart Haligonian merchant, and as a gesture of appeasement, the steamship motif was retained on the corporate seal. Approval secured, the solicitors obtained parliamentary sanction and, on January 2, 1901, sign-painters and stationers across the country went to work introducing Canadians to The Royal Bank of Canada.* Although nobody publicly declared as much, the Royal was now a Montreal bank. In private correspondence, bank officers acknowledged that the head office was now only "nominally" in Halifax and "that the management itself will likely emanate from Montreal."[59]

At this moment of ascendancy, Pease's strategy in Montreal faltered – and faltered badly. For years after, Royal Bankers would shudder at the mention of what in the autumn of 1900 became known as the Cold Storage Scandal. For die-hard Halifax bankers, it seemed to confirm the folly of abandoning the security of Halifax harbour; for Pease and his cohorts it instilled a sense of greater caution and due procedure.

Kenny made much of banking's "changed circumstances" in justifying the adoption of a new name. The same justification was increasingly true of the underpinnings of Canadian banking; the Cold Storage Scandal was the product of the fact that old banking methods no longer fitted new banking circumstances in an increasingly urbanized and commercialized economy. Since early in the nineteenth century, the financing of Canadian trade had hinged on the taking of warehouse receipts and bills of lading as surety for short-term loans. Such receipts and bills provided the lender with proof that goods had been received for shipment and for eventual consumption and could therefore act as collateral. Enshrined in legislation as early as 1859, the use of warehouse receipts had received its widest interpretation in the 1890 Bank Act. By the turn of the century, such receipts were routinely accepted by banks for transactions well beyond simple commodity movements.[60] Raw materials for industrial manufacture were, for instance, now secured by warehouse receipts for the goods in question. What had changed, however, was the volume and

(continued on p. 80)

---

* There is no documentary record of the choice of the word "Royal." It can be safely suggested that the choice was inspired by the much-respected model of the Royal Bank of Scotland and the prevalent Canadian infatuation with things imperial. Queen Victoria's long reign had imbued the word "royal" with deep emotional appeal. Such emotions flowed powerfully in Halifax. Pease also undoubtedly felt that, since the bank had just opened in New York and Havana, the Royal title would, as New York agent Stephen Voorhees later recalled, "clearly express the international character of our institution."

# ARMED AND DANGEROUS

## Bank Robbers and Bank Managers

JUST AFTER NOON ON MARCH 26, 1887, a stranger appeared in the Merchants' Antigonish branch and asked for a private interview with Robert Currie, the junior. Currie had no sooner closed the door than the stranger pulled a pistol and shot him in the head. A "death struggle" ensued, during which Currie was shot again in the side. By the time a posse of local merchants responded to the alarm, Currie had subdued the robber. A belt of fifty cartridges was found around the waist of the man. No money was lost, and Currie lived. The bank's directors in Halifax voted Currie a $100 raise and a gold watch and praised him for "his gallant defence of the valuables of the Bank."

In small-town, nineteenth-century Canada, a bank hold-up was the most traumatic of events. Canadians did not see the local bank as an inanimate institution; it was their bank. They had usually petitioned to have it open on their main street. It contained their money and was their financial lifeline to the outside world. Robbers invariably came from beyond the familiar bounds of the town and were spared little sympathy. Rough justice was dispensed on the spot. When the Union Bank of Canada branch (later taken over by the Royal) in New Hazelton, a railway construction town in the B.C. interior, was held up twice in 1914 by the same seven-man gang, the local citizenry, led by the Anglican minister with his Lee-Enfield rifle, took the law into its own hands. As the bandits left the bank, they were met by a hail of bullets. Three died. "All in all," the manager reported, "a really gory aftermath."

Banks armed themselves against robbery. Managers were issued revolvers – usually large-calibre Smith and Wessons – which they kept loaded in their desk drawers. Those with quarters above a branch often cut holes in the floor to allow them to fire at night intruders below. The revolvers were never an especially effective deterrent; in moments of high panic, managers frequently wounded themselves, not the crooks. However, they had their uses. One Prairie manager obliged his clients whenever they wanted an infirm animal despatched.

The late-nineteenth century saw more systematic attempts to foil robberies. Quality safes with time locks, sturdy tellers' cages, alarms, and Pinkerton agents were all employed to deter bandits. When hold-ups did occur, banks covered their losses with insurance from Montreal firms like Lukis, Stewart & Co. In the 1920s, the Canadian Bankers' Association introduced a centralized reward system for those who aided in the apprehension of robbers; from 1924 to 1948, $219,000 was paid out.

Urbanization and gasoline changed the nature of hold-ups. Cities provided crooks with greater anonymity, and gasoline made for faster getaways. In 1926, eight men in two cars snatched $42,000 from the Nanaimo branch, subsequently fleeing to the United States in a speedboat. The banks responded with the introduction of armoured cars; uniformed bank messengers, even

if armed, were too easy a target.

The courts meted out stiff justice to bank robbers who were apprehended; well into the twentieth century, long jail sentences were accompanied by twenty or thirty lashes. When a hold-up entailed the death of an employee or a policeman, the bank or the CBA made generous pension arrangements or donations to police benevolent funds. Banks have also introduced hold-up procedures for staff; employees are no longer encouraged to replicate Robert Currie's heroics. Deterrence and passivity are now the keywords. Discrete arrangements for the storage of cash have dramatically reduced the average loss during robberies; "white-collar" crime is now a far-more-insidious threat. The introduction of automated tellers in the 1970s meant that, for the first time, a bank "hold-up" could occur without putting a bank employee at risk. None the less, robberies – particularly in economic hard times – remain a fundamental concern.

*Aftermath of the New Hazelton shoot-out: armed citizens inspect a dead robber.*

complexity of such deals. Whereas a bank manager in, say, Lunenburg knew the "character" of those submitting receipts and could simply wander down to the wharf to inspect the fifty quintals of fish held against a loan, a city manager usually faced an unknown client and an unknown commodity. The possibilities for misrepresentation of the goods with a warehouse receipt were wide and tempting.

In hiring D. M. Stewart away from the Commerce in 1899, Pease knew that he had captured one of the brightest young stars of Canadian banking. A Bankers' Association essayist with an ambitious eye, Stewart quickly picked up on Pease's aggressive philosophy of developing a Montreal corporate clientele. Stewart had scored an impressive victory when Thomas Chisholm, the manager of the Montreal Cold Storage and Freezing Company, brought his business to the Merchants'. A huge refrigerated facility for the warehousing of butter and cheese prior to export, the Cold Storage lived on a generous float of credit, all based on warehouse receipts. Stewart was delighted to oblige. By the spring of 1900, however, William Torrance in Halifax became anxious over the bank's commitment to Chisholm. "The reserves are not as strong as I expected or Mr. Stewart led me to believe they would appear at his end," he warned Pease.[61] Chisholm, he had heard on the street, was "a very clever talker," who was heavily involved in gold-mining speculation. Within weeks, huge cracks began appearing in the Cold Storage account. Chisholm had succeeded in passing off fraudulent warehouse receipts for massive amounts of non-existent cheese in exchange for credit from the Merchants' Banks of Halifax and Canada and the Ontario Bank. After years of building up the Merchants' as a bold but safe new bank on the Montreal scene, Pease learned that Stewart's recklessness and Chisholm's dishonesty had exposed the bank he now wished to call Royal to a potential loss of $600,000.

News of the Chisholm scandal reached Halifax by telegram. It created consternation. A young manager visiting head office recalled seeing President Kenny walking the halls "with tears streaming down his face," pouring out his fears to the Maritime "old guard."[62] Clumsy efforts were made to keep the news from junior staff and the Halifax press. Pease in Montreal was less flappable. Throughout the bank's expansion he had taken the precaution of procuring the best available legal counsel; names such as Tupper, Lougheed, Borden, Bennett, and Casgrain had or would advise the bank as it moved into new regions. In this moment of crisis, Pease turned to Zebulon A. Lash, Canada's leading authority on warehouse receipts and counsel to the Bankers' Association. When the Cold Storage Company collapsed and sought a winding-up order, Lash counselled the bank not to seek its pound of flesh from the carcass, but to sue the perpetrators of the fraud and then try to resuscitate the business. Legal proceedings were thus brought against Chisholm and his co-conspirator, a dairy company manager named McCullough. The case was called in October 1900. Lash was brought up from Toronto to coach a jittery Kenny before he appeared on the stand. Pease and Stewart also gave testimony. The Merchants' prospects were immensely improved when Chisholm took to his heels in the midst of the trial, headed, the *Monetary Times* speculated, for South America.[63]

In December, a jury awarded the case to the bank. Pease immediately turned his attention to refinancing the Cold Storage Company; old losses on the account were quietly made good by sales of holdings in American railway bonds. If the bank had looked like a dupe of fraud artists before the verdict, it now appeared the champion of probity. The *Monetary Times* scolded the bank for its "relaxed methods," but added that its decision to tackle the swindlers and not the company "was a wise one for the community."[64] D. M. Stewart, Pease's star pupil, enjoyed no such rehabilitation in his colleagues' eyes. The next June he resigned from the bank and made it known that he would lend his talents to a new Toronto bank, the Sovereign. "He is clever in a way," Torrance noted, "but his judgement in regard to loans is not always sound. He is too optimistic."[65]

The Cold Storage crisis shattered the aging Kenny's executive will and, paradoxically, left Pease unchallenged to remake the bank entirely along Montreal lines. Although Kenny was the bank's largest shareholder, with over 1,200 shares, there was no likelihood of a family succession to the presidency. Only one Kenny son had entered the bank, and he had not progressed in the ranks. Nor were there any other promising Halifax candidates. The year 1900 had seen the death of Michael Dwyer and H. H. Fuller, two venerable Halifax directors. Neither was replaced, and at the 1901 annual meeting the board was actually reduced in size from seven to five members. Although he had broached the idea of introducing Montreal, Vancouver, and even Havana directors to the board, Pease in 1901 was content to see the matter "deferred." Why did Pease hesitate at this crucial juncture? The answer would seem to lie in the fact that he had not as yet found the kind of man he wanted to sit at the head of the board. For the Royal to capitalize on the momentum it had accumulated in the late-nineteenth century, Pease needed a president who would reinforce its new *national* status, a man who preferably came with a dynamic business personality and reputation. Such a man might work with him as the bank sought to consolidate its gains and expand in the Laurier boom. As early as 1898, Pease had begun to "groom" two men for Kenny's

*Herbert Holt in the 1890s*

job. The trouble had been that neither much wanted the honour.

Charley Hosmer was Pease's first pick. He possessed exactly the kind of "new wealth" credentials that a "new" bank like the Royal needed. In 1898, Pease began, with Halifax's knowledge, to entice Hosmer to join the Merchants board.[66] Hosmer held Merchants' shares, proffered it advice on strategy, and kept an account with it. None the less, his loyalties lay elsewhere, and in 1899 he joined the board of the Merchants Bank of Canada and nine years later that of the Bank of Montreal, the CPR's banker. "This is a sad blow to me," Pease wrote, "as I had counted so much on his assistance and support in our new departures."[67] Hosmer would continue to play an influential role in the shadows, but his name never moved further than the shareholders' list.

Hosmer led Pease to his second candidate, the shyer-but-no-less-accomplished Herbert S. Holt, an Irish-born railway contractor who had made a name and sizeable fortune helping to build the CPR. Holt had taken up residence in Montreal in 1892 and had gradually turned his talents to industrial promotion and the consolidation of Montreal's public utilities. His boldest stroke came at the turn of the century, when he moulded three local utilities into the Montreal Light, Heat and Power Company, which held an incipient monopoly over the city's gas and electric needs.[68] From an early date, Pease had befriended Holt, arranging bank loans for him and joining him in various investments. In 1897, for instance, Holt had joined Hosmer and Pease in syndicating Halifax Heat and Light bonds.[69] From Pease's perspective, Holt was cut from the same cloth as Hosmer. He was not alone in thinking so.

In 1901, Holt surprised the Montreal financial community by announcing that he had accepted the presidency of the new Toronto-based bank, the Sovereign. There was a galling double irony for Pease in the news. The Sovereign was the product of the same syndicate, spearheaded by J. P. Morgan in New York, that had earlier unsuccessfully approached Pease with an offer to join the American Bank of London. The Sovereign had also captured Pease's old protégé D. M. Stewart as its general manager. Holt gave the Sovereign just the dynamic image that Pease craved for the Royal and, with Stewart at the operational helm, the new bank quickly made a name for itself as an aggressive force in Canadian banking. It combined a rapid branch expansion with an easy credit policy; many commented on its "American" style of operation. Holt's role in the bank was shadowy; Stewart cut the bank's bold image. Suddenly, in December 1904, Holt quit the Sovereign's presidency and board. There could be simple explanations for this: Holt's businesses were predominantly in Montreal, while the Sovereign was Ontario-centred. It is worth noting, however, that while Holt was at the Sovereign, Pease left an opening at the Royal. No directors were appointed, and no other succession candidates were sought. Neither did Holt sell his holding of 350 Royal shares. Did Pease poison Holt on the Sovereign by feeding him damaging evidence of Stewart's Cold Storage adventures? The records are silent.

What is clear is that, within a month and a half, Pease had won shareholder consent to increase the Royal board to seven members and that two of those members were to be Montrealers who would constitute a committee of the board.[70] On February 8, 1905, Herbert Holt joined the Royal's board, together with local manufacturer James Redmond. Within a week, Holt was installed as chairman of the

Montreal committee, meeting every Tuesday and Friday to approve the bulk of the bank's credits. The committee's secretary was, predictably, Edson Pease. Thus, three non-Haligonians now effectively directed the bank's affairs; the Halifax board was relegated to approving Maritime loans alone. A year later, Frederick W. Thompson, Hosmer's partner in the 1902 Ogilvie Flour take-over, joined the board. Both Redmond and Thompson came to the bank through Pease, not Holt. In later years, when asked to comment on Holt's arrival at the Royal in 1905, senior bank employees invariably used the phrase "invitation" to describe the event.[71]

The Montreal committee of the board immediately became the pulse of the Royal. While Halifax made *pro forma* decisions on dividends, Holt and Pease cleared loans for a range of undertakings, from Cuban sugar operations to Mackenzie and Mann's new transcontinental railway, the Canadian Northern. The captains of Canadian industry appeared in its offices: Max Aitken (later Lord Beaverbrook), an aggressive young Maritimer, borrowed to support his ascendancy in the securities market. Sir William Van Horne relied on the New York agency to finance his Cuban railway ventures. Even federal finance minister William Fielding carried personal loans with the bank. The Royal became a bank to be watched; rumours spread along St. James Street that the Royal would take over the Ontario Bank and the Merchants Bank of Canada.[72] Relations with the Bank of Montreal mellowed; in 1902 a Montreal financier, William Stavert, had even tried to amalgamate the two banks.[73] Now the two shared large loan underwritings. Montreal society began to take note of Royal bankers; in 1898 Pease had commissioned city architect Edward Maxwell to build him a country home on the slopes of Mt. Bruno to the south of Montreal, where Pease was soon active developing a prestigious golf course. Early in 1906 the bank itself turned to American architect H. C. Stone with a commission for a new Montreal branch. A site was obtained at 147 St. James, just doors down the street from the Bank of Montreal, and no expense was spared on the building. When opened in 1908, its columns were adorned with four buxom classical statues depicting transportation, fishery, industry, and agriculture. They soon became known as the "giants of St. James Street."

The bold, new St. James building was intended to be more than a branch. Few were surprised when at the bank's annual meeting on February 14, 1907, a weary Thomas Kenny proposed a by-law change to the shareholders assembled in Halifax. The directors were empowered "to take whatever steps necessary to move head office to Montreal." The board was increased to twelve – including for the first time Pease and regional representatives from Winnipeg and Saint

*"The giants of St. James Street"*: The façade of 147 St. James Street.
Opened in 1908 as the Royal's first Montreal Head Office, the building was dominated by
statues representing agriculture, transportation, fisheries, and industry.
St. James Street is now rue St. Jacques, and 147, sold by the Royal in 1928, has been
redeveloped as an office-and-hotel complex. The façade remains.

John. Kenny and Pease arranged for A. K. Maclean, a veteran Liberal from Lunenburg and head of the "Bluenose caucus," to introduce a private member's bill in Ottawa sanctioning the shift. Despite sporadic opposition from Maritime loyalists,[74] the bill passed in June, and in July the Montreal committee of the board became the full board.

Thomas Kenny never presided over the board in Montreal. On April 28, he was stricken, probably by a stroke, while staying in Montreal's Viger Hotel. When his condition failed to improve, he was taken to Halifax on the private car of Thomas Shaughnessy of the CPR. There he lingered in ill health until, on October 26, 1908, he died. Later the same day, Kenny's old foes, the Laurier Grits, swept to another land-slide victory at the polls. Kenny's estate included 1,302 Royal Bank shares worth $240,000. Canada, the newspapers noted, had lost "the dean of Canadian bank presidents." The directors in Montreal passed a resolution that portrayed Kenny in quintessential Canadian terms: he had "breadth of view tempered by caution." At the funeral, Pease led the entire Royal Bank Halifax staff to Holy Cross Cemetery, where Kenny now joined his father, Edward Kenny, Sr., John Tobin, Michael Dwyer, and James Duffus.

With no fanfare, Herbert Holt assumed the presidency of the Royal Bank on November 16. Edson Pease was elected vice-president. Holt made $5,000 as president, and Pease $25,000 as general manager. Although Holt held 550 Royal shares and Pease 300, Pease was clearly the dominant force in the bank's affairs. Holt had an array of other business affairs, while Pease's life was consumed by the bank. Together they controlled an institution that was reaching its limits. The bank had sustained its spurt of growth since coming to Montreal by stretch-ing its manpower, its management, and its capital base to the break-ing point. Now, in 1908, there were worrisome signs of fatigue and instability in the ranks, and in those of Canadian banking as a whole. The more Pease pondered the future, the more he became convinced that a new strategy of corporate growth was in order. That strategy came to be expressed in one word: amalgamation.

# 1880-1930

# Working for the Bank

## "His Good and Faithful Behaviour"

H E WAS EIGHTEEN YEARS OLD, A LONG WAY FROM HOME AND VERY MUCH in love. It was also his first job. Hired by the Merchants' Bank of Halifax in Victoria at an annual salary of $200, Harold Penn Wilson had learned quickly that his first assignment would be as a junior at a newly opened branch in the province's northern interior. "I'm going up to Lake Bennett where a branch of the bank is being opened," he wrote his sweetheart, Mattie, from a Vancouver hotel room in February 1899, "and it must be kept secret until it's started so don't tell anybody." Sensing the distance growing between them, he added: "Send me that lock of hair in your next letter please." The next morning, Wilson joined James Fulton, his manager-to-be, and together they sailed north for Skagway, Alaska.

Wilson found Skagway locked in the grip of winter; he reported seeing men with frozen limbs being invalided onto their steamer as they disembarked. Three days later, Fulton and Wilson headed inland. They carried the bank's cash and documents in satchels and loaded revolvers in their pockets. A seven-hour train ride up White Pass was followed by three and a half hours of tough slogging on horseback down the other side. It was petrifyingly cold; "be sure the kisses are good and warm ones," he wrote Mattie, "or they'll freeze before they arrive." Bennett Lake was no paradise. Wilson found it "a dreary hole," a makeshift gold-rush town lacking in civility. Long hours in the bank were followed by the tedium of rooming-house life. To entertain himself, Wilson shot grouse with the bank revolver. In the spring, he fished. When a gentleman's club opened, he and his manager joined and "lived like princes": napkins and "nice people" had finally come to

*Harold Wilson (left) and James Fulton on the doorstep of their Bennett Lake branch in 1899.
Note the gold weighing scale in the window. Wilson: "The shack we are in at present and
where I sleep is so full of cracks you can hear the wind whistling through them."*

the frontier. The Merchants' branch was still, however, a "shack...so full of cracks you can hear the wind whistling through them." When Mattie's letters became infrequent, Wilson grew despondent. Although he was losing his sweetheart, he *was* becoming a banker. We have his photograph, captured on a spring day in March 1899, standing outside the branch. Fulton, a seasoned ten-year veteran, stands confidently on the doorstep, while Wilson, his junior, stares forlornly at the camera. Despite his emotions, Wilson already appears the banker: a dark suit, a tie, and a watch fob announce that he has become a novice in the growing ranks of Canada's turn-of-the-century professional class.[1]

Harold Wilson never married Mattie. Even if her affections had not turned elsewhere, Harold's masters at the Merchants' head office in Halifax did not allow the young males in their employ to marry until their salary reached $1,000. Above all else, the directors of the bank expected "good and faithful behaviour" from their employees; they had even written the expectation into their 1869 charter. The early years of banking demanded that career be placed ahead of affairs of the heart. Halifax rewarded Wilson's service at Bennett Lake with a $300 raise in July 1899. In a sense, he had married the bank. We last catch sight of him in the staff ledger in 1905, earning $900 a year as an accountant in Vancouver, after stints in Atlin, Washington State, and Victoria. James Fulton was by then a Royal Bank accountant in Santiago, Cuba. Few Canadians had ever seen far-flung careers like these. Thousands of "bank boys" would follow in their footsteps. "A bank officer, if loyal and wise," Edson Pease once observed, "goes where he is told to go. He does not choose his own position. If he did he would not get very far. All that we need to know is that he is a valuable officer, and advancement is sure to follow."[2]

From 1880 to 1930, the bank's staff grew from a meagre handful of twenty-five managers and clerks, spread thinly through the Maritimes, to 8,784 Royal Bankers scattered across three continents. Twelve "agencies" became 941 branches in these same years. In 1880, the staff thought of themselves as Maritimers, employed by a fledgling financial institution with a federal charter but no national exposure. Fifty years later, they saw themselves as Canadians and Royal Bankers. Some saw themselves as Cubans and Royal Bankers, or Puerto Ricans or Spaniards or Brazilians; over 2,500 members of staff, many of them non-Canadians, served beyond Canada's shores. What bonded them all together was a strong, homogeneous culture, which had been developed in them by unbendingly uniform training and which was displayed in a set of shared values and ambitions. If the Bank Act opened the way to a national bank system in Canada, the corporate culture that was bred in thousands of young bank employees fostered this wide national perspective. While enduring streams of Maritime nostalgia flowed through the bank, particularly for the Nova Scotia villages that had provided so much of its manpower, by the turn of the century the mental outlook of the organization was unshakeably national. When Stephen Leacock, in *Sunshine Sketches of a Little Town*, gave us Peter Pupkin, the teller of the Exchange Bank in Mariposa, he reminded us that, although Pupkin came from "somewhere down in the Maritime Provinces," he was in the eyes of the local citizenry a representative of a mobile, urban professional class. Pupkin might have found similar national prospects in the late-nineteenth century with the CPR, the Mounties, or possibly in religious ministry, but it was the banks that first moved large numbers of Canadians around within one institutional framework. That the banks were also able to place young Canadian Pupkins as far afield as Santiago, Cuba, and Lima, Peru, spoke even more convincingly of this new organizational ethos of mobility and nationality.[3]

The pervasiveness of Royal Bank culture by 1930 was widely evident; the pages of the *Royal Bank Magazine*, correspondence between branches and head office, the very look of bank employees as they stare out from their cages and ledger tables in photographs, all speak of a remarkably durable set of values and attitudes. The banker's world was Anglo, male, and predominantly Protestant. Catholics were not ostracized; T. E. Kenny was devoutly Catholic. Similarly, French-Canadians, often non-Quebec francophones from Cape Breton, New Brunswick, Ontario, and Manitoba, found employment in the bank's Quebec branches and in French-speaking international operations such as Guadeloupe. The Protestants were, none the less, in the ascendancy. Bankers also saw themselves as "British," and in doing so subscribed to an Anglo-imperialist code which would send them to the trenches of Europe in the First World War, and to the Conservative Party in politics. Canadian bankers were rural in origin and urban in aspiration. Bank officers were small-town boys who had "done well"; in the bank's entire history only one chief executive of the bank has *not* called a small town home.* Their careers embodied mobility, both geographic and social. Rhymed *The Grip* in 1892, "We bankers' clerks of Canada, / Are envied all throughout the land, / We are the true *jeunesse doree*, / And high in ladies' favor stand."

Wherever bankers established their homes, they cultivated middle-class respectability. After work, bankers disported themselves in manly ways; they took to the golf links, the curling rink, and the football field with near fanaticism. They became great "joiners": church groups, community clubs, and fraternal organizations were studded with bankers. They seemed charter members in the urban middle-class, fixed in attitude, yet mobile in career.

From their employers' point of view, this uniform bank culture produced a reliable, standardized bank employee whose loyalty to the organization was assured, after an initial period of testing and low pay was endured. Once trained, a Canadian "bank boy" could be despatched to the far corners of the earth, and head office could be assured of a favourable result. In return for such loyalty, the directors of the bank provided their employees with job security, reasonable remuneration, and a sense that, in adversity or retirement, their needs would be taken care of by their employer. Pensions, sick leave, and relocation allowances were provided with benevolent paternalism.

---

* The one exception, Rowland Frazee, born in Halifax in 1921, was city-born only because his banker father had been posted to Dartmouth; he would spend his youth in small towns as his father moved from one rural branch to another. The bank's present CEO, Allan Taylor, was born in Prince Albert, Saskatchewan, in 1932.

*"Bank boys" of the Charlottetown branch, 1928*

In this environment, bank employees were reminded that what bound them together was their quasi-professional status and their loyalty to their employer; unionization has never made an inroad into Canadian banking for both practical and emotional reasons. However boastful it might sound, there was ample truth in management's annual salute to the bank's rank and file. "The history of the progress of the Royal Bank of Canada," General Manager Sydney Dobson noted in his 1935 New Year's message, "is the story of initiative, staunch loyalty and co-operation of the members of the staff."[4] When Dobson – a Cape Breton boy who rowed across Sydney harbour every morning to work as a bank junior in 1900 – became president of the bank in 1946, the Canadian Press saluted him with the headline: "$100-a-year bank clerk now in president's chair."[5]

By the late 1930s, the culture that had propelled the bank so power-fully through its first seventy-five years was beginning to lose its potency. Always closely bound by its Anglo, male outlook, the bank's corporate culture found itself increasingly out of kilter with the ethos of a society that was now obliged to acknowledge significant ambitions elsewhere in Canadian society. A Canada in which women and a swelling multicultural population began to make their ambitions known announced the twilight of the old bank culture. It did not fade

*Bluenose bankers: Since 1864, six of the bank's eleven chief executives have been Nova Scotians. Maritime "boys" pervaded the Canadian banking system well into the twentieth century. Sydney Dobson (above, standing centre), a Cape Breton native who climbed to the bank's presidency in the late 1940s, returned home every summer for a cruise on his yacht,* The Eskasoni.

overnight, however, a testament to its strength and the devotion of the males who inhabited it. What then was at the heart of this golden age of banking? Who were Canada's "bank boys"? What kept them behind their wickets?

If there was a blueprint for the staffing of Canadian banks in the late-nineteenth century, it was drawn up in Scotland. Stimulated by the Industrial Revolution, Scottish bankers began displaying "a truly remarkable degree of banking initiative" in the early-nineteenth century, initiative aimed at creating a banking system that could move money to where industry and trade required it. By 1810, Scottish merchants had introduced the joint-stock bank, an institution which promoted stability by spreading ownership and branch coverage at the same time.[6] Scottish banking companies succeeded in introducing the circulation of uniform notes throughout Scotland, and in mobilizing savings and lending on a national basis. It was by no means an unblemished evolution; periodic bank failures and opposition from the established public banks in Glasgow and Edinburgh impeded the advance. The trend, however, was toward stability, induced by expansion. By the 1850s, Scottish regional banking entered a period of consolidation built upon legislative reform and upon the emergence of common procedures arrived at as a result of consensus between bankers. The result was a triumph of Scottish pragmatism. Names such as the Bank of Scotland, the Royal Bank of Scotland, and the Union Bank of Scotland became synonymous with stable, progressive banking. By the end of the century, the leading historian of Scottish banking has concluded that the "major Scottish banks were now so large, and under such strict management, and perhaps so careful, that none was ever threatened with liquidity problems."[7]

Scotland's branch-banking system rested on the perfection of standardized procedures and staffing. There could be nothing capricious about the taking and lending of money. Scottish banks thus introduced many innovations in the interests of stability and dependability. Clearing houses, overdrafts, limited liability for shareholders, and internal inspection all originated in Scottish banks. The central

## THE STRUCTURE OF
## THE MERCHANTS' BANK OF HALIFAX: c.1890

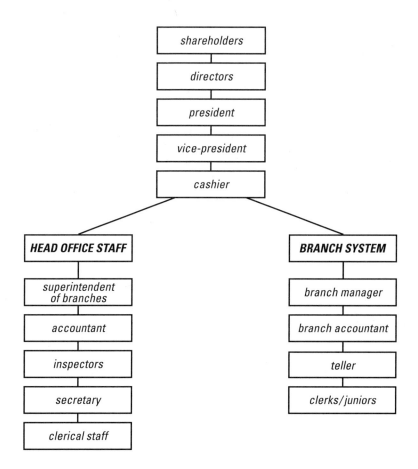

*Twenty-one-year-old James Muir, freshly arrived from Scotland in 1912, sits in his Moose Jaw rooming house shortly after joining the Royal. Muir epitomized the notion that hard work and Scottish methods lay at the heart of Canadian banking.*

connecting point was the bank head office. As branches spread out from Glasgow and Edinburgh, banks first sensed the difficulty of balancing the imperatives of "staff" and "line." Conformity with head-office procedure had to be ensured without extinguishing branch initiative. To achieve this, Scottish bankers became sticklers for on-the-job training and strictly defined job descriptions and hierarchies.

At the pinnacle of Scottish banking was the general manager. Once quaintly labelled a cashier,* the general manager emerged in the late-nineteenth century as a kind of "grandee" or "mandarin," the chief executive and strategist of the bank. Nominally responsible to a chairman and board of directors, the general manager was "virtually all-powerful within his bank, with the same kind of authority over his crew as the captain of a ship, for the rank-and-file employees had no trade union or organization of any kind."[8] Under the general manager, banks were organizationally segregated into a small head-office staff, comprised of a corporate secretary, an accountant, and a pool of clerk trainees, with a branch system of managers, tellers, and clerks, overseen by a supervisor of branches. Scottish bank clerks led a dismal life, enduring low pay, little prestige, and stiff discipline, all in the interest of job security and later advancement. The entire apprenticeship experience in Scottish banking was intended to build character – accuracy, probity, and loyalty being the key attributes of a tenured bank officer.

It was exactly these attitudes and experiences that young Scottish bankers like David H. Duncan, who had worked for the Bank of Scotland in the 1860s, brought with them when they emigrated to the new world. Well into the twentieth century, Canada imported Scottish bank clerks in the belief that they contained the seeds of "the sternest frugality and industry."[9] They also came as well-trained practitioners of the Scottish branch-banking system that seemed so ideally suited to Canada's vast expanses. As a consequence, Canadian banking is shot through with nostalgia for its Scottish connection. Like most nostalgia, this tends to romanticization, elevating the values of hard work and ambition while minimizing the mundane aspects of Scottish bank employment. James Muir, a craggy Scot who stepped off the boat in 1912 to a job at the Moose Jaw branch of the Royal, habitually harkened back to his Scottish origins. A fifteen-year-old lad "guid at tottin' up figures," Muir left high school at 1:00 p.m. one afternoon in 1907 and joined the Commercial Bank of Scotland an hour later as a clerk. Fifty-three years later, he died, president of Canada's largest bank.[10]

---

* Even today, the second-most-senior executive in the Bank of Scotland is called the chief cashier.

Immigration was not the only transmitter of Scottish banking practice. Would-be Canadian bankers devoured libraries of bank manuals published in the British Isles. This was a rich, practical literature, often written in epistolary form, full of moralistic axioms and heavy with "lessons" of prudent banking. The undisputed best-seller was George Rae's *The Country Banker: His Clients, Cares, and Work*, first published in 1850 under the pen name Thomas Bullion. "Bullion on banking" acquired almost biblical authority; a copy sat in the bookshelf of every Canadian bank manager's office. Scottish-born, Rae had become the general manager of the North and South Wales Bank in 1845 at the extraordinarily young age of twenty-eight. Aware of the danger of writing about banking in "dry and uninteresting details," Rae determined to convey the knack of canny banking in an appealing style. "Never," he wrote of the tricky task of assessing personal credit, "trust to a man's means or safety as seen through the telescope of rumour; you will find his truer diameter, as a rule, by reversing the glass."[11] Similarly popular was the work of English banker James Gilbart, whose *History, Principles and Practice of Banking* appeared in 1859. A friend of nineteenth-century reformers Edwin Chadwick and J. S. Mill, Gilbart presented banking in scientific, professional terms, accessible to members of the emerging middle class.

Rae and Gilbart attracted Canadian apostles. Most prominent among them was Homer Eckardt, a former Merchants Bank of Canada employee who published prolifically through the turn of the century for a burgeoning army of young bank recruits. "The author," he wrote in his 1913 *Manual of Canadian Banking*, "hopes that what he has written will help his fellow bank men climb the ladder." A bank was "a great training school," where "raw material is being taken in all the time and moulded into the desired shape, the refuse being thrown away." Eckardt's work echoed Scottish precedent; the general manager was "practically despotic" in his authority.[12] Eckardt's work was shadowed by the writing of Gordon Tait, who joined the Merchants' Bank of Halifax in 1900 and for two decades acted as the bank's first theorist of Canadian banking practice. Tait's many contributions to the *Journal of the Canadian Bankers' Association* would bring to Canada the Gilbart tradition of banking as a science. He acknowledged that Canada's great distances strained the relationship between head office and far-flung branches; he would pioneer the use of the concept of "systems," by which he meant cutting away the "deadwood" and imposing a national organizational structure.[13]

But for President Kenny and his directors back in the 1870s, the term "systems" had absolutely no meaning. The staffing and organization of their small bank proceeded along chaotic, *ad hoc* lines.

Inadequate training, an imprecise definition of the relationship of agent to head office, and the absence of checks and balances in financial management left the bank open to abuses. More than anything else, the Maclean defalcation of 1882 jolted the directors into action. If the bank was ever to expand, it needed reliable and loyal staff, rigorously standardized to bank-wide criteria. This David Duncan and Edson Pease delivered over the next two decades. Duncan, a Highland boy trained by the Royal Bank of Scotland in the 1860s, introduced the Scottish tradition, and Pease, inducted into Canadian banking by the Commerce, moulded it to Canadian circumstances. By 1900, their joint effort had provided the Merchants' with a steady supply of reliable bank clerks, the indispensable foot soldiers in the bank's campaign of expansion. In doing so, they created a corporate culture marked by an astonishing degree of standardization in pay and procedure, tremendous mobility, and durable loyalty. Charles Neill, the young Fredericton boy hired into this culture at $100 a year in 1889, later reflected on the purpose of the whole exercise by quoting Emerson: "When duty whispers low, Thou must, / The youth replies, I can."[14]

Standardization was the primary goal. In 1885, a book of *Rules and Regulations* was distributed throughout the bank. Employees were instructed to memorize the contents of the thin, psalter-like book; inspectors were told to quiz staff on the rules whenever they visited a branch. In time, the rule book would grow as the bank matured; by 1931 it was a bulky 170 pages, with companion volumes in French and Spanish. Between its covers, the hierarchy of duties and privileges of every bank officer was precisely defined; messengers, junior clerks, tellers, accountants, and managers could all position themselves in the bank's great chain. Duties great and small were laboriously spelled out, from balancing the ledgers and maintaining the "character book" of clients' creditworthiness to oiling the branch revolver. Hours of attendance – nine to four on weekdays and nine to two on Saturdays – were set; these were "bankers' hours," less onerous than work on the farm or in the factory and enviously regarded by the rest of society. Smoking was outlawed during business hours. The rules were laden with penalties: instant dismissal awaited any clerk accepting an IOU – or "kiting" – from another clerk. Verification and probity were of utmost importance: a daily "double check" was to be performed on the cash book. All cash-book vouchers had to be cancelled by sundering them with a "hammer and chisel." In true "country-banker" style, the rules concluded with a set of "hints to agents": bankers must not "allow amiability or weak desire to befriend a customer, to permit him to make a rash advance."[15]

# BANKERS IN MOTION: 1890-1940
## MOBILITY & THREE ROYAL BANKERS' CAREERS

**HAROLD EDWARD GIRVAN** b. 1881

| | |
|---|---|
| 1900 | Bathurst – junior |
| 1903 | Halifax – clerk |
| 1903 | Edmundston – clerk |
| 1904 | Camagüey, Cuba – teller |
| 1905 | Halifax – clerk* |
| 1905 | St. John – clerk |
| 1906 | Bathurst – accountant |
| 1906 | Winnipeg – accountant |
| 1906 | Plumas – manager |
| 1914 | Fort William – manager |
| 1922 | St. John – manager |
| 1940 | Retired |

*Doctor advises against return to Cuba*

**CHARLES EVERETT MACKENZIE** b. 1877

| | |
|---|---|
| 1892 | Pictou – clerk |
| 1899 | Truro – accountant |
| 1900 | Halifax – clerk |
| 1901 | Maitland – acting manager |
| 1902 | Sackville – acting manager |
| 1902 | Shubenacadie – acting manager |
| 1904 | Woodstock – manager |
| 1904 | Havana – manager |
| 1914 | Montreal – inspector |
| 1915 | New York – agent |
| 1919 | Barcelona – manager |
| 1921 | Rio de Janeiro – manager |
| 1922 | Cuba – supervisor |
| 1924 | Halifax – supervisor |
| 1940 | Retired |

**JAMES WILLIAM FULTON** b. 1867

| | |
|---|---|
| 1890 | Montreal – clerk |
| 1892 | Halifax – clerk |
| 1892 | Montreal – clerk |
| 1897 | Montreal – accountant |
| 1897 | Nanaimo – manager |
| 1897 | Bennett – manager |
| 1899 | Nanaimo – manager |
| 1901 | Montreal – accountant |
| 1904 | Santiago, Cuba – accountant |
| 1905 | Montreal – accountant |
| 1906 to 1909 | Peterborough – accountant<br>Burk's Falls – accountant<br>Porcupine – manager<br>Cobalt – manager<br>Quebec – manager<br>Rawdon – manager |
| 1909 | Montreal – manager |
| 1925 | Retired |

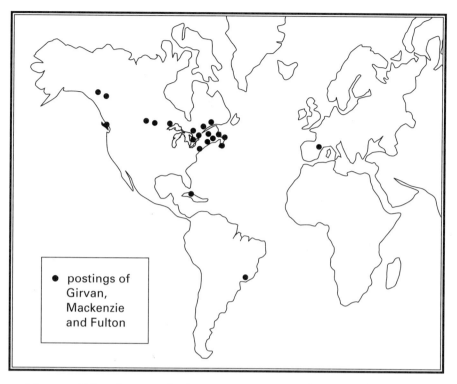

• postings of
Girvan,
Mackenzie
and Fulton

Most striking from today's perspective was the way the *Rules and Regulations* intruded into the bank employee's personal life. Managers were instructed to maintain a strict watch over the conduct of their clerks, both in and without the office. "Should it be found that an officer is involved in debt, or is engaged in speculations, or is dissipated in habits, he will be dismissed from the Bank's service," it stated. Marriage was seen as an impediment in the path of any ambitious young clerk and was summarily prohibited until an employee's salary reached $1,000 a year. Marriage encouraged a clerk to live in a manner "not becoming his position," and invariably led to debt, which in turn could lead to possible defalcation. Behind this paternalistic reasoning lay a more strategic objection: "An early marriage must retard the promotion of a clerk, as it prevents those frequent removals necessary for his proper training." Single men in the bank's employ were expected to live on the premises, frequently in small rooms above the branch or, in some primitive locales, downstairs in the bank itself. A junior posted to Erin, Ontario, in 1907 recalled acting as a human alarm by sleeping on a "folding bed which fitted snugly between the vault door and the teller's wire cage," with the bank revolver under his pillow.[16] Where accommodation was unavailable in the branch, juniors were farmed out to local rooming houses and given small living allowances.

99

Mobility was thus the fundamental determinant of a capable young banker's prospects with the bank. A junior could expect that, after a short stint of evaluation in the branch nearest his home town, he would be shipped out with little prior notice to a new branch, usually one closer to the frontier. Transfer orders were delivered with military arbitrariness; few questioned their fate. Bankers were expected to travel light, packing their clothes and little else. "Due economy" was to be exercised on the journey, the bank agreeing to pay for only one or two nights' hotel accommodation. The bank developed a uniform pay scale, so that bonuses could be used to differentiate responsibilities and performance. A basic clerk's salary in the 1880s and 1890s was $75 to $100 a year, regardless of location. Special allowances were paid for arduous postings, like Bennett Lake. As the bank pressed to develop its trade in the West and in Cuba in the new century, separate, more-generous pay scales were introduced for those accepting these distant assignments. A teller could, for instance, expect a handsome $300 increase on his $300 Maritime salary for relocating to, say, Nanaimo or Havana, although the ceiling on salary permitting marriage was raised to $1,200 in these areas. A return east or north brought a diminution in salary. Mobility had one other beneficial effect from the employers' perspective. It ensured that bank staff came to communities as strangers, free of emotional and personal bonds to the people they served. The prospect of imminent transfer minimized the temptation of marriage or local financial involvement that might lead to defalcation.

Management strove to condition its employees' behaviour and loyalty in a number of other ways. Guarantee funds, pensions, rudimentary training, and annual branch inspections were all introduced to ensure probity and improve efficiency. From the bank's inception, employees had been required to post bonds as a guarantee of honesty. Juniors were required to have their parents endorse such bonds until they reached the age of majority. In 1887, this process was systematized with the creation of an Officers' Guarantee Fund, for which monthly deductions were taken from juniors' pay. The fund indemnified the bank in the case of any "want of fidelity, mistake, negligence, or other misconduct" on the part of an employee. After an initial contribution by the bank of $10,000, an employee placed $\frac{1}{2}$ per cent of his annual salary into the fund until it reached $25,000, an amount that was raised to $50,000 in 1922.

The bank looked not only for mobility in its employees but also for longevity. With longevity came the need for pensions. At first, the directors dealt with the pension in an *ad hoc*, paternalistic fashion. Pensions were doled out at their discretion as circumstances dictated.

When the bank's Saint John manager drowned while fishing in 1904, the board voted his widow a monthly payment of $50 for seven years.[17] In 1895, a Superannuation Fund was established to acknowledge the "vigilance and fidelity" of bank officers. The directors voted to contribute up to $5,000 annually in light of "the necessity of having officers who will take an interest in the Bank and then encourage them to remain with us."[18] Not until 1909 was an actual Pension Fund established, into which employees paid 3 per cent of their annual salary. In 1935, the fund would acquire a separate legal identity when it obtained a federal charter, becoming only the second federally incorporated pension fund in Canada. Throughout these years, pensions were considered a perquisite of career officers and, as such, an exclusive male preserve. When women entered bank employment early in the new century, the perception that they were uninterested in a career meant their exclusion from pension rights. Similarly, the bank's trusted male messengers were excluded. These older men, frequently ex-military, served as liveried messengers and were well paid, but were not considered part of the bank's "family." They received *ex gratia* payments upon retirement. Messengers and women would not become contributing members of the pension plan until the 1960s.

Other benefits in the late-nineteenth century bore a similar stamp of paternalism; they were dispensed as a reward for meritorious service, not as a right of employment. Holidays were shoehorned into slack periods. Those willing to take winter leave were given three weeks, as opposed to summer's two. Young clerks relied on the humanity of their manager to get permission for an annual trip home; in many cases their work schedule or wages kept them away from home for years. As the bank expanded abroad, provision for paid home leave was unavoidable. Canadians stationed in Cuba had an extended trip home every second year, subsidized by the bank. Similarly, foreign service brought special dangers to body and health. In 1900, Cuban employees were given life insurance, paid for by the bank, with the bank as beneficiary. Head office would allocate benefits where they saw fit.[19] When bankers died abroad, they were brought home and buried at bank expense.

Uniformity and probity had two further guarantees: branch inspection and after-hours bank education. The inspector's annual visit was the most galvanizing event in the life of a branch. The inspector and his team of accountants always arrived unannounced around four o'clock, just after closing time. They came as emissaries of the superintendent of branches at head office and were all-powerful. Upon arrival, they sealed the safe, took over the ledgers, and set to work vetting every aspect of branch operation, from the state of its loans portfolio to the condition of the exterior paint. The manager's all-important bill case was scooped up and its telling contents – such as customers' promissory notes – examined for any irregularities. Through all this, the branch staff stood mutely by, unable to go home until the inspectors dismissed them or called upon their services. The vigour of this inquisition provided the banks with a ready response to outside critics who demanded government inspection of Canada's banks.[20] The inspectors were the master diagnosticians of the bank; they knew all "the worms in the woodwork," from the personal foibles of a manager to the strength of the local economy.[21] They identified promising young juniors and reported on their progress to head office; promotions, dismissals, and the very fate of a branch hung on their confidential reports.

Inspectors formed an élite corps within the bank. A stint of inspection became mandatory in the grooming of promising young Royal Bankers; Pease had prowled the Maritimes in the mid-1880s as an inspector, Charlie Neill did the same from Montreal in the 1900s, as did Graham Towers in the 1920s. Inspectors were respected, not liked. "An inspector is not usually a very successful manager," Pease once noted, "for the reason that he is so much given to measure with the square and act by the plumb line....We do not want a popular inspector."[22]

By the turn of the century, the ethos of on-the-job apprenticeship in Canadian banks was coming under pressure for change. As business in general became professionalized, the demand for autonomous training of business professionals grew. The first business schools emerged in the United States in the late-nineteenth century; in 1919, Queen's University in Canada began offering commerce degrees. Little provision was, however, made for the formal education of bankers. The *Monetary Times*, for instance, frequently drew attention to the lack of theoretical training in Canadian banks, urging clerks to better themselves by reading texts ranging from Adam Smith to banking manuals.[23] By 1909, even the Royal's own Gordon Tait complained that bank clerks "have no instructors, nor tutors nor schoolmasters...*nothing whatever* beyond severe and constant drilling with a view to regularity and uniformity in the carrying out of internal clerical routine."[24] Bank management met such criticism with ambivalence. On the one hand, the desperate need for new recruits made some measure of outside training enticing. On the other hand, academic-style training offended their deep-rooted intuition that banking was something one learned only as the result of long hours of practical experience. They believed that there was a "native judgement" in banking that no book could convey.[25] There was also the unspoken fear that external qualifications would boost junior bank employees' wage bargaining power and inter-bank job mobility.

By way of compromise, the banks turned to the Canadian Bankers' Association for educational assistance. In 1904, a Bank Clerks' Institute had been created in Montreal with management's blessing to provide after-hours courses for the large pool of aspiring young bankers in Canada's leading bank city. In Toronto, a Bankers' Educational Association pursued similar goals. Just before the First World War, the CBA began sponsoring courses on banking through Queen's and McGill universities. Evening lectures on banking were offered in Toronto and Montreal, drawing on the expertise of scholars such as Stephen Leacock at McGill and Toronto corporate lawyer J. D. Falconbridge.[26] Eventually, these initiatives solidified into a systematic program in which young bankers could attain to Associate and Fellow status in the association's affiliate, the Institute of Canadian

*Small-town boys enter the middle class: Alex Kearney (right)
in the Traders' Embro, Ontario, branch in 1909.*

Banking. Bank education, none the less, remained within the confines of the banking industry. Like a fraternal organization, one was taught its secrets only after a painstaking induction in which loyalty was assured.

Drilled, groomed, and inspected by his employer, the Canadian bank employee marched into the labour market with formidable efficiency. "A junior's loyalty to his bank," wrote *Saturday Night* magazine in 1908, "is a thing for the gods to marvel at, and comes but once in a lifetime."[27] Rule books, journal articles, and circular letters give us, however, only one side of the story: what the banks wanted their employees to be. We are left wondering what this edifice of regimentation looked like *from below*. Why did thousands of young Canadian lads take up banking and stick with it? Why did Charles Everett Mackenzie, whose forty-eight-year career is charted in this chapter, join the bank in Pictou, Nova Scotia, in 1892 and stay with it in "service" across three continents?

Almost without exception, bankers' careers began with nervous adolescent interviews with their home-town bank managers. They were quite literally pushed through the bank door by fathers who banked at the branch, by high-school teachers who saw promise in a graduating pupil, or, in isolated cases, by their own desperation for employment. A simple examination followed, a two-sided sheet that tested the candidate's proficiency at spelling and arithmetic. Potential bankers ranged in age from sixteen to twenty; Charles Mackenzie was a stripling of fifteen. Their roots were rural or small-town; they were very often the second or third sons of farmers, who foresaw little chance of inheriting the family homestead and were eager to find employment that furnished both security and a degree of social respectability. Many were of English or Scottish stock; most were above-average-but-not-brilliant high-school students. For many, banking was simply "a job."

Two examples suffice to illustrate the remarkable homogeneity of recruitment to Canadian banks. Allan Grant Mackenzie was an Ontario farm boy, born outside Kincardine, Ontario, in 1890. He was the sixth child in a family of staunch Presbyterians; his father left farming to become a local merchant and insurance salesman. Allan was a competent student and a conquering athlete – in 1907 he ran an eleven-second hundred yards. In February 1909, he was given a note by his science teacher and told to go and see the local bank manager. That evening the manager stopped by the Mackenzie home to speak to his parents, and the next morning Allan was a $150-a-year clerk with the Traders Bank. He decided to "try banking." Three years later, he became a Royal banker when the Traders became one of Edson

Pease's takeover targets. By then, Allan was in Saskatoon, well on his way to a career that would stretch to 1951.

Three months after Mackenzie joined the Kincardine branch, Alex Kearney took a break from his correspondence studies at the University of Toronto to spend the Victoria Day holiday with friends in Walkerton. There, on the holiday Monday, he peered through the window of the Traders to see the staff busy readying their month-end statements. A farm boy whose father had sold the farm, Kearney saw his opening: "I decided I was going to bank." Throughout his subsequent forty-one-year career he never doubted that he was "bank minded."[28]

A "job" at the bank fit into a broader social and economic transformation in Canadian life at the turn of the century. Although the country was still fundamentally a rural society, urbanization, driven by industrialization, was pulling Canadians into the towns and cities. This was also a society in which credentials and status carried increasing weight, where accreditation within professional ranks meant mobility and social and economic acceptance virtually anywhere in the nation. The term "middle class" has always proved very slippery in historians' hands, but in this context it was a middle class of trained, salaried employees and self-employed professionals that was at the core of the new Canadian society. When W. A. Rowat received an offer from D. M. Stewart to join the Sovereign Bank in 1903 as a $200-a-year clerk, he immediately quit his job in a cheese-box factory, "elated that I was now in the white collar class."[29] When the Union Bank of Canada transferred young Norman Nagle to its Smithville, Ontario, branch in 1908, he reported to his parents that the larger town contained people "of a much higher class." Although he lived in a cramped little room above the branch, he found himself invited to dances, polo matches, and concerts. He was, he wrote home, "glad that I went banking."[30]

Banking provided all the trappings of middle-class life. There was a uniform of sorts: a dark suit, a white shirt, a wing collar, and polished boots. Tellers sported colourful arm garters, often in bank colours, to keep their cuffs above the grimy business of dealing money. All this was a big change from farm dungarees. The deportment of employees was enforced by the management. "There is no worse blot on the landscape," the CBA *Journal* advised, "than an embryo General Manager with a cigarette in his mouth and his hat cocked on one ear."[31] Bank clerks *looked* modern; they were clean-shaven, shunning the beards of the nineteenth century. "We were all young gentlemen and addressed each other as Mister even at 16 years," C. W. Frazee recalled of his 1890s clerkship.[32] The social standing of bank employees was enhanced by the fact that they were always in the public eye. They

**HOCKEY!**

*This is not an attempt to caricature bank hockey in Canada and our artist assures us that he did not make the sketch from life—but felt that he wanted to contribute something to the Supplement, so took hockey as the motif for his contribution. One of our budding humorists was asked to suggest a title for the picture and submitted the following from which to choose : Pell-Mellism; A Mid-winter Night's Dream; Within the Law; Nocturne in B Flat; Shockey; The Hockey Strike; Three Up and Two to Go. We leave it to each reader to select the most appropriate. The Cartoonist is Armand Laflamme, who is on the staff of the Superintendent of Head Office Building.*

*A cartoon from the* Royal Bank Magazine *in 1922 presents an image of bankers at play. The Bank Hockey League in Montreal drew crowds of 6,000 during the 1920s.*

were among the first employees who were expected to embody and project a corporate personality. Just as a minister knew the secrets of a community's soul, so the banker knew its true financial worth. Thus the banker, however junior, had to act with discretion and rectitude. When the Ottawa branch manager was seen intoxicated in public, Pease reprimanded him, reduced his salary by $250, and gave him "another chance."[33] If the rule book prohibited "dissipation," management from an early date encouraged bankers to become pillars of the community, lending their talents to civic and religious groups. Bankers were never seen at the race track or the seamier saloons.

They were, however, paragons of amateur sport. "The bank officer in Canada is conspicuously of an athletic *genus*," Gordon Tait noted. "He is as much at home with paddle and tiller, and with rod and rifle during the summer and autumn months, as with hockey-stick and curling stone, with toboggan and snowshoe, enjoying to the full the delights of a vigorous winter."[34] Curling and golf attracted legions of bankers. Both were manly, outdoor pursuits. Both were Scottish in origin. They were socially respectable, excellent means of building up social and business contacts. They lacked any speculative element and,

*"Boys" will be "boys": The cocoon of regimentation in which a young bank clerk was expected to develop his skills invited occasional roguery. Here, a group of "bank boys" from the Republic, Washington, branch (c.1899) deliberately flouts the rules on a picnic. Liquor, games of chance, and big cigars are conspicuously displayed, but their ties – a badge of middle-class respectability – stay in place.*

like banking, were carefully prescribed by sets of rules. Hockey, and its companions soccer and baseball, provided a healthy outlet for the after-hours energies of young juniors. By the 1920s, the Bank Hockey League in Montreal was drawing crowds of six thousand to witness an excellent calibre of junior hockey. Across the St. Lawrence, Pease and other senior bankers were prime movers in building up the posh Mount Bruno Country Club. The Royal exported its athletic prowess; Canadian bank boys played baseball in Cuba and hockey in New York, and sailed in Vladivostok. Above all else, sports built character and kinship in Canadian banking. In 1916, as the Northern Crown Bank tottered near collapse, Finance Minister Thomas White wrote to his confidant Frederick Williams-Taylor at the Bank of Montreal for an assessment of the Crown's general manager. "Personally I would like to give Campbell a helping hand for the sake of old times," came the response. "He is not only an ex Bank of Montreal man, but he and I

*(continued on p. 110)*

107

# SUNSHINE SKETCHES OF A ROYAL BANKER

HE GOT "RATTLED" AND BECAME "AN irresponsible idiot" whenever he went near a bank. In the end, he decided to "bank no more," and elected to keep his silver dollars in a sock. He was, of course, Stephen Leacock, Canada's beloved humourist. It is from Leacock's *Sunshine Sketches of a Little Town* (1912) that most Canadians derive their quaint impression of turn-of-the-century banking. Few realize that Leacock drew his sketches from real life, from the staff of the Orillia branch of the Royal Bank.

A professor of political economy at Montreal's McGill University, Leacock was both an admirer of the Canadian banking system and a close friend of the Royal right up to his death in 1944. In the 1920s, he fed promising young economists from his classroom into the bank's economics department. He prompted the bank to offer an economics fellowship. During the Depression, he spoke out on behalf of the banks against Alberta Social Credit. "My Financial Career" was republished in the *Royal Bank Magazine*. Leacock also banked at the Royal.

When free of his McGill duties, Leacock retired to his summer home in Orillia, Ontario. There he enjoyed a weekly game of golf with George Rapley, manager of the Royal's branch there since 1899. A colourful banker with a penchant for aggressive representation of the bank's interests, Rapley was undoubtedly the model for Henry Mullins, manager of the Mariposa branch of the "Exchange" Bank. In fact, in the early editions of Sketches, Mullins was called "Popley," a name Leacock changed because of its similarity to Rapley's. Rapley died in 1931. "I wonder if it is on record that the Mr. Mullins in Stephen Leacock's *Sunshine Sketches of a Little Town* was our own unforgettable George Rapley?" a friend later wrote to the Royal's President Wilson. "The other banker in the tale was Scott of the Dominion Bank. Stephen once told me the story was true, which anyone knowing George well can readily believe."

It seems highly likely that Leacock acquired a good deal of his banking anecdotes and folklore from Rapley as they walked the golf course. There are striking similarities between reminiscences of various bankers now locked in the bank's Montreal archives and the exploits of characters in the Mariposa branch of the Exchange Bank. Let the reader be the judge.

---

*Stephen Leacock on the porch of his Orillia home in 1941 (opposite). With him is Dr. Robert Picard, a McGill graduate and future corporate secretary of the bank. Leacock directed many promising young men toward the banks of St. James Street. Back at McGill he lectured to others on behalf of the Canadian Bankers' Association.*

---

**From F. T. Walker's 1945 reminiscences:**

McKane got mixed up in a shooting in 1896, was removed to Montreal in a clerical position, resigned, and went to Rossland where gold mining had started, from there to Tonopah, Nev., where he made a big strike and cleaned up a million. Always spectacular, he made a trip to Scotland, scattering sovereigns from the top of his four-in-hand coach in his home town, returned to New Brunswick to live, bought one of the leading dailies in St. John and proceeded to drink himself to death.

**From *Sunshine Sketches*:**

Then presently young Fizzlechip, who had been teller in Mullins' Bank and that everybody had thought a worthless jackass before, came back from the Cobalt country with a fortune, and loafed round in the Mariposa House in English khaki and a horizontal hat, drunk all the time, and everybody holding him up as an example of what it was possible to do if you tried.

played football together side by side for several years. We never had a better captain, and my experience in life has been that a man who can successfully captain a football team has some of the qualities at any rate to run a Bank."[35]

A crucial ingredient of middle-class professionalization was the predictability given it by routine and standardized procedure – the same service dispensed over time with the same result. Bankers excelled at routine. Each rung in the bank hierarchy had its specific schedule of duties, but it was at the junior's level that the habit of routine first made its purchase. A junior's day began early. Many supplemented their meagre annual income with a $50 stipend from the bank for undertaking janitorial work around the branch. The day would thus either begin or end with a bout of sweeping and tidying, a task made easier by the fact that the junior lived upstairs. Before the other employees arrived at 9:00 a.m., the junior was expected to have filled inkwells, cut pen nibs, and changed blotters. It took a deft hand to chip frozen ink out of inkwells, thaw it, and then refill the wells, a chore that befell juniors in many a poorly heated branch. Many a clerk scorched his fingers learning to seal packets of notes with a stick of molten wax. The official day began with the entering of maturing bills in the accountant's ledger. To this task the junior was expected to bring meticulous chancery cursive handwriting. Juniors who "blotted their copybooks" were expected to initial their errors for subsequent entry in the manager's Discrepancy Book, a document that fell under the inspector's critical eye. His entries complete, the junior set out on his daily round of "peddling" or "slinging" drafts, the delivery of due bills of exchange and other notes. If cash was involved, the bank revolver and messenger joined the expedition. Peddling drafts required another item of uniform: a respectable cloth coat. A sandwich lunch, taken in the basement, usually followed the morning round. The afternoon was devoted to writing up notices of dishonour for bills refused in the morning, copying the mail, and journeying to the post office. Overtime was frequent, especially at month's end. For all this, a junior in 1900 received $8.33 monthly, from which 83 cents was taken for the Guarantee Fund.[36]

A junior's road to success rested on a foundation of loyalty, initiative, and consistency. As late as 1931, the *Royal Bank Magazine* published articles framed in the epistolary style of Rae's *Country Banker*. "Remember," a banker father told his would-be-banker son, "that your entire loyalty belongs to your employer as well as your entire time." He added, "Don't wait to be told everything but cultivate initiative." Initiative must not, however, usurp consistency. Well into the 1950s, James Muir, the archetypal bank clerk turned bank president, attributed success in banking neither to "spasmodic genius nor occasional bursts of energy," but to "sustained performance."[37] The handwritten staff ledgers attest to the qualities sought in a clerk: "steady and accurate," "a good penman," "trying hard to improve himself so as to be of greater value to the Bank," "faithful and is always at his post," and "very conscientious, willing & industrious. A plodder."[38]

If the bank expected "unflagging, self-denying devotion" from its employees,[39] it did not always get it. There was tremendous attrition in the ranks of bank clerks. Many young men simply refused to buckle down to the rigorous discipline; others would not leave their home region. "Not suited to banking" was the curt ledger entry placed at the end of many a short career. Others were summarily cashiered because they failed the test of performance, showing "carelessness" or "intemperance," and "keeping fast company." Salary cuts were meted out for poor penmanship or habitual lateness.

There was constant grumbling in junior ranks over poor pay. The first five to six years of bank employment were marked by subsistence wages; the attainment of a teller's or accountant's job brought a salary at the turn of the century into the $800 to $1,100 range, and offered the prospect of relative comfort and, of course, marriage. As early as 1878, the *Monetary Times* published letters complaining that "all bank clerks do not live in clover,"[40] and editorialized that, if clerks' pay were more generous, the incidence of defalcation might be lessened. With the new century, the issue became politicized every time the Bank Act came before Parliament for revision. "Go into any office in Toronto or Montreal, and you will find probably 200 young men from 16 to 20 years of age, white faced and anaemic, toiling over their ledgers" for $300 to $400 a year, one Tory MP complained in the Commons in 1911.[41] At times even Merchants' Bank officers winced at the low salaries they paid. "Many of them," Superintendent of Branches Torrance wrote of his Maritime clerks in 1900, "are getting only sufficient to keep body and soul together." Torrance sometimes slipped $50 bonuses to hard-pressed clerks. In general, however, senior management saw low starting salaries as part of the initiation to banking; the bank was teaching the clerks a profession that would sustain them for life, and their clerking was but a form of tuition. When confronted with one clerk's complaint of low pay, General Manager Duncan could bluntly reply in 1900: "Wait not one year, but a few."[42]

The bank's marriage rule involved similar postponement of ambition. Here the bank was somewhat more flexible; permission to marry was often granted to clerks whose parents agreed to supplement salaries up to the required $1,000 ceiling. The rule none the less attracted much criticism. In 1902, the *Monetary Times* reported that

"The Conscientious Clerk": The frontispiece to J. P. Buschlen's 1913
exposé of bank clerking.

the banks had been attacked by a Rev. John Langtry as "immoral tyrants" for their marriage prohibition; a decade later the policy was assailed in parliament as a "very unwise and an almost criminal interference with the personal right and personal liberty of our young men."[43] Bank managers replied that the rule existed to allow the clerks a period of concentrated training, uninterrupted by the responsibilities of family and debt. This logic found some resonance elsewhere in society. In 1909, Finance Minister William Fielding confided in Sir Edward Clouston of the Bank of Montreal that having "undertaken to marry, myself, on less money than that [$1,000 a year], and discovered my mistake in the financial calculations, I can more readily admit the soundness of the Bank's policy. I know," he concluded, "the necessity of discipline in all large organizations."[44] The marriage rule, adjusted for inflation, would last into the 1950s. When women began entering bank employment in the 1910s, an even stricter, though unofficial, marriage rule governed their employment: marriage meant retirement. Many skirted these rules by marrying secretly.

There was always the growing possibility that bank clerks would cease to subscribe to the notion of deferred gratification implicit in their early years of employment. In 1907, the *Monetary Times* carried reports of an English Bank Clerks' Union and then, three years later, the news that a Bank Clerks' Association of Canada was being organized.[45] Since membership in the union was rumoured to be secret, bank officials found it difficult to gauge the extent of its appeal, but the public's attention was aroused. "The wage scale of the young banker," *Saturday Night* editorialized in 1912, "has been little better than stationary in many instances."[46] Agitation for bank unionization received an added fillip in 1913 from the publication of a *roman à clef*, *A Canadian Bank Clerk*, written by a disgruntled Toronto bank clerk, Jack Preston. Using the pen name of J. P. Buschlen, Preston wrote to "enlighten the public concerning life behind the wicket and thus pave the way for the legitimate organization of bank clerks into a fraternal association." The novel portrayed the sorry career of Evan Nelson, an underpaid bank clerk subjected to long hours and frequent transfers, who eventually succumbs to "kiting" cheques and is fired. Stiff and didactic in style, *Bank Clerk* was a frontal assault on the culture that management sought to instil in Canadian banking. A year later, Preston described the book as "too serious" and published a more romantic picture of clerking under the title *Behind the Wicket*.[47] The object remained unchanged: the recognition and better pay of clerks as "specialists."

None the less, the early attempts to unionize bank clerks fizzled. Sporadic meetings in Montreal and Toronto failed to create much solidarity. The First World War and the fact that the majority of clerks were scattered across the nation in small pockets – and could be trans-ferred at management's discretion – meant that organization was impossible. Bank management was, however, rattled. The CBA president D. R. Wilkie saw "red flag people" behind the agitation, but counselled a passive response, trusting in the "loyalty" of most employees.[48] When talk of unionization reemerged after the war, the CBA hired a detective from the Thiel Agency to monitor organizational meetings in Montreal. The CBA president, however, assured the federal finance minister that the banks were not transferring troublesome clerks to distant branches. In June 1920, the American Federation of Labour brought Samuel Gompers to Montreal and, following his rousing convention speech, voted $15,000 to organize the bank clerks.[49] Again, in the face of a depressed economy in the early 1920s, unionization made virtually no progress. Whatever their frustrations, bank clerks saw themselves as entry candidates to the middle class, and viewed unionization as working-class activism, contrary to their long-term interests. They subscribed to the ethos of "loyalty" that management so forcefully promoted, since most had their eye on the next rung of the bank's ladder of promotion, not the rung they stood on.

The mettle of any banker was first tested in the teller's cage. In the years up to the Second World War, the interior of any Royal Bank was dominated by a formidable piece of bank furnishing – the teller's cage. A hulking, Baroque contraption of heavy-gauge wire, wood, and iron struts, the cage was the centre of all cash transactions with the public. Some were brassy and ornamented, others were stark metal cages; all were fitted with lockable doors and a wicket. In larger branches, there were two cages, one for "paying" and the other for "receiving." The fortress-like security of the cage served a twofold purpose: hold-up protection and character building. In the cage, the teller became a self-contained financial unit; character emerged from doing the job well. It was "foolish economy," the CBA *Journal* decreed, to provide tellers with "a poor, rickety, shaky cage."[50] The cage door had a knob only on the inside, and the teller was armed with a .38- or .45-calibre revolver. The cage was thus a formidable defence; a dead or wounded teller on the inside got the robber nowhere. The bank rule book stipulated that only "under absolute necessity" was a teller to exit his cage during business hours.

At 10:00 a.m. every morning, the teller stepped into his cage with his cash box, blotter, and revolver, and locked himself in. He stayed there until 3 p.m., taking a sandwich lunch at his post. Here he projected the bank's image to its clients; the cage was a visible signal that one's money was in safe hands. Its "isolation" from other bank activities meant that the teller's attention was undivided. A teller's first

*Ambition's box: Tellers' cages at Truro branch, 1915 (top), and Morse, Saskatchewan, 1926 (below). The pelican was not standard bank issue and would not have met with the bank inspector's approval.*

# We Make TELLERS' CAGES for BANKS
## ALL FINISHES.

*Supplying banks with furnishings was a flourishing business, as this advertisement from the* Monetary Times *of 1903 indicates.*

duty on closing the cage was to balance his daily blotter; all the monotony of a clerk's training was intended to bear fruit in his meticulous handling of the cash entrusted to him. Juniors, for instance, often studied the hand action of an adept teller when he was dispensing cash and copied his style. Arrayed in colourful sleeve garters and visor, a proficient teller looked "sharp" and authoritative.

A promising banker was expected to develop his banker's intuition in the cage. The cage was the bank's window on the world. Even the fictional J. P. Buschlen saw its worth: "My wicket was of burnished brass / And served me for a looking glass."[51] The teller was expected to be an acute observer of the community, of the "character" of the bank's clientele. If the community in turn invested the teller with respect and social standing, it was because he alone in the midst knew their financial circumstances.[52] As Leacock once flippantly remarked, one needed "the ABC's of banking" to get into the cage, but "once you get past the ABC you can learn a lot that is mighty interesting."

Given its importance to career and branch alike, Canadian bankers developed an immense devotion to the cage. Their first instinct on opening a new branch was to erect a cage, even if only symbolically. "I bought a shack," one manager recalled of pioneering Swift Current branch in 1911, "and built a cage out of chicken wire and scantling."[53] While some decried "being caged like monkeys" and having to handle filthy banknotes,[54] there was universal agreement that performance behind the grillwork of the cage set the course of a banker's career. Combined with a stint at the accountant's table behind the cage, success as a teller led to the manager's office, usually in a small Prairie or Ontario town out on the bank's frontier.

The manager "made" the branch. He was on his own, often tied to head office by no more than the telegraph. Rule books and circulars kept him abreast of bank policy, but it was his years of training that provided the stuff of branch leadership. Consequently, head office agonized over the choice of a manager – particularly those for new branches. "Spokane is likely to be the next branch," the superintendent of branches wrote in 1899, "if we can find the man."[55] Character had to be married to opportunity: "There are slow horses and fast horses, and in their proper place one is as valuable as the other," Pease once observed.[56] Once appointed, a manager had great autonomy and, aside from the inspector's annual visit, there was little to check his treatment of employees or clients. Mistakes were made, particularly during the headlong growth up to 1914; F. T. Walker recalled one British Columbia manager whom he could only describe as a "sadistic brute."[57] These were the exceptions. If there was one factor that propelled the Royal forward during its spurt of growth from 1900 to 1920, it was its ability to put the right men in the right places. Early on, the bank acquired a reputation as an "up and coming" institution that trained its men well, treated them well, and promoted them quickly.[58] As early as 1898, Pease quietly congratulated himself that "our service is considered a desirable one to get into."[59] Above all else, the Royal was a "young man's institution."[60] It gave promising young men plenty of leash; it trained them to be cautious and promoted them expecting boldness. In 1900, Pease, for instance, gave the crucial

*From "boys" to "girls": A typical staff portrait, Sydney, Nova Scotia, branch in 1910 (above).*
*The bearded manager sits surrounded by his clean-shaven male staff.*
*The messenger (back centre) is clearly older, and the lone female, probably a*
*stenographer, stands to the side. (Opposite page) Sydney branch in 1945:*
*A male manager and messenger, together with nine "girls," now in the middle.*
*Unlike the situation in the First World War, women did not abandon the bank when the men*
*returned. By 1945, 71 per cent of bank staff was female; in 1939 it had been 21 per cent.*

Vancouver managership to Charles Neill, who had been with the bank only eleven years and who had just turned twenty-seven. Neill would become general manager in 1916 at age forty-three, the same age at which Pease took the post in 1899. The pattern continued deep into the twentieth century: men in their forties have consistently taken the helm of the Royal.

The coordinating hub of the entire Royal network was head office on St. James Street in Montreal. Since the ethos of the bank rested on the hands-on training of men in the branches, head office played a low-profile role in bank operations. Its staff was small and largely relegated to administrative duties. Head office embraced: the general manager's staff; the central inspection, credits, and accounting staffs; the stationery and routine departments (to provide the branches with forms and circular letters); and the corporate secretary and staff to coordinate international operations. There was no training department; the inspectors maintained an informal watch on promising young officers. Montreal main branch, downstairs in the same building, served

as a proving ground for promising talent. Head office consolidated accounts, ensured consistent procedure throughout the bank, and vetted large credit applications sent in from the regions. A desk in national credits provided a window on the Canadian economy and a stepping stone to promotion.

The routine department in Montreal also controlled the pace of modernization in the bank. In terms of technology, that pace was slow. Reliance on machines was viewed with suspicion, since it eroded the basic skills which a banker was expected to master unaided. The first typewriter was purchased in 1879, but by 1937 there were only 1,981 machines in the entire system. Adding machines were cautiously introduced in busy urban branches by 1900, ledger-posting machines in 1918, and cheque-encoding machines in 1928. A year later the first Recordak machine for photographing batches of cancelled cheques appeared. Loose-leaf ledger books were introduced with reluctance; despite the ease they offered in posting balances, managers feared that their flexible spines might promote record tampering. Banking thus remained a labour-intensive profession, with head office strictly controlling technology.[61]

The dynamic centre of head office was the small office of the bank's general manager, and Edson Pease was the first of a long line of hard-driving occupants of that office. In true Scottish tradition, the general managers of Canadian banks ruled their charges with imperial sway. The general manager was the highest-paid officer of the bank; at the height of his career in the early 1920s Pease earned a princely $50,000 a year. Herbert Holt, as the bank's president in the 1910s earned an honorarium of $7,500 and seldom darkened the door of his bank office. The general manager, particularly Pease, travelled prodigiously: branch tours, CBA lobbying in Ottawa, and active involvement in international operations kept him constantly on the move. In photos of the early 1920s, Pease looks like a worn-out man.

While the general manager made the bank's strategic decisions, he was at least obliged to seek the approval of the board. In 1880, the board was still a tight group of six Halifax merchants; by 1930 it had become a regionally diverse group of twenty-seven, drawn from Canada's leading centres of commerce. The board met twice a week, the directors earning a small fee for attendance. In practice, Montreal directors monopolized the board after the head-office shift, although sub-committees operated in Halifax, Toronto, Winnipeg, and Vancouver. Certain boardroom rituals evolved: the directors were obliged by the charter to count the bank's cash quarterly. Their presence was also required whenever the bank destroyed worn-out banknotes, a duty fulfilled in front of a stinking furnace in head-office basement. Directors were expected to alert the bank to promising opportunities in their regions, but in reality the directors played a quiescent role in bank affairs. They acted on the advice given them by the general manager. Board meetings seldom lasted more than an hour, followed by a chatty lunch. Directors occasionally went on tours of inspection to Cuba and other far-flung reaches of the Royal network.

From the boardroom to the teller's cage, the Royal was thus a manly meritocracy. Ability, not social background or patronage, governed movement through the bank's ranks. Bankers were by nature careful gradualists in the administration of their industry; those prone to impatience or dramatic change were quickly weeded out. Within the framework of Canadian banking set out in the Bank Act, the loyalty that was developed in "bank boys" soon proved a powerful instrument of growth. Embedded in this culture were prominent characteristics – mobility, merit, and maleness – which would ultimately serve to shift and broaden the ground on which it so securely rested. Until the late 1930s, Canadian banking was thus an Anglo, male pursuit; after the 1930s it hesitantly opened its doors to women and a less Anglo-centric definition of Canadianness.

"Bank boys," for all their Scottish inspiration, saw themselves as "British." As historian Carl Berger has pointed out, being "British" in Canada at the turn of the century did not necessarily imply a denial of a distinctly Canadian identity.[62] Anglo-Canadians saw themselves as contributing members of an imperial federation of English-speaking peoples, sharing a common cultural, linguistic, and political heritage. In this, they found pride in being Canadian. Theirs was a narrow, exclusive view of Canadian nationhood, but it was one with a broad and powerful reach. It touched federal politicians, educators, and bankers. School curricula throughout the Maritimes and Ontario were redolent with lessons in the virtues of Britishness. High-school graduates carried these values with them into their banking careers. When asked who his role models were, Charles Neill, who had risen to the general managership in the 1920s, cited Canadian imperialists Sir George Parkin and poets Bliss Carmen and Charles G. D. Roberts. It was Parkin, the New Brunswick educator who headed the Rhodes Scholarship Fund, and George Foster, the well-known professor at the University of New Brunswick, who educated Francis Sherman, a leading Canadian romantic poet and the bank's assistant general manager in Cuba. Bank employee Allan Grant Mackenzie in Kincardine was, for instance, named for a distant relative, George Munro Grant, principal of Queen's University and a muscular Christian. In politics, Canadian bankers voted Tory, in large part because it was the British party in Canadian politics. When the Boer War erupted in 1899, the CBA *Journal* urged its readers to uphold "the cause of freedom in South Africa." It is perhaps no coincidence that Earle McLaughlin, the Royal's Ontario-born president in the 1960s and 1970s, possessed one the finest collections of G. H. Henty, a British writer of boys' adventure books set in the glory days of Empire.

In 1914, news that England was at war with the "Hun" brought out the jingoism of Canadian bankers as never before. They enlisted without hesitation. By 1918, 1,495 Royal Bank men had enlisted; 191 never returned. For a staff of 2,832 in 1914, this had far-reaching implications. It put the organization's maleness at risk. Women had traditionally occupied a peripheral role in bank life. As wives, they were "charming little wives," saluted at the end of letters between managers, companions in the social respectability of Canadian banking.[63] As clients, women were not seen by Canadian society as financially significant. By the early 1900s, some banks in affluent, urban areas were opening women's branches, fitted out to appeal to women's supposedly more delicate sensibilities.[64] By 1910, a trickle of single women had found employment in the Royal as stenographers and clerks. They worked, chaperoned, behind the scenes; the public expected men to deal with money. For bank "girls," the war proved an opportunity for advancement. As their male clerks rushed to the recruiting office, management reluctantly turned to the women in the back room and put them behind wickets. By 1916, "the question as to whether women are to obtain a foothold in banks" was "past the stage of debate,"[65] but after the war, the feminine mystique prevailed, and women abandoned the banks for the altar, while the "boys" repossessed their cages. But the watershed had been crossed. Banking was no longer a male preserve. Women would maintain a minority presence in the banks between the wars, and during the Second World War return in numbers to stay.

The "Britishness" of the bank, which had inadvertently opened the door to women, proved a more persistent legacy of the Royal's founding culture. Not until the 1950s did the Anglo cohesiveness of the bank find itself out of alignment with the increasingly diversified nature of Canadian society. By then, the retirement speeches and reminiscences of men who had served the Royal for the last half century carried a strong vein of nostalgia for a world of male camaraderie and banking adventure, a world, they believed, that was fast slipping away.

# Growth Through Amalgamation

## *"In Union There Is Strength"*

THE ROYAL BANK'S 1903 ANNUAL REPORT WAS, IN THE *MONETARY TIMES'S* opinion, "a dainty piece of book-making."[1] For the bank's 595 shareholders, there was ample evidence of a network of forty-nine branches spread from Cuba to British Columbia and profits of $373,252 generated from assets of $25 million. Financial performance had shown a handsome increase from the previous year, a pattern that would persist for the next twenty-five years. The *Monetary Times* would, for instance, report four years later that the Royal's "cheering profit" of $746,775 worked out to a 19-per-cent return on the bank's capital base, a figure "calculated to make some competitors pink with envy."[2] By the time the bank celebrated its fiftieth anniversary in 1919, it was Canada's second-largest bank; by the mid-1920s it would have assets of $583,789,509 and 654 branches and have overtaken the front-running Bank of Montreal. This was an unprecedented spurt of banking growth. "The Royal Bank has been in the habit, for a number of years," *Saturday Night* noted in 1920, "of establishing new records for Canadian banks."[3]

What made the 1903 annual report what the *Monetary Times* termed "dainty," was not so much the hint of future financial profit as the bank's association with national growth. A month after its publication in early 1904, Laurier proclaimed that the twentieth century would "belong" to Canada, a prophecy soon seconded by a crescendo of growth up to 1913. From the adoption of its new name in 1901, the Royal began accompanying its annual report with statistics of national growth. To the majority of bank shareholders – small investors scattered through the Maritimes – such statistics would hardly have been

123

a revelation. For the growing number of Montreal, New York, and British shareholders, the statistics would have vindicated their decision to invest in what seemed a dynamic young bank. Prospective immigrants were the real audience for the Royal's annual report; bundles of the reports were shipped to Canadian immigration offices in Europe and the United States. New Canadians would ultimately become new Royal customers.

In the first quarter of the new century, the institutional structure of Canadian banking jelled. By 1925, the corporate identity of Canadian banking would assume a form still recognizable three-quarters of a century later. In 1900 it had been an industry dominated by the Bank of Montreal and populated by a myriad of small regional banks struggling to carve out a national market share. Within this quarter-century, there was the paradox of immense growth in assets and facilities accompanied by a steady contraction in the number of banks. In 1900, Canada had thirty-six banks; by 1931 there were only ten. In the same period, 708 branches grew to just over 4,000. Canadians were pampered by this expansion; in 1900 there was one branch for every 7,600 Canadians; by 1920, this had risen to an astonishing one branch per 1,900 and by 1930 had somewhat relaxed to an average of 2,500.[4] Behind this swelling tide of branches, from 1900 to 1920, the assets of Canadian banks grew at an annual average of 9.45 per cent. Within this expansion, the Royal excelled. In 1900, it had 3.6 per cent of Canadian bank assets; by 1920, it had 18.7 per cent, and by 1930, 27.2 per cent. In an era when Canada's "big banks" emerged, the Royal emerged as the biggest. As Herbert Holt told the 1912 annual meeting, when Canada was "a country of small affairs, small banks sufficed, but that we must have banks to handle the large operations of the present day."[5] Seven years later the general manager of the Bank of Nova Scotia similarly reminded Finance Minister Thomas White that "[O]nly large and strong banks can expand."[6]

However, to ascribe terms such as "corporate strategy" to the turn-of-the-century deliberations of Edson Pease and the directors of the Royal would create a false sense of purposefulness. The corporate horizon of the bank was defined by day-to-day, *ad hoc* decision-making: a branch established here, personnel shifted there, or a dividend declared. The bank's corporate direction still bore the mark of the 1887 decision to establish in Montreal and to use it as a springboard for expansion. Over two decades, Pease had pursued this mandate vigorously, supplementing it with an effort to export the bank's expertise into the Caribbean. Ten years into the new century, the Royal was a *national* bank by virtue of this strategy, but it was still a relatively small bank with only 162 of the nation's 2,367 branches.

Further growth, Pease realized, would depend on an even-more-vigorous pursuit of internal growth or, possibly, on the adoption of a new approach to growth – the acquisition of other banks' assets. The years 1910 to 1925 would be marked by Pease's masterful blending of these two "strategic" options. On one front, the Royal continued to push its branch network out to the edge of Canadian development – in boom years such as 1909 and 1919, Royal branches proliferated in the West and in hinterland Ontario. At the same time, the Royal made five crucial mergers with other banks. More than anything else, mergers vaulted the Royal into the leadership of Canadian banking.

The Royal was by no means the only Canadian bank to embark on a merger campaign; Pease assured the Commons Banking and Commerce Committee in 1913 that "we are not the arch consolidators."[7] None the less, Edson Pease assembled the Royal's jigsaw of consolidation with incredible prescience. Each piece brought special advantage. The completed picture in 1925 revealed a stable national balance of regions, towns, and cities. Each amalgamated bank added new talent and exposure to the Royal's already well-defined culture. There was an undoubted element of luck in the whole process; several attempted mergers were in fact botched. But banking in Canada was becoming a much-more-complex process – an amalgam of public opinion, public policy, and competitive strengths. It was Pease's master stroke that he was able to plot the bank's path through this changed landscape. The Royal's amalgamation strategy was, on the whole, precisely targeted and cleanly executed; each infusion of new staff strengthened, not dissipated, the culture of the bank. Through all this, Herbert Holt, the bank's president, sat mutely by, tending to his other, varied, business interests. Given Pease's pre-eminence, there was natural sense in the bank's 1916 decision to create the chief executive post of managing director for Pease, freeing him from the bank's daily operational affairs (C. E. Neill became general manager) to concentrate on its strategic direction.

Canadian bank mergers have usually been seen as a response to external competition, a means of weeding out weak regional banks and buttressing emerging national banks. Edson Pease would come to subscribe to this rationale, but initially the thought of taking over other banks came in response to internal factors that were beginning to constrict the bank's growth. Principal among these was the bank's inability to generate a sufficient supply of reliable young bankers to staff its aggressive expansion, despite its success in training a small army of "bank boys." Again and again, head-office correspondence was punctuated by the persistent complaint that "we are pressed for good men." Given the gradualism implicit in the "bank boys'" education, it was difficult to accelerate the advancement of young staff. Hurried promotion courted sloppy banking and the risk of defalcation and error by men put in positions to which their talents and loyalty were as yet unequal. As early as 1899, the board was deferring branch openings because, as it admitted, "we find it difficult to find suitable men: our staff having been so heavily drawn on during the past year for our western branches."[8] Western expansion most overtaxed the bank's staff; isolated western branches placed a premium on a banker's resourcefulness and character. Much the same was true of the bank's growing international network. An untried manager could not, for instance, be sent to an isolated post in Cuba's Oriente Province. None the less, the Royal's reputation as a "young man's institution" reflected management's willingness to push recruits hard and early. Many buckled. Two years after opening a branch in the copper-boom town of Grand Forks, British Columbia, head office learned to its horror that their manager in the town had allowed himself to become personally embroiled in questionable loans and had succumbed to a nervous breakdown.[9]

The Royal devised various measures to alleviate the manpower strain. Halifax and, after 1908, the "marble palace" in Montreal were employed as incubators for young Maritime-born clerks, ideal locales for exposing staff to the pressures of urban banking. Staff reminiscences often dwelt on the image of "snowed-under tellers" in Montreal being hastily prepared for despatch westwards.[10] However, the board soon learned that many of these forced-growth bankers succumbed to the "get-rich-quick" opportunities of western boom towns and quit the bank. A surer bet, eastern bankers concluded, was to import proven staff from England and Scotland, paying a premium on salary to ensure loyalty, but even this did not meet the pressures of expansion. The only remaining option was to obtain staff from competing banks. Here the way was barred by an understanding between the banks that they would not raid each other's staffs, mainly out of a fear that a bidding war for manpower would drive up wages. This unwritten rule would last into the 1960s; one had to resign from a bank before seeking employment with another. Thus the prospect of the outright purchase of an entire bank with its staff was immensely attractive. Given the standardized nature of bank training in Canada, this meant that person-nel from either banks could be readily incorporated into the Royal's ranks. Furthermore, merger meant the acquisition of trained *managers*, not just clerks, and, since a merger usually meant the closure of dupli-cate branches in the east, it created an immediate pool of surplus labour ready for reassignment. "The consolidation," Pease confided in a friend of the 1916 takeover of the Quebec Bank, "will give us a hundred and fifty surplus men, who will be very welcome. Lack of men has prevented us from occupying some attractive new fields."[11]

Staff shortage was not the only factor keeping the Royal on a short leash. Competition was also inhibiting expansion. Given that the Bank Act capped interest on money lent at 7 per cent (on occasion 8 per cent) and that the rate on money deposited was set by consensus at 3 per cent, there was little scope in Canadian banking for head-on product competition. Competition was driven by location and service; the reward was a larger market share. In a country still predominantly made up of small towns, only a handful of larger centres could support vigorous bank competition. In smaller centres, the market was too small to be profitably shared. The Royal had, for instance, met tough competition from the Toronto-based Traders Bank of Canada in its attempt to penetrate rural Ontario. Managers had engaged in unseemly efforts to poach accounts from established Traders branches and, even when successful, such efforts seldom brought much profit. As early as 1898, CBA president D. R. Wilkie complained of this "delirium of competition." Soon after, the association began facilitating informal "saw-off" agreements, which stopped competition in smaller centres.[12]

The folly of over-ambitious expansion on thin ground was made abundantly clear to Pease and his colleagues by the ignominious collapse of the Sovereign Bank in 1908. Chartered in 1901 and guided by its general manager, ex-Royal Banker D. M. Stewart, the Sovereign had plunged headlong into rural Ontario, opening branches with a rapidity that drew the breath from Canada's staid banking community. With financial backing from New York and from the prestigious Dresdner Bank in Germany, the Sovereign was invariably described as being "very American" in its methods. Stewart introduced innovations such as the quarterly payment of interest on savings. By 1907, it boasted nearly ninety branches and assets of $25 million. But the panic of 1907, which rocked Wall Street and brought about a sudden contraction of credit, exposed the shallow roots of the Sovereign. A year before, the Ontario Bank had collapsed under a heap of unsecured loans. Its general manager quickly found himself in Kingston penitentiary. Now Stewart, who had already resigned his general managership at the Sovereign, fled the country when it became apparent that the bank carried huge bad debts in Alaskan and mid-western American railways and utilities. "It was born of ambition," the *Monetary Times* reported, "it lived on the fruits of ambition, nice but not nourishing; and it died as the result of ambition."[13] As it had for the Ontario Bank, the Royal participated in a rescue of the Sovereign, paying $300,000 into a liquidation fund set up by the CBA and eventually inheriting six Sovereign branches of dubious worth.[14]

The rubble of the Sovereign smouldered for several years as creditors fought for their rights, a constant reminder to more sober banks that expansion had to be broad-based and well-balanced. The essential lesson of bank failures early in the century was that banks that relied on a regional base were vulnerable banks. Regional banks got caught in cyclical downturns and commodity slumps; national banks, by contrast, hedged their bets through diversified savings and loans. Surplus savings in developed regions could be reapplied to immature regions. Nowhere was this more true than in the Canadian West. From the onset of the Laurier boom in the late 1890s, western farmers had displayed a voracious appetite for credit. This was "next year" country, where future prosperity depended on the application of sweat and a generous line of credit. Not only was capital scarce in the West, but the demands of western credit were peculiar. Potential borrowers had little collateral and invariably wanted loans geared to the seasonal rhythm of grain production. They wanted short-term credit to cover the period from spring seeding to fall harvest. As the Royal's Winnipeg manager lectured Pease in 1913: "we must remember that this is a grain growing country. One might broadly say that there is only one pay day in the year, that is when the farmer sells his grain. When we make a loan to a farmer during the winter or spring, we know perfectly well that we are not going to be paid until late the following autumn or during the winter."[15] Over the long run, farmers were prepared to bet on the rising price of grain and western land as the ultimate hedge against their indulgence in credit.

In the years of the Laurier boom to 1914, the wheat frontier and the bank frontier coincided. Pease incessantly prowled the Prairies on the outlook for promising locations for branches; by 1914 the ten Prairie branches that the Royal had in 1906 had grown to sixty-three. Back in the Montreal boardroom, the directors provided financing for western grain companies and for Mackenzie and Mann's Canadian Northern Railway. In 1906, the bank appointed James Lougheed (patriarch of what was to become a great Alberta Conservative family) and R. B. Bennett as its Calgary solicitors. Winnipeg directors followed in the 1910s. With characteristic flexibility, the Bank Act accommodated the West's banking needs; Section 88 of the Act was a marvellous testament to the ability of Canadian banking to meet the needs of a developing economy, short on capital and long on labour and resources. Under Section 88, a farmer might secure short term (i.e., three to six months') credit to purchase seed, fertilizer, or twine in the spring on the security of the crop in the ground.[16] Western branch managers soon became adept agriculturalists, hiking out to sodbusters' farms to check crop progress or run their fingers through harvested grain. In

*Banking at the "end of steel": A Union Bank of Canada branch in Foremost, Alberta, c.1914.*
*Bankers impatiently established ramshackle branches at the head of rail construction*
*to capture the business of construction navvies and win the confidence*
*of newly arrived immigrants. Such branches spawned a rich*
*folklore: language problems, ferocious winter weather, and loneliness.*

later years, Section 88 would be extended to cattle rearing. Just as they had moved fish and timber in the Maritimes, the banks now helped convert raw resources into finished commodity exports. But Section 88 had an Achilles' heel: farmers' ability to make good their own loans hinged on good crops and rising prices. Without these, bank debts might pile up as quickly as unsold grain. The commercial slump of 1913 hinted at this; the Depression would make it a chronic western condition.

In 1908, the Bank Act was amended to alleviate another obstacle in the path of western development. The seasonal nature of farming meant that the annual fall sale of the crop brought a surge in the demand for ready cash. Since the banks were limited in their note circulation to the extent of their paid-up capital, the West faced a seasonal cash drought every fall. Because this cash crunch tended to choke national development, Finance Minister Fielding seized the initiative in 1908 and permitted the banks to circulate notes equivalent to 115 per cent of paid-up capital in the crop-moving period, subject to a 5 per cent tax on excess circulation. It was a crucial precedent, because for the first time the government had found a direct mechanism to affect the volume of credit available in the country. In the 1913 Bank Act revision, this precedent was expanded by the creation of a Central Gold Reserve, by which banks might obtain excess circulation upon deposit of gold or Dominion notes with the Reserve.[17] While some bankers felt threatened by these government initiatives, Pease of the Royal welcomed them, realizing that they facilitated bank development in the West. The West was hungry for loans, and the Royal wanted as much financial reach into the region as possible. "Yes," he told the politicians in 1913, "our loans run from one, two, and three times as much as our deposits. ...Our loans are very much in excess of our deposits. I could not say definitely, but at least 150 per cent." Big banks, he argued, were better equipped to cater to the needs of the frontier. Despite high overheads and meagre deposits, western branches moved eastern savings to western opportunities. If an 8 per cent interest rate was sometimes charged, Pease believed that the accessibility of loan money warranted it.[18] He also believed that mergers offered the Royal a means of extending its western reach – mergers brought an expanded asset base and a broader net of branches.

Since the move to Montreal in 1887, the bank's paid-up capital had increased with exponential regularity. From a base of $2 million in 1900, it surged to $6.2 million by 1910. Each increase necessitated an elaborate *pro rata* distribution of shares to existing shareholders and a series of "calls" for the shares to be taken up. Maritimers remained very loyal to the bank and continued to constitute the majority of its shareholders. A steady stream of Royal dividends, which would peak at 12 per cent per annum in the 1911-31 period, flowed into the Maritimes. Since so much depended on the bank's capital base, Pease decided to broaden it forcefully. In Montreal, he induced friends such as Charley Hosmer to take large blocks of Royal shares. Herbert Holt maintained a modest-but-by-no-means-controlling block of Royal shares throughout his presidency, reaching 1,300 shares in the early 1930s.

As early as 1902, Pease had explored ways of expanding the shareholding base in more dramatic fashion. Since 1899, the bank had maintained an agency in New York and, although barred from American retail banking, the Royal had acquired a certain notoriety in New York as a Canadian bank that was making deep inroads into Cuba, the Americans' *de facto* sugar colony. Since American banks were legislatively restricted from exporting their services, the Royal had an inner track on the Cuban market. With this in mind, Pease headed for New York and Chicago in late 1902 with a proposal that prominent American capitalists take up stock in the Royal. Working through the New York financial firm of Blair & Co., Pease secured orders for 5,000 shares at a premium price of $250 a share. The takers came from the front rank of the American financial élite: Marshall Field, the Chicago retailer; J. Ogden Armour, the meat-packer; Ledyard C. Blair, a steel, railway, and financial-services capitalist, and others.[19] Pease's *coup* brought an extra $1.25 million in capital to the bank's books.

In later years, the notion grew up that what happened in 1902 was in fact an American takeover bid for the Royal. An editorial in the *Monetary Times* speculated at the time that the 5,000 shares "could" allow the new American shareholders "if they chose" to take control of the bank. The *Times* pointed out that one of the American share-holders was George Baker, president of the National Bank in New York and a friend of J. P. Morgan. The syndicate was thus, some historians have alleged, a Trojan horse for Morgan. There is no evidence for this fancy. The archival record reveals that Pease both initiated and controlled the whole exercise. The New Yorkers did not seek and received no board representation. They bought no more shares and remained passive investors. Had they moved for control, Halifax and Montreal directors could have easily mustered sufficient votes to destroy the Americans' pretensions. Instead, the placing of shares in American hands represented yet another aspect of the bank's search to circumvent the limits of its internal growth.

It is clear that, by about 1905, Pease and the Royal directors were also consciously entertaining the notion of growth by way of merger. Bank mergers were hardly a novelty. In the nineteenth century, failing or failed banks often sought refuge in the arms of an established bank. One of Edson Pease's first assignments on joining the Merchants' was to evaluate the assets of the troubled Maritime Bank in Saint John. A subsequent negotiation for a share exchange was aborted, and four years later, in 1887, the Maritime collapsed.[20] When successful, such mergers were little more than salvage exercises. Furthermore, they required a special act of Parliament to complete. The 1900 Bank Act revision dropped the provision for a special act and permitted mergers by mutual agreement and approval of the federal cabinet on recom-mendation of the Treasury Board. Failed banks would in future be dealt with by a CBA-appointed curator. Combined with the vigorous national economy, the Act now opened the way to mergers between relatively healthy banks intent on aggrandizing themselves. Merger fever began to creep into bank boardrooms: "Any amalgamation suggestion that comes to my notice," the superintendent of branches assured President

*A Union Bank of Canada branch in Strathmore, Alberta, c.1923 and a Northern Crown branch in Lloydminster, Saskatchewan, c.1918 (opposite page). In large urban centres, branches were the result of commissioned architecture (often executed by well-known Montreal or New York architects), but in small towns, branches were usually the product of "factory" architecture. The Royal's architecture department in Montreal (under S. G. Davenport from 1920 to 1942) produced set-piece designs for rural branches. Such designs usually incorporated classical features such as a pediment and pillars to give the branch a sense of solidity. Banks also experimented with prefabricated branches; the Royal took a fifty-seven-ton "knock-down" branch to Vladivostok, Russia, in 1919.*

Kenny, "will be mentioned to you."[21] Cautiously, the bank began to sniff out potential merger candidates. Tentative negotiations were held with the ailing Ontario Bank, but when the extent of the Ontario's indebtedness was discovered, the directors pushed the Toronto bank in the direction of the larger Bank of Montreal.[22] From the outset, it was plain that orchestrating mergers required a deft mixture of caution and decisiveness. Much to its chagrin, the board watched in 1905 as the Bank of Montreal snatched the Peoples Bank of Halifax out from under its nose. Edson Pease learned such lessons quickly.

Mergers made eminent sense in Maritime banking. Intuition had told Kenny and Pease in the 1880s that size and breadth were the surest guarantees of their bank's survival. Sooner or later, Maritime banks that did not grow became trapped in a regional economy that was slowly losing its dynamism. In 1902, John Stairs, Halifax's leading industrialist, confided to William Robertson, president of the Union Bank of Halifax, that there had been a "marked tendency on the part of the larger banks to increase still further their capital," and that trouble lay ahead for "small Maritime banks." If Toronto and Montreal controlled Canadian finance exclusively, the result would be "disastrous" for Maritime industry and commerce. The solution, Stairs believed, was for all Halifax banks to join "into one large and resourceful banking institution."[23] The die was, however, already cast. The Royal and the Bank of Nova Scotia had already shifted onto the national stage. Maritime banking was now an integral part of national banking; it was no longer, however, on the cutting edge. If Stairs hoped for decisive action from the Union Bank of Halifax, he was sadly misinformed. The Union was a quintessential old-style Nova Scotian bank, hugging its native shores and fearful of "foreign" adventures. By 1910, it had forty-five branches – all but seven within the province – and assets of $15 million. It had not opened in Montreal until 1909. Its one bid for boldness had come in 1902, when, egged on by budding financier Max Aitken, it had bought the Commercial Bank of Windsor. A handful of branches in Puerto Rico and Trinidad represented the bank's only other flicker of initiative. It was thus, by 1910, a solid, unimaginative, regional bank, perching on an increasingly narrow foundation.

From Pease's perspective, the Union was attractive in two respects. Its thirty-eight Nova Scotian branches offered the Royal a chance to consolidate its hold on Nova Scotia. An overlap with the Royal's sixteen Nova Scotia branches existed in only ten locations. The merger would thus make the Royal the largest bank in the province, an important status considering the continuing strength of some of its industries and the Maritimers' propensity for saving. Pease also cast an envious eye on the Union's staff. Here was a well-trained crew of Maritime bankers, who with the right handling might be persuaded to transfer their loyalty to a more-progressive bank with similar Halifax origins. The Union was noted for its good service and integrity: its officers prided themselves on their "democratic views," and the *esprit de corps* in the ranks had won the bank a reputation as a "bank of the people."[24]

Bank mergers early in the century were never hostile takeovers. They were instead smooth, secretly arranged affairs designed to present shareholders with a virtual *fait accompli*. Since shareholder approval was needed to sanction any merger, the terms of the deal – usually a share exchange – had to be advantageously framed. Shareholders had to be presented with a good deal and a good rationale. Since Ottawa's approval was needed after shareholder ratification, the deal had also to be cast as being in the public interest. From the outset, Pease proved an adroit merger manager. In the spring of 1910, he put out feelers to William Robertson, the Union's president. A Halifax merchant cut from the same cloth as Tom Kenny, Robertson lacked any ambition to carry his bank inland, and he proved a willing negotiator. The Royal's first acquisition was thus a model of expedition.

In late July, Robertson unveiled the deal he had struck with Pease. The Union was starved of capital, capital it needed to compete with the larger banks of Canada. Past efforts seemed to indicate that this capital was not forthcoming. A liaison with the Royal, then the third-largest Bank in Canada, promised salvation. Conscious of Nova Scotians' suspicion of central-Canadian designs, Robertson assured his shareholders that the Royal "may still be regarded as a Nova Scotian institution" whose shares were largely held in the province. To clinch their approval, Union shareholders were asked to exchange their stock at the rate of five Union for two Royal shares. Since Royal shares, nominally worth $100, were trading at nearly $250, and Union shares were nominally valued at $50, there was little reason for hesitation. To sweeten the deal, the Royal promised to boost its dividend to 12 per cent, to take Robertson onto its board, and to retain Union employees for at least a year at existing salaries.[25] At a special shareholders' meeting on September 7, 1910, unanimous approval was won for the deal. The next morning in Montreal, a special meeting of Royal share-holders approved an increase of $1.2 million in the bank's paid-up capital to cover the twelve thousand shares issued to Union share-holders. Ottawa offered no resistance to the merger, issuing its approval on November 1. Assistant General Manager Neill went so far as to write the Finance Department to thank it for its "special effort" and "courteous treatment" in reviewing the deal.[26] Almost immediately, an elaborate procedure clicked into operation: Royal inspectors appeared at Union branches, ledgers and vault keys were exchanged, and the Union Bank of Halifax ceased to exist.

The Royal's takeover of the Union and the Bank of Nova Scotia's 1913 acquisition of the Bank of New Brunswick sealed the fate of Maritime banking. Regional banking had little future "down east." Instead, the region increasingly became an integral part of the Royal's *national* system. After 1910, the Royal would look westward for further merger candidates. The Union, none the less, left a legacy: "Union boys" soon proved their mettle in the Royal. Many found more challenging horizons in the new bank. Charles Pineo, a Union accountant in Puerto Rico, excelled in the Royal's international operations. Another Union accountant, Rowland Frazee, would later introduce his son to the Royal "family." In 1979, Rowland junior would become the Royal's chief executive.

Canada's surge of economic growth peaked in 1912; a sharp commercial depression in 1913 and 1914 cooled the frenzy of immigration and industrialization. By then the economic face of Canada had been dramatically changed. Nowhere was this more evident than in Toronto's ascendancy as a centre of commerce. While St. James Street's primacy would remain intact for another forty years, Toronto's Bay Street and its Ontario hinterland were now a force to be reckoned with in Canadian economic life.[27] From the turn of the century the Royal had eyed Toronto with ambition. Stiff competition, a scarcity of labour, and the high cost of real estate had blunted its hopes. Toronto's own banks – the Commerce, Imperial, Toronto, Dominion, and Traders – dominated the city and the province. By 1912, the Royal had only 39 Ontario branches. The front-running Traders had 104. Pease knew that Ontario was an indispensable block in any attempt to build up the Royal's national reach, and he also knew that the cost would be high. Then luck intervened.

In 1906, the Traders had taken possession of its new head office – said to be the tallest commercial building in the Empire – at the corner of Yonge and Colborne in Toronto. Behind this magnificent façade, the Traders had problems. Its strength lay in its small-town Ontario network. In the 1890s, for instance, its inspector, Aemilius Jarvis, had canvassed the concession lines, dropping Traders "piggy-banks" off at farm homes and returning monthly to empty them. But the Traders never developed a strong urban network, and thus found its fortunes unduly dependent on the fortunes of agriculture. By 1910, it had only eight branches in Toronto and a single Montreal branch. Consequently,

*The Toronto-based Traders Bank was strongly rooted in rural Ontario. In the early 1890s, its inspector, Aemilius Jarvis, developed an ingenious cast-metal savings bank (above), modelled after the bank's Toronto Head Office (opposite page). The savings bank was left at farm homes, where savers deposited coins in slots along its roof line. Compartments inside could be designated for specific savings purposes. Once a month, bank officials visited the farm to unlock the roof and "deposit" the savings.*

it had little commercial exposure. Two of the business accounts it *did* have, a construction company at the Sault and a Kentucky coal-and-timber company, were in deep trouble.[28] Furthermore, the Traders had only a smattering of branches in the West and none east of Montreal. While there were no visible cracks, the Traders was in fact in precarious shape, and in the spring of 1912, a Toronto lawyer, D. Lorne McGibbon, quietly began to try to orchestrate a buy-out of the bank. In March, he brought together Stuart Strathy, the Traders' general manager, with the president of the Bank of Toronto. A tentative purchase agreement was signed. Strathy was promised $200,000 if he would facilitate the merger. When the deal collapsed, two young Toronto promoters, Albert E. Dyment and Douglas K. Ridout, stepped into the breach and began a search for another potential buyer. Dyment and Ridout were described by the Toronto *World* as being part of the "young element in local finance"; Dyment was a stockbroker with an interest in timber development and horse breeding and Ridout was in insurance. Their attention soon focused on Pease of the Royal.[29]

Acquiring the Traders appealed to Pease. Its strength was the Royal's weakness. The two banks overlapped in only eleven communities; acquisition of the Traders' Ontario system would give the Royal greater exposure than any other bank in the province. Once again, there was also the inviting prospect of additional staff. The price, Pease knew, would be steep, and the negotiations would be delicate. Traders' shareholders, unaware of any of their bank's problems and satisfied by its 8 per cent dividend, might be reluctant to surrender their shares, particularly to a Montreal bank. If the deal became public prematurely, or if Traders' management opposed it, the resultant publicity might spark a panic. Pease accordingly moved quickly. On May 8, Holt informed the board that a deal had been struck. Two days later, the Traders broke the terms of the deal to its shareholders: 33,600 Royal shares valued at $240 each in exchange for the Traders' assets. Three Traders directors on the Royal board, a boost in dividend to 12 per cent, and security for the staff rounded out the deal. The Royal would accommodate its new shareholders by increasing its capital base from $10 to $25 million. Traders management heartily endorsed the exchange: the two systems were supplementary and the merged bank would enjoy the stability of a well-managed bank, with large reserves and capital. The merger would produce increased confidence and security.[30] In Montreal, Holt assured his shareholders that the merger would eliminate waste and was in keeping with the pattern of consolidation that had made Scottish and English banking so efficient.[31] Early in July, shareholders of both banks happily approved the merger. The Traders' general manager, Stuart Strathy, became the Royal's Ontario supervisor, and in September three

Traders directors – E. F. B. Johnston, a prominent Toronto corporate lawyer, W. J. Sheppard, a lumber baron, and C. S. Wilcox, a Hamilton steel man – joined Holt's board. The election of a fourth director, Albert Dyment, an outsider with no previous obvious tie to the Royal or the Traders, must have struck many as peculiar.

In fact, Dyment's name was the only evidence of a huge corporate deal that had been slipped by the shareholders unannounced. Dyment was taking his part of the reward for delivering the Traders into Pease's hands. In April, he and Ridout had struck a secret deal with Pease and his assistant general manager C. E. Neill to ensure that "the President, Board of Directors and General Manager of the Traders Bank will agree to the conditions of the sale, and recommend same to the shareholders."[32] For this they would receive a "commission" of $600,000, an astonishingly generous sum. Dyment and Ridout subsequently agreed to pay Strathy, the Traders general manager, $150,000 to coax his shareholders into accepting the Royal's embrace.

The Dyment deal was unethical, but not illegal. Instead of being a love match, the Traders/Royal merger was in fact an arranged marriage. Although A. J. Brown, the Royal's corporate counsel and a director, assured the Finance Department that the deal was virtually the same as the 1910 Union Bank of Halifax acquisition, Finance Minister Thomas White was uneasy from the outset about the implication of the merger. His political instincts told him that Torontonians looked askance at the prospect of a Montreal bank swallowing a local bank. Sensing public concern over growing bank concentration, White also wanted to see the Bank Act revised before any further mergers were consummated. He told the CBA president that he favoured some form of prior notification of the minister before deals were ratified.[33] White's concern grew when the Toronto *World* attacked the merger as a "blow to Toronto."[34] A Toronto Tory, White became even more agitated when one of his constituents wrote him, alleging that the Royal was paying "bribes" to Traders officers.[35] White asked Brown for an explanation. If there was any truth in the story, he confided to Prime Minister Borden, "the public would be shocked to learn of a transaction such as this."[36] On August 7, Strathy made a solemn oath, stating that the $150,000 payment had initially been intended as a "retiring allowance," but this had been cancelled when it was decided to make him the Royal's Ontario supervisor.[37] On August 23, Treasury Board in Ottawa approved the merger, and Strathy shortly thereafter took up his new duties in the Royal. Almost a year later, in June 1913, A. J. Brown quietly arranged for $300,000, the unpaid balance of their 1912 commission, to be sent to Dyment and Ridout through the bank's New York agency, and $150,000 to

Strathy "in full payment of all claims against A. E. Dyment and Douglas K. Ridout."[38] Shareholders never learned of these payments.

While Pease was soon complaining about the "weak character" of much of the Traders business and that over a hundred of its men had quit,[39] the acquisition of the Traders made the Royal one of Canada's major banks at one stroke. It reinforced the growing impression that the Royal was a progressive bank.[40] It also coincided with a pronounced shift in Canadian attitude to the banking industry. The years from 1909 to 1912 had witnessed an unprecedented spate of mergers in Canadian business. Merger kings such as Max Aitken wheeled and dealed companies such as the Steel Company of Canada and Canada Cement into existence, working in a *laissez-faire* business environment of minimal government intervention and remarkable investor credulity.

The banks were at least obliged by Section 99 of the Bank Act to report their mergers to Ottawa for sanction, but even with this regulator in place, a public debate over the limits of bank concentration began to emerge. Canadian concern echoed a much-more-vigorous debate over the limits of the "money power" in the United States. The Wall Street "Money Panic" of 1907 had dramatically revealed the shortcomings of the decentralized American bank system: its fragmented nature was chronically prone to uncontrollable contractions in credit and in normal times worked inefficiently in moving money around the country and in rediscounting business notes. The American public was also more prone to see banking as the creature of a handful of secretive financiers. At the famous 1912 Pujo Hearings before the U.S. House of Representatives, the "money power" was put on political trial. "Muckrakers" provided a Greek chorus of opprobrium against big money in the press. In 1913, Congress moved to impose a measure of central discipline on banking by creating the Federal Reserve System, a chain of twelve regional banks designed to "rediscount" (i.e., influence credit creation through discounting for a second time commercial paper taken by retail banks) the credit of America's banks and to act as clearing house for financial transactions. Owned by the banks, the Federal Reserve was a *de facto* central bank. American banking had "reformed" itself.

In Canada, the debate was more muted.[41] With the spectacular exception of the Sovereign's collapse, Canadian banks had weathered the Panic of 1907 on a relatively even keel. Finance Minister Fielding had personally commended CBA president Sir Edward Clouston on the "good reputation" of Canada's banks and suggested that they capitalize on this by selling their stock in Europe.[42] As the ten-year revision of the Bank Act approached, however, Fielding began to detect voices of criticism. Bank failures drew demands for government inspection of banks, and mergers provoked calls for stiffer government policing of the merger process. The spectacular crash of the Farmers Bank in 1910 – brought on by fraudulent management and dubious mining loans – fanned the fires of criticism. Banks, concluded the *Monetary Times*, "should regard mining investments as a man would the handling of red-hot coal." Others demanded better recognition of shareholder rights; Farmers Bank shareholders had lost all. Bank mergers also excited regional jealousies; Halifax, Winnipeg, and Vancouver were sensitive to the growing commercial prowess of Montreal and Toronto.

The Liberal government remained, none the less, fundamentally sympathetic to the bankers; Laurier once described Canadian banking as "fair, just and equitable."[43] In January 1911, Fielding introduced a revised Bank Act that hinted at reform, with the inclusion of an independent shareholders' audit, but the bill was shunted aside when the government plunged the country into a heated debate over U.S. free trade, a debate which was to lead to a Tory victory at the polls that fall.

It was not until 1913 that Conservative finance minister Thomas White again turned towards Bank Act revision. White, a Bay Street financier, inherited Fielding's basic empathy for bankers. Other Parliamentarians were more sceptical. At the Commons committee hearings accompanying the revision, Canadian bankers were for the first time obliged to explain themselves publicly. Bank Act revision had ceased to be a cosy, predictable affair between bank general managers and the finance minister, and, no longer a small regional bank, the Royal found itself at centre stage. Pease, not Holt, spoke for the bank. Again and again, he affirmed his belief that bank mergers were in the national interest. Mergers removed "weak banks" and stabilized the banking industry. Merged banks profited from economies of scale; they reduced overheads "very largely." Large banks served communities – particularly the West – better by moving capital around the country. "I am not averse to strengthening the banks," Pease concluded. "I think 'In union there is strength' and that there is room for a great deal of economy, as there is a great deal of waste." By this standard, the Traders acquisition was a "good one." When asked how much the Royal had paid in commission to "outside agents" for the Traders, Pease declined all comment. He was sharply critical of any suggestion that mergers be submitted to Parliament for approval: "I think it would defeat the object in view....The good will of a bank would be dissipated before you could reach Parliament. Every bank would make a dead onslaught to get its business, leaving

*(continued on p. 144)*

# RELUCTANT SALESMEN

## The Beginnings of Bank Advertising

"THE BUSINESS OF A BANKER DOES not lead him to the public, but the public to him," wrote George Rae in his seminal Country Banker of 1850. "He does not cross the street to Brown to beseech him for a deposit, nor to Jones to implore him to overdraw his account." Canadian bankers studied their Rae well. In their view, there was something crass and unbankerly about advertising. At most, they placed innocuous notices of their hours, address, and services in newspapers, but these never exalted the quality of service nor disparaged the competition. When the McKim advertising agency solicited the bank's business in 1903, the board did not "view the proposal favourably." The bank was already well known throughout the Maritimes, it reasoned, and the expenditure "would not warrant the outlay."

By the turn of the century, the pressure of national growth obliged bankers to act less bashfully. With mushrooming branch systems and unprecedented population growth, it was crucial to keep a bank's name in the public eye, but the approach remained indirect: cultivate goodwill and associate the bank with national expansion. Within Canada, the Royal began distributing desk blotters and calendars aimed at various segments of society: university students, farmers, and Boy Scouts. The blotters carried tips on first-aid and fire prevention. Abroad, "reaching the foreigner" considering immigration to Canada was the priority.

Pamphlets in languages as varied as Hungarian and Yiddish were sent to Europe, extolling Canada's potential and the Royal's availability for foreign-exchange transactions. For new Canadians, the bank printed calendars and service information in Chinese, Portuguese, and other languages. All this was done in an ad hoc manner. The animus against direct advertising persisted. As late as 1918, Edson Pease told the CBA that "I am strongly opposed to any advertising that takes the form of direct solicitation."

The First World War opened bankers' eyes. The dramatic

Savings That Grow as the Child Grows
Assure Education and Success to the Man

*Advertising extolling saving, c.1930 (above) and advertising aimed at immigrants, c.1924 (opposite).*

effectiveness of government war-bond campaigns in drawing billions of dollars out of Canadians' pockets into the war effort convinced bankers that advertising was a potent force in Canadian society. In 1919, the Royal established an advertising department at head office. Under Gordon Tait, the department brought a system to the bank's bid to build good-will and recognition. A Monthly Letter was established to provide the general public with analysis of the Canadian economy. The bank undertook sponsorship of prizes at agricultural fairs. Guides to foreign trade were published. The blotters began carrying homilies that reflected the Presbyterian soul of Canadian banking: "What is Thrift?" "The Bondage of Debt," and "Your First $100." In the late 1920s, it seemed only natural that the bank's first "star" promoter should have been the Scottish tenor Sir Harry Lauder endorsing "thrift." Millions of Canadian school children began the annual ritual of wrapping their texts in manila covers emblazoned with the Royal logo and a brief lesson in history or saving that were supplied by the bank. The artwork in these advertisements was often striking. In 1930, poster advertising was initiated by the Norman Rockwell-like "Happiness through Savings" series.

Despite its conservative nature, bank advertising was well established by 1930. The Royal finally had an advertising agency – Cockfield Brown – and saw advertising as a means of expanding and defending its place in society. When Western

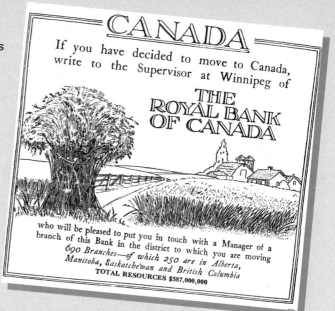

hostility to bank mergers began to mount in the mid-1920s, General Manager Charlie Neill penned a pamphlet essay entitled "Canadian Banks and Local Business," which was distributed free as a way of boosting the bank's legitimacy in the eyes of the public. On occasion, bank advertising hinted at products. The availability of safety-deposit boxes and travellers' cheques were "sold" on grounds of their security and convenience. There would, however, be no hard-sell of bank products until the 1950s, when personal chequing accounts were introduced. Similarly, marketing, advertising's hand-maiden, did not appear as a corporate function until the 1960s. Without marketing research to segment the market, advertising had to be applied in an undifferentiated fashion. Bank advertising appeared only in print. Radio advertising seemed huckster-ish, better suited to soap and tooth-paste. The banks did not take to the airwaves until the late 1960s, when advertising was called upon to change customers' attitudes: "Will that be cash or Chargex?"

nothing to the purchasing bank."[44] When asked if bank concentration had gone "too far," Pease said he thought not, pointing to the small number of Scottish banks: "I think they have the best banking facilities in the world."

The Bank Act revision of 1913 made two concessions to the public mood of reform. Shareholders were afforded the right of selecting an independent auditor to make an annual inspection of their bank's financial affairs. In early 1914, Royal shareholders selected Marwick, Mitchell, Peat & Co. to represent them. Government inspection was held at bay. Similarly, Parliament was given no sway over bank takeovers, but banks were now obliged to seek ministerial approval *before* finalizing any merger agreement through their shareholders. The finance minister was thus put in a better position to ensure that the public interest was served by a proposed merger. From the bankers' point of view, the critical path to a merger now became delicate; it was less possible to present the minister with a *fait accompli*. Management of both banks in a potential merger had to ensure that the minister was presented with an airtight case demonstrating public good. In later years, definition of "public interest" proved difficult. Did it mean the removal of weak banks or the building up of a national system? Timing and secrecy were now doubly important. A well-timed intervention from a foe of the merger might spook the minister or entice another party to the bidding or provoke panic in the clients of the bank about to be taken over. A deft touch would be needed. Just how deft Pease would learn in 1915.

The commercial slump of 1914 and the outbreak of war temporarily cooled the ardour of Canadian bankers for mergers. In the summer of 1915, Pease saw an opportunity to replicate his Traders *coup*. As early as 1907, a small Ontario bank, the Bank of Hamilton, had unsuccessfully sounded out the Royal on a possible merger. Like the Traders, the Bank of Hamilton was strong in rural districts and weak in the cities. Only 19 of its 124 branches were urban. It had no branches east of Toronto. It had developed some western exposure, and it was questionable loans on the Prairies, weakened by the slump in grain prices in 1914, that reawakened thoughts of a merger. "The amalgamation," the Bank of Hamilton general manager would later tell the finance minister, "has many points in its favour...as the Royal Bank supplies exactly what we lack – strong reserves, large earning power for dividend requirements and a chain of branches in the East."[45] By early July, Pease had a tentative deal, but before he could seek shareholder ratification he had to obtain Ottawa's blessing. Here Pease thought he had a trump card: Herbert Holt.

By 1915, Holt was *persona grata* in Ottawa. He fit neatly into the "nation building" school of capitalism, as a railway builder, utility capitalist, and now a bank president. He sat on scores of company boards and loomed large in the Anglo-Conservative business élite of Montreal. Prime Minister Borden in Ottawa looked on Holt as a "progressive" businessman, one capable of admitting the reforming power of the state into society while maintaining a fundamental belief in capitalism. In 1913, Borden had asked Holt to chair the Federal Plan Commission, an advisory panel empowered to divine a master plan for the development of the national capital. The commission's 1915 report – unacted upon in wartime – laid the capital out on a grand scale with broad boulevards and vistas.[46] War brought out Holt's jingoism, and he soon found himself congratulated by Borden for helping to finance a machine-gun contingent and for various bits of political advice.[47] Through all this, Holt was only minimally involved in bank affairs: his letters to Borden were not even written on Royal letterhead. Holt appeared punctually to chair the bank's weekly board meeting, but Pease ran the bank. Now Pease saw that Holt's stature in Ottawa might well help to facilitate the Bank of Hamilton merger. What Pease forgot was that to most Ontarians Holt was a Montrealer.

In mid-July, Pease and Brown drafted a letter to Finance Minister White for Holt's signature. Ottawa should approve the merger, Holt argued, because the Hamilton bank had "a comparatively small earning power" and had been subject to several "runs." Unlike the Royal, it had failed to shed the "local character" of its name and had little city business. It had "seen its best days." The letter concluded with as explicit a statement of the Royal's merger philosophy as would ever emerge: "I think that anything which tends to make the banks stronger and more powerful is of greater importance than the decrease in numbers, provided the reduction is not carried too far."[48]

The danger implicit in the revised merger-approval process was that a deal hung in the balance until the minister ruled on it. Secrecy was all-important and was virtually impossible to preserve. To his consternation, Pease discovered in early August that news of the merger had "leaked out in some unaccountable way" and that White believed that his authority had been circumvented.[49] The leak aroused the voice of Ontario provincialism; another Ontario bank seemed about to be devoured by a Montreal competitor. J. S. Willison, editor of the Toronto *Daily News*, told White that, although it was a "weak" bank, control of the Bank of Hamilton could not be allowed to leave the province. Willison suggested that a nation at war had other priorities than bank mergers and implied that A. E. Dyment was at the bottom of this "unnecessary" merger.[50] The general manager of the Hamilton bank fought back, attacking the "noisy newspapers." Pease joined in,

*The Royal's reputation as Canada's high-flyer of bank mergers was matched, on a recreational level, by its adventurous senior executives. Here a distinctly ill-at-ease Edson Pease (above, left seat) prepares for a seaplane flight, c.1922. A decade later Sir Herbert Holt took to the air (opposite page, front seat). When it came to bank mergers, Pease was always in the pilot's seat, with Holt sitting quietly in the passenger's seat.*

arguing that the general financial situation was conducive to a merger in the public interest. The final blow was landed when Hamilton City Council passed a resolution against the merger, and the local MP joined the chorus of opposition. The rapid politicization of the issue and the danger of provoking a run on the Bank of Hamilton prompted White to quick action: on August 20, he summarily denied permission for the merger. He told Pease that he had acted because of the "newspaper controversy." He told the Bank of Hamilton general manager that he believed his bank to be in "excellent standing" and not in need of a merger.[51]

Pease was livid. For years the whole episode rankled with him. White had not served the public interest: the Royal's "generous offer" would have rendered a "distinct service to the public in absorbing an institution which at best has a doubtful future."[52] The Montreal *Gazette* provided an obituary for the deal: "geographical prejudice and not a principle" had prevailed.[53] Although Pease and White became the closest of confidants as the war progressed, Pease refused to let the memory of the Hamilton fiasco fade. As late as 1920, he reminded the retired White that his 1915 decision had, among other things, hurt the Royal's ongoing attempt to secure "a large number of men without which we could not have extended our branches to the British West Indies and further South."[54] Banker and politician had, in short, arrived at different definitions of the public interest: Pease's was direct and was cast in terms of banking efficiency, and White's was political and coloured by circumstance. In 1923, the Toronto-based Bank of Commerce took over the still-wobbly Bank of Hamilton.

The Royal never again attempted to play the merger game in Ontario. The Traders had given it sufficient resources to rely henceforth on internal growth in Canada's richest province – 1919 would see the Royal launch a crusade of new branches in Ontario. Pease would complete his amalgamation jigsaw nearer home in Montreal and also in the West. The acquisition of the venerable Quebec Bank in 1917 and of the Winnipeg-based Northern Crown in 1918 consolidated the Royal in Anglo Quebec and made its presence pervasive on the Prairies. Both were indisputably "weak" banks, and their disappearance aroused little public or ministerial concern. By the mid-teens, it became a truism in Canadian banking that the stronger became stronger and the weak became more vulnerable to, and in some cases more desperate for, amalgamation. As the national economy malfunctioned in the pre-war slump and again in the lethargic early twenties, smaller banks either collapsed, as the Home Bank did so spectacularly in 1923, or simply folded their tents and moved peaceably into the camp of a larger bank. For Edson Pease and his big-bank confrères, amalgamation became cheaper and easier. By 1925, the cycle was virtually complete, and amalgamation ceased to hold much attraction for the managers of what now seemed a rationalized national bank system. The public accordingly readjusted its sensibilities, prompting Parliament to revise the Bank Act in 1923 and create the office of Inspector General of Banks in 1924, to police the system by making an annual inspection of each chartered bank.

The Quebec Bank was an Anglo-Quebec institution. Founded in 1818, it was Canada's second-oldest bank and had thrived throughout most of the nineteenth century on the fruits of Quebec City's wood-and-water economy. Although it initially attracted some French-Canadian participation, the Quebec Bank soon became a conservatively managed instrument of Anglo commerce in the Quebec–Montreal corridor.[55] As such, it failed to adjust to the decline of traditional Quebec City timber staple and the emergence of new opportunities in the continental interior. Only belatedly did it push westwards, establishing scattered branches in Ontario and across the Prairies. By 1916, it had a network of fifty-eight branches, twenty-six of which were in Quebec. In a bid to capitalize on its ties with Montreal hydro developers such as J. E. Aldred, it moved its head office to Montreal in 1912. The push for diversification was, however, weak and reckless. The bank was hit hard by bad loans to utilities developers and the impact of the pre-war slump on Quebec commerce. Late in 1915, the directors were forced to draw $337,000 from the bank's rest (a bank's reserve fund against bad debts) to shore up its profit-and-loss account.[56] Depletion of the rest account signalled the death rattle of a bank.

Twice before, the Quebec Bank had sought to merge with a larger bank. After fruitless negotiations with the Union Bank of Canada in 1907, the directors turned to Pease at the Royal and actually initialled an agreement before breaking off the deal.[57] By 1916, they had no such option. In September, the desperate board offered Pease a "full opportunity to examine the affairs of this Bank." A month later Pease offered them 9,117 Royal Bank shares and $683,775 cash for the assets of their bank. The bank's shareholders had little option but to ratify the merger at a special meeting a month later; John Ross, the president, provided a final prod by pointing out that the bank was so weighed down by bad debts that it could not even advance money to its best customers. On December 28, Ottawa approved the merger, and on January 2, 1917, the Quebec Bank ceased to exist – just a year shy of its centenary. The financial press praised the deal, pointing out that the Royal had acquired assets at a knock-down price, as well as "a large and welcome addition to its staff, which is badly needed on account of war conditions."[58] Quebec shareholders could comfort themselves that they had at least escaped with one Royal share and $75 for every three shares they had held in their beleaguered bank. Holt told Royal shareholders that they had finally secured a "valuable connection" in Quebec. In 1917, former Quebec Bank general manager B. B. Stevenson became supervisor of the Royal's fifty-one Quebec branches. In a private letter to his manager in London, England, Edson Pease showed his ego: the Quebec Bank gave him surplus men to open up "some attractive new fields," *and* it meant that the Royal now surpassed the Bank of Commerce in total assets.[59] Thirty years after its first appearance in the St. James Street financial district, the Royal was now hot on the heels of the Bank of Montreal.

Earlier in the same year the Quebec merger was finalized, Finance Minister White received a confidential letter from his cabinet colleague, Public Works Minister Bob Rogers. Rogers, a Manitoban, had heard rumours that the Winnipeg-based Northern Crown Bank was in trouble, the product of its own mismanagement. Most worrisome was the fact that the Northern Crown had paid a million dollars in dividends since its formation in 1908 – out of the Crown Bank of Toronto and Winnipeg's Northern Bank – and had neglected to build up its rest beyond a puny $150,000. Rogers wanted a thorough enquiry.[60] White instinctively turned to Frederick Williams-Taylor, the general manager of the Bank of Montreal, for advice; as the government's banker, the Bank of Montreal had both the ear and the trust of Ottawa. Williams-Taylor counselled patience and, remarkably, in 1917, buoyed by the wartime agricultural boom, the Northern Crown fought back. The rest was fattened to $715,000, and a 5 per

*Royal Bank branch in Whitemouth, Manitoba, in 1934*

cent dividend was restored. But the rot was in the timbers. Provision for bad debts continued to hamper the bank's lending and profits. When the bank's president resigned, rumours swirled and the shareholders became panicky, dumping the shares at depressed prices. Pease saw his opportunity: the Northern Crown's strategically located network of seventy-six Prairie branches offered the Royal a solid presence in Manitoba and Saskatchewan.[61]

Pease found a willing negotiator in the Northern Crown's new president, William Robinson, a Winnipeg lumber merchant. Robinson's persuasive letter to the finance minister won Ottawa's approval for the deal on March 8, 1918.[62] If nothing else, Northern Crown shareholders were enticed to ratify the merger by the prospect of the Royal's 12 per cent dividend. Their approval of the deal in early May also brought them 10,883 Royal shares and $576,970 in cash. The promise of seven Royal shares, plus cash, for every ten old shares would effectively double the income they received from their investment. Pease had learned to make his deals sweet to hasten their approval.[63] Robinson and two colleagues from the old board joined Holt's board. Suddenly, the Royal had 200 branches west of the Lakehead and 488 across the nation. Later that same year, the board in Montreal turned its thoughts to the upcoming fiftieth anniversary of the bank in 1919, and a decision was made to publish a pamphlet history of the bank, giving prominence to "its modest beginning, the development of its expansive policy, and its phenomenal growth."[64]

Edson Pease's "expansive policy" had other consequences. The Royal's emergence as a coast-to-coast bank was predicated on Pease's philosophical commitment to the virtues of *national* banking. A banking system with national scale and breadth assured stability and the efficient creation of credit for economic growth. Canadian bankers clung to this orthodoxy and resisted any hint that, as the Federal Reserve in the United States had done since 1913, the state or some outside agency might govern credit creation beyond the sway of the private bankers. As he surveyed the precarious condition of many of Canada's regional banks and witnessed the increasingly complex demand for credit generated by the diversified national economy, Pease began to question the received wisdom of his banking peers. Some form of central credit control, he concluded, was the natural outcome – not an obstacle in the path – of the vigorous consolidation of Canadian banking that he and the other managers of Canadian "big" banking were pursuing. By 1918, Pease would emerge as the first champion of a central bank for Canada.

The backbone of the Canadian banking system was the gold standard. The ultimate guarantee for anyone holding a Canadian banknote was that it was backed by gold or gold in the form of Dominion notes. While this ensured confidence and stability in the national currency, the reserves backing a bank's circulation were essentially non-earning and tended to crimp a bank's ability to expand credit in a buoyant economy. When Ottawa partially alleviated this strain by creating the Central Gold Reserve in 1913, Pease was strongly in favour of it as a means of expanding the Royal's credit. Extra circulation, made possible by the deposit of gold or Dominion notes in the central reserve, gave the bank added reach in the national economy.[65] The prospect of an unprecedented global conflict in 1914 unsteadied this system: Canadians frantically hoarded gold as a hedge against upheaval. Early in August 1914, Ottawa suspended the gold standard. To forestall a potential strangulation of bank credit, Ottawa offered advance money to the banks, taking securities (e.g., loans held by the banks) in return. This temporary measure – the Finance Act of 1914 – for the

*As the bank's managing director from 1916 to 1922, Edson Pease (opposite, in 1922)
dominated the Royal's strategic direction and was arguably Canada's most dynamic
banker. His $50,000 annual salary supported a bucolic, but luxurious, lifestyle.
At his country home, "The Pines," at Mt. Bruno, south of Montreal (above),
he entertained an association of Anglo-Montrealers, including his close
friends the Birks and the Drummonds. Pease was also instrumental in
establishing the nearby Mt. Bruno Country Club. He was
an adequate-but-not-avid golfer. Pease's social and professional
eminence in Montreal was testament to how far a "bank boy"
could go in Canadian society.*

first time put the power of expanding national credit in the hands of government, not private bankers. Pease found this piece of monetary *ad hocism* a "most effective and advantageous" means of providing credit for a wartime economy. It was, however, a makeshift, made possible by the draconian authority of the War Measures Act and not sustainable in peacetime.[66] It also, Pease suspected, set a trap for the Canadian economy when peace returned. The end-of-war production would cool the economy, depress commodity prices and thereby reduce bank deposits. At the same time, the reconstruction of the national infrastructure and of foreign trade would require plentiful credit. Some mechanism would be needed to assist the banks to stretch their credit; some favoured a return to the gold standard, others the perpetuation of the 1914 Act. Ever the "progressive" banker, Pease preferred a more innovative solution.

In 1916, Pease was elected president of the Canadian Bankers' Association. The CBA presidency embodied the consensus at the heart of Canadian banking: its incumbent took the sense of the banking community and carried it to Ottawa. War had invested the post with a heightened authority; all the intricacies of war finance from war-bond sales to currency controls were coordinated through the CBA presidency. The relationship between bankers and Ottawa, bonded by daily telegrams and incessant meetings, would be described by Pease at war's end as one of "perfect concord."[67] Late in 1917, with victory now a possibility, Pease decided to use this authority to tackle the dilemma of post-war credit creation. In July, he made inquiries as to whether the Bank of England might establish a branch for rediscounting in Canada, and then, in October, he used the Royal's New York agency to arrange an entrée to the Federal Reserve in Washington, where he befriended Paul Warburg, a confidant of President Woodrow Wilson and a Federal Reserve board member. Would Canadian banks, Pease asked, be permitted to join the U.S. Federal Reserve "to rediscount commercial paper and bills of exchange in an unlimited amount"?[68] Could the Royal become an agent of the Reserve in Canada? By mid-November, it was apparent that the answer was no. The Reserve would allow a foreign agent to handle only international transactions.[69] Pease would have to find his solution in Canada.

On January 10, 1918, Pease stepped to the podium at the Royal's annual meeting in Montreal and delivered a surprise. To an audience habituated to the smooth recitation of bank operations, he broached the question of establishing supplementary banking facilities for the post-war economy. "If we had a bank of rediscount patterned somewhat after the Federal Reserve Bank in the United States, it would render legitimately available millions of assets in the form of high grade commercial paper, now lying dormant in the portfolios of the banks, and thereby greatly increase our financial resources."[70] A committee of experts should be appointed by the government to investigate the proposal. Pease's foes would later charge that he was hiding behind his Royal Bank office to further his aspirations as CBA president, and should have waited for the CBA Council to approve his initiative. Pease responded that he spoke "in my individual capacity" to spark public debate.[71] Believing that "public criticism" of his proposal had been favourable, Pease took the idea to the CBA Council in late May. Here he succeeded in obtaining a resolution for the appointment of a "confidential committee" to study the proposal, subject to the finance minister's approval. Pease's gambit met a quick death when Frederick Williams-Taylor, general manager of the Bank of Montreal, voiced his staunch opposition to any form of central banking. The CBA could not act on a matter of "divided opinion."

For the next year, Pease butted his head against this wall of opposition. When, in July, White agreed to let the CBA draft legislation for a central bank, Williams-Taylor quickly enlisted Sir John Aird and Edmund Walker of the Commerce into his camp. Pease grew anxious: "unless you take hold of the scheme," he wrote White, "I think it is doomed to failure."[72] At the CBA's annual general meeting in November, he made an impassioned defence of his idea: "Serious problems will soon confront us in Canada in connection with the end of the war." Bankers could not continue to borrow from the government under the 1914 Act; it was not a "good principle," and it produced inflation. Far better to borrow for credit expansion from an impartial central bank. These arguments won Pease approval for a confidential committee. Again, Williams-Taylor objected. A central bank, he argued, would be open to "political influence and political patronage." The requirement that chartered banks pool their reserves in a central bank would penalize the strong banks and unduly protect the weak. A central bank would be a reckless experiment with "untried and possibly inexperienced managers." Better to continue to rely on the 1914 Finance Act and let each head office act as a central bank to its own branches.[73]

Pease persisted. In January 1919, he succeeded in convincing White to let the CBA, aided by Toronto's crack corporate lawyer, Zebulon A. Lash, continue to prepare draft legislation for a government-controlled central bank to manage the national debt (another of the war's "serious problems"), the floating of government loans, and "the lending to Banks of Dominion legal tender notes on securities."[74] In the end, it was Lash who finally dashed Pease's hopes. The war was over, and White had to act. The issues involved in establishing a central bank were, Lash reported, "so numerous and so susceptible of different kinds of treatment" that progress would be very slow. Early in February, the CBA's confidential committee advised White to put off such "drastic" change until the scheduled 1923 Bank Act revision. Pease did not attend the meeting; general manager Charlie Neill was sent to reiterate the Royal's belief in a "bank of rediscount." Shortly after, Bank of Montreal president Vincent Meredith suggested to White that it "is not too much to ask you to stand with the conservative and well-informed majority."[75] White duly extended the 1914 Finance Act into the post-war period. The April 1919 issue of the CBA *Journal* carried an article by Lash comparing the U.S. Federal Reserve and Canadian banking. The Federal Reserve, he concluded, was necessary because American banking was defective; the powers given to the Reserve "could always have been done and still be done by the banks of Canada."[76] Royal staff in Montreal would later recall that

Pease after this went to great lengths to avoid meeting and talking to Vincent Meredith.[77] Lash lived in Toronto and was easier to avoid.

There was an obvious sub-plot to the central-bank controversy. In 1917, Pease had attended the centenary festivities of the Bank of Montreal. He had always relished gentlemanly competition with Canada's senior bank: "You are the sun," he once wrote to Williams-Taylor, "and the rest of us are the stars revolving around you. Some of us may shoot to earth, but you will endure forever."[78] By 1917, however, Pease was entertaining thoughts of disturbing the cosmos. Creation of a central bank would have effectively ended the suzerainty of the Bank of Montreal as the government's banker. Since Confederation, the Bank of Montreal had been Ottawa's favoured banker, handling its affairs in London, managing its loans, holding its departmental accounts and, in the Great War, even acting as paymaster to Canadian troops in England. As the national debt burgeoned during the war, it seemed natural that the Montreal bank would be delegated to manage it in peacetime. Since early in the war, Bank of Montreal president Vincent Meredith had seen the Royal as a "persistent competitor" for its privileged trade.[79] Moreover, whatever its theoretical merits, a central bank threatened to be the Bank of Montreal's ultimate replacement, stripping it of all its perquisites as government banker. Pease, Meredith, and White all knew this: "the real question which is raised," White told Pease in 1919, "is whether the Bank of Montreal is to continue as the Government Bank or whether the Government's accounts are to be divided among all the Banks without exception."[80]

In 1919, the Royal lost out in its bid to create a central bank; the *status quo* prevailed. Despite his esteem for Pease, White in the end heeded the advice of the venerable Bank of Montreal. Later in the year, Pease's health collapsed and he headed for Victoria to recuperate. Throughout the 1920s, he appears haggard in photos, bags under his eyes. After he stepped down from the managing directorship in 1922, Charlie Neill took up the fight. Government accounts were won by mid-decade. Pease would go to his grave in 1930 before realizing his dream of a central bank. The Depression would vindicate him.

In December 1921, the Bank of Montreal stole a page out of Pease's playbook. It announced that it was merging with the four-hundred-branch Merchants Bank of Canada. The Bank of Montreal was no stranger to the merger game; however, most of its previous conquests had been relatively small banks – the Ontario Bank and Peoples Bank of New Brunswick, for instance. Now it had moved belatedly into the big league, taking over a major competitor. The Merchants was ailing; bad loans had necessitated a nearly $8-million reduction in the rest, and the president and general manager were subsequently charged with making false reports. The cry for government inspection of banks was again raised. Nevertheless, after the merger, with paid-up capital of $27,250,000 and 623 branches, the Bank of Montreal again seemed comfortably installed as Canada's largest bank.[81]

The fate of the Merchants Bank of Canada paralleled that of the nation in post-war – high hopes followed by a persistent depression. As Pease had warned the CBA, the armistice heralded a period of serious problems: falling commodity prices and industrial demand brought on a severe recession that lasted deep into the 1920s. Many misjudged their chances in the period and stumbled. One such reversal of fortune would once again prompt thoughts of merger at the Royal's head office. The Union Bank of Canada – founded in Quebec in 1865, but prescient enough to relocate its head office to Winnipeg in 1912 – celebrated the peace with a binge of expansion. From 1918 to 1920, its branch network grew from 299 to 393. It pursued an easy-lending policy, taking quick profits to boost its dividend to 10 per cent and investing in a joint venture in Oriental banking with a New York bank. All this fit neatly into a corporate culture that emphasized exuberant expansion: the Union had been the first bank into Alberta. During the Laurier boom, it prided itself on being first at the "end of steel." But by 1922, as the depression bit deeper, the Union began to regret its culture. Too exposed on the Prairies, it began reaping a harvest of bad debts. Branches were closed, the Oriental adventure was abandoned, and the dividend was trimmed. When shareholders showed signs of panic, the directors asked the Bank of Montreal to inspect the bank's assets. The news was grim: "there is too large a proportion of lower-grade business on your books; credits should be granted on a more conservative basis."[82] It was a familiar story: a regionally based bank caught off base. The rest was reduced $4.25 million in 1923, management was shaken up, and the arduous task of reconstruction begun.

Edson Pease's absence from daily management had not dulled the Royal's own merger instincts. General Manager Neill saw a marvellous opportunity for rounding out the bank's western presence: 204 of the Union's 320 branches were in the West. When Neill intimated to J. W. Hamilton, the Union's general manager, that a merger was possible, the Union board leapt at the chance. In less than three weeks, an agreement was hammered out: 40,000 Royal shares in exchange for the Union's $99 million in assets. The cost to the Royal was covered by the issue of $2,100,000 in new capital stock. Five Union directors came over to the Royal board, together with the entire staff. Given the precarious condition of the Union, Liberal Finance Minister James

Robb obligingly approved the merger on May 22. Few protested. One of those who did was former Union director R. T. Riley, now on the Royal board, who quietly noted to Arthur Meighen, the federal Tory leader, that "the Union is the only Bank of any size with its headquarters in the West, and it is being lost sight of."[83] With the Bank of Montreal's acquisition of the Molsons Bank later in 1925, the cycle of big-bank mergers ended and the new geographical pattern of Canadian banking was apparent. Vancouver, Winnipeg, Hamilton, Ottawa, Quebec City, Fredericton, and Halifax had become satellites in a net of national banking that radiated from Montreal's Place d'Armes and the corner of Yonge and King streets in Toronto.[84]

The success of the Royal's takeover campaign between 1910 and 1925 is of fundamental importance in understanding the bank's emergence in the mid-1920s as Canada's leading financial institution. By 1925, the Royal had branches in 801 Canadian communities. Four years later, it became the first Canadian bank with assets in excess of $1 billion. Other factors propelled this advance: vigorous overseas growth, a strong corporate culture, and personnel practices that encouraged youthful promotion and innovation. But it was the vision and verve with which Edson Pease conceived and executed the bank's amalgamation strategy that separated the Royal from its competitors. The Royal neither invented takeovers nor held an exclusive patent on them; as Pease told the Commons' committee: "we are not the arch consolidators." The Royal *was*, however, arguably the most skilled practitioner of the takeover. Pease selected each takeover candidate with cold, clear-headed deliberation. Each acquisition served to fill another gap in his jigsaw of national expansion. Each piece brought a special regional advantage – greater reach into western farming communities, a fuller blanket of urban branches, or service to special niches in the economy. With each takeover, the Royal soaked up the strengths of the amalgamated bank. Union Bank of Halifax bankers became legendary in the Royal for their Maritime resourcefulness and stamina. Northern Crown and Union of Canada veterans allowed the Royal to move with confidence and acceptance on the western concession lines. Such was the homogeneity of Canadian banking that bankers might transfer their allegiance with ease. The culture of the acquiring bank seldom looked threatening to those taken over; in fact, most were only too willing to attach their personal fortunes to a bank that was widely perceived as "up and coming." Pease's urge to merge was powerfully driven by the need to provide the Royal with a steady supply of reliable, pliable, and work-ready young men. Again and again, he celebrated his merger triumphs in terms of men acquired and the vistas their availability opened up. The Royal's pre-eminence as Canada's leading international

# THE AMALGAMATION NUMBERS GAME

Keeping track of total branch numbers for any bank is a perilous game. Branches open and close with annoying regularity, seldom on neat year-end dates. Other branches are moved and others change function (e.g. a sub-branch becomes a full branch). The merging of the Royal Bank's system with that of five other banks between 1910 and 1925 complicated this ebb and flow of branches, although the overall effect was a massive addition. Each amalgamation was thus subject to a "shake down" during which duplicate branches were weeded out. Sometimes an existing Royal bank was closed if the amalgamated bank offered a better location. What follows is a close approximation of the net statistical impact of the Royal Bank's growth through merger from 1910 to 1925.

*1910*:   126 RBC branches are joined by 42 Union Bank of Halifax branches (excluding 3 international branches) and, after 10 duplicate branches are eliminated, the Royal Bank emerges with a consolidated total of *156*.

*1912*:   *101* Traders Bank branches join the Royal Bank system. After 16 duplicate locations are eliminated, the system stands at *314*.

*1917*:   58 Quebec Bank branches bring a net gain of *38* branches, thus giving the Royal Bank a total of *375* branches.

*1918*:   *110* Northern Crown Bank branches are trimmed to a net gain of *96* branches, thus boosting the Royal Bank's total to *526*.

*1925*:   217 Union Bank of Canada branches are pruned by 51 to give a net gain of *166* branches thus bringing the Royal Bank's branch system to a total of *792*.

banker was in large measure rooted in its ability to muster sufficient manpower at home to realize its ambitions abroad. As one of the "merged" noted in a piece of doggerel poetry dedicated to his "merger-brethren" in the *Royal Bank Magazine* in 1925:

> You have released us. We, whose future lay
> In the broad spaces of this Northern clime–
> You have released us. Now let Fancy stray,
> Leading me through the lands of summertime.[85]

Business historians can provide ample evidence of the dangers of a strategy of growth by merger: huge debts, wounded morale, and a refusal of two hitherto-separate entities to meld into one efficient whole. Yet the Royal Bank's merger campaign of 1910 to 1925 was a sterling success. Above all else, it solidified the foundation of a bank that was now the largest and most regionally diverse in the country. Why?

In addition, none of the takeovers was hostile. The five acquired banks all approached the negotiation from a position of declining competitiveness. Some, like the Union Bank of Canada, were in fact in dire straits. Others were living out a precarious existence, trapped in regional markets and unable to diversify nationally. In all instances, the directors and staff of these banks welcomed the Royal's blandishments: merger offered a chance for survival and a chance to join what was seen as the country's most progressive bank. There was almost universal eagerness to slip on the coloured sleeve garters of the Royal Bank – only in the case of the Traders did any significant number of staff refuse to come over to the Royal. The diminished circumstances of these banks also meant that their assets came relatively cheap. The only chink in Pease's takeover strategy was in Ontario. His miscalculation of Toronto's determination to keep sway over its regional banks denied him control of the Bank of Hamilton. As a consequence, the Royal Bank was for years to be underrepresented in the Ontario market, a fact he frequently reflected on with bitterness.

But for all its evident success by 1925, the merger movement did have an Achilles' heel. In their eagerness to avoid head-to-head competition in innumerable small towns where there was scarcely enough business to sustain the business of a single branch, banks had merged in the name of better economies of scale and lower overheads. While this may have controlled the further multiplication of Canadian banks, it did little to rationalize the overexpansion of the Laurier boom. By 1925, the Royal was the leading bank in each of the Prairie provinces. The influx of Northern Crown and Union branches, for instance, gave it exposure in 148 Saskatchewan communities, a ratio of one branch for every 6,100 persons. Changes in technology – most notably, the mobility given small-town Canadians by the automobile – and the ever-present possibility of an economic downturn made small-town banking a very marginal activity on the Prairies and in many areas of rural Ontario. Within a decade, the Royal would pay a painful price for its merger exuberance in the West.

If the Royal was overexposed on the Prairies, the merger movement had only slightly improved its presence in French-Canada. Its sixty-eight branches in Quebec were largely confined to urban, Anglo districts, a pattern accentuated by the acquisition of the Quebec Bank. This was largely a deliberate outcome. Like the other Montreal and Toronto banks, the Royal had surrendered its pretensions in French-Canada to francophone banks and the vigorously successful *caisse populaires*. To some degree, the assurance of an ethnically exclusive clientele tended to cancel out the dangers of regional specialization for the French-Canadian banks. But it also made them small banks, and they too sought safety in merging: in 1925 the Banque Canadienne Nationale emerged as the province's leading bank. Not until the 1950s would the Royal systematically turn its energies to the Quebec market; not until the 1970s would Quebec's banks venture across the Ontario border in any numbers.

However, the dangers of overexpansion were largely dormant in 1925; more apparent was the Canadian public's changed attitude to their banks. Pride in the widespread strength of Canadian banking was now accompanied by a muted, but abiding, concern over the power of the "big banks" and their position in Canadian economic life. On the morning in 1925 that the Union merger was announced, Prime Minister William Lyon Mackenzie King received a cable from the worried editor of the Vancouver *Sun*: the merger was the "only thing that could be done under the circumstances...[but] will be deeply resented by Canadian public who fear bank monopoly resulting from banks getting into too few hands and controlled entirely from eastern Canada."[86] Pease had seldom had to concern himself with managing the public consequences of his corporate policies. His successors would find themselves increasingly preoccupied with the way their actions were viewed by Ottawa and by Canadians at large. In this regard, Sir Herbert Holt's varied business activities outside the bank would soon become a liability.

Thus, via merger and expansion, the Royal had become a national institution. With each merger, the once-dominant Maritime character of its shareholder base became more diluted. Each merger brought faces from new corners of the Dominion to the boardroom table. When the directors commissioned the New York architects York and

Sawyer to design a new head office – taller than the Bank of Montreal's – on St. James Street in 1926, they instructed them to decorate the gilded ceiling of the main banking hall with the provincial crests of *all* the provinces, not just the coats of arms of Halifax and Montreal.

1899-1930

# International Banking

*"Deep in the Gulf Stream"*

IN THE SPRING OF 1882, THE DOUR, DILIGENT ACCOUNTANT OF THE Merchants' Bank of Halifax, David Duncan, broke his Presbyterian routine in two uncharacteristic ways: he got sick and, consequently, took a holiday. A bout of "rheumation," brought on by the damp Halifax March, prompted Duncan's doctors to advise a convalescence in sunny, semi-tropical Bermuda, a British colony warmed by the Gulf Stream, nine hundred miles to the south of Halifax. The directors were quick to approve Duncan's request for a leave of absence; they were also quick to sense opportunity in Duncan's infirmity. Duncan was "authorized by the Board, in the event of his finding suitable opening, to establish an agency of the Bank at Hamilton," the small colony's capital. A month later the rejuvenated accountant returned to report that "after considerable difficulty, and misgivings as to success owing to the opposition of the business people" in the colony, he had struck a deal with the mayor of Hamilton, Nathaniel Butterfield, to act as the Merchants' agent "as an experiment" for a year.[1] Halifax now had a bank with an international affiliation; other Canadian banks had established New York and London offices, but the Merchants' was the first to establish itself beyond these traditional roadsteads of Canadian finance.

Bermuda was a natural oceanic extension for the fledgling Merchants' Bank. Like Halifax, the little colony lived by its wits in foreign commerce. Its political and social life was dominated by a close-knit commercial élite which had the ear of the Governor, and Nathaniel Butterfield was prominent in this colonial coterie as a shipowner and trader. Bermudian merchants were a wily crew. As

Haligonians had done, they had prospered in the American Civil War as blockade runners. Their colony was bound in many ways to Halifax; Bermuda was a first stop for many a Haligonian vessel heading south. British troops and warships moved between the two ports as part of the Imperial shield around North America. The Anglican and Catholic bishops of Halifax both counted Bermuda in their dioceses; as a prominent Halifax Catholic, Thomas Kenny, the bank's president, would have heard much of Bermuda from his bishop. Like Kenny in the 1860s, Butterfield realized that his business stood to be made more profitable if it could be extended into trade financing.[2]

The directors treated the Bermuda agency like any other. Butterfield's son, Harry, was brought to head office in Halifax to apprentice in banking. In 1883, Kenny visited Hamilton and reported that the senior Butterfield was a model banker, "cautious, correct and trustworthy."[3] Although profits "would barely suffice to cover expenses," Kenny remained hopeful of future success. In 1884, a small profit of £300 seemed to indicate that the bank's skill as a financier of trade could be exported. The same spirit prompted the Merchants' to open a second foreign agency in the French fishing port of St. Pierre off Newfoundland in 1886. This time Edson Pease did the scouting. But the scent of profits soon soured; St. Pierre was "expensive" and its bankruptcy laws "dangerous." As for Bermuda, the directors soon began to suspect that Butterfield was using their affiliation to further his own commercial ambitions, that he had sent his son to Halifax simply to learn the ropes of banking, and that his aim was to establish his own bank. Continuing meagre profits seemed to demonstrate his lacklustre commitment. In 1886, Duncan was again sent southward to break the arrangement. For the next three years, the Merchants' maintained its own agency on Front Street, but without the good offices of a Bermudian to help it penetrate the local market, the operation was stillborn and was closed in 1889.[4] St. Pierre followed a year later.

Bermuda, however, continued to entice. In 1918, there was a fruitless negotiation to purchase an established Bermuda bank.[5] As late as 1930, a holidaying Prime Minister Mackenzie King could report that the thought of the Royal acquiring a local bank aroused "a good deal of feeling" in Bermuda.[6] The message was clear: an entrenched commercial élite would fight to exclude foreign bankers if they felt they could capture the trade for themselves. The Butterfields *did* incorporate their own bank in 1904. Before that, in 1890, another local syndicate had opened a bank – the Bank of Bermuda – out of the remnants of the Canadian agency. In their House of Assembly, the same merchants quickly moved to pass legislation insulating their banks from foreign competition. To this day, Bermudians bank with Bermudians.

The Halifax bank learned a lasting lesson in Bermuda. Just as it had discovered that appointed agents in Maritime towns like Truro were liable to indulge in local politics or commerce contrary to the bank's interests, it had now learned that any foray into foreign banking would have to be closely guarded. In future, head office instinctively knew that its foreign branches must be established and operated as extensions of its domestic branch system. After all, the purpose of such branches was to apply the bank's expertise in financing Maritime exports to similar needs in foreign lands. By the 1880s, that necessity was becoming undeniable.

Oceanic trade was second nature to the men behind the Merchants'. The early directors and shareholders of the bank – Kinnear, Tobin, Taylor, Cunard, and Mitchell – were practised in despatching ships southward, laden with dry and pickled fish. They returned bearing Caribbean sugar and molasses.[7] Haligonians lived in constant hope that more could be made of this trade. In 1879, they seized on the protectionist National Policy to establish the Halifax Sugar Refinery;[8] the bank promptly extended credit to the enterprise. Throughout his tenure as an MP in Ottawa, the bank's president, Thomas Kenny, persistently lobbied for better steamship service between Halifax and the West Indies.[9] Like a supporting chorus, Merchants' directors joined the Halifax Board of Trade to echo the demand. There was always, however, the sense that Halifax was contending with forces beyond its control: the price of sugar, the dominance of American and British shippers, and the vagaries of trade finance. Halifax would ultimately fail in its contest with the ports of the American seaboard, and Montreal would take its place as the seat of Canadian sugar production (one of the bank's first Montreal clients was the St. Lawrence Sugar Refinery). Only in financing its oceanic trade did Halifax build a legacy.

Newfoundland was a natural first step abroad. As early as 1866, pro-Confederation forces in the rocky colony had held up "the need of a branch of a *good* Canadian bank" as a compelling argument for union with the mainland.[10] Newfoundland, however, doggedly clung to its independence, and, as a result, in the late-nineteenth century, found its banks tied to English finance and dependent on a narrow colonial economy. In December 1894, a "panic" crippled St. John's two banks – the Commercial Bank of Newfoundland and the Union Bank of Newfoundland – leaving the colony without a circulating currency. To save the economy from paralysis, three Canadian banks, including the Merchants' and the Bank of Nova Scotia from Halifax, stepped into the breach. Within three days of the panic, Pease had despatched his inspector to St. John's, and by January, the Merchants' had an agency in operation.[11] Within months, the bank's new Newfoundland agent, F. H. Arnaud, had aggressively acquired accounts with some of the Water Street commercial élite. Bowring Brothers would become an enduring client, soon to be joined by merchants Tasker Cook and John Chalker Crosbie. Edson Pease always held up the "rescue" of 1894 as proof positive that big banks had the sustaining power lacking in small, regional banks: in 1913, he boasted that "the island was never so prosperous as at the present time" on account of its link with mainland banking.[12] By then, he could make the same claim in warmer reaches of the hemisphere.

As early as 1837, the Colonial Bank, a British bank operating in Jamaica, had appointed the Halifax Banking Company as its northern agent to facilitate the passing of bills of exchange.[13] As in the actual shipping of goods, merchants sought to bypass London and New York in the negotiation of trade finance. Intermediaries took commissions for handling bills of exchange and foreign exchange. The pull of metropolitan commercial centres was, none the less, inescapable. Canadian banks thus began establishing agencies at these crossroads of international finance, beginning with the Bank of Montreal in New York in 1855. Other Canadian banks followed – the Bank of Commerce and the Merchants' Bank of Canada in the 1870s.[14] In the 1890s, Canadian banks appeared in other centres of American commerce – Chicago, Minneapolis, and into California. Once the Merchants' Bank of Halifax opened in Montreal, some form of New York affiliation was unavoidable, and in 1888 Pease negotiated a correspondent agreement with the Chase National Bank in New York, giving the Canadians foreign-exchange and credit facilities.[15] The president of the Chase National, Henry W. Cannon, was to become Pease's trusted ally south of the border.

New York opened other doors to Canadian banking. Since Canada lacked any kind of workable money market – a means of investing in short- and long-term financial instruments – New York, as did London, allowed foreign banks an opportunity to invest their liquid reserves profitably. By the 1890s, for instance, the Merchants' of Halifax was building up a solid portfolio of American railway and utility bonds. Although New York agencies of foreign banks were prohibited from acting as retail banks, Canadian banks soon sensed a kernel of international advantage planted in the centre of American finance. While the Canadian Bank Act encouraged Canadian bankers to "open branches, agencies and offices" wherever they saw fit, American bankers were severely curtailed in pursuing their expansionist urges. The 1864 National Bank Act had stipulated that American banks must draw their directors from the narrow precinct in which they operated.

The fact that a state bank charter generally imposed less-stringent incorporation and reserve requirements gave American bankers further latitude – which they used.* It was ironic therefore that in the very years in which America was building the most powerful national economy in the world, its banks remained localized, limited in any hope of effective national coverage, let alone international expansion. Although barred from buying into American banking or from issuing notes or taking deposits, Canadian agencies were situated to attach themselves to America's overseas trade and thus act as *de facto* American bankers. A shrewd American banker, or promoter, would at the same time realize that a liaison with a Canadian correspondent might offer an escape from the constraints of American banking.[16] Late in the 1890s, Edson Pease of the Merchants' and Henry Cannon of the Chase National found themselves thinking along these lines. The lines converged on Havana and the fabled sugar fields of Cuba.

Urbanization and industrialization fuelled the world's appetite for sugar. In the first quarter of this century, world sugar production increased 150 per cent and one country, Cuba, soared to the top of the producers' list. In 1900, Cuba fed 2.7 per cent of world demand, but by 1925 it accounted for a dominant 21.1 per cent.[17] Cuban sugar production surged forward under the stimulus of large-scale, mechanized processing of cane and the opening of the insatiable American market for sugar. This transformation was born out of the convulsions of the Spanish-American War. Sugar has found an habitual place in history as a commodity that begets political and economic dependence and turmoil. Just as fish, fur, and timber drew European traders to Canada and coloured its political evolution, so too has sugar fundamentally shaped Cuban nationhood. "As sugar goes, so goes Cuba," Cubans are fond of quipping.

In the years 1895 to 1905, Cuba passed from outright colonial dependence on Spain to a quasi-colonial dependence on the United States. A Spanish plantation colony since the fifteenth century, Cuba by the late-nineteenth century was an island of discontent. Its agricultural mainstay, sugar, had benefited in mid-century from the advent of large-scale sugar mills, or *ingenios*, and from railway access to ports,

---

* A. P. Giannini, an Italian immigrant whose Bank of Italy in San Francisco would ultimately become BankAmerica, drew inspiration from the Canadian branch-banking system. Noting the success of Canadian agencies in California, Giannini toured Western Canada in the first decade of the century and was impressed: "These safe, well-conducted, economically operated institutions were at the other end of the pole from the speculative, loosely run banks of the American frontier, including San Francisco in its early days." (M. and B. R. James, *Biography of a Bank: the Story of Bank of America*, New York, 1954, p.43). Giannini soon covered California with branches.

but was now becoming stalled in its bid for further mechanization by lack of capital and the ineptitude of Spanish administration. Cuban land was encumbered by an archaic royal land-grant system and sugar financing was complicated by interest rates as high as 20 to 25 per cent, which prevailed as a result of perverse lien provisions of Spanish law – the *privilegio de ingenios* and the *retracto convencional* – which fortified the interests of the borrower at the expense of those of the lender.[18] Cuban banks were consequently small and incapable of stimulating commerce. Even the largest, El Banco Español de la Isla de Cuba, was also confronted with a chaotic monetary system that mingled various currencies and made trade transactions awkward. The anaemic economic and financial condition of the colony was but one of the many frustrations that fed the Cuban hunger for independence. An earlier nationalist uprising in the 1870s had ended in a stalemate that had seen many Cuban nationalists go into exile. Their return in 1895, under the leadership of poet José Marti, brought down the curtain on Spain's influence in the Americas.

The United States was no disinterested bystander in this conflict. Already Cuba's largest trading partner, America clearly saw Cuba as falling under the Monroe Doctrine – America's self-declared right to order the affairs of the hemisphere. Once the insurrection had begun, it took little to provoke the Americans to action. Faced with national hysteria over the loss of the USS *Maine* in Havana harbour in April 1898, President McKinley recognized Cuba's right of independence and went to war with Spain. Victory was quick and decisive. Aid to the Cuban Army of Liberation and direct military intervention – forever etched into the American psyche by the charge of Teddy Roosevelt's Rough Riders up San Juan Hill – forced a Spanish capitulation in July and the signing of the Treaty of Paris in December. Cuba acquired its independence, and the United States acquired Puerto Rico, the Philippines, and Guam, plus a substantial *de facto* suzerainty over its newly independent neighbour. "In their struggle for independence, Cubans had confronted two metropolitan centres - Spain and the United States," an historian of the war has noted. "Cubans emerged from the war victorious, but only over one metropolis."[19]

The United States moved quickly to secure Cuba's loyalty. Even before Spain's capitulation, Americans spoke openly of their hopes of drawing the island into their diplomatic *and* economic net. The U.S. Vice-Consul in Havana, Joseph A. Springer, prophesied that, under American protection, "a reciprocity in trade will doubtless be sanctioned and all the riches of the most fruitful and productive bit of ground on the globe will flow into our markets. Cuba will become a source of great profit to the people of the United States."[20] To ensure this, Cuba was cocooned in American protection. Within a month of the Treaty of Paris, President McKinley had appointed an American military governor for the island and had decreed that all official trans-actions in the "new" Cuba be undertaken in U.S. dollars. The appoint-ment of General Leonard Wood, a Rough Rider sidekick of Roosevelt, as the second military governor in 1900 marked the real beginnings of Americanization. Massive rebuilding of roads and railways and an assault on malaria were undertaken, opportunities that attracted swarms of foreign builders and promoters. To stimulate the sugar economy, Cuban sugar was given preferential access to the American market. Although in 1902 Cuba elected its first democratic president, Estrada Palma, the United States continued to cast a long shadow across the Straits of Florida.

The capstone of this new Cuban–American relationship was set in place by Senator Orville H. Platt. An outspoken expansionist, Platt had been instrumental in the American annexation of Hawaii in 1898. Platt now wanted Cuba pulled firmly into the American baili-wick, and his Platt Amendment – a rider to the Army Appropriation Bill of 1901 – did just that. Reluctantly ratified by Cuba, the amend-ment gave the United States the right of intervention to protect prop-erty and liberty, forbade the Cubans to enter treaties which might impair its Treaty of Paris obligations, and set strict limits on its fiscal policy. Although repealed in 1934, the Platt Amendment set the tone of Cuban–American relations right down to the day in the late 1950s when, like José Marti before him, Fidel Castro waded ashore from exile to lead an insurrection.[21]

The Treaty of Paris was signed on December 10, 1898. Three days earlier, Edson Pease, the Montreal manager of the Merchants', had advised the bank's board in Halifax that "Cuba might be a desirable place for an Agency." The board was sceptical, but authorized Pease to visit Havana "with authority to open."[22] Just as he had sensed the potential of positioning the bank at the cutting edge of Canadian devel-opment, Pease now sensed another beckoning frontier, this one to the south. Just as he had hurried into the B.C. interior in 1897, Pease, accompanied by the bank's inspector, W. F. Brock, now darted to New York to catch a steamer to Havana. At dockside in liberated Havana, the Canadians found chaos. The last of the Spanish troops and adminis-trators were crowding aboard ships ready for repatriation; American and Cuban liberation troops ruled the city. Pease toured the city in a horse-drawn carriage lent to him by a local merchant banker.[23] The evidence of four years of turmoil was everywhere. The war had wrecked Cuba's urban and economic infrastructure: streetcars, tele-phones, bridges, and warehouses needed a massive renovation. In the countryside, the sugar industry lay in ruins: of the estimated 1,100 mills processing cane in 1894, only 207 still operated. A million-ton output in 1895 had fallen to 300,000 tons by 1900.[24] Given the guerilla nature of much of the war, railways and storage facilities – the all-important arteries of sugar export – had suffered heavily.[25]

Amid the wreckage, Pease could see opportunity. If Cuba was ever to be rebuilt, it would need ready access to capital, and the Cuban banks were in no position to provide it. Mortgage debt had been under moratorium since 1895. There was no reliable currency. The two largest banks – Banco del Comercio and Banco Español – had suspended operations. A hodgepodge of private banks in Havana survived, but, lacking branches, could not move money to the provinces. With the blueprint of Canadian branch banking fresh in his head, Pease could see a place for the Merchants' in Havana. After all, the bank had cut its teeth moving Maritime fish and timber to foreign markets. Why not Cuban sugar? He also knew that he had a special advantage: America's myopic banking laws made it unlikely that an American competitor would materialize. An American trust company had set up shop in the southeastern city of Santiago de Cuba, but its compatriots had not followed. Pease also knew that opening in Cuba was a leap in the dark. His "bank boys" did not speak Spanish. The bank lacked any feel for the market; there was no Dun and Bradstreet for ready credit checks. Furthermore, before the bank could lend, it would have to build up a deposit base. Foreign exchange, profitable elsewhere, was problematic as long as Cuba lacked a stable currency. Lastly, since Cuban sugar depended on the American market, some better form of financial intermediation would be needed in the United States, preferably in New York.[26]

Time was of the essence. Rumours – undoubtedly confirmed through Pease's new-found friendship with American consul Joseph Springer – indicated that the Americans were poised to initiate financial reform; a report on Cuba's financial and economic woes had been presented to McKinley. This was confirmed when the president announced that the *peso* would now be pegged to the American dollar; trade financing now became a more lucrative prospect. Later, the *retracto convencional* would be scrapped, giving the sugar grower surer access to capital. Anxious to capitalize on these changes, Pease hurried back to Montreal to prepare a report for the board. There is reason to believe that Pease also feared that the Bank of Nova Scotia, which had operated in Jamaica since 1889, might leap into the Cuban breach. Pease, however, had a special advantage in Montreal. The Merchants' ascendancy in the city was in large part the product of Pease's ties with prominent local capitalists. Charley Hosmer, the telegraph wizard, had led Pease into friendship with Van Horne of the Canadian Pacific and other Montreal promoters, such as Charles and Edwin Hanson. The Hansons were, for instance, not only bank clients but also provided Pease with a bell-wether of Canadian investment activity. In Halifax, a regular bank client, lawyer/promoter B. F. Pearson, had joined Pease's informal circle, as had director David Mackeen, another Halifax promoter. Van Horne, the Hansons, and Pearson had all been active in the promotion of Canadian urban utilities, principally streetcars and power generation, and they, too, now sniffed profit in the warm Cuban wind.[27]

Van Horne, an American by birth, led the Canadian business invasion of Cuba; in January 1900, he visited Havana to inspect the Havana tramway system. While there, he hit on another idea, an idea born out of his experience in the Canadian West. Direct business promotion by foreigners was made difficult in Cuba by the Foraker Amendment, which forbade the acquisition of franchises by foreigners. Foreigners *could*, however, buy land. Why not, therefore, buy land and use it to build a railway and then use the railway to push agricultural development into eastern Cuba?[28] Thus, Van Horne's Cuba Company, with a head office in New York, was born. "It is believed on the part of the Company," Van Horne told Senator Platt, "that, as with wheat and corn in the Western States, sugar must before long be produced in Cuba by those who work with their own hands."[29]* Just as the banks had been at the "end of steel" in the Canadian West, Edson Pease would oblige his Montreal friends with banks in eastern Cuba.

Through the Christmas week of 1898, Pease hurriedly prepared a report for the board on his Cuban expedition. It was typical of his growing impatience with the conservatism of the Halifax directors that he simply submitted the report in writing on January 3. The sceptical directors would not oblige Pease with a quick decision, and "it was thought best to ask Mr. Pease to visit Halifax." On January 14, "prolonged discussion" led to agreement that Pease should revisit Havana before a final decision on opening was taken.[30] This time he did not hesitate; space was leased on Obrapia Street in downtown Havana. Although some of the Halifax directors remained "strongly averse" to an agency in Cuba "upon the ground that it was too far away from home,"[31] Pease pressed his suit. However, without a New York connection, Havana made little sense, and on February 18 he predicted that a New York agency "in time would do a very profitable business." Henry

---

* The investment mania that swept through Mariposa in Leacock's *Sunshine Sketches of a Little Town* was sparked by the "Cuban Land Development Company," from its offices in New York. Local investors were enticed with "coloured pictures of Cuba, and fields of bananas, and haciendas and insurrectos with machetes and Heaven knows what." The Mariposa lily was Cuba's national flower.

Cannon at the Chase National, the bank's American correspondent, "very much approved of the new venture and promised his assistance to make the business a success."[32]

Clearly, in the early weeks of 1899, Edson Pease was pushing both the Halifax bank and his own authority in it to their limits. The Havana–New York initiative was entirely his own; it is likely that, had the board disappointed his ambition, Pease would have left the bank. He was no longer a small-city banker, and his vigour and vision had attracted wider attention (it was later in the same year that the New York syndicate would seek out Pease to head the mooted American Bank of London).[33] As it had when Pease advocated an agency in Montreal in 1887, the Merchants' faced a momentous decision in pondering a move south in 1899. Would it cling to Canadian shores or strike out abroad into unknown-but-promising territory? What tipped the balance in Pease's favour was the willingness of bank president, Thomas Kenny, to share in his vision. Kenny had traded into the Caribbean for decades. As an MP, he had championed better trade and transportation links with Canada's southern trading partners. Like other Halifax merchants, he saw the American intervention in Cuba as a golden opening for trade; the first Cuban consignment had left Halifax within a month of the Spanish capitulation.[34] If other directors swooned at the thought of Havana, Kenny backed Pease wholeheartedly. Not coincidentally, the decision to open in Cuba and New York was accompanied by Pease's elevation to joint general manager. By the end of 1899, Pease was sole general manager. Without Kenny's backing, Pease would probably have spent his energy battling with the board and departed, leaving the bank to its conservative Maritime devices.

In the spring of 1899, Kenny proved his mettle. He realized that the real opportunity in Cuba lay not only in the financing of improved Canadian trade, but in capturing Cuban–American trade, and that this meant establishing the bank in New York.[35] Kenny was no stranger to New York; in 1856 he had married Margaret Burke, daughter of a prominent New York family. In March, Kenny accompanied Pease to New York, where they rented space on Broadway and employed an American, Stephen Voorhees, as their first agent. A former Chase National banker, Voorhees was a prize catch and was duly paid $5,000 a year. Before Voorhees could open the agency, however, an obstacle emerged. Pease had known that New York law precisely prescribed the limits of agency banking in New York – no retail banking, in particular – but had hoped that the Merchants' would find acceptance as an agency, just as other Canadian banks had done earlier in the century. Some doubt was thrown on this assumption by the news that the Toronto-based Bank of Commerce, already comfortably established in

New York, was planning to challenge the right of the Merchants' to open in the city under the provisions of an 1892 New York law. The law allegedly exempted new banks from entering the city without state incorporation. Those operating prior to the law were precluded. Pease sensed a messy battle; rumours indicated that the Commerce was planning to enter Nova Scotia, and New York offered an opportunity for a pre-emptive strike.[36]

Pease and Kenny rushed to New York. Hurried consultations with Cannon and the Chase National lawyers brought the opinion that the 1892 law "was not intended for such banks as ours." Its purpose was instead to deter individuals from presenting themselves as banks. Still uneasy, Kenny played his trump card. He would go directly to Governor Teddy Roosevelt in Albany and ask him for a definitive clarification. He would go not as an unknown Canadian banker, but as a relative of the illustrious governor. Kenny's mother-in-law was a Roosevelt. "I had not met Teddy for 15 years," Kenny scribbled in his trip diary. "I wired him on Friday if he could see me on a matter of public business on Saturday – yes – come to dinner at 7 o'clock." Dinner was a convivial affair: "the conversation was the war – the Rough Riders – State and Federal politics." On Monday, Roosevelt introduced Kenny to the attorney-general, who assured him that the state welcomed foreign banks – "the more the better." After a considerable legal minuet, Kenny learned that no legal obstacle lay in the way of the Canadian bank making loans on collateral or in making foreign exchange. The lifeblood of the New York agency had been assured.[37] Cuba now beckoned.

On March 8, 1899, the Merchants' Bank of Halifax opened at the Obrapia address in Havana. Even before the New York agency was secured, Pease was determined to make the gambit succeed; it was "his" project. Over the next two decades, he would visit the island regularly, often towing Kenny or a director along. Bank clerks at head office recalled Pease's triumphant returns from the south, bearing fine Cuban cigars, some of which he proudly distributed to staff and the rest of which he stored in the bank's vault.[38] Beyond these pleasures lay a carefully plotted strategy for the Cuban venture, a strategy devised and compulsively supervised by Pease himself, which rested on a triad of shrewd personnel, political, and business policies. It resulted in the bank rapidly becoming the island's largest financial institution; by the mid-1920s Pease had built a network of sixty-five branches. By then, the Canadian bank acted as Cuba's *de facto* central banker. When Graham Towers, a young Montrealer who was sent south as an assistant accountant, arrived in Havana in 1922, he

# THE ROYAL BANK IN CUBA: 1925

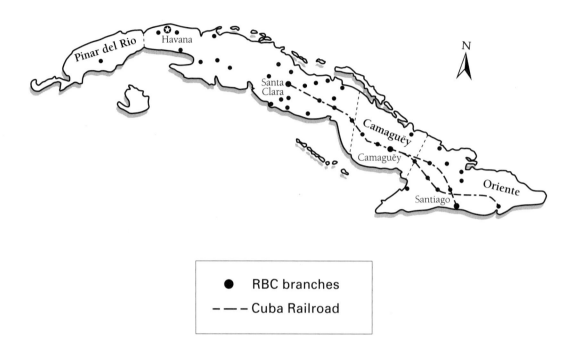

● RBC branches

– – – Cuba Railroad

instructed the cabbie at dockside to take him to "El Banco Real de Canada." "He corrected me at once, 'Banco de Canada,' and started off."[39] The whole impressive edifice of Canadian finance in Cuba, however, rested on sugar and, when the price of sugar plunged in the 1920s after two soaring decades, "Banco de Canada" would find its fortunes much straitened.

Pease's first concern in Havana was to put the right men on the job.[40] He faced the almost impossible challenge of finding men reliably versed in Canadian banking procedure and at the same time adept at winning Cuban business. The bank's appointment of joint agents in Havana in late February 1899 was thus a brilliant *coup*. The first agent was W. F. Brock, the head-office inspector who had accompanied Pease to Havana in 1898. Brock would run the bank. His partner as joint agent was Joseph A. Springer, the American vice-consul in Havana. Fluent in Spanish, Springer was *persona grata* with both the Cuban authorities and the American military government: "his duties were to introduce prospective clients and to obtain general and financial information."[41] In keeping with its inclination to bring on young talent quickly, the bank sent the twenty-eight-year-old Fredericton branch manager, Francis Sherman, south as second agent.

It was an effective combination, but Brock soon buckled. Heat, Spanish, and the topsy-turvy world of Cuban reconstruction killed his spirit, and he was transferred to New York. Sherman succeeded him and, more than any other man, pioneered the bank's presence in Cuba. For the next twelve years, Sherman combined his talents as a charming-yet-aggressive banker with a lifelong passion for poetry. While his romantic verse regularly appeared in northern periodicals, Sherman learned Spanish and became a genial presence in Cuban social and business circles.

Sherman and Springer immediately realized that Canadian "bank boys" might ably erect the girders of the Cuban system, but that Cubans would soon have to be brought into the branches. Young Spanish-speaking staff began appearing at the Obrapia Street branch almost immediately. The guide who had shown Pease around Havana on his initial visit was, for instance, hired.[42] Hispanic Americans were hired in New York and brought to Havana.[43] As the bank gained stature, Cubans began seeking employment there as a promising step up the ladder of post-revolutionary advancement. Sometimes such requests promoted the bank's own ends. One of the bank's earliest accounts was that of the Bacardi distillery and, when a Bacardi son, José, presented himself to Sherman in 1903, he soon found work as a junior in Santiago branch.[44] Turnover in Cuban staff was high; the ways of Canadian banking did not come easily to Cubans. None the less, a core of Spanish-speaking "bank boys" began to emerge within a few years, and the first Cuban managers appeared in a decade. Despite this, the New York or Miami steamer seldom docked without disgorging another small expedition of Canadian "bank boys." The Canadian Bankers' Association soon began offering Spanish courses, and in some years the course catered solely to Royal Bankers.[45]

The North Americans brought an undeniable ethnocentricity with them to Cuba. When things went awry, the bank's senior managers chalked it up to "the excitability of the Latin races."[46] Realizing that Cuban service was onerous for many North Americans, the bank altered its *Rules and Regulations* to suit the circumstances. The marriage-rule ceiling was raised to discourage marriage, and salaries were increased to reward those who took southern assignments. Holiday trips home were paid for by the bank every two years. In addition, from the outset, international service in the bank carried a degree of glamour unattainable in Canada. Few Canadians had jobs like these. For most, however, service in Cuba was seen as a short-term

*Our men in Havana: The pleasures of a southern assignment. Canadian "bank boys" relax on a Havana Beach, 1919 (above); picnicking in the Cuban Hills (opposite) – note the ties and bank revolver.*

means of acquiring seniority and saving money before returning to marriage and a branch managership in Canada.

"Bank boys" in Cuba were housed in guest houses, the most famous of which was Vedado in Havana. Here sports (and other high jinks) flourished. Managers sent to rural branches enjoyed a less-gregarious existence. An inspector, arriving at an isolated branch in Oriente province, reported that he found the manager, the son of a Maritime Presbyterian minister, and the only English-speaker in the district, morosely fulfilling his duty. He had written on the wall above his desk: "How long, O Lord, how long?"[47] This strange mixture of Anglo sojourners and Cuban nationals, overseen by a small core of Cuba veterans headed by Francis Sherman, manned a branch system that expanded almost without interruption from 1900 to 1925.

Pease not only found the men, but also a political strategy for the bank in Cuba. From the outset, the Canadians saw themselves as an "American" bank in Cuba. Before his first trip to Havana, Pease asked Cannon of the Chase National to "smooth the way through the American authorities."[48] Until the Federal Reserve Act of 1913 permitted American banks with federal charters to establish foreign branches and to provide financing for the import and export of

goods, the Royal Bank had the Cuban field virtually to itself. A Cuban rival, the Banco Nacional de Cuba, established with American backing in 1900, enjoyed the privilege of holding the government's account, but it was poorly managed. The Bank of Nova Scotia did eventually enter Cuba in 1906, but never developed a branch network. Only after 1914 did the American National City Bank seriously challenge the remarkable sway given the Royal Bank by Pease's bold dash to Havana in 1898.[49]

In the interim, the Canadians acted as surrogate American bankers and, as such, saw themselves snugly covered by the protective blanket of the Platt Amendment. "The United States authorities have the affairs of the island well in hand at the present time," Pease told the *Financial Post* in 1907. "Every effort will be made to provide for the perfect autonomy of the island but if all efforts fail and it is found impossible to secure peace and harmony, there is little doubt as to the final destiny of the country being brought into union with the United States."[50] When trouble brewed – as it did in 1906, 1912, 1917, and 1920 – an American battleship in Havana harbour or a Marine contingent restored political calm. As late as 1933, the British Ambassador in Havana could report to London that the Canadian bank had a "special" place in Cuba and that it "always expected that the United

*A farewell dinner for Graham (third on left) and Molly (far right) Towers under the palms, 1929. Beside Molly is Harold Hesler of the Havana supervisor's staff and a bank expert on sugar*

States Government would accept also the disadvantages and responsibilities which it entailed."[51]

If Pease saw the bank's role in Cuba as one of responding to American-created opportunity, Sherman sensed the Cuban opportunities. In its first years of Cuban operation, the bank pursued a cautious loaning policy, intent on attracting deposits to make the bank self-supporting. This proved difficult; Cubans had traditionally not seen banks as a place for their savings. In 1900, the Merchants' Havana branch loaned $517,000, but took in savings of only $300,000, for a slim profit of $11,000.[52] Sherman was determined to increase both savings and profits, and in 1902 he saw his chance. On taking office in May 1902, Cuban President Estrada Palma inherited a political problem: the troops of the Army of Liberation had been promised $1 a day for their patriotic services. The bill – some $60 million – was now due. Uneasy at the prospect of an unpaid army, Estrada Palma floated a bond issue in New York and prepared to pay the troops. Sherman instantly began lobbying to act as paymaster; he realized that each soldier paid was a potential deposit account for the bank.

Working through Van Horne's Havana attorney, Sherman strove vigorously for the contract and, in September 1904, he won the right to distribute what would eventually total $56 million. The bank's small branch network – five branches in 1904 – allowed it to make payment throughout the island. Each payment brought a commission and the prospect of a new client. "I do not think the question of direct remuneration for the bank's services in paying the Cuban Army is of the least consequence," Van Horne wrote Pease, "as compared with the standing it must give your bank throughout the country."[53] The Liberation Army payroll proved an immense fillip to the expansion of the bank's branches and staff in Cuba.* Henceforth, the Royal Bank was to enjoy a favoured relationship with successive Cuban governments; both democrat and dictator turned to the Canadians for financial support.

Just as the Royal Bank cultivated the political good will of the new Cuban government, so too did it seek out a solid base of business clients. With its New York agency, the bank was excellently situated to capture the boom in Cuban–American trade and investment. The bank consciously established its branches wherever it could facilitate the spread of foreign investment entering Cuba. In this respect, its best customer was Van Horne's Cuba Company and its offspring, the Cuba Railroad. In 1903, a branch was opened in Santiago de Cuba, and a year later in Camagüey; both were crucial junction towns in the expansion of Cuban sugar and cattle production. As Van Horne's Cuba Railroad pushed down Cuba's central spine, Royal Bank branches sprouted up in the wake of construction. "I take pleasure in repeating my assurance that the bank accounts of the Cuba Company and the Cuba Railroad," Van Horne wrote Pease, "will be continued with your branch at Camagüey." Van Horne went so far as to lecture Pease on the need for an "impressive" building in Camagüey – his railway headquarters – to build Cuban confidence in the bank. Van Horne, a gifted amateur artist, even sent along a sketch of a façade for the building, and he suggested a corner location.[54] Through its New York office, the

(continued on p. 182)

---

* Note that the three young bankers featured in the "Bankers in Motion" chart in Chapter Three were all despatched to Cuba in 1904 to help with the Army payroll operation. One of them, C. E. Mackenzie, remained in international banking and remembered Sherman as "a man of unusual attainments...and engaging personality and a fine intuition."

# LEDGERS AND LAUREL LEAVES

## *Poet/Banker Francis Sherman*

IS THERE POETRY IN BANKING? PERHAPS. There have certainly been poets in banking. Banking and literature have intersected frequently in the bank's history. The Royal Bank has had among its staff not only Sinclair Ross, an outstanding Canadian novelist, but also Francis Sherman, a distinguished poet. We tend to stereotype poets as impractical artists, remote from the world of business or action. The career of Francis Sherman (1871-1926) proves us wrong. Poems and ledgers dominated Sherman's short life.

Sherman was one of the bank's pioneers in Cuba, a banker so capable that, for many of the sugar planters who formed Cuba's economic élite, the bank was simply "Sherman's Bank." By the time he was appointed as joint agent to Havana in 1899, Sherman's career was already a model of a Maritime "bank boy's" path of advancement. Born of Loyalist stock in Fredericton in 1871, Sherman fell under the powerful influence of George Parkin, an outspoken admirer of Empire, at the Collegiate School in Fredericton. Later instrumental in establishing the Rhodes Scholarship, Parkin obliged his students to broaden their parochial horizons. So too did Sherman's mentor at the University of New Brunswick, George Foster; Foster himself would go on to prominence in federal politics. Many of Sherman's adolescent friends were destined to distinguish themselves: Frederick Williams-Taylor as general manager of the Bank of Montreal and Charlie Neill in the same role at the Royal Bank.

Sherman loved literature, and by the time he joined the Merchants' Bank's Woodstock branch in 1887 as a junior, he was already writing poetry. Influenced by Maritime poets Charles G. D. Roberts and Bliss Carman, Sherman published his first book of verse, *Matins*, in 1897. That same year he became the bank's youngest manager, taking over the Fredericton branch at the age of twenty-six, living proof of the bank's reputation as a "young man's institution." In 1899 he was called to Montreal to work under the discerning eye of Edson Pease. Pease liked what he saw and despatched Sherman to Cuba.

Charming and generous by nature, Sherman was ideally suited to winning Cuban confidence. He had a keen eye for potential accounts; he learned Spanish and mingled freely in local society. Among his friends were José Bacardi, William Van Horne, and General Leonard Wood, the American military governor. He "made" the bank in Cuba and was, in 1907, promoted to assistant general manager. Cuba also inspired Sherman's muse. Although he had less time for poetry, he was able to pen a few poems exalting Cuba's tropical landscape. Caribbean gold dominated Sherman's working day at the bank. In his poems, the "gold" became a metaphor for a Caribbean sunset:

> More gold than Cortes, even,
> Touched in any dream
> Sank half-an-hour ago
> Deep in the Gulf Stream:
> Like fine dust of it
> The few clouds seem.
>
> —"IN THE SOUTH"

In 1912, Sherman returned to head office and, like so many of his confrères, harkened to the patriotic call in 1915 by joining the army. He was soon a major. By the time he rejoined the bank in 1919, he had worked his heart out. Suffering from a heart condition, he was compelled to retire and went to live in balmy Atlantic City.

There was a last touch of romance in his life. In his youth, Sherman had fallen in love with a girl who, stricken with polio, became a chronic invalid. Devoted to his beloved during her years of invalidism, Sherman never married, and returned to Fredericton annually to visit the love of his youth. After her death – and his own retirement – Sherman married at last. Five years later, on June 16, 1926, he died. One of his last acts was to order red roses for Ruth, the wife with whom he had found domestic happiness at last.

*(Opposite) Major Francis Sherman, 1916.*
*(Above) Canadian "bank boys" at play at the bank's Vedado guest house in Havana.*

Cuba Company drew large advances on the Royal Bank. When Pease and the bank's president, Herbert Holt, toured Cuba in 1913, Van Horne instructed his staff to roll out the red carpet; the Royal was "our Banker."[55]

With its New York agency and growing branch network, the bank soon attracted other prominent clients engaged in building up Cuban agriculture and infrastructure. The Swift and Armour meat-packing companies established accounts, as did Minor C. Keith, whose United Fruit Company was fast binding Central American fruit plantations to the American market. Another early account was that of Sosthenes and Hernand Behn, brothers from the Virgin Islands who graduated out of Puerto Rican sugar into Caribbean utilities. The bank won their Havana Telephone and Havana Docks business; in 1919 the Behns melded their various interests into International Telephone and Telegraph (ITT).[56] The umbrella of the Platt Amendment also made it possible for the bank to attract prominent Cuban clients. Along with the Bacardi distillery, Romeo y Julieta, the renowned cigar-maker, was soon a client. Similarly, up-and-coming Cuban promoters such as José Miguel Gomez and José Miguel Tarafa turned to the bank for financial support. Gomez, an unsuccessful presidential candidate in 1905, became involved in railway building, which the bank helped under-write, until he was elected Cuban president in 1908. Tarafa looked to the bank to finance his Cuba Northern Railway and his Central Cuba Sugar Company, a kind of Cuban carbon copy of Van Horne's venture.

Flowing inexorably below these prestige accounts was a constant ebb and flow of sugar financing. The Sugar Reciprocity Treaty of 1902 initiated a two-decade crescendo of Cuban sugar production; the price of refined sugar rocketed by 266 per cent. Under such pressure, the nature of Cuban sugar production changed dramatically. Railway development such as Van Horne's Cuba Railroad pulled sugar produc-tion eastward into Camagüey and Oriente provinces, which by 1919 produced 60 per cent of the country's sugar. Contrary to Van Horne's hopes, production did not fall into the hands of small producers as wheat farming had in the Canadian West; huge *centrales*, or sugar estates, dominated the industry. While Cuban mills participated in this concentration of production, American-owned mills perfected it. From 1902 to 1924, American investment in Cuban sugar production leapt from $50 million to $600 million.[57] The Royal Bank held the accounts of many of these huge American enterprises – loans to the Río Cauto, Antilla, and United Fruit mills punctuate the directors' minute book. There were also Cuban sugar accounts of nationals such as José I. Lezama or locally owned mills like the Central Borjita.

*"If the word cane was changed to wheat and the language used changed to English, you might almost imagine it to be one of those farming-ranching districts in western Canada," wrote a Royal Bank employee in the Dominican Republic. Decades of financing the movement of Canadian fish, timber, and wheat prepared the bank well for the Caribbean sugar trade. A Cuban cane field.*

If sugar production was revolutionized, so too was sugar financing. In effect, the Royal Bank simply applied the principles of Section 88 of the Canadian Bank Act to Cuban sugar production. The cycle of sugar production was not dissimilar from that of Canadian timber or wheat. Producers needed credit to put the crop in the ground and were prepared to carry the debt in hopes of retiring it on the proceeds of the harvest. "Dead season" financing carried the industry from one crop year to the next. In an industry in which prices pushed steadily upward, the "hypothecation" – or pledging – of the crop in the ground was a tailor-made opportunity for profits and expansion. Here were the roots of what Cubans would come to call the "Dance of the Millions," the headlong bull market in sugar. Throughout Cuba, millions of bags of sugar were pledged as surety against Royal Bank loans.[58] To ensure that pledged sugar was of promised quality, the bank created the post of "sugar inspector" and empowered him to

*Since so much lending in Cuba was secured by sugar destined for market, the bank was obliged to check its existence and quality on site. This man is a sugar inspector. Inspecting sugar was an unpopular and dangerous job – note the revolver.*

travel to far-flung warehouses to verify the worth of mountains of sugar. For all concerned, it was a highly lucrative trade. Similar financing evolved for the production of tobacco in Pinar del Río province and for the Cuban iron-ore industry.

In all of these commodities, the bank stood to make money both in lending and from the inevitable foreign-exchange transactions that commodity trading generated. In 1919, the bank established a separate foreign-exchange department in New York. In the same year, a Foreign Trade Department was set up at head office in Montreal. When the department's first head, a former Canadian trade commissioner, Dana Wilgress, unexpectedly quit, the bank looked to McGill University for a replacement. There it found a young honours economics graduate, Graham Towers, and set him to work promoting trade. "The growth of Canadian foreign trade, and the expansion of this bank in other countries," Towers wrote in the bank's *Financing Foreign Trade* a year later, "is making increasingly necessary a knowledge of the details of import

*As in Canada, the branch system in Cuba tended to follow the railway. Van Horne's Cuba Railway led the bank into eastern Cuba, where large-scale sugar production flourished. When Van Horne made his headquarters in Camagüey, Oriente Province, the bank quickly opened a branch in 1904. Van Horne suggested the corner location and even sketched the facade of Camagüey branch (above).*

and export finance."[59] In 1922, Towers was sent to Havana to gather some first-hand knowledge of his own.

Under these marvellous auspices, the Royal Bank experienced luxuriant growth in Cuba. Beginning with the Santiago and Camagüey branches in 1903-4, the branch network steadily expanded, to eleven by 1908, twenty-seven by 1918, and a peak of sixty-five in 1923. In 1903, the bank acquired the Banco del Comercio in order to enhance its reach into Havana's commercial and municipal banking market. In 1905, it joined forces with Norman Davis, an American promoter, and several Cuban merchants to form the Trust Company of Cuba in an attempt to provide the kind of fiduciary financial services that accompanied banking elsewhere. Wherever it went in Cuba, the bank attempted to present itself as a progressive, modern bank. It heeded Van Horne's advice and sought prominent locations for its branches and equipped them handsomely. In 1919, a new, seven-storey head office was opened in Havana, designed by the bank's architect, S. G. Davenport. The building was consciously designed to be a model

*Canadians had a knack for branch banking in the Caribbean. Unfortunately, moving between those branches was not always easy. Since inspection was the crucial check in branch banking, inspectors soon became intrepid travellers. Here an inspector contends with Puerto Rican mud, while another fords a Jamaican river (opposite).*

of North American modernity.[60] The Canadians thus furnished Cuba with a model of branch banking: branches throughout Havana connected the city to its export markets and its hinterland, particularly Oriente and Camagüey provinces, where Canadian and American enterprise was so evident. By 1914, Cuba was the jewel in the Royal's international crown. It gave the bank profits and prestige. When called before the Commons' Banking and Commerce Committee in 1913, Edson Pease told the politicians that the bank's business in the south was "conducive directly to the great advantage of Canada as well as to the bank." Deposits outweighed loans by 40 per cent. Was it profitable? he was asked. "Yes, it is so much so that four or five years ago we received an offer from an American syndicate of no less than $1,000,000 for the goodwill of the business if we retire."[61] Pease did not bother elaborating on his response to the Americans.

Cuba was the test ground for the Royal Bank's Caribbean and Latin American proliferation. In 1907, Francis Sherman was promoted to Supervisor of Cuban Branches and instructed to sail to Puerto Rico to

investigate its potential for business. Like Cuba, Puerto Rico had fallen under American sway in the wake of the Spanish–American War, a fact capitalized upon by the Union Bank of Halifax when it opened in San Juan in 1906. Sherman reported that the island's sugar, tobacco, and coffee crops might well support profitable banking and, early in 1907, the bank opened in San Juan. Other branches in Ponce and Mayagüez followed. Almost immediately, important accounts were won: Puerto Rico Telephone Company, a promotion of the ubiquitous Behn Brothers, and the Porto [sic] Rico Railways, a promotion of the brash, young Montrealer Max Aitken.[62] Commodity financing flourished. In 1910, the Union Bank of Halifax branch was taken over; its accountant, Charles C. Pineo, was to become a stalwart of international banking at the Royal Bank. Men like Pineo and Sherman would over the next two decades carry the Royal throughout the Caribbean and Latin America. By 1925, the bank was Canada's leading international banker, with 121 branches in 28 countries.

The Royal Bank was far from alone in the south; by 1926, there were 114 branches of Canadian banks in Cuba and the West Indies, of which an overwhelming seventy-two were Royal branches. Another Halifax-born bank, the Nova Scotia, was the bank's closest Caribbean rival. American banks, with forty-four branches by 1926, and a smattering of British banks completed the foreign presence. In South America and Cuba, however, the Royal Bank and the National City Bank of New York had the field virtually to themselves.[63] The Royal Bank was, as its advertising boasted, "a great international bank."[64]

The bank's success abroad hinged on two crucial conditions. Given Canada's fledgling presence on the world stage, the Royal habitually donned the *de facto* identity of other nationalities. Hence, the Platt Amendment had allowed it to assume American protection in Cuba, Puerto Rico, and the Dominican Republic. In the British West Indies, it was a "British" bank. In Guadeloupe, it was a "French" bank. Only in South America did it develop a more autonomous identity, although the British ambassador was usually its best friend in town. If its external identity was tinted by other nationalities, the Royal Bank's internal strength in these areas – the second condition of growth – bore a strong Canadian stamp: Canadian "bank boys" and bank methods travelled the world.

This amalgam of trade financing, retail banking, and Canadian manpower placed the bank's international operations on a sturdy foundation, but the foundation did have some cracks. Much of the trade financing rested on *laissez-faire* commodity economics, which could be imperilled by several forces. Commodity prices were capable of sudden slumps, slumps that could become prolonged or even

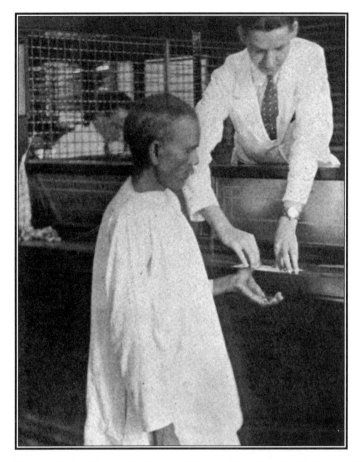

*Many of the bank's Caribbean clients were illiterate. Since Rule 95 (d) stipulated that all customers have a "dependable" means of identification, many managers resorted to taking fingerprints. Above, a Trinidadian provides prints in 1926.*

permanent if new sources of production or new technologies were involved. Prices could also leap upwards if other producers exited the market; such was Cuba's happy fate in the First World War when European sugar-beet production halted. Similarly, as commodity-producing regions gained economic headway, they would frequently try to restrain their reliance on exports in the hope of stimulating commodity-processing at home, and Cuban exporters were extraordinarily favoured by the unbroken rise in the price of sugar from 1900 to 1920. Everything depended on sugar: there was little crop diversification to provide insurance.[65] Commodity production was also vulnerable to other cruel variables: war, pestilence, and political upheaval. In effect, commodity production could rapidly become a trap for producer and banker alike. Most of the Royal's Caribbean

*The success of Canadian banks abroad flattered national pride. The above advertisement appeared in the* Canadian Geographic Journal *in the late 1920s.*

operations were established in colonial societies or in societies, like
Cuba, which lived a kind of semi-colonial existence. As the century
progressed, especially after 1945, the urge to decolonize would alter
the political mood in many of the Royal Bank's host countries. The
bank countered these tendencies by hiring nationals wherever it operated and by remaining sensitive to the political sensitivities of its
hosts. In the years down to 1930, however, these trends manifested
themselves as little more than periodic upheavals. In only one country,
Panama – where the bank opened in 1929 – did the Royal Bank pull
out as a result of changed political circumstances, a 1939 law requiring banks to invest in government bonds.

The Royal Bank's Caribbean network was generally complete by the
early years of the First World War. In 1910, a branch in Trinidad was
acquired as a result of the takeover of the Union Bank of Halifax.
Jamaica and Barbados were added in 1911, British Honduras in 1912,
Grenada in 1913, British Guiana in 1914, and Antigua, Dominica, and
St. Kitts in 1915. Nevis, Montserrat, and Tobago joined the family in
1917 and St. Lucia in 1920. Since the trade and foreign-exchange
energies of these colonies were focused on Europe, particularly on
England, the Royal opened in London in 1910.

The London branch assumed all the duties hitherto performed by
the Royal's correspondent banks in the City. For the first time, the
bank found itself at work in a city that prided itself on being "the
world's banker." Senior staff donned morning coats and top hats; tea
was served at 4:30 sharp every afternoon. Royal Bankers were acutely
conscious of the Bank of Montreal's prestige in the City; it had long
been established as the Dominion's fiscal agent in London. In 1915,
the bank's ambitions in London were dented by the discovery of a
£15,850 defalcation on the part of the branch manager, who was
unceremoniously cashiered.[66] None the less, the London branch
flourished. By 1920, it had a staff of over a hundred and an evenly
balanced portfolio of loans and deposits averaging $20 million. In
1928, a West End branch would open off Trafalgar Square, and in
1931 S. G. Davenport would design a splendid new main branch in
Lothbury, opposite the Bank of England in the City.

In 1914, Pease became aware of another piece of the colonial patch-
work in the Caribbean, the French colonies of Guadeloupe and
Martinique. The British consul in Martinique provided a succinct
rationale for opening a branch of the Royal there: "The colony is prosperous, there is a good deal of money lying around for investment,
and our banking institution, the sole one, namely the 'Banque de la
Martinique' seems to me to be behind the times."[67] With cocoa, coffee,
vanilla, and rum exports flowing mainly to France, here seemed another

*"Bank boys" relax in San Juan, Puerto Rico, 1917.*

opportunity to capture a rich colonial trade. The outbreak of the First World War (making trade dangerous and straining bank manpower) postponed the bank's entry into Martinique and Guadeloupe until 1919. In the same year, a branch was launched in Port-au-Prince, Haiti. To complement these branches, an office was opened in Paris on the prestigious rue Scribe and, to avoid onerous French taxation, the French operation was given a separate French incorporation. Paris quickly became a lively office, allowing the bank to capitalize on post-war reconstruction in Europe. Success came more slowly in the Caribbean.

From the outset, Montreal realized that the two French colonies had special needs: "The neighbouring British islands are as different from the French islands as they could be from islands at their antipodes."[68] When initial results proved disappointing, French-Canadian staff were sent south, notably H. L. Gagnon, a Franco-Nova Scotian, who acquitted himself so well that he would be sent in 1923 to the bank's fledgling branch in Barcelona. Martinique and Guadeloupe continued to labour under ineffective management – attributed in one bank report to the persistence of "Anglo-Saxon" attitudes – and the impact of the Depression. When the Second World War cut the colonies off from metropolitan France in 1940, the branches were closed.

War in Europe or local political upheaval always placed the Caribbean operation at risk. While commodity prices may have risen, so too did the risks of doing business. In 1914, the rush of Canadian "bank boys" to the colours and the appearance of German submarines in the Atlantic cooled the bank's overseas expansion. In 1916, the fragility of the Caribbean system was amply demonstrated in the Dominican Republic. The Royal Bank had entered the Dominican Republic in 1912, eager to capture its sugar and cocoa export trade, and by 1916 it had pushed three branches into the hinterland. Assassination, the repudiation of foreign debt, and a pattern of foreign occupations had, however, given the Republic a very "uncertain nationhood."[69] In 1905, the Americans had stepped in and obliged the Dominicans to settle with their creditors and when, in 1916, President Jiminez was toppled and replaced by the army, the U.S. Marines again came ashore. "Most decent people are not only resigned to the Americans being here," the manager in Santo Domingo wrote to his branches, "but appear to be afraid that they may go away before straightening things out....If there is any fighting, close the Bank and keep as far away as you can."[70] The Americans stayed until 1924, thereby bringing the Dominican Republic into the fold of its other sugar "colonies." American occupation brought land reform, U.S. stewardship of Dominican customs, preferential access to the American sugar market, and the creation of a National Guard, on whose coattails Rafael Trujillo would ride to dictatorship in the late 1920s.[71] A similar American intervention in Haiti from 1916 to 1934 brought similar reforms and dependency.

If the First World War created a hiatus in the bank's international expansion, it also witnessed two important developments. In the first place, competition materialized. Freed by the Federal Reserve Act of 1913 and out of the war until 1917, American banks now sprinted abroad, led by the National City Bank of New York. In James Stillman, the National City found a chairman as dynamic as Edson Pease. Stillman forged alliances with prominent American companies operating overseas – Standard Oil and W. R. Grace – and began opening foreign branches, beginning in Cuba, Argentina, and Brazil.[72] The Royal Bank now had head-to-head competition. Some years later, a Royal manager forced out of his Aux Cayes, Haiti, branch by National City competition grimly reported that he "never liked the smiles of the American bankers in Haiti which seem to be the same smiles offered by the cats to the mice."[73]

Prospective American competition was intensified by a second pressure: the need to formulate a post-war strategy of expansion. Prompted by the optimism that an Allied victory would herald a post-war boom, head office began early in the war to scan the foreign horizon for opportunities. There was an automatic assumption that peace would bring new offices in Europe – Barcelona did open in 1918 and Paris in 1919. At the same time, curiosity, not assurance, ruled the bank's attitude to the Orient and Latin America. Early in 1916, the bank's British Columbia supervisor urged head office to look to the Far East: "Japanese goods are here to stay."[74] Two months later, the Canadian trade commissioner in Shanghai urged the bank to open in "Shanghai, Hong Kong, Manila and Yokohama, for in this direction real opportunity lies."[75] In Ottawa, Prime Minister Robert Borden made it clear that he would like to see the banks open Latin America for Canadian trade. The completion of the Panama Canal had created "wonderful possibilities" on the west coast of South America.[76] Edson Pease was alive to all these notions. He already had his eye on Honolulu as a branch site and, now assured, began giving "immediate attention" to the Far East. He was in good company; there were clear indications that the National City was also readying itself for a post-war dash.

The scramble began in earnest in the early fall of 1918; up to then Pease felt constrained by the wartime shortage of men. With peace imminent, however, the Royal Bank struck out in two directions. It was not alone in concluding that Siberia offered Canada an attractive field for commercial expansion. In the wake of the Russian Revolution, Ottawa had wagered that the Bolsheviks could not cling to power and had despatched troops to assist the White Russians. Trade commissioners followed, including the appointment of Dana Wilgress to Vladivostok in October 1918. Within days, General Manager Charlie Neill inquired of Trade Minister George Foster whether the bank "could be of service to the Dominion Government...our aim is to foster international trade." Foster replied enthusiastically.[77] Over the next three weeks, the bank engaged in a headlong charge to transplant a Toronto branch manager, D. C. Rea, onto the virgin soil of revolutionary Russia. "The whole situation bristles with difficulties," Neill confided to Rea, "and we are to a great extent unfamiliar with conditions and risks."[78] On November 28, Rea left Vancouver on the *Empress of Japan*, accompanied by a small staff and a fifty-seven-ton prefabricated bank building. He had instructions to open in Vladivostok and then to scout opportunities in Shanghai and Hong Kong. On December 21, Rea presented his credentials to Wilgress in the winter-bound Russian port; the National City Bank had already been open a week.

Vladivostok proved a quixotic disaster. Canadian officials had greatly overestimated its trade potential; its only vitality came from supplying the White and Allied troops, which moved through it up the Trans-Siberian Railway to counter Trotsky's Red Army. Rea

*On guard for thee: Bank officials in Havana greet Prime Minister Mackenzie King (second from right) and his external affairs advisor O. D. Skelton (far left), 1939.*

complained that the rouble was "worthless" and looked "like the label on a beer bottle." The "mañana habit" pervaded the city. The branch eked out a paltry existence on foreign exchange. Gunfire kept the staff awake at night and "in the morning there'd be 5 or 6 dead bodies in the street." Rea prevailed on the Canadian commander to post troops around the branch. In inimitable "bank-boy" fashion, Roy East, the acting manager after Rea departed for Shanghai, spent his weekends sailing on the Japan Sea in a yacht he dubbed the *Minnetonka*.[79]

By the spring of 1919, the end was near. The Canadian contingent pulled out, and the Red Army drew ever closer. Rea later claimed to have received a telegram signed by Lenin and Trotsky, protesting the bank's "financial guardianship" of the Whites. "The Red Guard," Trotsky warned, "will hungrily await your arrival."* In July, East reported that Bolshevism was rampant in the city and, when the Whites failed to gain representation at the Versailles peace talks, the Royal Bank announced on October 15 that Vladivostok branch was "temporarily closed." The bank would not reopen in the Far East until 1958, when a representative was posted to Hong Kong; in the interim, the mysteries of Far Eastern commerce kept the Canadians at bay.

Central and South America aroused greater hope. Branches in Costa

---

* The whereabouts of this cable (and one of welcome from Provisional Government leader Kerensky) are unknown. Although quoted verbatim elsewhere, the original is not in the archive files on the Vladivostok fiasco. One can only assume that Rea kept it as a memento.

# EXPORT BANKING:
# ROYAL BANK BRANCHES ABROAD 1882-1930

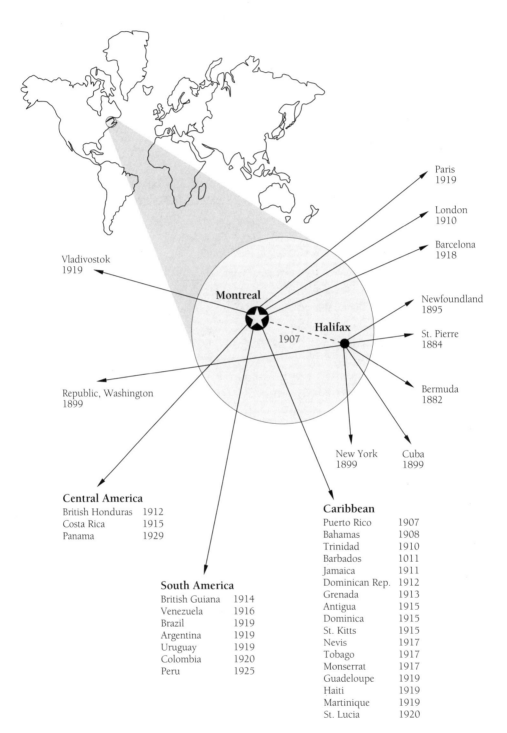

Paris
1919

London
1910

Barcelona
1918

Vladivostok
1919

Montreal

Newfoundland
1895

Halifax

St. Pierre
1884

1907

Republic, Washington
1899

Bermuda
1882

New York
1899

Cuba
1899

**Central America**

British Honduras   1912
Costa Rica         1915
Panama             1929

**Caribbean**

Puerto Rico     1907
Bahamas         1908
Trinidad        1910
Barbados        1011
Jamaica         1911
Dominican Rep.  1912
Grenada         1913
Antigua         1915
Dominica        1915
St. Kitts       1915
Nevis           1917
Tobago          1917
Monserrat       1917
Guadeloupe      1919
Haiti           1919
Martinique      1919
St. Lucia       1920

**South America**

British Guiana  1914
Venezuela       1916
Brazil          1919
Argentina       1919
Uruguay         1919
Colombia        1920
Peru            1925

Rica and Venezuela, opened in 1915 and 1916, had given the bank an initial toehold. Late in 1918, Pease decided "to proceed energetically" into Latin America.[80] Instinctively, his first move was to ensure that he had men who were up to the challenge. In 1915, the National City Bank had "raided" the Royal Bank, hiring away the very capable Charles Pineo to manage their Brazilian business. In any other circumstance, such behaviour would have put Pineo on a blacklist, but now Pease wanted him back for the sally into Latin America. Pineo spoke Spanish and had an encyclopedic knowledge of the continent. The task of winning him back fell to the redoubtable F. T. Walker, now the bank's New York agent. Walker succeeded and, in April 1919, the two men set off on a grand tour of Brazil, Uruguay, and Argentina. Walker's elaborate report on the expedition gave Pease every reason to forge ahead. Walker found ample banking prospects in the trade of all three countries: "I have come to believe that there is a sort of special opportunity for us to fit in between the English and American banks." The British banks were perceived by Latin American traders as too conservative and the American banks too aggressive – "American brass bands," Pineo called them.[81] All the Canadians had to do was to demonstrate their ability to finance trade and to handle foreign exchange between the ports of South America and the docks of Europe and America. Canadian trade would constitute a part of this, but the bulk was destined to go elsewhere. "There is a tendency in these South American Cities to think that we came chiefly to foster Canadian trade. This will have to be gotten over by judicious propaganda," Walker noted. What had been mastered in Cuba would now be applied to South America: "There is a big opportunity to do some very fine team work with our branches at New York, London, Paris and Barcelona. One must help the other in securing collections and exchange business."[82]

Pease acted quickly. Late in 1919, branches were opened in Buenos Aires, Rio de Janeiro, and Montevideo, followed early in 1920 by Barranquilla, Colombia. Success was almost immediate. Despite problems with organizing staff, Pineo could report that in just over a year that the Brazilian exchange business was "exceedingly well run...the cleanest and most satisfactory...in Brazil."[83] Other branches were added in Brazil at Santos and Recife, to capture the coffee and cocoa trade, and in São Paulo, where the bank began loaning to Brazilian industry. New branches were opened in Venezuela, and in 1925 the assets of the American-owned Bank of Central and South America were purchased, bringing twelve new branches in Costa Rica, Colombia, Venezuela, and, for the first time, Peru. Only in Mexico, where the Bank of Montreal was well established and the legacy of the bloody civil war of 1910-20 remained strong, did the Royal Bank play a retiring role.

The breadth of the Royal Bank's international system served it well throughout the 1920s: branch systems were meant to induce stability. Inevitably, the unpredictable warp and woof of Latin American politics would occasionally impinge on the bank's operations. The seasoned Pineo summed it up best when he talked of "the jolts that must come from time to time" when doing business in Latin America.[84] In 1919, for instance, President Tinoco, the unpopular revolutionary leader of Costa Rica, fled into exile, taking with him a fraudulently obtained draft for U.S.$200,000 drawn on the bank. Despite international arbitration, the money was never recovered.[85] On the whole, however, the international system was stronger than the sum of its parts. The international branches contributed solidly to the bank's profits throughout the 1920s. Aggregated profits for the years 1922-31 reveal that Rio and São Paulo in Brazil were the chief profit-makers, contributing just over $2 million in these years. Colombia ($593,000), the Dominion Republic ($645,000), British Honduras ($313,883), and Jamaica ($236,000) were also consistently profitable. High overheads in Argentina made Buenos Aires a weak link in the chain. Elsewhere the profits were respectable, with one conspicuous exception – Cuba.

In 1920, the price of sugar collapsed – plummeted or nose-dived would be more accurate. The First World War had made the already-overheated Cuban sugar economy even hotter. With European sugar-beet production cut off, the Allies created the International Sugar Committee in 1917 to coordinate the purchase and distribution of the entire Cuban crop. All actual purchasing was undertaken by the United States Sugar Equalization Board. Under such controlled conditions, prices leapt upwards. Production mushroomed to nearly four million tons in 1919. Canadians were not immune to the virus; the Cuban-Canadian Sugar Company was promoted – "Bankers: Royal Bank of Canada" – to acquire the assets of the Río Cauto sugar plantation in Oriente.[86] In Cuba, the banks, particularly local banks such as Banco Nacional de Cuba, indulged sugar speculators with reckless lines of credit. The suburbs of Havana became studded with the homes of the *nouveaux riches*, and the Cuban playboy acquired his mythic reputation. And then the Dance of the Millions ended.

At war's end, European sugar-beet production began to resuscitate, and Far Eastern sugar reappeared on the market. Sensing the return of a normal market in sugar, President Wilson abandoned sugar controls in December 1919. Initially, heightened speculation gripped the market as the price jumped to 12.50 cents by year's end. By next May, it was

*Sir Herbert Holt on the deck of the Imperial Oil tanker Albertolite in Colombia in 1926. Imperial was an early Toronto corporate account of the bank, and Holt had been active in promoting Colombian pipelines. The bank's entry into Colombia and Venezuela in the 1920s was partially intended to serve the oil trade.*

flirting with 22.50 cents. Then the free market prevailed, and the price plunged until December, when it bottomed at 3.66 cents. The Cuban economy was devastated. Harold Hesler, a Royal Banker returning from a Canadian furlough in October, found Havana a "city wrapped in gloom." On October 9, withdrawals from the banks reached panic proportions and the government declared a moratorium on all debts until December 1. Representatives of foreign financial interests, including Edson Pease, rushed to Havana for consultations. Early in 1921, the mopping-up began. A commission was appointed to oversee the liquidation of banks caught overextended by sugar's collapse. Worst hit were the Cuban banks; sixteen were wound up by 1925. Banco Nacional de Cuba suffered catastrophic losses, its president committed suicide, and it was reduced to a shadow operation.

The Royal Bank weathered the crash, although deposits plunged from $73 million in October 1920 to $32 million by the next July. These vanished $41 millions were very evident in the drop in the bank's overall deposits from $455 million to $376 million between 1920 and 1921. On the surface, loans declined less dramatically: a drop from $64 to $62 million in the same period. The real impact was less obvious. Sugar loans negotiated in the heyday of the boom became non-performing, obliging the bank to take possession of assets backing the loans. Thus, the Royal Bank went into the business of producing sugar. Huge mills such as the Borjita, Antilla, and Río Cauto in effect became operating subsidiaries of a Canadian bank. In 1922, the Sugar Plantations Operating Company was created to oversee these valuable-but-unwanted assets. When sugar rebounded, the bank reasoned, the mills would be sold; few could have known that the last sale would not occur until 1950.

As the Cuban bank industry buckled in the 1920s, the National City and Royal Bank consolidated their hold on Cuban banking. Both carried the burden of bad sugar debts and both began trimming their branch networks on the island. The Canadians actually acquired a few

*Directors' Latin America tour, 1925:*
*Neill, Holt, and Smeaton White (right to left) beside an Andean train.*

small Cuban banks, but by 1930 there were only thirty-eight branches in Cuba, down from a high of sixty-five five years earlier. Despite the fact that the so-called "sugar mill accounts" sat like a time bomb at the heart of the bank – one that was to tick very loudly in the Depression – the bank still had a healthy retail system in Cuba, one that on average generated a $2-million-dollar annual profit through the 1920s. None the less, the bloom was off Cuba by 1920, and henceforth the bank tended to downplay its presence there to its shareholders. To Cubans, however, it remained Banco de Canada.[87]

Despite the sting of the Cuban collapse, Royal Bankers knew that their adeptness in transplanting Canadian branch banking to the Caribbean and Latin America had contributed mightily to their bank's ascendancy. It had handsomely supplemented profits, provided off-shore investment opportunities, developed Canadian trade to some degree and, perhaps more than anything else, provided them with a magnificent adventure. When Canadian tourists, trade missions, and even prime ministers stepped ashore in foreign lands, more often than not it was a Canadian banker who greeted them. There was lots of hard work and lots of good fun. "I hardly think it is worth while to take our golf clubs to South America," Pease concluded on the eve of a 1922 tour of the South American branches.[88] Three years later, in early 1925, the bank's president, Herbert Holt, General Manager Neill, and four of its directors headed off on a two-month Royal tour of Latin America. "We shall take golf clubs for Buenos Aires," Neill instructed his colleagues. Accompanying them was Smeaton White, editor of the Montreal *Gazette*, who later published an account of their stately trek through Cuba, Brazil, Uruguay, Argentina, Chile, and Peru. Holt, he reported, delighted in guiding the group across the Andes, bragging of his exploits as a youthful engineer in search of Chilean contract work in the 1890s.[89]

Many a Royal Banker serving south of the equator could have echoed Holt's nostalgia. They too were taking a chance on a foreign shore. C. R. Beattie, the manager in Belize, British Honduras, loved telling the story of how, in 1912, he learned that a shipment of chicle – the key ingredient in chewing gum – had been seized and taken down river by corrupt government officials. Since the chicle was security for a Royal Bank loan, Beattie gave chase. Donning his royal-blue bank hockey sweater with its rampant lions' crest, he chartered a launch and closed in on his prey. Believing that the Royal Navy was on their tail, the pirates meekly surrendered to the "Royal Bank Navy."[90]

Others were less fortunate. Head office had always been aware that service in the south entailed special dangers. The threat of yellow fever and malaria in Cuba had, for instance, prompted the directors in

1900 to take out life insurance on their staff in the south.[91] The first issue of the *Royal Bank Magazine* in November 1920 noted that Guy Cameron, who had just opened Barranquilla branch in Colombia, had dropped by head office. "He claims that he has been in more God-forsaken countries than any other man in the service of the bank."[92] Eight years later, Cameron died in the fever ward of a Lima hospital, while inspecting the bank's Peruvian branches. The bank brought his body home for burial in his home town of Strathgartney, P.E.I.[93] If there was glory in foreign banking, there was also sorrow.

# The Challenge of Maturity

## "The Top of the Tree"

T HERE WAS MUCH TO CELEBRATE. IT WAS NEW YEAR'S EVE, 1911, AND Charlie Neill, the bank's bright young assistant general manager, had crossed the Atlantic to visit the newly opened London branch. Norman Hart, the branch accountant, recalled being invited to "a very gay party" that evening in Neill's Savoy Hotel suite. His host exuded a "boyish gaiety": Hart shared most peoples' impression that Charlie Neill "often appeared to be lucky."[1] Three years later, Neill, very much Edson Pease's hand-picked successor, would be made a director of the bank and then, in 1916, its general manager. Pease in 1916 would assume the title managing director, an echo of English banking, and would busy himself with plotting the bank's strategic direction. Neill would run the bank's day-to-day affairs until 1929, when he would assume Pease's old title of managing director. He was thus the first chief executive of the Royal Bank to have spent his entire working life within the bank; to all concerned his success epitomized the rewards that awaited a dutiful "bank boy." When he became president of the Canadian Bankers' Association in 1925, he told the *Monetary Times* that banking was no longer a "rich man's art."[2]

Like so many of his confrères – notably his fellow assistant general manager Francis Sherman – Neill, as mentioned, was a Fredericton native. For $100 a year he had become a Merchants' Bank clerk in 1889. His formal education ended in high school. Thirty-five years later, he would advise the graduating class at the University of Fredericton that success came to those with "a well-considered ambition."[3] Neill first displayed his talent in the rough and tumble of British Columbia banking in the late 1890s – his manager's assessment of him as "a very promising lad"[4] gained him the Vancouver manager-ship in 1900 at the age of twenty-seven. By the time he returned home for his honorary degree in 1924, he was earning $50,000 a year. Every Saturday night in Montreal, Charlie now joined cronies from the city's financial élite for "the best dinner which the Mount Royal Club could provide" and high-stakes poker to midnight.[5]

Charlie Neill's New Year's Eve celebration in 1911 reflected the success of the bank as a whole. Through the first decade of the century the bank had ridden a crescendo of growth. Six months after Neill returned from London, Herbert Holt won shareholder approval to increase the bank's capital from $10 million to a dramatic $25 million.[6] For the first time, also in 1911, the bank reported a million-dollar profit – $1,152,249 – and it inaugurated an era of 12 per cent dividends that would last two decades. With assets of $110 million, a staff of 1,510, 207 branches, and a healthy rest account, the Royal Bank of Canada was coming of age. In 1909, Holt had helped to round out this expansion by engineering the takeover – at arm's length – of the Montreal Trust Company. The trust company acted as a useful ally, providing the bank with ready access to the services of a financial fiduciary.[7] Building on this foundation, Edson Pease's aggressive strategy of fortifying internal growth with amalgamations and vigorous foreign growth would now propel the bank through an exuberant adolescence to maturity.

Like any adolescence, the Royal Bank's was punctuated by celebrations of achievement. Throughout the 1910s and 1920s, Holt, Pease and Neill cut ribbons and made speeches. In 1919, the bank celebrated its fiftieth anniversary with a slim historical text describing its "phenom-enal growth" and a 20 per cent salary bonus to staff. Eight years later, a copy of the history was sealed into the cornerstone of the bank's new head office on Montreal's St. James Street, a twenty-three-storey skyscraper, designed by York and Sawyer of New York to be Canada's tallest building. As age crept up on the senior managers overseeing this growth, they began commemorating themselves. In 1929, the directors commissioned a portrait of Herbert Holt, twenty-one years their president. Pease presented the portrait, pointing out that since Holt had come to the bank its assets had multiplied eighteen-fold and it had outstripped every other bank in the country. "To-day there are only ten existing banks, most of them having disappeared through consolidations and otherwise, and this bank stands at the top of the tree."[8]

With maturity, however, came responsibilities and vulnerabilities. If amalgamations and international banking were the glory of the bank in these years, there were also signs – disturbing signs – that maintaining a national bank entailed huge risks and obligations. The

*Charles Ernest Neill, general manager from 1916 to 1929, provided another example of a Maritime "bank boy" who rose to prominence. Neill grew to love Montreal social life. (Above) The Neills are pictured at a 1924 costume ball at the Mount Royal Hotel.*

Depression of the 1930s would lay these bare; in the interim, Pease, Neill, and their staff were exposed to the initial implications. At the heart of the matter was the relationship of Canadian banks and the creation of national credit and its application to Canada's varied regions and industries. Banks were not just mechanisms for moving money around the country; Canadian branch banking was indisputably efficient at doing this. But banks were also expected to minister to economic opportunity, to furnish credit for the creation of national wealth. "What is in the interest of the country," Neill glibly told a Commons committee in 1924, "is in the interest of the banks."[9]

As the breadth and complexity of the Canadian economy increased in the Laurier boom, divergences occurred between the "interests" of the banks and those of the nation. Several factors conspired to this end. The strictures of Scottish–Canadian banking emphasized probity and stability, not unsecured credit creation. Since every banknote had to be redeemable in gold or Dominion notes, the whole credit system was tied to the security of the gold standard. In prosperous times – such as the 1896-1913 boom – credit tended to expand as foreign capital poured into Canada and the banks constantly built up their capital bases. In economic downturns, Canadian credit creation atrophied.

The notorious vulnerability of Canada's trading economy to external shocks further complicated the credit process. The banks' scramble onto the Prairies had been predicated on the steady appreciation of grain prices and of the value of the land on which it was grown. The same was, for instance, true on the mineral frontier of northern Ontario – in 1911 the bank had opened in the silver-boom town of Cobalt. Wherever the bank established itself on the frontier, it quickly found its loans outstripping its deposits. Once again the superiority of national-branch banking seemed evident; American unit banks found their credit in the slow accretion of local wealth, while Canadian banks imported their credit. The Canadian process could, however, backfire if land and commodity prices went into prolonged decline. In these circumstances, Canadian bankers instinctively moved to protect their solvency by restricting credit. Lacking any central bank to act as a lender of last resort, the banks saw themselves as the nation's financial front line. If they faltered, then the nation would falter.

Ensuring the solvency of the banking system was therefore bankers' unavoidable response to troubling times, even if the immediate effect was to deflate the national economy or regions of it, thereby inflicting hardship on many of those who depended on credit to make their livelihood. Both the bank and its borrowers suffered in differing ways from the same deficiency in Canada's financial system: there was no formalized control over the system's liquidity. In fact, the bank's diversification out of the Maritimes in the late-nineteenth century represented a gradual response to signals – bankrupt sugar and textile firms – that indicated that the Maritime economy was no longer a sure credit bet. The Canadian West was capable of transmitting even sharper signals and, once the Laurier boom began to lag, tensions would begin to grow over the western farmer's access to credit. Regional grievance, long a threat to Canada's political unity, would soon begin to fray the fabric of national banking. During his tenure as general manager, Charlie Neill would see the banker's image in the West radically changed from that of the friendly Easterner with the satchel of money to that of an insensitive Eastern "big shot."[10]

Whenever the credit process came under strain, the high risk implicit in Canadian banking came to the forefront. The risk lay in the danger that unserviced loans might provoke a crisis of liquidity, and that this might in turn bring on the ultimate crisis of a "run" on the bank. Clients naturally saw the credit process in a different light. The banker was a capricious lender, who withdrew credit at the least sign of an economic downturn, thereby exacerbating the decline. Thus, Canadian banking lived in ever-present danger of a confidence-rattling credibility crisis. Protection of the national stability of the system often entailed some cruel twists for the local client; any banker's intuition of a national liquidity crunch might result in a local retraction of credit. Bankers protected this prerogative vigorously. An aggrieved farmer-politician buttonholed Neill before a Commons committee in 1924 and demanded to know if it was better "that we have an uncontrolled credit system."

"I would say so," Neill answered.

"Just left any way it wants to be?" the MP shot back.

"The bankers, as bankers, must exercise their intelligence," Neill confirmed.[11]

The financial turmoil engendered by the First World War and the economic hard times of the early 1920s would pry this credibility gap open even wider. In the absence of any alternative guarantee for their liquidity (somewhat along the lines of the U.S. Federal Reserve), Canadian bankers continued to exercise their "intelligence" as they saw cautiously best; their clients continued to grumble about the effect of such cautious lending on their livelihoods. Typically, Edson Pease foresaw the whole shift to a state-controlled credit process long before his colleagues. The vehemence with which they greeted his lonely 1918 campaign for a central bank of rediscount testified to the conservatism of Canadian banking, and Pease concluded that his idea of central control of credit by an agency independent of the banks was "premature."[12] As Pease receded into the shadows in the 1920s,

Charlie Neill would be left to defend a malfunctioning credit system. By the time a national consensus had formed around the idea of an independent central bank in the early 1930s, the Royal Bank was ready to volunteer one of its own – Graham Towers, hired by Pease in 1919 – as its first governor.

The first intimations of strain in Canadian banking appeared in the West just before the First World War. Ironically, the initial crack developed over railway financing, not farm lending. In the wake of the creation of Alberta and Saskatchewan in 1905, eastern banks had rushed to finance the building of the new western economies. In 1909, the Alberta government had given its guarantee to the Alberta and Great Waterways Railway, a pioneer line from Edmonton to Fort McMurray. When $7.4 million in bonds for the line were successfully floated in London, the Royal Bank and two other banks agreed to create construction accounts in New York for the proceeds. A political scandal derailed the project, leading the provincial government to demand that the banks divert the railway construction monies into general revenues. The banks refused, arguing that the sanctity of an account could not be breached and that the bondholders' rights must be respected. When Alberta passed an act in 1910, upholding its demand, both sides headed for the courts. Suddenly, the bank found itself in a very public squabble with a provincial government, its reputation and a huge account at stake. The Alberta Supreme Court was unsympathetic, awarding $6.5 million to the Liberal government of Arthur Sifton in Edmonton. Pease was apoplectic.[13] Much of the bank's lucrative London business was rooted in the tremendous flow of English capital to Canadian opportunities. Any hint that English capital was subject to the whims of provincial governments could spoil investor confidence.

In desperation, the bank instructed its Alberta solicitor, R. B. Bennett, to appeal the case. Bennett was the Calgary promoter-lawyer whom the bank had retained, together with his partner James Lougheed. Both were Tories; the Sifton government in Edmonton was Grit. In the fall of 1912, Bennett earned his retainer. He carried the bank's appeal to the Judicial Committee of the Privy Council in London, arguing that the province had acted *ultra vires* by denying the bondholders their civil rights. The court agreed, and even awarded the bank costs.[14] Bennett had provided the bank with its first practical demonstration that the federal power – Section 91 of the BNA Act – was banking's ultimate guarantee in the face of a regional challenge. The West would try again. In 1913, however, Pease was ecstatic. He got the news from London while lunching at the Mount Royal Club. "I want you to come into Birks with me," he told his companion. "I am going to buy a fine watch

*A rare shot of four Royal Bank general managers together. Between the two golfers stand (left to right) Sidney Dobson (1934-45), Charlie Neill (1916-29), and Edson Pease (1899-1916). The golfer on the right is James Muir (1945-49). Muir was always hungrily ambitious; he was the winner at this 1921 tourney at Mount Bruno.*

for Bennett and have it suitably engraved as a tribute to his work in this case. When he gets it he'll be so flattered that he'll take $5,000 at least off his bill."[15] Bennett's ties with the bank would last another thirty-five years as lawyer, client, director, and political confidant.

Regional challenge was quickly followed by regional collapse. In 1913, the Bank Act had once again been revised to facilitate production on the farm. Section 88 had been expanded to permit the securing of farm loans on the security of threshed grain, and now directly favoured the farmer as well as the grain wholesaler, since they could now receive their money earlier. Previously, farmers had relied on short-term credit notes, which they had rolled over. While Pease was privately uneasy about taking grain as a "security over which we would have practically no control," he acknowledged its political necessity: "In the event of a farmer being unable to borrow upon wheat in the granary there would be a great howl against the banks."[16] In a similar move to aid farm output, the 1908 provisions allowing the banks excess note circulation in the crop-moving season were institutionalized in a Central Gold Reserve, a fund secured by gold or Dominion notes. For its part, the bank extended its reach in the West by appointing two Winnipeg merchants, G. R. Crowe and W. H. Thorne as directors. In the spring of 1913 this felicitous relationship of eastern banker and western grower suddenly became strained. The Laurier boom finally faltered in the face of a sharp slump in the North Atlantic trading economies; grain demand slackened, and credit contracted in London. Drought accelerated the collapse: wheat yield per acre in 1914 was only 74 per cent of its 1913 level. The downturn soon reverberated throughout the banking industry.

Pease reacted immediately. Reduced capital from England and the imbalance of the bank's western loans over deposits convinced him that "stormy weather" lay ahead. "Our only course," he instructed T. R. Whitley, his Winnipeg supervisor, "is to retrench in every direction and try to live within ourselves." Demand notes should be called and not extended; marginal branches should be closed.[17] Whitley protested: "This is a grain growing country. One might broadly say that there is only one pay day in the year, that is when the farmer sells his grain. When we make a loan to a farmer during the winter or spring, we know perfectly well that we are not going to be paid until the following autumn."[18] Patience and a few losses would build up business in the long run, he stressed. Pease clung to the tenets of Canadian banking. If the foundation – gold and capital inflows – contracted, then the banks had no option but to deflate the demand for credit.

There were natural political and social consequences. Saskatchewan, for instance, established a royal commission on agricultural credit.[19] By the summer of 1914, the federal finance minister, Thomas White, told the bank general managers that members of Parliament were complaining of their "very drastic policy towards the farmers of the West." Cattle were being repossessed, and farmers were being driven into the hands of loan sharks by "young and inexperienced branch managers." If well-founded, White concluded, such behaviour was "a serious indictment of the Canadian banking system." Pease, however, stood his ground: the bank was pursuing "a conservative policy," while not "unduly" restricting credit. Managers had been instructed to act "leniently" in collecting debts. To Whitley in Winnipeg, Pease wrote that it was "very important that we should look after our own interests and not allow debtors to pay other creditors to our prejudice." Before all else, the bank must protect its liquidity. The interests of a national-banking system and the sectional interests of farmers no longer invariably coincided.[20]

And then Canada went to war. If the recession of 1913 had given the Canadian financial system a fit of palpitations, the rumblings of

war in July 1914 threatened cardiac arrest. A "world war" in Europe
would batter the two key pillars of Canadian monetary policy: the
convertibility of Canadian currency into gold and the steady inflow of
investment capital into Canada. As the news from Europe worsened,
Canadians became panicky and began raiding their deposit accounts,
using the proceeds to buy gold. European money markets contracted,
and the stock markets twitched; rumours spread that the Canadian
government was unable to back its currency with gold. Others foresaw
a moratorium on debts. To make matters worse, the Bank of
Vancouver was tottering on the edge of collapse.[21] On July 28, 1914,
the financial panic forced the stock markets to close. Only gold
seemed capable of calming public nervousness. The finance minister, vacationing in New Hampshire, abandoned his golf clubs and
rushed to Ottawa. On August 4, Canada went to war.

Instinctively, White turned to the Canadian Bankers' Association for
assistance. Like every one of his predecessors, he knew that the CBA
Council – embracing the general managers of the banks – provided
a standing consensus of the industry, ready to consult and act without
compulsion.[22] It was crucial that the announcement of war not trigger
a financial stampede; the banks simply did not have the liquid reserves
to sustain a massive "run." Early on August 3, Edson Pease had joined
a delegation of general managers from the other banks and had taken
a special train from Montreal. By lunch they were in conference with
White in Ottawa. In the space of hours, White and the bankers pulled
the linchpin of Canadian monetary policy – the currency would no
longer be directly convertible into gold. Instead, banks would create
credit up to 15 per cent of their paid-up capital by borrowing Dominion
notes from Ottawa and securing the advances with collateral of high-
quality securities, such as municipal, utility, and railway bonds.
Furthermore, the banks would be allowed "excess circulation" beyond
the traditional crop-moving period of the year. Through the afternoon,
White and the bankers worked the proposals into a written document.
As the agreement gelled, it was glaringly obvious that the reforms ran
counter to the Bank Act; they were in fact illegal. Time was of the
essence. Alerted to the obstacle, Prime Minister Borden called a
cabinet meeting for eight in the evening, at which an order-in-council
would be passed ratifying the changes. A four-member Bankers'
Protective Committee, including Pease, would be formed to imple-
ment the agreement. White alerted the King's Printer to prepare for
a late-night press run of a special edition of *The Canada Gazette*. The
next morning Canadians awoke to find their banking system backed
by the confidence of the federal government. The solvency of the
banks was assured. Hours later war broke out, and financial calm

prevailed in the land. When Parliament convened later in August, "An Act to Conserve the Commercial and Financial Interests of Canada" – the Finance Act – made the whole exercise legal.[23]

Back in Montreal, head-office officials scurried to evaluate the quality of the bank's holdings of high-grade securities as backing for advances from the government. By early September, Holt was in a position to assure White that the bank intended "to make an immediate application for an advance."[24] Small wonder that, at the same time, White wrote to Pease and his fellow general managers to express his thanks for their "invaluable counsel during the critical financial conditions from which we are now gradually emerging."[25] Almost overnight, Canada had regeared its national credit from one that relied on external capital and gold to one now reliant on internal credit creation. The practicalities of Canadian bankers once again displayed itself. Eventually, there would be a price to pay in inflation, but in the short term Canada had the credit to fight the "Hun." Late in 1915, Pease could assure White that "you can count, I think, upon the hearty cooperation of all the banks."[26]

The Finance Act of 1914 became the new dogma of the Canadian banking community. As the war progressed, the Bank Act was tinkered with to stimulate production: Section 88 was expanded to allow banks to lend on the security of seed grain and cattle. When the war ended and the emergency of war finance eased, the bankers found themselves habituated to the 1914 Finance Act – with the exception, as we have seen, of Edson Pease. Pease argued that it was "not a good principle for the government to engage permanently in the banking business." An independent bank of rediscount, similar to the U.S. Federal Reserve, would provide better credit for the peacetime economy. Frederick Williams-Taylor of the Bank of Montreal disagreed; the 1914 Act had "satisfactorily performed the functions of a bank of rediscount" during the war and "American principles" did not apply in Canada.[27] White, exhausted by the war, avoided conflict by extending the Finance Act for two years; in 1923, his successor renewed it, saying that it had become a "permanent part of our financial system."

By 1919, the returning soldier-banker would also have detected a real change in the daily life of Canadian banking. The social impact of the war had affected the culture of the bank – "bank-boy" veterans now found "girls" working efficiently in their once-hallowed cages. The war had also greatly expanded the volume and variety of services. The banks had found themselves at the crossroads of an immense wartime financial effort to convert personal savings into war production, and branch banking was ideally suited to national, grass-roots war finance. Tellers learned to pay out a huge volume of savings, to take back war-bond orders, and in due course to pay out interest on bond coupons. If tellers found the microcosm of banking changed, so, too, did their general managers find changes in the contours of national banking. The centralized control of Canadian banking allowed great leverage over the national economy. War loans to government, controls on gold, and loans to accommodate Britain's appetite for Canadian wheat and munitions had put bankers at the centre of the war economy. The national banking system had responded to a national crisis with its usual pragmatism.

Pragmatism had been born out of the unprecedented and unpredictable nature of the war: the "bank boys" who rushed to the colours in August 1914 had not been alone in thinking that they would be home by Christmas. Even a short war, however, presented problems: how was Canada to pay for the conflict at a time when its depressed economy was generating meagre tax revenues and when access to the capital market of London was closed. "All we can do," Finance Minister White wrote late in August, "is to take matters up from day to day and accomplish what is possible to us."[28] In an initial flush of naïveté, the British government had promised to finance the cost of Canada's military operations overseas. A $60-million advance from the British Treasury was accordingly arranged, but by March 1915, British generosity was exhausted. Ottawa responded by literally printing money to pay its way and by imposing new taxes, including user taxes on financial, railway, and telegraph companies. A two-cent War Stamp was, for instance, to be affixed to any cheque or savings-account withdrawal.

Such taxes changed bank routine but did not fill the national coffers. With the national debt burgeoning – by the end of 1915 it totalled $580 million, up $131 million that year alone – White again turned to the bankers.[29] In November, he called the CBA Executive Council to Ottawa and broke the bad news. Any further foreign loans could only "be transferred to Canada at a very heavy loss" in exchange. The cost of the war was growing exponentially; White estimated that the bill for 1916 would top $200 million. The only alternative was to borrow from the people of Canada. White suggested a war loan of $50 million. The bankers agreed. Edson Pease told the minister that he had no doubt at all the banks would cooperate as long as the bonds yielded as well as other first-class securities.[30] In retrospect, Canada's national debt can be traced to this momentous meeting; from this date the national debt became a permanent fixture of Canadian fiscal policy. So, too, can the oft-mentioned fact that Canadians owe themselves their own national debt: between 1915 and 1920 all but $200 million of Canada's $2.2-billion borrowing was raised *in* Canada.[31] Much of this debt would be routinely negotiated as war bonds at the wickets of Canadian banks.

# The Canadian Bankers' Association

## Invites the Co-Operation of the Public on Behalf of the Banks

---

### Staffs Heavily Reduced by War

MORE than half the men in the banks of Canada are now on military service, and the number which remains is being steadily reduced.

Women clerks have been employed in thousands and have done splendidly, but they have not the experience of the men they replace. It would be out of the question to expect them to work as rapidly or with the same knowledge of banking as officers of many years training in the profession.

The drain upon the number of experienced officers has now reached a point where it is necessary to ask the public to take into consideration this decrease in efficiency, and to lighten, as far as they can, the burden thus thrown upon those left to run the business. Canada was never so busy as now and the volume of banking business is greater than ever before.

### How the Public Can Help

Transact your banking business in the morning as far as possible, and as early as possible. Try to avoid a rush at closing time.

Do not draw any more cheques than are absolutely necessary. Instead of paying small accounts by cheque, draw the money in one amount and pay in cash.

### Change in Banking Hours June 1st.

On and after June 1st banking hours will be: 9.30 to 2.30; Saturdays 9.30 to 12.00.

This arrangement will give the staff more time to complete the large amount of work which cannot be taken up until after the office is closed to the public.

### Special Services Discontinued July 1st.

Certain services must of necessity be discontinued, for a time at least.

On July 1st banks will discontinue receiving payments for tax bills and the bills of gas, electric and other public service corporations.

*The banks desire to render all essential services including many special ones arising out of the war. In order to do this they make this appeal for co-operation in the manner suggested above*

*During the war, the Canadian public was bombarded with financial publicity. The bank maintained its traditional advertising, adding a patriotic tone to its calendars. The* Monetary Times *extolled the necessity of subscribing to victory loans, while the Canadian Bankers' Association informed the public of the effects of labour shortages on bank operations.*

Just as Canadian troops in Europe fought their way through a series of grim campaigns, so Canadians at home met the challenge of successive War Loan and Victory Bond drives. Two War Loans – in November 1915 and September 1916 – introduced Canadians to the idea of lending their own government money. Their success prompted four Victory Bond campaigns in 1916, 1917, 1918 and 1919. Banks underwrote each bond drive on a *pro rata* basis, reflecting their respective asset bases. For smaller savers, $50 million in low-denomination War Savings Stamps were issued. In all, $1.7 billion was raised. In each instance, the finance department and the banks, brokers, and insurance companies that were actually selling the bonds were astounded by the avidity with which Canadians patriotically devoured them. The 1915 War Loan was modestly set at $50 million. When purchases soared to $78 million, the total was raised to $100 million, and a $50-million loan was made to the Imperial Munitions Board to underwrite the cost of British munitions purchases in Canada.[32] The 1917 Victory Bond target was nominally set at $150 million, but quickly captured $420 million from 874,000 subscribers. One in ten Canadians bought a bond. "Without exception," the staid CBA *Journal* noted, "this is the most ambitious financial transaction Canada has ever undertaken."[33] The 1918 target of $300 million was overshadowed by a $690 million result from over a million subscribers. "That we are able to handle these gigantic sums is amazing," Pease confided to a friend. "It is proof of the great increase in the wealth of the country since the war began. It is hard to believe that in addition to taking care of the Government requirements and the flotation in Canada of $350,000,000 of domestic loans, the deposits of the banks today are $500,000,000 greater than they were before the war began."[34]

The war-bond drives both burdened and profited the banks. Each drive swamped the branch system with applications. Long hours of overtime were needed to bring order to the ensuing chaos. The pattern was repeated every time a bond-interest coupon came due and, while patriotic fervour predisposed Canadians to buy, the bonds still had to be sold. Branches were decked out in bunting and patriotic posters, and one legacy of the war for bankers would be a knowledge that advertising clearly paid. Prominent bankers gave speeches at war-bond rallies and set themselves up as patriotic examples. Holt, for instance, bought $100,000 of the 1915 War Loan.[35] Initially, the banks feared that war-bond subscriptions would drain their deposit base and crimp their ability to lend. They quickly learned, however, that war-loan saving was cyclical in nature: money removed from the banks to buy bonds soon found its way back as government spending, reinvested coupon interest, or British purchases in Canada. Furthermore, the government paid a commission of $\frac{1}{4}$ per cent to $\frac{1}{2}$ per cent on each bond sold. This, White believed, was only fair to the banks in light of the "substantial special outlays" entailed in selling bonds.[36] Public holding of bonds also whetted clients' appetite for safety-deposit boxes; purchasers of a $1,000 bond at the Royal Bank were given free storage for a year.

As the war dragged on, Ottawa and the bankers drew closer. Early in 1917, White told the CBA Council that he would probably have to "lean more heavily upon the banks towards the close of the War."[37] As president of the Bankers' Association from 1916 to 1919, Edson Pease was at the fulcrum of this relationship. Pease had a knack for divining the minister's wishes, conveying some sense of the banking industry's tolerance to Ottawa, and then ensuring "a loyal observance of the Minister's wishes."[38] One is struck by the cosy, informal-yet-effective quality of the relationship between Pease and White: meetings hastily arranged by telegram brought a candid exchange of views and prompt action. Pease even felt free to approach Prime Minister Borden, whom he had earlier known as a Halifax lawyer. In the conscription crisis of mid-1917, Pease was quick to apprise Borden of the Anglo–Montreal view of political tensions running through Quebec.[39] Within days of the 1918 Armistice, White cabled his "most earnest thanks" for the bankers' "fine and splendid support"; Pease replied by praising their "perfect accord."[40] After the war, White left politics and, among other assignments, became a paid advisor to the Bankers' Association.

The tight harmony of Canada's political and financial élites allowed Canada to win the fiscal war. There were, however, consequences. Wartime expansion of the money supply unleashed inflation, which was to have grave effects on farmers and workers whose prices and wages were largely controlled. The war encouraged western farmers to heighten their reliance on grain production and, consequently, through Section 88, on the banks. As early as 1917, Pease saw "great problems to solve after the war": "a terrific burden of debt" that only a vigorous policy of resource development and open immigration would allevi-ate.[41] In the interim, the Royal Bank prospered. The war awakened profits from their pre-war depression: they climbed from $1.8 million in 1914 to $5.3 million in 1919. Assets similarly ballooned from $179 million to $533 million by war's end. Deposits outstripped loans, tripling to $419 million by 1919. Loans increased from $114 million in 1914 to $284 million in 1919. Viewing these results, the financial press attributed them to the savings attendant on the bank's shrewd amalgamation strategy – the Quebec and Northern Crown Banks were wartime acquisitions – and its ability to contain its management expenses.[42] Everything would now hinge on post-war prosperity.

The First World War thus introduced Canadians to the age of mass banking. Banks no longer simply catered to a narrow commercial clientele. By the end of the war, Canada was a predominantly urban nation. Canadians lived in a cash society; their wage cheques, consumer bills, and, as the war had demonstrated, their small savings, gave them every reason to frequent a bank. How many Canadians first darkened the door of a bank clutching $100 in savings intent on buying a war bond? Even more would have appeared at a teller's cage to purchase a $5 War Savings Stamp. Some came to obtain money orders for their kin overseas and others to stash savings in case depression returned with peace. Chances were that these new clients would have been served by fresh faces – female faces – in the bank; the war produced the first cracks in the monolithic "bank-boy" culture of Canadian banking.

If the outbreak of war sent bank general managers hurrying to Ottawa, it sent "bank boys" to the recruiting posts. Canada's "bank boys" had cheered the British crusade – "the cause of freedom" – against the Boers at the turn of the century and, by 1914, had no doubt that the "Hun" deserved similar treatment. Initially, they shared the universal belief that the war would be a brief, jolly junket. So did their managers. Royal Bankers who enlisted were given leaves of absence and promised that their jobs would be there when they returned. By September 1915, the war had become persistent, and staff losses unrelenting. The Royal's board halted further leaves of absence. Men enlisting were told to resign and promised their jobs back "if their services can be utilized." In 1914, the Royal Bank had 1,900 men of military age; by the end of 1915, 404 had enlisted. By March 1, 1916, 523 were gone. "And more resignations coming every day" scribbled a bank officer in the margin of the annual report that recorded the fact.

In the branches, chaos reigned. Managers complained that no sooner had they replaced a teller or accountant gone soldiering with a hastily trained junior than the new incumbent enlisted. Stopgaps were tried: retired managers were coaxed back into the branches to serve their country behind a wicket. Bank hours were shortened. The crunch remained. The banks found themselves competing for a diminishing pool of labour with the army and a booming war industry. Powerful stereotypes stood in the way of recruiting bank labour from one obvious and ready source of labour: young, single women.

Women had been present in Canadian banks since the turn of the century. To say that they "appeared" in branches would be misleading. As mentioned earlier, women were invariably given behind-the-scenes

*After the First World War, women were a permanent feature of Canadian banking,
but their roles were strictly prescribed. Marriage meant immediate retirement. None the
less, the bank was no longer a male preserve. This librarian worked at Head Office.
Library work became a niche in which women could make a career in the bank.*

jobs, as stenographers, clerks, and switchboard operators. Although
the records are not conclusive, the first woman in the employ of the
Royal Bank was probably Jennie Moore, hired in 1902 as Charlie
Neill's secretary in Vancouver. In the nineteenth century, it was
commonly accepted that men and women inhabited separate
"spheres." As Canada urbanized and industrialized, women began
drifting into the workforce. The banks reacted cautiously. In large
cities, some banks provided special women's branches, where women
– mostly middle-class matrons – could do their banking in decorous
surroundings.[43] Only in these few branches could women deal with
women in money matters – the first female manager was appointed at
a Banque Provinciale du Canada branch in 1904.[44] Management

generally believed that clients felt ill at ease with women in the bank, and that women lacked the skill to cope with money. "A woman's heart generally rules her head," wrote the female manager of the Crown Bank's woman's department in 1907. "Her intuition is keen, but it exercises itself upon people – not affairs." At head office, women employees were chaperoned by older women; the stenographic pool worked on a balcony screened from the eyes of male employees and the public.[45] Women had a separate lunchroom and were given car fare home if they worked overtime. Banking thus offered career opportunities for women, but only within prescribed limits. Starting salaries for women were higher than male juniors' salaries, but tended to reach a plateau early and stay there. Like the "bank boys," "bank girls" were not to marry. Unlike the "boys," they were never considered mobile. There was an unspoken assumption that female "careers" ended with marriage. Even then, a bit of bank training would pay a dividend: "It will make her a companion for a brainy man – and that is worth more than all things else."[46]

Old attitudes died hard. As males deserted the banks for the army, management tried to shore up the system by squeezing the most out

*Ladies hockey team in Toronto, 1923*

220

of the remaining males and allowing women to occupy more clerical jobs behind the scenes. The general managers worked through the CBA in the hope that the government would "protect" their employees from enlistment: bank work was a "grave and responsible" patriotic duty.[47] Approaches to Sam Hughes, the hawkish militia minister in Ottawa, brought no special treatment. Why not hire more women? one cabinet minister asked the CBA president. Replied the general manager of the Union Bank: "We are engaging a great many ladies, but there is a certain class of work [i.e., tellers'] which they cannot, of course, satisfactorily perform."[48] Such qualms soon disappeared as the labour market continued to tighten. Reluctantly, the banks moved women into the front line of banking. Women tellers now looked out through the grillwork at the Canadian public. By 1916, almost 25 per cent of staff were women.[49]

Women, it turned out, excelled in the male sphere of banking. "She is giving to the public," the CBA *Journal* reported in 1916, "just as speedy, just as efficient, and – may we hint it? – a more cheerful service than that heretofore received."[50] Arguments once used to justify keeping women out of the cages were now turned to their defence: a woman's "nimble fingers," once suited only for work around the home, now served her well in the counting of cash. Yet, the old stereotypes persisted. Women were not put on the accountant's stool, nor were they installed in the manager's office, and, in spite of their success as tellers, women bankers were a wartime aberration. With peace, they would return to the home as the men took up their rightful place in the cage once again. This did not reflect only a male attitude; some women themselves echoed it. Women, wrote one woman banker at the Dominion Bank, found bank routine "very wearing" on their "nerves." "Be very sure, therefore," she concluded, "that when the opportunity offers the most successful banking woman amongst us will cheerfully retire to her own hearthstone, preferring the love of a husband and little children to thousands a year and a seat in the council of the mighty!"[51]

The exodus of women from the banks began when the troopships returned from Europe. The staff ledgers for 1919-21 are therefore punctuated with the phrase "services not required" beside many a female name. Others left of their own volition: "required at home," "to be married," and "to take up nursing."[52] By the early 1920s, the bank was again overwhelmingly male. The war experience of women in banking was not, however, a false revolution. Women had disturbed old myths; they had proved themselves in the workplace. A core of female bankers remained throughout the inter-war years – though they were all single and largely confined to the traditional niche of

*The Chinese–Canadian staff of the Vancouver East End branch in 1925*

clerical work, although new niches opened up at head office in the library and in pension administration. Ironically, women remained excluded from the pension plan. Nor could they entertain any hope of managerial responsibility. Perhaps the best-known woman on staff was the redoubtable Miss Frances Montgomery. A Queen's graduate, Montgomery joined the bank in 1905 as a steno and rose to head the bank's circular-letters department. She remained there until her death in 1937.[53] She never married; other women married secretly in order to keep their jobs. To all concerned, they were the "girls," just as the men were "boys." Even bankers' wives were instructed by the *Monetary Times* to listen to their husbands' financial news with "rapt attention."[54] It would take another war to dislodge the "bank-boy" majority in retail banking; even after that, executive power long remained a male prerogative.

Of the 1,495 Royal Bankers who went to war, 191 never returned. The bank commemorated the loss by erecting plaques to "Our Sacred

Dead" in the branches where the fallen had served. Those lucky enough to return alive almost invariably looked to the bank for their old job. Neatly typed paragraphs on the back of staff cards testified to innumerable "honorable discharges" and "satisfactory medicals," followed by a curt "re-engagement recommended." Gordon Parker, who had left Tillsonburg branch in 1916, returned from the war with "no bad habits" and was still considered a "steady boy." Joe Demers exchanged his pilot's seat for a $1,200 annual salary at an accountant's stool in St. John's. Throughout the 1920s, the ethos of the bank was still fundamentally male, dark-suited, and hierarchical. On-the-job training still prevailed; juniors fixed their ambition on "the next stool up the line."[55] In the spring, golf clubs appeared, followed in the fall by curling brooms. Even the women who now worked beside the men conformed to the male culture of the bank: they too organized golf and curling tourneys. There were at the same time, however, subtle but persistent changes in the life of the bank. In the post-war decade, the bank would see change in its branch system, in the way it treated and trained its staff, and in its relations with government.

Through the 1920s the Royal Bank continued to grow. Wartime austerity had slimmed the staff to 4,218 by the Armistice. A surge of post-war expansion in the international system – 60 foreign branches in 1918 became 121 by 1925 – and steady domestic growth pushed the staff total to 6,548 by the end of 1920. Canadian branch growth slackened early in the decade, but the Union Bank of Canada amalgamation in 1925 and late-decade prosperity pushed the total to 8,656 by 1929. Despite this doubling in staff, mobility in the bank was not quite as important as it had been in the heady years of initial expansion. There was still a bank frontier in Canada; wherever the Canadian economy moved, the bank followed. Branches were, for instance, opened in the Quebec mining towns of Rouyn and Noranda in mid-decade, while in 1929, branches opened in the grain port of Churchill and in Fort St. John in the B.C. interior.

These were tough assignments. For most Royal Bankers, however, the city was now the frontier. Throughout the 1920s, Canadian banks vied to capture an urban clientele. Most-coveted were busy corner locations, but there was growth out along the streetcar tracks and paved streets into the suburbs. By 1929, the Royal Bank had forty-four branches in Montreal, thirty-seven in Toronto, and twenty in Vancouver. Within the cities, specific clienteles were sought out; in Vancouver, the bank's first Chinese-speaking staff, headed by manager Wong Ow, manned the East End branch. Staff were still expected to accept transfers without question, but there was less of the frenzied mobility that had typified the turn of the century. The bank was now divided into six domestic regions, and it was possible to plot a career within any one of these – in effect, to stay close to home. Promising young bankers were still, however, challenged with frequent and distant transfers.

If the stability of bank employment improved, so too did the benefits. Starting salaries remained low, and junior staff were still expected to prove their loyalty before salaries improved. The fact that the nation was locked in recession through much of the early 1920s removed pressure on wages and made banking seem a stable career in lean times. When an $800-a-year clerk in Saint John complained in 1927 of penury, an assistant general manager in Montreal haughtily replied: "While we appreciate that on your present salary you cannot afford to be extravagant, and that you would have difficulty in saving any substantial amount, we do feel that you should be able to live within your income without any great hardship to yourself."[56] Despite its early financial deprivations, a career in banking none the less brought security and respectability. A job in a bank was a *salaried* job, free from the uncertainties of having to sell one's wares or labour daily or seasonally in the marketplace.*

Sporadic efforts to unionize bank staff invariably fizzled, aided, some alleged, by the banks' penchant for posting troublesome clerks to distant branches.[57] Those who persevered found that the bank offered better benefits as the decade progressed. In 1895, the directors had established a superannuation fund, financed out of bank profits; in 1909 this pension plan became contributory, employees putting in 3 per cent of annual salary.[58] In the 1920s, the directors fattened the scheme considerably. A $50,000 surplus from the Officers' Guarantee Fund (the reserve built up in the nineteenth century out of bonds posted by bank officers) was transferred to pensions in 1922. Every year the directors siphoned money from bank profits into the pension fund, and the bank magazine soon began displaying photos of retired bankers tending their gardens in Victoria.

In 1926, the bank also introduced group life insurance for staff over twenty-one years of age, the bank paying the difference between the premium paid by the employee and the cost of the insurance. Similarly, the bank paid all income tax – another legacy of the war – and municipal taxes payable by employees. Each Christmas the board

---

* Comparing wages is always an inexact science, but comparisons to a bank clerk's $800-a-year salary in the 1920s may be made using Department of Labour statistics. In 1921, a male telephone operator made $728 a year, a male garment cutter $1,560 annually, and a male farmhand $669 a year. It can be argued that the bank clerk had greater scope for wage growth. A small-town bank manager in 1921 earned between $2,000 and $2,900.

routinely approved a general staff bonus, usually 5 per cent of salary. Staff at or above the accountant and branch-manager level also became eligible for reduced-rate loans. There was no systematized performance review, except branch tours by regional supervisors and inspectors. Once a year the board approved a package of salary increases; promising young bankers were tracked at head office and groomed, as if by an invisible hand, for greater things. For the seasoned employee, the bank thus provided a comfortable blanket of benefits, largely furnished at the discretion of management. Such benefits tended to promote loyalty and longevity in employees, while at the same time allowing tellers, accountants, and managers to live in the middle-class style that their professional status demanded. As CBA president in 1927, Charlie Neill boasted that banking offered "a pleasant occupation and steady employment, a life of reasonable comfort and, on retirement, a fair pension which is available for his wife and children in the event of his death."[59]

As banking gained in comfort and remuneration, Canadian bankers increasingly came to see themselves as professionals. Even before the war, there had been agitation for more formal education of young bankers. An arduous apprenticeship was not enough, some argued, to prepare the junior for management; "theoretical training" was now in order.[60] The banks strongly resisted this demand – so effectively, in fact, that banking has never found a place in Canadian post-secondary education. Bankers would become professionals on the job: "Many things," noted the CBA *Journal*, "can be learned from text books – sound judgment can only be gained through experience, and experience through patience in doing your allotted tasks with cheerfulness, understanding and intelligence."[61] None the less, young bankers were soon able to avail themselves of summer courses offered by the Canadian Bankers' Association.

Professionalization also entailed specialization. Winning and serving clients in an increasingly urban and global marketplace demanded special skills. Bankers, for instance, began to apply cost accounting to their services.[62] New head-office functions appeared: in 1919, a foreign-trade department was started, followed a year later by the advertising department. Foreign trade soon begat the economics department and the library. For each of these functions, specialists were groomed; there was a sense that the bank was adopting new skills to break "ultra-conservative" habits.[63] On the administrative front, the routine and the stationery departments grappled with the growing complexity of a bank that now served over twenty countries and

(*continued on p. 228*)

# FROM NUMBERS TO NUMBER CRUNCHING

## *The Bank Economists*

DURING THE LAURIER BOOM, THE BANK had fattened its annual report with a compendium of statistics of national growth – population, grain shipments, immigrant arrivals. This regurgitation of raw statistics underlined Canada's belief in its potential for exponential growth. The recession of 1913-14 shattered this confidence: the economy suddenly became something capricious. The war then provided a demonstration that the economy could be crudely measured and controlled. By 1919, it was apparent that success in the post-war economy would depend on understanding how the economy functioned and in tracking its performance over time. In the 1920s, Ottawa responded by establishing the Dominion Bureau of Statistics, and the banks began hiring economists, the first outside professionals to break into the world of the "bank boys."

In 1919, the Royal Bank established a Foreign Trade Department to furnish Canadian traders with reliable statistics on the economies of Caribbean and Latin American countries where the bank had branches. In 1920 a *Monthly Letter* began publication, edited by Graham Towers, fresh from his economics studies at McGill. Towers also published the more-theoretical, book-length *Financing Foreign Trade* in 1921 and later turned his attention to Canada's economic potential in *Canada of the Future*. He also supplied Holt and Neill with economic data and trends for use in their speeches. In the 1920s, economics as a profession was in its infancy. For many it was still *political* economy, what Stephen Leacock, for instance, taught at McGill. Economics by itself tended to focus on current analysis; it lacked the tools to predict furture trends.

In 1925, the bank hired its first university-trained economist, Dr. D. M. Marvin, and created the Economist's Department. Marvin produced a regular *Report on Canadian Business Conditions* and a *Latin American Report*. Two years later, the Royal Bank Fellowship in Economics was established to provoke "serious discussion of Canada's economic problems." University students were set topical questions: "Does Canada need a federal farm loan system?" Jurors included Prime Minister Mackenzie King and one-time Queen's economists Adam Shortt and O. D. Skelton. "Let me say again," Leacock wrote from McGill, "how much this department appreciates what your bank is doing for Canadian Economics."

The Depression further blighted Canadians' trust in their economy. The thought of another unpredicted economic earthquake was seldom out of mind. Although the Economist's Department felt its share of depression austerity, the need for making sense of the economy grew. If the market economy was malfunctioning, new norms of economic behaviour were required. Bank management reacted conservatively, but bank economists sensed a new role for the state. Two graduates of the bank's foreign-trade group, Graham Towers and Randolph Noble, would become personal friends of John Maynard Keynes, the prophet of interventionist economics. Towers became the first governor of the Bank of Canada in 1935, while Noble remained with the bank and championed monetary expansion in a deflationary depression.

The Second World War provided a more convincing lesson in the art of analysing and controlling the economy. Noble, for instance, went to Ottawa as Canada's sugar controller, drawing on his Cuban sugar experience with the bank. The war also gave economists a new tool: econometrics – which gave the ability to project varied economic scenarios into the future. As econometrics was perfected after the war, especially as computers made complex "models" of the economy possible, bank economists began to "forecast" the economy. It now seemed possible to alter economic reality, not just adapt to it. After the war, the bank's economist was Donald B. Marsh, an avowed Keynesian whose *Taxes Without Tears* (1945) argued that taxes in good times allowed governments a cushion in bad times. In 1952, the Royal Bank's Economics Research Department was established. Its publications – today, typified by *Econoscope* – were directed at various audiences: bank clients, senior management, bank officers dealing with specific sectors of the economy, and the general public. From the 1950s, the bank's chairman became a forceful, and well-briefed, commentator on the national economy. What had begun to provide straightforward trade statistics in the 1920s had become a complex, modern science by the 1960s.

FINANCING
FOREIGN TRADE

*By*
GRAHAM F. TOWERS
*Superintendent, Foreign Trade Department*
THE ROYAL BANK OF CANADA

*Prepared for the use
of the Staff.*

HEAD OFFICE
MONTREAL
1921

*Graham Towers, a Royal Bank employee from 1920 to 1934,
and the title page of one of his publications*

colonies. Every spring, for instance, boxcars and steamers bore tons of bank forms and updated rules and regulations to branches as disparate as Rio and Prince Rupert. Forms were the lifeblood of banking, and a thick catalogue allowed branches to order these directly from the stationery department.

Head-office staff was rounded out by departments of inspection and national credit approval, the traditional central-control mechanisms of the bank. It was to these pivotal offices that promising young bankers were brought to prove their mettle and to gain an instinct for banking. The bank developed a hierarchy of credit approval, by which loan applications were referred upward as their size grew, the largest eventually finding their way to Montreal for approval by the board. Inspection revealed the anatomy of the branch system, and national credit the working of the country's regional economies.

As banking grew more specialized and departmentalized, it also grew more mechanized, but machines did not conquer Canadian banking overnight. Given the "bank-boy" ethos of the industry, there was extreme reluctance to surrender to machines any of the manual tasks that had always been deemed part of a banker's competence. As the volume of daily work burgeoned, however, especially in urban branches, some measure of mechanization became unavoidable. In 1895, the first typewriters had appeared at head office. The board minutes and the general manager's correspondence were now typed. In the branches, where copperplate handwriting was considered indispensable in a "bank boy," typewriters were shunned until after the war. Adding machines had begun appearing in busy city branches in 1900, followed in 1913 by machines for mechanically updating customers' passbooks. The arrival of ledger-posting machines in 1918 diminished the ledger-keeper's job – now one machine allowed the teller to enter, or "post," his daily transactions and balance them in one swift operation. The 1920s brought electric appliances to banking: coin counters, cheque-endorsing-and-cancelling machines, and Recordak machines. The Recordak could provide a photographic record of eight thousand cheques for storage in a hand-sized carton. The teller's job was also eased by the creation of proof departments, which validated all the teller's non-cash transactions *after* the customer had departed. Machines thus increased the speed, accuracy, reliability, and integration of Canadian banking, but they were introduced stingily and were not intended to reduce labour costs, which were low at the junior levels anyway. Machines made banking more service-oriented and error-free.[64] "Bank boys," though, still dealt with bank clients.

Hard on the heels of the bank's 1919 jubilee came the news that the Royal Bank was now Canada's largest bank. The May 1920 returns of

The Patricia, Alberta, branch in 1922 (above).
Back to the Frontier: The return of prosperity in the late 1920s once again prompted
bankers to look to the frontier. Discoveries of natural resources drew the banks north.
In 1929, the Royal Bank opened in the new grain port of Churchill on Hudson Bay (below).

the chartered banks to the minister of finance showed that, for the first time, the Bank of Montreal had been surpassed in assets by another Canadian bank. This emergence as Canada's largest bank aroused a consciousness of corporate identity. In 1920 the *Royal Bank Magazine* began publication. An otherwise straightforward employee publication, the magazine gained colour and distinctiveness from the inclusion of news of the international branches – such as Graham Towers writing on Cuba – and contributions from some of the bank's literary friends, notably Stephen Leacock. What emerged from its pages was the sense that the Royal Bank was becoming an organization of national, at times international, cohesiveness and significance. Each year at the annual meeting, promising managers from across the country were brought to Montreal, where they were wined and dined and asked to respond to the annual vote of thanks to the bank's scattered staff. The Royal was retreating from its image as the bumptious Halifax bank that had stormed out of the Maritimes at the turn of the century – a gang of bluenose "bank boys" clambering onto the national stage. As if to symbolize its new dignity and prominence, the bank made frequent use of the stark silhouette of its new Montreal head office in its literature and advertising. As the tallest building on Montreal Island, 360 St. James reminded anyone arriving in the city that the nation's largest bank, with its 944 branches spread around the world, was headquartered in Canada's largest city.

If the Royal Bank emerged as Canada's largest bank in the 1920s, it also found itself part of a national banking industry that was constantly off balance. Economically, the twenties was a decade of fits and starts. Hopes of post-war prosperity quickly faded into a recession that mired the Canadian economy until mid-decade. Freed from wartime constraints on manpower, the bank sprinted to open new branches: from 1918 to 1920 almost two hundred were opened. But in the face of a faltering economy, branch growth halted, and in fact receded. By 1924, the bank had shed seventy-seven branches. The takeover of the Union Bank of Canada again fattened the system to a record 944 branches by 1929, a total it would not touch again until 1960. Despite the return of prosperity in the late decade, there was ample evidence that the system was occupying some pretty marginal ground, particularly in the West. Equally apparent was the fact that the banks now faced a more-complex national economy, one which had developed distinct regional rhythms that often failed to coincide with each other. Credit risk varied dramatically across the nation; the days when credit could be supplied to a uniformly growing national economy were over. Furthermore, the deflationary inclination of the Canadian banking system – the impulse to curtail credit and thereby ensure a bank's solvency during downturns – increasingly made trade-exposed regions of the country think that Canadian banking was biased in the interests of central Canada. As farmers took to direct political action – in 1921, a farmers' protest party, the Progressives, sent sixty-five MPs to Ottawa, giving Canada a three-party system for the first time – banking became ever more politicized. Farmers wanted "easier" credit.

Amid these pressures, banking found itself awkwardly placed to defend itself. The old argument that Canadian banking was self-regulating was wearing very thin. For the first time since the Sovereign Bank debacle of 1907, Canadians encountered the phrase "bank scandal." Late in 1921, shareholders of the Merchants Bank of Canada learned that their president had allegedly misrepresented the condition of the bank's loan portfolio. The Merchants Bank desperately reduced its rest by $8 million, and then staggered into the merger arms of the Bank of Montreal. Although its blue-blood president, Sir Montagu Allan, was later acquitted of any malfeasance, the Merchants fiasco deeply damaged Canadian bank credibility.

The 1923 revision of the Bank Act was consequently a fractious affair. Farmers agitated for more-generous-and-assured access to credit. Progressive MPs hammered away at the bank general managers in the Commons' Banking and Commerce Committee; the United Farmer government in Alberta set up a royal commission on farm credit. Much of what farmers alleged was true: the banks were charging in excess of the 7 per cent ceiling on loan interest stipulated in the Bank Act. Some farmers were paying interest as high as 12 per cent. The banks countered that the cost and risk of credit in the West was high. Henry Ross, secretary of the CBA, told Finance Minister Fielding that it cost 2 per cent more "to carry on banking in the West than in the East and in the remoter districts the difference in cost is much higher than that."[65] If the 7 per cent ceiling was religiously adhered to, branches would have to be closed and credit further restricted. Bank-bashing flourished in the Commons and on the Prairies. "Unfortunately, attacks on the banks, and incidently on eastern interests generally," a miffed Sir Frederick Williams-Taylor of the Bank of Montreal noted privately, "are not confined to certain incompetent or unreasonable farmers, but important men of affairs and certain politicians have not hesitated to try to achieve cheap local popularity by baiting these interests."[66]

The anguish of western credit was not the product of "evil" bankers or ignorant farmers who habitually abused credit. It was the natural outcome of the combination of a boom-and-bust farm economy and a credit system that provided short-term credit, secured by the very means of production – tractors, ploughs – as well as the produce itself – cattle and crops.* In an expansionary economy, credit and production thrived mutually; in a faltering economy, the sanctity of credit worked against the sanctity of life on the farm. An overzealous bank manager, an incompetent farmer, or even a hailstorm could upset the delicate balance of credit. Those unable to meet short-term credit obligations soon found themselves labouring under an accumulating burden of debt that increasingly hindered their ability to put next year's crop in the ground. Farmers saw a solution in American-style unit banks, local credit for local needs. This the bankers decried as unstable, inflationary, and even "socialistic."[67]

In 1923, the bankers' credibility held in Ottawa. The Bank Act was tinkered with, but not fundamentally altered. Banks were required to register liens taken under Section 88, and provisions for outside auditing of banks were stiffened. Two months after the 1923 act was passed, the Toronto-based Home Bank crashed spectacularly, the victim of its own reckless lending and deceitful reporting. A public inquiry and the necessity of federal restitution for Home depositors soured public esteem for the banks further. If bank directors could not be trusted – and there was further disquieting news of debt writedowns at the Union and Standard banks – then the government itself must inspect the banks. The Commons committee duly reconvened. While some hard-liners maintained that the state had no place in the banking hall, Neill of the Royal sensed the inevitable: the Home Bank was a "sad commentary" on the industry and, as long as it was "efficient," government inspection was welcome.[68] In 1924, the office of Inspector General of Banks was created and empowered to inspect the banks with an eye "to the safety of the creditors and shareholders." The inspector had power to take charge of a mismanaged bank's assets. In what was to become a tradition, a Royal Banker, Charles S. Tomkins was appointed to the post – when the time came to surrender some piece of authority to the state, the Royal Bank acknowledged the necessity of federal inspection by proffering one of its capable own to staff the position. This would guarantee the "efficiency" that Neill had spoken of and minimize bankers' fears of political interference.

Skirmishing with farmers and rectifying the Bank Act were part of a broader politicization of banking in the 1920s. Banks were coming

---

* Banks did *not* hold mortgages on farms. The Bank Act prohibited banks from lending monies on the security of "lands, tenements or immovable property." Only the trust companies had this fiduciary right. The commonly held notion of the bank repossessing the homestead is misplaced. Bankers might take possession of cattle, tractors, or grain, all of which might have been used under Section 88 as surety for the loan.

to realize that other groups were pressing their attentions on government. Bankers could no longer simply rely on their confabs with the finance minister to ensure their legitimacy in the public forum. Consequently, they began to speak out, both to defend themselves and to inform the national agenda. The Royal Bank, for instance, began publishing pamphlets addressing public criticism of the banks: in 1926, Neill's views on the strengths of national branch banking were printed in response to farmer demands for unit banking.[69] Each year at the annual meeting, Holt used his speech as president to address the issue of the national economy. The banker's agenda for national prosperity invariably featured lower taxes, open immigration, a return to the gold standard, and the development of Canada's trade and basic industries. There was a natural tendency to see Canada's future in terms of a re-creation of the glory days of the Laurier boom. The return of a vigorous wheat economy and industrial expansion in the late 1920s seemed to fulfil Holt's prescription.

The 1920s found the Royal Bank active in Ottawa for other reasons. As the place of government grew in Canadian life, so too did the attractiveness of government accounts to Canada's bankers. They represented a huge cash flow that regularly washed through the economy from coast to coast. There were also special accounts, such as the new government-owned railway, the Canadian National. What troubled the Royal Bank was that, if precedent held, the government's long-time official banker, the Bank of Montreal, stood first in line for these plums. As mentioned, Pease's 1918 campaign for a central bank had as a clear secondary motive the disruption of the Bank of Montreal's privileged position in Ottawa. Finance Minister White wavered, but in the end clung to the *status quo*. All the banks were Tory, but the Bank of Montreal was more Tory than the rest.

In 1921, the rules of the game were changed. The Canadian people turned on the Tories and made Liberal Mackenzie King their prime minister. Charlie Neill immediately headed for Ottawa. King directed Neill to his finance minister, W. S. Fielding. Although Fielding was a Haligonian and had long associated with Royal Bankers at the Halifax Club, he had never been overtly friendly to the bank, perhaps because of the memory of Thomas Kenny's Tory ties. Fielding told Neill that "as a general principle he was entirely opposed to the diversion from the Bank of Montreal of any part of the Government's business."[70] An enraged Neill complained to King. Never a man for precipitous action, King replied that it would "take time," but that he was determined to break the Bank of Montreal's "monopoly."[71] Neill therefore persisted, using the bank's Ottawa manager, Charles Gray, as a political pointman. Gray lobbied the railways minister, William Kennedy, and by November

**ROYAL BANK EDUCATIONAL SERIES**

MAKERS OF CANADA

Sir ISAAC BROCK
(Born 1769 · Died 1812)

Was Lieutenant-Governor of Upper Canada and defended
that province against United States forces in 1812.
Compelled General William Hull to surrender at Detroit.
Was killed in the battle of Queenston Heights.

**The Royal Bank
of Canada**

SERVING CANADA SINCE 1869
A 5

**The Royal Bank
of Canada**

Protect your Victory Bonds by
Renting a Safety Deposit Box.

Deposit the coupons every
six months in a Savings
Account and earn interest
upon the bond interest at
3% per annum, compound-
ed half-yearly.

If this is done regularly with
(say) a 15 year bond, you will
accumulate more interest than
principal.

CAPITAL AND RESERVES  $35,000,000

TOTAL RESOURCES  -  $535,000,000

625 BRANCHES

*(Above and opposite) Prompted by the remarkable success of the war-bond drives, bank
advertising became more adventurous in the 1920s. Actual products were advertised.
Safety and savings were the predominant themes. Non-English-speaking clients saw the
first advertising in their own language. Old-style image advertising, such as the
"Makers of Canada" series of blotters, continued.*

he could report that he had secured the Canadian National's telegraph
and express accounts, with an annual turnover of $42 million.[72]

The Liberals also had their eye on the Royal Bank. King knew that
all St. James Street was solidly Tory, but appreciated that the Grits
needed more business support. Holt was "as strong a Tory partisan as
there is," but King liked Neill very well. The political opportunity lay
in breaking the Bank of Montreal's grip on government business and
pushing "some distribution of the Government's patronage" towards
the Royal Bank. King was encouraged in this hope of befriending
the Royal by his friend Philip Larkin, a Liberal bagman and High

Commissioner to Britain. As owner of Salada Tea, Larkin had won a reputation as the Tea King of America, and had been a long-time client of the Royal in Toronto. He had met Pease in London, dined him, and pointed out how "foolish" it was for all the great banks to fly Tory colours. He "dangled" a senatorship in front of Pease, whom he regarded as Canada's most dynamic banker, and even suggested that Pease become ambassador to Washington.[73] Pease accepted neither offer. None the less, the ice was broken with the Liberals. In 1925, the bank helped Ottawa renegotiate the West Indies Trade treaty. Soon after King won the 1926 election, Neill redoubled his efforts to have the government "recognize our friendship," and won a bigger share of the CNR account.[74] In 1929, Sir Henry Thornton, the government-appointed president of the railway, joined the bank's board.

Despite these inroads, the senior echelons of the Royal Bank remained Tory blue. Holt continued an ardent admirer of Conservative leader Arthur Meighen and, when King drubbed Meighen, the Tories turned in 1927 to R. B. Bennett, the bank's Calgary solicitor since 1908 and a director since 1924, as their new leader. Although he left the board, Bennett continued to counsel the bank on business opportunities in the West.[75] Neill himself was linked to the Tories through his brother-in-law, New Brunswick MP Richard Hanson. Neill's achievement in the 1920s was not so much in remaking the bank's politics, but in balancing its presence in Ottawa. Senior executives of the bank could now be assured of receiving a hearing in the corridors of power regardless of whose offices lined that corridor. In passing, he had also groomed Charles Gray – who served as Ottawa branch manager until 1941 – as the Royal Bank's first "government affairs" man.

The bank directors who gathered just after noon on April 22, 1927, to lay the cornerstone for the bank's new head office on St. James Street projected an image of bankerly solidity. Homburgs, great coats, and sober expressions dominate the official portrait. This, after all, was the cornerstone of Canada's largest bank. Charles Tompkins, the Inspector General of Banks, had come down from Ottawa to join his former employers; R. B. Bennett would soon leave for Ottawa to take up his duties as Opposition leader. The bank had levelled a small city block to make room for the skyscraper and, as the girders rose throughout the summer, so did the bank's sense of self-esteem. Edson

*In April 1927, the cornerstone of the new Head Office was set in place by Herbert Holt. Among the guests were: The Hon. R. B. Bennett (left bottom in dark coat), A. J. Brown and Hugh Paton (beside stone on left), C. E. Neill and E. L. Pease (on right of stone).*

Pease – who looks haggard and ill in the portrait – was in virtual retirement. Although he retained his title of vice-president, the bank that Pease had built now seemed securely in Neill's hands. Holt continued to play out his role as a figurehead president, chairing weekly board meetings, delivering his annual-meeting speech, and touring the Latin American branches, but he spent most of his time over at his Montreal Light, Heat and Power office. Later in the year, Neill told the Liberal finance minister in Ottawa, James Robb, that the country seemed to be "on the upward grade."[76] The same seemed true for the bank in Montreal.

There were, however, three barely visible cracks in this magnificent new façade, cracks the historian with the benefit of hindsight can now see were capable of working their way to the bank's very foundation. They could be summed up in these words: the West, Cuba, and Holt. The return of western prosperity in the late 1920s masked the bank's overextension in the region. There were, none the less, too many branches serving too thin and unpredictable a market. Much the same was true in Cuba. Despite good operating profits, the bank was highly exposed in Cuba. At the beginning of the decade, Cuba had constituted roughly 16 per cent of both the bank's overall loans and deposits. The sugar "crash" of 1920 had diminished this somewhat, but, carrying massive "sugar estate" debts, the bank still lived a precarious existence on the island, one dependent on the price of sugar and on Cuba's ability to preserve its enormous share of the American market. In the spring of 1925, the bank was caught in a "panic" when rumours spread through Havana alleging that the Canadian bank would be trapped by a debt moratorium. Only the intervention of Cuban president Geraldo Machado, who appeared on the doorstep of the Havana main branch to announce that the government would display its confidence in the Canadians by depositing $7 million on its account halted the panic. Machado then sent a Cuban destroyer to Miami to collect $18 million in cash, which the bank had rushed from New York.[77] It was clear that if either the price of sugar or Machado's government – which had embarked on an ambitious public-works program – faltered, the bank was in deep trouble.

Any prescient observer of Canadian banking in the late 1920s would, of course, have had some sense that trouble in the West or in Cuba – most likely, a downturn in commodity prices – might damage any Canadian bank active in these regions. Few had the slightest notion of the true state of Herbert Holt's affairs. At the 1927 CBA annual meeting, Charlie Neill used his presidential speech both to celebrate the nation's return to prosperity and to sound a warning about guarding against "boom conditions" and the "violent fluctuations" that

booms precipitated. To make his point, Neill noted that call loans made by Canadian banks in 1926 had shot up 41 per cent. Much of this was prompted by investors speculating in the expansion of Canadian commerce and industry. "Speculation is undoubtedly being overdone," Neill cautioned, "… over-optimism concerning the immediate future must eventually be followed by an unfavourable reaction."[78] What Neill did not disclose to his CBA colleagues was that, back in the Royal Bank boardroom, he and his colleagues had been encouraging another kind of late-1920s speculation: industrial consolidation. And the bank's own president, Herbert Holt, was the biggest borrower.

Herbert Holt's reputation as a captain of national industry was rooted in his ability to build consolidated companies. At the turn of the century, during Canada's first great bout of merger-mania, he had welded together Montreal Light, Heat and Power out of disparate local utility companies. He had shown similar business artistry as a participant in other companies such as Calgary Power and the Steel Company of Canada. There was nothing reckless about Holt in these years of the Laurier boom; he has been described as "a very cautious and rather unimaginative business technocrat," who "cherished" control of "promising" companies.[79] His arrival at the bank in 1905 and his friendship with such moguls of Montreal finance as J. W. McConnell of St. Lawrence Sugar and T. B. Macaulay of Sun Life fit

The breathtaking ceiling of the main banking hall at 360 St. James (right). Designed by York and Sawyer of New York, the building's sparse, heavily rusticated façade (opposite) was reminiscent of another York and Sawyer commission, the Federal Reserve Bank of New York (1919).

*Herbert Holt and his wife on shipboard, 1923*

*E. L. Pease*

this pattern perfectly. When the pre-war merger mania died, Holt settled down to managing his companies and to building up his collection of corporate directorships. The Royal Bank minute books in the years from 1913 to 1925 show that Holt's companies virtually never turned to the Royal Bank for financing. Holt was, in effect, a fine ornament at the top of the bank's list of officers; his name and contacts alone acted as a magnet in attracting corporate clients to the bank. In 1924, for instance, Holt brought in the Calgary account of his friend from railway days, Pat Burns, now a successful meat-packer.[80] Except for making such introductions, Holt took little active interest in the bank at all. In the late 1920s, all this changed. Merger-mania returned, and Holt came to life again as an industrial promoter.

As the economy revived in mid-decade, Canadian industry responded. At the heart of the revival was the pulp-and-paper industry, aroused by the prospect of capitalizing on the hungry American market. Eastern Canadian paper producers rushed to add capacity, and financiers rushed to tout the industry as a quick road to sure-fire gains. Added capacity, however, meant added competition and, as a consequence, the industry soon felt the first twinges of merger fever. In this climate, Holt immediately saw an opportunity to practise his old consolidation magic. He aligned himself with Toronto financier J. H. Gundy of Wood, Gundy & Co., a long-time Royal client. Together they

241

formed Holt, Gundy & Co., a closely held investment company designed to capture control of existing paper companies, to refinance them, and to place them under unified control. Acting through a shadow agent, Consolidated Investment Company, Holt and Gundy became the kings of Canadian pulp and paper. In 1923, they acquired the bankrupt Bay Sulphite Company; in 1925 they acquired and merged the St. Maurice and Belgo-Canadian paper companies, and a year later they won control of the Canada Paper Company. In 1928, Holt and Gundy folded the collection into the Canada Power and Paper Company, which was hailed as the world's largest paper company. The whole edifice sat on a foundation of watered stock – each takeover offered an opportunity to pump up the purported value of the components – and on the hope of continued strong demand for paper products.[81] Similar consolidations were taking place in America and Europe, where trusts were being assembled to control and restructure huge chunks of the steel, electrical-goods, and synthetic-materials industries.

Holt, Gundy & Co. required vast amounts of capital, mostly held over the short period of market operations, to realize their ambitions. Although he would later tell a parliamentary inquiry that he "personally

*After visiting Barcelona branch in the late 1920s, three Royal Bank directors continued on to Madeira. (From left to right): Edson Pease, aged but still capable of savouring one of his beloved Cuban cigars; Albert J. Brown, a Montreal corporate lawyer and director from 1912 to 1938; and Hugh Paton, Holt's brother-in-law and a Montreal businessman. Paton contributed little to the board; Brown was its legal brains.*

made it a rule never to borrow from the bank,"[82] it is clear that Holt, Gundy & Co., Wood, Gundy & Co., and Consolidated Investments were heavily dependent on the Royal Bank. The sums were staggering, in amounts never before brought before the board for approval. In December 1926, the borrowing peaked with a special call loan of $16,744,104, secured by St. Maurice Paper shares.[83] Throughout the last years of the decade, a board meeting seldom passed in which a loan to one of the Holt–Gundy family of companies did not find its way to the boardroom table.

There is no written record of the directors' deliberations in these years – board minutes are always cryptic and consensual. One can therefore only speculate on what ran through the minds of the bank's officers as they brought these unprecedented credit approvals forward. Neither the Bank Act nor the bank's by-laws had anything to say about such loans. They were in no way illegal. Industrial consolidation was in the air, and Holt was its most-vaunted Canadian practitioner. The board reacted accordingly. The late 1920s saw other Montreal clients, like T. B. Macaulay and Ward Pitfield, aggressively staking out new territory in the Canadian economy. These were years of financial expansion. In 1927, the bank had increased its own authorized capital by $10 million to $40 million. But nothing matched Holt's corporate adventures. Neither did any other industrialist sit in the president's chair of a bank boardroom. The board even began approving credit to Holt's son Andrew, now a budding financier in his own right. One can perhaps conclude that the prevailing optimism overcame the better judgement of men like Charlie Neill and Edson Pease – a booming economy would quickly remove the risk of the seeming overindulgence in pulp-and-paper loans. In 1927, Neill had become general manager; two years later he assumed Pease's old role as managing director. Pease was always in evidence but was fading fast, as his shaky signature in the minute book attested. A new generation of senior management, slowly groomed by the "bank-boy" culture, began to appear. In 1929, Morris Wilson, a Lunenburg lad trained by Martin Dickie at Truro branch, moved into the general manager's office. If things went wrong, many must have assumed, the bank had the men to handle the situation.

In the fall of 1930, Edson Pease left Montreal to winter on the warm shores of the French Riviera. Norman Hart, now the bank's Paris manager, found him there, "a lonely, sick man, but lion-hearted withal." He beseeched Hart to tell Montreal that all was well and gave him a photo to send home. "It showed him smoking a cigar and holding a tennis racquet as if he had just finished a game" – a true "bank-boy" pose.[84] In December, he died. Less than a year later, the doctors at Royal Victoria Hospital in Montreal told Charlie Neill that he had stomach cancer. By December, he too was gone. "The fact remains that what little I may happen to know about banking," Morris Wilson confided in a friend, "I learned from him."[85]

As the Depression broke around him and opened up the cracks in the bank's foundation, Wilson must have looked down the boardroom table and prayed that Pease and Neill had trained him well. The test was now at hand.

# The Depression

## *"No glory in being head of a bank"*

LAVOY, ALBERTA, WAS NO BANKER'S PARADISE IN THE DEPRESSION. A DECADE before, when it opened, the Lavoy branch might have offered an ambitious young banker a promising first managership. The Royal Bank opened more branches – a neat one hundred – in 1919 than in any other year in its history. Lavoy, a grain-elevator stop 130 kilometres east of Edmonton on the Canadian National, was one of them. For the hardy Ukrainian immigrants who had settled around it, Lavoy was similarly a land of promise. But by 1931, Lavoy was a financial ghost town.

For Sam Halton, the manager in Lavoy since 1930, life in the branch was dreary and depressing. With $30,000 in bad debts on the books, customers seldom darkened his door. From ten in the morning, when the branch opened, until the three-o'clock closing, Halton and his junior, Norm Stewart, marked time. Only on Saturdays and during the crop-moving season did the pulse of business quicken slightly. Loan demand was moribund, and the dead hand of the Depression lay on deposits. On many days, Halton balanced the books long before closing time, knowing that there would be no more business that day.

The real banking day began when the branch closed, and Halton and Stewart headed out of town in the manager's Chevy. "We buy a lot of gasoline for our managers," General Manager Morris Wilson told the Royal Commission on Banking and Currency two years later.[1] Lavoy was no exception. Halton would bump along the back roads, pulling into the yards of farmers who owed money to the Royal Bank. Stewart vividly recalled the nervous encounters that followed. Against a backdrop of rural poverty – "apple boxes for furniture," he remembered – Halton engaged in broken half-Ukrainian, half-English conversations that touched on everything but the farmer's financial

*Sam and Dorothy Halton stand proudly in front of their new Chevy, shortly after Halton took up the Lavoy managership in 1930. Drought crippled Lavoy.*

condition. "How are the kids?" "Does the crop look any better this year?" Despite his suspicion that there were small caches of money buried behind the shed or under the floorboards, Halton could not bring himself to demand any form of payment. There seemed little point in seizing cattle or tractors, as Section 88 of the Bank Act allowed him to do. The Depression made them virtually unsaleable, and Sam Halton was too humane a man to force the issue. Back at the branch each evening, he would duly enter a cryptic report of his visit – such as "we appear to have his goodwill" – in his loans ledger.

Neither Lavoy nor Halton were to remain long in the Royal Bank fold. When Sam had returned from the First World War, he had hurried to take up the tellership the Union Bank of Canada offered him in Pincher Creek. British-born, he had first "gone banking" in 1913. Banking offered him a future in his new country. In 1925, the Royal–Union merger gave him a new employer.[2] His daughter remembers him as a man who was "born to bank," but the Depression crushed Sam Halton's enthusiasm for his profession. In the 1920s, banking had given him prestige and a sense of purpose in small prairie towns; now he found himself vilified, a creditor rather than a giver of credit. Prairie managers were, for instance, instructed to scrape the gold letters that advertised the size of the bank's assets off their branch windows. What had provided customers with an assurance of stability in the 1920s, now smacked of excess and bred distrust. Sam's brother, Matthew, had opted for a career in the fledgling broadcasting industry, and would soon win fame as a foreign correspondent for the CBC. Sam must have reflected on the irony of this; by the mid-1930s the airwaves of Alberta were crackling with condemnations of the banks and of the eastern "big shots" who ran them.

Despite the radio talk of bank profits, however, Lavoy made a meagre profit of $1,256 in 1931, and in May of the next year head office instructed Halton to close the branch. He was posted to nearby Holden, and then to Edmonton, but his zest for banking was gone. In 1935, the Calgary supervisor concluded that "there did not appear to be much future for him in banking" and requested his resignation. With a retirement allowance of a year's salary in his pocket, Halton joined an oil company. He never relished the work, and died two years later, a broken man. For Norm Stewart, the future was rosier. He was transferred to Bellevue when Lavoy closed and went

*Lavoy, Alberta, branch, opened 1919, closed 1932.*

on to help pioneer the bank's stake in the oil patch in the 1950s.[3]

Sam Halton's agonies were largely a private matter, poignant to his family but unremembered elsewhere. It was left to another Royal Banker to give Canadians their most enduring literary remembrance of the "dirty thirties." Like Halton, Sinclair Ross came to the Royal Bank as a result of the 1925 Union Bank merger. He began as a junior in Abbey, Saskatchewan, in 1924 and served across rural Saskatchewan through the Depression. By day he was a banker, but in the evenings he became a writer. In 1941, his first novel, *As for Me and My House*, appeared.[4] It is not about banking; it is instead an evocation of the emotional desolation of small-town prairie life in the grip of drought and depression. If prairie towns had central figures, they were invariably ministers, bank managers, or station and elevator agents. Ross chose the local minister. He called his town Horizon; it could have been Halton's Lavoy, or Eyebrow, or Didsbury, or any one of the hundreds of towns where the Royal Bank had positioned itself to help build the West. In each of these communities, the Depression tested not only men's bank balances but also their souls.

The Depression was not just a Prairie phenomenon. It reached, for instance, thousands of kilometres east into the office of the prime minister. In 1930, R. B. Bennett, former Royal Bank director and solicitor and still-prominent shareholder, had vanquished Mackenzie King and the Liberals with promises of protectionism and special relief from the hard times that had engulfed the country. If the banks thought that they had a friend in Ottawa, they were quickly disabused of the notion. From his caucus, constituents, and Canadians at large, Bennett had daily reminders that something was amiss in the world of Canadian banking. "It is idle to expect any member of Parliament or Canadian citizen for that matter," he bluntly told the president of the CBA in 1933, "to justify some of the acts of the banks in driving customers to the wall who are unable to liquidate their liabilities under existing circumstances."[5] When a Saskatchewan MP told the prime minister that the Royal Bank manager in Borden was "simply taking the shirts off the backs of the people" by exercising his Section 88 prerogatives, Bennett warned the bank's head office that such incidents fed political radicalism – "the nourishment upon which the Woodsworth faction feeds."[6] When, in 1933, J. S. Woodsworth and his allies established the Co-operative Commonwealth Federation – the forerunner of today's NDP – they gave prominence in their manifesto to a demand for the nationalization of banks. Morris Wilson was obliged to acknowledge that "certain managers did go too far" and instructed his prairie supervisors not to give "justifiable cause for complaint."[7] Clearly, not every Royal Banker had the sensitivity of a

Sam Halton. Loan collectors and inspectors sent out by regional offices often descended on small-town branches intent on shaking out loan payments that the local manager knew were unshakable. The old trusting bond between manager and townsfolk was thus broken, and bad blood was left in its place.

The credibility of Canadian banking sagged elsewhere as well; loans were written off in downtown Toronto, managers presided over dormant branches in Cape Breton, and even at head office the hard times reverberated – staff defalcations jumped dramatically. As commodity prices tumbled and protectionism strangled world trade, the international system began to falter. In Cuba, political turmoil complicated the situation. As President Machado's reformist zeal succumbed to political corruption, nationalist ferment grew in Cuba. Foreign banks offered an inviting symbol of the island's woes; in 1931 a "heavy bomb" blew the doors off the bank's Havana main branch.[8] A year later, the staff at São Paulo branch in Brazil were caught behind the barricades when the state rose in insurrection.[9] The Spanish Civil War engulfed Barcelona branch in 1936; the bank pulled out all but two of the Canadians on staff, leaving the manager, H. L. Gagnon, to live out three hellish years of dive-bombing and street fighting. When asked what had sustained him through the ordeal, the Nova Scotia-born Gagnon replied: "Sam Slick's formula: human nature and soft sawder – we worked wonders."[10]

Despite all the trauma inflicted on its customers and staff by the Depression, Canadian banking survived. Unlike the United States, where banks fell like bowling pins, there was not a single bank failure in Canada's Depression. The American banking system, dominated by small regional banks, was obliged to take a "holiday," to close down completely in early 1933 and to endure a dose of stiff reform in the Glass–Steagall Act. Canada's "big banks" survived because they were big; they wobbled but they did not topple. The system entered the 1930s broad and stable enough to absorb even the most brutal of regional reverses – but only just. Yet, as the system creaked from Lavoy to Havana in the early 1930s, Canadian bankers were astute enough to know that change was in the wind, that the time had come for a little of Sam Slick's "soft sawder" to be applied to the national banking system. They were reluctant converts, the Royal Bank being perhaps a little less reluctant than others. There was grudging recognition that the time for the central bank that Edson Pease had proposed in 1918 had finally come. Slowly, but only slowly, it came to be realized that the banks were not in a position to manage the monetary system, that a central bank was needed for this, and that without a central bank, the banking system, for reasons of sheer survival, would always sharply restrict credit in tough times. Their own survival would come first.

When Bennett created a Royal Commission on Banking and Currency in July 1933, the bankers' first instinct was to have CBA president J. A. McLeod of the Bank of Nova Scotia present a historical sketch of Canadian banking to remind the commissioners that Canadian banking was "extremely strong and singularly flexible."[11] Even in the face of its severest test, Canadian banking instinctively stuck to the gradualism that had served it so well since the first Bank Act was passed in 1870. But, if they had only tinkered with the act in earlier revisions, bankers were soon obliged by a sceptical public in the 1930s to make some major structural renovations.

The Royal Bank of 1939 showed the ravages of the Depression. It had shed over two hundred branches and seen its staff decline from 8,784 to 7,016. Its assets, having peaked in 1929 at a billion dollars, sagged as low as $729 million in 1933 and only recovered the billion mark in 1939. By decade's end, the Royal Bank was still Canada's largest bank, but its primacy had been eclipsed by the Bank of Montreal in the years from 1932 to 1935. Similarly, profits slid from their 1929 high of $7.1 million and languished between $3 and $4 million through the decade. An 8 per cent dividend was maintained – reasonable, but lower than the 12-per-cent-plus-2-per-cent bonus that prevailed in the "roaring twenties." The bank's statistical shifts in the decade were hardly out of keeping with the national trends in banking. What was fundamentally different by 1939 was the relationship of all the Canadian banks with the country's fledgling central bank. By 1935, the private banking system found itself working in partnership with an independent and active central bank in the setting of national credit, rather than with a passive and directionless Finance Act. The gold standard was really dead and the banks' power to issue their own notes was fast expiring. The Bank of Canada now set the conditions of the money market, and the federal government was experimenting with ways to use the banking system to stimulate the economy into recovery.

For the Royal Bank, as for many others, the first hint of depression had come with the news of drought in the West in the summer of 1929. Managers in Saskatchewan and Alberta began reporting that loans made for spring seeding were in jeopardy as the parched soil destroyed crops. The stock-market crash of October created a whirlwind of rumours about the Royal in the east. The Toronto tabloid *Hush* began spreading the rumour that a prominent Toronto client, the brokerage firm of Solloway Mills & Co., was guilty of "bucketing" –

# Stock Market Tips

Cartoon by C. Fleming

**BEWARE OF THE BULL**
*A risky support on a narrow margin.*

*Belated advice: A cartoon in the* Royal Bank Magazine *of May 1930*

speculating in marginal stocks – and that the bank was suffering heavy losses as a result. Morris Wilson in Montreal quickly moved to squelch such rumours by assuring his managers that "not one dollar has been lost by the bank through stock loans during the recent panic."[12]

In its public pronouncements the bank had initially sought to portray the economic downturn as simply "a breathing spell in the long-term trend of expansion and constructive development" of Canada. Throughout the 1920s, the bank had championed an economic strategy for Canada based on aggressive trade and vigorous exploitation of natural resources. Bank presidents traditionally played the role of national confidence-boosters. Every year Sir Herbert Holt had used his annual-meeting address to extol the latest increases in mineral, forest, and farm production. For him, this "nationalism" entailed an open-immigration policy and open access to the American market. The events of 1929 and the onset of protectionism undermined this whole outlook. None the less, the bank persisted in viewing the hard times as an aberration, a moderate recession, as Holt told the shareholders, brought on by the speculative enthusiasm of the late 1920s. "Prudence and conservatism" were the order of the day. Again and again in the early Depression, bank officers called for the nation to return to what they perceived as the fundamentals of national economic life: a balanced budget, reduced taxes, and orderly market-ing. Wasteful competition between the CPR and the CNR must, for instance, be eradicated by the creation of one railway. Above all else, Canada must begin with the "exorcising of the spirit of extreme nation-alism" in trade. Well into the Depression, the Royal Bank remained committed to these "corrective forces."[13]

A more anxious mood prevailed in the bank's executive offices. Behind closed doors along the walnut-panelled corridors of 360 St. James, a handful of the Royal Bank's most senior men wrestled with matters that struck at the very heart of the bank. The thick, red carpets outside their doors muffled any report of their conversations long before they might have reached the street below. The fact was that what *Hush* gossiped about and what Prime Minister Bennett suspected was true: the Royal Bank technically tottered on the brink of insolvency throughout 1932-33. If there was a miracle for the Royal Bank in the Depression, it was that the knowledge of its precarious financial state in the early 1930s never became known outside 360 St. James. The mortal blow to confidence that public disclosure might have brought was never landed.

Bankers had no inside track on understanding the Depression. Like other Canadians, they had experienced nothing that would have prepared them for its severity and persistence. There had been other economic slumps – like that of 1913-14 – which had etched themselves into the Canadian psyche, but the Great Depression quickly pushed aside all that had gone before. It rolled unevenly across the country, hitting first the regions most exposed to slumping commodity markets and then creeping into the more protected industrial heartland of central Canada. Nobody knew where it would end, how deeply it would erode the national economy. The decline was at its worst from 1929 to the spring of 1933. Unemployment peaked at 32 per cent in the bleak winter of 1932-33. The gross national product contracted by an astounding one-third. The price of wheat plunged 53 per cent in 1933 alone. Auto production dropped 75 per cent in the same years. Base-metal mining slumped, leaving the boom towns of the "roaring twenties" virtual ghost towns. Only gold sparkled; precious metals seemed an elixir for insecurity. Immigration, the traditional feedstock of Canadian growth, dried up. With demand moribund, the cost of living shrunk by 23 per cent by 1933 as deflation took its toll.[14]

Two forces unleashed by the Depression pushed the bank toward the brink: a dangerous accumulation of bad debts and the stifling effects of tight money across the country. Drought and plummeting prices for Canada's export commodities provided the first jolt. The problems of western farmers contending with a faltering wheat economy were just the most visible symptom. In the east, for instance, the mammoth pulp-and-paper industry that Holt and Gundy had built up vigorously in the 1920s suddenly found itself facing slumping prices, huge overcapacity, and a surly mood of protectionism in its principal market, the United States. And the bills were coming due, as companies like Holt's Canada Power and Paper struggled to service a mountain of funded debt.

Declining commodity demand placed the Royal Bank in global double jeopardy. The crown jewel of its international system, Cuba, lived and died on the fortunes of sugar. The sugar crash of 1920 had already dragged the bank deeper into Cuban sugar than any bank would have ever normally tolerated. The so-called "sugar-estate accounts" represented the bank's actual operation of sugar mills that had collapsed and been taken over by the bank. Thus, for both the bank and for Cuba itself, sugar was the be all and end all; and, in the early 1930s, the end again seemed near. As the world's largest producer, Cuba had to have access to the American market. From a peak of 4.1 million tons in 1929, American imports of Cuban sugar fell to 1.6 million tons in 1933. Sugar producers desperately sought to control the market. Agreements such as the Chadbourne Plan of 1931 tried to dispose of huge surpluses and rationalize the market. Despite such quotas, the Cuban sugar industry was in contraction and creditors looked on with alarm. The bank's Havana main branch bore the brunt of the austerity. Lending, which had peaked at $43 million in 1926, had shrunk to $5.2 million a decade later. In 1932, this key branch actually reported an operating loss. Similar contractions took place in Brazilian coffee, Grenadian cocoa, Antiguan cotton, and many other Caribbean and Latin American commodities which the bank had traditionally financed. Only in Cuba, however, was the risk of catastrophic proportion.

The Depression brought other unpleasant international repercussions. Throughout the 1920s, the bank had tried to establish itself in Germany, lending to German banks through its New York, London, and Paris offices. The recuperating German economy seemed like a natural new frontier for the bank, but hyper-inflation and growing social instability soon obliged the now-cautious Canadians to apply the brakes. By 1930, the bank was still owed $9.4 million by German banks such as the Dresdner and Deutsche. A year later the German debtors began defaulting. "Unfortunately," Paris office reported, "the problems to be faced proved to be far beyond the most pessimistic anticipations."[15] Late in 1931, all Germany's creditor banks signed a Standstill Agreement, which effectively froze the country's foreign obligations and placed its creditors on an equal-preference footing. Although there was perpetual talk of better times, Norman Hart, the Paris manager, grimly acknowledged that the German debt situation had become a political one. The better times that Germany was to get in the 1930s were not the kind that saw debts to foreign bankers settled. As late as 1952, the Royal Bank was still grappling with the Standstill Agreement.[16]

The Depression thus exposed the bank's over-indulgence in the financing of Canadian merger mania, in Cuban sugar and in German reconstruction in the 1920s. What had seemed normal lending decisions in the "roaring twenties" became abnormal liabilities in the "dirty thirties." It also triggered a liquidity crisis that jeopardized the bank's stability. As the national economy soured, head office instinctively tried to minimize the bank's exposure to liabilities by adopting tight money policies. From a 1929 high of $640.5 million, loans were reduced a dramatic 40 per cent to $384.6 million by 1933. This was partially the result of a natural falling away of loan demand, but it was also the outcome of hard-nosed lending policies. Even though deposits in the same 1929-33 period fell only 22 per cent, the bank strained to make provision for its liabilities. New loans were vigorously scrutinized, old loans vigilantly policed, and interest rates boosted above the usual 7 per cent. With no central bank regulating the nation's appetite for credit, the banks were the sole masters of their fiscal fate. Thus, whatever the social and economic cost of squeezing the availability of credit, banks saw preserving their solvency as their first duty.

It was this duty that provoked the political outcry. When Prime Minister Bennett complained in late 1932 that Peace River District farmers were, for instance, being charged 9 per cent interest,* Morris Wilson acknowledged the fact, defending his managers by citing the burden of increased taxation: "In the very nature of things they, like other business people, attempt to pass these increased charges on to the public."[17] Branches could also be closed, but this, too, brought political outrage. There was always the bank's rest account if the bad-debt situation became precarious, but any resort to the rest account would be viewed as a desperate measure by the public, a final, frantic grab at the life raft. Through the early Depression, the Royal Bank thus enforced a regime of tight credit to protect its solvency. Few realized that this banking orthodoxy seriously deflated the national economy by denying it capital to grow. The bankers' concern was survival: to protect the stability of the bank by limiting its exposure. Without a central bank to ensure adequate liquidity, there was no other way – as Pease had earlier realized.

But, no degree of tight money or corporate austerity could get around the Royal Bank's over-exposure to certain cyclical types of credit dispensed in the late 1920s. In January 1932, the bank's accountants broke the bad news. In a codicil to their annual report on the bank's financial condition, Peat, Marwick, Mitchell and Price, Waterhouse warned the directors that they found the condition of "certain loans...unsatisfactory." In Cuba, interest on $33.7 million in loans to the sugar companies had fallen into arrears. The accountants called on the directors to materially increase the reserves set aside for these loans. Closer to home, there were $23 million in questionable loans on the Canadian books "where the securities held as collateral, on the basis of quoted market values at November 30, 1931, were insufficient to cover the amount of the loan, or for other reasons the loan appeared unsatisfactory."[18] The day of reckoning had arrived.

The mortal danger of nearly $60 million in doubtful loans was heightened by a fresh gust of rumours about the personal precariousness of Herbert Holt. Rumours are a banker's nemesis, and work to dissolve the public's trust in a financial institution. By the early 1930s,

---

* Banks could charge whatever interest they liked on loans, but the Bank Act only allowed them to legally recover 7 per cent.

Holt's name had become synonymous with that of the bank and with that of St. James Street corporate capitalism. If the banking community construed the Royal Bank in terms of Pease, Neill, and now Morris Wilson, the man on the street thought of Holt when he thought of the bank. Pease had brought Holt to the board in 1905 and to its presidency three years later because his status as a captain of industry gave substance to the bank's drive for national prominence. The Depression, however, torpedoed Holt's ship of capitalism. Not only did the pulp-and-paper industry, which Holt and his Toronto partner, Harry Gundy, had so vigorously promoted in the late 1920s, collapse into debt and idleness, but the public came to associate Sir Herbert with the problems of "big business" in Canada.

In the previous decade, counting Holt's corporate directorships had become a national pastime. These ranged from his personal hold on Montreal Light, Heat and Power to his presence in the boardrooms of companies as influential as Canadian Pacific and Sun Life. He was "Mr. Capitalism" in many a Canadian mind. Most assumed that he was Canada's richest man. This he was not; his power consisted of control, not extent of wealth. Throughout the 1930s, Holt, for instance, held only 4,217 of the over 350,000 shares in the bank.[19] None the less, as Canadians reached the conclusion that their market economy had faltered in the early Depression, delivering them into unemployment and uncertainty, they drew a bead on Holt. The unchecked speculation and interlocked power of corporate titans like Holt was the root of Canada's misery, they decided. "Large, taciturn, surrounded by the traditional insignia of the very biggest business," the *Canadian Forum*, the small but outspoken voice of Canadian radicalism, noted in 1934, "he has become for many the fearful embodiment of reaction."[20] And it was not just for the man on the street that Holt became the shibboleth of greed. In 1932, W. E. J. Luther, the president of the Montreal Stock Exchange, became distraught over his own losses in Holt stocks and attempted to assassinate Holt. Thinking he had succeeded, Luther went home and killed himself. Holt was only grazed and soon recovered. Luckily, the story never came to light in the press.*

Holt's precipitous decline in public esteem soon had implications for the bank. The Winnipeg supervisor had, for instance, reported that one North End client had closed out her account: "she had been told by a financial friend...that the bank was unsafe and that the Holt interests owed us $250,000,000. The gossip is rife amongst all classes here, but withdrawals in the main are by wage earners and professional

---

* The Toronto tabloid *Hush* alone covered the story. It alleged (without evidence) that Holt's bodyguard had in fact gunned Luther down as he attempted to shoot Holt, and later took his body to his Oka home, where a suicide was staged.

people."[21] The Regina supervisor complained that "false statements respecting this bank are matters of discussion in barber shops and women's social functions."[22] The New Glasgow, Nova Scotia, manager, E. G. MacMinn, reported that local shareholders of the bank were being panicked into selling their stock by the woes of Holt's Canada Power and Paper. To make matters worse, just two months before the auditors' report was received, the prominent Montreal brokerage house of McDougall & Cowans, a frequent recipient of Royal call loans, went spectacularly bankrupt. To cover its liabilities, the bank collected the cash value of Percy Cowans's personal insurance policies.[23] In Toronto, the bank participated in a hasty reorganization of the debt-laden Wood, Gundy & Company.

There was, however, no way to cover all the rumours. Fortunately for the bank, the public did not even have an inkling that another pillar of the Montreal Anglo business community was dangerously near the financial rocks. Thomas B. Macaulay, president of the redoubtable Sun Life Assurance Company, had relied on the bank for call loans to support Macaulay Securities, a private holding company. By October 1931, Macaulay Securities was $10 million in debt and not meeting its payments. Two million of this was owed to the Royal Bank. By the spring, Morris Wilson concluded that the situation was "highly unsatisfactory" and could not "be allowed to continue."[24] Unfortunately, continue it did – for many years.

By February 1932, the directors knew that something had to be done to alleviate the debt load, but their options were very limited. Among the $23 million in questionable domestic loans were the businesses of some of Canada's premier financiers: T. B. Macaulay, Harry Gundy, and, indirectly, Herbert Holt. Any attempt to force liquidation of these accounts would provoke a major crisis of confidence in Canadian business. Who in the bank, after all, would have the temerity to demand repayment of a $2.9-million loan to the Consolidated Investment Corporation, a 1929 Holt holding-company creation? But more worrisome was the knowledge that much of the marketable assets supporting these loans were in fact Royal Bank stock. Any forced liquidation of these accounts would have the effect of flushing a huge volume of the bank's stock onto an already depressed market; from a 1929 high of $298, Royal Bank stock had slipped to a low of $120 in 1932. An investor panic would undoubtedly follow any mass sell-off of Royal stock. From the outset, therefore, secrecy was imperative – even the whisper of a rumour might create a crisis.[25]

The crisis was managed by a team of bank directors working with

(*continued on p. 260*)

# GOOD MEN AND BAD DEBTS

## *The Saskatchewan "Outlawed" Loans Book*

ROYAL BANK'S ARCHIVE IN MONTREAL contains shelf after shelf of neatly filed documents, millions of them, reaching as far back as 1818. This is the stuff of history. No one document in this vast collection makes history come alive more than the "Saskatchewan District Register of Written-Off Debts" from the Depression. An "outlawed" debt was one which the bank resigned any hope of ever recovering. A debt first fell into arrears and was later "outlawed." Most of these Saskatchewan loans were Section 88 loans, made to farmers to support their annual crop, and they were secured by chattel mortgages on possessions, but never on land. When a loan became non-performing, the branch manager began tracking it on the back of the loan sheet. The record over time presents a heart-wrenching piece of history. This is the tale of one such loan.

On May 28, 1929, Charles W., a farmer, contracted a $282.50 loan at Sedley branch. The loan was for spring seeding and was due on September 4. Drought hit the area that summer, and Charles W. failed to meet his obligation. The bank did not press for repayment. The loan was labelled a "carry-over." A year later, on November 29, 1930, he managed a small payment, and then fell into complete arrears. Two years later, on December 29, 1932, head office wrote off a total of $408.73 in principal and accumulated interest. The manager's notes complete the sad tale.

**Jan. 5, 1933:** "a married man aged 43...secured by chattel mortgage covering twelve horses, three cattle, McCormick tractor, Chevrolet truck and a Star car. The horses and cattle could not be located and the tractor, truck and car were brought in...by the bank...in poor condition... stored." The truck and car were then sold for $10 and the tractor offered for $50. Charles W. moved to Hudson Bay Junction "and has been out of employment for some time and is in very poor condition."

**Feb. 15, 1934:** Tractor sold for $65. "No further security held...debtor...reported to be worthless." The bank thus recovered $64.77 after costs from Charles W.

**March 19, 1935:** Charles W. has "partial employment doing odd jobs...on Relief...very little likelihood of W. ever improving his position to such an extent as would permit of him looking after his old obligations."

**March 12, 1937:** "Recovery of the account seems hopeless."

**Jan. 4, 1944:** "This man is now the Village scavenger...should be contacted from time to time."

**Feb. 4, 1947:** "We have been authorized by the supervisor to accept $300 in settlement... payable in monthly instalments of $10."

**Feb. 4, 1948:** "This claim is outlawed and we are inclined to think W. has no intention of arranging a settlement."

*The Depression brought out Westerners' resourcefulness. In 1933, J. M. Windsor, the manager in Spirit River, Alberta, took these pictures of improvised winter transportation.*

General Manager Wilson and his four assistant general managers –
S. G. Dobson, C. C. Pineo, S. R. Noble, and G. W. Mackimmie. Only
three directors – Holt, A. J. Brown, and G. H. Duggan – appear to have
been actively involved: Holt because he had so much at stake, Brown
because he was the bank's indispensable corporate counsel, and
Duggan, chairman of the Dominion Engineering Works and a director since 1916, probably because of his intimate ties with Montreal
business. The group immediately recognized the need for secrecy. The
auditors' codicil was not printed in the annual report, but it was
appended to the annual statement sent to the minister of finance in
Ottawa, who was required by the Bank Act to receive each bank's
annual statement. Prime Minister Bennett, who acted as his own
finance minister, thus knew of the bank's predicament and later
confided that the issue "gave me more concern than any other single
matter that I had to deal with during my term of office as Prime
Minister."[26]

Throughout the spring of 1932, the team at head office groped for
a means of extricating the bank from its predicament. The Bank Act
prohibited a bank from purchasing or dealing in its own stock. This
therefore precluded any direct bail-out, whereby the bank might
relieve its debtors by taking over their holdings of bank stock. Some
arm's-length arrangement was therefore necessary.

In April, inquiries were made of F. T. Walker, the New York agent,
about establishing an American shell corporation "to act as nominee to
hold shares of the bank for account of customers and/or correspon-
dents."[27] This bore no fruit, and all the while, the economic situation
continued to blacken. By most indexes, the Depression hit bottom in
the winter of 1932-33. At this darkest hour, a solution was found. The
architect was probably Albert Brown, the director drawn from the
Montreal law firm of Brown, Montgomery and McMichael and a master
of corporate law. A holding company, Islemont Securities Corporation,
was established in December, using $5 million of the "private
resources" of Holt, Duggan, and Brown. Islemont then turned to the
bank for a loan of $7,993,780,[28] which it secured with $8 million of its
own twenty-year collateral trust bonds. Thus, Islemont itself became
"one of the largest debtors of the Bank." With this capital, Islemont
then bought large blocks of Royal Bank shares from the bank's beleaguered debtors, thereby easing their indebtedness. Morris Wilson later
noted that Islemont bought these shares "at a time when such a
purchase would not normally have been considered; and paid for them
about $4,000,000 in excess of their then market value."[29]

Islemont's immediate effect was to loosen the corset of debt around
several of the bank's most prominent debtors. The tactic was quickly

mimicked to relieve the pain of debt elsewhere in the bank's portfolio. Exchequer Securities, for instance, was formed "to take over loans and securities of Wood Gundy & Co." totalling $8.3 million.[30] The Islemont companies were given a cubbyhole office in 360 St. James and had a lawyer from Brown's firm as their titular president. Islemont's long-term strategy was to gradually retire its debt by selling its holdings of Royal Bank stock onto what was hoped to be an improving market. The plan worked. While the Islemont loan stayed on the bank's books until well after the Second World War, by 1946, for instance, the principal was down to just under $3 million.[31]

Islemont Securities was the creation of perilous times. Given Albert Brown's canny sense of corporate legal affairs, it broke no law. Behind all the secrecy, it was in fact an early example of debt restructuring. In late 1934, two years after Islemont's creation, Morris Wilson prepared a secret affidavit in which he outlined his view of the Islemont affair. The debt crisis of 1932, he wrote, threatened "most serious repercussions" for the bank. Holt, Brown, and Duggan acted out of altruism, and senior management was beholden to them for their secret intervention. From the outset, management felt an "obligation...to collaborate by all available means" to help Holt, Brown, and Duggan "withdraw their capital from that company [Islemont] without loss." To assist this, management agreed to waive or "materially reduce" interest on Islemont's loan. Wilson and his four assistant general managers duly signed the affidavit and consigned it to the secret file of Islemont documents, which was quickly stored in the president's vault. Islemont remained the Royal Bank's best-kept secret. Prime Minister Bennett clearly knew about it, and there was a good deal of scuttlebutt "on the street" about it, but public confidence in the bank was never fundamentally shaken. It is probably no coincidence that, in 1934, the Bank Act was revised to prohibit a bank director from voting approval of any loan to a concern in which he held an interest.

While Islemont quietly stood guard over the bank's troubled corporate loans, the Cuban debt problem and the accumulating losses from normal Canadian operations continued to exert pressure. Early in the Depression these had been accommodated out of the bank's inner reserve, an undisclosed contingency fund built up out of operating profits. But this tactic had two unfortunate outcomes: it depleted the inner reserves dangerously, and it gave the public the impression that the bank had bottomless pockets. By the summer of 1933, the bank was on the leanest possible financial diet; salaries had been cut by 5 per cent, the dividend had been cut, the 2 per cent bonus to shareholders had been stopped, and branches had been closed. Bank accountants were prophesying – rightly – the worst annual profit in ten years.

The news from Cuba was even worse. President Machado had been toppled and had fled the country, coming briefly to Montreal. In his wake, labour unrest and rural insurgency engulfed Cuba. This time the United States did not intervene; the Platt Amendment would be repealed in 1934. In September, for instance, a mob of five hundred, carrying red flags and clubs, laid siege to the bank's Palmira sugar mill near Cienfuegos.[32] As the Machado regime crumbled, there was sporadic violence in Havana. When a bomb exploded near a branch, "one of our tellers got so excited that he took a revolver of the bank's and went out to the back and finished himself off."[33] News that the bank's Havana supervisor was reduced to pleading with the British ambassador for protection of foreign property convinced head office that the end was near in Cuba, and faint rumours that a strongman, Colonel Fulgencio Batista, was beginning to restore order did little to reverse the pessimism. Facing a possible Cuban fiasco and accumulated Canadian losses, the bank finally turned to its $35-million rest account – the proud symbol of the bank's solidity, the fruit of careful husbandry since the days of Edson Pease.

The Royal Bank was not alone in feeling the pinch of the Depression. In September 1933, Prime Minister Bennett told the president of the Bank of Montreal that he was "very anxious that the banks take

*Many Canadians were unsure exactly which bank Herbert Holt headed. On this crude counterfeit $5 bill, Holt is mistakenly portrayed (see signature) as the president of the Bank of Montreal. Holt's successor as president, Morris Wilson, enjoyed less notoriety. After attending the Coronation in London in 1937, Wilson went on to Paris, where (opposite) he met with H. L. Gagnon (left) and Paris manager E. G. Groning (centre). The bank magazine noted that Gagnon had temporarily escaped "the tragic conditions" under which he had been managing the Barcelona branch.*

some definite action in connection with appropriation of reserves for unforeseen demands."[34] By December 1933, a "standing committee" of the Royal Bank board – consisting of five Montreal directors – recommended that $15 million be drawn out of the rest account to reimburse the inner reserves for "appropriations made therefrom during the past few years of disturbed business conditions and consequent abnormal depreciation in values, and to provide for future contingencies."[35] The transfer from the rest account was not an act of desperation. During the course of the Depression, six of Canada's nine banks reduced their reserves. Since the shareholders would have to be informed, the transfer could not be hidden from the public. From the outset, it was presented as "conservative and constructive" banking. Wilson was quick to point out that financial results for 1933 showed a distinct improvement over 1932; profits were up from $3.9 million to $4.4 million, and assets were again on the rise. The uncertain Cuban situation made it prudent, however, "to make liberal allowance for contingencies." Equally important, depletion of the published reserves would counter the public impression that the bank had a deep well of undisclosed profits – its inner reserves – that it had built up "through excessive profits during good times."[36] With a revision of the Bank Act looming in 1934, the bank had no wish to appear falsely as a "fat cat," untouched by the Depression.

In advance of the January 1934 annual meeting, Wilson carefully briefed his managers on the transfer. The announcement should be "treated in a very matter of course way," so as not to arouse undue comment.[37] After decades of assuring its customers that its rest equalled its paid-up capital, the bank was now letting its rest slip well below its $35-million capital. The annual meeting brought no adverse comment; it was, after all, still a small, cozy affair, commanded by the proxies held by the directors. The inspector general of banks in Ottawa heard isolated criticism: a disgruntled former Royal Banker demanded to know "just how much was written off the books from the year 1933."[38] The financial press was unperturbed; the ability to write off bad debts was a sign of Canadian banking's stability. "They have faced what some might call the worst and faced it successfully," the Monetary Times noted. "It was necessary to make certain write-offs and they have done so…Canadians will continue to regard the banking structure of the country as one of its bulwarks."[39] Privately, Morris Wilson sensed that a crucial challenge had been met: "We can now hope for better things."[40]

And things did get better. In January 1935, the bank's auditors quietly reported that "the improvement in the status of some of the larger loans is quite marked and the Cuban situation has changed for

*An aged-but-still-jovial Herbert Holt arrives at 360 St. James in his limousine, c.1934.*

the better owing to the increase in the price of sugar over that of last year."[41] Even Macaulay Securities began to whittle down its debt. A more positive tone crept into the annual meetings of the late decade. Profits – still depressed by weak commercial demand and low interest rates – stabilized around $3.5 to $4 million annually. More encouraging was the steady growth in deposits from a nadir of $600 million in 1933 to $911 million in 1939.

With this slow improvement came a sense that change was now inevitable, both for the Royal Bank and for banking in general. The Depression had severely dented the credibility of Canadian banking and probably the deepest dent had been provoked by the unsavoury perception the public held of the Royal Bank's president, Sir Herbert Holt. "I do not see why I should be picked out and the Royal Bank is being made the devil in the piece," Holt lashed out in 1934.[42] Morris Wilson knew why. Holt's octopus-like reach in the Canadian economy meant that an early reputation as a "builder" could easily be turned inside out in hard times. Not just to the narrow readership of *Hush* or the *Canadian Forum*, Holt was a convenient target for discontent. He had restructured the pulp-and-paper industry to the point of monopoly and overcapacity. His grip on Montreal's public utilities was felt every time a utility bill was dropped in a mailbox. And, although Wilson tried his best to deny them, the country was awash with rumours that Holt was hanging by a financial thread – a thread tied to the bank. While Islemont remained a hermetic secret, most in the financial know suspected that Holt had somehow been "bailed out" by his friends. Even R. B. Bennett was quick to make the allegation. When a Calgary constituent complained that the bank was taking legal action against her to recover a $6,100 loan, Bennett asked general manager Dobson to "think of the losses that the Bank has experienced through some of the 'pirates of finance' and 'captains of industry' and then remember the toil and suffering which that woman has passed."[43] To friend and foe of the bank alike, it was clear that Holt had to go.

By 1934, Holt's health was deteriorating. Now well into his seventies, the reclusive millionaire appeared gaunt and haggard in the few photos that the press managed to take of him. Holt increasingly pleaded poor health in his attempts to shun public scrutiny. When the Commons Committee on Banking and Commerce called him to Ottawa to give evidence in the spring of 1934, Wilson obtained an opinion from the dean of the McGill medical school, saying that he was "absolutely and irrevocably opposed to his going up"; the limitations on the president's heart had reached "an extreme degree" and he had suffered brain "spasms."[44] The committee obliged Holt by travelling to Montreal. There was little to hold Holt in the president's office. His $25,000 salary had been cut 10 per cent in token resistance to the Depression; he collected another $4,000 in director's fees, and then paid taxes on the lot. "I cannot imagine anybody but a bank in Canada being able to secure a man of his ability for the average rate of $14,000 a year," Wilson told the Commons committee. That's what MPs earned, a politician gibed. "Yes," Wilson retorted, "but there is honour and glory there and there is no glory in being the head of a bank."[45]

If he could not find glory, Holt was determined to find the sun. One of the few bright spots for the Canadian economy in the Depression had been gold mining; precious metals assuaged troubled investors. Canada's gold king was Harry Oakes, the irascible millionaire proprietor of Kirkland Lake's Lake Shore Gold Mines, a solid bank client since the 1920s. Like his friend Holt, Oakes was eager to escape the Depression limelight, and he fled his Niagara Falls home in the early

1930s for the Bahamas, where the Royal had been active since 1908. Holt followed.* During 1934, the finishing touches were put on Holt's splendid mansion on the outskirts of Nassau. At the annual meeting in January 1935, shareholders learned that, for the first time since 1914, Holt would not preside over their assembly. He was wintering in the Bahamas. More surprising was the news that, after twenty-six years, Holt was no longer the bank's president. A month earlier, Holt had told the board that the time was "opportune" for him to step down. In true Royal Bank tradition, Holt said that he had "always been a strong believer in appointing younger men" and that the new president, Morris Wilson, was "the outstanding banker in Canada." Holt would remain in the new – and completely titular – position of chairman. As president and managing director, Wilson would run the show, backed up by General Manager Sydney Dobson.[46]

Holt's departure was a watershed. For the first time in its history, the bank had as its president a banker born and bred. The tradition of an outsider president, begun by Kenny in Halifax, had died, and the Royal Bank would from now on groom its own presidents. Banking had become too involved, too professional, to entrust its leadership to amateur, part-time presidents, especially if their personal business adventures might drag their banks down. In Wilson and Dobson, the bank now had two Nova Scotia "bank boys" at its helm. They had both pursued remarkably similar paths, Wilson's starting in Lunenburg in 1897 and Dobson's in Sydney in 1900. Both had been trained under the redoubtable Martin Dickie in Truro. Both had been posted to Vancouver. Both had been called to head office young to serve as the bank's chief inspector. They were not captains of industry; they were trained practitioners of banking. They had worked long, long hours to get where they were, and neither had lost the "natural kindliness or friendliness" of a Maritimer.[47] "I am just one of the 'common herd,'" Wilson told one of his managers in 1937. "I recall that Abraham Lincoln once said that God must like the common man because he made so many of them."[48]

In a jocular salute to Wilson, the *Canadian Banker* noted that, in 1934, "he finally escaped from all worry by being appointed President." Certainly, Wilson had been instrumental behind the scenes in orchestrating the Islemont rescue on behalf of his predecessor. Barring a catastrophic relapse into deep depression, after 1934 the bank could rest assured that its internal affairs had been shored up. For Wilson, the worry was to lie in rebuilding the bank's external credibility. From 1934

---

* Sir Frederick Williams-Taylor, general manager of the Bank of Montreal until 1929, also frequented the Bahamas but was by no means a friend of Holt's.

*When Morris Wilson became president of the bank in 1934, he was the first "professional" banker to head a bank in Canada. Another Maritime "bank boy," Wilson was toasted (with coffee) by the staff of Wolfville branch when the news reached them.*

to the onset of war, Canadian banking lived with constant challenge and change. Public antagonism and an economy starved of credit led to a royal commission on banking and, ultimately, the creation of a central bank. Eager to pump purchasing power into a still-faltering economy, Ottawa followed these initiatives with schemes to enlist the banks in financing home and farm improvement. Impatient with piecemeal reform, the West exploded in protest and embraced populist schemes for radical economic reform of the banks. The CCF call for bank nationalization and Social Credit assaults on eastern "big shots" – like Holt – shook the pillars of Canadian banking. These were to be Morris Wilson's worries, and they had found their roots in the early Depression.

As the economy collapsed around them, Ottawa and the bankers had clung to their orthodoxies. They did so in no coherent fashion, indulging in piecemeal renovation, but never pursuing coordinated action in the face of economic hardship.[49] Amid this chaos, government and the banks tried to shore up the economy in *ad hoc* ways. In 1931, the banks had helped Ottawa raise $180 million in a National Service Loan, a campaign modelled on the wartime victory loans. As the price of wheat spiralled downward, the western wheat pools found it increasingly difficult to arrange forward financing of the annual crop. Initially, the three Prairie governments enhanced their guarantees of these loans to the banks. When wheat fell further, Ottawa stepped in and, under the 1931 Unemployment and Farm Relief Act, furnished its own guarantee. Thus, the Canadian financial system's fundamental obligation to move the crop to world markets was maintained.[50]

In the east, other obligations were also met in *ad hoc* ways. When the giant Beauharnois power project on the St. Lawrence near Montreal faltered in 1931, the Royal Bank joined the Commerce and Bank of Montreal in providing advances to the beleaguered project. Once again, Prime Minister Bennett intervened, providing a federal guarantee to the banks. Despite the fact that it was bathed in political controversy, Beauharnois was reorganized and completed without the banks ever having to draw on Ottawa's guarantee – "without it having cost the country one cent," as Wilson told Bennett in 1934.[51] (Coincidentally, Beauharnois fell under the sway of Holt's Montreal Light, Heat and Power.) Similarly, the bank took a $12.2-million share of a $60-million loan to Canadian Pacific in 1933 to rescue it from defaulting on a series of short-term obligations that could not be refinanced on troubled Wall Street. This too was backed by a federal guarantee.[52] The loan was successfully retired in 1936 when the CPR returned to the bond market. When Price Brothers Paper defaulted on its loans, the bank became embroiled in a longer and less-fruitful attempt to reorganize the company with British press barons Beaverbrook and Rothermere.[53]

*Ad hocery* was by no means capable of solving the fundamental malaise that had been brought on by the Depression – the chronic deflation of the economy. In the wake of the "crash," risk aversion and tight credit became the bywords of Canadian banking. In 1929, the Royal Bank had $640.5 million in loans on its books. It would not regain that level of lending again until 1948; lending bottomed out in 1937 at $338.4 million. Canadian bankers continued to see themselves as the nation's lender of last resort. "Cheap money" was reckless money, money that would simply rekindle the fires of speculation and thereby endanger the solvency of the banks. In 1933, the banks shaved a per cent off their loan rate for farmers and municipalities to 7 per cent, a decrease soon echoed by a fall in the savings rate to $1\frac{1}{2}$ per cent.[54] Even then, the vigilance of most managers in assessing potential borrowers' collateral and prospects tended to militate against any quick flush of cash reserves into the banking system. In 1932, Ottawa had tried to inject some credit by *obliging* the banks – under the 1914 Finance Act – to borrow $35 million in Dominion notes from Ottawa at 3 per cent. The banks then lent a similar amount back to the government at 4 per cent. Under the Finance Act, this was the limit of monetary expansion and it had little or no impact on credit conditions.

The banks' tight credit policies soon inflicted grievous damage on their public credibility. However natural a policy of limiting dangerous exposure to loss in lending seemed to the banks, the borrowing public saw tight credit as slow strangulation. In August 1931, for instance, the branch manager in Plenty, Saskatchewan, reported that his clients were seething over the bank's "conservative loaning policy." At one meeting, an eavesdropping branch manager reported that a speaker called Scarlet of Saskatoon made "some very damaging remarks about our institution and...stated that the Royal Bank of Canada was no doubt head of the Capitalist System in Canada and for this reason it was difficult to obtain credit."[55] The Canadian Bankers' Association responded to such assaults by sending B. K. Sandwell, a former McGill economics professor and now editor of *Saturday Night*, on a western swing to suggest "propaganda" that might be directed against "socialistic" criticism.[56] Back east, however, there was a growing recognition that "propaganda" was not the answer to Canada's credit woes.

As early as 1931, Prime Minister Bennett had asked the CBA to consider "some form of central bank"; such an organization would make dealing with the U.S. Federal Reserve easier. Sensing the opposition, Bennett conceded that such an "institution would have to be owned by the banks."[57] The bankers balked. A central bank might regulate national credit, but it would undoubtedly fall under the thrall of politicians. If political appointees governed national credit, Canadian banking would be at the mercy of the least populist whim. "This is quite contradictory as it is impossible," Holt complained, "as in the case of the railways, to do away with politics if the directors are to be appointed by whatever government may be in power at the time."[58] Whatever its shortcomings, bankers argued, the present system at least ensured stability.

A few lonely bankers were beginning to think otherwise. Within the Royal Bank, there was the memory of Edson Pease's ill-starred campaign for a central bank in 1918. Pease had argued that "supplementary banking facilities" might ease the problems of post-war adjustment. Pease left apostles. Most prominent among them was Randolph Noble, assistant general manager since 1922. Another Fredericton "bank boy," Noble oversaw the bank's foreign branches. In Montreal, he had become a self-taught economist, taking evening courses at McGill from Leacock. Through his colleague Graham Towers, he fell in with a group of academic free-thinkers, notably McGill law professor Frank Scott. Together, they questioned the *status quo*. What if, Noble suggested, the private banks were relieved of their duty on the nation's financial front line by a central bank? Would a central bank have eased the financial pain of the Depression? Would it have helped to stimulate the national economy? Avoid the Islemont predicament? Put credit in farmers' pockets? Such ponderings did not ingratiate Noble with his superiors;

at a board meeting a prominent Montreal director – probably the arch-conservative A. J. Brown – once openly berated him for consorting with a "radical" like Scott. Noble learned to segregate his daytime banking and his nighttime philosophizing.

The social and economic disintegration of the Depression prompted Noble and Towers to question the received wisdom of their profession. As the bank's chief inspector since 1929, Towers daily saw the financial carnage of a nation starved of credit. Noble concluded that this credit strangulation was not a cure but a perpetuator of the Depression; he would later write of the "misguided financial policies" pursued by governments caught in the grip of the Depression. "The Canadian experience shows," he wrote, "that so long as bank reserves were deficient, deposits steadily declined and liquidation proceeded apace."[59] Noble began to sense that monetary expansion, not contraction, was the way out of the Depression. The unveiling of the Roosevelt New Deal – "Roosevelt magic," he called it – in 1933 seemed a move in this direction; Noble visited New York to share ideas with "New Dealers" such as Dean Acheson and a circle of secret Roosevelt admirers on Wall Street, including several J. P. Morgan partners. The ideas of John Maynard Keynes, the English economist who advocated the forced injection of purchasing power into a lagging economy by government, began to attract Noble and Towers.[60] "I think Mr. Keynes is right," Noble wrote to a prominent Toronto businessman in 1934, "when he says in his *Treatise on Money*…'Booms and slumps are simply the expression of the results of an oscillation of the terms of credit about their equilibrium position.' Monetary management must devote itself to maintaining the equilibrium position and when this becomes possible it will be the greatest single thing that has ever been done for the good of mankind. It will eliminate the agony of depressions and the stupid waste of resources and effort always connected with them."[61] In 1937, Noble joined Keynes in contributing an essay to a book on the monetary experience of the Depression.

Closer to home, Noble piqued the curiosity of Prime Minister Bennett, another New Brunswick boy grappling with the meaning of the Depression. "I was the centre of all the propaganda for an inflationary policy from the beginning of 1930," Noble wrote to a leading American economist. "Without assistance from anyone, I sold the idea to the Prime Minister of compelling the banks to borrow under the Finance Act, although I wanted him to make it fifty million dollars, not thirty-five."[62] Noble's musings found little resonance in senior management at 360 St. James; the bank economists proved a more receptive audience. In May 1933, Donald Marvin, the chief economist, praised the Roosevelt New Deal as being of "utmost importance in restoring prosperity." In particular, Marvin pointed to the powers given to the Federal Reserve to bolster commercial bank credit.[63] Then good news came from Ottawa. The Bank Act was slated for its decennial revision in 1933, but, rather than face an onslaught of protest and half-baked reform, the government moved to postpone the revision for a year. In the interim, a royal commission on banking and currency would perform a "complete and detailed examination" of the act *and* study "the advisability of establishing in Canada a central banking institution." Headed by the British jurist Lord Macmillan, the commission set out in early August on a brutal schedule of coast-to-coast hearings, returning to Ottawa to present its report in September. Canadian banking would never be the same again.

*High River, Alberta, lives up to its name in a 1932 flood.*

In city after city, the Canadian banking system was found wanting. Never was the fatal gap between the banks' insistence on their solvency and the public's need of credit more apparent. A spontaneous coalition of farmers, labour, and political agitators pummelled the banks, and the temperature rose as the commission moved westward. "The farmer was educated to do his business on credit," the president of the United Farmers of Alberta complained. Now he could not get that credit. There was "no intelligent or systematic regulation of the volume of purchasing power…we are faced with the tragic paradox of our times – a lack of financial means to distribute to our people the goods and services which can be provided in superabundance."[64] There was no credit because there was no competition in banking: "Here was a fine machine for concentrating control in a few hands," one Alberta farmer MP claimed.[65] Eastern reformers joined the chorus: in Toronto, the League for Social Reconstruction – the brains trust of the CCF – called for the "complete social control of the machinery of finance."[66] This would begin with an end to "the very low salaries paid to junior workers in the commercial banks."

In an effort coordinated by the CBA, the banks defended themselves as best they could. If Westerners could not get credit, it was because Section 88 loans, secured by chattels, made no sense in falling commodity markets. Even in the best of times, a crop in the ground was a precarious security. "The only thing is that loaning money on anything covered by a chattel security to a farmer," the Royal Bank supervisor in Regina noted, "is like loaning on a watch in the other man's pocket."[67] In Winnipeg, the banks argued that their western loans outweighed their deposits by $106 million in 1932. Morris Wilson told the commissioners that 99.6 per cent of Royal Bank loans were approved on the spot in the West, not in the East. Banking profits, Wilson added, were not lavish: in 1932, 42.3 per cent of Canada's 3,263 branches lost money. But this was all a rear-guard action; the bankers were defending a system that virtually everybody agreed was in need of fixing.

It fell to Morris Wilson, as a progressive industry leader, to concede defeat – grudgingly – on behalf of the banking community. The heads of the chartered banks each presented briefs on aspects of banking to the commission, but Wilson addressed the crucial questions of bank control of national credit, the banks' note-issuing privilege, and the effectiveness of bank directorates. Canadian bankers, he maintained, believed that the 1914 Finance Act still provided an adequate means of creating excess credit. Furthermore, the profits they garnered from circulating their own notes helped to pay the cost of running a national branch system. While banks' boards were "representative of the entire country," they oversaw a marvellously decentralized credit system that distributed credit efficiently around the nation. A state-appointed central bank would dismantle this entire arrangement. It would demand a monopoly on note issue and would appropriate the right of divining the volume of credit in the economy. Wilson did his best to stress the dangers involved. The "moral force" of its advice would initially be weak; its "prestige must inevitably be the product of slow growth." Unlike the commercial banks, it would lack the network of sensors into the community that the branches provided. Its officers must be "men of the very highest calibre," not political hirelings.

Wilson proceeded to outline his views on how a central bank *might* operate. Canada had never had a short-term money market, a place where the placing of money bills established the going rate of credit. The commercial banks had maintained reserves in New York and London so that they could play these markets. A Canadian central bank might, however, control domestic credit in four ways: moral suasion (i.e., the influence of a top-notch staff); the purchase of bonds on the open market; intervention in the foreign-exchange markets; and the use of open-market operations to establish a bank rate for credit. Use of these mechanisms, Wilson concluded, would "necessarily be somewhat crude" and it would be "visionary" to suggest that even a very capable central bank could enforce its will by these methods.[68] Despite this, Wilson made it clear that the fledgling central bank would have the support of the commercial banks.

In its report, the Macmillan Commission was quick to praise the achievement of the private banks – "admirable evidence of security, efficiency and convenience" – but was equally quick to prescribe a central bank.[69] Facing both an election and immense public unpopularity, Prime Minister Bennett acted quickly. "No purely profit-making institution operating in a competitive system," Finance Minister Edgar Rhodes told the Commons, "can afford to place social interests before its own in regard to credit policy." National credit would now be set impartially. This was "but another stage in the natural evolution of our banking system" – "Canada's coming of age financially."[70] The central bank would be empowered to regulate internal credit and foreign exchange, and would also give the government impartial financial advice and use monetary action to mitigate economic fluctuations. The commercial banks would surrender their right to issue notes and the gold reserves that anchored these notes to the central bank. Ottawa would now guarantee the Dominion's note circulation and assume the risks attendant on national credit creation. Within five years, the medley of distinctive private banknotes would disappear from Canadian wallets to be replaced by a uniform national currency. On March 11, 1935, the Bank of Canada opened for business. The bank was one of Bennett's few lasting achievements. When Mackenzie King swept back to power later in the year, he embraced the central bank and promised to bring it completely under national control. This King completed by 1938.

The Royal Bank lost more than its notes and gold to the Bank of Canada. Throughout the commission hearings, Wilson had made much of the need for a high-calibre staff for the new central bank. As its head, the bank's governor would also have to be free of any political taint. Once the Bank of Canada Act was passed in July 1934, Bennett turned his thoughts to the task of finding a governor. His thoughts naturally turned to the Royal Bank, a bank he had been intimately involved with for four decades. Despite frosty exchanges with Morris Wilson over Depression banking, Bennett was still close to him. Bennett also knew that the bank had a tradition of promoting men young, of testing their ability. The Royal Bank had always been quick to the frontier. A central bank was a new kind of frontier and, one senses, Wilson wanted one of his own at its edge. In 1924, C. S. Tompkins had left the bank to become the inspector general of banks. Now Graham Towers would follow him to Ottawa. At thirty-six, Towers was young, dashing, and already committed to the idea of central banking. After several meetings with the prime minister, Towers accepted the post on September 6. His $14,000 bank salary more than doubled; so did his challenge – not only to make the bank work but to build its credibility.* Six years later, his friend "Ran" Noble would follow him to Ottawa.[71]

The Depression had a few bruises left for the bank. Despite the creation of the Bank of Canada, the Bank Act still had to be revised. Through the spring of 1934, Wilson was obliged to hear yet again the litany of faults laid before the banks by their parliamentary critics. The charge was led by C. G. "Chubby" Power, a Quebec Liberal, and G. G. Coote, an Alberta United Farmer. Together they dragged out issues as disparate as interlocking directorates and the mechanics of bank mergers. Power persistently quizzed Wilson on the bank's support of the Holt–Gundy paper companies in the 1920s. He often got dangerously near the truth. "I have never," Holt declared, "borrowed a cent from a bank in my life."[72] If Holt had not, then his holding companies had. To some degree, Wilson was aided by the fact that the chairman

---

* In September 1936, Ogema, Saskatchewan, branch hired seventeen-year-old Gerald Bouey as a junior. After taking leaves for military service and university, Bouey left the bank in 1947 and eventually joined the research staff of the Bank of Canada. In 1973, he became the Bank's fourth governor.

*"He's the man to photograph," Montague Norman, Governor of the Bank of England told the press when Graham Towers arrived in London just days after leaving the Royal Bank to become Governor of the Bank of Canada in 1934.*

of the Commons committee was R. B. Hanson, Charlie Neill's brother-in-law.[73] The revised act was duly passed, sanctioning the end of the banks' note-issuing privilege.

The Depression brought the final curtain down on the banks' direct personal relationship with politicians. The banks were soon caught in a scrum of pressure groups. They could no longer count on their informal confabs with the finance minister to make sure that their views were understood in the capital; Canadian finance was now too complex for such intimacy. By the end of the decade, bankers found themselves using paid lobbyists, radio "propaganda," and advocacy programs to preserve their stake in Canadian society. Much of this public-relations effort was administered in Alberta. Just as the battle was subsiding in Ottawa and the new landscape of Canadian banking was taking form, the West exploded in regional protest. If Chubby Power had demanded a reformed banking system, Alberta's Social Credit movement wanted a *different* banking system. If the League for Social Reconstruction attacked the banks on the basis of class, Social Credit attacked on the basis of *region*. It was a root-and-branch challenge that did not lend itself to compromise.

Banks were but one obvious target for western political alienation. Even as Lord Macmillan and the Bank Act committee deliberated, Westerners were abandoning another form of what they saw as eastern control of their lives – traditional politics. In the summer of 1933, a farmer-worker coalition had come together in Regina to form the CCF, which, among other things, promised to nationalize the banks. Randolph Noble's Montreal friend Frank Scott helped to write their ringing manifesto. The startling prospect of socialized banking was somewhat blunted by the fact that the CCF failed to win office anywhere in Canada in the Depression; Saskatchewan would finally elect a "socialist" government in 1944. The threat from Alberta Social Credit was far more immediate.

The landslide victory of William "Bible Bill" Aberhart at the Alberta polls in August 1935 reverberated down Bay and St. James streets. Social Credit fanned smouldering western discontent into a raging brushfire of protest. A high-school teacher and hot-gospeller from Calgary with a flair for stump rhetoric, Aberhart played on Westerners' belief that their destinies were controlled by "fifty big shots" in the east. Fields went unplanted because the financiers would not risk their capital on the "little guy." There was more profit to be made in speculation. There was also enough gossip in the daily press to make Herbert Holt one of the biggest of the "big shots." Since eastern bankers were clearly in "cahoots" with eastern politicians, Aberhart told Albertans, then the time had come to break the manacles of outside control.

Aberhart embellished his populism with theory. In 1923, the Commons committee revising the Bank Act had given short shrift to an English monetary theorist, C. H. Douglas, who believed that the way to stimulate a faltering economy was to inject purchasing power – "social credit" – into it. Adequate purchasing power was a right of all citizens; its absence was the result of the manipulations of financiers. Douglas's rejection in the 1920s paved the way for Aberhart's triumph in the Depression. Social Credit, he claimed, would restore the purchasing power of Albertans by seizing control of the banking system and then using it to distribute a "prosperity certifi-cate" to every citizen. The danger of inflation never entered Aberhart's rhetoric. The eastern press promptly attached the label "funny money" to the certificates.

From Lavoy to Calgary, Albertans believed in Social Credit because it made sense of the topsy-turvy Depression world; it restored their sense of self-worth by seeming to give them control over their personal destinies. Above all else, Social Credit promised to banish debt. Aberhart made brilliant use of his Sunday radio Bible show to

**JAUNTY STEP** is performed by S. Randolph Noble, the head of Canada's Industrial Development Bank, who likes to be called "the Keynes of Canada."

*High-stepping banker:* Life *magazine published this photo of S. R. Noble at the 1949 Montreal St. George's Ball.*

reach the grass roots. The eastern banks were horrified. Ironically, some aspects of Social Credit were theoretically moving in the same general direction as men like Noble, Roosevelt, and Keynes – it sought to restore economic health by injecting purchasing power into the economy. It was on the question of *how* this was to be done that Aberhart and Keynes differed. Rather than controlling the levers of credit creation through a central bank, Social Credit would simply print money. The result, as bankers saw, would be rampant inflation and monetary chaos. Would the certificates be secured by reserves? Would they have any value outside the province? More worrisome for the bankers was Aberhart's implicit threat to provincialize the banking system, to trespass on Ottawa's monopoly over bank regulation. Lurking in the background was the grotesque fear that the province might default on its debt.

In 1936, "Bible Bill" made his initial move. The Social Credit Measures Act – "to bring about the equation of consumption to production" – introduced the prosperity certificates, and the Provincial Loans Refunding Act capped interest payable on the provincial debt.[74] Sensing the challenge to national banking, the CBA executive council decided to take "every effort…to prevent the spread of a desire for this type of legislation into other provinces."[75] Assured that the prosperity certificates were worthless as circulating currency, the bankers focused on the more potent threat of debt adjustment. Alberta's attempt to limit interest on municipal bonds at 3 per cent, even on existing debt, seemed to tamper with the central tenet of creditor-debtor relations. In January 1936, Wilson used the bank's annual meeting to transmit his alarm: "Almost all the important relationships in life are based on the sanctity of contracts." Aberhart seemed oblivious to this.

In the face of Aberhart's threats, the banks sensed that they had an ally in Ottawa; they could find protection in the federal government's clearly defined monopoly over national banking. Ottawa could simply knock down Aberhart's acts by disallowing them. Not yet, cautioned the banks' Edmonton legal advisor, H. R. Milner. Disallowance would "be playing into Aberhart's hands. It would give him a grievance and spread the present insanity."[76] Instead, the banks decided to fight fire with fire.

From the outset, the banks had greatly underestimated Aberhart's psychic appeal to debt-ridden Albertans. A little common sense, they thought, would make Albertans see the error of their ways. In 1935, the banks had sponsored a special issue of *Saturday Night* on "The Banks and the Average Man." The banking industry's old friend Stephen Leacock then took up the torch. In the fall of 1936, Sydney Dobson of the Royal Bank, soon to be CBA president, secured

# *Next* YEAR'S HOLIDAY

● This can be you a year from now. Impossible? Not at all—if you start saving for it now.

Saving money can be thrilling if you save for such a purpose, and a real holiday is well worth saving for.

## To Help You SAVE

The Family Budget Book, published by The Royal Bank of Canada will help you to save. It contains sample budgets for your guidance, and a section for each month's accounts. Thousands of householders use this handy Budget Book each year. A copy is yours for the asking at your nearest branch.

By the way . . .

A home of your own; a new car; an education for your child—these also are objectives that will give new life to your savings programme, help you in your natural desire to get ahead in the world.

Don't worry if your savings are small. Saving regularly is the important thing.

You will find it's as easy to save as to spend—when you save for a *purpose*.

P.S.—*Don't forget . . . the one who gets the bargains is the one with ready cash.*

## THE **ROYAL BANK** OF CANADA

OVER 600 BRANCHES IN ALL PARTS OF CANADA

*The Depression changed bank advertising. The old ideal of saving remained, but "consumerism" now sometimes became the objective. The 1938 ad above emphasized short-term saving and was designed to counter the notion that bankers were "coldblooded, impersonal 'money-changers'." (Opposite) brochures for the Home Improvement Loan Plan of the late Depression. Note the prominence given to the federal government's guarantee of the plan.*

a princely $10,000 from CBA members to finance a western speaking tour by Leacock. The Port Arthur-to-Victoria tour was arranged at arm's length by the bank's advertising agent, Cockfield Brown, although Leacock must have had no doubt about who was footing the bill. "I spoke," Leacock reported, "on literary, humorous and college stuff, and on Social Credit." In Vancouver, Aberhart actually showed up at one of Leacock's lampoonings.[77]

The CBA complemented Leacock's tour by hiring a publicity director, Vernon Knowles of the *Winnipeg Tribune*, to carry the banks' case to the West. Knowles, in turn, hired a lobbyist in Edmonton to sniff out political intelligence. Later in 1937, Knowles attempted to put "some plain facts" before Albertans in six radio lectures on banking broadcast from Edmonton. James Muir, the Royal Bank's ambitious assistant general manager, was the "star."[78] Eastern wit and preachy broadcasts hardly put a dint in Aberhart's popularity. Social Credit back-benchers continued their pressure for a real assertion of provincial control over the banks. Fearing the worst, the bank began drawing up contingency plans to withdraw from the province. If Aberhart tampered with bank powers, Albertan clients would be served from "shadow branches" in British Columbia and Saskatchewan.[79]

By August, the banks' lobbyist in Edmonton reported that Aberhart was "floundering wildly." His attorney-general had advised him that any action against the banks would be ruled *ultra vires* by the courts. Fearful of losing his credibility, the premier plunged ahead and staged what amounted to a *coup d'état* against the Canadian banking system. The so-called "August Acts" asserted provincial power over bank credit policy, promised Albertans interest-free loans for homes, and set up an Alberta Credit House. The banks were forbidden to challenge the legislation in provincial courts, bank employees would have to be licensed by the province, and, to prevent adverse press comment, press liberty was limited to ensure "accurate news." When the provincial Tory leader portrayed the legislation as an assault on civil rights, he was labelled a "bankers' toady." A libel suit followed. So did Ottawa's massive disallowance of the whole package as *ultra vires*. Canadian banking would not become balkanized like its American counterpart.

Having won his defeat, Aberhart would continue to pound the banks. As the banks' lobbyist reported in 1938, "It now appears that Alberta will, for some time to come, be a hunting ground for every type of political adventurer."[80] But Social Credit reverted to a role of vociferous regional protest, and the nation again turned to Ottawa and the *national* banks for a solution to its economic ills. Neither possessed Aberhart's flair for the dramatic. They did, however, share the belief, vaguely realized by Aberhart and now championed by Keynes and his apostles, that the Depression might be banished by the injection of purchasing power into the economy. The power of money grew with its velocity. If the banks entered the "dirty thirties" trapped in a deflationary role, the creation of a central bank allowed them to entertain ideas of credit expansion at the end of the decade.

At first, the experiments were small and hesitant. R. B. Bennett's ignominious ejection from the prime ministership in late 1935 had left the Mackenzie King Liberals to grapple with the Depression. King applied his usual caution to the situation. He asked Montreal businessman Arthur Purvis to study ways of stimulating employment. Inspired by the American New Deal, Purvis's National Employment Commission suggested that the broadly based construction industry was an ideal candidate for a nudge from the state. Late in 1936, Finance Minister Charles Dunning announced a "home improvement" loans scheme that would allow home owners to borrow up to $2,000 from the banks to renovate their homes. Ottawa guaranteed the loans up to 15 per cent of the aggregate loans made by each bank. The loans could be repaid on instalment, and interest of 6.20 per cent was levied.[81] All the details aside, the home-improvement loans were simply intended to put paycheques in builders' pockets – to boost spending power.

The banks eagerly participated in the home-improvement plan. The plan diminished the bankers' credit risk and brought business to the branches. The CBA worked closely with Ottawa to introduce the loans; in 1938, for instance, the association president Dobson urged member banks to give prominence to the loans in their spring advertising. The Royal Bank quickly became the leading home-improvement lender, with 26 per cent of loans made by the end of 1937. The plan was a great success; by 1940, $50 million had been dispensed under the scheme. It had brought the state and the banks together in an unprecedented manner. The scheme worked because the government shouldered some of the risk involved in lending in hard times, risk the banks alone carried at the decade's outset. It did not, however, revolutionize Canadian banking overnight. Together with the establishment of a central bank, the Canadian financial system was discovering new ways of facilitating economic growth. In 1936-37, for instance, agreements were made with the Alberta and Saskatchewan governments to allow the banks to finance farmers' annual purchase of seed grain under a government guarantee.[82] In themselves, none of these measures would have ended the Depression. They did, however, point to a different future for banking. The outbreak of war would deliver a huge injection of purchasing power into the economy; the banks would help to administer its application. As the war economy began to subside, Ottawa and the banks returned to the banking innovations of the late 1930s – a government-guaranteed farm-improvement loan scheme was introduced. This was banking for a more-complex, precarious national economy. Always a bank undaunted by new frontiers, the Royal Bank had been quick to establish itself on this new frontier of banking, not without initial hesitancy but ultimately reconciling itself to change in the spirit of Edson Pease.

In May 1941, John Maynard Keynes quietly slipped into wartime Ottawa. As a consultant to the British Chancellor of the Exchequer and a director of the Bank of England, he had just come from consultations with the U.S. Federal Reserve. Now he wanted to see Graham Towers at the Bank of Canada, but he did not want the Americans to learn of his visit. Knowing this, Towers proposed a private dinner party to fill their evening. It would be a surprise birthday present for Randolph Noble, Keynes's ardent Montreal admirer, who now found himself on leave from the Royal Bank as Sugar Administrator in the wartime bureaucracy.[83] We can only speculate what else they celebrated that evening.

# 1939-1949

# Banking for Victory and Peace

## "Our Patriotic Duty"

MORE THAN ANYBODY ELSE IN THE BANK, HENRY GAGNON KNEW THAT WAR was inevitable. Even before he arrived as the bank's Paris manager early in 1939, there were worrisome signals. The 1938 inspection report had noted that "local conditions" around the rue Scribe office were "unsatisfactory, principally it would seem because of lack of confidence in the present Government, fear of strikes and the general political situation in Europe."[1] Gagnon needed no reminding that Europe was in turmoil: he had just spent three years as the Royal Bank manager in war-torn Barcelona.

When the Spanish Civil War erupted in 1936, Gagnon and his assistant manager were the only "British" bank employees to remain at their posts; the rest were hastily withdrawn. For thirty months, they endured the siege of Barcelona, as General Franco's forces – with German aid – pummelled the city. Gagnon endeavoured to pursue a policy of "neutrality," but his car was none the less commandeered and he was periodically taken in for interrogation. Because the Loyalists who controlled the city lacked air defences, Barcelona was subjected to merciless bombing raids. On one day, Gagnon recalled, eighty bombs fell within five hundred metres of the bank. Employees at the bank's New York and London offices passed the hat and arranged for a food hamper to be smuggled into the beleaguered Spanish branch at Christmas, 1938.[2] At the bank's annual meeting in 1938, Gagnon became the first staffer ever to be commended by name – "exhibited a rare sense of responsibility to the Bank" – before the shareholders. In January 1939, Franco took the city, and Gagnon left for Paris: two years later the Royal Bank sold its Spanish operation to Banco de Aragon.

Paris was meant to be a reward for Gagnon. Born at Arichat, Cape Breton, he was the bank's senior francophone. Since joining in 1910, Gagnon had been posted to places where his language skills mattered: rue St. Denis in Montreal, sunny Martinique, and now Paris. Paris was unique among the bank's international operations, a legally separate subsidiary, with its own board and considerable autonomy for its manager. The mainstays of its business were trade finance to the French West Indies and middle-European finance. Both were threatened by war; furthermore, the frozen German loans of the 1920s still hung over the branch.

Across the Channel, Gagnon's counterpart at London branch had less to worry about. As late as September 1, 1939, Blake McInerney blithely reported to head office that a "way out will be found."[3] Spain had taught Gagnon to be less sanguine. He despatched securities in the branch's safekeeping to Cognac in southern France and settled into an uneasy watch over the "phoney war." By late September, McInerney in London was bomb-proofing his windows and duplicating his records.

Late in May of the next spring, the tension broke. As the German *blitzkrieg* raced across the North European plain, Gagnon reported "exceptional withdrawals." By June 10, the Germans were just twenty-five kilometres outside Paris, and Parisians began a hasty exodus southward. Gagnon was ready. Several weeks before, he had bought a truck and parked it behind the branch. At nine that evening, he loaded the signature-verification cards, cash, and negotiable securities into his car and joined the slow crawl out of Paris. At four the next morning, the truck, loaded with branch records, and two cars crammed with the branch staff and their families, departed. On June 13, The Royal Bank of Canada (France) reopened in a small house in Jarezac outside Cognac. The Germans kept coming. A day later, the German regional commandant, General von Falkenhausen, exercised his new-found authority over France by issuing a decree placing all foreign-exchange transactions under his control and embargoing all safety-deposit boxes. Head office cabled Gagnon, telling him to close the bank and escape. Without a foothold in France, Gagnon feared the bank would have no post-war prospects on the Continent. Disobeying his orders, Gagnon signed over corporate control of the bank to the French nationals on his staff and fled across the Channel. On the morning of June 24, the staff awoke to find German tanks on the lawn outside their temporary branch. Their crews wanted accommodation. "They were all exceedingly polite, gentle and correct....They did not ask much, only a dining room and some bedrooms for their officers."[4]

A week later, the Germans ordered all foreign banks back to Paris.

Led to believe that the bank still had access to foreign exchange, von Falkenhausen allowed the Royal Bank to reopen behind enemy lines. "Les canadiens sont malins," he is said to have muttered. "Would he not be a German," the *pro tem* manager reported, "you would say that he is a gentleman."[5] But there was no foreign exchange – the bank closed its Martinique and Guadeloupe branches in 1940 – and the Paris branch went into an unprofitable hibernation for the rest of the war. Montreal wrote the Paris operation off its books. Despite his insubordination, Gagnon returned to a more tranquil assignment in Canada, managing the main branch in Sherbrooke, Quebec. Thanks to his initiative, he told his superiors, Paris would be there for the bank when the war ended. The Royal Bank in Paris would live out the war in a kind of profitless limbo, tolerated by the Nazis but cut off from head office and the normal arteries of international finance.

Towards war's end, in August 1944, as the Allied armies recaptured France, W. H. Hayne, a young Royal Banker serving in the RCAF, found himself on the outskirts of liberated Paris. He commandeered an army jeep and headed for rue Scribe. Rifle in hand, he bounded up the stairs to confront a startled receptionist and ask if the manager was in? The manager dutifully surrendered four years of balance sheets and made one emphatic request: coffee. Hayne returned to London, from whence a generous supply of coffee and a crate of accumulated circular letters were despatched to a rejuvenated Paris branch.[6]

The headlong retreat and subsequent return to Paris provides an apt metaphor for the Royal Bank's overall experience in the Second World War – initial shock, followed by adept adjustment, eventual consolidation, and post-war growth. The bank's international system was the first to feel the full brunt of the war; the impact was immediately evident, as trade, foreign exchange, and even physical safety were jeopardized. With its strong concentration on the Caribbean and Latin America, the bank's international system was vulnerable to any disruption in transatlantic commerce. The London, New York, Paris, and Barcelona offices had all been established to service the European and American ends of a lucrative trade in southern commodities and the return trade in finished goods, but after 1939, a variety of factors – U-boats, exchange controls, and American neutrality – sliced deeply into these arteries of trade and finance. "Since the outbreak of war," the supervisor in Trinidad typically complained of Martinique and Guadeloupe, "the situation has been complicated by the various exchange regulations and their interpretation often changing from day to day in these Islands."[7] The pattern was general. The first years of the war witnessed dislocation of trade already laid low by the Depression. Cut off from French, German, and other European markets, many of the Caribbean islands that the bank served languished.

Only the British West Indies initially prospered. Brought under the umbrella of British emergency-powers legislation, the British colonies found an assured and controlled market for their staples – sugar, cocoa, petroleum, and tobacco. Caribbean coconuts, for instance, found a ready demand as an edible-oil substitute for butter. In some ways, life in the British West Indies maintained its sunny gentility. The bank's chairman, Herbert Holt, still wintered in the Bahamas, near Harry Oakes, the gold millionaire. Both banked at Nassau branch; neither outlived the war. Holt died in Montreal in September 1941. Despite fulsome eulogies, he quickly slipped out of the bank's corporate culture. Oakes died in a grisly, unsolved murder in 1943. Nassau branch had an even-more-famous client, the Duke of Windsor. Appointed as governor of the colony as a kind of princely exile from wartime England, the Duke found Nassau branch's connection with the bank's New York agency ideally suited to his personal finances. He also found the branch assistant manager, Paul Potter, ideally suited as a golf partner. When he departed in 1945, he saluted the bank's "efficient and courteous" service.[8]

America's entry into the war in 1941 galvanized the economies of the Caribbean and Latin America and in turn revived the bank's international system. Nowhere was the turnaround more evident than in Cuba. Sugar led the way. In 1944, Cuba harvested its largest crop in fifteen years – 4.25 million tons. So great was the demand that the sugar quota system, imposed in the Depression to control production in a shrinking market, was abandoned. Tobacco and iron-ore mining also responded to American demand. Economic vitality promoted political stability and, in 1944, Cubans re-elected Grau San Martín as their president. San Martín had been ejected from office in a 1934 army *coup* led by Fulgencio Batista, who quickly set himself up as Cuba's kingmaker. A decade later, Batista promised Cubans an "honest election," and they took the opportunity to show their displeasure at the country's rampant corruption and to bring back San Martín. Although now reduced to seventeen Cuban branches, the Royal Bank both shared and promoted Cuba's prosperity. Long-time clients like Bacardi and Sun Life relied heavily on the bank. New clients, such as the Cuban department of public works and the Quartermaster General, looked to the Canadian bank for financing as San Martín pushed to modernize Cuba; the Cuban branches boasted large cash balances. Above all else, Cuban prosperity finally allowed the bank to liquidate some of the notorious "sugar estate" accounts that had weighed it down since the 1920s. As sugar recuperated, bankrupt sugar plantations could pay down their debt, and the bank in turn could free itself from the onerous task of operating them. In 1948, the largest plantation, the Antilla, was sold, and the sombre atmosphere of the international credit department at head office temporarily gave way to an impromptu celebration.[9]

Latin America also succumbed to the magnetic pull of America's war economy. The bank's operations in Argentina, Brazil, and Peru flourished through most of the decade. Clients such as W. R. Grace, the American trading conglomerate that dominated the economy of South America's west coast, drew on the bank's traditional strength in trade financing; elsewhere the bank financed industrial development. In Brazil, for instance, trade finance was provided for exports of coffee, cotton, and rubber, but industrial loans were also furnished to Brazilian industrialists like the Matarazzo family of São Paulo and to foreign enterprises like Esso and Ford do Brasil.

Canadian trade to the southern hemisphere trailed along in the slipstream of America's growing importance – during the war, Canada established embassies in Brazil, Chile, and Argentina. For the bank, however, the overall effect of the war was to accentuate the importance of its New York agency as the fulcrum of its international system. With London trapped under a blanket of war regulation, New York prospered. Despite the fact that American law barred it from taking direct deposits, the bank's William Street office gained immense stature, because it positioned the bank on the doorstep of the New York money market and ensured access to global trade and corporate accounts. The bank retained many of its oldest American accounts, like that of Sosthenes Behn, now chairman of ITT, but it also acquired a stable of prestigious new clients like Sun Oil of Philadelphia. Later, in 1951, to capitalize on its enhanced position, the bank would establish a trust-company affiliate in New York. The RBC Trust Company would enable the bank to act as registrar and paying agent for corporate and governmental clients issuing bonds on the New York market.[10]

The American shadow fell even over the bank's more northern operations. The construction of American military bases in Newfoundland drew the Royal Bank deeper into the colony: branches were opened in Goose Bay, Stephenville, Gander, and Argentia. Similarly, a branch was established at Montreal's Dorval airport to service the crews ferrying newly made Canadian and American aircraft to the European theatre of war. Across the Atlantic, London remained the bank's crucial beachhead in Europe. The West End branch in London found itself across the street from the Canadian Army Headquarters, and it soon became a hub of activity for Canadians overseas. The bank captured a large portion of the Canadian servicemen's accounts, thereby creating a huge cash flow. While there was little scope for lending, and many European accounts were embargoed by the Custodian of Enemy Property, London branch did see its deposits grow handsomely during the war. Miraculously, it also escaped serious bomb damage. At the height of the Blitz in late 1940, the London assistant manager reported, with bankerly aplomb, that the constant rain of bombs around the branch "was rather trying to one's nerves."[11]

The Royal Bank in London thus emerged from the war unbombed and well-positioned for the bank's post-war European strategy. For instance, former Prime Minister Bennett, now retired in England as Viscount Bennett, rejoined the bank's board and headed its London committee. But senior men at head office, particularly the aggressive new general manager, James Muir, knew instinctively that New York would be the real magnet of post-war finance for Canadian banks. "Personally," Muir confided in the London manager some years later. "I have lost neither love nor loyalty for the old kingdom but I do think I see its plight rather more clearly than those who live too close to the forest."[12]

But for all its drama, the dislocation and reorientation of the international system paled beside the fundamental and lasting changes wrought in banking on the home front. The war economy yanked Canada out of its persistent slump. Mindful of the experience of the First World War, Finance Minister J. L. Ilsley, Bank of Canada Governor Graham Towers, and the bank general managers came together in a cooperative triad to finance the war economy and to control inflation, consumption, and foreign exchange. "I think," said Deputy Minister of Finance W. C. Clark, during the 1944 Bank Act revision, "you are talking about a system that is entirely different from the system that exists today...a system in which there was no central bank."[13] Retail banking snapped out of its Depression lethargy under the stimulus of an unprecedented volume of transactions: victory loans, ration coupons, and burgeoning national savings filled the teller's day with activity. From the end of 1940 to the end of 1945, the assets of all Canadian banks ballooned from $3.73 billion to $7.79 billion; of this the Royal Bank saw its share more than double, from $955 million to just over two billion.[14]

Once victory was in sight, politicians and bankers turned their attention to the building of bridges to post-war prosperity: farmers and urban consumers were given good reason to support their post-war dreams with bank credit. War production had given Canada a solid new base of industrial strength; it also gave the banks the kind of dynamic corporate clients they had so lacked in the Depression.

In 1918, the bank had greeted the coming of peace with exuberant expansion. The early 1920s had exposed the naïveté of this optimism:

the war's legacy of inflation, social unrest, and depressed trade under-
cut its chances of success. In 1945, the optimism was more realisti-
cally rooted in Ottawa's determination to ensure post-war growth in
prosperity and employment. In the First World War, Canadians *hoped*
for a prosperous peace; in the Second World War they *prepared* for it.
The preparations began almost as soon as did the war itself.

In 1914, only crude mechanisms existed to control the creation of
credit for the war effort – the minister of finance, informally supported
by the general managers of the chartered banks, tinkered his way
through the conflict. The 1914 Finance Act, for instance, furnished
the banks with "excess circulation" to feed the economy. In 1939, the
challenge was far more complex, but the resources at the nation's
disposal were also somewhat more versatile. From the outset, Ottawa
fixed on three goals: to finance war expenditures, to restrict civilian
demand for goods and services, and to ensure that the economic
burden of the war fell equitably on all Canadians.[15]

In August 1914, the finance minister had hurriedly assembled the
bank general managers in Ottawa for a mixture of advice and compulsion. The war was subsequently financed on a basis of institutionalized *ad hocery*. In 1939, there was a much surer sense of the way
ahead. The Depression had produced a central bank, which provided
a convenient spigot for the flow of credit. Inflation and the application
of credit could thus be controlled. Almost instantly, a literature on war
finance sprung up, furnished by academics eager to supply the
"lessons" of the First World War.[16] Similarly, the banks were ready
participants in this technocratic response to the challenge of managing the war economy. There was clear understanding of the danger
of succumbing to the temptation of letting inflation finance the war –
the strikes and social turmoil of 1919 had underlined the folly of this
option. The banks thus became willing participants in the system of
controls that Ottawa stretched over the economy. Bankers reported for
duty in the wartime bureaucracy. Donald Gordon, for instance, trained
at the Bank of Nova Scotia, headed the Wartime Prices and Trade
Board. Those who remained in the branches carried memories of First
World War rationing and Victory Bond drives as blueprints for
controlling expenditure and capturing savings. Exchange controls also
resurfaced. The banks thus did not scramble to war in 1939 as they
had done a generation before; they marched to war in an orderly
column.

Like the war itself, there was a brief, initial phoney war on the
financial front. The industrial slack of the Depression economy
provided room for the first throes of war production. Unsure of the
ultimate costs of the war, Ottawa turned initially to the banks for

short-term financing, borrowing $200 million from the banks early in 1940, of which the Royal Bank took almost a quarter. By the time Allied troops fled Dunkirk and Henry Gagnon fled Paris, however, Ottawa was quickly readjusting its fiscal sights on long-term borrowing from Canadians at large. From 1939 to 1946, Canadians devoured two war loans and nine victory loans, furnishing Ottawa with $14.9 billion. While the banks continued to supply some short-term credit, the general public provided Ottawa with 85 per cent of its wartime borrowing. The banks indirectly encouraged and benefited from this immense transfer – by acting as vigorous salesmen for war bonds. If clients initially drained their savings to purchase the bonds, the money soon returned as coupon interest or as government spending. Consequently, the number of savings accounts – a record 1,450,000 for the Royal by 1944 – grew dramatically and government securities became the largest component of a bank's asset base, larger than its loans portfolio.

Through all of this, the Bank of Canada acted as orchestra leader, with Graham Towers meeting regularly with the bank general managers, much as Finance Minister White had done in the last war. The difference was that Towers now controlled the note issue of the nation (the last Royal Bank notes were issued in 1943*) and could, through open-market operations, influence the supply of money to the economy. Towers was thus in a position to guide the chartered banks informally into cooperation with the war effort. From Towers, the banks learned everything, from what Ottawa's borrowing intentions were to what their commission for selling war bonds would be. Towers even wandered into non-financial domains, urging the banks to close unprofitable branches to conserve national manpower.[17]

Ottawa and the banks acted as partners in other respects. Canada's trading economy depended vitally on ample and liquid foreign exchange. Any shortage or misappropriation of exchange might hinder Canada's ability to interact with the British and American war economies. In September 1939, Ottawa therefore established the Foreign Exchange Control Board, under the ubiquitous Towers. Its primary mission was to conserve Canadian holdings of precious American dollars. To do this, the U.S. dollar was pegged at a ten-cent premium on the Canadian, and the branch system, with its unified central control and uniform procedures, was employed to enforce

---

* In January 1943, the Royal Bank issued the last commercial banknotes in Canada. The batch of $5 bills was inadvertently released, contrary to the banks' agreement with the Bank of Canada, and were hurriedly recalled. Some fell into collectors' hands. Pre-1943 bills are still occasionally presented at the bank and are promptly exchanged for Bank of Canada notes.

currency control. Rigorous prohibitions and exemptions were established, backed up by paperwork procedures for every branch transaction. Before Pearl Harbor, the Royal Bank even tried to draw American exchange to Canada by advertising for American tourists – "As One Good Neighbour to Another."

The centralized character of Canadian banking also made it a natural mechanism through which to administer wartime rationing. Ottawa had created the Wartime Prices and Trade Board to control consumption of goods as varied as butter and rubber tires, and Canada was soon awash with ration coupons, which were not only spent but had to be collated and redeemed by merchants. To alleviate the chaos created by the millions of these coupons, Ottawa and the banks introduced "coupon banking" in March 1943. In effect, the coupons became a kind of surrogate currency, and merchants were permitted to establish accounts at banks, where coupons could accumulate. Eventually, consolidated vouchers would be issued, allowing the merchant to reorder new stocks of the rationed commodity. The banks received a small commission for each coupon account. By the spring of 1944, Royal branches were taking in four hundred million coupons annually, resulting in one and a half million ration-account entries a year.[18]

Just as the war changed Canadian banking, it also changed how the banks were staffed. With the news of conflict in Europe, Canadian "bank boys" once again abandoned their cages and rallied to the colours. By 1945, 2,321 bank employees had enlisted; 193 never returned. Head office did not resist the call; if Canadian banking was anything, it was still Anglo to its core. Within weeks of the outbreak of war, the board approved a policy granting a leave of absence to any employee enlisting for military service. Soldier bankers would get a month's salary on enlistment and their pension and life-insurance benefits would be kept up by the bank.[19] Once the grim news of the spring of 1940 – Dunkirk and the fall of Paris – made it apparent that this was to be no brief skirmish, the board agreed to supplement bankers' military pay to a level of 75 per cent of their peacetime pay, for married men, and 66 ⅔ per cent for single men.[20] Implicit in all these arrangements was the guarantee that a bank job awaited all "warrior bankers" when Hitler was beaten.[21] One aspect of the old paternalism did end. As the cost of war grew and Ottawa hiked taxes, the board voted in 1941 to stop paying employees' income tax, a once relatively inexpensive benefit that had been instituted in the First World War.[22]

Almost overnight, the *Royal Bank Magazine* was overflowing with news of warrior bankers. The air force was the bankers' service of preference – 46 per cent chose it. Unlike the army and navy, the air force demanded high-school matriculation; so did the banks. One suspects that air-force recruiters snapped up young bankers because they were proven organization men. They were also good with figures and calculations, excellent material for a service that demanded precision and small-unit teamwork. From the bankers' perspective, the air force offered the glamour of being part of the élite. Again, one suspects that aviation allowed young bankers to live out the Walter Mitty side of their personalities – the routine of banking was supplanted by the adventure of flying. Certainly, the bank magazine soon began overflowing with "before" and "after" photos of young tellers transformed by the dashing garb of pilots – goggles pushed back on the forehead, gaze fixed on the wild blue yonder. And Royal Bankers excelled in the air. Jack Boyle, a junior from Spadina and College in Toronto, won a Distinguished Flying Cross for downing seven German aircraft. On Christmas Day, 1944, he became the first Spitfire pilot to down a German jet, an Me 262. Other bankers were miraculously lucky. Bob Utting, a Niagara Falls junior, walked away from the spectacular crash of his Marauder bomber on Ascension Island. Both Utting and Boyle returned to banking after the war.

Back on the home front, bank management was fighting its own battle to maintain staff levels in the branches. During the Depression, the bank had allowed its staff level to dwindle, not through lay-offs, but through attrition. In 1933, salaries had been cut by 5 per cent.

*Three banker pilots: R. G. C. Pagett (left) of Bahamas branch joined the RAF, while G. C. Stalker and T. W. Trewin (opposite, left and right respectively) of Winnipeg joined the Canadian Air Force. Trewin died over Germany in 1945.*

*In 1939, Jack Boyle was a junior at Toronto's Spadina and College branch. By 1944, he was an allied ace, the first Spitfire pilot to down a German jet.*

As branches, particularly in the West, were closed, redundant staff was brought into regional offices such as Vancouver, where work was found for them. Very few were let go, mostly out of loyalty and the fear that they might sign on with competing banks.[23] In 1939, therefore, there was a small cushion of surplus staff. If banking was to play its crucial role in regulating the war economy, service had to be maintained. As this feedstock of young male bankers quickly dried up, retired managers were brought back into service. More branches were closed: 639 Canadian branches in 1939 became 592 by 1945. In the words of the *Canadian Banker*, "the staff situation was the No.1 bank headache." Unlike their behaviour in the previous war, however, the banks did not try to plead for special privilege in Ottawa in hopes of retaining their male work-force. Instead, they looked without hesitation to women. It was apparent that the bulk of wartime banking would entail mountains of routine work – processing war loans, ration coupons, passbook entries – "and so, to the high schools the banker went for routine recruits." The war thus permanently changed the face of banking by feminizing its daily life. As the men went off to war, the "girls" moved out of their traditional, immured roles in banking – as stenographers and behind-the-scenes clerks – and into the front line

*The Hastings and Homer branch staff picnic in Vancouver, 1940*

of branch work. "It was the young woman, thus recruited, who saved the situation. A mere bobby-socker, she traded her stool at the soda fountain for one in the bank."[24]

Women had an immense impact on the bank. In 1939, they made up only 21 per cent of the bank's staff; by 1945 they represented 71 per cent, and that level held steady in the post-war era. Women enlivened life in the bank. The bank magazine was no longer monopolized by pictures of all-male dinners and sports tourneys; pictures of mixed staff picnics, where the men actually removed their ties and laughed for the camera, began to materialize. Women finally began to figure in the bank's advertising; the "girl" behind the wicket soon came to dominate the image of service projected. During the war, bank women tended to be cast in the role of patriotic citizens doing their bit on the home front while the men were away. As peace became likely, patriotism was superseded by a ready acknowledgement in the bank's magazine that women had "special" talents as bankers: they were "alert, polite, tactful, understanding...calm and unruffled." Viewed from today's perspective, women in the bank fell victim to stereotyping. "She is our Filing Clerk," one male banker informed the magazine in 1943, "and she sure knows how to file (her nails)."[25] The *Canadian Banker*, the voice of professional banking, was less flippant. "The intensive training of the past few years has made them a valuable asset," it noted shortly after the war, "and women have by their wartime performance established for themselves a permanent place in banking."[26] These mixed attitudes would persist, and would govern women's place in the world of post-war banking.[27]

Despite their growing numbers and accomplishment behind the wicket, women still found themselves in a segregated workplace. On the staff ledgers, they were entered as "temporary" employees. The cards also recorded their fathers' names and occupations. They were predominantly young and single – invariably referred to as "Miss" – although, given the severity of the labour crisis, some married women were hired, usually as older, more-experienced clerks. Women were

*The return of the "girls": Tellers display their tired legs in Montreal main branch, 1944.*

paid the same as the men they replaced: a steno earned $800 annually in 1943, a clerk $600, and a page-girl $600. Salaries for women, however, tended to peak at about $1,350; there was a clear sense that women were not career employees and that only men should be encouraged to aspire to management positions. Marriage still generally meant retirement, although wartime exceptions were made. There was an unspoken expectation that peace would lure most women back to the home, but few at the same time expected banking to ever again be a totally male precinct. Women were not members of the pension scheme; in 1945 the board approved *ex gratia* retiring allowances for women. These were to be "fair and reasonable," but entailed "no contractual obligation."[28]

The influx of female staff also freed the men of the bank for wartime vocations beyond the trenches and cockpits. The bank's pre-war inclination to cooperate with the state as it pioneered a new role in the economy found added impetus in the war. Where Tompkins and Towers had gone in the previous two decades, others now followed. As the challenge of war production reached crisis proportion in 1940, Ottawa looked to the business community to supply the expertise to "get the job done," and bankers, with their financial and managerial skills, were obvious candidates. In May 1940, Prime Minister Mackenzie King briefly toyed with the idea of inviting Royal Bank President Morris Wilson to join his wartime cabinet, but rejected the idea because Wilson had no political experience.[29] Wilson soon found wartime employment elsewhere.

One of Churchill's first acts on assuming the British leadership after the fiasco of Dunkirk was to appoint the feisty and hard-driving Canadian Lord Beaverbrook as his minister of aircraft production. In June 1940, Beaverbrook, a long-time bank client and Maritime-boy-done-well in London, called in turn on the Lunenburg-born Wilson for help in expediting the shipment of North American aircraft to Europe. Wilson had worked with Beaverbrook in the 1930s in trying to refinance the debt-ridden Canadian paper industry. What Beaverbrook needed now was a capable man in still-neutral Washington to chivvy the flow of American planes to British pilots. "He keeps his desk-top clean," the Montreal *Standard* noted of Wilson, "and is not afraid to fill his wastebasket."[30] Wilson approached Canadian Pacific – a company accustomed to dealing with great distances – and, with its assistance, established the Atlantic ferry command – ATFERO. Hundreds of new bombers travelled the resultant air bridge, stopping at Dorval, Goose Bay, and Gander for fuel, meals, and possibly a quick visit to one of the Royal Bank branches opened to serve the air crews. In 1941, ATFERO became the Royal Air Force's Ferry Command.

In the words of the *Financial Post*, Wilson became "a big-time international commuter."[31] Mondays and Tuesdays saw him at his desk in the president's office on St. James Street, then the night train carried him to New York or Washington for the rest of the week. He became one of London's most trusted men in America. When the Packard Motor Company agreed to produce the famous Merlin aero engine, London despatched Wilson on a secret mission to Halifax to collect the blueprints from a British warship. Wilson naïvely brought along his briefcase to receive the plans and was consternated when a two-ton crate was delivered into his safekeeping.[32] In 1941, Wilson became vice-chairman of the British Supply Council in North America and, when its chairman, Montreal businessman Arthur Purvis, died in an air crash, Churchill quickly appointed Wilson to assume the chair; he kept the post until the spring of 1942. In recognition of these services, Wilson was made a Companion of the Order of St. Michael and St. George. At home, he became chancellor of McGill University in 1943, and, as such, he helped to arrange the conferring of joint honorary degrees on Churchill and Roosevelt after the Quebec Conference. More importantly, the chancellorship brought him into frequent contact with the university's principal, Cyril James, an economist charged by Ottawa to start drawing up the plans for Canada's post-war "reconstruction."[33] Amazed at his prodigious drive, friends noted Wilson's efforts, worrying that he was "working himself to death." It was to prove an apt prophecy.

Other Royal Bankers harkened to Ottawa's call. Most prominent among them were S. R. Noble and C. C. Pineo, both seasoned international bankers. With his experience in the bank's Cuban sugar accounts, Ran Noble was a natural appointee as Sugar Administrator in October 1939. Noble also brought his reputation as a free-thinking economist to the assignment. When the head of the Social Credit party claimed that Noble's strict control of sugar production smacked of socialism, a young Tory MP from the West, John Diefenbaker, rose to the sugar administrator's defence in parliamentary committee. Afterwards, Diefenbaker asked the grateful Noble to tell him something of Keynes, whose name he had heard bandied about Ottawa. Not long into his discourse, Noble was amused to discover that Diefenbaker, a prairie lawyer fresh to the Commons, did not realize that Keynes was an economist.[34]

Noble became a quintessential "dollar-a-year man," receiving a token dollar for his services as a businessman-turned-bureaucrat; later Ottawa assignments took him to the Commodity Prices Stabilization Corporation and the Wartime Prices and Trade Board. Noble never returned to the bank; Charles Pineo, Noble's successor as assistant general manager for international banking, never left it. None the less,

*Selling war bonds at Montreal's Stanley Street branch, 1945.*

Pineo lent his tremendous experience in foreign banking to the work of the Canadian Inter-American Association and to the establishment of the Exports Credits Insurance Corporation in 1944. Retiring from the bank in 1945, Pineo moved on to become the first loans director at the International Bank for Reconstruction and Development – today, the World Bank – and later financial advisor to Nelson Rockefeller.

If bankers went to Ottawa to help secure *victory*, they lingered there – as Noble and Pineo illustrated – to prepare the way for *reconstruction*. Hard on the heels of the German menace was the fear that depression might again stalk the land. In 1942, Principal James of McGill had given Ottawa its first glimpse of a planned and prosperous future in a report that advocated government support of key national industries like housing and agriculture. A year later, another McGill academic, Leonard Marsh, presented an even broader blueprint for peacetime "social security." The central thread of both reports was the avoidance of unemployment through the deliberate stimulation of prosperity. Government fiscal and monetary policy should be used to craft prosperity and to

*Red Deer, Alberta, in 1945*

prevent any return to the social calamity of the thirties. "I profoundly disagree with your theory that the rehabilitation of the world can be left to the haggling of the market," Noble wrote to an American friend in 1944, "in other words, to free enterprise."[35]

At first glance, the banks seemed ambivalent about the prospect of reconstruction. Ideologically, they were wary that a controlled economy might represent the Trojan Horse of socialism. Given the CCF's surge in wartime popularity, Wilson seldom let a public opportunity slip by without stressing "the danger of socialism."[36] Such "visionaries" might be "honest and sincere" but their naïve plans would lead to the "complete regimentation of Canada." With the practical implications of the James and Marsh reports, however, the bankers had little quarrel. In the fall of 1943, the Canadian Bankers' Association began to position its members for the dual challenge of the upcoming Bank Act revision, due in 1944, and the broader prospect of reconstruction. A Parliamentary Committee on Reconstruction and Re-establishment had been deliberating for two years, and the banks wanted to be ready with suggestions for "practical bank action" when called upon by Ottawa. Chaired by the Royal Bank's James Muir, the CBA subcommittee focused on specific ways in which banking could stimulate the post-war economy: the financing of rural electrification and small business. Muir quickly concluded that "the banks are in rather a unique position with respect to post-war reconstruction and re-establishment" and were "likely to be interested to some extent at least in almost every phase of post-war reconstruction."[37] The early steps in the direction of stimulating the national economy that were taken in the late Depression – such as Home Improvement Loans – would become bolder as peace neared. At the 1944 annual meeting, Morris Wilson assured shareholders that "we shall consider it our patriotic duty to play our full part in assisting business generally in becoming re-established."

Given the urgency of post-war planning, there was common agreement that the revision of the Bank Act could not be postponed as it had been in the Depression. Ottawa and the banks both recognized that there could be no repetition of the Depression's strangulation of short and medium credit to Canada's farmers, small businessmen, and consumers. Given stable and affordable access to credit, farmers would mechanize their farms, business would retool for peace, and consumers would indulge their pent-up dreams of the "good life." There were solid political reasons for what Muir of the Royal Bank called a policy of "graceful acquiescence" in the face of the government's plans for an activist peace.[38] The banks' public credibility was still bruised from the Depression. While Finance Minister J. L. Ilsley was quick to praise the banks' wartime record and their instinct for self-regulation, others carried forward different memories of the

*As chancellor of McGill, Morris Wilson (standing on right) oversaw the granting of honorary degrees to Churchill and Roosevelt (seated middle) in 1944.*

Depression. The leader of the CCF, M. J. Coldwell, pushed for bank nationalization, arguing that the creation of national credit should not be left in the hands of "irresponsible boards of directors." From the other end of the ideological spectrum, Social Credit arrived at the same conclusion. Both zeroed in on the banks' inner reserves, which they portrayed as a means of secreting unseemly wartime profits, thereby shielding them from taxation. Ilsley defended inner reserves as a normal operating procedure, a means of providing for losses. Both the shareholders' auditor and the inspector general of banks had the right to determine whether they were excessive.

Despite such criticism, the 1944 revision provided another timely example of the way in which the Bank Act was aligned with changing Canadian needs.[39] Ilsley described it as "a very serious effort to build up in this country a well-rounded and highly integrated financial structure."[40] The financial reforms of 1944 were designed to offer consumers a menu of financial products appropriate to post-war needs. Most of these emanated from the banks; some, however, were to have an existence of their own. Ottawa thus introduced a kind of pragmatism into the Canadian financial marketplace. This began with the Bank Act itself. In a bid to democratize ownership and control of the banks, the par value of bank shares was reduced from $100 to $10 and the shareholding qualification for directors ($3,000 to $5,000) was lowered by half for up to a quarter of the board. Small investors and directors of small means might now be heard in the "big" banks. Although, in reality, this reform did little to change the boards of most banks, it did help to broaden the base of bank ownership. By 1950, the Royal Bank had more shareholders than any other Canadian bank – 15,642 – and for the first time more shareholders were registered in Montreal and Toronto than in Halifax.

Far more important in the 1944 revision were new provisions for farmers and small borrowers. Section 88, so crucial to Canada's annual cycle of agriculture, was enhanced to allow the giving of credit for the purchase of farm implements, the cost of farm electrification, and general farm improvement. Pledge-taking procedures for collateral were at the same time greatly simplified.[41] In its eagerness to see small consumers partake in the post-war economy, the government proposed that the act be amended to allow the making of hitherto risky small loans under $500. Significantly, this initiative was brought forward by the government and not the banks. Since the late 1930s, consumer loans had been available from some banks, notably the Commerce, but the effective rate of interest on these loans had been as high as 12 per cent. The government had turned a blind eye to this. By 1944, the Royal Bank had 125,000 small loans under $500. General Manager

Sydney Dobson none the less admitted that the Royal Bank had always been "rather fearful" of public criticism of an officially sanctioned higher rate of interest – a suggested 9¾ per cent – that such small and riskier loans would carry. He also felt that there would not be much profit in the business. Instead, Dobson advocated a broad-front lowering in the Bank Act's long-standing 7-per-cent ceiling on lending rates; this would stimulate post-war borrowing. "You give us a rate of 6 per cent," Dobson told the revision committee, and "we can give you this assurance that we, the Royal Bank, will go all out to try to increase the personal loan business."[42] The government did just that, lowering the rate to 6 per cent. The banks were thus brought to the edge of a new frontier: consumer loans. The finance companies still, however, had an advantage in consumer lending, because their rates were completely ungoverned by the Bank Act.

The revised Bank Act was designed to minimize the chance of a sharp contraction in credit when peace came; the whole ethos of post-war planning in the allied democracies was driven, as Noble told a New York friend, by a desire to "save the world from a depression."[43] At the same time, Ottawa was busy building other financial bridges to the post-war period. Remembering the success of Home Improvement Loans, it brought in a Farm Improvement Loans scheme. If Section 88 provided short-term credit, this provided intermediate credit through the banks under a government guarantee. Now a bad crop year would not necessarily trap a farmer in a vicious circle of short-term debt. By 1951, $255.4 million of these loans would be made, some spread over as much as ten years. Similarly, Ottawa struck out on its own in 1944 when it established the Industrial Development Bank as a subsidiary of the Bank of Canada. The IDB was designed to provide capital to small businesses over longer periods than the banks were prepared to offer. As its first president, the IDB was given dollar-a-year man Ran Noble, whose only condition was that the new bank's head office be situated in Montreal, where he had so long worked for the Royal Bank.

In its determination to spread a blanket of available and dependable credit across the land, Ottawa also sponsored the Export Credits Insurance Corporation in 1944 to protect Canada's all-important exporters from the tribulations of trade. Here C. C. Pineo of the Royal lent his advice. And finally, in 1946, loan-guarantee legislation was introduced to allow the banks to finance the business or professional plans of veterans. "Consult your banker would be a good slogan," the bank's *Monthly Letter* advised, "for businessmen, private individuals, and service men."[44]

(continued on p. 308)

# SPREADING THE WORD
## *Royal Bank's* Monthly Letter

CLOSE TO THE HEART OF THE Scottish–Canadian banking tradition one always senses an unwritten code of personal integrity and social responsibility. Bankers were expected to be "pillars of the community." While they have long since ceased holding up their services in moralistic terms – saving as a "virtue" – Canadian bankers have continued to contribute their views to the discussion of public affairs. Although they have focused narrowly on issues which touch on their own self-interest – the Bank Act, the economic management of the nation – they have also found themselves engaged by issues of the broadest social relevance – citizenship and culture. The latter finds no better illustration than the bank's seventy-year commitment to its *Monthly Letter*.

After the First World War, the bank established a Foreign Trade Department under S. R. Noble. To promote trade, Edson Pease advised Noble to start "a monthly commercial letter reviewing trade and business conditions." Noble hired Graham Towers as editor and, in 1920, the first issue appeared. The focus was on economic matters – exports, markets, leading indicators – and the readership (about eight thousand by the early 1940s) was specialized.

In 1940, the bank hired a veteran newsman, Irish-born John Heron, away from the Toronto *Star* as a public-relations advisor, and immediately lent him to Ottawa to assist in war publicity. When Heron returned to head office in 1943, he was button-holed by assistant general manager Muir: "Why in God's name can't we write something that will interest people?" Muir persuaded the board to "humanize" the *Monthly Letter*, to let it address broad social and ethical issues, in a readable format unfettered by any "official" line. Heron got the assignment.

Heron produced the *Monthly Letter* with elegant simplicity. The letter became a four-page essay, unsigned, unillustrated, and devoid of advertising. His themes were simple: "The Public Library," "Growing Old Successfully," or "Conservation of Soil." The prose was beautifully crafted and unpretentious. Produced in both English and French, the letter was on occasion translated into Portuguese and Spanish. It was not sold, but was made available in the branches or upon request.

Success was immediate. By 1949, circulation had reached 150,000 per issue. Head office was inundated with requests for copies from readers as disparate as U.S. congressmen and Argentinean naturalists. Compendiums of Heron's essays were subsequently produced; since its publication in 1950, one of these compendiums, *The Communication of Ideas*, has "sold" 390,000 copies. The letter became arguably the most-read English periodical in Canada. By the 1960s, the press run touched 750,000; one in every thirty-eight Canadians received the letter. It was quoted in *Forbes* and *Business Week*.

*Saturday Night* praised it as a "social document, with never a graph or business forecast, covering a range of interests as wide as life itself." Heron, said the *Star Weekly*, was "the conscience of Canadian public relations."

Heron's only tools were a battered typewriter, a pipe, and a library of over seven thousand books. In 1976, he retired, and his place as the bank's wordsmith was ably taken by Robert Stewart. With a circulation of 350,000, the Letter remains a fixture in every Royal Bank branch and in many a Canadian life. Its abiding popularity, one can speculate, rests on superb writing, clear, concise logic, and its appeal to the positive side of human nature. In a world cluttered by jargon, fads, and loose thinking, it talks plainly of self-knowledge and self-help.

*John Heron at his desk, 1973*

Ottawa kept the banks busy in other ways. Committed to avoiding any repetition of the social agony of the Depression, the federal government began to unfurl the umbrella of the welfare state. Unemployment insurance and family allowances were in place by 1945. For the banks, this meant a monthly surge of cash passing from government to the citizenry, most of which worked its way into the economy through the banks. To handle this dependable business, the bank established a Government Department at Ottawa main branch, where government cheques were "batch processed" in huge volume by code.

Like Ottawa, head office had begun to plot its post-war strategy early in the war. Unlike the 1918 Armistice, when the bank had greeted peace with headlong geographic expansion, this peace required conscious planning. Markets – farmers and consumers, for instance – could be targeted and products could be developed for them. Nobody in senior management in the 1940s used terms such as "corporate strategy," but it was clear that the time-worn geographic, quantitative approach to banking – the simple multiplication of branches offering the same undifferentiated services – would be a poor guide into the post-war world. As early as late 1940, branch mangers were surveyed to discover their views on ways to build up branch business. A symposium was then held, and late in 1941 all managers received a copy of *What Our Branch Managers Say About New Business*. For the first time, Royal Bankers were told that they would actually have to *develop* a client base: "The day of waiting for business to arrive in the bank is nearing an end."[45] Business would come to branches where the staff went out and found it and then retained it with good service. Managers should, for instance, make a point of joining service clubs and dining at local eateries. Tellers should smile at customers, remember their names, and try to ascertain their business needs.

The cities would be the crucial post-war frontier for banking; the war put wages in people's pockets, and it was relatively easy to capture their business. The farmer was a more problematic potential customer. The Depression had not treated farmers kindly, and neither, the farmers believed, had the banks. As peace neared, the bank turned its attention to rebuilding the once-trusting relationship it had had with farmers. The Farm Improvement Loan scheme, with its promise of medium-term credit, aroused hope of new business. As soon as Ottawa approved it, the bank circulated a confidential brochure, *The Bank and Its Farmer Customers*, to managers. Bankers must get out on the farms and build trust by taking an active interest in farmers as businessmen on the land. "Much can be done by such courtesy to overcome an incipient feeling that banks are fair-weather friends of the farmers." To encourage the relationship, the bank began publishing a series of instructional booklets for farmers – *Water Systems for the Farm, Feeding and Better Livestock* – which managers freely distributed.

While the farmer and the urban consumer loomed large in the bank's post-war ambitions, corporate Canada was already much in evidence on the loan books before the peace. The Depression had been a trying time for corporate lending. The growth industries of the twenties – pulp and paper, in particular – had become mired in debt. The bank's energies were thus principally focused on shoring up and reorganizing ailing corporate clients. Some new ground had been won in the Depression: the booming precious-metals industry brought some substantial new clients, such as Jules and Noah Timmins and J. P. Bickell. As reorganized industries rose out of ashes of the early Depression, other clients emerged. E. P. Taylor, a Toronto-lawyer-turned-beer-industry-consolidator, brought the Canadian Breweries account. Sir James Dunn, the tyrannical president of a reorganized Algoma Steel, sought Royal Bank support for his plans to resurrect steel-making in Northern Ontario. It took the pressure-cooker of war production, however, to turn these hesitant beginnings into a solid corporate base.

The war reinvigorated many of the bank's traditional clients. Production reached fever pitch between 1940 and 1943. Base industries responded first; power, food, raw metal, transportation, chemicals, and construction all came alive and began devouring huge amounts of capital. As the appetite for industrial capital swelled, the bank's board meetings, where large loans were approved, became longer and longer. Familiar accounts – Acadia Sugar, National Drug & Chemical, Price Brothers, Shawinigan Water & Power – dramatically increased their borrowing. Whole new areas of borrowing quickly opened up. Since coming to Montreal in 1887, the bank had had a reputation for the aggressive pursuit of corporate clients. The war years proved no exception. When, for instance, the Aluminium Company of Canada embarked on its huge Shipshaw project at Arvida in the Saguenay, it turned to the Royal Bank for credit and foreign-exchange hedges. Similarly, the bank became prominent in backing Canada's fledgling aircraft industry with loans to a long list of producers: Fairchild, Boeing, de Havilland, Federal, Noorduyn, Fleet, and Reliance.

As the country geared up for reconstruction, the bank began to attract corporate accounts well placed to capitalize on the unfolding "baby boom." Companies like H. J. Heinz, Dominion Electrohome, National Grocers, Polymer, Pepsi-Cola, Continental Can, Standard Brands, and Motor Coach Industries all seemed well positioned to serve the technological and consumer cravings of Canadians. Construction companies like that of Fred Mannix in Calgary joined the list. Some of these linkages were undoubtedly enhanced, or possibly inspired, by the bank's extensive exposure in the wartime bureaucracy. Morris Wilson, for instance, would have encountered E. P. Taylor; both had been called by Beaverbrook to serve Britain in Washington. After the war, Taylor returned to the bank with not only his brewery account but also the business of his new holding company, Argus.* Argus would allow Taylor to win control and tap into the profits of post-war growth industries. Thus company names such as Honey Dew, British Columbia Forest Products, and, eventually, Don Mills Developments began to appear for board credit approval.

If names such as Mannix and Taylor indicated that the bank was putting down roots in corporate Calgary and Toronto, there was also no mistaking that Montreal still ruled corporate Canada. Although the bank's board contained broad representation from coast to coast, its dynamic centre was built out of the Montreal-Anglo business community – Harold Crabtree of Howard Smith Paper, William Angus of Canadian Car and Foundry, and Arthur Wood of Sun Life, were but a few of the twelve Montreal directors in 1945. The Montreal connection of the bank was reinforced in many ways. The Royal made generous donations to McGill, where Wilson presided as chancellor, and to the Royal Victoria Hospital. The brightest stars of the city's financial and industrial community – Sir James Dunn, Ward Pitfield, I. W. Killam – were frequently entertained in the bank's executive dining room. To symbolize the bank's pre-eminence in the city, the lantern in the high tower of 360 St. James was replaced in the 1950s by four rooftop spotlights which dramatically pierced Montreal's night sky.

Depression did not return to the land after the war. Nor did the bank falter in its post-war expansion. The problems that Canada had in the late 1940s were the problems of growth; foreign exchange, for instance, had to be conserved, and inflation had to be monitored as demand pushed constantly up against supply. Victory at war and carefully planned reconstruction had opened the door to "baby-boom" prosperity. The bank's annual meeting became a yearly celebration of growth. In 1945, the Royal Bank became the first Canadian bank to post assets of $2 billion; by 1950, assets touched $2.3 billion. Although demand for corporate and commercial loans was strong, overall lending grew less spectacularly. In large measure, this reflected the chartered banks' inability to capitalize on the nation's ballooning consumer debt. These were years in which Canadians learned to indulge their dreams on the "never-never" plan. Yet, it was the finance

---

* Taylor had another connection with the bank. When he was a boy in Ottawa, his father had been manager of the bank's Rideau Street branch.

companies and trust companies that were the principal beneficiaries of this consumerism – the trust companies because they alone had the right to hold residential mortgages and the finance companies because of their proficiency in matching goods to potential buyers. The bank's boast in 1946 that it had placed loans of under $500 in the pockets of over 150,000 Canadians paled beside the advances of the finance companies.[46] The banks remained bashful and inexperienced consumer lenders. There was, however, a silver lining. It was to the banks that the finance companies turned for their initial float of capital. The Royal Bank thus acquired the steady patronage of Household Finance and General Motors Acceptance.

Nothing spoke louder of post-war success than profits, which soared from $3.8 million in 1945 to $11.8 million by 1950. Late in 1945, the $15 million taken from the rest account in the Depression was restored, together with another $5 million for good measure. In 1948, a dollar-a-share dividend was instituted. The return of peace also saw the return of branch expansion. A hundred branches were added up to 1950, many fleshing out the bank's city network. Neither did the bank neglect Canada's new frontiers, opening branches in mining towns like Wawa and Mayo. The drive westwards, which had propelled the bank at the turn of the century, was now superseded by a drive northward, as new minerals sparked Canadian development. Aluminum smelting at Kitimat and uranium at Port Radium would draw bankers further north in the early 1950s. In 1957, the Royal Bank would open Canada's most northern branch – in Frobisher Bay.

Another promising frontier opened for the bank in the late 1940s: oil. In a small way, the Royal Bank had always prided itself on being first in Canada's oilfields. In 1928, a branch had been opened in Turner Valley, where the prospect of plentiful oil had drawn exploration since 1914. Shortly thereafter, the bank began the practice of appointing the president of Imperial Oil in Toronto to its board; Imperial had spearheaded western oil exploration. By 1935, the Royal Bank had 51 per cent of the accounts of the companies listed as active in Alberta oil.[47] Ernie McLean, the bank's Calgary manager, took a crusading role in galvanizing head office to the day-to-day financial needs of the oil patch. As the war invigorated the search for energy, the bank kept a watchful eye on Alberta. McLean toured the United States, trying to lure American investment northward; oil had great foreign-exchange potential. In 1947, Ray Milner, an Edmonton lawyer who had advised the bank during the Social Credit crisis of the 1930s and who was now president of Canadian Western Natural Gas, joined the board.

On February 14, 1947, Imperial's long-held hunch paid off: oil gushed from the ground at Leduc, Alberta. As the media stampeded to the site, Ernie McLean quietly slipped into town – "so as not to alert our competitors" – rented space in the local council chamber, and opened for business on February 15.[48] When the council met, the bank went on a long coffee break. Two years later, further oil branches opened in Redwater and Devon. Oil brought back some of the adventure to western banking: in 1959, for instance, the Royal Bank became the first bank to open in Swan Hills after its truck and trailer managed to race into town first, because the Bank of Commerce rig slid into a ditch on the outskirts of town.*

Oil generated business for the bank in the form of payroll deposits, foreign exchange, and real estate. Back in Calgary, Jack Bankes arrived from the Winnipeg Supervisor's Office to head a business-development office. The hastily transferred Bankes, a bachelor, took a room in the Palliser Hotel, where he soon found himself befriending the army of Texas and Oklahoma oilmen who were scouting out Canada's new oil patch. Although bank-transfer regulations stipulated that bankers could stay only for a few days in hotel accommodation before cheaper housing was located, Bankes lingered on in the Palliser for months, reeling in lucrative accounts.

Financing exploration proved more forbidding. Given the highly speculative nature of oil exploration, it proved difficult to lend on the basis of Section 88 of the Bank Act. Hydrocarbons in the ground were not considered plausible collateral until proven. Companies with functioning wells might pledge these, but junior companies were often refused credit. Not until 1954 was the situation rectified by the inclusion of Section 82 in the act, which allowed hydrocarbons in the ground as collateral.[49] In the interim, Calgary main branch continued to champion oil development, often in the face of indifference from head office. In the early 1950s, Assistant Manager Bankes worked hard to establish the business-development department for oil and gas; two years later this became the bank's Oil and Gas Department. The bank's first oil-production loan, given in 1948, set the precedent for a growing relationship with a succession of colourfully named oil companies: Jupiter, Atlantic, and Pan Western. Frank McMahon, president of Pacific Petroleum, became a prominent client and, later, a director. By the 1950s, the bank would start styling itself the "R-oil Bank" in its western advertisements.

The Leduc gusher provided an apt metaphor for post-war Canada:

---

* Trailer branches became popular in the 1940s and 1950s as a quick means of establishing a branch. Because the Bank Act was construed to mean that a bank branch had to be fixed, and because it was felt that clients wanted some assurance of permanence, the wheels on the trailers were knocked off when the "branch" opened.

*Maritime boys going places: Sydney Dobson at the helm of his beloved yacht.*

careful and exacting preparation had produced prosperity undreamed of a decade earlier. The 1950s would open the floodgates. Prosperity and profits were also fundamentally changing the culture of the bank. The predictable, comfortable world of Canadian banking – still redolent of its nineteenth-century origins – died a slow, dignified death in the two decades after the war. By the 1960s, Canadian banking would face a "culture shock," as it struggled to align not only its products but also its staff with the dramatically altered nature of Canadian society.

Change crept up on the bank in many ways. By the late 1940s, the Royal Bank was no longer a Halifax bank gone national, and the days when Maritime "bank boys" smiled out from tellers' cages from coast to coast were disappearing. Gordon Owen, a West Coast boy who joined the bank in 1922, recalled the staff's consternation when, in 1940, he became the first non-Maritimer to manage the Edmonton branch. Eight years later he compounded his transgression by becoming

313

the first non-Nova Scotian to manage Halifax main branch.[50] None the less, some of the old Halifax mercantile names still appeared on the board – Stairs, Black, and Mackeen. Particularly influential was Halifax lawyer J. McGregor Stewart, whose legal erudition and Maritime reputation would echo through the boardroom from 1931 to 1955. In 1948, J. L. Ilsley, the former federal minister of finance, added to Halifax's lustre on the board, but, by 1950, only four of thirty-three directors were Maritimers.

As Bluenose banking faded, the Royal Bank became more cosmopolitan. Winning post-war business in Toronto and in western cities like Calgary and Vancouver became increasingly important. While the board remained essentially a loans-approval committee, directors were appointed in the expectation that they would drum up regional business. E. P. Taylor's election to the board in 1950, for instance, gave the bank its most powerful ally in Toronto. Similarly, as the names of prominent Jewish Montrealers like Sam and Allan Bronfman and Sam Steinberg began appearing on the loans list, the board reduced its exclusivity. It found an astute Jewish director in Lazarus Phillips, the Bronfmans' legal advisor, who joined in 1954.* There were other forces that could no longer be ignored in Montreal. In 1946, the first French-Canadian director was appointed. Raymond Dupuis, head of the department store Dupuis Frères, was elected, largely at the urging of former Prime Minister Bennett.[51] Soon after, head-office staff members were offered lunchtime lessons in French.[52] But despite these small steps, senior management remained fundamentally Anglo; only in large French-speaking centres like Sherbrooke did francophones dominate branch management. The bank's expansion beyond the St. Lawrence Valley in the 1950s would increase the pressure for change in Quebec.

Language lessons and a broadened board of directors were hardly a revolution, of course. Real change was evident in the rank and file of the bank. The average branch in 1950 looked much different than its 1939 predecessor. After the war, many of the "warrior bankers" had not returned to the bank. Many sensed that the peace offered other avenues of professional advancement. Generous veterans' benefits lured many banker veterans to university and law school. There were also more-generous starting salaries elsewhere in the post-war economy. Those who returned to the bank came with expectations of advancement – a managership or a chance in a new area of banking, like consumer loans. Few wanted to return to the monotony of the

---

* Phillips was in fact the bank's second Jewish director. The first, Sir Mortimer Davis, the flamboyant president of Imperial Tobacco and an important early Montreal client, sat on the board in the early 1920s.

teller's cage. Banking was a changing industry, and males set their sights on its new prizes. At the same time, the post-war economy created a demand for part-time or short-career employment among women of the "affluent society," which retail banking was ready to fill. Here the "girls" thrived. In 1949, the bank magazine reported that all ten cages at Halifax main branch were "manned" by women.

But although women were now in the majority in banking, they remained corralled in tight job compounds. By the late decade, management was beginning to complain about the high turnover of female employees: were women simply treating banking as a way station on the road to marriage or as a means to part-time income or were they conforming to the gender roles imposed on them by males? In banking, as in the rest of Canadian society, women would soon begin asking themselves about the role they played and how they might better assert themselves.

International banking still remained a male bastion; here celibacy and mobility still mattered. In 1950, the new general manager, Ted Atkinson, told the annual meeting that "young men of courage" could still find great opportunity abroad. Many went. Yet, international banking was itself feeling the first stirrings of change. The war had ushered in the post-colonial age, and in many of the areas where the Royal Bank had traditionally prospered abroad the urge for national self-determination had begun to assert itself, usually quickly followed by the idea of financial sovereignty. For the next three decades, the Caribbean and Latin America would be awash with political change, as colony after colony shed its colonial ties – and in some cases its ties with foreign banks. As early as 1939, the Royal Bank had pulled up stakes in Panama after the republic passed legislation requiring banks to make compulsory purchases of state bonds. In 1946, Argentina nationalized its central bank and obliged all banks in the country to act as its agent. This severely crimped the Royal Bank's Argentine operations, but it did not retreat. Four years later, Cuba created a central bank and ceased to accept the American dollar as legal tender. The Royal Bank welcomed this, lending technical advice and, in fact, becoming a part owner in the Banco Nacional de Cuba. Despite these cracks, international banking remained strong; Latin American industry and trade generated good profits, and Caribbean retail banking flourished. By the decade's end, the Royal Bank was still Cuba's largest bank, with annual deposits averaging over $100 million.

The coexistence of prosperity and incipient change in the late 1940s put a premium on leadership. Banking was becoming more competitive in a more lucrative marketplace. While the Canadian financial-services industry continued to be strictly segregated, there were more products for more uses at the disposal of Canadians. As the success of the finance companies in attracting consumer loans had demonstrated, the spoils went to the aggressive or to those who ensured that the Bank Act served their ends best. There was even competition for labour. In the late Depression, a job in a bank was a prize – it represented security and the promise of social and economic advancement. A decade later, it still promised these advantages – but so did other professions. And, as banking diversified, simple on-the-job training was increasingly becoming a less-effective means of grooming and retaining young employees. Everything in the culture of Canadian banking predisposed its leadership to change gradually; everything about the late 1940s indicated that unprecedented rapid change was necessary.

Since 1934, Morris Wilson had navigated the bank through the shoals of depression and war. In war, he lent his prodigious energies to the Allied cause as a "bottleneck buster."[53] In January 1945, the victory won, the sixty-three-year-old Wilson told the shareholders that he had "no fear of the future" – with "imaginative leadership" the country and the bank could prosper. As the bank's first professional-banker president, Wilson was mindful of executive succession and, in the previous December, had shuffled his senior executives. His old friend and fellow-Nova Scotian Sydney Dobson, general manager since 1934, became executive vice-president. The same age as Wilson, Dobson had joined Sydney branch in 1900 and had followed in Wilson's footsteps out of the Maritimes to Montreal, Vancouver, Winnipeg, and back to Montreal, where he had flourished as an assistant general manager since 1922. Sydney Dobson was the epitome of the gentleman banker. Kindly, intelligent, and unflappable, he had carried much of the bank's executive burden while Wilson laboured for Beaverbrook in Washington. Dobson did this out of friendship, not executive ambition; there is little sense that he hankered after the president's office. Age was against him, and his heart was at times closer to the helm of his Nova Scotia yacht than the helm of the bank.

Wilson made two other crucial appointments that December. Sensing Toronto's post-war importance, he despatched Burnham Mitchell there as a resident vice-president. More importantly, Wilson made James Muir, an assistant general manager since 1935, Dobson's successor as general manager. Fifty-four years old, energetic, and relentlessly ambitious, Muir was the epitome of post-war leadership. Wilson hoped a few years as general manager would prepare Jimmy Muir for a smooth presidential succession. Wilson planned to be the first Royal Bank senior executive to die in retirement. His unexpected death in May 1946 – the result of a heart attack – foiled the entire plan.

Dobson reluctantly acceded to the board's request that he assume the bank's presidency; Muir was too untried as general manager to warrant the risk of an accelerated appointment. The press made much of Dobson's ascendancy from a $100-a-year clerkship to the presidency – at $50,000 a year – of the country's largest bank. His love of the sea and his addiction to golf fit him perfectly for the role of Maritime "bank boy" made good. He walked to work and, each summer, motored in the bank limousine to Cape Breton, stopping en route at Royal Bank branches to chat with the staff. It is no cliché to say that he was universally liked by the staff, a modern embodiment of Thomas Kenny's Halifax paternalism. He brought order and competence to the bank, but lacked the drive and vision daily demanded by post-war change. Muir, on the other hand, was thriving as general manager, travelling extensively, winning corporate clients in Toronto, and asserting his views to the board. A Scottish "bank boy" who had emigrated to Canada at twenty after a five-year apprenticeship, Muir burned with Presbyterian zeal for advancement, and Dobson could soon feel Muir's hot breath on his neck. Muir began to insinuate himself into the affairs of the president's office, intercepting junior executives and impressing his growing authority upon them.

Among the many aspects of old-school banking to which Sydney Dobson remained true was the notion, always prevalent in the Royal Bank, that the organization had a duty to bring on young men. Young men brought new ideas and new energy. Although Dobson never relished Jimmy Muir as a friend, he saw in him a powerful force of advancement for the bank. In 1937, for instance, when Dobson, as president of the CBA, had moved to counter Social Credit, it was Muir whom he seconded to go to Edmonton to join the public-relations effort against Premier Aberhart. During the war, Muir represented the bank on the CBA reconstruction committee. He best seemed to understand the new Canada of corporate growth and consumer spending; Dobson felt ill at ease in it. In October 1949, he announced to the board that he was stepping down "to make way for a younger man." The board acknowledged what seemed inevitable: new times required new bankers. Dobson was asked to remain as chairman. James Muir moved into the president's office, and Ted Atkinson became general manager. The age of the stately gentleman banker was fast waning.

Shortly after Muir became president, the board ratified plans for the redecoration of the boardroom at 360 St. James. Wood panelling was refurbished, new leather furniture was bought, and the portraits of past presidents were reframed. A portrait of Jimmy Muir was commissioned and hung. Early in 1952, the new boardroom stood ready. George Goodman, a bank electrician, remembers being called to the president's office days before the reopening. Goodman reported "on the double." Go to the boardroom, Muir told him, and replace all the bulbs in the lights above the presidential portraits with bulbs weaker than the one above his own portrait. "I had to make his picture brighter than S. G. Dobson,"[54] remembers Goodman. For the next decade, Jimmy Muir would shine very brightly.

# 1950-1960

# Jimmy Muir's Royal Bank

## *"The Wave of Optimism"*

HE NEVER EXPECTED TO DIE. IN 1960, DEATH CAUGHT HIM AT THE WHEEL of his Rolls-Royce during a Sunday drive in the Lowlands of Scotland. There, on a low, gorse-covered hill above his native Peebles, Jimmy Muir was carried away by a massive heart attack at the age of sixty-nine. On a nearby hill four years previously, he had been installed as Warden of Neidpath Castle. Before that, in 1952, he had been made a Freeman of the Royal and Ancient Burgh of Peebles. His friend Roy Thomson had called him to the board of Scotland's great newspaper, *The Scotsman.* These honours were but punctuation marks in Muir's annual pilgrimages to his homeland, treks intended to refresh his immense self-regard and indulge a nostalgia for his Scottish roots. Here was a Scottish laddie, "aye guid at tottin' up figures," who had left school at age fifteen, joined a bank, immigrated to Canada in 1912, and now found himself president of Canada's largest bank. The boy who once earned £10 a year as a junior in the Commercial Bank of Scotland now oversaw assets in excess of $4 billion. In Muir, such success bred a sense of invincibility and imperiousness. Few liked him, most respected him. William Zeckendorf, the New York developer who helped Muir conceive Place Ville Marie in Montreal, likened him to the "chieftain of a fighting clan."[1] Even George Goodman, the bank electrician who had indulged the president's boardroom egotism, had to admit that Muir was "a hard, but fair man...he made the bank."[2]

The news of Muir's death caused consternation at 360 St. James. He had interjected his domineering personality into every crevice of the bank's affairs, *except* executive succession. Muir had been congenitally unable to delegate authority. Who would now step into the president's office of a bank that Canadians had come to think of as "Jimmy Muir's bank"? For the time being, however, there were more pressing matters. Muir's body was flown to New York, where the bank's Viscount aircraft picked it up. When the plane was halfway back to Montreal, somebody phoned a bomb threat into the Dorval control tower.[3] Nothing happened; police concluded that it was the work of a crank.

Muir's funeral was a testament to his stature in the Canadian business community. At the Church of St. Andrew and St. Paul, the spiritual bastion of the Montreal business community, the Rev. R. J. Berlis reminded the mourners that there was "no royal road to the Presidency of the Royal Bank, no substitute for determination, ability, and concentration. James Muir was a great Canadian because he deserved to be a great Canadian."[4] Honorary pallbearers included Mayor Sarto Fournier of Montreal, C. D. Howe, "Rip" Powell of Alcan, Donald Gordon of the CNR, and Sydney Dobson, who had outlived the man who had shunted him aside in 1949. Muir was buried high up in Mount Royal cemetery, close to Edson Pease, Herbert Holt, and other luminaries of the bank.

By the 1950s, Scottish "bank boys" had been coming to North America for a century. David Duncan had introduced the species to the Merchants' Bank of Halifax in the 1880s. Many others followed.[5] Even after the Second World War, young Scots were disembarking from liners at Montreal's Victoria Quay, walking the few blocks to the bank's head office on St. James, and reporting for work.[6] The bank usually paid a small salary premium to such Scots: there was the assurance that they were well trained and hungry for advancement. Jimmy Muir fit this tradition exactly, only he elevated it to the level of a cult, and, as with most cults, fact often became distorted by striving ego and nostalgia. Once Muir had occupied the president's office, there was little to moderate his self-made image. An uncritical and overawed press was fed an anecdotal diet of stories by the president himself and his obedient publicists in which Muir was cast as a Scottish Horatio Alger. The shelves of the corporate archives still sag under the weight of volume after leather-bound volume of Muir's press clippings; the same wire-service story was clipped and filed regardless of whether it had already been saved from twenty other papers. If a particularly striking new photo of Muir was received, the president passed it to his secretary after attaching a small note: "Put this in book A2 - *first page*."

Muir's vanity even affected his birth date. He originally told his would-be employers in Glasgow that he was born on November 11,

1890, thereby ensuring his acceptance into a banking system that demanded a Scottish lad be at least sixteen before he took his perch on a clerk's stool. But, as his career blossomed, Muir realized that youth would now serve him better by allowing a later retirement. The birth-date on his Royal Bank personnel card was thus subsequently altered to November 11, 1891 – a handwritten note explained, "Changed on instructions from Mr. Muir." He never spoke in public or in correspondence of his parents, but one can infer that his early surroundings in Peebles were humble. He constantly invoked the image of the "little cottage" of his birth, but provided no details. There was also much talk of his love of reading – biographies – and rugged sports. But it was his acute memory and nimbleness with figures that pointed him towards banking. He later relished telling high-school and university graduating classes that he finished his high-school education at 1 p.m. on July 17, 1907, skipped lunch, presented himself at the Peebles agency of the Commercial Bank of Scotland,* and an hour later found himself on a junior's stool making ledger entries. Within three years, his annual salary had risen to £30 and he determined to take the London road to greater opportunity.

London offered the metropolitan connections that could carry a young man with ambition to foreign success. Muir's initial thoughts turned to the Far East; he joined the Chartered Bank of India, Australia, and China. A chance meeting with a young Canadian in London aroused Muir's interest in Canada and prompted him to pay a call on the newly opened Royal Bank of Canada branch in London. James Mackie, the joint manager, hired Muir – on the condition that he get himself across the ocean. (This was unusual. The bank usually furnished passage for such emigrants.) Late in January 1912, Muir landed in Halifax and headed west. He got off the train in Moose Jaw, Saskatchewan, where he began work as a ledger-keeper at $700 a year.

"I set myself no other goal than hard work," he told a CBC interviewer four decades later.[7] Muir sincerely believed in Canada as a land of opportunity, rich in resources and open to the ambition of immigrants. It would be an attitude ideally suited to the heady expansionist mood of Canada in the fifties.[8] It seemed to Muir that his family motto – "Relentlessly Pursuing" – applied to both himself and his adopted country. Unlike the vast majority of "bank boys," Muir made no effort to enlist in the First World War. The same would be true in the Second World War. When Prime Minister Mackenzie King sought

---

* The Commercial Bank of Scotland trained another young Scottish banker who was later to emigrate to Canada: the poet Robert Service. The bard of Yukon gold, Service joined the Bank of Commerce in Victoria in 1902 and was sent north to Whitehorse.

his services as a "dollar-a-year" man in 1942, Muir responded that he was "not temperamentally suited" to such work.[9] Instead, Muir pursued his banking career.

Four years in Moose Jaw were followed by a year at the crucial Winnipeg Grain Exchange branch, and then a call to head office in Montreal in 1917, a sure sign of preferment. Muir excelled in national credits, and was soon sent out as an inspector. Another stint in Winnipeg led in 1925 to an assistant inspectorship at New York agency. Here Muir formed a lifelong appetite for the city's delights and an abiding sense of its financial importance. Here, too, he befriended another of the bank's inspectors, Graham Towers. In 1926, Muir and Towers gallivanted through Guatemala and El Salvador on a mission to scout out possible new branches. "It is difficult to settle down," Muir complained after the trip with Towers, "when one's mind is filled with visions of 'Thirsty Apfels,' 'Adenoid Aggies,' and 'Fair Evangelinas' [all drinks], to say nothing of the plethora of bananas which surrounded our sleeping quarters."[10] That same year, Muir became marooned at a snow-bound train station in the Andes while inspecting South American branches.[11]

Muir's early career exemplified the mobility demanded of any "bank boy." It also gave evidence of the bank's reputation as a "young man's institution." By 1931, at the age of forty, Muir was general inspector at head office, and four years later he was appointed assistant general manager.[12] Muir won promotion in the face of the Depression – grim banking years – and, given his long familiarity with the West, he was called upon to try to shore up the bank's sagging credibility on the prairies. Here too he perpetuated a Royal Bank tradition: speaking out on public issues. Pease had championed a central bank long before its time. Holt had advocated open immigration in the twenties. Now Muir picked up the traces. Bankers, he told the Advertising Club of Montreal in 1935, were not, as many Canadians in the Depression believed, "a body of men sitting Midas-like upon a hoard of money"; they, instead, rendered Canadians "a devoted, faithful and intelligent service."[13] When "Bible Bill" Aberhart threatened to run roughshod over the banks in Alberta, the Canadian Bankers' Association seconded Muir to Edmonton to participate in six radio broadcasts designed to counter the Social Credit challenge with "plain facts." Compared to Aberhart's flamboyance on the airwaves, Muir's efforts were ineffectual, but the episode did leave him with a vivid awareness that the stuffy ways of established banking offered a poor defence in the age of radio.[14] A few years later, Muir persuaded his colleagues to transform the bank's *Monthly Letter*, as we have seen, from an economic commentary into a renowned public-affairs essay.

Muir was remembered by his colleagues during these years as a man in a hurry. Morris Wilson's elevation to president in 1934 sent the signal that the "bank-boy" meritocracy now extended to the bank's highest office. Holt was the last titular president. Loyalty and ambition could now carry a bank veteran right to the top of the organization. The old chummery of senior management began to be infected by a degree of personal ambition. If the bank was a place in which young men made their mark early, then one had to move quickly and aggressively. By the late 1930s, Muir's experience in inspection had given him an instinctive grasp of retail banking, although, ironically, he had only once been a manager himself – in Winnipeg, from 1928 to 1931. New York and the south had exposed him to international banking. At head office, he had seen the ebb and flow of corporate lending through the national-credits department. Nobody was better positioned to succeed.

A bank's sucess, Muir was convinced, was built on securing as large a base of retail banking as possible and using it aggressively to pursue corporate business. In the Depression, this seemed irrelevant. After the war, it would be a lodestar. Muir never cast a backward glance at the Depression; he seemed to lack the flywheel of Depression-induced conservatism that checked the strategies of many of his fellow bankers. A contemporary remembered his judgement as "so swift and so right as to make unthinking people regard him as somewhat psychic." He possessed "a mind of razor keenness."[15] But there was a mean side to Muir's genius. He jealously kept tabs on his colleagues' perks and rewards. One recalled tears in Muir's eyes when he learned that his annual bonus had been cancelled as a Depression austerity measure and guessed that others had been luckier.[16] His competitiveness was evident in other aspects of his life, as well. Muir took up golf with a vengeance in the 1920s. He won the first tournament he entered, the 1921 Montreal bank championship. He triumphed again in Winnipeg. One has the sense that Muir played golf not because he liked the game, but because he liked the competitive stimulus.

Morris Wilson's frequent wartime absences and Sydney Dobson's reserved approach to post-war banking left the door open for Jimmy Muir. The war represented a vast challenge to the daily working of the bank as a retail system and Muir met the challenge. Of the bank's five assistant general managers, Muir alone had the inside track to post-war growth. Nobody had his finger so firmly on the pulse of retail banking. Even before Wilson's death, Muir was general manager. A director in 1947, a vice-president a year later, and then the only "younger man" Dobson could reluctantly see as his successor in 1949 as president. The change in style that he brought to the office was immediately evident. At the same meeting he assumed the presidency, Muir briefed the board on the bank's progress in retail banking: the Royal Bank had opened more branches since the war than any other Canadian bank. The directors were then told of the need for new corporate accounts of "major importance."[17] Muir led the directors to believe that they *too* were to play a role in bringing in new business. Muir soon began making it a practice at board meetings to thank individual directors for their efforts on behalf of the bank.[18] Within a month of arriving, Muir brought a new activism to the president's office. He *left* Montreal to pay calls on Premier Duplessis of Quebec, Prime Minister St. Laurent, and his old friend Towers at the Bank of Canada. In New York, he appeared at J. P. Morgan, Standard Oil, the National City Bank, and General Motors Acceptance. Back in Montreal, Muir wined and dined the influential – the chairman of Hydro Quebec, the president of Canadair – in the bank's executive dining room.[19] James Muir was introducing a new aggressiveness to the placid world of Canadian banking.

It might be inviting to conclude that the fifties were an easy decade in which to practise banking; Canada boomed. In 1951, there were 13.7 million Canadians; by 1961 there were 18.2 million. The gross national product virtually doubled in the same years, from $21.6 billion to $39.6 billion. Urban sprawl acquired its modern meaning. Montreal remained Canada's largest city, but Toronto was hard on its heels with 1.9 million inhabitants. In cities and in the country, Canadians fell in love with consumer technology: cars, televisions, refrigerators, and hi-fis were the accompaniments of a persistent housing boom. And money – saved and borrowed – set the pulse of the economy. Early in the decade, the Korean War intensified the pressure on the economy. If the previous two decades had seen Canadians trying to stimulate their economy, the fifties saw them grappling with the problems of growth, of directing increasingly scarce capital to where it was most needed, and of waging a constant battle with inflation. Despite all this raw economic energy, the decade demanded new skills from Canada's bankers.

Unlike the Depression, the commercial banks were not alone on the economy's front line. The Bank of Canada now tried to regulate the nation's appetite for credit. Every three months, Graham Towers met with the banks' general managers to exercise his right to "moral suasion" over their affairs. And throughout the decade, that message was usually one of credit restriction. In November 1950, Ted Atkinson of the Royal Bank came to Ottawa to tell Towers that "the wave of optimism" sweeping the Canadian economy was "still fairly high." The governor of the central bank responded that the banks had better cool consumer and commercial demand for credit. Towers would habitually urge the general managers to "weed out some of the less urgent demands on our resources."[20] When James Coyne succeeded Towers as governor in 1955, the message remained unchanged: "a remedy must not be sought in monetary expansion or deficit financing."[21]

In this environment of controlled credit and a surging national economy, banking became more competitive and versatile. The chartered banks found themselves increasingly challenged by other financial intermediaries – trust companies and finance companies – and, in fact, lost ground to them in terms of their assets as a percentage of total gross national product. Within the banking industry, competition intensified. As they had in the boom years at the turn of the century, Canadian bankers scrambled for advantage. Canadians encountered a greater range of bank products. For the first time, the "average" Canadian had *two* bank accounts; the traditional low-interest savings/chequing account was displaced by a separate savings account and a personal chequing account. The concept of service fees appeared, as "user pay" now became the rationale for bank service. Like the trust and finance companies, banks began to offer investors short-term deposit notes. Consumers found that they could turn to the banks for instalment loans, and banks made their first, tentative sortie into the field of home mortgages.[22]

Competition did not come easily to the banks. Despite the relatively smooth and profitable transition from war to peace, there remained a powerful undertow of conservatism flowing from the Depression, a fear of getting caught off-base. None the less, some banks proved more aggressive than others. The Royal Bank, for instance, took an early lead in mortgage financing. Amalgamation once again provided an avenue for growth. In 1955, the Toronto and Dominion banks merged, followed five years later by the marriage of the Imperial and Bank of Commerce. Real growth, however, could only be had by winning business. A bank was only as big as its asset base; deposits were the foundation of that base. The larger the pool of deposits, the greater the possibilities of lending to consumers and corporations. Here lay Jimmy Muir's genius: he galvanized the bank's retail network and drew on its strength in his vigorous pursuit of corporate clients. He told staff that the Royal Bank would be "the bank with a thousand front doors."

Muir was not alone in understanding the changing rules of competitive banking. Other banks, notably the Bank of Nova Scotia, prospered in the fifties; others, such as the Bank of Montreal, lost ground. By decade's end, the Royal Bank was still the country's largest bank, its $4.3 billion in assets representing a quarter of the whole industry's assets. More importantly, Muir had positioned the bank for tremendous future growth. Historians are wont to debate whether the times make the men or men make the times. In Jimmy Muir's case, the times were undeniably propitious, but he pounced on the opportunities they threw up and stretched them to their utmost. On occasion, as his trips to Russia and China would reveal, he could audaciously go against the trends of his times and still win.

At the 1952 annual meeting, Muir told the shareholders that since "its earliest days, the pioneering spirit has been part and parcel of this bank." Throughout the decade, he relentlessly strived to keep that spirit alive on the bank's three crucial frontiers: domestic banking, corporate banking, and international banking. The domestic branch system was the foundation of the bank and, by the 1950s, its "frontier" was in the cities. During Muir's presidency, 237 new branches were added, bringing the Royal Bank domestic network to 917 by 1960. Muir's ambition of "a thousand doors" was not, in fact, reached until 1962. Much of this growth comprised a filling out of the urban market. The crosshatch of suburbia and Canadians' love affair with the car tended to alter the geography of Canadian banking. As Canadian cities

*Moving to the suburbs: A new branch is planned on Ottawa's Riverside Drive.*

had emerged in the first half of the century, banks had hurried to establish themselves at busy downtown intersections. Corners were prized
locations. By the 1950s, Canadians still worked and shopped downtown, but they increasingly lived on the edges of the city and
commuted by car. Downtown banking was easy on foot, but difficult
by car. Parking at a busy intersection was often harrowing; it was much
easier at any of the plazas that were springing up in the suburbs. In
1951, the bank therefore opened its first plaza branch, at Norgate
Shopping Centre in St. Laurent, a satellite city of Montreal. Others
followed: in the Montreal suburbs of Dorval and Anjou, and further
afield at Ottawa Westgate, Greater Hamilton Centre, Vancouver
Oakridge, and Quebec Ste. Foy. In some instances, the bank even
provided financing for the plaza development. Similarly, when bank
director E. P. Taylor conceived and developed the Don Mills area of
Toronto, the bank again provided financing and, in 1954, opened a
branch.[23] In another attempt to capture the car-borne client, "drive-in"
branches were developed.[24]

The Anjou and Ste. Foy plaza branches hinted at another departure
from established practice. For the first time, the bank made a

*The new look of banking: Banking became more accessible and less intimidating in the
fifties. (Above) A plaza branch in Montreal North.*

concerted effort to penetrate the broader Quebec retail-banking market. Since its acquisition of the Quebec Bank in 1917, the Royal Bank had limited its Quebec exposure to the Montreal–Quebec corridor; its clientele tended to be drawn from the Anglo commercial community. Although a base of francophone business had been steadily built up, it had been difficult to counter the competitive advantage of the two Quebec-based francophone banks and the pervasiveness of the *caisse populaire* movement. Wartime production of pulp and paper, aluminum, and hydro power had, however, brought prosperity to many of Quebec's smaller cities. This prosperity finally prompted Montreal-based banks to look to the Quebec hinterland. Royal Bank branches opened in towns like Baie Comeau, Alma, Chibougamau, and Sept-Iles. In 1950, the bank had 90 Quebec branches, the same number it had in 1930; by 1960, it had 128.

Quebec began to impinge on the bank's consciousness in other ways. Competitive service off Montreal Island demanded more French-speaking staff. In an article carried in *Le Soleil* in 1957, Muir noted that the bank had 3,000 employees in the province, of whom 1,400 were francophones.[25] Head office, however, remained an anglophone bastion; Muir spoke no French. Like much of the Anglo business community, he did befriend Quebec's redoubtable Premier Maurice Duplessis. Duplessis saw in Muir a valuable conduit to the kind of financiers and industrialists who, in the 1950s, were so active in integrating the province's resource base into the continental economy. For the bank, this represented a continuation of its longstanding relationship with those in the inner sanctum of Quebec business and politics. Since the turn of the century, the bank had done business with leading Quebec financiers such as the Forget Brothers. Now Quebec was about to change. The base of business would have to broaden. Duplessis's death in 1959 would unleash pressures for change that would swell into the "Quiet Revolution" by the 1960s, Quebec's great leap forward in terms of social and economic modernization. The bank, too, would feel this surge, and would be obliged to acknowledge its pressure: in 1961, the bank's annual report appeared in French for the first time, and in 1968 the bank magazine began appearing in French.

In some respects, Quebec was a banking market like any other. The whole of Canada was responding to the "baby-boom" economy. Growth occasionally hiccuped, but consumer confidence remained buoyant. Depression memories faded. In 1952, the bank upgraded its Economist's Department into an Economic Research Department in an effort to be able to plot and predict economic performance more accurately. Although Muir often poked fun at "the gobbledy-gook of economic forecasting" in public, in private he relied heavily on the advice of the bank's chief economist, Donald Marsh, to gain a sense of the economic outlook. In the fifties, that outlook consistently showed that Canadians were saving, spending, and moving money about in unprecedented amounts. Their financial needs and habits were changing. The traditional low-interest savings/chequing account no longer served the needs of clients who now had varied short, medium, and long-term uses for their money; utility bills had to be paid at the end of the month, the summer vacation had to be saved for, and a new car would be needed next year. The market for bank "products" (the very term seemed alien) was fragmenting and for the first time since mass consumer banking had emerged at the turn of the century the banks felt the pressure to respond.

In 1957, the bank introduced "personal chequing accounts" (PCA). The old savings/chequing account had allowed customers a couple of "free" cheques per month, after which a fee was imposed for additional cheques. Chequing on savings accounts had been a Canadian oddity; even with an 8-cent-per-cheque service charge, the service operated below cost.[26] Personal chequing gave a customer a separate account for chequing, while savings were now segregated in an account that had no chequing privilege. The PCA also introduced most customers to the concept of ongoing "user-pay" service fees. The bank had long had service fees – rental fees on safety-deposit boxes and per-cheque charges for cheques written beyond set limits – but now service charges bore a direct relation to the actual cost of bank service and the burgeoning use of cheques by "average" Canadians. A monthy all-inclusive PCA charge was soon offered to customers.

Personal chequing had several immediate implications for retail banking. First, consumer resistance had to be overcome. The product had to be sold. Consequently, in the fifties, bank advertising became more product-oriented and somewhat more aggressive. It was designed to do "a real selling job."[27] The PCA, for instance, was launched with the "2-Account Plan" campaign. Advertising was accompanied by training sessions to familiarize staff with the new account. Secondly, because other banks were busy entering the same field, an eye had to be kept on the competition. Service charges were market sensitive, so either the quality of delivery or the actual service charge had to be perceived as better than the competition. Advertising of the PCA focused on saving "time, trouble, and expense" in daily banking.[28] A monthly statement replaced the bother of updating a passbook.

Retail banking became attuned to changing consumer needs in other ways. If people were now generally more in a hurry, the banks would oblige them with faster service. The old system of separate "paying" and "receiving" tellers was abandoned. Now a customer could enjoy "one-stop" banking; a single teller accepted deposits, updated passbooks, and dispensed cash. Tellers were also now equipped with coin-counting machines and, especially on paydays, "Fascash," bundles of pre-counted bills. Other services were added: "around the clock banking" came closer to reality in larger centres as night depositories were installed on the outside walls of branches. Behind the scenes, the ballooning volume of transactions was handled by improved daily "proof" procedures. In large branches, designated staff worked on "deferred posting" after business hours; by 1957, for instance, Toronto main branch's eight proofing machines made sixteen thousand postings – verifying, or "posting," the branches' transactions after the day's closing – a day. In Montreal, McGill students worked as bank employees through the night, clearing "that day's harvest of cheques." On average, "the knights of the night" posted one hundred thousand items at a sitting.[29] Microfilming of items "in transit" to other branches was introduced, as was a private teletype circuit between principal branches.

Even bank architecture changed. As banking became more competitive, bankers realized that doing one's weekly banking had to be made a pleasant, as opposed to a necessary, task in customers' minds. New branches were designed to admit more light, tellers' cages were stripped down to ornamental grillwork, and chairs and writing tables were placed for clients' convenience. Older branches were modernized. "What's happened to the Bankers?" asked *Maclean's* in 1955. "Modern bank interiors have changed from gloomy, forbidding places in which employees lurked behind iron bars and frosted-glass barriers," the magazine observed, "to bright cheerful spots where customer and employee face each other across blond maple counters."[30]

Muir knew that the remodelled branches were only as good as the staff in them. "It cannot be denied," he admitted, "that the cold, formal and unimaginative attitude of previous generations of bankers did much to antagonize many people and make most feel ill at ease in their dealings with the banks."[31] He became a stickler for service; Stephen Leacock would not have been rattled in one of Muir's branches. When a ten-year-old girl in Montreal asked if she could have savings account #1 at the bank's new Pointe Claire branch, Muir picked her up in his car, took her to the branch, and personally opened the account for her. On other occasions, Muir was more surreptitious. In the mid-1950s, he hired a young Scottish immigrant reporter in Vancouver, Jack Webster, to snoop around the bank's branches in the B.C. Interior. "I'd ask to see the manager," Webster recalled, "clock the time it took before he saw me and then gauge how

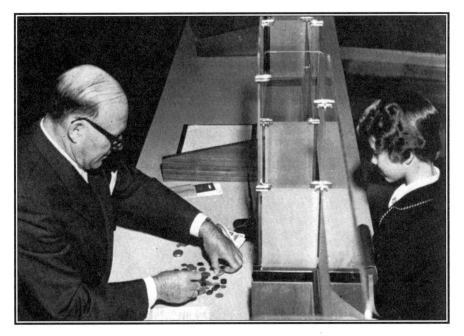

*Serving the client: Muir acts as teller as ten-year-old Nancy Clapham opens a savings account at the Pointe Claire, Quebec, branch. Twenty-five years later, Rowland Frazee, the bank's CEO in the 1980s, would escort Nancy, by then married and still an account-holder, to the branch's anniversary celebrations.*

I was treated."[32] Webster got $50 a day. He reported directly to Muir; nobody at Vancouver regional office was told of the arrangement.

Under Muir's vigilant eye, retail banking grew vigorously throughout the 1950s. The first post-war decade from 1945 to 1955 saw a million new depositors come through the bank's doors. The bank's 2,557,909 accounts in 1955 grew to in excess of three million by 1960. Deposits of $2.3 billion in 1950 were just nudging $4 billion by 1960. Taking deposits was, however, only half of retail banking. In the boom economy of the 1950s, Canadian consumers also had borrowing on their minds, and they did not always think of the banks as their lender of first resort. Other lenders beckoned. The "near banks" – trust and mortgage companies, finance companies, *caisse populaires*, and credit unions – were often better positioned to meet consumer demand. While the Bank Act still constrained banks to a 6 per cent interest ceiling, the "near banks" were free to lend at whatever rate they found remunerative. The banks, therefore, became disinterested lenders whenever the prime rose to levels that denied the banks sufficient "spread" between the actual cost of lending and the 6 per cent ceiling allowed by the Bank Act. The "near banks" simply adjusted

331

their rates upwards. To make matters worse, the banks were the chosen instruments of the Bank of Canada's credit policy. The "near banks" were not. In 1954, for instance, the Bank Act was revised to oblige the banks to keep at least 8 per cent, and, if requested, as much as 12 per cent, of their deposits with the Bank of Canada as a cash reserve. Previously, the required ratio had been 5 per cent, but in practice was held to about 10 per cent. The central bank could now restrict national credit with greater certainty by adjusting the banks' cash-reserve requirement.

Under this regime of interest-rate ceilings, the banks not surprisingly became reluctant lenders. This became particularly evident in the late 1950s when the Bank of Canada boosted the short-term interest rates so that prime went as high as $5\frac{3}{4}$ per cent in an effort to cool inflation. "They had little or no incentive to take risks," one observer of Canadian banking has noted, "nor any immediate incentive to compete vigorously for savings or money market funds, against institutions which could invest in mortgages or make term loans at much higher rates."[33] Beyond legislative constraints, "bankers' preferences"[34] also cramped the banks' lending performance. Because of the First World War, Canadian bankers in effect had been required to reorient their asset base from loans, the backbone of their business in the late-nineteenth century, to more liquid security holdings. The shift was particularly evident in the banks' acquisition of federal government securities during the Second World War. The shift peaked in the late 1940s, but even in the 1951-55 period, securities still represented 37.3 per cent of bank total assets, while loans made in Canada and abroad totalled 38.4 per cent of assets.

The banks' more limited room to lend, together with the legal interest-rate restrictions they faced in consumer lending, opened the way for the "near banks" to fatten themselves on loan expansion. Companies like Household Finance offered small instalment loans to consumers, while captive finance companies like General Motors Acceptance offered credit on the purchase of automobiles. The "near bank" proportion of total assets of the Canadian financial-services industry consequently grew steadily in the post-war economy: in 1945, the banks had 48 per cent of these assets, but by 1968 this would slip to 29 per cent. By 1954, for instance, the banks supplied only 15.6 per cent of Canadian consumer credit; the "near banks," led by the finance companies with 26.1 per cent, and various "point of sale" retail dispensers of credit, such as department stores, purveyed the rest.[35] By the mid-1950s, therefore, the banks were at the point where their ability to grow with the economy was in doubt. Greater legal flexibility, together with innovation in lending and in taking deposits, would be the key to meeting the "near-bank" challenge and to giving the banks a more dynamic place in the national economy.

Part of the very first changes came from the banks themselves, and part came from without. In the late 1950s, for instance, the banks moved aggressively into the short-term money market. Led by the Bank of Nova Scotia, the banks introduced deposit notes for large amounts; these were transferable and paid competitive interest that moved with the prime. Term deposits stimulated term lending, allowing the banks to lend large amounts to individuals over the medium and long term. Similarly, the 1954 Bank Act revision had given the banks the power to make chattel mortgages secured by household property or automobiles. The banks had hitherto only been able to make personal loans on the basis of a personal guarantee. Thus in 1958 the banks – led by the Bank of Nova Scotia's Scotia Plan – began to compete for personal loan business and, through the next decade, would see their share of national consumer credit grow steadily.[36] What had been a 17 per cent share in 1958 became a 38.8 per cent share a decade later.

Personal loans were not the only new lending frontier. In 1954, the Bank Act was amended to remove its age-old injunction against bank lending secured by real estate. The parallel proclamation of the National Housing Act created the means for banks to make mortgage loans. It was not a frontier that bankers crossed eagerly. Over and above the Bank Act prohibition, Canadian banks had always been uneasy about lending on real estate. Mortgages were not very liquid. Property values were mercurial; the disasters that had befallen American banks in the Depression were largely brought on by real-estate loans. From their own experience with Section 88 farm loans that were in default, Canadian bankers knew that they would reap a whirlwind of ill will if they should ever have to foreclose on bad mortgages. As the *Financial Post* suggested, "They might be cast in a Simon Legree role."[37] From a practical angle, they would also have to train staff to administer mortgage lending. Others were less reluctant. Since the middle of the nineteenth century, building societies, insurance, and trust companies had furnished Canadians with mortgages, learning to cover their risk through such practices as maintaining a high equity-to-debt ratio.[38]

Since home-building was a powerful stimulus to a healthy national economy, government had not been shy in facilitating residential finance. As early as 1918, Ottawa had made money available to municipalities to stimulate home construction. In the Depression, Ottawa saw home construction as a way to prime the nation's economic pump and, under the National Housing Acts of 1938 and 1944, offered the banks minority government participation in loans to new home buyers.

In 1945, the Central Mortgage and Housing Corporation was established as a crown corporation to regulate these NHA loans. The "baby-boom" economy stretched this arrangement to the limit.[39] If there was one thing post-war Canadians wanted, it was a house. Since trust and insurance companies could lend only to the extent of their paid-in capital, the housing industry soon found itself knocking its head on the financial ceiling. By the early 1950s, Canada was facing a housing crisis. Despite 106,000 new home starts in 1953, the National Home Builders' Association was lobbying Finance Minister Douglas Abbott to loosen the strictures on mortgage lending.[40] In September 1953, the inspector general of banks reported to Abbott that it appeared "unlikely that existing sources of private mortgage funds will be sufficient to finance a satisfactory volume of new housing building in the future."[41] What followed was a curious role-reversal in the traditional relation of Canadian bankers and politicians.

Up to the 1950s, the legislative structure of Canadian banking had been shaped by a discreetly formed banker-politician consensus. Change took place by mutual consent, along lines usually laid out by the bankers. By the early 1950s, however, Ottawa had grown impatient with the banks' conservatism. The housing crunch had the makings of a political crisis. With a federal election looming, the Liberal government of Louis St. Laurent decided to act. Abbott informed the banks that the National Housing Act (NHA) would be amended to allow mortgage lending by banks. Although he assured the banks that consultation would follow and that there would be "no compulsion," Abbott made it clear to the executive council of the CBA that the goal of broadening the mortgage market was beyond debate.

The bankers initially balked at the government's initiative. Royal general manager Ted Atkinson then took it upon himself as CBA president to turn the tide, pointing out that the move was a *fait accompli*, coming straight from the prime minister's office, and that the banks should therefore turn their energies to obtaining "the most workable arrangements possible."[42] Back in Montreal, Jimmy Muir picked up the message immediately and despatched a promising young assistant general manager, W. Earle McLaughlin, to Ottawa with instructions to master every detail of mortgage financing as the National Housing Act unfolded. McLaughlin was to make himself "Mr. Mortgage," and then return to Montreal in a position to guide the bank in an early sortie into the mortgage field.

Throughout the late fall of 1953 and into the winter, McLaughlin parked himself at the Central Mortgage and Housing Corporation (CMHC) and immersed himself in the intricacies of making the new act "workable." At the same time, another Royal Bank assistant general manager, Charles B. Neapole, took the chair of the CBA's Bank Act revision committee. The bankers had many anxieties. Would mortgage lending leave them short of precious liquidity? How could they avoid the awkwardness of foreclosure? Was there an easy way of taking "vacant possession" of a property in default? The answers to these questions soon came to constitute what the *Financial Post* called "the Big 'If' in Housing for 1954." Bankers, Muir told the *Post*, were "rather notorious for resisting change," but promised that once "the machinery is set up…a useful job can be done."[43] The bankers received assurance from various quarters. "The main job of the Bank of Canada," Graham Towers assured them, "is to see that the chartered banks have enough resources to meet the demands of borrowers including mortgage loans." Existing customers were in no danger of being hurt.[44] By March 1954, the new NHA was law; an amended Bank Act followed in July. Within weeks, the first Royal Bank mortgage advertisements were in the newspapers.

Banks were now "approved lenders" for new homes, and their lending was backed by a CMHC guarantee of payment. Borrowers were obliged to take out CMHC insurance to cover their liability. A ceiling of $5\frac{1}{2}$ per cent (later dropped to $5\frac{1}{4}$ per cent) was set for CMHC-insured mortgages. McLaughlin protested, arguing that, if the prime rate rose, mortgages might become unattractive to banks.[45] Initially, McLaughlin was wrong in his prophecy. The banks were finally part of the fast, expanding mortgage debt market; in 1945, mortgages were only 5 per cent of outstanding primary debt in Canada, but by 1962 they comprised 20 per cent. From nothing in 1953, NHA mortgages rose to 7.2 per cent of Canadian bank assets by 1959. And, thanks to Muir and McLaughlin, the Royal Bank led the pack. Indeed, the Royal Bank went so far as to reduce its mortgage lending rate to 5 per cent, below the required rate. Immediately on returning to Montreal, McLaughlin set up a mortgage school, at which staff from across the country were trained to appraise property and to write up mortgages. McLaughlin then set out on a coast-to-coast briefing tour. The results were soon evident: by 1958, the Royal Bank had 38 per cent of all mortgages held by banks.

But, as McLaughlin had suspected, the new mortgage scheme had an Achilles' heel. Late in the decade, the Bank of Canada began to pursue a tight-money policy, boosting the prime to cool growing inflation. The NHA mortgage rate followed in its wake. In 1959, the federally sanctioned NHA mortgage rate crossed the 6 per cent border beyond which the banks were legally unable to lend. From a 33 per cent share of the NHA mortgage market in 1958, the banks quickly

*(continued on p. 338)*

335

# THE MEN AT THE TOP

OF THE NINE MEN TO OCCUPY THE bank's senior executive office since its federal incorporation in 1869, none has left as rich an anecdotal legacy as James Muir (1949-60). Mention Muir's name to anyone who joined the bank in the fifties, and the phrase "Did you hear the one about...?" soon arises. The anecdotes usually divide between those intended to display Muir's dark side and those intended to bring out his kinder side. When Westmount boys made sport of stealing the bulbs off Muir's outdoor Christmas tree, Muir had an electric trip-wire alarm set up around the tree. On the other hand, when he read in the New York press that the power had been cut off in a slum tenement, he forwarded a cheque for its restoration. Learning that the Russian translator who served him on his 1956 Russian trip had a schizophrenic uncle, Muir sought the advice of Dr. Ewen Cameron of the Allan Memorial Institute in Montreal. Muir then forwarded the drugs given him by Cameron to Russia. Muir prevailed on other friends: when he visited Turkey in 1955, Allan Bronfman ensured that the bank president had "a beverage supply" available for him in Moslem Istanbul.

In some respects, the anecdotes obscure Muir's normality. The men who have reached the bank's highest office have displayed a remarkable homogeneity in many respects. The titles have changed over the years. The term "chief executive officer" has been used only since 1960.

Before that the "president" was the bank's highest officer; from 1870 to 1934, however, the title was largely honorific. Under Thomas Kenny (1870-1908) and Herbert Holt (1908-1934), effective executive direction of the bank rested with the cashier (David Duncan) and then with the general manager (Edson Pease and then Charlie Neill). The office of chairman existed as a non-executive post for Holt from 1934 to 1941 and for Dobson from 1949 to 1954. Muir was president and chairman from 1954 to 1960. Earle McLaughlin (1960-1980) became president and CEO in 1960 and then in 1962 chairman and CEO. Rowland Frazee and Allan Taylor have both carried this same title.

If one takes the nine men who have carried the title of president/chairman, the average age at which this highest office was attained is fifty-three years. The youngest was Kenny at thirty-seven; the oldest Dobson and Madison Walter at sixty-three. If one considers the professional bankers (i.e., Wilson onward, plus Duncan, Pease, and Neill), on average the bank's senior executive joined the bank at age seventeen. With the exception of Rowland Frazee, they have been small-town boys. Frazee was born in Halifax because his banker father was posted there from small-town New Brunswick. Only Kenny came from an affluent background, but he was never a full-time banker.

Counting the nine chief executives, four were Nova Scotians, two

*Jimmy Muir (right, with ball) and fellow juniors stage a baseball confrontation, Moose Jaw, 1914.*

were Ontarians, and Scotland, Ireland, and Saskatchewan have each contributed a single president. All completed high school; only two – McLaughlin and Frazee – held university degrees. Holt claimed to have a degree from Trinity College, Dublin, but did not. Frazee and Walter saw wartime service; Wilson and Holt lent their talents to war governments. Eight have been Protestants; only Kenny was Catholic. They all have been unilingual Anglos. All married, and all had children. There have been no divorces. Like most bank managers, they have been prolifically active in community work, graduating as bank president to support national charity and advocacy work. With the exception of Kenny, all were addicted to golf. Most excelled in their youth as amateur athletes. Four presidents and one chairman have died in office; the others have retired in their mid-sixties.

They were, in short, men who fulfilled the promise of the Royal Bank as a "young man's institution." They bought into its culture early, worked with unbending energy, and came to enjoy the ultimate reward held out to young "bank boys."

retreated to a 0.2 per cent share of new mortgages by 1961.[46] The mortgage issue went into a kind of limbo in the early sixties, a constant reminder that the Bank Act was in need of a major revision before the banks could proceed further into consumer financing. Although the Bank of Canada now effectively controlled the terms of national credit, the banks were still captive to a 6 per cent interest ceiling that smacked of nineteenth-century usury laws. Without flexible interest rates, such as the finance companies enjoyed, the banks entered the marketplace with their hands tied behind their backs.

If the road to consumer finance had its obstacles, Muir was quick to remind himself that corporate lending offered more-immediate rewards. In 1957, for instance, personal loans represented only 13.8 per cent of chartered bank loans, whereas loans to industry and retailers totalled a healthy 38.8 per cent[47] Muir knew that the Royal Bank prided itself on the aggressive pursuit of corporate clients. Edson Pease's ability to snatch corporate accounts out from under the nose of the redoubtable Sir Frederick Williams-Taylor of the Bank of Montreal was the stuff of corporate legend. Wilson had picked up where Pease left off – until the Depression chilled corporate borrowing. The war and the post-war spurt reawakened industry's borrowing instincts. The most persistent theme in Muir's public speaking in the fifties was the need to open Canada up to the power of business investment. At his first annual meeting as president, he declared that he was a proponent of "a greater Canada, one capable of exploiting its potential."[48] A year later: "a new spirit of enterprise is abroad in the land." Trade, foreign investment, and industrial capacity must all be built up, taxation, regulation, and political squabbling closely held in check. Muir was also shrewd enough to sense that bankers must be a dynamic element in this process.

Muir approached corporate Canada with gusto. Whereas previous Royal Bank presidents had conducted stately annual tours of the West or Cuba, Muir barnstormed Bay Street, Wall Street, and London. After Muir, to be president of the Royal Bank meant a life on the road. Late in the decade, the bank bought a four-engine Viscount airliner which shuttled Muir around the continent. Time was money and Jimmy Muir wanted to arrive ahead of the crowd – and in style. In New York, a Rolls-Royce was at his disposal.* To cater to small and

---

* Muir never lost his sense of Scottish frugality. In his view he had earned his luxuries; others had not. In 1954, his eagle eye noticed that the odometer on the New York Rolls showed many more miles than was warranted by the weekly trip to La Guardia to fetch him. The chauffeur had been joy-riding! "There is no use pussyfooting longer!" he blasted the bank's New York agent. Use of the car was summarily placed on a work-sheet basis.

medium businesses, the bank revamped its Business Development Department, which would pump practical advice for potential business clients to the branches. Foreign businesses considering Canada could, for instance, be briefed on markets or possible factory sites. Special business-development offices were opened in Montreal, Toronto, Calgary, Vancouver, New York, Chicago, and London. Trade representatives were posted throughout the Caribbean and Latin American system to help bring buyers and sellers together.[49] In 1961, the bank joined a syndicate of banks to acquire the Export Finance Corporation, an agency designed to furnish traders with credit.

Muir realized that pulling in large corporate accounts required a more personalized effort. Through his friendships with men on the commanding heights of the Canadian economy – men like C. D. Howe, Ottawa's ubiquitous trade and commerce minister[50] – Muir was quick to spot the strategic opportunities in the Canadian economy. His first step towards seizing these was through the boardroom. Muir looked for activist directors, each chosen to bring special advantage in a particular industry or region. In Toronto, he relied on Eric Phillips and E. P. Taylor. In Montreal, there was the traditional circle of client directors from Dominion Bridge, Canada Steamship, Imperial Tobacco, and others, but it was corporate lawyer Lazarus Phillips to whom he turned most frequently. From the booming oil industry, Muir attracted Frank McMahon of Calgary, J. R. White of Standard Oil in New York, and Bill Twaits of Imperial Oil in Toronto. Muir learned to mix and match directors and potential clients in the interest of developing business. His desk book bristles with such appointments: "The object of that lunch," he noted in 1953, "was to introduce me to Mr. William Woodward, Jr., one of the directors of the Hanover Bank and a very wealthy man. He is contemplating the investment of very substantial sums in real estate in Canada and I wished to make sure of the bank having the business."[51] When Muir encountered Bud McDougald, E. P. Taylor's partner in the Toronto-based Argus Corporation, on a 1952 crossing of the Atlantic on the *Queen Elizabeth*, he set up shop at McDougald's dinner table each evening and reeled in potential clients.[52] In 1958, Graham Towers, who had retired from the Bank of Canada, joined the board.

Muir's assiduous development of a corporate clientele touched many bases. He maintained the bank's strong presence in the economy's heavy industrial base – Alcan, Noranda, K. C. Irving, and Algoma Steel were frequent customers. Muir was particularly alive to the needs of the post-war growth industries. Here was another frontier with potential. The media were, for instance, soon well represented on the board's credit-approval agenda, represented by names such as Jack Kent Cooke, Howard Webster, Lord Thomson, Foster Hewitt, and Senator

*Muir loved the prestige that being head of Canada's largest bank brought. (Above) At the Queen's plate with Col. R. S. McLaughlin (centre) and E. P. Taylor (right). (Opposite page) Being initiated as "Chief Eagle Ribs" by Alberta's Blackfoot tribe, 1954.*

Rupert Davies. Aviation loans remained prominent: Avro, Okanagan Helicopters, and Pacific Western Airlines. It was in the oil patch, however, that the bank attained its greatest prominence. The Oil and Gas Department in Calgary pulsated with activity; so much so that its staff frequently chafed at their obligation to refer major credits back east for approval. From this beachhead, the bank made quick inroads into the petroleum industry – Pacific, Husky, Federated, Great Plains, Royalite, and Westcoast Transmission were typical clients. The "R-oil" once again began styling itself as Canada's leading energy lender in its advertising. To capture the American oil connection, a representative was posted in Dallas in 1958. Muir cemented these relationships by accepting directorships – on McMahon's Westcoast Transmission, for instance – with some of these clients.

Although the Royal Bank had had a presence in Toronto, New York, and London since the first decade of the century, it took Jimmy Muir to bring their potential fully alive. He knew how to position himself at the crucial intersection of business and pleasure. The Queen's Plate with E. P. Taylor or an evening at the Folies Bergères with European clients saw Muir at his charming and persuasive best. Above all else, Muir acquired a taste for New York. A former Royal Banker, Isaac Atkin, had become a partner in J. P. Morgan, and he gave Muir a superb entrée into New York's highest circle. Prominent American accounts – First Boston, U.S. Steel, Merrill Lynch – began appearing in the loan approvals. New York was also ideally situated for capturing promising off-shore accounts. In 1957, for instance, the bank provided financial support for Aristotle Onassis's shipping activities and the Gulbenkian Middle-Eastern oil empire.[53] In 1951, the bank expanded its activities in the city by incorporating a trust company that would allow it to act as agent for Canadian companies making bond issues there. New York became Muir's second home, a glamorous and profitable backdrop for the Scottish lad from Peebles who had come so far.

On the move: Muir knew that bankers could not rest quietly on their laurels in the prosperous fifties. They had to go out and get business. Muir became a prolific world traveller.

Since it had been opened in 1899, New York agency had been the bank's stepping-off place for the Caribbean and Latin America. In the fifties, this role continued, as the bank's international operations enjoyed a healthy decade. Growth was along established lines – the provision of efficient retail banking and trade financing throughout the Caribbean and Latin America. From 61 branches in 1950, the network grew to 101 by the decade's end, thanks mainly to modest expansion in Cuba and South America. By 1960, the Royal Bank's 27 South American branches gave it overwhelming dominance over Canadian banking on the continent. Profits were good, partially because commodity prices were buoyant throughout the decade, but also because the bank's international operations were less regulated than its domestic retail operations. The 6 per cent ceiling on loan interest did not, for instance, exist abroad. As a consequence, the growth of Canadian bank assets abroad in the decade and a half after the war far outstripped growth of their domestic assets.[54]

There were trouble spots. In Haiti and the Dominican Republic, the bank found itself locked into countries where dictators – François "Papa Doc" Duvalier and Rafael Trujillo – treated their local economies as fiefdoms, and made doing business a capricious affair. The situation was compounded by the fact that both dictators chose to do their banking at the Royal Bank. Trujillo, for instance, used the bank's Paris branch to deposit money abroad. Far from solidifying the bank's position in the republic, the president's favour placed it in a precarious corner, ever subject to the whims of one man. By the mid-1950s, Cuba began displaying similar signs of instability. The Batista regime was mired in corruption and still unduly reliant on sugar, and the Royal had little choice but to cooperate with Batista's central bank, Banco Nacional de Cuba. The news that an insurgency had broken out in Cuba heightened the bank's anxiety, as did Batista's insistence that the bank invest 10 per cent of its deposits in Cuban government securities.[55] Trouble was clearly brewing in the Caribbean.

The day-to-day administration of foreign banking was the one area of the bank's sprawling activities into which Muir did not intrude. Senior executives elsewhere in the bank lived in daily fear of Muir's unannounced visits and calls, but international banking was left to Art Mayne, who in 1955 was appointed associate general manager (non-domestic). A small-town Ontario boy who had joined the bank in 1925, Mayne had devoted his career since 1943 to foreign banking. He had a brilliant facility for international banking and made it clear that he would not brook Muir's interference. Atypically, Muir obliged him. International was a relatively well-oiled and profitable machine and, except for his brief New York sojourn in the twenties, Muir had little front-line experience with it. Muir instead fixed his attention on the far-distant horizon. The Caribbean had been a logical frontier for Canadian banking, but the post-war world was throwing up new and more-lucrative opportunities for global banking. Muir would spend his time abroad positioning the bank for these eventualities. As Edson Pease had done in Cuba in 1899, Muir would turn the bank to the emerging markets of the 1960s. In short, Muir became the bank's "international travelling billboard."[56]

In the wake of the First World War, the bank had scouted the Far East as a possible new frontier; there was a sense that Canadian trade might penetrate these exotic markets and that the bank could capitalize on the result. At the time, the ill-fated Vladivostok branch was the only outcome of this vision. Sugar problems in Cuba, a dedication to Latin America, and the damper of the Depression combined to limit the bank's expansionist urges for the next thirty years. Besides, the curtain of communism descended over Russia and, by the 1950s, China. The chill of the Cold War banished any thought of trade behind the Iron Curtain. The West fixated on communism as the antithesis of free enterprise; Morris Wilson and Muir himself had frequently used the presidential address to the shareholders to castigate the evil of a "planned economy." Imagine, therefore, the consternation of Canadians in late May 1956 when they saw the Toronto *Star* headline: "Royal Bank Head to Meet Soviet Financiers in Moscow."[57] A few days later, Muir and his Ottawa branch manager, Jack Bankes, headed behind the Iron Curtain. Two years later, the pair would pack their bags again, this time for communist China. The photographic images of these ventures are remarkable: Muir, resplendent in his banker's blue suit, sipping tea with denim-clad Chinese central bankers or posing under red stars in Moscow. Neither the Russian nor the China trip added significantly to the bank's short-term bottom line – they provided some grain-trade financing and a representative office in Hong Kong – but they speak volumes of Muir's vision and his ability to move beyond prevailing stereotypes.

Muir's trip to Russia began in the manager's office of the Royal's Ottawa office. For years, Ottawa main branch had carried the account of the Soviet embassy and, in late 1955, when the Soviet ambassador had casually mentioned to Jack Bankes that a senior official of the bank would be welcome in Moscow, Bankes passed the message on to Muir. Muir snapped at the bait. Ambassador Dimitri Chuvakhin was invited to lunch in Montreal. Muir wanted a "chat" in Moscow with the Soviet finance minister and the head of the central bank and a chance to see the sights.[58] All this was arranged and, in June, Muir was off. He always insisted that this was a "private visit," paid for by himself. Canada's leading banker was, however, hardly a normal tourist, especially at a time when western tourists in Russia were an oddity. For two weeks, the Canadian banker was paraded through ministry offices by day and entertained by night. His only complaint seemed to be the lack of good scotch.

Muir was obviously no "fellow traveller," but neither did he react to Russia with ideological blindness. "I must say," he told the CBC, "I found in the places I visited a degree of economic development beyond anything that had been indicated to me and anything I previously heard." Russian banking was "efficient in the narrowly technical sense." There was certainly an opportunity for trade and the exchange of ideas: "I think it is only realistic to concede that it is impossible to confine, to ostracize, or to ignore a rapidly expanding country of some 225 million people."[59] It is worth noting that Muir visited the Soviet Union *before* any Canadian minister of external affairs did so. Here, perhaps, was the visit's principal outcome: as a prominent Canadian – what would today be called an opinion leader – Muir helped to turn Canadians' thinking on the Soviet Union. "Though Mr. Muir is not the first to say, in effect, 'it just isn't so,'" wrote the *Anglican Outlook*, "his is an important contribution to a sound rapprochement between East and West."[60] Muir's Russian journey also caught the attention of prominent

*Behind the Iron Curtain: Muir's 1956 trip to Russia and 1958 China visit helped to establish Canada's presence in the communist world. (Above) Muir with Chinese children in Canton.*

# Chapter Nine

*Muir takes tea with the assistant manager of the Bank of China.*

business and political leaders, many of whom wrote to commend his views.[61] Moscow did not forget Muir's boldness; Canadian wheat shipments to Russia in the late fifties were arranged with temporary loans from the Royal Bank.

The China trip in 1958 set a more startling precedent. The itinerary was similar: visits to the Bank of China mingled with tourism. For a nation still fearful of the menace of "yellow" communism, the message that Muir brought home with him was almost heretical. The "vast majority of the people of China have a government they want," Muir reported, "a government which is improving their lot, a government in which they have confidence, a government which stands no chance of being supplanted."[62] Similarly, Muir did not slip into the prevalent narrow western habit of upholding the nationalist government of Chiang Kai-shek on Formosa and focusing alone on its potential.[63] Instead, he saw the region as a whole; the Far East had immense economic potential. "Somehow," he told the Vancouver Board of Trade, "it has to be brought forcibly home to us that, comparatively, we are an indolent, pleasure-seeking and soft section of humanity as opposed to the endlessly toiling, fanatical, ambitious and dedicated hordes in other lands who seek first to equal and then surpass the productive powers of the Western world."[64] To support Muir's message, the bank opened a representative's office – to help finance trade – in Hong Kong. In typical style, Muir made the decision on the spur of the moment; a somewhat bewildered Jack Smith, manager in Port-of-Spain, Trinidad, received a cable in which he was simply *told* that he was being transferred to Hong Kong. Even before Smith could scramble into position, the board in Montreal was approving letters of credit for the Bank of China to cover purchases of Canadian wheat.[65]

Under Jimmy Muir, the Royal Bank's boardroom became a more exciting place. There can be no denying that Muir in fact ruled the board. On the other hand, he picked his directors for their connections, insights, and ability to attract business. He also used the directors as a sounding board as he pursued his three-pronged strategy of expanding the bank's retail, corporate, and international activities. If the Royal Bank had risen to national pre-eminence, it was because in times of national expansion, such as the Laurier boom, it had a deliberate policy of capitalizing on the potential of growth. Pease vigorously pursued domestic and foreign growth before adroitly switching to a strategy of merging with other banks. Four decades later, Muir picked up the formula, resisting the natural inclination to conservatism in Canadian banking.

In Muir's mind, Montreal was by no means simply the static centre of the bank, a place for unavoidable board meetings and a hangar for the Viscount. For all his efforts to build up business in Toronto and Calgary, Muir knew that St. James Street was still Canada's financial mecca. In 1887, the bank had come there to make its mark. Since then, it had celebrated its growth with the erection of two splendid head-office buildings. The completion of 360 St. James in 1928 provided the bank with a grand trophy of its ascendancy over the Bank of Montreal. In the mid-1950s, Muir reinforced the point by installing four 900-watt beacons on its roof to pierce the night sky. And then, in an audacious move, he decided that the time had come for the bank to take its leave of St. James Street and move its head office. In doing so, he would shift the centre of financial gravity in Montreal, forever breaking the suzerainty of St. James Street. The "Quiet Revolution" in Quebec would finish the process.

Like any self-respecting member of Montreal's Anglo business community, Muir was a member of the St. James's Club, which sat magisterially at the corner of Dorchester and University, a quick limousine ride up the hill from St. James Street. The club perched precariously on the edge of a huge, grimy hole, a legacy of the Canadian Northern Railway's once-grand vision for downtown Montreal. The railway had punched a hole under Mount Royal to bring trains into the heart of the city. War and the depressed twenties had stalled any attempt to mask the scar with development. The hole now belonged to Canadian National. The railway's president was another craggy Scot, Donald Gordon, who was cut from the same cloth as Jimmy Muir. Gordon had come from Scotland, risen as a banker with the Bank of Nova Scotia, served in the wartime bureaucracy, and emerged in peacetime as one of Ottawa's trusted fix-it men.

In the 1950s, he had been sent to fix Canadian National. Hard-drinking, egotistical, and profane, Gordon was a man of action, and he soon wanted something done about the hole. Construction of a modern hotel above Central Station across the street was a first step – a controversial first step, since many Montrealers, not surprisingly, objected to the hotel's name, The Queen Elizabeth. Urban renewal was none the less in the air. If New York could have a Rockefeller Center, why couldn't Montreal have a similar grand development?[66] To do this, Gordon would need a partner who could bring to the project the skills of a developer and the ability to pull in the prestigious tenants that make any office development pay. Nobody seemed interested; the Bank of Montreal had, for instance, just committed itself to an expansion of its St. James Street head office, a signal that the centre of Anglo business gravity was not about to shift.

A dispirited Gordon turned to Lazarus Phillips, lawyer to the Bronfman family, in the hope that he might find a partner in the Jewish community. Seagram's, the Bronfmans' huge liquor conglomerate, had just completed a stylish office complex in downtown New York. Phillips came up with nothing, but the contact would later prove crucial. Unable to find a way around Montreal's lethargy, Gordon looked to New York. Here he finally found his partner in William Zeckendorf, a galvanic American developer. Zeckendorf had joined a small management company, Webb and Knapp, in 1939 and since then had pushed the company to the cutting edge of American property development. At first, Webb and Knapp simply acquired property – the Chrysler Building in New York, for instance – but by the 1950s, it had moved on to the challenge of actually *developing* properties. Zeckendorf soon asserted himself as America's most aggressive urban redeveloper. He would buy downtown real estate cheap and redevelop it with verve, drawing on a stellar team of associates. His star was the brilliant Chinese–American architect I. M. Pei. When two of Gordon's Montreal friends showed up in Zeckendorf's New York office with maps of Canadian National's twenty-two-acre site in Montreal, Zeckendorf saw not a hole, but a development possibility.[67] Late in 1955, Webb and Knapp formed a Canadian affiliate. John McCloy, the chairman of the Chase Manhattan, suggested that, for a Canadian bank, Zeckendorf choose the Royal Bank, and went so far as to introduce him to James Muir. The die was cast.

Throughout 1956, Gordon and Zeckendorf defined their intentions. Working closely with Montreal mayor Jean Drapeau, Zeckendorf's planners, sparked by the genius of Pei and his associates, devised a plan for a massive, forty-storey skyscraper, which would sit atop the hole and dominate Montreal's skyline. The building was to be cruciform in shape, a complement to the cross which symbolized the city's origin and identity on nearby Mount Royal. It was to be called Place Ville Marie. Drapeau fought for the project in city council and even obliged Zeckendorf with permission to expropriate the St. James's Club. Zeckendorf was, however, having a harder time demolishing the conservativism of the club's members, who regarded him as an outsider and resisted his attempts to sign their companies up as charter tenants for Place Ville Marie. Even with the hearty backing of Gordon and Drapeau, Zeckendorf remained an American and a Jew. Without tenants, Place Ville Marie would remain a hole in the ground.

The Zeckendorf–Gordon–Drapeau trio soon became a quartet. Once in Montreal, Webb and Knapp had become fast clients of the Royal Bank. They had borrowed, for instance, to purchase the Dominion Square Building, another downtown Montreal location.[68] Muir watched Zeckendorf at work, a New Yorker on his own doorstep. He was intrigued. But there was so much that was wrong with the project from the bank's perspective. Place Ville Marie did not look like a bank building: there were no pillars, there was no grand banking hall. The bank would not own the structure, and the public expected a bank to own its head office. It would not even be called the Royal Bank Building. Yet, there was something compelling in Zeckendorf's dynamism. More than anything else, Muir was inched towards the project by Lazarus Phillips, who was probably his closest confidant on the board. Phillips spent his days in his Montreal law office, but over lunch or on the telephone each evening, he and Muir mulled over the auguries of corporate Canada. In the spring of 1958, their conversation more and more turned on Zeckendorf's project. Phillips's election to the Webb and Knapp board intensified the confidences.

Some things were obvious. The building at 360 St. James was aging. There was no air conditioning, nor much space for employees' cars. St. James Street was too cramped to entertain any thought of expansion of the old head office or a new site in the immediate vicinity. Place Ville Marie – a twenty-minute walk away in the city's retail district – offered shops, parking, and easy access to train commuters. But did it offer prestige? Could the bank risk being the first to sign a lease, only to discover that its customers and the competition had stayed in their St. James Street warren? "Undoubtedly," a confidential bank study concluded, "the tower building will become equally as well known as such developments as Rockefeller Centre and the Empire State Building."[69] Muir then became convinced that the bank, not Canadian National, must own the ground on which its new head office would stand. The idea of an emphyteutic lease (one which provided long-term rights to land owned by another) was raised. Zeckendorf and Pei tried to tantalize the bank president: a spectacular penthouse would be added to the top of the building for Muir to live in, and the bank would have its grand banking hall on the ground level.[70] By mid-April, Muir finally told Gordon that he was engaged in an "honourable" negotiation with Webb and Knapp for "an important amount of space" in Place Ville Marie. I. M. Pei hurriedly began preparing a mock-up of the project so that Muir could brief his directors.

On May 26, Muir broke the news to the board. It was a typical Muir *tour de force*. So confident was Muir that a press release had been prepared in advance announcing that the bank would lease 300,000 square feet of Place Ville Marie on a ninety-nine-year emphyteutic lease. At the end of the lease, ownership of the site would be fully vested in the bank. Although the overall project would be called Place Ville Marie, the actual building would be named for the bank. There was no penthouse for Muir (a restaurant took its place) and the external façade was not altered to give the bank its grand entrance.[71] The 360 St. James building would be sold to the developers of PVM and leased back as a branch. In 1960, a management company, Trizec, was formed by Webb and Knapp and English capital to hold the investment. Construction finally began, and other tenants soon materialized, many of them Royal Bank customers. In return for a lease, Zeckendorf, for instance, promised Alcan that the building would be clad in aluminum. The banking competition also started marching up the hill from St. James Street; the Bank of Commerce announced plans to build its own skyscraper on nearby Dominion Square. Once the Commerce's plans were fixed, the Webb and Knapp architects added three floors to the PVM design so that Muir could boast that he had the tallest building in the Commonwealth. The Commerce retaliated with a radio mast.

Place Ville Marie was the product of one of the most unlikely entrepreneurial liaisons in Canadian business history: two tough-minded Scots, a visionary New York Jew, and a populist French–Canadian mayor of Montreal. In the May press release, Zeckendorf declared that the negotiation had been one of "realism and goodwill." This presented the picture in a rather rosy light. Relations were always explosive. Muir and Gordon had chosen to deal with a New York developer and a Chinese–American architect, both of whom were conspicuously outside the pale of the Montreal establishment. The stakes were high – the Royal would be the first Canadian bank not to actually own its head-office building. There was thus often unavoidable friction. Zeckendorf later admitted in his memoirs that his Montreal project was "no honeyed love feast." In anger, Muir assailed

*Muir inspects I. M. Pei's architectural model for Place Ville Marie.*

Pei as a "goddamn Chinaman" (this from a man who had just returned from communist China). Yet, for all the friction, these powerfully egotistical men, bound up in Place Ville Marie's genesis, found common purpose and emerged full of respect for each other. "Each of these leaders laid something, sometimes something as subtle and precious as his reputation, on the line to make our project go." By 1962, the result was a "massive imaginative building" – Canada's first modern skyscraper – that not just changed the face of Montreal but also altered the way in which all Canadians saw their downtown cores.[72] What was first evident at the corner of Dorchester and University soon spread across the nation.

When the news of Jimmy Muir's death reached Montreal from Scotland in April 1960, Place Ville Marie was still an incomplete steel shell. It is not surprising that Donald Gordon and Jean Drapeau's successor as mayor, Sarto Fournier, acted as pallbearers at the funeral. Zeckendorf was busy in the American West, but remembered Muir as the head of Canada's "most aggressive" bank. Everybody

*Place Ville Marie: A conscious effort to shift the centre of Montreal's financial district. (Above) The "hole" at Dorchester and University, with the St. James's Club centre right. (Below) Construction progress, 1961.*

352

praised the man who had built up the bank with $4 billion in assets. But there was something fittingly metaphoric in the unfinished state of Place Ville Marie.

For all his dynamic leadership, there was something lacking – something unfinished – in Muir's post-war reformation of the Royal Bank. There are persistent hints of this in the reminiscences of the men who served the bank under Muir. For all their praise of Muir's vision and supercharged drive, there is also a common denominator of criticism: "Jimmy was a throw-back to the old one-man rule," "a despot," and "If God had horns, he would be James Muir."[73] Earle McLaughlin, who eventually succeeded Muir, reached the same conclusion, perhaps more tactfully: "He did a great deal for the bank, a dynamic man, a driving man who stayed too long. He would have carried on until he was 75 had he lived. That would have been a mistake." Muir was inveterately incapable of delegating authority at a time when the growth of Canadian banking was leading inexorably towards challenges that were beyond the kind of rigid hierarchy that Jimmy Muir tried to impose on the bank. "I remember," McLaughlin recalled, "in the old building they were lined up almost twenty deep outside Muir's office, you know a piece of paper in their hand, and you spent more time waiting in the hall than you did at your desk."[74]

Muir was the epitome of the "bank-boy" approach to management. He was a banker for fifty-three years. "I think one of the most important requirements for success is to form a very definite idea of what you want to be, and to do so at an early age,"[75] he once said. He saw banking as a hierarchy that one scaled on the rungs of loyalty and proficiency. The top of the ladder was only accessible to those who first mounted it on its lowest rung. Pease, Neill, Wilson, and Dobson all believed that a generous measure of autonomy had to be afforded those below them on the ladder. The system worked because it trusted that character would develop within the parameters of carefully honed procedures; a bank system that was by law and nature centralized could still be slackened to accommodate the diversity of a country as large as Canada without jeopardizing the integrity of the whole. Jimmy Muir's boundless ambition upset this delicate balance. The higher he climbed, the less he trusted the system below him. He ruled by "fear mechanism."[76] He pulled the bank's entire stream of decision-making across his desk; the bank still abounds with tales of men summarily fired (and usually rehired after an agonizing penance) for forgetting Muir's omnipotence. When Muir went to China or London, head office stood in a state of paralysis. The Oil and Gas Department in Calgary waited days for credit approvals that they needed to get within hours if they were to build up business.

Muir's dogmatic centralization came at a time when banking found itself under structural stress. Its market had expanded dramatically, competition had grown, and even the legislative framework within which it operated was being liberalized. More changes were undoubtedly in the wind; the 6 per cent interest ceiling on its lending activities was clearly cracking under the pressure of consumer demand. In some things of great strategic importance, Muir's post-war aggressiveness overrode any hesitancy that lingered from the Depression experience. His quick reaction to mortgage financing in 1954 proved this. In other respects, however, he stifled innovation in the bank, stifled the free play of his subordinates' imaginations. The old system was still pushing "young men" to the forefront of the Royal Bank. There was, for instance, young Earle McLaughlin, whom Muir had appointed assistant to the president. Art Mayne was masterful in international banking, where he was backed up by Whit Shannon. John Coleman was excelling as general inspector. Jim Cornish worked efficiently as staff supervisor. There was lots of talent, but by the late 1950s it was becoming frustrated talent. In 1954, Sydney Dobson resigned the chairmanship, sensing that he had become a fifth wheel. Muir was quickly dubbed president and chairman. A year after Muir had taken over as chairman, Ted Atkinson had stepped down as general manager, exasperated with Muir's interference. Muir would not tolerate challengers: he developed, an upcoming executive in head office recalled, the ability "to cut men off at the knees."[77]

Thus, as Muir chalked up his victories in retail, corporate, and international banking, there was an undercurrent of anxiety in senior management that he was cutting the bank off from the currents of change in Canadian society. Modern banking required modern methods. Muir's obsession with on-the-job training closed the door to any systematic attempt to prepare staff for new challenges in banking: administering personal loans, writing up mortgages, or mastering the new technologies of banking. Muir's idea of advanced training was to distribute a copy of C. N. Parkinson's *Parkinson's Law* to every branch manager and insist that he read it. In desperation, area managers began organizing clandestine training sessions for staff and hiding the costs in their expense accounts. Training, salaries, and promotion still hinged on the *ad hoc* judgement of supervisors and an antiquated system of personnel cards which were simply passed around by senior management. Similarly, there was no marketing department to help position the bank in the marketplace. Only in 1959 was an assistant general manager finally given responsibility for the bank's public relations. In all these matters, Muir simply assumed that new challenges could be met from the president's office.

Steeped in a world of male banking, Muir also missed other shifts in Canadian society in the fifties. After the war, Canadians wanted to settle down. They wanted permanence and affluence. The old "bank-boy" culture dictated mobility and low starting salaries, and banking was ceasing to be a coveted career. In 1954, the marriage rule was finally dropped. Other changes, however, came slowly. Muir never saw women as career bankers, and did little to accommodate them. Women spent the decade consigned to specific niches in the bank as tellers, stenos, and clerical workers. It "never crossed our minds," one executive remembered, "that women wanted a viable banking career."[78] Many in fact did not. Banking was the perfect part-time job for women trying to balance the awkward demands of raising a family and supplementing the family income. None the less, women were excluded from management. They had become front-line bankers with no hope of generalship. "Royal Tops in Pulchritude," reported the bank magazine. Another article, "How To Drive the Manager Crazy," advised "Royal Bankerettes" on office deportment – such as how to sit properly at a desk.[79] Forty per cent of women bankers were now married, and there was an assumption that they were not mobile and therefore not promotable.[80] The Royal Bank had ridden to prominence because it had groomed a loyal, efficient, and well-disposed work-force. By the late 1950s such lifelong loyalty was in question. As Muir himself admitted to Percy Saltzman of the CBC in 1958, "Our great problem in the bank is to get – *to get* – able men."[81]

There were other unresolved challenges by 1960. The Bank Act, and indeed the whole financial-services industry in Canada, needed reform to align it with the needs of a post-war, urban-industrial, consumer society. Muir might have handled this, but he would have been at sea in coping with Quebec's aroused sense of social and economic distinct-ness in the years after Duplessis's death in 1959. There would be a first, symbolic hint of this when *Le Devoir* complained that, while the signage on the ground floor of PVM was bilingual, it remained unilin-gual English on the upper floors.[82] The news from Cuba indicated that the old order was crumbling elsewhere. All of this change would have to be managed, and Jimmy Muir's one-man show would in all proba-bility have buckled under the strain.

And then, suddenly, he was dead. The board hurriedly gathered and passed a motion of sympathy. Madison Walter, the bank's vice-presi-dent since 1955, reluctantly accepted the directors' offer of the pres-idency. Banking, he told *Canadian Business*, was not the "placid, genteel occupation" he had learned in his adolescence. It was now "a rugged game, highly competitive." "Management," he concluded, "has to be better, more perceptive; there is much over-capacity, competition is keen and probably will stay that way."[83] The directors evidently agreed. Within a month of Muir's death, they voted to sell his Viscount and to create a remuneration committee of the board to determine executive salaries in the bank.[84] There was a sense that Canada's largest bank was in for some changes, but, with Muir's firm control lifted, there was also considerable uneasiness about how it would handle them.

CHAPTER TEN

# Royal Banking in a Changed Canada

*"The Right People ... in the Right Spots"*

$F$OR CANADIANS AND FOR THEIR BANKERS ALIKE, 1967 WAS AN *annus mirabilis*. On April 28 of that wonderful year, Expo 67, Canada's glittering celebration of its centennial, opened its gates for a summer that would etch itself into Canadian consciousness as a high point of national self-confidence. Four days later, on May 1, a radically revised Bank Act – praised by bankers as being "market-freeing" – went into operation. Radical was not a word traditionally associated with Canadian banking, but this *was* fundamental change. Gone was the 6 per cent interest ceiling on bank lending. Lower cash-reserve requirements would allow the banks to compete more effectively with the "near banks." Conventional mortgages, worth up to 75 per cent of the value of new *and* existing homes, were finally available at the local bank. The revised Bank Act seemed to release, directly or indirectly, a flood of new banking "products." Chargex cards, mutual funds, a wide range of consumer loans, and electronic banking quickly began to figure in Canadians' financial calculations.

Thus, the "winds of competition" were transforming the local bank into "a centre of diversified retail financial services for the man of ordinary means."[1] Canadian banking faced another new frontier in the sixties, its most important since the creation of a central bank in the 1930s. And the Royal Bank faced it without Jimmy Muir and prospered. It did so by reverting to two of the mainstays of its history: it found a "young man" as its new president and it employed "progressive ways" to preserve its place as Canada's largest bank. Like the nation at large, the bank was emboldened by the headiness of the sixties, and the Royal's transformation was already apparent at Expo in Montreal.

357

Throughout the summer of 1967, millions of "ordinary" Canadians pushed through the turnstiles of Expo 67. Montreal became Canada's mecca, and on their way to the fair, many tourists visited Place Ville Marie, Canada's most famous skyscraper. There, in the foyer, the Royal Bank established an Expo Centre, where hostesses fluent in nine languages dispensed maps, information, and financial services to a steady stream of visitors. Many ventured up to the forty-second-floor observation deck, where they took in the breathtaking view of the St. Lawrence as it curved around the island of Montreal. Each night the four Royal Bank beacons – moved from 360 St. James – swept the city's skyline, while dinner was served in Altitude 747, the building's spectacular rooftop restaurant. The bank also found other ways to reach out to the Canadian public in the centennial year. On April 3, the Royal Bank became the first Canadian bank to advertise on radio; radio "spots" were followed in the fall by television ads.[2] Print advertising by itself seemed stolid, out of step with the electronic age. The airwaves were the fast route to improved market share.

"Riding the airwaves" soon had another meaning. On April 1 of the next spring, the CJAD traffic helicopter in Montreal took off bearing Royal Bank colours. The JetRanger – the "Flying Lion" – carried an unlikely passenger: an avuncular, mustachioed businessman in his early fifties, clad in sombre dark blue, pipe clenched between his teeth, peered down through his heavy frame glasses at the streets below. W. Earle McLaughlin had become the first Canadian bank president to fly traffic watch. "We bought the helicopter to identify us with a useful public service," the bank's sales-promotion manager declared, "and we also feel that it further identifies us with a highly sophisticated, modern technique, which banking is today."[3] McLaughlin's early-morning helicopter sortie provides a telling metaphor for his years as the chief executive of Canada's largest bank. For almost twenty years, he proved capable of rising above the hurly-burly of the changing financial world. Unlike Jimmy Muir before him, McLaughlin also learned to share and delegate power; his cockpit was a place for teamwork – not one-man heroics.

McLaughlin's arrival in the president's office in 1960 was by no means preordained. Muir's death left the board caught in a dilemma. The fifties had seen the bank's Toronto business grow significantly. Montreal directors, once accustomed to an unchallenged control in the boardroom, now found themselves rubbing elbows with strong-willed Torontonians like E. P. Taylor, J. S. D. Tory, and W. E. Phillips. In addition, the bank had responded to Toronto's growing economic eminence by parachuting top executive talent into the city. Two seasoned Nova Scotians led the way: Burnham Mitchell and Ken

Sedgewick soon became fixtures in corporate Toronto. Sedgewick became the bank's general manager in 1955 and, five years later, he assumed the idiosyncratic title of vice-chairman and chief executive officer in Ontario. Mitchell's untimely death in 1959 left fifty-eight-year-old Sedgewick the bank's top man in Ontario. Patrician in manner, Sedgewick was none the less well received in Toronto business circles, a "friendly banker" in the eyes of the Toronto *Telegram*, carrying on the bank's "splendid tradition" in the city.[4] The bank's presidency, he assumed, awaited him.

Back in Montreal, there were other contenders. Associate General Manager Art Mayne was handling the bank's international operations very competently. A skilled corporate politician, Mayne, however, suffered from poor health and his ambition was consequently in abeyance. Flanking him was Madison "Matt" Walter, the bank's gentlemanly vice-president. A former assistant general manager, Walter had sat on the board since 1955 and was much respected in Montreal business circles. Walter's charm emanated from his adherence to sedate "old school" banking; he was closer in style to Sydney Dobson than to the aggressive Jimmy Muir. Nor did he much hanker after the top job. That left young Earle McLaughlin. McLaughlin had shone as Montreal main-branch manager in the early 1950s before becoming an assistant general manager in 1953. Muir saw in McLaughlin, unlike Walter and Sedgewick, signs of his own drive and ambition. In 1954, he turned to McLaughlin to spearhead the bank's entry into the mortgage field. Inasmuch as Muir ever tipped his hand, he did so in 1959 when he made McLaughlin his "assistant" and then, early in 1960, appointed him general manager when Sedgewick was promoted to Toronto. McLaughlin had talent in abundance, but he was only forty-five and virtually unknown beyond the bank. Three months later, the selection of McLaughlin, Walter, Sedgewick, and Mayne as honorary pallbearers at Muir's funeral seemed natural; less automatic was the selection of his successor at the bank's helm.

With Muir at rest near the summit of Mount Royal Cemetery, the board met on April 26 to broach the delicate issue of his replacement. Despite Sedgewick's ambitions, it was soon clear that the Montreal directors still held sway, and they would go with the familiar Walter. He was best known to them, and his warm-heartedness had made him many allies. An Ontario lad who had joined the bank in 1912, Walter seemed the safe bet – his polished ways undoubtedly a welcome prospect after Muir's abrasiveness. The bank magazine portrayed him as a "very human man, good-humoured, considerate" who had "grown up in the 'Royal' family."[5] Matt Walter was now sixty-three years old and unenthusiastic about the challenge set before him by the

*Madison Walter: The bank's first Ontario-born president and also the office's briefest incumbent (above). Elected in April 1960, Walter died the next December of a brain tumour. (Opposite) As his successor, Earle McLaughlin inherited Walter's ease in public. Prime Minister John Diefenbaker cuts the ribbon at the new Ottawa Main Branch. The ribbon is held by Mayor Charlotte Whitton of Ottawa (right) and Samuel Short (left), a customer since 1899.*

directors. None the less, when Montreal lawyer W. H. Howard and Graham Towers nominated him, he acquiesced.* Sedgewick, thirteen years Walter's junior, was given to understand by his Toronto supporters that his time would come.[6]

Walter's personality immediately showed itself in a new collegiality in senior management. He let McLaughlin brief the board on Place Ville Marie's construction. Mayne alone reported on international. Not only was Muir's airplane sold in short order, but in another clear signal of change, the board created a compensation committee to bring some system to executive salaries. In choosing Walter, the board had, perhaps unconsciously, defied a Royal Bank tradition – that of the "young man's institution." Younger men brought change and energy. Whether Walter would ever have recaptured Muir's dynamism outside head office is, alas, conjectural. Fate cut short his opportunity. Late in October 1960, five months into his presidency, Walter called his secretary into his office and asked her to investigate the source of the persistent ringing that was tormenting him. She could hear nothing. Walter had a brain tumour, and on December 9, the Royal Bank lost its second chief executive in eight months.

---

* As it pushed more and more onto the international stage, Canadian banking was fast shedding its archaic Anglo–Scottish titles. Walter would be elected president *and* chairman, a style that made it easier to move in American banking circles.

Acute anxiety spread through the Royal. Canada's largest bank seemed bereft of leadership. Adverse comment in the financial press might tend to undermine the bank's strategic prospects and provoke a crisis of confidence. Jim Cornish, the assistant GM in charge of staff, recalled the incipient panic: "You know the other banks were almost prepared to go out to pass tin cups up and down St. James Street to help us out."[7] The trepidation was heightened by the news that the Commerce and Imperial banks were amalgamating; the Royal Bank was no longer comfortably Canada's largest bank.* Fortunately, the bank was enjoying a good year – profits in 1960 were up 14 per cent, and deposits had set an all-time record – which tended to soothe the anxiety. But, when the board met on December 19, the directors knew that they faced one of the toughest decisions ever. And they entered the room with little sense of consensus over the leadership.

Not since it had agonized over Pease's 1887 proposal to open a branch in Montreal had the board found itself so divided. Toronto directors, led by Eddie Taylor and Jack White of Imperial Oil, believed that Sedgewick's time had come. The Montrealers, led by W. H. Howard and R. D. Harkness of Northern Electric, had their doubts. Sedgewick, although relatively young, lacked verve, and seemed unpopular with the staff. The logical Montreal alternative was the skilful international banker Art Mayne, but he remained in uncertain health and had written himself out of the running. An expectant Sedgewick had come up from Toronto and had booked into the Ritz-Carlton. At ten in the morning, the directors filed into the boardroom, and an uneasy hush spread through head office.

The issue was forced when Harkness, as chairman of the new compensation advisory committee, tabled a report recommending that Earle McLaughlin be given the nod. Now the Toronto directors took their stand, and for four and a half hours the battle raged. McLaughlin was too young, too unknown, the Torontonians argued. We'll take the chance, the Montrealers replied – the bank could not afford to coast in such heady times. A sandwich lunch was sent in. A delegation was despatched to Mayne's home to ascertain his stand. A handful of Torontonians dashed up to the Ritz to confer with Sedgewick. By mid-afternoon, the Montrealers had the upper hand. The bank would go with the forty-five-year-old "young man." To placate Toronto over McLaughlin's inexperience, it was agreed that the new president would defer to the experience of Art Mayne (who became a director) and C. B. "Charlie" Neapole (who became full general manager) in

---

* For one brief quarter in 1961, the CIBC actually surpassed the Royal Bank in asset size.

setting up shop as president.

"My strong advice to you now," E. P. Taylor wrote privately to Sedgewick two days later, "is to become 'a good soldier' in spite of your personal convictions and natural disappointment."[8] Sedgewick had been offered a vice-presidency and a chance to become a "full member of the executive team." Despite Taylor's advice, Sedgewick resigned. He had, he told McLaughlin, "lost heart and, to a degree, lost faith in some ideals which heretofore, were to me beyond doubt."[9] Sedgewick quickly became a director at Pitfield Mackay, Ross & Co., and McLaughlin began his tenure as president mending fences. To fill what one director called "a hole in our Toronto set-up,"[10] he appointed Donald Anderson as Ontario general manager and promoted John Coleman to back him up.* Mayne became executive vice-president, and his international banking duties were taken over by Whit Shannon as associate general manager. General manager Neapole acted as chief operating officer. McLaughlin was thus well buttressed with executive talent; he had a "team," and never lost sight of the need for their support and advice. There was always a folksiness about McLaughlin: he had an ability to "energize" those about him and to eschew the majesty that engulfed many a bank president. Looking back on these early months from the perspective of 1979, Jim Cornish – whom McLaughlin came to trust implicitly in personnel matters – generously credited his boss with "one of the greatest changes in corporate leadership that you can find in all the corporate history."[11]

The challenge to the new order was not confined to the domestic front. Even before the new president had devised a strategy for modernizing Muir's one-man bank, a crisis rocked the Royal Bank's once majestically stable international network. Late on a cold Friday afternoon in December 1962, Earle McLaughlin received three unexpected visitors. The American consul in Montreal, Jerome Gaspard, he knew from the cocktail circuit. But the other two needed introductions. They also needed a favour from the Royal Bank. Nicholas Katzenbach was the deputy attorney-general of the United States, first lieutenant to Robert Kennedy. With him was James B. Donovan, the New York lawyer who had won wide publicity in the late 1950s for defending Soviet spy Rudolf Abel. Donovan now acted as the emissary

---

* The Montreal–Toronto tension remained. In the 1970s it would resurface when politics in Quebec prompted certain Toronto directors to urge that the bank position itself more prominently in their city. McLaughlin remained adamantly committed to Montreal; only an outright declaration of sovereignty would force such a move to protect the bank's federal charter. Ironically, the actual concept of most head offices in an age of electronic communication and jet travel was being steadily eroded in strategic terms. McLaughlin would later transfer select corporate functions to regional centres elsewhere in Canada.

*Cuban farewell: After six decades in Cuba, the bank sold its assets to the revolutionary government of Fidel Castro in 1960. The parting was amicable, unlike the expropriation of the American banks that same year. (Above) R. K. Mennell, the bank's manager in Camagüey, presents a trophy for Best Bull in Show to a Cuban army captain at a 1959 cattle show. After the pull-out, the bank continued to finance Cuban trade and kept a representative's office in Havana.*

of a committee of Cuban–American families whose men had been caught in the ill-starred invasion of Cuba the previous April.

Of the ragtag army of liberation that had waded ashore at the Bay of Pigs, 1,200 now languished ignominiously in Cuban jails. Relations between Washington and Havana were at Cold War loggerheads. The revolutionary government of Fidel Castro was prepared to release the hostages – for a price. Castro would not, however, deal directly with the American government. Any release had to be privately negotiated. Nor would the Cubans deal through American banks. In October 1960, Castro had nationalized all but two foreign banks operating in

Cuba: Canada's Royal Bank and the Bank of Nova Scotia. Both escaped the taint of economic imperialism that had spelled the downfall of their long-time American rival, the First National City Bank of New York. Castro needed a financial outlet to the outside world, and Canadian bankers had always been *persona grata* in Cuba. If the Americans wanted their prisoners, they would have to pay through the Royal Bank.

Katzenbach and Donovan needed a means of paying a ransom of almost $60 million – in the form of medicines and foodstuffs supplied by the American Red Cross – to the Cubans. The request ruined the weekend plans of senior Royal Bankers in Montreal, New York, and Havana. Whit Shannon, head of the bank's international division, coordinated arrangements between the bank's New York agent, Bob Utting, and its Havana representative, Harry Berry. At the height of these negotiations, Castro and the head of Banco Nacional de Cuba, Ernesto "Che" Guevara, arrived at Berry's apartment and spent several hours impatiently pacing his floor. Berry later confided how uneasy he had been at the sight of the pistols strapped to the belts of the two revolutionary leaders; at one point, Guevara had unbuckled his gunbelt and plunked it down on the desk beside an unnerved Berry. Within days, the bank had a *modus operandi*. It would issue an irrevocable letter of credit to Banco Nacional de Cuba, allowing it to draw down monies from the American Red Cross, acting on behalf of the Cuban–American families, as hostages were repatriated from Cuba. On December 20, Donovan and Banco Nacional de Cuba officials signed an agreement, and the first prisoners arrived in Miami on Christmas Eve.

The repatriation continued into 1963. When it was finally over, Bobby Kennedy wrote to Earle McLaughlin to praise the bank's "speed of decision and action." Katzenbach echoed this, citing "the gracious attitude of Canadian banking officials." Amid the fanfare, the bank quietly waived all fees for the transaction, notably the $70,000 fee for the letter of credit, the largest the bank had ever issued.[12]

The Bay of Pigs episode, however, could not disguise the fact that the bank had reached the end of the road in Cuba. It also provided a kind of symbolic swan song for the bank's retail system in the Caribbean and Latin America. There would still be opportunity and profit in exporting Canadian prowess in retail banking throughout the region, but the frontier was contracting. Even before Castro's dramatic seizure of power, the Cuban branch system was ailing. The Batista regime had stifled the Cuban economy. Banco Nacional de Cuba had begun demanding that the island's commercial banks make compulsory investments in government treasury bills. Rebel insurgency plagued branch operations; late in 1958, for instance, Contramaestre branch had been summarily closed after government aircraft strafed the town.

Castro's entry into Havana early in 1959 brought relief. The system had regained some stability. But an anti-American backlash soon set in; in October 1960, all American banks in Cuba were expropriated. Despite the exemption of Canada's two banks from this order, Art Mayne, then head of the bank's international operations, had soon reported that "profitable" operations in Cuba seemed unlikely, as Banco Nacional de Cuba under Guevara began to assert a monopoly over all banking on the island. Thus, in the last month of 1960, even as the bank's board was grappling with the thorny issue of finding a new CEO, the Royal Bank had negotiated a remarkable exit from Cuban retail banking. Unlike its American counterparts, the bank managed to repatriate its Cuban investment – about U.S.$8.8 million – by transferring all its assets and liabilities to the Banco Nacional de Cuba. Non-Cuban nationals were permitted to leave the island, and local employees were guaranteed employment with the Cuban central bank. A representative office was opened in Havana to give Cuba a financial outlet to the non-communist world. Through it, the hostage negotiation would be handled. It would close in 1965, but the bank continued to finance Cuban trade. In Montreal, the bank retained the accounts of the Cuban consulate and a growing number of Cuban *émigrés*.

There was upheaval elsewhere in the Caribbean during McLaughlin's early years. In the Dominican Republic, the collapse of the Trujillo regime in 1961 relieved the bank of a government rotted by cronyism, but left it locked in an unseemly battle with the assassinated dictator's family over off-shore assets. At the other end of Hispaniola in 1965, "Papa Doc" Duvalier of Haiti expelled the Royal Bank's manager in Port-au-Prince on trumped-up charges. In most Caribbean countries, however, the bank was crimped in less dramatic ways. Profit repatriation laws, demands for local participation, and volatile local currencies all made operating in the South difficult. In some instances, the bank would seek local incorporation – for instance, the Banco Royal Venezolano C.A. in 1971 – and during the 1960s it even forged ahead with a string of Caribbean trust companies in Jamaica, Trinidad, Barbados, Guyana, and the Caymans. Similarly, in 1965 the bank joined several prominent partners, including Westminster Bank and Morgan Grenfell, to form RoyWest Banking Corporation in Nassau to undertake mortgage and international investment banking in the British West Indies. But the overall trend in the South was towards gradual – and for many Royal Bankers and clients, sorrowful – divestment.

While events in Cuba and the Caribbean had been startling, the ultimate new shape of international banking – powerfully moulded by

Euro and Petro dollars – would emerge less dramatically through the sixties and seventies. At the same time the pressure for change at home was more immediate. Muir had stretched the bank's potential to the utmost limits of the existing Canadian banking system. He did so by managing the bank in a hierarchical, authoritarian style: decision-making moved in an upward linear fashion. Muir was the last man who can be said to have "ruled" the Royal Bank; his tenure marked the last hurrah of the old "bank-boy" school of management.

Earle McLaughlin was a different kind of "bank boy" for a different age. He, too, had polished his trousers on the stools of the branch system, but only after graduating from Queen's University. He had come to the bank in the Depression and had seen it inch towards new roles during the crisis of the Second World War and the boom of the fifties. He knew the limits of Canadian banking: Muir had sent him to Ottawa in 1954 to help establish the bank's presence in mortgage lending, only to see the initiative asphyxiated in the late 1950s by the 6 per cent blanket on bank lending. He had seen the rise of the "near banks," the finance and trust companies, which vied in an increasingly crowded financial marketplace for business that had often traditionally been the banks' alone. By 1960, there was no escaping the necessity of structural change in Canadian banking. Muir would have fought it; McLaughlin would welcome it.

Now, just as Edson Pease had embraced "progressive ways" to assert the bank's primacy in the Laurier boom at the turn of the century, McLaughlin's intuition for change would carry the bank into new territory over varied paths. In doing so, he would change the bank's culture dramatically. It was by no means a flawless transition; in later years, McLaughlin likened the bank to "a big ball of jelly" that elastically resisted change.[13] There were shortfalls, miscalculations, and crises. Women, for instance, found that they had to pound hard on the bank's door for attention. All the while, international banking changed fundamentally and bankers long inured to the rhythms of retail banking in the Caribbean now confronted the dizzy, unfamiliar world of Eurodollars and merchant banking.

Despite all this, McLaughlin learned to cope with change. He decentralized and resisted Muir-like interference. He joked that he always knew "a little about a lot." A colleague likened him to a "surfer" always riding the crest of a wave.[14] By the time he stepped down as chairman in 1980, the Royal Bank was a different place. "The imperial chief executive, lonely and alone, is no more," wrote *Maclean's*. "He has been replaced by strategic planning, management committees, productivity flow charts, squads of consultants and computer technology. Seat-of-the-pants management has, quite simply, worn thin."[15]

*A new building in Quebec: The "Topping-Off" ceremony at Place Ville Marie, 1960 (top), which featured a Mohawk flag erected by Mohawk high-steel workers. (Bottom) The September 1962 inauguration of the building provided evidence of the cross-currents flowing in Quebec society: Premier Jean Lesage, doyen of the "Quiet Revolution," addresses the guests.*

Growth was on McLaughlin's side. Pushed ahead by prosperity and inflation, the bank's assets ballooned from $4 billion to $62 billion during McLaughlin's twenty years from 1960 to 1980. Under McLaughlin, 1,018 domestic and international branches in 1960 had become 1,592 branches by 1980. Behind these statistical advances, there were seismic shifts in the nature of the bank's growth. The energy boom in the West quite literally pulled the bank's centre of gravity westwards. If Toronto had gained in stature in the fifties, Calgary and Vancouver asserted themselves in the seventies and early eighties. In 1971, 55.5 per cent of the bank's loans portfolio was lodged in Ontario and Quebec; 23.5 per cent was in Alberta and British Columbia. By 1980, the central Canadian provinces would have a 48.5 per cent share and the two Pacific provinces would surge to 35 per cent. While Muir would have gloated over such growth as a personal triumph, McLaughlin measured such success in collegial terms. He restored the morale and sense of cohesiveness in senior management that had so powerfully driven the bank since the days of Pease, Neill, Wilson, and Dobson, and which had lapsed under Muir. "It was not done overnight," he told the *Canadian Banker*. "We saw that the right people were appointed in the right spots and gave them responsibility and left them alone. That's the way I tried to run the bank."[16]

The need for delegation was apparent from the start. Like Walter, McLaughlin almost instantly realized that procedures dictated by Muir's need for total control had to be changed. Late every afternoon, for instance, the bank's treasury officials appeared at his door seeking approval of their plans for overnight placements, T-Bill purchases, and foreign-exchange deals. McLaughlin quickly grew frustrated; he knew little about such transactions. "I don't want to make that decision any more," he told them, "keep me posted if you're in trouble, let me know when you're borrowing from the Bank of Canada, there's no harm in that, but not every day. Gradually, gradually we delegated."[17] It soon dawned on the new president that *ad hoc* delegation might ease the pressure on his office and reduce some of the rigidity in the bank's management. If the national banking marketplace was changing, so too must the bank's organization. Starting slowly at first, the momentum of change built over the next few years, cresting in 1967, when, for the first time since 1899, the bank consciously reorganized itself.

If McLaughlin seemed unperturbed by the prospect of change, it was because he brought a different attitude to the top job in the bank. He lacked Muir's fundamental insecurity in power. In his mind, delegation did not imply diminution in his stature. Some of this might have stemmed from the fact that he was the first university graduate to head the bank. Joining the bank after college, even in the

Depression, offered a less-daunting challenge than a Scottish boy immigrant or a Nova Scotia farm boy might have earlier experienced. McLaughlin had been born into relative affluence in small-town Oshawa. Emigration was not necessary for advancement. He was a cousin of Col. Sam McLaughlin, the carriage-maker turned car-maker – but "a distant enough cousin that I had to work," he once quipped.[18] He always said that his first ambition had been to be a lawyer, but instead he took history and economics at Queen's. There he studied under some of the few Canadian academics who actually wrote about the Canadian banking system. From Clifford Curtis and Frank Knox, he learned about Canada's new central bank. Good marks got him a tutorship for the banking courses offered by Queen's for the CBA – at 25 cents a paper marked. In Depression Canada, however, good marks did not guarantee him a job. He tried the Bank of Canada and the finance department in Ottawa before Professor Curtis suggested he try the Royal Bank. Curtis sent him to see Mr. Travers, the Kingston manager of the bank. McLaughlin had heard that the banks hired only high-school grads. What future could banking hold for a university grad? "Look at Graham Towers," Travers shot back.

Ten days after McLaughlin received the gold medal in economics at Queen's in the spring of 1936, he reported for duty as a junior at a Yonge Street branch in downtown Toronto. His salary was $750. He was immediately struck by the fact that there was no training beyond what rubbed off from the accountant who sat beside him. What McLaughlin did not know was that the bank was consciously experimenting with university grads as trainees. He was being paid $250 more than high-school recruits, and his name was on a secret "to be watched" list. A year later, Whit Shannon also left Queen's and joined the same list. Their careers were accelerated. They were moved more frequently and promoted aggressively. By 1945, McLaughlin was on the Canadian credits desk at head office, and a year later he was assistant manager at Montreal main branch, both crucial testing grounds. Here he came under Jimmy Muir's eye.

By the time McLaughlin reached the president's office, he could find ample evidence that the bank could no longer sustain itself on a diet of "on-the-job" training. Muir had adamantly clung to the notion that the "boys" could learn all they needed as they climbed the bank's ladder of advancement. Extension courses from the CBA might assist the climb. Yet everything about banking by 1960 indicated that specialized training was increasingly the order of the day. The volume of transactions, for instance, was becoming punishing – every day Toronto and Montreal branches cleared a half million cheques.[19] Mechanization was one response. A universal system of cheque coding – Magnetic Ink

*Schooling bankers: Earle McLaughlin sensed the need to provide bank staff with formal training. In 1954, he travelled coast-to-coast to brief regional managers on the working of residential mortgages. Here, McLaughlin (centre right) looks on as western branch managers socialize under canvas.*

Character Recognition – was introduced. Electronic posting, using "Post Tronic" machines, was introduced in large centres. To bring order to this skein of financial transactions, the bank began to consider computers, but there was hesitancy. "Number-crunching" machines seemed a direct threat to the virility of "bank boy" banking. They were "robots" and "highly talented morons."[20] None the less, in 1961 the bank became the first Canadian bank to install a computer – an IBM 1401 – at its head office. Machines reduced costs and speeded service. The tedious chore of calculating monthly interest on accounts was, for instance, now within the grasp of computers. But machines, and the growing range of products they processed, underscored the need for staff specialization.

Even with mechanization, staff numbers were growing. From 16,600 in 1960, the Royal Bank "family" would grow to 36,900 by the end of

McLaughlin's tenure in 1980. McLaughlin had no doubt that they had to be trained. He immediately capitalized on the underground sessions that Toronto-area managers had instigated to circumvent Muir's ban on training. Training would now be backed by deliberate policy. McLaughlin and Jim Cornish, his AGM for personnel, shared the view that the bank was only as good as its staff: training, not the old "bank-boy" philosophy, was the key. George McFarlane, one of the Toronto guerilla trainers, was appointed Senior Training Officer. Courses on subjects ranging from the writing of business letters to understanding computers were organized, and staff, mainly middle management, was pulled into seven regional centres to take them. Within a year, 1,500 officers had been "on course." In 1962, an educational-leave program – ironically named for Muir – was introduced to release selected male employees for university education.[21] At the same time, the bank moved away from its old, paternalistic performance-review process – across-the-board pay increases every May 1, based on notes scribbled on staff cards by managers and inspectors, with bonuses used to reward strong performers. Cornish and Hal Wyatt, his supervisor of staff, now brought in systematic salary review, job descriptions, and some sense of career planning. Appointments and transfers, however, remained management's prerogative; mobility of staff was still thought crucial to the system.

Over the next two decades, it was the swelling ranks of junior staff who were the first to sense the need for change in the corporate culture. Here the majority was female, and aspects of the old culture – frequent transfers, for example – grated. Refusal of a transfer had always cut off an employee from promotion. McLaughlin's relative youth and open personality allowed him to tap into the frustrations of junior employees and set the bank on a new course. In 1963, women and maintenance workers were, for instance, finally allowed to contribute to the bank's pension fund. How, McLaughlin asked, could an organization run a pension fund which was closed to the majority of its employees? What made changing the bank's culture so arduous was driving these policies and principles through a cadre of male middle management to connect with the staff below. Here was the bulwark of the bank, men long loyal to the organization, efficient in their work but now threatened by change.[22]

The commitment to systematic training unleashed further forces of change. Training implied a shift towards specialization, but it was not always the magic solution. The old bank generalist could only be stretched so far. For the first time – with the exception of the bank's economists and librarians – "experts" were added to staff to run computers and administer "systems." "I am in the hands of my

*New means and messages: Chief General Manager John Coleman (top)
inaugurates the Computer Age at the bank by pushing
the "start" button at the Montreal Data Centre in 1963.
(Below) Automation in 1960.*

experts" was a favourite McLaughlin response. By the late 1960s, there would be MBAS, marketing specialists, and economic analysts who focused exclusively on narrow sectors of the economy. Many had university educations and did not necessarily see themselves as Royal Bankers for life, so the enticements of benefits, salaries, and career development therefore became doubly important. Head office ceased to be simply a small praetorian guard around the president's office, approving large credits, preparing circulars, and minding the staff cards. It performed crucial "staff" functions for the organization.

Ironically, the changes set in motion under McLaughlin had the parallel effect of creating *decentralizing* pressures in the bank. Computers, regional training, and more career latitude all tended to eat away at central control. Similarly, the growing diversity of bank products, especially after 1967, reinforced the tendency to greater local autonomy; to meet the competition, managers needed more latitude to react quickly to customers' needs. The better McLaughlin came to understand the challenge of modernizing the bank for the marketplace of the sixties, the more he realized that he was attempting to pour new wine into old bottles. The time-proven linear authority structure of the bank could no longer bear the strain of the decade.

And the strain was about to increase. In October 1961, the Conservative government of John Diefenbaker asked the Chief Justice of Ontario, Dana Porter, to lead a royal commission "to enquire and report upon the structure and methods of operation of the Canadian financial system." Porter was to spread his net not just over the banks but also over the "near banks," and to make recommendations "for the improvement of the structure."[23] Not since the Macmillan Commission in the Depression had Canada's financial system been so thoroughly dissected, and there seemed little doubt that the outcome would be a liberalization of the entire system – a breaking down of the rigid demarcations that had kept bankers and near-bankers in separate, and, some alleged, unequal, spheres. Porter reported in April 1964; attention then shifted to the revision of the Bank Act, a laborious process that would stretch out another three years. Throughout this long gestation, it was clear that any liberalization would place a premium on organizational flexibility within the banking community. There would be an unprecedented opportunity for new products and new careers within the banks. Until this, the banks had met change by adhering to their gradualist instincts – slow internally dictated adjustment.[24] Once again, McLaughlin went against the grain. Gradualism simply could not work in the narrow window between the Porter Report and the emerging new Bank Act.

In the fall of 1964, it took little to persuade McLaughlin and his senior executives to import "management" into the bank. The bank had a 1920s structure for a changing 1960s marketplace. There was, for instance, no marketing department, no capability of developing the market that was about to be liberalized. The bank had not a single chartered accountant or lawyer on staff. Similarly, the on-the-job methods of bank training offered little hope for the speedy introduction of computer skills. Yet, there remained a tremendous resistance to outside advice in Canadian banking: outsiders did not understand bankers' ways. They were their own "experts." As we have seen, McLaughlin began to doubt this. There was an inkling of this doubt in 1962 when he approved the hiring of outside consultants, Lippincott and Margulies of New York, to revamp the bank's corporate image. As a first step, the bank's venerable rampant-lions logo was replaced by a lion-and-globe motif – the famous "Leo." With the promotion of John Coleman to chief general manager in 1964, McLaughlin and Executive Vice-President Art Mayne found a reformation ally, and together they ushered in the age of "management" as a conscious corporate function at the Royal Bank. Time and time again, McLaughlin would turn to Coleman to buttress his resolve for change; what McLaughlin decided, Coleman carried throughout the organization.

*Advertising bankers: In September 1967 the bank broke tradition and began advertising on television. The above cartoon promoted Termplan Loans. A shipwrecked sailor approaches his bank manager about "floating" a loan. The bank estimated that this commercial reached fourteen million viewers in its first week.*

Marketing proved the thin end of the management wedge. The bank's auditors, P. S. Ross & Partners in Montreal, had hired a young consultant, Hugh Hardy, who in 1964 had just returned from New York after a stint with an American marketing research firm. Hardy tried to persuade his new bosses to introduce him to the bank, where he might furnish what he could see was some much-needed marketing savvy. Fearful of souring their lucrative auditing contract, the firm told Hardy to back off, but he persisted, this time cultivating Royal Bank executives on his own. Through Brian Champion, the bank's novice "marketer," Hardy gained access to Coleman. Coleman's decisiveness in commissioning a study of the bank's marketing needs saved Hardy from a summary dismissal by his employers.

What the Ross consultants found was not very flattering. The bank marketed itself in the dark. It lacked any precise knowledge of its present and potential customers, it had no means of measuring the effectiveness of its advertising, and it used "unscientific" means of deciding on its new branch locations. The poor marketing led the consultants to bolder conclusions about the bank's overall management: no orderly reporting procedures and too little delegation of responsibility from head office. All this persisted in a decade brimming with change: computers, increasingly affluent retail customers, and corporate clients daily becoming "more sophisticated and more demanding." The bank simply conformed to the market after the fact. What was needed was a more proactive attitude to change. A formal marketing division, staffed by experts, and "formal plans for guiding and controlling future growth" were imperative. Above all else, "planning and development must be the responsibility of senior management," and it must drive a sense of the bank's direction down through the organization. The bank must, in short, become market-driven, not guided solely by adherence to the dictates of the Bank Act or of its own book of rules and regulations. "It will put the Royal Bank in a strong position to stress the offensive strategies – to *cause* change rather than simply *react* to change, which is defensive."[25]

McLaughlin, Mayne, and Coleman were provoked to action. In March 1966, they commissioned a full-scale organizational study of the bank to assist in the development of a five-year corporate plan. They also offered Hardy a position as head of the fledgling marketing department. The ensuing Ross study was a startling shock for the bank's corporate culture. Teams of consultants moved right into Place Ville Marie and began to prowl through head office. They quickly sensed opposition: barricades of "conservative people," who were "hesitant, if not opposed, to any thing new or different or likely to result in changes in the established order of things."[26] The Royal

Bank's structure in 1966 bore an uncanny resemblance to its organization in 1914: decision-making in the key corporate functions – Canadian credits, personnel, accounting, and investments – all converged on the general manager's office. Only international banking and a vice-president for Ontario stood apart, with direct access to the president. The consultants advised the bank to jettison this authority pyramid. Adopt instead a "functional team concept" approach to managing the bank. Push operating authority down into functional divisions and let head office concentrate on the strategic horizon. To drive home the point, their report came replete with a *flat* organization chart that neatly chopped administration of the bank into functional bailiwicks.

The whole process culminated in the September 1967 reorganization, probably the most dramatic organizational watershed the bank has ever crossed. Employees were told that banks now lived in "an environment of rapid change," in which agility in the face of competition was imperative. Their bank must become "a strong, flexible organization capable of banking leadership at home and abroad." To highlight the point, the Ross plan contrasted the past trend in management culture with the "proposed shift." Management on a day-to-day basis would be replaced by "management through established plans." "Heavy reliance on intuitive judgement" would give way to "provision of formal management information." Senior management would be given "narrower" spans of control, and would concentrate on strategic goals, not broad-ranging interference in the operational life of the bank. In short, it would now be a bank in which Jimmy Muir would feel out of place.

The "new" bank was cleanly broken into four divisions, each headed by a general manager. Two were essentially head-office support divisions. An Administrative Division acted as an umbrella for all those functions – personnel to computer operations – which by definition required central oversight. Similarly, Loans and Investments managed the central credit and financial functions of the bank, including economic research. The two "field" divisions – Canadian Districts and International – would operate the all-important retail network, "the *action* role in the bank." Coleman told the shareholders that the shift was the result of some "careful thinking about the basic principles of our business." The bank was a service business dedicated to its customers. It must have a structure that put it closest to its customers *and* derived the fullest benefit from its people and from available technology.[27]

There is a temptation to provide a glib report card on the 1967 reorganization as a success or failure. Certainly, it met with a jaundiced reaction from many staff members.[28] Department heads complained to Coleman that the new organization would "add consultants, add staff, add to overhead."[29] Others would later admit that the new structure relied on "too much paper and system, not enough corporate culture."[30] The real legacy of the 1967 reorganization was, however, that it introduced the idea of organizational change into the bank, not as a one-shot affair but as an ongoing process. Coleman saw the 1967 exercise as the first step in "a continual process of adjustment." Throughout the 1970s, the bank continued to reorganize. In 1974, a fifth division – for Canadian corporate banking – was added to the 1967 structure. A set of "corporate objectives" was developed to place the bank's organizational structure in the context of its corporate strategic goals. Bankers grew familiar with the jargon of modern management and began to apply buzzwords and catch-phrases to their business: "getting closer to our markets," "a bank that tends to be lean." Organizational issues made frequent appearances on the agenda of the Chief General Manager's Committee, the fulcrum of the bank's weekly executive decision-making.[31] By the end of the decade, new growth and market shifts would dictate continuing reorganization.

Organizational change broke down the homogeneous nature of "bank-boy" management in other ways. Management was no longer personality-driven; it was team-driven. The emphasis on reducing spans of management in 1967 tended to accentuate the definition of authority in management. The days in which a *general* manager and a cohort of assistant general managers could manage all they surveyed were gone. Soon their titles were gone as well. By the late 1970s, the old Anglo–Scottish nomenclature of banking had disappeared and banks were managed by an array of vice-presidents whose titles reflected regional and functional responsibilities. Over all this, McLaughlin presided beneficently, always aware of shifts in the bank's strategy and structure but seldom present at their forging. One of the benefits of the new executive ethos of the bank was that careers as well as structures could be planned. Men could be shifted to where their talents were best used or best developed. A straight linear progression from teller's cage to president's office would no longer prepare a man for computer-age banking, but throughout the McLaughlin years, there was always the sense that capable men were being groomed in the wings.

Whether of men or of structures, planning was now an integral part of banking. Bankers could no longer simply define their future in terms of the next decennial revision of the Bank Act. Demographics, economic "shocks," and shifts in the regulatory climate could all push banking in unexpected directions.[32] The early 1970s would, for instance, deliver in quick succession an unprecedented energy crisis, followed in Canada by a federally imposed blanket of wage-and-price controls. Long-range, or strategic, planning to anticipate the environment in which business would have to operate became an unavoidable aspect of managing any business. The bank responded by pulling Warren Bull, a former head-office inspector, out of the personnel department and making him the bank's director of compensation and organization.

Bull took to strategic planning with messianic fervour and was, by 1975, appointed AGM of Corporate Planning and Organization. It was an uphill battle. The purpose and process of strategic planning was alien to bankers habituated to hard "results" and defined procedures. Planning consumed valuable time, many complained, and the "plans" often seemed to miss the mark. Bull persisted: strategic planning was an aid to the bank's development, not a blueprint for it. In 1977, for instance, Bull convinced Rowland Frazee and Jock Finlayson, McLaughlin's most promising senior executives, to follow him to California for a two-day confidential session with American management guru Peter Drucker.[33] When Frazee took over operational control of the bank that same year, he created a presidential committee on the bank's strategic direction. In 1979, an annual Strategic Planning Conference was initiated for the bank's fifty top executives. As the "turbulent" seventies faded, Royal Bankers were asked to divine some "manageable probabilities" for the eighties.[34]

A good deal of the "turbulence" in Canadian banking in the seventies was the natural consequence of the 1967 Bank Act revision. Canadian banking had suddenly become more competitive and less hidebound. When Earle McLaughlin was called before the Porter Commission in January 1963, he left no doubt in the commissioners' minds that the Royal Bank was in favour of liberalizing Canada's financial industry. Much of the regulatory framework surrounding the banks "originally arose to correct abuses in the early days of banking" and to serve as a bolster to the public interest. In more recent years, the banks had become instruments of federal monetary policy – squeezing or freeing credit – while many of their "near-bank" competitors operated in a less-stringent environment. Most irksome of these "special rigidities" were the 6 per cent ceiling on bank-loan rates and the 8 per cent cash-to-deposits reserve. "The right policy," McLaughlin concluded, "is not to impose handicaps on the near-banks; but to ensure the fullest degree of competition in the market for credit by extending near-bank freedom of action to the chartered banks."[35]

McLaughlin's was not a lonely voice. By the time the commissioners reported in April 1964, there was a strong consensus that Canada's financial-services industry must be placed on what is today called a "level playing field." Their report found the system full of "illogical and inequitable restrictions" that penalized the consumer; "a more open and competitive banking system" would "encourage creativity and efficiency and offer the public the widest possible range of choice of financial services."[36] To promote the "free flow of funds" and "equal treatment," the 6 per cent interest ceiling should be scrapped and the banks allowed full access to the conventional mortgage market. The near-banks should be brought under the Bank Act and, like the banks, be required to maintain a fixed ratio of cash-to-deposits on reserve with the Bank of Canada. A 10 per cent limit should be placed on banks' ownership of near-banks as a precaution against undue concentration in the industry.* McLaughlin echoed the general delight of the banking industry when he praised the "market-freeing" aspects of the report. No longer would the banks be obliged to act as "rationing boards" for credit; instead, their clients would have access to a wider range of loans, with less-onerous collateral requirements.[37] Given the magnitude of these recommendations, Ottawa postponed the revision of the Bank Act, slated for 1964, for a year.

Porter's recommendations were soon snagged on the rocks of political intrigue. Unable to muster a parliamentary majority, the Liberal government of Lester Pearson harkened to the political allure of economic nationalism. The issue was precipitated by Finance Minister Walter Gordon's perception that Canada's financial sector was vulnerable to foreign control. Citibank's 1963 purchase of Mercantile Bank of Canada, a decade-old, Dutch-owned trade bank, provoked Gordon to impose limits on foreign ownership of Canadian financial institutions – 10 per cent by any single shareholder and 25 per cent *in toto*.[38] Political squabbling over the Mercantile Bank engulfed the entire Bank Act revision throughout 1965 and early 1966. Gordon's 1965 attempted revision also failed to abolish the 6 per cent interest ceiling; its removal would, Gordon said, allow the banks to penalize borrowers with higher interest rates. This incensed McLaughlin, who complained to Prime Minister Pearson that the banks were no longer "the dominant giant in the financial system"[39] that Gordon imagined them to be.

It took all the political finesse that newly appointed finance minister Mitchell Sharp could summon to bring the Bank Act revision to a successful conclusion in the spring of 1967.[40] The spirit of the Porter Commission finally found legislative form. Not only could the banks

---

* From the days of Herbert Holt, the bank, for instance, had had an affiliation with the Montreal Trust; this would now come to an end, as the 1967 Bank Act severed all ties between banks and trust companies. Financial deregulation in the early 1990s would, ironically, undo this segregation and allow the banks to create their own trust companies.

make conventional mortgages, but they were permitted to raise capital by issuing five-year debentures. A lower cash-to-deposit reserve reduced the proportion of bank assets on which no interest could be earned. Bank shares could be split to broaden share ownership. Above all else, the 6 per cent interest ceiling was finally lifted. Viewed strategically, the 1967 revision positioned the banks to stage a counter-attack on the near-banks, the finance, trust, and loan companies that had done so well since the war in the unevenly regulated world of Canadian finance. And it was just such a strategic opportunity that McLaughlin's remaking of the bank's structure was intended to capture. Competition meant speed of reaction and quality of service.

The competitive instinct was evident in much of what the Royal Bank did in the 1960s; by decade's end the bank offered an array of products that would have startled clients and employees alike at its beginning. The notion that a bank could develop uniform products to blanket all its customers faded. Retail banking would, of course, always concentrate on common-denominator products – savings and chequing – but beyond this lay a fragmenting financial landscape, opening up market niches that required special products for special needs. Not all these sprang phoenix-like from the 1967 revision, but they cumulatively served to move the bank into hitherto uncharted financial territory. Like auto-makers, bankers now found themselves identifying consumer preferences and developing models to satisfy them.

In 1962, TermPlan consumer loans were introduced – life-insured, consumer instalment loans. Capped at $3,600, TermPlan loans were aimed at consumers in search of money to finance a trip, a car, or home improvement. University Tuition Loans were introduced. The small-business borrower was another target. In 1961, government-guaranteed Business Improvement Loans were offered. A year later, the bank joined the Banque Canadienne Nationale, Montreal Trust, and Canada Trust to form RoyNat in order to furnish medium-sized businesses with growth capital. Banks had traditionally provided such companies with working capital; capital markets delivered long-term capital. Now the banks could offer intermediate term financing to companies – especially family concerns – that wished to avoid the capital market. To finance its operations, RoyNat itself borrowed from the capital market. Computers and specially trained staff also allowed the bank to open up other services for business and retail clients. Payroll processing, business-accounting systems and consulting, pre-authorized payments, and mortgage accounting all emerged on the frontier of computer-assisted banking.

*(continued on p. 384)*

# "ANYTIME BANKING"
## Automating the Cash Box

IN THE LEXICON OF NINETEENTH-CENTURY banking, no term was as hallowed as "the cash." The daily round trip of the teller's cash box from the vault in the morning to the cage and back, neatly balanced when the branch closed, epitomized the business of banking. For the public, the quick delivery or receipt of cash was the essence of service. The good teller, his sleeves held up by colourful garters, dispensed cash with panache, his fingers crisply flicking down bills at his window. On that flow of money the public built its trust in a bank; any hesitancy might provoke a "run." Competency in handling "the cash" was also the first major test of responsibility for an aspiring young banker. A properly balanced blotter and neatly bundled piles of bills were the mark of a day's work dutifully done.

A half century later, the cages were gone and the tin cash box could not contain Canadians' burgeoning appetite for cash. Between 1961 and 1981, the assets of Canadian banks exploded from $19 billion to $350 billion; at the same time Canadians availed themselves of all sorts of new ways of spending their money and settling their accounts. By 1980, the volume of payments issued in Canada by the general public – excluding federal government payments – exceeded two billion items, an eightfold increase from 1965. Behind the scenes, computers were increasingly employed to "batch process" these transactions or to transmit them "on line." But, as long as the actual dealing of cash to clients remained a largely manual affair, a costly labour-intensive bottleneck remained in the branch itself. Furthermore, cash-related services were confined to the hours in which the branch was actually open. After the 1967 Bank Act revision, the bank began experimenting. In 1968, a mini-branch with an on-line computer was opened in a shopping mall, open as long as the stores were. "Fasteller," "Fascash," and "One-Stop Customer" followed, all dedicated to getting cash into clients' hands quicker. But only with the creation of its Automated Customer Services Group in 1969 did the bank begin to think of more dramatic alternatives.

Would people take money from machines? Would they trust the machines? Did machines contravene the Bank Act? The complexity of machine banking explained its initially cautious appearance. In 1972, fourteen Toronto branches were equipped with "Bankette" machines. They were activated by a customer identity card and only dispensed cash. "Tomorrow morning at 9:00 a.m.," the ads read, "the Royal Bank will open and never close again." Vice-President Frazee assured the press that the Bankettes were designed to lighten workload, not to strip jobs out of the branches. In 1977, the first free-standing machines (i.e., independent of a branch) were introduced. Unlike Leacock's famous nervous depositor, Canadians did not seem to get "rattled" in front of the impersonal machines.

Positive initial reaction to the machines led to a broadening of the services they could perform: transfers and deposits. Since a client might now deal one day with a customer-service representative (CSR) and the next with a machine, the bank introduced its "client card" to give its customers a universal identity. In 1981, Personal Touch Banking (PTB) was launched, and within a year, 400 PTB machines were operating. The Royal Bank had found another frontier. By 1985, there were 900 machines in 740 Canadian communities; by 1990 the bank maintained its lead with 3,127 machines. By 1992, 65 per cent of Royal Bank retail banking was done through what had become North America's largest automated banking network. At the same time, over-the-counter banking maintained its 1982 volume. Like Chargex, the machines dramatically changed Canadians' daily financial habits; for routine financial needs, anytime banking had become a reality. "Bankers' hours" have become any hour. Despite their high initial cost, the machines reduced the bank's fixed costs and allowed staff to concentrate on servicing niche markets on a person-to-person basis. Men and machines were not mutually exclusive: a combination of lean staff and machines has allowed the opening of twenty-four-hour, drive-in "superbranches" and supermarket branches.

*Renowned Canadian pianist Oscar Peterson at the keyboard of a Personal Touch Banking Machine, 1981. Peterson composed a musical theme, "My Personal Touch," for the advertising of machine banking.*

Since the Laurier boom had peopled the West, the bank had catered to farmers' needs. The days of the sod-buster on a quarter-section were, however, long gone by the 1960s. Western agriculture had become agribusiness. In 1967, the Royal became the first Canadian bank to dedicate staff to the service of the Prairie farmer. Simple Section 88 loans or Farm Improvement Loans no longer met farm finance needs. A year later, FarmPlan was introduced to provide "one-stop, fully integrated credit" for "the progressive commercial farmer who conducts his operation in a business-like fashion."[41] Life-insured loans amortized over as long as ten years were made available for needs ranging from farm buildings to breeding stock. Over the next decade, these were supplemented with specialized services to assist farmers with their mortgage, retirement, and financial-management needs. The bank developed farm-oriented information programs, like the *Farm Business Review* and "Farmchek." The galvanizing force behind FarmPlan was Doug McRorie, an agricultural economist hired in 1967 by General Manager Frazee to help the bank understand the complex underpinnings of agribusiness. A good example of the kind of expertise initially brought into the bank by McLaughlin to broaden its reach, McRorie would guide FarmPlan for over two decades.[42]

The West played another, more fundamental, role in the bank's affairs during the McLaughlin years. The hothouse growth of western energy created a new Laurier-style boom in the late 1960s and through the tumultuous 1970s. Since the 1950s, the bank had prided itself on being the "R-oil" Bank, the leading bank in the oil patch. By 1953, it had the accounts of 47 per cent of the companies listed in the Alberta oil directory; by 1967 this had risen to 53 per cent. Despite this success, the bank had had to train itself to cater to western needs. Staff in the West complained that head office often gave them the impression that they were second-class citizens – loan approvals in what was a yeasty industry took too long. Once, when Jimmy Muir visited Calgary, a staffer asked why this was so. "Read your circulars," Muir barked back. Slowly, the situation changed; rigid procedures set out in circulars were ill-suited to the demands of competitive banking. Turn-around on loan approvals improved dramatically. In 1962, McLaughlin convened a board meeting in Calgary for the first time. By the mid-sixties, the Royal Bank was capturing 75 per cent of the new business in the oil patch. The soaring price of energy in the 1970s reinforced the trend.

The two oil "shocks" in the early seventies had a galvanic effect in drawing bankers to Calgary. In this respect, the Royal had always been well served by its Alberta directors. Frank McMahon and Fred Mannix had done much since the fifties to introduce the bank to good energy clients. In the seventies, their efforts were supplemented by men like

Don Getty.* The west also found champions within the ranks of the bank's staff; Hal Wyatt, the Moose Jaw boy who had been with the bank since 1939, agitated for a greater active presence for the bank in his native region. With oil prices bounding upwards in the seventies, there was little resistance to such pressure. By the decade's end, Calgary main branch had become the bank's second-busiest branch in the country, surpassing Montreal and trailing only Toronto. In 1971, Alberta interests comprised 11.3 per cent of the bank's loan portfolio; by 1980, they commanded 16.4 per cent. In the same year, energy lending constituted 20 per cent of all the bank's business lending.

As the bank came alive to energy lending, petroleum engineers were brought on staff. What started in Calgary was quickly carried abroad. Oil and gas representatives were posted to London and representative offices were opened in Houston and Denver. The bank began participating in international energy syndications as far afield as the North Sea, Mexico, Iran, and even Brazil. Back in Canada, the bank took a leading role in financing some of the energy megaprojects that had come into vogue. In 1979, for instance, the Royal Bank joined the Polar Gas Project and helped syndicate financing for PetroCanada. To exemplify Calgary's new financial stature, the bank created a vice-chairman's post in Calgary in 1978, appointing Hal Wyatt to the position. And then, in 1980, a Calgary-based global-energy and mining group was created to spearhead the bank's services to the energy industry. Later in 1980, the bank joined with the CIBC and Trizec to unveil plans for a huge Bankers' Hall on Calgary's 8th Avenue. The Royal's share of the project, a forty-nine-storey tower, would, Hal Wyatt announced, help it "to better serve the growing needs of this very dynamic marketplace."[43]

The western energy boom finally broke the central Canadian suzerainty over the bank's affairs. Ever since migrating from Halifax to Montreal in the 1880s, the bank had managed itself according to the managerial dictates of central Canadians. McLaughlin's willingness to decentralize the bank's management thus coincided with strong western pressures that pulled the bank out onto the prairies and, in an operational sense, made it a real national bank for the first time. There were, however, hidden dangers in energy lending, as the eighties would amply reveal. In retrospect, it would become apparent that the

---

* When Getty assumed the Alberta premiership in the 1980s, his place on the board was taken by the retiring premier, Peter Lougheed. Lougheed's election to the board in effect rounded a circle for the bank. His legal firm, Bennett Jones Verchere, had been connected with the bank since the first decade of the century, when R. B. Bennett, its founding partner, did legal work for the bank. Bennett, too, of course, joined the bank's board.

headlong rush to finance energy development in the West bred what one Calgary Royal Banker called a kind of "collective virus" in bankers, which over time affected the credit culture of the banks. If the banks had been slow and stingy in energy lending in the early 1950s, they became overquick and careless in the late 1970s and early 1980s. But in 1980, the consequences of this largesse were not as yet apparent.

Energy entrepreneurs, farmers, small business, and employers were thus developed by the bank as new or revamped clients. But the rock bed of the bank's health was still its retail-branch network: a thousand domestic branches generating 60 per cent of the bank's deposit base. Breadth in the retail base supported, and fed, more specialized banking. The challenge in the sixties was to maintain the bank's retail vigour by improving service – hence the importance of training – and adding new products. Mortgages were a crucial step in this direction. Other forms of more accessible consumer credit beckoned. In 1959, Bank of America had given consumers the first glimpse of a "cashless" society when it introduced its BankAmericard in California. In 1961, it began to advertise the card on television, and its use exploded. By 1967, BankAmericards were in 5.1 million American wallets. When Hugh Hardy came to the bank in 1966, he brought with him memories of marketing research in New York. As he told General Manager Coleman: "It is generally accepted that a well-run credit card scheme can be a highly profitable venture." Other Canadian banks were toying with the idea of introducing cards, and a Montreal-based finance company, Credico, was about to launch a national card. Failure to seize the initiative would leave the Royal Bank, as Canada's largest retail bank, in an extremely vulnerable position.[44]

Credit cards required a real leap of faith by bankers. McLaughlin opposed them strongly. In late 1966, Hardy persistently urged McLaughlin and Coleman to consider buying Credico's nascent card network, thereby positioning the bank on the frontier of this new field. There were rumours that the Toronto-Dominion was negotiating for a BankAmericard franchise, and that other banks were working up feasibility studies. Yet, when the proposal was taken to the general manager's committee, McLaughlin emerged with a "final and irrevocable" decision: no credit cards. After decades of extolling the virtues of "saving" to Canadians, how could bankers turn around and tell Canadians to "charge it," to take on debt? McLaughlin also worried that credit-card interest rates could easily become a volatile public issue. Might the banks run afoul of the Bank Act by "factoring" receivables (i.e., receiving debts at a commission) when it accepted merchants' credit slips? Within the bank, credit cards would require vast systems support, more reliance on computers, and specialized training. Given the banks' traditionally tame advertising methods, how would they ever "sell" the cards to sceptical merchants and clients? In the face of this rebuff, Hardy was encouraged when General Manager Coleman told him *sotto voce* to keep an eye on credit-card developments elsewhere.

It was a mark of McLaughlin's management style that, unlike his strong-willed predecessor, he could change his mind. By the spring of 1967, there was evidence that, for all their reluctance, other banks were looking at credit cards and that the Royal Bank stood to be scooped. Coleman told Hardy to reopen his investigations. The inspector general of banks was, for instance, contacted by bank lawyers about the issue of factoring. Given the fluid nature of consumer spending, it was also clear from the outset that a "go-it-alone" strategy – insisting that merchants carry one bank's brand of card – would not work. A joint venture was in order – a common card serving several affiliates. Hardy reported that the Toronto-Dominion Bank had done "a good deal of thinking about and preliminary planning" and its Deputy Chief General Manager Dick Thomson was eager to negotiate.[45] McLaughlin was now convinced, and created a special task force to expedite preparations. In December, a delegation of Canadian bankers trekked to San Francisco to see the BankAmericard operation. Barclays Bank in England had become the second franchisee of the highly successful American card. In August 1968, a Canadian consortium of the Royal, Commerce, BCN, and T-D banks would become the third.

Credit cards were a novel product for the banks. Profits stood to be made from a transaction fee payed by merchants and from interest charges on unpaid client credit balances. American experience had shown that the cardholders carried an average balance of $140 on their cards. To give the card national recognition, a bilingual name was needed. Why not "Chargex," a BCN executive suggested? A two-pronged sales effort would then be needed to sell the card, first to merchants and then to clients. This would require that "aggressive, well-informed, ethical salemanship" be developed in Chargex sales staff.[46] Card "activation" – actually getting people to use the cards – would be the next challenge. On top of all this, a complex system of purchase authorization and billing tailored for the Canadian scene had to be established.

During the summer of 1968, Montrealers and Torontonians were introduced to Chargex. Spreading westward and eastward through the fall and winter, the card was initially delivered unsolicited to promising existing bank clients. Consumer protests soon forced the banks to adopt direct marketing of the cards through branch promotions and the mail. The cards quickly found their way into Canadian wallets. By 1971, the Royal Bank led the competition with 571,000 Chargex customers, 80 per cent of which were existing bank clients. Activation remained a problem; only 40 per cent of cardholders actually used their cards. The bank redoubled its promotional efforts. A concerted attempt was made to sign up strategically located merchants, such as service-station chains. By 1980, there were 1.7 million Royal Bank cards, 70 per cent of which were in regular use. There were changes en route. In 1977, the globally ubiquitous (and still bilingual) "Visa" name was adopted. Card procedures were polished; the Royal Bank was the first to adopt "descriptive" monthly billing – a computer listing – instead of the old "country-club" billing, in which loose receipts were attached.

Within a decade, the credit card had affected a remarkable revolution in Canadian banking. Chargex put $300 – the initial personal ceiling – of instant credit into millions of Canadian hands, either in terms of the thirty-day billing hiatus until payment or as a cash advance. No other financial product had such a democratic reach in society. None has ever changed Canadians' spending habits more. For the banks, Chargex overheads were high, but fraud and bad debts – another of the early fears – never rose above 1 per cent of volume. Consequently profits were steady and good. At the same time, Chargex did much to drive computer data systems deep into the heart of bank operations.

Chargex succeeded not just because it was a timely companion to Canadian consumerism but also because banks made a market for it. It was a testament to the power of advertising. "Will that be cash or Chargex?" etched itself into the popular culture of the late sixties. The concept of card credit had to be sold,[47] and then, since Chargex was a generic term, each bank had to work to develop its own Chargex clientele. Advertising Chargex was thus the cutting edge of a broader remaking of the bank's advertising effort. Old-style bank advertising – static print and poster promotion – seemed impotent in the face of this dynamic challenge. Despite spending over a million dollars a year on print advertising, the bank felt that it occupied a rather shadowy position in most consumers' minds. A study in the fall of 1966 revealed that only 7 per cent of those interviewed could recall "anything that was said in Royal Bank advertising." On the other hand, 30 per cent of the same respondents could recall the advertising of a "near-bank" rival, Household Finance. The difference lay in the fact that HFC spent nearly all of its much-smaller advertising budget on television and radio advertising.[48] Canada's bankers politely had long abided by a long-standing gentlemen's agreement that electronic advertising was off-limits. Having committed itself to a fully fledged marketing effort, however, the Royal decided that it could no longer afford to be a gentleman, and in March 1967, General Manager Coleman informed the CBA that the Royal Bank would begin experimenting with radio "spots" the next month. The 1966-67 advertising budget was increased 16 per cent to allow $250,000 to be spent on broadcast media.[49] Although billed as "a flirtation rather than a marriage" with radio, "live" advertising was instantly seen to be banking's most potent ally in the liberated marketplace of the late sixties. Despite its cost, the bank quickly moved onto the television screen.

Having broken down the wall of convention, the bank needed something to fix its new, moving image in the consumer's mind. *All* banks were offering mortgages and most had credit cards. Friendly, efficient service seemed to be the key to a distinctive reputation and improved market share. If this could be established, then the promotion of all the bank's products could be "driven" off this central image. That image emerged in the summer of 1968 when the bank decided to build its radio identity around "Mary," a "dream teller," who would give the bank a more consumer-oriented face. Since customers were now dealing with a bank that was predominantly female, Mary was to be the "girl-next-door" bank employee, a friendly, attractive, and efficient embodiment of the corporate culture. Mary was launched on the radio in 1968 and won instant recognition. The voice of Mary on radio was soon reinforced by a "visual" Mary in print ads. In 1970, the Mary of the print ads began appearing on television, using the dubbed voice of an actress. An intensive search was then launched for one Mary, whose voice and appearance suited her to all media. Success came in the person of Kathleen Flaherty, a vivacious, bilingual Ottawa "girl" with acting training. Kathleen received some branch training as a teller, and then stepped into her role as Mary. Mary was to be pleasantly "average," "not a worldly sophisticate and she is not an egghead."[50]

As an advertising strategy, Mary was a phenomenal success. For the next six years, "Mary of the Royal Bank" was one of the best known – arguably *the* best known – advertising personalities in Canada. She was the first woman ever chosen to carry a high-profile corporate message to the Canadian public. "The Royal Bank is as Canadian as maple syrup. And so is our Mary." Mary unified the bank's growing array of products in the public's mind; her face appeared on posters and in TV ads, and Mary was present at branch openings and public functions to which the bank lent its name. By 1973, the bank's advertising manager, W. L. Robinson, concluded that "the terms 'Mary' and 'Royal Bank' have become virtually synonymous."[51] In 1966, "top of the mind" recall of Royal Bank advertising in English Canada was only

*Mary of the Royal Bank sells consumer loans (top)*
*and joins the Grey Cup Parade in Vancouver in the early 1970s (below).*

3 per cent; by 1973 it had soared to 59 per cent, 14 per cent higher than its nearest rival. Similarly, the bank received an 8 per cent higher rating for "good advertising" than any other bank.[52] So successful was Mary that, in 1973, negotiations were undertaken – ultimately unsuccessfully – with Mattel, makers of the Barbie doll, for a Mary doll.

The Mary marketing plan had an Achilles' heel. Her rise to national prominence coincided with that of a growing concern over the place of women in Canadian society. These were the years of "women's liberation," and by the mid-seventies Mary was to become a lightning rod for the early feminist movement. For all her media success, Mary still came to symbolize what many saw as the predicament of women in Canadian society and within the bank. In the case of the Royal Bank, Mary brought into the open social changes and frustrations that had been simmering below the surface of Canadian banking for over two decades. By 1968, 64 per cent of Canada's 82,921 bank employees were women. They occupied the capacious service niches of bank employment. The 1966 Ross study of the Royal Bank found that 75 per cent of women in the bank were under twenty-five years of age. For many, bank work as a teller provided ideal supplemental employment, a second income for a baby-boom family. Other women, however, bridled at the lack of long-term prospects in the bank. A "glass ceiling" hovered above their heads. The male executives for whom they worked had long concluded that women were not mobile employees, and were therefore best deployed in service roles in fixed locales. Since other demands on their lives often cut short their employment, they reasoned – the Ross study found a 35 per cent turnover rate – there was no point in training women for management. It was, of course, a Catch-22. Mary therefore fell into the role of the teller – there to serve. During the negotiations with Mattel, for instance, discussion of a male companion doll for Mary arose. Predictably, Mary's "male friend" would be "her manager." Banking was admittedly but one screen onto which these social roles were projected, but the gender differentiation was statistically striking. A study undertaken for the Royal Commission on the Status of Women discovered that, in 1968, only 29 of Canada's 5,147 bank managers were women.[53] The Royal Bank had appointed its first woman manager – Georgette St. Cyr in Longueil, Quebec – in 1968, but there were as yet no women in the bank's executive or on its board.

In 1973, Mary was on location at Queen Mary Road branch in Montreal to film a thirty-second commercial. Mary was depicted serving a mother and her son. Short five seconds of dialogue, the producer had the little boy *ad lib* that he wanted to be a doctor when he grew up. Answered Mary: "I wanted to be a nurse." The ad went to air.

*The sixties and seventies saw women begin to break out of their traditional service niches in the bank. Tellers remained the bank's front line of service, and the always-genial McLaughlin frequently carried that message into the branches (above). Slowly, women eroded men's monopoly on management. In 1979, Suzanne Labarge (seen opposite in 1978 on inspection in Montreal) became the bank's first woman executive.*

Shortly thereafter, the bank issued an educational booklet on banking, *Let's Pretend We Work in the Bank*, in which little girls played teller and boys played manager. The balance finally tipped. Ontario had just established a Status of Women Council to promote equal employment opportunity in the province. Its head, Laura Sabia, drew a bead on the sexual stereotyping in the bank's advertising, bought a single Royal Bank share, and showed up at the bank's annual meeting the next January. When, she demanded of Earle McLaughlin, would the bank take "that idiot advertisement" featuring Mary off the air?[54] Later the same day, Sabia and McLaughlin met privately to address a longer list of women's concerns: pensions, treatment of female clients' credit needs, and managerial training for women. Male bankers, Sabia asserted, needed to be "sensitized" to women's frustrations. McLaughlin admitted some shortcomings and outlined efforts that were under way to place men and women on an equal footing in the bank.[55] After the meeting, *Let's Pretend* was withdrawn from circulation.

Henceforth, women's issues would be an explicit part of the corporate agenda. Mary and Sabia had combined to draw public attention to the role of women in Canadian banking. The time had come, McLaughlin admitted, for bankers "to take a long and careful look at ourselves."[56] There was now an expectation both inside *and* outside the bank that some sort of employment-equity process would be initiated. And it was, although the male culture of Canadian banking approached the transition rather clumsily at first. Old attitudes die hard. In 1976, for instance, McLaughlin ill-advisedly told a reporter that the bank's forty-eight-member board contained no women because women lacked the "qualifications in the areas we need." A "simple housewife" would not do. Again, the public reacted. So did McLaughlin. Two women – Mitzi Dobrin, a Steinberg's vice-president, and Dawn McKeag, president of a Winnipeg investment company – soon joined the board. The year 1976 also saw Mary's "retirement" from the bank. Royal Bank advertising shifted from being personality-oriented to being product-oriented.

The momentum of equal-opportunity employment for women was slow in the late 1970s. The solidly entrenched male cadre in management could not be shunted aside overnight. There were limits to reform in large organizations.[57] In 1978, an American sociologist was brought in to conduct "awareness sessions" to sensitize senior management to the interests of women. Word-association exercises, for instance, were used to make managers aware of sexual stereotyping ("woman are…men do…"). At the same time, women within the bank began agitating on their own for change. In Montreal, where head office provided a high concentration of female employment, women in middle management began meeting after hours to discuss their frustrations as woman bankers. The 1976 appointment of Gwyn Gill as the bank's RSVP Coordinator served to bring their discontent into the open. The RSVP coordinator was to act as the employees' ombudsman on any issue of discontent, enjoying direct access to senior management. Gill, who had risen from a Halifax tellership to branch management in Montreal, seemed well situated to carry the concerns of her colleagues to her vice-president and eventually to Chief General Manager Rowland Frazee. She agreed to take on the job. Torn between their loyalty to the bank and their frustrations, the women knew that they were forcing management to move from rhetoric to action. Frazee soon responded by creating an Advisory Task Force on the Status of Women in the Royal Bank.[58]

After probing the bank's staff with interviews and questionnaires, the task force reported that while there was "no discrimination in the Bank's policies," there were "in fact inequities in practice." Mobility was a bugbear for men and women alike. Advancement in the bank could no longer depend solely upon willingness to relocate. Allow employees to indicate their willingness to move and then channel men and women alike into appropriate career streams, the task force suggested. Tailor training to these ends, create an Equal Employment Opportunity (EEO) Coordinator to ensure that women were trained for executive advancement and drive the equal-employment message through the organization with vigour. There were some sharp differences of opinion within the task force. Should the bank set quotas for women in management? Were the quotas attainable? Should the existing personnel department or senior management monitor the overall progress towards affirmative action? In the end, the bank adopted a program of incremental change, based on the equal-employment concept. An EEO Coordinator was appointed in 1977. Guidelines were established, and close attention was paid to the progress, accelerated by designated training and "fast-tracking," of promising, university-educated women up the management ladder in the bank. Explicit quotas, in the end, were not established. Goals were, however, set in hiring, to ensure that "feeder" populations of promotable women were created in the management hierarchy. There would be no quantum leaps for women in the bank, only a steady ascent up the ladder.

From the late seventies through the eighties, women steadily expanded their presence in the lower echelons of the bank's management pyramid. In 1977, women comprised only 8 per cent of bank middle and upper management. By 1982, this was 16 per cent, and by 1988 it was 29 per cent.[59] The more junior management-support cadre – considered the "feeder population" for future management generations – was, however, 75 per cent female by 1988. But despite its increasingly feminized base, the pyramid still narrowed dramatically at its apex. In 1979, Suzanne Labarge, a bilingual, Harvard-trained MBA, had become the bank's first woman executive. Her appointment as assistant general manager, international loans, was followed in 1984 by Gwyn Gill's promotion to vice-president, organization planning and development. Women who broke through the "glass ceiling" reported that they had brought a "very aggressive" attitude to their career and had acquired a "thick skin" to deal with some male colleagues and clients. Women, for instance, generally lacked mentors in male senior management, nor did they easily fall into the networking patterns – built largely around golf – of male banking. Consequently, by 1988, only 4 of the bank's 176 senior executives were women; two years later this had crept up to 8 executives, or 5 per cent.

The management pyramid sat on top of an even broader base of administrative support (AS) personnel, which was still overwhelmingly female – 93 per cent in 1988. Here were the people who actually serviced the customer on a day-to-day basis. As the bank's product line grew, so did the complexity of branch administration. The venerable title of "teller" disappeared, replaced by "Customer Service Representative" (CSR). Ironically, these years saw the reappearance of males as "tellers." As the bank's principal entry-level position, that of the CSR offered the kind of thoroughgoing exposure to practical banking that remained fundamental to the shaping of a banking career. None the less, the female-dominated AS group became associated with three gender-related employment issues in these years – computerization, unionization, and part-time employment.

Computers stripped away much of the traditionally menial work of banking. "Busy-hands" routine work, once so central to a bank clerk's daily life, were now smoothly automated, and there was much debate over the ultimate consequences of the spread of computers from strategic functions in head office into the daily life of the branches. Would computers "de-skill" clerical employees, making them mindless automatons?[60] Would computers push women employees further into a job ghetto? By the mid-1980s, it was apparent that computers did not throw branch staff out of work, nor did they "de-skill" them. Staff numbers grew steadily through the decade and the microcomputer not only reduced the tedium and workload of banking but also enabled CSRs to "handle a broader range of transactions and perform more complex financial services."[61] The bank soon learned that computerization was not a one-time adjustment, but a rolling revolution, which demanded constant retraining of staff. The more it invested in such training, the more valuable and less dispensable its staff became.

These same years also saw sporadic attempts to unionize bank support staff. Ever since the fitful unionization movement of the years between 1910 and 1920, bank employees had remained one of the largest blocks of non-unionized labour in Canada. The strong corporate culture, the latent promise of professional status, and the scattered nature of employment had successfully militated against unionization. The persistence of a female majority within the bank since the Second World War had worn down this immunity, since, in many ways, women felt excluded from the corporate culture that had rewarded men for shunning unions. At the same time, unions elsewhere in the Canadian economy began to turn their fraternal attention on the banks. In 1977, the Canadian Labour Congress backed the creation of the Canadian Union of Bank Employees and sponsored its drive to unionize banks. Much of the campaign was fought out before the Canadian Labour Relations Board. The union won the right to organize at the branch level and to "freeze" branch staff at the moment that a certification vote was requested. Management, in turn, won the right to exclude unionized branches from across-the-board salary and benefit increases given to non-union staff.[62]

Once again, unionization fizzled. By 1979, about fifty branches of various banks had been organized, few of them in the Royal Bank. A study done for the Centre for Industrial Relations revealed that unions attracted bank workers not primarily on account of wage demands, but on account of "poor management" practices, such as constant job shifts and lack of summer relief. The same study suggested that the Royal Bank was least susceptible to these dissatisfactions because it "had a well developed employee relations group long before unions came on the scene." The bank's improved training of management since the sixties had broken down much of the "legacy of paternalistic management" on which unionization thrived elsewhere.[63]

Increased competition between banks in the wake of the 1967 Bank Act revision greatly multiplied the number of part-time employees. Longer branch hours and the predictability of peak-service demand (such as paydays) bred demand for occasional staff. By 1980, 5 per cent of bank employment in Canada was part-time. Most part-timers were women. Critics argued that the banks were consciously creating an expendable pool of cheap labour; the banks replied that part-time labour was necessary to maintain a competitive edge, and that full-time employees were not being displaced by it. Besides, changing Canadian lifestyles had created growing demand for part-time employment in Canada.[64]

Computers, unions, and part-time employment were all aspects of a broad movement, beginning in the 1960s, by which bankers were sensitized to the needs of Canadian society. As the once-impervious maleness of Canadian banking began to dissipate, the banks were obliged to accommodate the interests of other groups in society on which they depended for clients and staff. There was a good deal of groping on the part of the banks towards these frontiers, and a good deal of pushing by government and interest groups. On balance, the Royal Bank fared well in this adjustment; it was served well by the long-held sense that it was a "progressive" institution. The scant representation of women in senior management revealed shortcomings in this progressiveness. None the less, the bank's culture had proved durable *and* adaptable. In 1986, the Royal Bank was the only bank ranked in *The Financial Post's 100 Best Companies in Canada*. The bank had the lowest staff-turnover rate in the industry – 2 per cent in management and 8 per cent in support staff. Above all else, the *Post* reported, the Royal Bank took care of its people.[65]

It was a measure of Earle McLaughlin's shrewdness that he did nothing to impede the transformation of the bank's culture. On occasion he misspoke himself – about women directors, for instance – but his inclination to delegate and decentralize had smoothed the way for change. McLaughlin was not, however, left alone in his executive suite to ponder the horizon. He remained at the centre of what was probably the greatest challenge to the bank's orientation during his twenty-year tenure as chief executive: the need for the bank to explain itself in society. The president of the Royal Bank saw more and more of his time dominated by the need to communicate to the external world. In a country that was growing daily more complex in its social, political, and economic relations, the bank had to discern the social, political, and economic priorities of Canadians, devise strategies to meet them, and then frequently defend these decisions in the public forum. Banks had become one of many interest groups in society, albeit large and well rooted. The days of privileged access to government were gone.

Within months of taking office, McLaughlin began roaming the corridors of power. In February 1961, he paid a courtesy call on Prime Minister Diefenbaker and received a lecture on the newly formed New Democratic Party. The banks, Diefenbaker told him, were "sitting ducks for nationalization."[66] Over the years, McLaughlin never retreated from

public debate. He became a persistently outspoken advocate of a floating exchange rate for Canada; Canada lived by trade, and its dollar
must reflect this fact. Similarly, he argued that the nation must not fall
into the "banana republic syndrome" of economic nationalism; foreign
direct investment had *built* Canada, not enslaved it.[67] Later, he would
scold Prime Minister Trudeau for imposing wage-and-price controls on
the national economy in the mid-1970s. McLaughlin thus brought an
outspoken economic liberalism to the public forum, an antipathy for
anything that constrained the market's freedom of action.

McLaughlin knew that he could not face society alone. These were
unruly years. Vietnam had troubled the western democratic conscience.
The public mood was sceptical about "bigness" and the credibility of
authority; the banks were perceived by the public as "fat and sassy."[68]
Business must become "socially responsible"; McLaughlin grew fond of
responding that bankers had "responsibilities," not "power." None the
less, he also knew that speeches were not enough in this age of protest.
The bank now had to anticipate social and political change and position itself to act effectively. It must become, in the parlance of the day,
"proactive"; it could no longer rely on simple, after-the-fact public *relations*, but must be aware of its public *affairs*. A 1975 reorganization of
head-office public relations was designed to shift the bank towards
"planned, preemptive and preventative public relations."[69] Again,
McLaughlin turned to outside experts. New methodologies – polling,
"tracking" issues – helped to "place" the bank in society. In 1976, an
Ottawa lobbyist, Intercounsel, was retained to help guide the bank
through what had become the policy-making maze in the capital. A
year later, the bank became a charter member of the Business Council
on National Issues. Although ties with the Canadian Bankers'
Association remained strong, the bank soon established its own
"government affairs" office on the Sparks Street Mall. These sophisti-
cations were complemented by enhanced corporate philanthropy. In
1967, for instance, the Royal Bank Award – today worth $100,000 –
was established to honour outstanding contributions "to human
welfare and the common good."

Of all the outside social and political issues that swirled through
McLaughlin's two decades, none was as vexatious as the national-unity
"question." The euphoria of centennial year was soon displaced by
national anxiety: Quebec flirted with separation and a strident mood
of discontent emerged in the West. Both issues threatened to strike at
the heart of Canadian banking. It was, after all, a *national* banking
system that reaped its efficiencies on a coast-to-coast basis. Any
sundering of the nation would in turn incapacitate the banking system.
With its head office in Montreal, the Royal Bank felt vitally exposed

to any shift to independence in Quebec. Beyond its own practical problems – by 1977, the bank had 7,700 Quebec employees – the Royal Bank also had to contend with its stereotypical image as a pillar of the Montreal Anglo business world. None the less, as such crises as the 1976 election of the Parti Québécois (PQ) and the passing of Bill 101 broke around the bank, McLaughlin proclaimed the bank's "deep wish" to stay in Quebec "given conditions which will enable us to do so."[70]

In this regard, one of the ironies of McLaughlin's decentralization was that the location of head office was of increasingly less relevance to the daily working of the bank. Telecommunications, a corporate jet, and delegated authority had in effect shrunk the bank's domain. Authority could go where the business was: Toronto, Vancouver, and Calgary were soaking up bank staff. Nothing better symbolized this than the opening in 1976 of Royal Bank Plaza in Toronto. The plaza relied on its architectural elegance – twin towers of gilded glass – rather than crass height to establish its presence. A year later, three head-office functions – investments, international money markets, and corporate marketing – were moved from Montreal to Toronto. None the less, head office in Montreal remained important. Crucial integrating functions, like foreign exchange, were performed there. Thus, when Quebec began consideration of language legislation that would promote "francization" of the workplace, the bank was quick to react. Although federal regulation insulated most of the bank's operations from Bill 101, the bank made it clear to the PQ government that successful international banking would be difficult in a Montreal where the linguistic freedom of some citizens was restricted.

In the face of Bill 101, the bank vigorously defended its role in Quebec. At the operational level, Quebec district had 4,822 employees, of whom 88 per cent were bilingual. Since the early 1960s, all circulars had been issued in both languages. Recruiting was conducted at Quebec universities and high schools. Despite this, the bank maintained a firm belief that "merit, qualifications and experience," not legislated quotas, must govern hiring. In terms of clientele, the bank was no longer an Anglo island in the province. A full 51 per cent of its personal accounts were francophone; 66 per cent of its government accounts were also francophone. Two-thirds of its "industrial" accounts were, however, Anglo.[71] Quebec was "the most important beneficiary of the activities of the Canadian chartered banks, if one considers it an advantage to have more loans than deposits."[72]

Events in Quebec none the less delivered another jolt to the bank's culture. Its Montreal corporate head-office staff of 2,158 was 98 per cent fluent in English in 1977, but only 49 per cent had a working knowledge of French. The bank's Quebec district staff was, on the other hand, overwhelmingly francophone. The problem therefore lay in drawing francophones into the national and international management of the bank. As had been the case with admitting women to the bank's culture, a gap needed to be closed between the bank's practice and the new realities of Quebec. The bank's 1979 marketing study of the province concluded: "We are perceived as a big English bank, particularly friendly to big industry."[73] McLaughlin responded in his habitual manner: he increased pressure on the bank to accommodate the "French fact." Language lessons for senior executives were stepped up. More French–Canadian names began appearing in senior management; in 1978, for instance, Pierre Frechette was appointed senior vice-president, government affairs, to help head office in its "highly sensitive dealings" in Ottawa and Quebec. Instructions were issued to staff for compliance with Bill 101, and the bank found a good working relationship with the PQ government in matters of provincial finance. At a CBA dinner early in 1979, Finance Minister Jacques Parizeau told bank vice-president J. G. R. Bénard that the province was "especially appreciative" of the bank's support of Quebec's Eurodollar borrowing.[74] Thus, the bank remained a vocal federalist, while trying to remake its image and mentality within Quebec.

In the late 1970s, the bank tried to readjust itself regionally in other ways. Throughout the decade, McLaughlin had shuffled his executive talent, trying to balance ambition and ability. Unlike Muir, he had cultivated a rich stock of talent at the senior levels of the bank and deployed it according to his decentralizing instincts. Senior executives were moved throughout the organization to build their expertise in the expanding world of Canadian banking. Ironically, McLaughlin failed to combine these shifts with plans for his own executive succession. Although he often quipped that he had no intention, like so many of his predecessors in the president's chair, of leaving his office "feet first," McLaughlin did not make the issue of his own successor a priority.

Official retirement in the bank was supposed to come at age sixty, but McLaughlin had crossed this divide in 1975. On the question of retirement, the bank's chief executive had always made his own rules. However, since Morris Wilson had become the first professional banker to serve as president, nobody had occupied the presidency longer than McLaughlin. The bank's evident success and McLaughlin's genial style seemed to protect his tenure. None the less, the board was beginning to exert some pressure for a change; nobody wanted to face the kind of wrenching dilemma that had been produced by Muir's untimely death in 1960. The first divestiture of power came in 1977, when, at a Calgary board meeting, McLaughlin was requested to drop the title of president; henceforth he would style himself chairman and CEO. The presidency would go to an heir-apparent who would assume operational control of the bank.

The contest for president was as close a race as the Sedgewick/ McLaughlin decision of 1960, but without the friction and drama. The leading contenders, Rowland Frazee and Jock Finlayson, each brought the kind of layered experience that an ambitious "bank boy" could acquire even after the Second World War. It was still possible that a candidate for the bank's top job could boast practical experience in virtually every key facet of the bank's operations. Finlayson had international experience; Frazee, like McLaughlin, had been to university. Finlayson had been deputy-chairman and an executive VP since 1972, Frazee chief general manager and an executive VP since 1973. Both were born in 1921, and thus had at least a half-decade of solid executive service still before them. In the end, McLaughlin settled on Frazee, but he immediately buttressed the new president by appointing Finlayson a vice-chairman. The bank's crucial Toronto business would be shepherded by a second vice-chairman, Doug Gardiner, in Toronto; Gardiner had proved a great business builder in the all-important Ontario market. Further depth was added by Deputy Chief General Manager Robert Utting, who brought rich international experience, and by Tommy Dobson and Bev McGill as executive vice-presidents.

By 1979, a still-reluctant McLaughlin and the board had refined their succession strategy. Frazee assumed the CEO's title, and McLaughlin had become "non-executive" chairman. Frazee moved quickly to spread the burden of authority among the bank's senior executives. The old one-man-at-the-top executive pyramid had left little room to reward multiple ambitions. The "top-tier system" announced in 1980 attempted to spread authority as widely as possible at the highest level of an organization that could put only one man at a time in the CEO's office. Frazee served now as president and CEO, backed up by Finlayson in Toronto overseeing worldwide corporate banking, with the title of vice-chairman. Hal Wyatt, who had long advocated the necessity of meeting western banking needs *in* the West, became vice-chairman resident in Calgary. Chief General Manager Utting became a vice-chairman in Montreal overseeing financial strategies on a worldwide basis. When McLaughlin exited the executive floor later in 1980, Frazee would become chairman and CEO, Finlayson would become president, and Chief General Manager Utting would join Wyatt as a vice-chairman. Given the stakes, it was a remarkably smooth transition of power. The *Wall Street Journal* saw the hand of management guru Peter Drucker at work and noted that the "layered approach" to senior management was much like that adopted

The right men: Earle McLaughlin cultivated capable lieutenants. For the first time,
Westerners rose to the bank's highest echelon. Nanaimo-born
Jock Finlayson (top, in 1969) would rise to the bank's presidency in 1980.
Moose Jaw-born Hal Wyatt (below) believed that the bank needed a higher executive
profile in the West and in 1978 was appointed vice-chairman, resident in Calgary.

by Citicorp in New York.[75] "What we've done, in effect," Frazee told the press, "is anchor key banking areas with top management. We feel this will give us greater flexibility and better capability to meet the banking needs of our clients as we move into the 1980s."[76] Throughout his presidency, Frazee would make executive succession a priority; executive leadership was no longer simply allowed to germinate, it was to be "groomed."

In September 1980, Earle McLaughlin celebrated his sixty-fifth birthday and punctually stepped down from the chairmanship. His time would quickly fill up with directorships, charitable activities, collecting G. H. Henty boys' adventure books, and golfing and relaxing in the Bermuda sun. He remained on the bank's board to within a year of his death in 1991. He left behind a bank that had vastly changed. The bank, and what it did, had changed more in his twenty years than it had in the previous half century.

If by some magic in 1960, McLaughlin could have conjured up a pre-First World War "bank boy" and dropped him into a Royal Bank branch, he would not have been surprised in the least to find that, within days, the young lad was performing efficiently. At its core,

*In 1977, the bank got another Bluenose president, Rowland Frazee, the Halifax-born son of a Royal Bank manager. Here, McLaughlin greets his successor (right).*

Canadian banking had changed little since it had hit its national stride at the turn of the century. Products, procedures, and colleagues would all have had a familiar cast. But had anyone parachuted a 1960 banker into the daily world of a 1980 customer-service representative, the result would have been bewilderment. Charge cards, mortgages, electronic banking, RRSPs, mutual funds, and consumer loans had no roots in the world of the "bank boy." Neither would many of his (or her) new colleagues have had "bank-boy" kin. He would have found the idea of working for a woman manager absolutely astounding. And the term "global banking," with all its resonance of electronics and deregulation, would have left him perplexed.

# Banking in the Global Village

EARLE McLAUGHLIN WAS A TRAVELLING MAN. THE MAN AT THE TOP IN THE Royal Bank had always been a man on the move. As president of the bank in the 1880s, Thomas Kenny had been obliged to travel up and down the Intercolonial Railway from Halifax to Montreal and then on to Ottawa. Edson Pease led as dizzy a life as early-twentieth-century transportation would permit him: steamers to Cuba, overnight trains to New York, and chauffeured limousines through eastern Canada. Jimmy Muir became the first president of the bank to circle the globe. But all this paled in comparison with McLaughlin's globetrotting.

As retirement neared in 1980, McLaughlin relished telling reporters that, during his tenure as president, he had logged 2.4 million kilometres of air travel. By his count, he had 2,456 take-offs and landings to his credit. He had visited every continent except Africa and India. "I've got friends on a first name basis from Sydney, Australia, to Helsinki, Finland, and a lot of places in between. We're an international bank and it's extremely important to be seen and to be known," he told the *Canadian Banker* in 1980. "When I travel I am the Royal Bank." Although, in 1960, the board had hastily disposed of Muir's Viscount airliner, deeming it an unbankerly frivolity, in the 1970s, the bank quietly went back into the airplane business when a corporate jet was again bought, not just to ease the strain of travel on its executives but also to give them greater flexibility and privacy in their travel.

But the travel destinations changed. Pease, Holt, and their generation had made inspection tours of the bank's sprawling international network – sweeps through Cuba, the Caribbean, and Latin America. Muir's sorties to the Soviet Union and China had hinted that the horizons of international banking were changing. Certainly, the Royal Bank's exit from Cuba in 1960 had shown that the foundations of traditional export banking were weakening. McLaughlin's years saw the process continue; Canada no longer enjoyed the same success in exporting its skills as a retail banker to the south. The overall trend was towards divestment in the Caribbean and parts of Latin America. Parts of the region suffered from deteriorating economic conditions – Jamaica's mercurial economy, for instance – while others wrapped their new-found political independence in legislation which restricted foreign access to their economies. In 1971, for instance, the bank was obliged to take out local incorporation in Trinidad, and by 1978, majority control was held by Trinidadians. By the mid-1980s, operations would cease in Guyana, Jamaica, St. Vincent, Haiti, and the Dominican Republic. In Latin America, the bank had already closed in Uruguay in 1963 and in Peru in 1971. By 1986, the *Financial Times* of London could proclaim that the Canadian banks' "Caribbean holiday" was over. As late as 1992, the bank's Puerto Rican retail system – established in 1907 and enlarged in 1980 by the acquisition of Banco de San Juan – was sold, leaving only a corporate banking presence. All these were painful decisions. They touched the lives of people who had worked for the bank in the Caribbean through decades – and sometimes through generations. At head office there was a sense of a loss in the "family."

In some areas of Latin America, the promise of growth held. In 1969, the bank had incorporated in Brazil as Banco Real do Canada S.A. As Brazil's "economic miracle" hit its stride, retail banking flourished. Two years later, Bank of America joined the Canadians in Brazil in a joint venture which was eventually given the name Banco Internacional. To coordinate these activities, an area headquarters for the Caribbean and Latin America was established in Coral Gables, Florida, in 1980, just in time to see Latin America deliver some rude shocks to the northern banks' unbounded optimism about the continent.

The slippage and reorientation of the bank's traditional retail strength in the south was, however, but a subplot to far greater shifts in international banking. After the Second World War, prosperity had restoked the fires of world trade. For the banks, this had meant a return of the lucrative ebb and flow of foreign exchange, something the Royal Bank had always relished. The same prosperity had also made the American economy the locomotive of the world economy. By the 1950s, a rising tide of liquidity lapped against the shores of world financial centres. Jimmy Muir's frequent treks to New York were prompted by much more than relish for the city's hedonistic delights; he sensed that New York was at the crossroads of powerful new currents of global finance – and that the bank had to be there. McLaughlin followed suit. Traditional international banking, well rooted in the nineteenth century, linked nations and banks together along relatively straightforward bilateral lines. Now banking abroad was becoming a complex skein of multinational and multilateral ties. Hence, McLaughlin made a point of making his name known at the annual meetings of the IMF and World Bank, post-war agencies designed to facilitate world trade and finance.

At the centre of this new financial order was the Eurodollar. A Eurodollar can innocuously be defined as a U.S. dollar liability on the books of banks anywhere outside the United States. Its power was, however, far from innocuous. As one wag put it, the Eurodollar was, in fact, neither European nor exclusively for dollars. It was, instead, a versatile new medium of exchange which began to emerge in the late 1950s as European and North American banks began to accumulate large deposits of trade-generated "hard" currencies, largely American dollars. These deposits allowed the emergence of a Eurocurrency market – an international market for short- and medium-term capital. Euroloans were usually denominated in currencies other than that of the borrower or host country. In the late 1950s, for instance, the Royal Bank helped to pioneer the Eurodollar market by taking U.S. dollar deposits of the Moscow Narodny Bank in Toronto.

The Russians did not want to bank in New York and, on a less-ideological basis, were aware that Regulation Q of the Federal Reserve Act placed a low ceiling on the interest paid in New York on offshore deposits. Offshore deposits made in Eurodollars in, say, Toronto offered a higher rate of return. As Eurodollar deposits grew, the possibilities of drawing on them to make Euroloans to multinational companies and governments also grew. The booming prosperity of the 1960s served to fatten the Eurodollar markets. Prosperity also drove energy prices upwards, bringing a windfall of U.S. dollar deposits – largely from the oil-rich Middle East – to western banks. International banking now became a business of "recycling" these deposits into Euroloans; both the potential profits and the risks were immense.

Towards the end of his presidency, Earle McLaughlin reflected that the Eurodollar was "a pretty good invention. I don't know what we would do without it." Twenty years before, in 1960, he had found them a little intimidating. Euroloans and Eurobond issues were of unprecedented size – well beyond the boundaries of lending familiar to single banks. Not only were the risks seemingly higher, but Eurodollar banking was peculiarly footloose, unconstrained by traditional regulatory and political pressures. Samuel Hayes and Philip Hubbard, in their 1990 study of global investment banking, have aptly described the Eurobond market as "the first marketplace without a home base." As investment banking became "globalized," so did its clients. Banks were now confronted with the huge capital needs of sprawling multinational corporations. If the banks failed to meet the multinationals' needs, they stood the danger of corporations going directly to the capital markets themselves. Faced with the need to satisfy these new demands, banks instinctively attempted to spread their risk through consortia. Here McLaughlin did not shy away. (Neither can today's historian, habitually wary of judging the recent past, back away from the momentous developments of these decades. However tentative the historian's judgements may be, the magnitude of the shift cannot be denied.)

In 1962, Arthur Chesterfield, the chief general manager of London's Westminster Bank, approached McLaughlin with a proposal that his bank and the Royal Bank form a joint venture to penetrate the world of European banking. The idea, McLaughlin reported, "set my mind awhirling," but when Britain backed away from entry into the European Common Market, so did the Royal Bank from the Westminster's offer. New York soon beckoned. In 1963, the National City Bank had bought control of Canada's smallest bank, the Dutch-owned Mercantile. The subsequent political furore had seen Ottawa cap foreign control of the stock of any Canadian banks at 25 per cent. Control by any one individual was limited to 10 per cent. American bankers, however, remained interested in an expanded base in Canada.

At a summer school for international bankers at Queen's University in 1967, a Chase Manhattan Bank vice-president informally floated the idea of his bank and the Royal Bank undertaking a straightforward swap of 10 per cent of each other's shares. McLaughlin was not interested, but the idea of some kind of alliance with the Chase intrigued him. "Both our banks were rather sizeable," he recalled, "and we decided that there were many deals that we could see were going to come along which would be too big for us individually and (we wondered) should we get together some time?" That fall, at the Reserve City Bankers' meetings in Phoenix, McLaughlin and David Rockefeller, president of the Chase, began to thrash out the details of a consortium bank that would move both of them comfortably onto the stage of global banking.

Both Rockefeller and McLaughlin were spurred in their discussions by the aggressive international expansion of the Chase's principal rival, First National City Bank of New York. In 1967, the head of National City's overseas division, Walter Wriston, had taken over as its president and launched a crusade to make his bank a global financial-services company. Two years later, Wriston created a worldwide Corporate Banking Group in a bid to service its business clients on a flexible, multinational basis. A year later, Wriston changed the name of his bank to Citibank. The Royal Bank was no stranger to Citibank's vigorous policies; in the 1920s, National City had competed head-to-head with the Canadian bank in Cuba, Latin America, and even in Vladivostok. In the 1960s, the old rivalry re-emerged, with Wriston clearly in an early decisive lead. Through the next decade, where Wriston went, other international bankers were sure to follow.

In October 1970, Orion Bank Ltd. was born. McLaughlin and Rockefeller succeeded in finding two European partners – National Westminster in London and Westdeutsche Landesbank in Germany – to join them in this new international merchant bank. A year later, Credito Italiano joined, and finally, in 1972, Mitsubishi Bank of Japan rounded out the consortium. Each parent would refer international business to Orion, which in turn would put together deals that spread the risk of lending. Orion offered a triad of services: merchant banking for international underwriting and consortium loans, a termbank to provide medium-term Euroloans, and a management-services group. With headquarters on the prestigious London Wall in the City, Orion joined the swelling ranks of consortium banks, and, given its lineage, quickly became a leader. By 1976, it had financed over U.S.$7 billion in loans. Orion's loan announcements had a truly global flavour: Shipping Corporation of New Zealand, the Kingdom of Sweden, the Province of Quebec, and Massey-Ferguson Credit Corporation, for instance, all came to Orion for financing.

Orion was but the most visible aspect of the Royal Bank's reinvigorated international presence. In 1970, the bank took a page out of Walter Wriston's book and decentralized its international operations, breaking them into regional bailiwicks, best suited to the needs of an increasingly diversified global marketplace. The staff newsletter, *Between Ourselves*, justified this "new closeness" by noting that "McLuhan's 'global village' has gone from catch phrase to reality." Once again the bank was seeking "new frontiers – Beirut, Tokyo, Frankfurt, Brussels." Under this umbrella, the Royal Bank would grow through the 1970s and the early 1980s to an impressive array of two hundred branches and other operating units in forty-five countries.

In the United States, the bank's traditional beachhead in New York was supplemented with actual branches – in New York and in Portland, Oregon – and an array of representative offices and agencies in San Francisco, Denver, Houston, Pittsburgh, Miami, Dallas, Los Angeles, and Chicago. These allowed the bank to tap into American corporate business, most notably in the booming energy field. The Caribbean and Latin American system was anchored in Coral Cables, Florida. Responding to the new-found vitality in parts of Latin America, the bank in 1972 joined another consortium bank – Libra Bank – dedicated to mobilizing European, North American, and Asian capital for Latin American purposes.

Across the Atlantic, London coordinated the bank's activities in England, Ireland, and the Nordic countries. A trade-financing subsidiary, Royal Bank of Canada Trade Finance Ltd., was added, and retail exposure was gained through the acquisition of Western Trust and Savings in Plymouth. In 1988, the Queen honoured the bank by opening its new London offices in the City. On the other side of the Channel, the bank attempted to penetrate European retail banking by acquiring control of three small German banks and the Banque Belge pour l'Industrie S.A. in Belgium and establishing The Royal Bank of Canada (Suisse). By the mid-1980s, the map of Europe from the Isle of Man to Madrid was dotted with Royal Bank affiliates and subsidiaries. From London, the bank ventured into the Middle East and even Africa. After the opening of a subsidiary in Beirut in 1971, other representative offices and subsidiaries had been added in Cairo, Dubai, Athens, and Bahrain. In 1975, the bank became a shareholder

On the Pacific Rim: In 1958 the bank opened a representative's office in Hong Kong. In 1962, R. A. "Bob" Utting, the bank's representative in the Far East, posed by Hong Kong's crowded harbour (opposite). Other Royal Bankers followed. In 1981, an office was established in Beijing; CEO Rowland Frazee (above) pays a courtesy call on Wang Dao-Han, the mayor of Shanghai, where the bank soon opened a second China office.

411

in Equator Bank, a consortium bank catering to the needs of post-colonial Africa.*

In the Far East, the bank picked up where Jimmy Muir had left off in the late 1950s. The Hong Kong representative's office became a full-service branch and, in 1981, the Royal Bank became the first Canadian bank to open a representative office in Beijing. In the Chinese capital for the opening, bank CEO Rowland Frazee remarked on the growing volume of Canada–China trade, but noted that the office's chief role would be to give China access to syndicated Eurodollar and Euro-currency loans. Further Chinese offices were opened in Shenzhen and Shanghai. Along the edge of the Pacific Rim, the bank expanded its influence through a majority participation in InchRoy Credit Corporation and a mixture of branches and representative offices in Sydney, Bangkok, Taipei, Seoul, Tokyo, and Singapore. A 1986 joint venture with the National Mutual Life Assurance Association of Australasia gave the bank access to retail banking in Australia. Finally, in 1986, the bank completed its embrace of the globe by opening a representative office in New Delhi.

There was a heady optimism behind the bank's sweeping global expansion. "Everything we do now," Frazee told the *New York Times*, "we think globally no matter what type of business we're dealing with." The bank proceeded on the instinctive, but untested, assumption that it could simply translate its traditional expertise in exporting retail banking into international eminence in merchant and investment banking. If the bank could prosper in Caribbean retail banking, then surely it could repeat the feat in Germany or Belgium. The bank's strategy throughout these years of international growth was therefore to establish "little footholds" wherever it could find them, and then to hope that it could pry these niches open to establish lucrative positions in far-flung foreign markets. Through the 1970s, there was much to sustain this belief. International banking profits outstripped domestic profits by a healthy margin; by the early 1980s international banking comprised 38 per cent of the bank's assets, but contributed 51 per cent of its profits. In 1980, for instance, the bank's domestic operations – strictly regulated by the Canadian Bank Act – returned 50 cents per $100 of assets, while international operations posted an 84 cent return. There was, however, an illusory quality to these gains.

---

* Back in Canada, the bank found itself under pressure from anti-apartheid groups concerned about Canadian financial support of the South African regime. In 1976, the Royal Bank stopped all lending – hitherto small – to the South African government, but refused to impose a blanket embargo on South African lending, lest projects with a humanitarian benefit suffer.

Initially, Orion found lucrative hunting in the Euroloans game. A window of opportunity opened for it in the mid-seventies, and it briefly ran near the front of the financial pack in Euroloans. But there were soon signs that all was not well at No. 1 London Wall, Orion's head office. From the outset, there were tensions in the bank's management. With each participating bank appointing a managing director to Orion, and with overall leadership left to a chairman, there were almost instantly "too many cooks" hovering over the Orion pot. Resignations and jealousies soon emerged. Adverse comment in the financial press began to tarnish Orion's initial lustre – one prominent financial publication took a catty delight in portraying Orion as a "clumsy quadruped in the nimble world of global finance." Even more damaging was the tendency of some of the participating banks to compete against their own creation in bidding for Eurocurrency business. As bankers' unfamiliarity with the new Euromarkets diminished, there was a natural tendency to pull this profitable line of business back within the confines of the parent bank and launch independent

*In March 1988, the bank opened a new banking centre in London's financial district. The centre incorporated much of Beaver House, the London Headquarters of the Hudson's Bay Company, and was inaugurated by Her Majesty the Queen. (Above) A beaming Allan Taylor accompanies Her Majesty around the centre.*

*Allan Taylor participates in the rituals accompanying the earlier opening of the bank's Bangkok office; Buddhist priests blessed the branch and were in turn honoured with food offered by a bank executive.*

merchant-banking activities. The late 1970s brought further resignations, increasing overheads, and a dividend that refused to budge upwards. Finally, in 1981, the Royal Bank bought out its partners and rechristened Orion as Orion Royal Bank, its own merchant bank. As *Newsweek* quipped, a consortium bank had "recycled" itself.

Throughout the 1980s, Orion remained the centrepiece of the bank's international strategy. Through it and the six regions into which it had decentralized its global banking activities, the Royal Bank pursued a goal of "worldwide marketing of a full range of financial services." "The Royal," CEO Rowland Frazee told *Euromoney* in 1982, "was international before it was national." The bank backed this boast with an array of services specially designed for the global marketplace. An international-banking division coordinated the now-decentralized network of branches, representative offices, and agencies. From 1977 to 1983, the bank's international efforts were directed by Executive Vice-President Allan Taylor. Taylor's education as an international banker had begun in 1965, when he was appointed as the bank's senior assistant agent in New York. Complementing this network were functional units, dedicated to select sectors and clients. World corporate banking, under Executive Vice-President Vince Kelly, targeted multinationals. It was flanked by an internal merchant-banking group, a trade-financing group, a global-energy group, and a net of private banking facilities for wealthy clients. All this was backed up by the bank's perennial strength in foreign exchange – the Royal Bank dominated international trading of the Canadian dollar and was ranked sixth in 1983 in total worldwide volume of all currencies traded. The sustained success of this impressive grid of international services depended on the exponential hopes of the 1970s extending into the 1980s. Vigorous expansion abroad hinged on a healthy domestic investment base, capable of feeding Orion and its affiliates, and the continued ebb and flow of a generous tide of Eurocurrency. Events of the early 1980s brought disappointment on both counts.

The energy shocks of the 1970s had spelled economic dislocation for the western economies, but they brought a windfall of "petrodollars" to the OPEC cartel. Finding themselves awash with these energy-driven deposits, banks in Europe and the United States began recycling them to the growth opportunities in the developing world. Third World governments and corporations crowded bankers' waiting rooms, usually returning home with petrodollar loans to feed their economic development. Photographs of Brazilian steelworks and Mexican railway construction found prominence in bank annual reports as evidence of petrodollars at work.

Two assumptions underlay this huge commitment to what would soon be labelled LDC – Less Developed Country – debt. Any sense of the high risk of lending to the less disciplined economies of the developing world was soothed by the assurance that this was "sovereign risk," that money lent to governments was unshakeably secured by the integrity of the borrowing government. It was also syndicated lending; it was assured that no Latin government, for instance, would risk offending the whole banking establishment of Europe and North America. (Nobody seemed to remember that Brazil and Argentina had both defaulted before – in the 1890s and 1930s). Once again, Walter Wriston at Citibank set the tone. "For the first time in history," Wriston would tell the *New York Times*, "it is within the power of a less developed country to obtain from external savings the capital needed for growth. One by one, those countries are finally breaking through the vicious circle of poverty." Armed with this brash confidence, Citibank put itself at the cutting edge of LDC lending. Other bankers' willingness to follow Citibank was, in the second place, a reflection of the belief that it was appropriate business for commercial banks to finance developing economies. This view was heartily endorsed by finance ministers in the developed world, particularly since their own efforts to develop petrodollar recycling mechanisms through the IMF and the Organization for Economic Co-operation and Development bore little fruit. Bank lending therefore became a vital component of the overall effort of the developed world to help the developing world pull itself up by its bootstraps. Royal Bankers were soon rubbing shoulders with American and European competitors in the waiting rooms of Latin American finance ministers.

The pervasiveness of these two assumptions soon tainted the credit culture of northern banks. What one Royal Bank executive later described as "a creeping type of disease" etherized the credit-approval process. The high rate of return on LDC debt disguised the fact that the debt was not the kind of long-term bonded debt – underwritten by merchant bankers – that Latin America had traditionally relied upon, but short-term debt, subject to what were to prove volatile interest rates and even-more-volatile economic performance. There were contradictions buried in the LDC loan portfolio; energy-poor Brazil was, for instance, extremely vulnerable to the very oil shocks that generated the petrodollars on which its foreign bankers depended. In the late 1970s, the Royal Bank began to recognize the extent of its exposure and started to withdraw from further participation in syndicated LDC loans. By mid-1982, all LDC lending would dry up completely; the damage was, however, already done. The onset of a global recession in 1981 hastened the day of reckoning. Ironically, the bad news was delivered right on the doorsteps of the Canadian banking industry. As the world's finance ministers assembled in Toronto for the 1982 IMF meetings, rumours spread that Mexico was defaulting on its debt payments. Even as Prime Minister Pierre Trudeau welcomed the delegates – with a speech rumoured to be written by a Royal Bank executive – news of a Mexican default spread through the outside corridors. A sense of shock gripped the delegates; action at the conference hastily shifted out of the conference and into the back rooms. A decade of trust in the sanctity of lending to sovereign states evaporated instantly. The sense of shock and confusion that replaced it would last for years.

"Non-performing" and "restructuring" became the bywords of the LDC debt crisis. As the crisis peaked in 1983-85, the statistical picture became daunting. In 1983, international loan losses were $318 million; a year later they touched $362 million. Such losses immediately took the glow off once-luxuriant international earnings. By the end of its 1984 financial year, the bank had made a net cumulative provision for loan losses of $2.7 billion. Of this, $832 million came out of the Latin American and the Caribbean situation. By way of comparison, the recession of the early 1980s produced $1.68 billion in non-performing loans by 1984 in Canada and the United States. Slow economic recovery, some tough IMF medicine, and agonizing restructuring negotiations brought the LDC debt situation under control by the late 1980s. Provisions for bad debts inched downward; by 1988 net provision for loan losses was down to just over a billion dollars, of which $293 million reflected the LDC situation. A further $1.9 billion was set aside for sovereign loan exposure, mainly in Brazil and Argentina.

Several facets of the LDC crisis bear examination. The Royal Bank had been active in Latin American lending for many decades, and was not prepared to abandon its stake in the region. From the outset, the bank therefore refused to give ground on the issue of absolute forgiveness of the debt. It would restructure debt, but not write it off entirely. "Brazil's the eighth biggest industrial economy in the world," Taylor told Canadian Press, "and to think in terms of forgiveness of the debt…. Where would you stop?" Restructuring negotiations thus dragged on throughout the decade, not ending in the case of Brazil until 1992. Restructuring, however, allowed the bank to leave the door open in the developing world. Other banks chose to withdraw completely from Latin America, but the Royal Bank maintained its presence with offices in Buenos Aires, Caracas, Mexico City, and São Paulo.

Despite the unprecedented loss provisions, it is worth remarking on the overall ability of the Canadian banking system to weather the debt storm. Even at its height, the LDC loan portfolio never equalled 10 per cent of the bank's total earning assets. In 1986, for instance, the Royal Bank's $1.6-billion exposure in Brazil amounted to only 1.8 per cent of the bank's earning assets. Canadian banks – long inured to the nineteenth-century habit of building up their rest accounts – were able to bring down their LDC debt exposure far quicker than their American counterparts. The same ability of the system to absorb the costs of other shocks – the energy slump of the mid-1980s, the fallout from the leveraged buyouts of the late decade, and the real-estate downturn of the early 1990s – provided a painful but salutary demonstration of the stability of Canadian banking. None the less, the LDC debt crisis exacted a heavy toll in damaged public credibility and depressed profits, and obliged the bank to adopt a much-more-selective international strategy – one concentrating on its strengths.

The LDC debt crisis also revealed the cohesiveness of the bank's senior management; the team spirit that had helped the bank weather

(continued on p. 420)

417

# BANKING ON THE PAST

ONLY A FOOLHARDY HISTORIAN WOULD insist that the past can in any direct way predict the future. The past can, however, illuminate the present, and thereby help to inform our options for the future.

Beyond all the dates, personalities, and strategies, the history of the Royal Bank leaves us certain "lessons," certain values or ways of doing things that explain the bank's rise and resilience. Canada's banks have thrived in large measure because they have built these values into strong corporate cultures. From the teller's cage to the president's office, one can detect these values throughout Royal Bank's 125 years. Canadian banking has by its very nature bred a conservative culture. Its knack has been to modify this culture continuously, under the pressure of social, economic, and political events. There is surely no more Canadian instrument of change than the decennial revision of the Bank Act – slow, sure, unexciting, but none the less progressive. The same rhythm is detectable within individual banks.

Out of the Royal Bank's history, five of these abiding "lessons" seem to emerge:

• *Royal Bank has been a bank quick to the frontier*: The bank has never shied away from making bold moves when bold moves offered new growth. The Royal Bank has succeeded because, in the words of America's pre-eminent business historian Alfred Chandler, Jr., it has tended to be a "first mover," the first to capture new territory and new methods. Edson Pease's dash

into Cuba in 1899 and Jimmy Muir's unprecedented visit to China in 1958 typified this spirit. In the 1980s, the bank took an early lead in electronic banking and has never relinquished it.

• *Royal Bank is a "young man's institution"*: The bank has grown because it has challenged its employees hard when they were young. It has always been prepared to take a chance on youth. It sent its "bank boys" to the mining-boom towns of northern British Columbia and to the sugar towns of Cuba, and gave them ample scope for initiative and ambition. In 1960, it made young Earle McLaughlin – at forty-five – the president of North America's fourth-largest bank. Since 1960, the bank has confronted the necessity of remaking itself into a "young woman's institution," of opening itself to visible minorities, and of recognizing Canada's multicultural reality.

• *Royal Bank has always cast itself in national terms*: Ever since its dramatic decision to open in Montreal in 1887, the bank has construed itself in national terms. A national framework has given it a diversity of clients, which has enabled it to withstand the uneven rhythm of regional development in Canada and at the same time develop a broad and flexible range of products. Banking's transcontinental evolution has also bred a natural nationalism in Canadian bankers and a consequent willingness to take on a prominent role in national affairs. The bank's first president, Thomas Kenny of Halifax, went to Ottawa as an MP in the 1880s to support Sir

John A. Macdonald's National Policy. In the 1980s, Rowland Frazee and Allan Taylor have been outspoken on the need to consider Canada's prospects – such as Quebec's place in the nation and free trade – in a national, not parochial, context. Taylor has recently likened some Canadians' talk of national dissolution to a "march of folly." "In union there is strength," Edson Pease said of the Royal Bank's amalgamation with five regional banks between 1910 and 1925. Without a solid national foundation, the Royal Bank could not – and cannot – venture abroad with confidence and competence.

• *Royal Bank has been a "progressive conservative" organization*: Canadian banking has succeeded because it is a national industry, carefully constructed and regulated to ensure a balance between dependability and responsiveness to Canadians' needs. Royal Bank has always tested this slow-evolved consensus to its outer limits and has been quick to advocate progressive change in its perimeters. As early as 1918, the bank acknowledged the necessity of a central bank in Ottawa. When the Bank of Canada finally emerged in 1935, the Royal Bank offered one of its own – Graham Towers – as its first governor.

• *The strength of Royal Bank has been its people*: From paternalism in the nineteenth century to a contemporary meritocracy, the bank has never strayed far from realizing that an efficient and well-motivated staff is the key to success. Corporate culture at Royal Bank is, as one forty-three-year veteran said, "a composite of a million things that *we* do." The bank has also learned to adapt to the social and economic ambitions of its employees – systematic training in the 1960s came to supplement the old on-the-job ethos of educating "bank boys" for their work. Successful management in the bank has drawn on the synergies of team effort; there has always been the sense that it is "a most marvellous association of people." Consequently, the bank has never been an "establishment bank." From President Thomas Kenny's avuncular inquiries after a young teller's folks back home on Cape Breton to an employee share-ownership plan in the 1980s, Royal Bankers have been made to feel that they have a stake in their bank. On this foundation, the bank has been able to build a tradition of good service.

These are not "lessons" of unbroken success. The values embedded in any corporate culture can play varied roles over time. What might drive an organization powerfully forward in one period – the maleness of the "bank-boy" culture at the turn of the century, for instance – can prove an obstacle in a later era. Similarly, the bank has not always flourished on the frontiers it has chosen – such as revolutionary Russia in 1919, or consortium banking in the 1970s and 1980s. But as in any education, it has learned the wisdom of modifying the lessons of its past. Early in its history, Edson Pease taught the Royal Bank that there was nothing to be gained from clinging to the status quo, and since then it has consistently embraced "progressive ways."

the bad loans of the mid-1880s and the dark days of the Depression reasserted itself. A Special Loans Group, under Executive Vice-President Brian Gregson, was created to handle the restructuring, thereby removing the anxiety generated by the problem from the day-to-day administration of the bank. The crisis also provoked a thorough reassessment of the bank's international strategy, and it abandoned those niches in global banking where it lacked a strategic advantage. Unprofitable Caribbean operations – such as Guyana – were sold; German, French, and British retail-banking operations were closed. There was a general recognition that the international system, which had spread so exuberantly in the optimistic 1970s and early 1980s, had to be given much sharper focus. The bank had learned that there was no easy transference of skills from the world of traditional trade and retail banking in the South to the crowded stage of global banking. This was a complex, volatile, high-risk financial world, in which the competition was keen and well honed.

The confusion over the bank's best international strategy persisted well into the late 1980s. Much energy and money was poured into trying to improve the footing that Orion gave the Royal Bank in global investment banking, and to link it with the bank's investment-banking activities in Canada. In 1986, Orion took advantage of Britain's "Big Bang" – its dramatic, overnight deregulation of its financial services – to acquire full ownership of the renowned London brokerage house of Kitcat and Aitken. Long practised in drawing English investment to Canada, Kitcat and Aitken allowed Orion to link its expertise in international debt markets with that of a seasoned player in the secondary share market. On the other side of the globe in Australia, the bank plunged into another joint-venture bank. In 1984, the Australians had opened up their banking industry to foreign entrants and, sensing an opportunity to gain access to a new retail market, the Royal Bank soon struck a deal with the National Mutual Life Association of Australasia to operate the National Mutual Royal Bank. With this affiliation also came access to Australian investment banking through the Capel Court stock brokerage. These initiatives looked good on paper. The Royal Bank would be placed in what seemed to be an emerging tri-cornered global financial marketplace, stretching from the Pacific Rim through New York to London. Back in Canada, the bank took advantage of Canada's own "big bang" of deregulation to acquire a 75 per cent interest in Dominion Securities to act as the Canadian anchor for Orion's investment activities. By mid-decade, the bank declared its objective of "being a round-the-clock, global financial institution."

In reality, Orion and the other bold initiatives of the 1980s had seriously overloaded the bank's credit culture. The bank found itself making loans in markets for which it lacked any intuition. At the same time, Orion generated extravagant overheads trying to penetrate markets that were already extremely competitive. High costs were accompanied by confusion in Orion's London executive suite, as senior executives continued to exit with alarming frequency. There were always "too many cooks" at Orion. Once again, the bank discovered that, as global finance became more homogeneous and instantaneous, it also became more crowded. Other banks – like the Canadian Imperial Bank of Commerce and Citicorp – were laying the same bets, building international investment-banking grids. Their experience in Britain would be the same. In London, Kitcat and Aitken found itself trying to promote investments in an overcrowded

*"It's been nuts. These are the three busiest days I've ever had," Royal Bank money trader Joe Cortese told the* Globe and Mail *when European currencies rode a financial roller-coaster in September 1992. "We've had a brilliant, brilliant time." Foreign exchange is the oldest of the bank's international activities. Once a simple matter of receiving and selling foreign-exchange drafts, it has now become a nerve-wracking electronic game. Cortese and his colleagues in the bank's Toronto Trading Room trade billions of dollars every day on global money markets.*

equity market. Orion's loan portfolio became littered with non-performing debts. Back in Canada, Dominion Securities enjoyed a healthy trade in domestic equities, but could not provide a sufficient investment base for the bank's international ambitions.

By the end of the decade, the writing was on the wall. Senior Vice-President Paul Taylor had been despatched from international corporate banking in Toronto to act as vice-chairman of Orion. There he joined Orion's new chairman, John Sanders, and its new director, David Pritchard, the man credited with inventing the "swap" market. Together, they had a mandate to fix Orion. They quickly concluded that Orion was pursuing an unpursuable strategy. Orion was chasing business in Europe that in no way complemented the bank's strengths back in Canada. Why should Orion seek to underwrite the Finnish pulp-and-paper industry when some of the bank's best clients back home in Canada were in the same business? It was hard news for head office to swallow, but changes followed. In 1987, Orion abandoned the Eurobond market, a market which now offered slim pickings. The acquisition of Dominion Securities that same year gave Kitcat and Aitken a stay of execution; it might serve as the Canadian brokerage's European arm. Kitcat and Aitken still, however, found itself in a tight and unprofitable market and, in 1990, it was closed, followed a year later by Orion itself. In 1990, the bank also divested itself of its share in the National Mutual Royal Bank in Australia; here at least it could boast of a $31-million after-tax gain. The heady global optimism of the last two decades was exhausted. In the future, the bank's global ambitions would be measured in terms of its realistic abilities; expansion would flow into strategic niches, not across broad plains of ambition.

On the surface, the bank had paid an expensive price for its tutorial in global banking. Orion became an uneasy memory. People grimly referred to the "O" word. Royal Bank had, however, by 1990 learned its strengths and weaknesses and was still well positioned abroad. The rationalizations of the late 1980s and early 1990s still left RBC International with a "global reach" of 125 operating units in 32 countries. These units provided corporate and institutional clients with corporate, investment, and private-banking services in virtually every major financial centre around the world. Foremost among its exportable strengths were the bank's long-polished prowess in rate-risk management, investment management, investment banking, private banking, correspondence banking, and trade services. It also continued to excel as Canada's leading foreign-exchange dealer. Foreign exchange was the one truly global market, free of any regulation and working by a twenty-four-hour clock. On an average day in 1992, for instance, Royal Bank trading rooms in Toronto, New York, and London would handle $13 billion in exchange transactions. Since global investment banking was crowded with major leaguers, perhaps, the financial press began to speculate, Royal Bank might again take what it did best – retail banking – abroad. Would, many asked, the bank find its next frontier in the American retail market?

If the Royal Bank spent much of the 1980s trying to establish itself in comfortable foreign niches, it was also busy conceding a place for foreign banks on its own turf. The 1980 Bank Act revision opened the door to the granting of charters for foreign banks to operate in Canada. Although their participation in Canada was capped at 8 per cent of total bank assets "booked" in Canada, over fifty of the now-so-called "schedule II" banks soon established themselves in Canada. At a time when it was seeking to penetrate foreign markets itself, the Royal Bank saw this foreign invasion as a fair reciprocity, and in fact was soon arguing for the lifting of the 8 per cent ceiling. The schedule II banks were indicative of the continued opening-up of Canadian banking in the 1980s. The slow creep of competition, first evident in the 1967 Bank Act revision, became a gallop. By mid-decade, the strict old demarcations in Canadian finance – the famous four pillars that supported separate banking, trust, insurance, and securities industries – crumbled, allowing new financial constellations to emerge. Here the Royal Bank moved with authority and confidence, surer of its skills and advantages than it had been in the turbulent world of international banking. The Royal Bank entered *and* left the decade as Canada's leading purveyor of financial services.

The decade began with heady optimism. Earle McLaughlin's successor, Rowland Frazee, brought a mixture of traditional "bank-boy" charm and modern management skill to the bank's executive direction. Frazee's father and uncle had been Royal Bankers. As a junior in Harvey Station, New Brunswick, he had acquired a wonderful reputation for his ability to put hockey pucks in nets. The story is told that, one night, young Frazee was detained at the Harvey Station branch balancing his ledger under the watchful eye of the inspector. Across town, the local hockey team was being thumped by a visiting team. A local businessman, incensed by the bank's insensitivity to the town's pride, appeared at the branch and threatened to pull his account if the "star" junior was not allowed to strap on his skates. Young Rowland duly hurried across town and pumped six goals into the opponents' net to ensure a come-from-behind home-town victory. His luck continued on the European front lines in the Second World War; as a young officer in the Carleton and York Regiment, he escaped death when a piece of German shrapnel deflected off his cap badge. Promotion to major came at the tender age of twenty-three. He emerged from the war a devotee of T. E. Lawrence, in whose writings he claimed to find inspiration for a leadership style that blended charisma and the common touch. Peace brought no automatic return to the teller's cage; Frazee felt the lure of higher education and took a commerce degree at Dalhousie University in his native Halifax before returning to the bank in 1949.

His career over the next three decades blended proficiency in the workings of Canadian retail banking and an acknowledgement of the need to break down the walls of tradition in banking. An apt student of McLaughlin, Frazee was an ardent decentralizer and strategic planner by the time he took the CEO's seat in 1980. Affable and polished, he seemed to be the man who could *plan* the bank's way to a better future. Like McLaughlin, he was not averse to seeking outside expertise. From the Department of Finance in Ottawa, he recruited E. P. Neufeld as chief economist. Pollsters and political consultants were retained to discern the public's perceptions of the bank and to help "manage" the bank's public affairs. At the bank's annual strategic-planning symposium, executives confidently discussed scenarios which made the attainment of a $200-billion asset base by the mid-1980s seem assured.

Domestic banking would, however, prove no golden road. Just as the LDC debt crisis derailed international banking, the Canadian economy slipped into its deepest recession since the thirties. Business and personal-banking volumes lurched downward. Energy prices plunged, and interest rates soared. Almost overnight, Frazee was faced with conditions his predecessors would have thought impossible. Public concern over bank profits and service charges, plus all the social consequences of banking in a recession, suddenly impinged on the CEO. Frazee joined Canada's other bank presidents as witnesses before a 1982 Commons Committee on bank profits, which ultimately concluded that the banks were "efficient instruments" of Canadian finance which returned "average" profits. None the less, it was clear that, in an environment of volatile interest rates, the social and political implications of banking in Canada had become "hot" issues. The return of prosperity in 1983-84 diminished these anxieties, only to see them replaced by the bad debts of the Canadian energy sector. As Canada's leading energy banker, the Royal Bank now found itself embroiled in restructuring the indebtedness of many energy companies in western Canada.

While decentralized management may have been a shrewd policy in the prosperous McLaughlin years, a more hands-on style was demanded by the "shocks" of the early 1980s. Frazee quickly realized that he had to pull management back towards head office; in doing so he tapped into the collegiality that had always been the mark of Royal Bank senior management. The Special Loans Group – dedicated to unravelling and restructuring LDC and energy bad debts – typified this sense of cooperative action.

Through all this, Frazee kept his eye on the horizon. The work of remaking retail banking continued. The sleepy world of old-style retail banking had been awakened by the 1967 Bank Act revision. In the fifties, branch managers concerned themselves with polite service and covering their exposure to loans; by the 1980s branch managers saw themselves as profit centres, which contributed to regional and national performance goals. For the first time in the bank's history, retail staff found that their daily performance in the branch could be reflected in their salaries. The "Great Performances" program could, for instance, bring a quarterly bonus or a Caribbean cruise to a CSR who excelled. Even the branches looked different: machines provided twenty-four-hour service, seniors were provided with sit-down lounges, and private banking centres sprouted under separate roofs. Saturday banking returned.

Remodelling its retail banking base presented the bank with an immense challenge. Banking became geared to the lifestyles of an increasingly segmented market. The goal, in the words of Reg Mac-Donald, who spearheaded retail banking through the decade, was to provide "cradle-to-grave" banking, tailor-fit to the saving, spending, investment, and retirement needs of Canadians through their entire "life cycle." The days of a person carrying only a savings and a chequing account through his or her whole life were gone. The bank thus began trying to enhance its services by segmenting them into products targeted at distinct consumer groups. "Relationship banking" would allow the individual needs of particular client groups to be precisely served.

As the decade progressed, the bank consciously began styling itself as a "financial services centre," Canada's largest. To this end, it accelerated its efforts to introduce automated banking; the Royal Bank jumped out to an early lead in the number of banking machines installed, and it has never surrendered that lead. In 1984, a $50-million research-and-support facility for electronic banking was announced for Toronto. Credit cards with various add-on features could, for instance, be offered. Innovative consumer products – like the launch in 1984 of "Buy-Back" car loans – would allow the bank to capture increased market share. RoyFund quickly expanded from its simple 1960s roots into a wide array of mutual funds, available at any branch. Separate private banking facilities were developed – the first of which opened in Vancouver in 1984 – providing personalized, expert advice for people with complex financial needs. In all these instances, the goal was to emphasize the quality of retail service by

*The "Superbranch" that was opened in Burlington, Ontario, in 1991 epitomizes the new wave in retail banking. Amongst many other services, customers can bank from their cars on a twenty-four-hour-a-day basis.*

backing it with solid training and by pushing responsibility for it right down to the branch level. From the corporate point of view, quality service would broaden the base of the bank's fee-driven income. It would also give the bank a competitive edge in a marketplace that showed every sign of being deregulated as the decade progressed.

If retail banking became more geared to the varied social and economic needs of Canadians, so too did banking become even more involved in Canadian public affairs. Frazee's experiences in the early decade taught him that bank presidents had to spend more and more time "outside the plant fence." Frazee acquired a reputation for "speaking out" on public issues. He attacked the National Energy Policy for "damaging Canada's reputation abroad and fomenting wasteful bickering at home." He championed the need for corporate philanthropy. Toronto director John Tory was asked to study the workings of the bank's board; one of his recommendations was the creation of a public-policy committee to advise on the bank's "social responsibility."

Frazee applied these same instincts to the bank's 42,000 employees. Throughout the decade, corporate employment policies became proactive. The bank learned, after decades of reacting to social change *after* the fact, to anticipate its employees' needs. An ACCESS substance-abuse program was introduced. Later, employees were, for instance, offered "Eldercare" counselling to ease their concern over aging parents. In 1985, a Royal Employee Savings and Share Ownership Program was introduced. For the first time, bank employees were encouraged to invest in their own bank. Within a year, 17,800 did; by the early 1990s, 85 per cent of Royal Bankers owned shares in their own bank. Similarly, Frazee warned that women would no longer tolerate "empty propaganda" on their employment prospects in the bank. The work of the Equal Employment Opportunity program continued; the bank committed itself to 50/50 male-female hiring at the trainee level. Women's progress in the bank was steady, but slow at the top. In 1991, only 5 per cent of the executive cadre was female; lower down in the corporate structure, women registered much more impressive gains. Perhaps as a reflection of all these efforts, the Royal Bank was the only major bank listed in the first issue of *The Financial Post's 100 Best Companies in Canada*.

Frazee's turbulent ride in the early 1980s seemed to underscore several paramount lessons. Despite the shocks of LDC and energy debts, the Canadian financial system had illustrated its stability in the face of adversity. The failure of two regional banks – the Northland and the Canadian Commercial – in 1985 seemed to illustrate the wisdom of breadth rather than narrowness in national financial services. For the larger banks, the 1980s had provided a painful lesson in the necessity of a disciplined credit culture. The body blows landed in successive rounds of troubled LDC, energy, and, in the early 1990s, real-estate lending and concentrations in large loans to single borrowers like Olympia and York revealed the folly of straying from a balanced loan portfolio. These lessons were taught not only in Canadian bank classrooms. Banks everywhere were learning to refocus their strategies, to avoid the overenthusiasms that could lead to undue exposure in any one company or industry. Canadian banks would have to find roles appropriate to their strengths on the world stage. At the same time, they were coming to realize that they could no longer regard their own national banking turf as sacrosanct.

The tremendous opening up of international banking in the previous decades had accentuated the compartmentalized, regulated nature of Canadian banking. Throughout these same decades, for instance, Canadian banks had slipped steadily down the list of the world's largest banks, as the Asian banks emerged in force and as European banks engaged in activities that were off-limits to banks in Canada. The debate over the future of Canada's financial-services industry therefore came to focus on balancing existing efficiency and public confidence in the system with the need to allow these same institutions a broader base of activities. It was a complex calculation. If deregulation was the answer, the public would want their confidence in the new more-open system assured by continued ceilings on ownership, controls on self-dealing, and deposit insurance.

As early as 1969, a provincial study group in Quebec, headed by Montreal economist Jacques Parizeau, had reported that the banks' age-old prerogative of deposit-taking could now safely be spread among the entire financial-services industry, while the banks might at the same time take on some of the segregated fiduciary and investment privileges of the other three pillars. Throughout the seventies and early eighties, initiatives towards any measure of deregulation tended to bog down in the usual crosshatch of Canadian jurisdictions. Ottawa, for instance, regulated the banks, but the provinces oversaw the investment industry. By the early 1980s, however, the banks began to grow restless. Their ability to marry banking and investment functions off-shore heightened their sense of exclusion from the Canadian securities industry. Orion's 1985 affiliation with Kitcat and Aitken in London made little sense if the bank was unable to build similar bridges at home. Although he urged "extreme caution" in reforming Canada's financial services lest competition be decreased, Rowland Frazee became outspoken in favour of deregulation, "as long as we all play by the same rules." The first bank to actually try to break the logjam was the Toronto-Dominion, which in 1983 began offering a discount-brokerage service to its customers and managed to defend its initiative before the Ontario Securities Commission.

The dam actually broke in 1986. Robert MacIntosh, the president of the Canadian Bankers' Association at the time, has argued in his memoirs, *Different Drummers*, that the four pillars were finally brought down by an elemental federal-provincial squabble. Since the turn of the century, Montreal and Toronto had been jealously eyeing each other's financial prerogatives. The Royal Bank had first encountered the intensity of this rivalry when it unsuccessfully attempted to take over the Bank of Hamilton in 1915. The fever never really subsided, but in the decades after the Second World War, Toronto had clearly gained the upper hand. By the early 1980s, Montreal was eager to reassert its financial prowess and began pressuring Ottawa to allow it to become a mecca for off-shore banking, a kind of "New York North," where international bankers could shelter from taxes. Few had really thought out the actual economic benefit of such a centre, but its genesis quickly became political, and by the time Ottawa announced its go-ahead for the scheme in 1986, Vancouver had been added as a second international banking centre – to balance, as it were, the political ticket.

Toronto's reaction to Montreal's gain was predictable. Within months, Queen's Park announced that it would slacken its investment-industry guidelines to allow banks, trust companies, and even off-shore financial companies to acquire up to 30 per cent of investment companies domiciled in the province. Financial deregulation had arrived in Canada through the back door. The integrity of the Canadian financial system was at risk; the agenda of reform was being set and altered by political caprice. In September 1986, Ottawa finally stepped into the breach. Michael Wilson, the federal minister of finance, flew by helicopter into the Quebec resort of Montebello, and there, in conference with the heads of Canada's six big banks, acceded to the banks' demand that the barrier between commercial banking and investment banking be taken down.

Wilson's decision was made easier by the knowledge that the investment dealers themselves were asking for the 30 per cent restraint to be lifted. Three months later, a federal policy paper, *New Directions for the Financial Sector*, unveiled the blueprint for a financially deregulated Canada. Within a year, all the Canadian banks but one – the Toronto-Dominion – had bought a controlling interest in a Canadian brokerage house. The Canadian financial industry now stood on a new, broader, more-integrated foundation. The bank's December 1987 purchase of a controlling interest in Dominion Securities would soon allow Royal Bank to refer its clients to RBC Dominion Securities for their investment. Dominion Securities clients would be but a telephone call away from the services of a banker.

One of the men waiting for Michael Wilson's helicopter at Montebello that fall weekend in 1986 was Allan Taylor, the Royal Bank's new CEO. Throughout the Montebello consultations, Taylor had spoken forcefully on the need for new "ground rules" in Canadian finance, rules that would preserve public confidence and, at the same time, make Canada's banks globally competitive. Three months earlier, Frazee oversaw a smooth transfer of executive authority. Perhaps sensing that change was on the horizon, the board used the changeover to restructure the bank's executive. The emphasis was on breaking down the old truncation between the bank's domestic and international operations. Taylor would be served by two vice-chairmen, Mike Michell and Geoff Styles, and a president, John Cleghorn. A native Montrealer, Cleghorn was a relative newcomer to the bank, but he brought the kind of wide-ranging experience that would equip the bank well for the rapidly changing world of global and domestic banking. McGill-educated, Cleghorn was also a chartered accountant, with experience as a sugar-futures trader and banker at Citibank's Montreal, New York, Winnipeg, and Vancouver operations. In 1974, the limitations of working the restricted base of a foreign bank operating in his native land convinced Cleghorn that his future lay with the Royal Bank, the "bankers' bank."

Cleghorn, Styles, and Michell were all given "worldwide" mandates, which stressed the need to push quality of customer service down into the grass roots of the organization, wherever the bank operated. Mindful of balancing national obligations, Taylor placed the CEO's office in Toronto, and asked Cleghorn to run the bank's operational life out of Montreal.

Like banking itself at the watershed of the mid-1980s, there were hints of the old and the new in Allan Taylor. A thirty-seven-year veteran who had joined the bank in 1949 at age sixteen in his native Prince Albert, Saskatchewan, Taylor had become a banker the traditional way: on a stool in a small-town branch, as an inspector working out of Regina, and then poring over credit approvals in Toronto in the mid-1950s. He toyed with the idea of a college education. When friends asked why he stuck with the low-paying bank in the salad days of the fifties, he simply replied that he liked the work. In 1957, he married Shirley Ruston, a secretary at the bank's Saskatoon branch. The bank took him out of Saskatchewan, but he never lost the Saskatchewan touch: a low-keyed mix of warmth and directness. In 1965, the broader vistas of banking began to open up for Taylor when he was posted to New York as senior assistant agent. For most of the next eighteen years he found himself at the heart of the bank's attempt to remake its international operations, becoming head of its international division in 1977. By the time he was appointed president and chief operating officer in 1983, Taylor was intimately aware that global banking was a nervous, fast-changing affair, a world apart from the secure world of domestic banking of the fifties.

Taylor inherited a bank that faced some major challenges. Profits had sagged under the weight of energy-loan write-offs; the Royal Bank was still first in assets and in overall profits in Canada, but it had slipped to second in profitability and fourth in loan quality. A note of scepticism often tinged reports on the bank in the financial press: "stiff challenges at Royal Bank," wrote the *New York Times*. But Taylor quickly brought certain bank traditions to bear on these challenges. At fifty-three, he too was another Royal Bank "young man," and he too had a new frontier before him – to make the Royal Bank Canada's leading financial-services company. At his first annual meeting as chairman, he told the shareholders to expect "ambitious goals." He would maintain the quality that had always been the mainstay of Canadian retail banking and at the same time open it up to new products and new competition. In doing this he knew he had one trump card to play: the breadth and stability of Canada's national banking system. "You've got banks as big as ours," he told *The Times*, "but find one that has the diversity as well." The Royal Bank had a "hard-rock backbone" of $35 billion in consumer deposits. On this he would build a bank that was domestically progressive and "a prominent force in selected international markets." Such ambitions, Taylor knew, invited risks; his exposure to the "shocks" of the seventies and eighties had shown him that global banking was unavoidably volatile. But when, in 1987, the bank passed the $100-billion milepost in assets, there was a sense that Taylor had set it on the right course. There would be further shocks – the fallout from real-estate overdevelopment in the late eighties – but once again the innate stability of Canadian banking prevailed. As the decade of its 125th anniversary appeared on the horizon in 1990, the bank could report that its asset base was keeping pace with its age – $125 billion.

By 1993, Taylor would have his eye on the twenty-first century. Pursuing the logic of financial deregulation, Royal Bank reached an agreement in principle to buy one of Canada's oldest and best-established trust companies, Royal Trust. The press made the predictable play on this "Royal marriage," but shrewd financial observers were quick to note that the bank was once again placing itself on a bold new frontier: the combination of traditional banking with the fiduciary services of a trust company. "Royal Bank gains a huge block of assets," the *Financial Post* was quick to note, "and becomes the fourth-largest financial institution in North America." Business columnist Peter C. Newman reached a blunter and more-flattering conclusion in *Maclean's*: it was "the deal of the century."

"What a serious trade it has become!" wrote Stephen Leacock in a 1939 issue of *Banking*. Gone were the days when a "bank manager was supposed to turn up with the key of the bank about ten; the clerks dropped in soon after." Yet, for all its foibles, banking was "a profession calculated to enlarge the amenities of life," and it was something Canadians did well. By some measures, banking had become just that much more "serious" by the 1990s. At its core, however, the bank told its employees, shareholders, and clients, banking was still a matter of "quality service, quality people, quality leadership, quality assets, and quality earnings."

Some of the bank's 57,000 employees and some of its 7.5 million customers live in Truro, Nova Scotia. Five days a week, Al Keilty, the

*The Truro branch, c.1900. Since 1871 Royal Bank has served the Nova Scotian town of Truro. Few towns have enjoyed as long a relationship with the bank; two bank presidents – Morris Wilson and Sydney Dobson – trained as juniors in this branch.*

area manager at the bank's Truro main branch, shows up with the key. Shortly thereafter, Keilty, a thirty-nine-year bank veteran out of Canterbury, New Brunswick, and his full-time staff of thirty set to work serving the daily financial needs of the people of downtown Truro. Royal Bankers have been doing this in Truro, as we have seen, since 1871 – very few other branches have been so closely tied to one community for so long. On March 4, 1871, the Truro agency first opened its doors. Its doors were in fact the doors of John Dickie's general store. Dickie, whose career had wandered through ship-building, farming, teaching, and even a stint as the town coroner, had struck a deal with Thomas Kenny, the Halifax wholesaler who had long supplied him with dry goods. Kenny now offered Dickie a banking

432

affiliation. "Banking services," Dickie later recalled, were "of a very primitive nature." Customers were served at a counter in the rear of his store. Dickie's ambitions soon shifted to politics. In 1874, he was elected to the Assembly in Halifax as the member for Colchester; his son, Martin, assumed charge of the Merchants' Bank agency three years later. He remained as manager in Truro until 1926.

John Dickie lived a lonely life as a banker, connected only by infrequent circulars to what must have seemed a distant head office in Halifax. The old "head office" on Bedford Row in Halifax is now long gone, but Royal Bank still operates on Truro's Prince Street, just up the block from where Dickie once operated his general store. As its manager, Al Keilty today lives a much livelier existence, connected by a net of telecommunications and couriers to a banking industry that straddles not just his own country but the world. Keilty's staff also offer the people of Truro a range of financial services that would have astounded John Dickie, whose understanding of banking extended no further than the intermittent financing of local trade.

Today, Truro main branch is one of the most venerable members of a Royal Bank "family" that wraps around the globe. Electronic communication, staff transfers, frequent training, and computer banking can make this family seem very small – a flicker on a screen away. But each branch or unit still serves the peculiar needs of the community in which it resides. As the staff in Truro locks the door each evening, the staff in Shanghai – where in 1993 Royal Bank became the first Canadian bank to open a full-service branch in China – are preparing to unlock theirs. Some branches never close: in Burlington, Ontario, Royal Bank's Drive-Thru Superbranch services clients in their cars at any time of the day – or night. Wherever Royal Bankers find themselves – in the front line of the branches or maintaining the structure that supports them – history seems to have bred in them an instinct for the social worth of what they are doing. Today they are encouraged to see this role in terms of "quality service" and "quality people." But some may still see themselves and their bank more in Leacock's terms – "enlarging the amenities of life."

# Appendix

ROYAL BANK IS TODAY CANADA'S LARGEST FINANCIAL INSTITUTION; IN 1864 it was a relatively insignificant copartnership on the Halifax waterfront. The following statistics are intended to provide a bold picture of the bank's tremendous growth – both domestic and international – over the last 125 years. Some areas of the bank's record-keeping in its earliest decades were rudimentary, a fact that is indicated in explanatory notes accompanying this table. By the late decades of the nineteenth century, the statistical series became more consistent and were reflected in the figures reported every year in the bank's annual report. These figures in turn reflect an annualized compilation of the bank's monthly submission of operating statistics to the Minister of Finance, an obligation stipulated in the Bank Act.

---

**SYMBOLS USED IN TABLES**

(a)  Pre-1883 share prices inconsistent

(b)  In certain years the bank paid a bonus dividend, shown following the + sign

(c)  10-for-1 stock split

(d)  Bank Act of 1944 terminated note-issuing privileges of Canadian banks

(e)  5-for-1 stock split

(f)  Full-time equivalent from 1978

(g)  2-for-1 stock split

---

# ANNUAL STATISTICS

($ thousands, except Dividends, Share Prices, Branches, and Employees)

| | Loans | Assets | Deposits | Royal Bank Notes in Circulation | Net Income | |
|---|---|---|---|---|---|---|
| **MERCHANTS BANK** | | | | | | |
| 1864 | No Record | No Record | No Record | No Record | Average | |
| 1865 | " | " | " | " | of | |
| 1866 | " | " | " | " | 9% | |
| 1867 | " | " | " | " | on | |
| 1868 | " | " | " | " | Paid-Up | |
| 1869 | " | " | " | " | Capital | |
| **MERCHANTS' BANK OF HALIFAX** | | | | | | |
| 1869 | $ 267 | $ 729 | $ 285 | $ 90 | $ – | |
| 1870 | 792 | 954 | 288 | 199 | 18 | |
| 1871 | 1,102 | 1,336 | 424 | 364 | 42 | |
| 1872 | 1,279 | 1,792 | 486 | 583 | 83 | |
| 1873 | 1,870 | 2,392 | 779 | 645 | 110 | |
| 1874 | 2,384 | 2,912 | 1,022 | 724 | 107 | |
| 1875 | 2,202 | 2,595 | 869 | 486 | 97 | |
| 1876 | 2,165 | 2,599 | 913 | 528 | 75 | |
| 1877 | 2,383 | 2,963 | 1,291 | 503 | 82 | |
| 1878 | 2,241 | 2,826 | 1,203 | 443 | 82 | |
| 1879 | 2,093 | 2,668 | 1,097 | 414 | 62 | |
| 1880 | 2,087 | 2,875 | 1,232 | 479 | 70 | |
| 1881 | 2,745 | 3,395 | 1,616 | 626 | 74 | |
| 1882 | 3,219 | 3,729 | 1,777 | 777 | 68 | |
| 1883 | 3,098 | 4,162 | 1,928 | 870 | 98 | |
| 1884 | 3,226 | 4,356 | 2,258 | 782 | 83 | |
| 1885 | 2,854 | 3,761 | 1,743 | 745 | (45) | |
| 1886 | 2,558 | 3,848 | 1,741 | 824 | 76 | |
| 1887 | 3,251 | 4,559 | 2,294 | 955 | 93 | |
| 1888 | 3,845 | 5,286 | 2,901 | 993 | 112 | |
| 1889 | 4,185 | 5,569 | 2,972 | 1,032 | 124 | |

| | Retained Earnings | Capital Stock | Average Share Price | Dividends per Share | Number of Branches | Number of Employees |
|---|---|---|---|---|---|---|
| | No Record | $ 160 | N.A. | N.A. | 1 | 3 |
| | " | No Record | " | " | 1 | 3 |
| | " | " | " | " | 1 | 3 |
| | " | " | " | " | 1 | 3 |
| | " | " | " | " | 1 | 3 |
| | " | " | " | " | 1 | 3 |
| | $ 20 | $ 300 | | N.A. | 1 | 4 |
| | 20 | 400 | | 4.5% | 2 | 4 |
| | 20 | 400 | | 6.5% | 7 | 12 |
| | 60 | 600 | | 7.5% | 8 | 13 |
| | 100 | 798 | | 8.0% | 10 | 15 |
| | 150 | 800 | | 8.0% | 11 | 17 |
| | 180 | 900 | | 8.0% | 11 | 19 |
| | 180 | 900 | | 8.0% | 11 | 19 |
| | 180 | 900 | | 7.5% | 12 | 19 |
| | 180 | 900 | | 8.0% | 12 | 22 |
| | 180 | 900 | | 7.5% | 12 | 23 |
| | 180 | 900 | | 7.0% | 12 | 24 |
| | 180 | 900 | | 7.0% | 13 | 29 |
| | 180 | 900 | (a) | 7.0% | 22 | 43 |
| | 200 | 1,000 | $ 123.50 | 7.0% | 22 | 55 |
| | 200 | 1,000 | 114.00 | $7.00 | 22 | 59 |
| | 120 | 1,000 | 102.00 | 7.00 | 22 | 61 |
| | 120 | 1,000 | 101.75 | 6.00 | 22 | 64 |
| | 160 | 1,000 | 109.00 | 6.00 | 25 | 64 |
| | 200 | 1,000 | 117.50 | 6.00 | 25 | 69 |
| | 275 | 1,100 | 125.25 | 6.00 | 24 | 84 |

| | Loans | Assets | Deposits | Royal Bank Notes in Circulation | Net Income | |
|---|---|---|---|---|---|---|
| 1890 | 4,435 | 5,849 | 3,278 | 996 | 144 | |
| 1891 | 4,799 | 6,264 | 3,485 | 949 | 143 | |
| 1892 | 5,665 | 7,602 | 4,252 | 1,020 | 127 | |
| 1893 | 5,732 | 7,641 | 4,273 | 1,014 | 180 | |
| 1894 | 6,328 | 8,539 | 4,966 | 941 | 159 | |
| 1895 | 7,135 | 9,812 | 6,199 | 1,001 | 188 | |
| 1896 | 7,874 | 10,759 | 6,328 | 1,185 | 208 | |
| 1897 | 7,498 | 10,967 | 6,927 | 1,187 | 200 | |
| 1898 | 8,499 | 12,682 | 8,275 | 1,387 | 187 | |
| 1899 | 11,813 | 17,102 | 11,324 | 1,854 | 249 | |
| 1900 | 12,282 | 17,844 | 12,016 | 1,833 | 182 | |

## ROYAL BANK OF CANADA

| | Loans | Assets | Deposits | Royal Bank Notes in Circulation | Net Income | |
|---|---|---|---|---|---|---|
| 1901 | 13,261 | 19,377 | 13,363 | 1,847 | 209 | |
| 1902 | 14,132 | 21,870 | 13,929 | 1,921 | 280 | |
| 1903 | 16,342 | 25,107 | 16,087 | 2,304 | 373 | |
| 1904 | 18,198 | 31,184 | 21,945 | 2,535 | 435 | |
| 1905 | 22,489 | 36,374 | 26,436 | 2,821 | 492 | |
| 1906 | 28,669 | 45,438 | 32,465 | 3,780 | 604 | |
| 1907 | 29,816 | 46,351 | 33,265 | 3,654 | 742 | |
| 1908 | 30,661 | 50,470 | 37,443 | 3,556 | 747 | |
| 1909 | 43,839 | 67,051 | 50,822 | 4,580 | 838 | |
| 1910 | 60,586 | 92,510 | 72,080 | 5,926 | 951 | |
| 1911 | 73,631 | 110,529 | 88,295 | 6,338 | 1,152 | |
| 1912 | 124,240 | 179,211 | 137,892 | 12,585 | 1,527 | |
| 1913 | 122,536 | 180,247 | 138,178 | 13,177 | 2,142 | |
| 1914 | 114,812 | 179,404 | 136,051 | 13,505 | 1,886 | |
| 1915 | 126,023 | 198,299 | 154,976 | 14,225 | 1,906 | |
| 1916 | 157,779 | 253,261 | 200,228 | 18,178 | 2,111 | |
| 1917 | 183,227 | 335,574 | 252,987 | 28,159 | 2,328 | |
| 1918 | 218,190 | 427,513 | 332,592 | 39,381 | 2,810 | |
| 1919 | 284,083 | 533,647 | 419,121 | 39,837 | 3,423 | |
| 1920 | 344,705 | 594,670 | 455,017 | 41,673 | 4,254 | |
| 1921 | 290,185 | 500,648 | 375,616 | 31,290 | 4,038 | |
| 1922 | 291,548 | 479,362 | 372,004 | 26,646 | 3,958 | |
| 1923 | 311,096 | 538,359 | 421,334 | 31,227 | 3,909 | |
| 1924 | 291,477 | 583,790 | 461,829 | 29,822 | 3,879 | |

| Retained Earnings | Capital Stock | Average Share Price | Dividends per Share | Number of Branches | Number of Employees |
|---|---|---|---|---|---|
| 375 | 1,100 | 130.75 | 6.00 | 25 | 97 |
| 450 | 1,100 | 131.63 | 6.00 | 24 | 101 |
| 510 | 1,100 | 132.00 | 6.00 | 25 | 105 |
| 600 | 1,100 | 138.50 | 6.50 | 25 | 113 |
| 680 | 1,100 | 145.25 | 7.00 | 25 | 115 |
| 975 | 1,500 | 156.00 | 7.00 | 26 | 118 |
| 1,075 | 1,500 | 161.50 | 7.00 | 27 | 123 |
| 1,175 | 1,500 | 171.25 | 7.00 | 30 | 138 |
| 1,250 | 1,500 | 185.00 | 7.00 | 36 | 151 |
| 1,700 | 1,985 | 183.50 | 7.00 | 42 | 210 |
| 1,700 | 2,000 | 177.50 | 7.00 | 40 | 245 |

| Retained Earnings | Capital Stock | Average Share Price | Dividends per Share | Number of Branches | Number of Employees |
|---|---|---|---|---|---|
| 1,700 | 2,000 | 175.00 | 7.00 | 41 | 256 |
| 2,500 | 2,481 | 183.75 | 7.50 | 42 | 276 |
| 3,000 | 3,000 | 213.25 | 8.00 | 47 | 316 |
| 3,000 | 3,000 | 204.63 | 8.00 | 52 | 378 |
| 3,400 | 3,000 | 219.13 | 8.25 | 59 | 404 |
| 4,390 | 3,900 | 234.75 | 9.25 | 80 | 514 |
| 4,390 | 3,900 | 230.00 | 10.00 | 97 | 629 |
| 4,600 | 3,900 | 222.38 | 10.00 | 109 | 719 |
| 5,700 | 5,000 | 222.50 | 10.00 | 130 | 887 |
| 7,000 | 6,200 | 234.75 | 11.25 | 179 | 1,264 |
| 7,056 | 6,251 | 233.00 | 12.00 | 207 | 1,500 |
| 12,560 | 11,560 | 227.00 | 12.00 | 340 | 2,408 |
| 12,560 | 11,560 | 220.50 | 12.00 | 378 | 2,823 |
| 12,560 | 11,560 | 223.50 | 12.00 | 392 | 2,855 |
| 12,560 | 11,560 | 261.00 | 12.00 | 380 | 2,671 |
| 12,560 | 12,000 | 216.13 | 12.00 | 380 | 2,733 |
| 14,000 | 12,912 | 211.00 | 12.00 | 434 | 3,474 |
| 15,000 | 14,000 | 211.50 | 12.00 | 548 | 4,218 |
| 17,000 | 17,000 | 213.25 | 12.00 + 2.00 (b) | 662 | 5,294 |
| 20,134 | 20,134 | 211.25 | 12.00 + 2.00 | 745 | 6,548 |
| 20,400 | 20,400 | 199.25 | 12.00 + 2.00 | 722 | 6,241 |
| 20,400 | 20,400 | 200.50 | 12.00 + 2.00 | 687 | 6,136 |
| 20,400 | 20,400 | 215.25 | 12.00 + 2.00 | 684 | 6,555 |
| 20,400 | 20,400 | 225.75 | 12.00 + 2.00 | 668 | 6,665 |

| | Loans | Assets | Deposits | Royal Bank Notes in Circulation | Net Income | |
|---|---|---|---|---|---|---|
| 1925 | 409,286 | 788,479 | 641,678 | 41,497 | 4,082 | |
| 1926 | 440,445 | 766,377 | 612,860 | 39,171 | 4,516 | |
| 1927 | 534,650 | 894,664 | 722,636 | 42,556 | 5,370 | |
| 1928 | 543,203 | 909,396 | 707,467 | 43,830 | 5,881 | |
| 1929 | 640,503 | 1,001,443 | 772,088 | 43,566 | 7,145 | |
| 1930 | 552,984 | 889,917 | 695,589 | 36,730 | 6,573 | |
| 1931 | 502,356 | 825,702 | 647,303 | 33,237 | 5,448 | |
| 1932 | 432,744 | 765,513 | 619,094 | 28,734 | 4,862 | |
| 1933 | 384,666 | 729,260 | 600,448 | 29,350 | 3,902 | |
| 1934 | 386,889 | 758,424 | 637,479 | 33,222 | 4,398 | |
| 1935 | 379,286 | 800,920 | 688,367 | 32,568 | 4,341 | |
| 1936 | 341,252 | 855,588 | 746,764 | 29,525 | 3,504 | |
| 1937 | 338,360 | 869,538 | 756,090 | 28,645 | 3,711 | |
| 1938 | 347,456 | 908,065 | 804,109 | 26,397 | 3,696 | |
| 1939 | 355,882 | 1,014,708 | 911,519 | 26,028 | 3,725 | |
| 1940 | 351,637 | 955,570 | 852,398 | 25,103 | 3,527 | |
| 1941 | 363,223 | 1,075,120 | 956,104 | 22,326 | 3,536 | |
| 1942 | 366,967 | 1,291,616 | 1,181,217 | 18,271 | 3,390 | |
| 1943 | 400,340 | 1,509,098 | 1,399,891 | 12,851 | 3,426 | |
| 1944 | 420,174 | 1,790,252 | 1,676,885 | 9,580 | 3,812 | |
| 1945 | 493,925 | 2,007,547 | 1,888,757 | 7,007 | 3,828 | |
| 1946 | 486,593 | 2,131,974 | 1,963,104 | 5,679 | 6,906 | |
| 1947 | 615,742 | 2,093,641 | 1,934,186 | 4,761 | 8,725 | |
| 1948 | 664,855 | 2,222,488 | 2,067,489 | 4,321 | 9,517 | |
| 1949 | 660,723 | 2,334,985 | 2,192,141 | 3,704 | 10,918 | |
| 1950 | 792,896 | 2,497,376 | 2,337,503 | 250 | 11,845 | |
| 1951 | 854,725 | 2,515,645 | 2,350,314 | 156 | 12,983 | |
| 1952 | 987,303 | 2,691,457 | 2,527,510 | 101 | 14,745 | |
| 1953 | 1,149,308 | 2,895,856 | 2,734,644 | (d) 83 | 18,953 | |
| 1954 | 1,217,846 | 3,026,896 | 2,797,548 | | 20,914 | |
| 1955 | 1,350,639 | 3,284,144 | 3,062,220 | | 10,858 | |
| 1956 | 1,654,460 | 3,571,298 | 3,278,375 | | 12,467 | |
| 1957 | 1,895,367 | 3,760,545 | 3,426,683 | | 13,920 | |
| 1958 | 1,781,482 | 4,133,559 | 3,782,069 | | 15,868 | |
| 1959 | 2,186,000 | 4,129,659 | 3,777,620 | | 17,119 | |

| Retained Earnings | Capital Stock | Average Share Price | Dividends per Share | Number of Branches | Number of Employees |
|---|---|---|---|---|---|
| 24,400 | 24,400 | 241.38 | 12.00 + 2.00 | 922 | 8,532 |
| 24,400 | 24,400 | 259.25 | 12.00 + 2.00 | 901 | 8,457 |
| 30,000 | 30,000 | 300.50 | 12.00 + 2.00 | 903 | 8,422 |
| 30,000 | 30,000 | 383.50 | 12.00 + 2.00 | 912 | 8,366 |
| 35,000 | 35,000 | 341.00 | 12.00 + 2.00 | 944 | 8,656 |
| 35,000 | 35,000 | 293.50 | 12.00 + 2.00 | 941 | 8,784 |
| 35,000 | 35,000 | 276.00 | 12.00 | 909 | 8,217 |
| 35,000 | 35,000 | 145.50 | 11.00 | 860 | 7,717 |
| 20,000 | 35,000 | 153.00 | 8.50 | 817 | 7,331 |
| 20,000 | 35,000 | 150.00 | 8.00 | 789 | 6,956 |
| 20,000 | 35,000 | 153.50 | 8.00 | 766 | 6,877 |
| 20,000 | 35,000 | 184.00 | 8.00 | 737 | 6,849 |
| 20,000 | 35,000 | 195.75 | 8.00 | 728 | 6,877 |
| 20,000 | 35,000 | 178.50 | 8.00 | 716 | 7,046 |
| 20,000 | 35,000 | 166.50 | 8.00 | 712 | 7,016 |
| 20,000 | 35,000 | 167.63 | 8.00 | 705 | 7,180 |
| 20,000 | 35,000 | 157.75 | 8.00 | 705 | 7,280 |
| 20,000 | 35,000 | 135.00 | 7.50 | 667 | 7,803 |
| 20,000 | 35,000 | 141.13 | 6.00 | 653 | 7,788 |
| 20,000 | 35,000 | (c)  14.73 | 0.60  (c) | 652 | 8,034 |
| 20,000 | 35,000 | 17.69 | 0.60 | 654 | 8,823 |
| 40,000 | 35,000 | 22.88 | 0.80 | 669 | 9,640 |
| 40,000 | 35,000 | 23.50 | 0.85 | 692 | 10,427 |
| 44,000 | 35,000 | 24.57 | 1.00 | 709 | 10,567 |
| 44,000 | 35,000 | 26.38 | 1.00 | 727 | 10,983 |
| 50,000 | 35,000 | 28.75 | 1.00 | 751 | 11,720 |
| 52,000 | 35,000 | 28.00 | 1.00 + .20 | 761 | 12,409 |
| 55,000 | 35,000 | 29.75 | 1.00 + .25 | 778 | 12,580 |
| 70,000 | 35,000 | 35.13 | 1.20 + .20 | 793 | 13,291 |
| 103,620 | 41,810 | 44.25 | 1.425 + .10 | 813 | 14,077 |
| 108,918 | 42,000 | 56.88 | 1.575 + .20 | 851 | 14,510 |
| 136,403 | 50,299 | 62.50 | 1.80 + .25 | 872 | 15,214 |
| 151,603 | 50,400 | 66.00 | 2.00 + .10 | 903 | 15,760 |
| 189,323 | 60,422 | 65.50 | 2.00 + .25 | 935 | 15,869 |
| 195,541 | 60,480 | 83.75 | 2.025 + .30 | 969 | 15,870 |

| | Loans | Assets | Deposits | Royal Bank Notes in Circulation | Net Income | |
|---|---|---|---|---|---|---|
| 1960 | 2,209,030 | 4,296,822 | 3,884,134 | | 19,504 | |
| 1961 | 2,357,165 | 4,954,610 | 4,501,789 | | 20,760 | |
| 1962 | 2,622,186 | 5,128,750 | 4,673,708 | | 21,492 | |
| 1963 | 2,872,277 | 5,713,936 | 5,191,490 | | 22,580 | |
| 1964 | 3,166,714 | 6,231,598 | 5,655,230 | | 23,757 | |
| 1965 | 3,771,999 | 6,571,055 | 5,921,645 | | 23,239 | |
| 1966 | 3,940,142 | 6,935,931 | 6,304,215 | | 27,432 | |
| 1967 | 4,402,748 | 7,779,659 | 7,028,816 | | 30,279 | |
| 1968 | 4,739,084 | 8,743,218 | 7,955,074 | | 35,324 | |
| 1969 | 5,752,525 | 10,196,159 | 9,308,225 | | 40,530 | |
| 1970 | 6,166,013 | 11,368,623 | 10,303,212 | | 44,620 | |
| 1971 | 6,973,914 | 12,953,578 | 11,772,301 | | 44,052 | |
| 1972 | 8,111,053 | 14,767,516 | 13,537,382 | | 51,399 | |
| 1973 | 9,972,051 | 18,363,535 | 16,800,301 | | 56,047 | |
| 1974 | 12,713,031 | 21,669,880 | 19,441,373 | | 63,879 | |
| 1975 | 15,816,493 | 25,211,131 | 22,870,875 | | 103,936 | |
| 1976 | 17,825,430 | 28,831,586 | 26,290,831 | | 101,050 | |
| 1977 | 23,066,315 | 34,275,159 | 31,874,374 | | 184,727 | |
| 1978 | 26,977,407 | 40,603,054 | 37,564,356 | | 271,105 | |
| 1979 | 32,714,333 | 50,675,587 | 45,574,896 | | 309,691 | |
| 1980 | 40,805,248 | 61,482,111 | 55,833,184 | | 334,032 | |
| 1981 | 57,131,133 | 85,359,452 | 76,865,388 | | 458,176 | |
| 1982 | 60,284,459 | 88,455,992 | 78,405,462 | | 181,648 | |
| 1983 | 58,066,890 | 84,681,823 | 74,389,208 | | 312,993 | |
| 1984 | 59,014,248 | 88,002,708 | 77,588,345 | | 385,085 | |
| 1985 | 63,830,803 | 96,016,863 | 83,542,969 | | 454,104 | |
| 1986 | 65,934,201 | 99,606,565 | 84,253,271 | | 452,037 | |
| 1987 | 69,292,539 | 102,170,201 | 85,811,030 | | (287,686) | |
| 1988 | 77,781,339 | 110,054,340 | 87,238,280 | | 712,318 | |
| 1989 | 83,238,785 | 114,659,558 | 89,186,275 | | 529,073 | |
| 1990 | 92,694,057 | 125,938,027 | 99,167,997 | | 964,929 | |
| 1991 | 98,344,455 | 132,352,007 | 105,022,395 | | 983,466 | |
| 1992 | 99,527,473 | 138,292,738 | 112,222,064 | | 107,355 | |

| Retained Earnings | Capital Stock | Average Share Price | Dividends per Share | Number of Branches | Number of Employees |
|---|---|---|---|---|---|
| 225,429 | 66,434 | 72.50 | 2.125 + .25 | 1,018 | 16,662 |
| 239,856 | 66,528 | 78.69 | 2.20 + .30 | 1,040 | 16,541 |
| 244,716 | 66,528 | 73.88 | 2.25 + .25 | 1,084 | 17,602 |
| 251,332 | 66,528 | 75.50 | 2.40 + .15 | 1,110 | 17,670 |
| 257,792 | 66,528 | 75.50 | 2.40 + .20 | 1,146 | 18,495 |
| 263,734 | 66,528 | 77.13 | 2.60 | 1,184 | 19,436 |
| 271,207 | 66,528 | 72.25 | 3.00 | 1,202 | 20,090 |
| 281,528 | 66,528 | (e) 15.48 | 0.60 (e) | 1,221 | 20,597 |
| 293,567 | 66,528 | 20.25 | 0.70 | 1,241 | 21,737 |
| 308,484 | 66,528 | 23.00 | 0.77 | 1,264 | 23,181 |
| 324,497 | 66,528 | 21.38 | 0.86 | 1,312 | 24,306 |
| 341,316 | 66,528 | 26.19 | 0.88 | 1,366 | 24,435 |
| 375,781 | 66,528 | 33.63 | 0.96 | 1,393 | 25,701 |
| 424,746 | 66,528 | 35.59 | 1.02 | 1,409 | 28,225 |
| 450,258 | 66,528 | 31.75 | 1.10 | 1,470 | 31,094 |
| 570,326 | 72,951 | 31.25 | 1.23 | 1,524 | 32,464 |
| 657,721 | 73,181 | 27.19 | 1.305 | 1,567 | 34,429 |
| 781,049 | 73,181 | 25.69 | 1.38 | 1,595 | 35,335 |
| 1,005,686 | 73,181 | 32.07 | 1.565 | 1,600 | (f) 37,746 |
| 1,219,329 | 73,181 | 41.32 | 2.18 | 1,604 | 38,895 |
| 1,605,621 | 80,243 | 49.57 | 2.52 | 1,592 | 39,439 |
| 1,908,263 | 233,128 | (g) 28.32 | 1.70 (g) | 1,574 | 42,040 |
| 1,992,544 | 438,871 | 22.75 | 2.00 | 1,568 | 42,904 |
| 2,019,893 | 1,278,972 | 29.75 | 2.00 | 1,536 | 42,321 |
| 2,094,484 | 1,646,751 | 30.06 | 2.00 | 1,510 | 41,888 |
| 2,328,842 | 1,839,009 | 29.94 | 2.00 | 1,494 | 41,951 |
| 2,444,081 | 2,217,561 | 31.38 | 2.00 | 1,496 | 43,229 |
| 1,806,622 | 2,557,208 | 32.31 | 2.02 | 1,517 | 42,839 |
| 2,171,766 | 2,915,258 | 31.31 | 2.08 | 1,560 | 46,096 |
| 2,322,361 | 3,459,593 | 41.25 | 2.20 | 1,607 | 47,989 |
| 2,857,333 | 3,596,089 | (g) 22.72 | 1.16 (g) | 1,665 | 50,106 |
| 3,374,899 | 4,386,716 | 24.00 | 1.16 | 1,747 | 50,547 |
| 3,001,757 | 4,503,930 | 25.25 | 1.16 | 1,744 | 49,628 |

# Notes

## LIST OF ACRONYMS USED IN NOTES

CBA  Canadian Bankers' Association
CBAA  Canadian Bankers' Assocation Archives
CHA  Canadian Historical Association
CL  Circular Letter
CMHA  Canada Mortgage and Housing Corporation
JCBA  Journal of the Canadian Bankers' Association
MBH  Merchants' Bank of Halifax
NAC  National Archives of Canada
NHA  National Housing Act
PANS  Public Archives of Nova Scotia
RBC  Royal Bank of Canada

## Introduction

[1] Royal Bank of Canada, Minute Books, RBC-2 31-el, Aug. 6, 1907.

[2] F. T. Walker, "Neck and Neck Banking–How Branches were Established in the 'Good Old Days,'" *Royal Bank Magazine*, vol. 176, Aug.-Sept. 1937, pp. 8-9 and 23. Walker Reminiscences, RBC 4 Wa.

[3] *Debates of the House of Commons*, July 26, 1944, p. 1296.

[4] Robertson Davies, *The Enthusiasms of Robertson Davies*, Toronto, 1979, p. 314.

[5] The *Monetary Times*, Oct. 8, 1910, Supplement p. 3.

[6] R.M. Breckenridge, *The Canadian Banking System 1817-1890*, Toronto, 1894, p. 3. See also: "As Others See Us" (editorial), *JCBA*, vol. 16, #1, Oct. 1908, pp. 4-5 and Adam Shortt, *History of Canadian Currency and Banking, 1600-1880*, republished by CBA, Toronto, nd.

[7] J. M. McPherson (Molsons Bank), *JCBA*, vol. 1, Sept. 1893, p. 59.

[8] W. W. Swanson, "Canada's Remarkable Banking Record," *Monetary Times*, Sept. 27, 1918, p. 46.

[9] Halifax *Chronicle*, March 4, 1875.

[10] Eva Innes, Jim Lyons and Jim Harris, *The Financial Post 100 Best Companies to Work for in Canada*, Toronto, 1990, pp. 235-58.

[11] See, for instance: R. Craig McIvor, *Canadian Monetary, Banking and Fiscal Development*, Toronto, 1958, pp. ix-x.

[12] See: A. B. Jamieson, *Chartered Banking in Canada*, Toronto, 1953, J. A. Galbraith, *The Economics of Banking Operations*, Montreal, 1963 and E. P. Neufeld, *Bank of Canada Policy Appraised*, Toronto, 1958 and *Money and Banking in Canada*, Toronto, 1964 and *The Financial System of Canada: Its Growth and Development*, Toronto, 1972.

[13] R. J. Gould, "Training the Man," *JCBA*, vol. 16, #1, pp. 174-75.

[14] Kenny to Thompson, July 27, 1889, Thompson Papers, MG 26 D, NAC.

## Chapter One

[1] For port information, see: Luke Hutchinson, *The Halifax Business Directory*, Halifax, 1863, David McAlpine, *Halifax City Directory 1869-70*, Halifax,

and *Halifax and Its Business: Historical Sketch and Description of the City and Its Institutions*, N.S. Printing Co., Halifax, 1876.

[2] A. G. Jones Reminiscences, Halifax *Morning Chronicle*, Jan. 4, 1892.

[3] T. & E. Kenny & Co. postcard, April 6, 1880, James Dickie Papers, Dalhousie University Archives.

[4] See: Dickie and Frieze Papers in the Dalhousie University Archives, especially: T. & E. Kenny to Frieze & Roy, March 1, 1877, and May 25, 1882, Frieze Papers.

[5] *Monetary Times*, March 7, 1873, p. 775.

[6] Johnston to Jones, April 8, 1864, A. G. Jones Papers, MG 1, vol. 523 PANS.

[7] See: D. A. Sutherland, "Sir Edward Kenny," *Dictionary of Canadian Biography*, vol. 11, pp. 480-82 and T. M. Punch, *Some Sons of Erin in Nova Scotia*, Halifax, 1980.

[8] See: A. C. Dunlop, "John Barnhill Dickie," *Dictionary of Canadian Biography*, vol. 11, pp. 262-63.

[9] See: G. F. Butler, "The Early Organization and Influence of Halifax Merchants, *Collections of the Nova Scotia Historical Society*, vol. 25, 1942, Julian Gwyn, "'A Little Province Like This': The Economy of Nova Scotia under Stress, 1812-1853," in D. Akenson, ed., *Canadian Papers in Rural History*, vol. 6, Gananoque, 1983, and David Sutherland, "Halifax Merchants and the Pursuit of Development 1783–1850," *Canadian Historical Review*, vol. LIX, 1978.

[10] *The Weekly Citizen* (Halifax), Dec. 31, 1864, and various petitioners to J. Howe, July 5, 1866, Jones Papers, vol. 523, PANS.

[11] *British Colonist*, July 2, 1867.

[12] *Monetary Times*, Aug. 16, 1872, p. 124.

[13] F. H. Bell, "The Nova Scotia Act Respecting Assignments and Preferences," *JCBA*, vol. 7, #3, April 1900.

[14] R. G. Dun & Co. mercantile ratings, vol. 11, p. 324, NAC.

[15] *Acadian Recorder*, Sept. 16, 1874.

[16] Halifax *Herald*, Feb. 18, 1880.

[17] *British Colonist*, June 10, 1869. Tobin left an estate of $270,000.

[18] All quotations taken from Dun's mercantile ratings for Halifax, 1852-1880, *Op. cit.*

[19] Connolly to J. A. Macdonald, Sept. 16, 1868, cited in F. J. Wilson, "The Most Rev. Thomas L. Connolly, Archbishop of Halifax," *Canadian Catholic Historical Association Report*, 1943-44, pp. 84-86.

[20] Kenny to Macdonald, May 30, 1878, Macdonald Papers, #160732-3, NAC. For T. E. Kenny biography, see: Halifax *Morning Chronicle*, Oct. 26, 1908.

[21] R. M. Breckenridge, *The Canadian Banking System, 1817-1890*, New York, 1895, p. 205.

[22] R. Craig McIvor, *Canadian Monetary, Banking and Fiscal Development*, Toronto, 1958, pp. 59-63.

[23] *Ibid.*, p. 61. See: Joseph Schull and J. Douglas Gibson, *The Scotiabank Story: A History of the Bank of Nova Scotia, 1832-1982*, Toronto, 1982.

[24] See: Acadia Fire Insurance Co. file, MG 100, vol. 155, file 5, PANS.

[25] Breckenridge, *Op. cit.*, p. 210.

[26] *Halifax and Its Business: Historical Sketch and Description of the City and its Institutions*, Halifax, 1876, p. 51.

[27] Minute Book of the Union Bank of Halifax, Feb. 4, 1864, RAB 4 B-1.

[28] *Acadian Recorder*, Sept. 24, 1872.

[29] Halifax *Morning Chronicle*, April 26, 1864.

[30] R. G. Dun & Co. Mercantile Ratings, *Op. cit.*

[31] Merchants' Bank of Halifax, *Prospectus*, April 1869, MBH-1 Ab-2.

[32] "Resolutions adopted by the Halifax Banks," *Monetary Times*, May 13, 1869, p. 615.

[33] See: E. P. Neufeld, *The Financial System of Canada: Its Growth and Development*, Toronto, 1972, chap. 4.

[34] See: Adam Shortt, *History of Canadian Currency and Banking 1600-1880*, reprinted by CBA, Toronto, nd, pp. 560-82

[35] Neufeld, *Op. cit.*, p. 88.

[36] Through the 1870s, T. E. Kenny acted as a confidant to Macdonald's Nova Scotia political lieutenants. See, for instance:

Kenny to Charles Tupper, Dec. 15, 1872, Tupper Papers #1878, NAC.

[37] MBH 1 Ab-2.

[38] An Act to Incorporate the Merchants' Bank of Halifax, chap. LIX, 32-33 Victoria.

[39] *Monetary Times*, May 13, 1869, p. 615.

[40] MBH Minute Book, Oct. 18 and Nov. 10, 1869.

[41] *Ibid.*, March 10, 1870.

[42] *Monetary Times*, March 25, 1870, p. 503.

[43] *Debates of the House of Commons*, March 4, 1890, p. 1411. Kenny's salary as president in 1872 was $800 a year.

[44] W. M. Botsford Reminiscences, RBC 4 Bo.

[45] MBH Minute Books, March 9 and 10, 1870.

[46] MBH Minute Book, March 5, 1879.

[47] MBH Minute Book, April 26, 1875.

[48] *Ibid.*, March 3, 1875.

[49] Halifax *Recorder*, July 5, 1877.

[50] Kenny to Jones, Oct. 3, 1883, RBC 5 Ken-3. Amazingly, Kenny was wrong in placing the bank at Granville and George; it was actually at Hollis and George.

[51] Petition of Shediac merchants to MBH, June 23, 1886, MBH 2 D-19.

[52] MBH Minute Book, July 25, 1870, and Chisholm and Dickie Reminiscences, RBC 4.

[53] *Royal Bank Magazine*, vol. 3, #1, Dec. 1923, p. 86.

[54] For a glimpse into these early agencies, see: Frieze & Roy (MS-4-57) and Dickie Papers (MS-4-63) at the Dalhousie University Archives.

[55] See, for instance: MBH Minute Book, Sept. 5, 1882.

[56] MBH Minutes, May 26, 1875.

[57] Maclean to Frieze, March 31, 1877, Frieze Papers, *Op. cit.*.

[58] MBH Minute Book, Dec. 11, 1974.

[59] *Monetary Times*, Jan. 2, 1874, p. 636 and Jan. 24, 1874, p. 722.

[60] Halifax *Morning Chronicle*, Feb. 9, 1887.

[61] Northup to Frieze, April 12, 1877.

[62] MBH Minute Book, April 23, 1873 and *Monetary Times*, April 25, 1873, p. 939.

[63] MBH Minute Book, Sept. 4, 1874.

[64] MBH Minute Book, Nov. 28, 1881. See: Douglas Baldwin, "The Growth and Decline of the Charlottetown Banks, 1854-1906," *Acadiensis*, vol. XV, #2, Spring 1986.

[65] *Ibid.*, Oct. 17, 1883. The Maritime Bank went into voluntary receivership in 1887.

[66] *Monetary Times*, March 28, 1884, p. 1089.

[67] *Monetary Times*, Sept. 12, 1879, p. 331.

[68] MBH Minute Book, Jan. 3, 1882 and *Monetary Times*, Feb. 17, 1882, p. 1004.

[69] MBH Minute Book, Dec. 19, 1882.

[70] *Ibid.*, April 20, 1883.

[71] *Ibid.*, Dec. 12, 1883.

[72] *Ibid.*, Nov. 28, 1884.

[73] Good examples of early circulars are available in the Frieze and Roy Papers at Dalhousie.

[74] MBH Minute Book, June 7, 1886.

[75] *Ibid.*, Oct. 22, 1886.

[76] *Ibid.*, May 10, 1886.

[77] *Ibid.*, Feb. 25, 1885.

[78] *Monetary Times*, Feb. 13, 1885, p. 910 and p. 916.

[79] *Monetary Times*, March 19, 1886, p. 1065.

[80] MBH Minutes, July 23 and Nov. 28, 1883.

[81] *Monetary Times*, July 10, 1887, p. 465.

[82] *Ibid.*, March 12, 1886, pp. 1042-43.

[83] Nov. 20, 1885. The interaction of industry and finance in post-Confederation Atlantic Canada has been extensively researched. Two excellent articles are: T. W. Acheson, "The National Policy and the Industrialization of the Maritimes, 1880-1910," *Acadiensis*, vol. 1, Spring 1972 and James Frost "The 'Nationalization' of the Bank of Nova Scotia, 1880-1910," *Ibid.*, vol. 12, Autumn 1982.

[84] Kenny to Macdonald, Jan. 31, 1887, Macdonald Papers, NAC.

[85] *Debates of the House of Commons*, May 6, 1887, p. 300 and April 20, 1887, p. 1413.

[86] MBH Minute Book, July 15, 1885.

[87] *Ibid.*, Aug. 4, 1887.

# Chapter Two

[1] Excellent sources exist for Canadian bank architecture. See, in particular: Susan Wagg *et al.*, *Money Matters: A Critical Look at Bank Architecture*, New York, 1990, and Kelly Crossman, *Architecture in Transition: From Art to Practice, 1885-1906*, Montreal, 1987. Leacock quotation from Marion Scott, "Banking Halls," Montreal *Gazette*, Dec. 17, 1990.

[2] E. P. Neufeld, *The Financial System of Canada: Its Growth and Development*, Toronto, 1972, p. 99.

[3] See: Merrill Denison, *Canada's First Bank: A History of the Bank of Montreal*, 2 vols., Montreal, 1967.

[4] F. T. Walker Reminiscences, RBC 4 Wa.

[5] Torrance to Pease, Jan. 31, 1900, MBH 2 D-14.

[6] MBH Minute Book, Sept. 17, 1891.

[7] Duncan to Pease, April 4, 1888, MBH 2 D-14.

[8] S. G. Dobson, *The Royal Bank of Canada, 1864-1945*, Montreal, 1954, p. 63.

[9] Pease to Duncan, Jan. 8, 1889, MBH 2 D-10-11.

[10] *Ibid.*, April 12, 1890.

[11] Duncan to Pease, May 28, 1888, MBH 2 D-10.

[12] For Pease's reforming zeal, see: G. R. Chisholm and C. E. Mackenzie Reminiscences RBC 4. The systematization of the Merchants' procedures and particularly its branch network was fundamentally influenced by Scottish banking practice. See: S. G. Checkland, *Scottish Banking: A History, 1695-1973*, Glasgow, 1975, parts three and four.

[13] *Monetary Times*, Feb. 17, 1888, p. 1034.

[14] *Monetary Times*, Dec. 28, 1888, p. 788, and John Knight, "The Montreal Clearing House: Its History and Mechanism," *JCBA*, vol. X, #1, Oct. 1902.

[15] A good survey of each revision is available in A. B. Jamieson, *Chartered Banking In Canada*, Toronto, 1953, chap. 2.

[16] Bank Act Revision 1880 - Minutes of Meeting with Government Officials, Mar. 18, 1880, CBAA, file 87-505-02. The Merchants' did not send a representative to Ottawa in 1880.

[17] Pease to E. Clouston, CBA president, July 11, 1910, CBAA, file 87-505-05.

[18] *Monetary Times*, Jan. 20, 1905, p. 982 and Jan. 26, 1906, p. 968.

[19] R. L. McCormick Reminiscences, RBC 4.

[20] Pease to G. Hague, Sept. 24, 1887, MBH 2 D-14.

[21] Pease to Duncan, June 18, 1888, *Ibid.*

[22] Duncan to Pease, Aug. 28, 1888, *Ibid.*

[23] Pease to Duncan, Jan. 25, 1888, *Ibid.*

[24] *Ibid.*, Aug. 2, 1888.

[25] Pease to Duncan, June 18, 1888, MBH 2 D-14. In a marvellous touch of irony, Pease and the two Merediths are buried in facing plots along bankers' row in Montreal's Mount Royal Cemetery.

[26] Torrance to Pease, April 9, 1900, MBH 2 D-16. By the early twentieth century, "progressive" seems to have become the adjective of choice in public commentary on the Merchants'/Royal: "this progressive bank" (*Monetary Times*, Sept. 14, 1912, p. 441) and "careful and progressive direction and management" (*Ibid.*, Jan. 16, 1914, p. 175).

[27] See: Ronald Rudin, *Banking en français: The French Banks of Quebec, 1835–1925*, Toronto, 1985.

[28] Pease to Duncan, Feb. 6, 1889, *Ibid.*

[29] N. G. Hart Reminiscences, RBC 4.

[30] H. A. Porter, "Christmas, 1903", *RBC Magazine*, Oct.-Nov., 1945, p. 6.

[31] *Morning Chronicle*, May 20, 1896.

[32] Kenny to Macdonald, July 16, 1891, Macdonald Papers, NAC.

[33] *Monetary Times*, Jan. 8, 1904, p. 871, and Jan. 15, 1904, p. 916.

[34] See: Alfred Chandler, *The Visible Hand: The Managerial Revolution in American Business*, Cambridge, Mass., 1977.

[35] Hosmer entry, *Who's Who*, 1910.

[36] *Monetary Times*, Nov. 12, 1897, p. 633.

[37] For a portrait of Montreal's "Square Mile" society, see: Donald MacKay, *The Square Mile: Merchant Princes of Montreal*, Toronto, 1987.

[38] John Heron, "Sgt. Vines…Chauffeur Par Excellence," Royal Bank Magazine, April-May 1949, p. 15, and Victor Ross, *A History of the Canadian Bank of Commerce*, vol. 2, Toronto, 1922, p. 72.

[39] F. Wolferstan Thomas, *JCBA*, vol. 5, #2, Jan. 1898.

[40] Van Horne Register #6, incoming letter #28911, from C. R. Hosmer, June 12, 1890, Canadian Pacific Archives, Montreal.

[41] Pease to Kenny, April 19, 1889, MBH 2 D-14.

[42] Torrance to Pease, Oct. 12, 1888, MBH 2 D-10.

[43] Schull and Gibson, *The Scotiabank Story*, *Op. cit.*, p. 70.

[44] Pease to Kenny, April 22, 1890, MBH 2 D-10.

[45] Statement of Bond Account, May 25, 1899, MBH Minute Book. The account also contained Canadian municipal bonds.

[46] MBH Minute Book, Feb. 9, 1898. For an example of the sudden fever of eastern interest in western resources, see: "Animated Banking Proceedings," *Monetary Times*, Nov. 25, 1898, p. 704, and a description of "boosterism" in Rossland, *Ibid.*, p. 706.

[47] Botsford Reminiscences, RBC 4 and "A Bank at Bennett," *Monetary Times*, April 14, 1899, p. 1368.

[48] See: Torrance to G. H. Bayne (Homestake Mine, Rossland), Dec. 8, 1899, MBH 2 D-16.

[49] B. E. Walker, "Banking in Canada", *JCBA*, vol. 1, #1, Sept. 1893.

[50] Torrance to S. Voorhees, Oct. 23, 1900, MBH 2 D-16.

[51] Profit and Loss Statement, June 1902, RBC Minute Book, July 1902.

[52] See: W. Pinder, Arthur manager, to Pease, Nov. 29, 1909 and Strathy to Pease, Nov. 27, 1909, RAB 5 D-25.

[53] J. A. Terrace Reminiscences, RBC 4.

[54] See: W. S. Fielding to E. S. Clouston, Nov. 5, 1906 and June 19, 1908, Fielding Papers, PANS, vols. 458 and 467, and Jeremy Adelman, "Prairie Farm Debt and the Financial Crisis of 1914," *Canadian Historical Review*, LXXI, 4, 1990.

[55] MBH Minute Book, Feb. 3, 20, 21, and March 27.

[56] *Monetary Times*, Sept. 1, 1899, p. 274, and MBH Minute Book, July 11, 1899.

[57] Pease remarks at annual meeting, *Annual Report*, 1922, p. 18.

[58] *Ibid.*

[59] Torrance to W. F. Brock, Nov. 2, 1899, MBH 2 D-16.

[60] See: Z. A. Lash, "Warehouse Receipts, Bills of Lading, and Securities Under Section 74 of the Bank Act of 1890," *JCBA*, vol. 2, Sept. 1894.

[61] Torrance to Pease, April 9, 1900, MBH 2 D-16.

[62] G. R. Chisholm and Martin Dickie Reminiscences, RBC 4.

[63] For coverage of the scandal, see: *Monetary Times*, Aug. 31, Oct. 12 and 16, and Dec. 12, 1900.

[64] *Ibid.*, Dec. 12, 1900, p. 768.

[65] Torrance to Pease, June 15, 1900, *Ibid.*

[66] Pease to Duncan, Sept. 22, 1898, MBH 2 D-15.

[67] *Ibid.*, Feb. 22, 1899.

[68] See: T. D. Regehr, "A Backwoodsman and an Engineer in Canadian Business: An Examination of Divergence of Entrepreneurial Practice in Canada at the Turn of the Century," CHA *Historical Papers*, 1977.

[69] *Monetary Times*, Sept. 12, 1904, p. 760, and Oct. 17, 1908, p. 647.

[70] RBC Minute Book, Feb. 8, 1905.

[71] See, for instance: J. A. Terrace Reminiscences, RBC 4. "the greatest stroke of his career was in getting H. S. Holt…as president."

[72] See, for instance: *Canadian Annual Review*, 1904, p. 509.

[73] Torrance to Kenny, Nov. 24, 1902, MBH 2 D-16.

[74] See: *Debates of the House of Commons*, June 1, 1906, p. 4389, and June 25, 1906, p. 6022.

## Chapter Three

[1] All Wilson quotations from: Harold P. Wilson Papers, Provincial Archives of British Columbia, E/C/W692. See also: Victoria *Daily Colonist*, April 11, 1965, and Wilson and Fulton entries in List of Officers, MBH 2, D-12 and 13

[2] Pease to T. R. Whitley, RBC Winnipeg, Aug. 30, 1912, RBC 5 Pea-5.

[3] To suggest that nineteenth-century Canadians rooted their identities in locality is not to suggest that transience was not also a factor in their lives. As demographers such as Michael Katz have shown for cities such as Hamilton, Canadians, especially young men, were constantly in motion. Large numbers of low wage, unskilled labourers ebbed and flowed across the land in a chaotic, seasonal search for work. What bank employment pioneered was mobile, professionally oriented employment within the confines of one national employer. Furthermore, while work as a "navvy" offered little upward mobility, a "bank boy" who persevered had a good chance of moving up the ladder of middle-class advancement.

[4] *Royal Bank Magazine*, Jan. 1935.

[5] Toronto *Star*, June 6, 1946.

[6] S. G. Checkland, *Scottish Banking: A History, 1695-1973*, Glasgow, 1975, pp. 711-15.

[7] *Ibid.*, p. 502.

[8] *Ibid.*, p. 502.

[9] *Monetary Times*, Oct. 13, 1905.

[10] The Muir Papers in the Royal Bank Archives are packed with evidence of Muir's mania for things Scottish. In 1952, he was made a freeman of his home town, Peebles. See: *Royal Bank Magazine*, Dec. 15, 1952, p. 15. See: H. B. Selwyn, "Bonnie Laddie, Hielan' Laddie," *JCBA*, vol. 31, #2, Jan. 1924, pp. 194-200.

[11] George Rae, *The Country Banker: His Clients, Cares, and Work*, Scribner's New York edition, 1886, p. 9.

[12] H. M. P. Eckardt, *Manual of Canadian Banking*, Toronto, 1913, preface, p. 191 and p. 183. For a synopsis of Eckardt's career, see: *JCBA*, vol. 26, #2, Jan. 1919, pp. 88-89.

[13] Gordon Tait, "The Branches: From the Vantage-Point of Head Office," *JCBA*, vol. XIII, #3, April 1906, p. 215.

[14] C. E. Neill, "Address to the Graduating Class-University of New Brunswick, May 15, 1924," RBC 5 Nei-2.

[15] All quotations from Merchants'/RBC *Rules and Regulations*, 1885, 1901, 1916, 1921, and 1931 versions.

[16] A. C. Hoffman Reminiscences, RBC 4.

[17] RBC List of Officers, MBH-2 D-12 and 13.

[18] *Ibid.*, Feb. 13, 1895.

[19] MBH Minute Book, Dec. 10, 1900.

[20] See, for instance: "Bank Auditors and Inspection," *Monetary Times*, Nov. 3, 1906, p. 633, and G. J. Nutt, "The Canadian System of Branch Inspection," *Royal Bank Magazine*, June 1921, pp. 828-32.

[21] Interview with Warren Bull (Feb. 14, 1991).

[22] Pease to Kenny, nd, c. 1895, MBH 2 D-14.

[23] *Monetary Times*, May 15, 1896, p. 1478.

[24] A. G. Tait, "John Jarvis, Banker?" *JCBA*, vol. 16, #3, April 1909, p. 223.

[25] E. R. Campbell interview, April 9, 1991.

[26] *Royal Bank Magazine*, vol. 1, #1, Dec. 1920, p. 18.

[27] *Saturday Night*, April 18, 1908.

[28] All quotations from Allan Mackenzie interview, Oct. 17, 1990, and Alex Kearney interview, Aug. 29, 1990. Mackenzie and Kearney were by 1990 both centenarians; no historian could find more charming and lucid voices from the past.

[29] W. A. Rowat, "Backward Glances (Memoirs of a Minister's Son)," nd., np., RBC 4.

30 Norman Nagle letters, 1908-09, RBC 14 D-34.

31 Victor Heron, "More Hints to Juniors," *JCBA*, vol. XIII, #1, Oct., 1905, p. 72.

32 C. W. Frazee Reminiscences, RBC 4.

33 MBH Minute Book, July 31, 1900. See also: W. S. Fielding to T. E. Kenny, Feb. 12, 1902, vol. 438, Fielding Papers, PANS. "Hope you will be able to give him a further chance...conditional on total abstinence."

34 *RBC Magazine*, Oct. 1906, vol. 14, #1, p. 42.

35 Williams-Taylor to White, Jan. 25, 1916, MG 27 II, D 18, NAC.

36 Details taken from T. B. O'Connell Reminiscences, RBC 4.

37 "On Commencing a Banking Career," *RBC Magazine*, April 1931, p. 19, and *James Muir: 1891-1960*, *RBC Magazine*, March-April 1961, p. 13.

38 All quotations from: Merchants' Bank of Halifax and Union Bank of Halifax staff ledgers, MBH 2, D-12 & 13 and RAB D-12, 1890-1910. Such ledgers were kept until the 1920s when a more scientific system of card records was introduced. The comments in the ledgers reflect the views of a junior's manager.

39 C. E. Neill, "Banking as a Profession," *The Canadian Banker*, vol. 34, #2, pp. 178-80.

40 *Monetary Times*, Dec. 6, 1878.

41 *Debates of the House of Commons*, May 10, 1911, p. 8698.

42 Torrance to D. M. Stewart, Jan. 6, 1900, and Torrance to M. Dickie, Feb. 23, 1900, MBH 2 D-16.

43 *Monetary Times*, vol. 36, #4, p. 114, and *Debates of the House of Commons*, May 10, 1910, p. 8699.

44 Fielding to Clouston, Feb. 26, 1909, vol. 469, Fielding Papers, PANS.

45 *Monetary Times*, May 4, 1907, p. 1724, and Nov. 26, 1910, p. 2214.

46 *Saturday Night*, March 25, 1912, p. 24.

47 J. P. Buschlen (pseud), *A Canadian Bank Clerk*, Toronto, 1913 and *Behind the Wicket: Short Stories Relating to Life in the Canadian Banks*, Toronto, 1914. Preston probably worked for the Bank of Toronto.

48 Wilkie to H. B. Shaw, Feb. 16, 1914, CBAA file 87-516-17.

49 See: CBAA file 87-516-17 and "Bank Employees' Association," *Union Bank of Canada Monthly*, Jan. 1920.

50 *JCBA*, vol. VII, #2, Jan. 1900, p. 142.

51 Buschlen, *Behind the Wicket*, Op. cit., introduction.

52 See: "The Opportunities of the Telling Box," in *Practical Suggestions for Bank Officers*, CBA, Toronto, 1918.

53 B. B. Carter reminiscences, RBC 4.

54 W. D. Melvin Reminiscences, RBC 4 and "Filthy Lucre," *JCBA*, vol. XI, #3, April 1903. There is persistent complaint from tellers that the greasy, worn bills in circulation endangered their health.

55 Torrance to M. Dickie, Dec. 9, 1899, MBH 2 D-16.

56 Pease to Duncan, April 12, 1890, MBH 2 D-14.

57 F. T. Walker, "British Columbia, 1899-1912," RBC 4.

58 R. L. McCormick Reminiscences, RBC 4.

59 Pease to Duncan, Dec. 13, 1898, MBH 2 D-14.

60 This phrase appears with uncanny frequency in reminiscences and commentaries on the bank's progress. See, for instance: W. H. Malkin to annual general meeting, *RBC Magazine*, Jan. 1936, I. R. Carlin to S. G. Dobson, Jan. 7, 1954, and C. H. Hunt to Dobson, Jan. 23, 1954, RBC 5 Dobson.

61 Thomas Craig, "Streamlining Routine Methods and Procedures," 1944, RBC 4. See also: A. J. Wilkins and R. M. Woollatt Reminiscences, RBC 4.

62 Carl Berger, *The Sense of Power: Studies in the Ideas of Canadian Imperialism, 1867-1914*, Toronto, 1970.

63 See: Edith Davis, "A Word to the Wives," *Canadian Banker*, vol. 34, #4, July 1931, pp. 402-04.

64 See: *Monetary Times*, Feb. 20, 1903, p. 1133.

65 *JCBA*, vol. 23, #4, July 1916, p. 294.

# Chapter Four

[1] *Monetary Times*, March 11, 1904, p. 1218.

[2] *Ibid.*, Jan. 18, 1908, p. 1166.

[3] *Saturday Night*, Jan. 10, 1920, p. 15.

[4] All banking statistics in this section taken from E. P. Neufeld's *The Financial System of Canada: Its Growth and Development*, Toronto, 1972, chap. 4. Also useful are: R. Craig McIvor, *Canadian Monetary Banking and Fiscal Development*, Toronto, 1958, chap. 4, and A. B. Jamieson, *Chartered Banking in Canada*, Toronto, 1958, chap. 2.

[5] *Monetary Times*, July 13, 1912, p. 135. The sentiment is echoed in an October 20, 1913, letter of Nathaniel Curry, a Nova Scotian industrialist, to Finance Minister Thomas White: the scale of Canadian development in the Laurier boom made it "absolutely necessary to have large banks." White Papers, NAC.

[6] H. A. Richardson to Thomas White, Feb. 17, 1919, White Papers, NAC.

[7] House of Commons, Committee on Banking and Commerce, *Journals of the House of Commons*, vol. XLVIII, 1912-13, p. 544.

[8] Torrance to R. P. Foster, Nov. 24, 1899, MBH 2 D-16. The branch deferred was Saint John, N. B.

[9] See: Smith-Craig correspondence, 1900, RBC 6 British Columbia-Grand Forks.

[10] J. A. Terrace Reminiscences, RBC 4.

[11] Pease to T. R. Whitley, October 16, 1916, RBC 5 Pea 5.

[12] *Monetary Times*, Oct. 28, 1898, p. 568-69.

[13] *Monetary Times*, Jan. 25, 1908, p. 1213.

[14] Minute Book, RBC, Oct. 16, 1906, and Jan. 21, 1908. T. D. Regehr, "The Sovereign Bank," unpublished paper.

[15] Whitley to Pease, April 17, 1913, RBC 5 Pea 5. See: Jeremy Adelman, "Prairie Farm Debt and the Financial Crisis of 1914," *The Canadian Historical Review*, LXXI, 4, 1990, pp. 491-519.

[16] W. D. Melvin, "Section 88," *Canadian Banker*, vol. 61, Feb. 1954, #1, pp. 22-35, and A. B. Jamieson, *Chartered Banking in Canada*, Toronto, 1953, pp. 243-72.

[17] See: Fielding Papers, vol. 467, PANS and McIvor, *Op. cit.*, pp. 82-85.

[18] *Journals of the House of Commons, Op. cit.*, pp. 535-49.

[19] RBC Minutes, December 12, 1902, Torrance to Kenny, Nov. 24, 27, and 28, 1902, MBH 2 D-16, and shareholders' list in 1903 *Annual Report*.

[20] MBH Minutes, Oct. 22 and Dec. 12, 1883.

[21] Torrance to Kenny, Mar. 16, 1902, MBH 2 D-16.

[22] *Monetary Times*, Oct. 20, 1906, p. 568.

[23] J. F. Stairs to W. Robertson, July 14, 1902, RAB 4 DI-7.

[24] C. N. S. Strickland Reminiscences, RBC 4.

[25] RBC Minute Book, July 14, 1910, and Union Bank of Halifax *Minute Book*, circular dated July 26, 1991.

[26] C. E. Neill to T. C. Boville, Nov. 15, 1910, RG 19, vol. 488, NAC.

[27] See: "The Emergence of Corporate Toronto," Plate 15 in *Historical Atlas of Canada: vol. III—Addressing the Twentieth Century, 1891-1961*, Toronto, 1990.

[28] F. T. Walker Reminiscences, RBC 4.

[29] Amalgamation documents, RAB 5 D-10. Before the Commons Banking and Commerce Committee a year later, Pease stated that the Traders "sought us" through "outside agents." *Journals, Op. cit.*, pp. 545-8.

[30] Amalgamation proposal to Traders shareholders, May 10, 1991, RAB 5.

[31] *Monetary Times*, July 13, 1912, p. 135.

[32] Neill to Dyment and Ridout, April 18, 1912, RAB 5-Traders.

[33] All quotations from RG 19, vol. 489, NAC.

[34] The Toronto *World*, April 30, 1912.

[35] Peter Ryan to T. White, May 28, 1912, RG 19, vol. 489.

[36] White to Borden, Aug. 2, 1912, MG 26 H, NAC.

[37] Solemn Oath, Aug. 7, 1912, RG 19, vol. 489.

[38]Strathy to ?, June 18, 1913, RAB 5 D-10.

[39] Pease to T. R. Whitley, Aug. 28, 1912, RBC 5 Pea 5.

[40] *Monetary Times*, Sept. 14, 1912, p. 441.

[41]For examples of Canadian commentary, see: H. M. P. Eckardt, "What Will Check the Merger Movement?" and "Competition That Persists in Spite of Bank Mergers," *Saturday Night*, May 5 (p.24) and June 22 (p.24), 1912.

[42] Fielding to Clouston, Dec. 6, 1907, Fielding Papers, vol. 464, PANS.

[43] Laurier to W. B. Hamilton, Feb. 27, 1903, Laurier Papers, NAC.

[44] *Journals of the House of Commons, Op. cit.*, p. 545.

[45] J. P. Bell to White, Aug. 19, 1915, White Papers, MG 27 II D 18, vol. 1, file 4a.

[46] See: John Taylor, *Ottawa: An Illustrated History*, Toronto, 1986.

[47] See, for instance: Borden to Holt, Aug. 14 and Oct. 8, 1914, Borden Papers, NAC.

[48] Holt to White, July 15, 1915, White Papers, vol. 1, file 4a. Pease and Brown personally took the letter to Ottawa.

[49] Pease to White, Aug. 16, 1915, *Ibid.*

[50] Willison to White, Aug. 7, 1915, *Ibid.*

[51] All foregoing quotations from White Papers, vol. 1, file 4a. See: *Monetary Times*, Aug. 27, 1915, p. 11.

[52] Pease to White, Aug. 23, 1915, *Ibid.*

[53] *Ibid.*, p. 24.

[54] Pease to White, Oct. 26, 1920, RBC Nei 5.

[55] See: R. Rudin, *Banking en française: The French Banks of Quebec, 1835-1925*, Toronto, 1985, and B. B. Stevenson, "The Quebec Bank, 1818-1916," typescript RBC Archives.

[56] P. S. Ross & Sons report, Dec. 20, 1916, RAB 9 C-3 and *Monetary Times*, Dec. 10, 1915, p. 14.

[57] Quebec Bank Minute Book, May 28–Aug.21, 1908, RAB 9 B-14.

[58] *Monetary Times*, Oct. 13, 1916, p. 24B.

[59] Pease to T. R. Whitley, Oct. 16, 1916, RBC 5 Pea 5.

[60] Rogers to White, Jan. 26, 1916, White Papers, vol. 1, file 4a.

[61] The Northern Crown duplicated the Royal in fourteen Prairie locations. These were closed. The merger also brought twenty-four Ontario and seven British Columbia branches. Because of duplicate branches and the yeasty growth of the Royal's own branch network, it is always difficult to calculate the *net* gain in branches from each merger.

[62] See: Robinson to A. K. Maclean, March 1, 1918, and G. M. Holbrook to T.C. Boville, March 25, 1918, RG 19, vol. 488.

[63] Pease to Robinson, May 21, 1918, RAB 11 D-1.

[64] *The Royal Bank of Canada, 1869-1919*, n.a., Montreal, 1919, introduction.

[65] *Journals of the House of Commons, Op. cit.*, p. 540.

[66] E. L. Pease speech, Minutes of the Annual General Meeting of the Canadian Bankers' Association, Nov. 14, 1918, and Pease to Z. A. Lash, Dec. 2, 1921, CBAA file 87-524, file 87-524.

[67] Cables, White to Pease and Pease to White, Nov. 13, 1918, White Papers, vol. 1, file 3b.

[68] See: R. Craig McIvor, *Canadian Monetary, Banking and Fiscal Development*, Toronto, 1958, p. 110 and Pease to F. T. Walker, Oct. 19, Warburg to Pease, Oct. 30, and Pease to Warburg, Nov. 3, 1918, RBC 5 Pea 6.

[69] Pease to Walker, Nov. 5, 7 and 8, 1918, *Ibid.*

[70] *Monetary Times*, Jan. 18, 1918, p. 27.

[71] CBA Minutes, Nov. 14, 1918, *Op. cit.*

[72] Pease to White, July 19 and Aug. 8, 1918, White Papers, vol. 1, file 2.

[73] Williams-Taylor to White, Dec. 5, 1918, White Papers, vol. 1, file 3b. See also: Z. A. Lash to Pease, Nov. 30, 1918, RBC 2 29A 17.

[74] Minutes of Toronto meeting of Z. A. Lash and Henry Ross (CBA Secretary), Jan. 28, 1919, *Ibid.*

[75] Minutes of Meeting of Confidential Committee, Feb. 3, 1919, and Meredith to White, Mar. 4, 1919, *Ibid.*

[76] Z. A. Lash, "The United States Federal Reserve Act and the Canadian Banking System with Some Contrasts," *JCBA*, vol. 26, #3, April 1919, p. 243.

[77] Walker Reminiscences, RBC 4.

[78] Pease to Williams-Taylor, Nov. 7, 1917, RBC 5 Pea 3.

[79] Meredith to White, July 21, 1915, White Papers, vol. 1, file 1.

[80] White to Pease, May 14, 1919, White Papers, vol. 2, file 5a.

[81] Merrill Denison, *Canada's First Bank*, vol. 2, Toronto, 1967, pp. 345-46.

[82] Jackson Dodds, "General Position of the Bank," May 26, 1923, RAB 14 D-7.

[83] Riley to Meighen, June 2, 1925, Meighen Papers, #061472-3, MG 26 I, NAC.

[84] For an excellent graphic representation of this concentration of Canadian banking, see: "Financial Institutions," Plate 9 in *Historical Atlas of Canada, Op. cit.*

[85] RBC *Magazine*, Nov. 1925, p. 606.

[86] Cable R. J. Cromie to Mackenzie King, May 23, 1925, King Papers, MG 26 J, NAC.

# Chapter Five

[1] MBH Minute Book, March 30 and May 1, 1882. Bermuda was a popular destination for wealthy Canadians in search of a salubrious climate; a year later the Governor-General's wife, Princess Louise, wintered in the colony making it a fashionable resort.

[2] See: H. C. Butterfield, *Butterfield's Bank: Five Generations in Bermuda*, Hamilton, Bermuda, 1958, pp. 82-84, and *Bermuda Pocket Almanac*, Hamilton, 1890, p. 144. The N. T. Butterfield Papers in the Bermuda Archives (Accession # 2246) indicate that Butterfield was trading to the West Indies and Halifax as early as the 1840s.

[3] MBH Minute Book, May 9, 1883.

[4] MBH Minutes, Nov. 22, 1888.

[5] S. R. Noble Reminiscences, RBC 4.

[6] W. L. M. King to James Malcolm (Minister of Trade and Commerce), May 19, 1930, #151428, King Papers, NAC.

[7] *Monetary Times*, Jan. 8, 1886, p. 772.

Trade statistics were reported in an awkward mixture of quintals, barrels, and hogsheads, making aggregation difficult. McAlpine's *Halifax and Its Business* (Halifax, 1876) estimated 1875 exports at $2.5 million and imports at $1.9 million.

[8] *Ibid.*, July 23, 1880, pp. 92-93.

[9] See, for instance: Kenny to J. A. Macdonald, Oct. 22, 1889, Macdonald Papers, MG 26 A, NAC.

[10] Ambrose Shea to A. T. Galt, Feb. 20, 1866, Galt Papers, MG 27 I D8, NAC.

[11] MBH Minute Book, Dec. 13, 1894, and Jan. 15, 1895. *Monetary Times*, Feb. 2, 1895, p. 1068. *Monetary Times* later portrayed the Newfoundland bank panic as the product of "mushroom banking" practices by unscrupulous directors in a volatile regional economy (June 28, 1895, p. 1686).

[12] Minutes of Committee on Banking and Commerce, *Journals of the House of Commons*, vol. XLVIII, 1912-13, p. 547.

[13] E. P. Neufeld, *The Financial System of Canada: Its Growth and Development*, Toronto, 1972, p. 125.

[14] *Ibid.*, pp. 123-25.

[15] MBH Minute Book, May 25, 1888.

[16] See: Mira Wilkins, *The History of Foreign Investment in the United States to 1914*, Cambridge, Mass., 1989, pp. 454-63, and H. van B. Cleveland and T. Huertas, *Citibank, 1812-1970*, Cambridge, Mass., 1970, chaps. 2 and 3.

[17] *Anuario Azucarero de Cuba*, 1959, cited in: Cuban Economic Research Project, *A Study on Cuba*, University of Miami, Coral Gables, 1965, p. 333.

[18] I am indebted to the work of Harold G. Hesler, a gifted amateur historian and Royal Bank official in Cuba from 1919 to 1930, for his exhaustive, typescript history of "Cuba: Banking and Currency, 1492-1950," in RBC Archives. See also: Louis A. Perez, Jr., *Cuba Between Empires 1878-1902*, Pittsburgh, 1983, and *Cuba Under the Platt Amendment, 1902-1934*, Pittsburgh, 1986.

[19] Perez, *Cuba Between Empires, Op. cit.*, pp. 377-78.

[20] Cited in Perez, *Cuba Between Empires, Op. cit.*, p. 345.

21 See: Jules Robert Benjamin, *The United States and Cuba–Hegemony and Dependent Development, 1880-1934*, Pittsburgh, 1974, and Leland H. Jenks, *Our Cuban Colony: A Study in Sugar*, New York, 1928.

22 MBH Minute Book, Dec. 7, 1898.

23 Hesler Diary, p. 43.

24 Perez, *Cuba Between Empires, Op. cit.*, p. 347, and Hesler Diary.

25 See, for instance: Franklin Matthews, "The Reconstruction of Cuba," *Harper's Weekly*, July 15, 1899.

26 Pease was not alone in sensing these possibilities. In October 1898, CBA President D. R. Wilkie had urged Canadian bankers to rise to the challenge of banking beyond their borders. See: "Spanish-American War," JCBA, vol. 6, #2, Jan. 1899, pp. 140-41.

27 Staff reminiscence files frequently comment on the closeness of this relationship. See, for instance: R. W. Forrester, RBC 4 Fo 1-7. Hesler credits Hosmer with initially turning Pease's attention to Cuba. *Op. cit.*, p. 40. For an overview, see: Christopher Armstrong and H. V. Nelles, *Southern Exposure: Canadian Promoters in Latin America and the Caribbean, 1896-1930*, Toronto, 1988.

28 Jenks, *Our Cuban Colony, Op. cit.*, pp. 150-51, and "Canadian Capital in Cuba," *Monetary Times*, Oct. 19, 1900, p. 501.

29 Van Horne to Senator Platt, nd. c. 1901, vol. 9, Van Horne, Letterbooks, NAC, MG 29 A60.

30 MBH Minute Book, Jan. 3 and 14, 1899.

31 R. W. Forrester Reminiscences, RBC 4.

32 *Ibid.*, Feb. 18, 1899.

33 *Ibid.*, July 11, 1899, and *Monetary Times*, Sept. 1, 1899, p. 274.

34 *Monetary Times*, August 19, 1898, p. 250.

35 See: Neil C. Quigley, "The Bank of Nova Scotia in the Caribbean, 1889-1940," *Business History Review*, Winter 1989, vol. 63, pp. 797-838.

36 Notes on April 1899 trip to New York and Albany by T. E. Kenny, RBC 3. The Bank of Commerce did eventually enter Nova Scotia in 1903, when it bought the Halifax Banking Company.

37 Kenny notes, *Op. cit.* See: S. H. Voorhees, "Looking Back," *Royal Bank Magazine*, June 1942, pp. 2-5, 13.

38 *Royal Bank Magazine*, Oct.–Nov., 1945, p. 11.

39 Graham Towers, "A Trip to the South," *Royal Bank Magazine*, September 1922, p. 378.

40 "The chief question of course is, where are we going to get men for this important branch…it will be essential to have the best men we can find." Pease to D. H. Duncan, Dec. 8, 1898, MBH 2 D-15.

41 R. W. Forrester Reminiscences, RBC 4.

42 *Royal Bank Magazine*, March, 1950, p. 10.

43 Fredrico Mejer, "A Havana Old-Timer," *Royal Bank Magazine*, July/August 1950, pp. 4-5.

44 Staff ledger, MBH 2 D-13, p. 25. Bacardi stayed with the bank only a year.

45 JCBA, July 1, 1926, vol. 33, #4, p. 528.

46 Torrance to Kenny, November 26, 1902, MBH 2 D-14.

47 C. E. Mackenzie Reminiscences, RBC 4.

48 Pease wanted accreditation with the War and State Departments. Pease to H. W. Cannon, Dec. 8, 1898, MBH 2 D-15.

49 See: Cleveland and Huertas, *Citibank, Op. cit.*, chap. 5.

50 *Financial Post*, Feb. 9, 1907.

51 Grant Watson to Sir John Simon, Oct. 14, 1933, #144115, Bennett Papers, MG 26 K, NAC.

52 Hesler Diary, p. 57-8.

53 Van Horne to Pease, Oct. 19, 1904, Van Horne Letterbooks, vol. 6, NAC. Pease boasted that the bank had paid no bribes – "subsidizing" – to win the contract.

54 Van Horne to Pease, April 2, 1905, Van Horne Letterbooks, vol. 8, NAC.

55 Van Horne to D. A. Galdos, Jan. 6, 1913, *Ibid.*, vol. 32.

56 See: Robert Sobel, *ITT: The Management of Opportunity*, New York, 1982.

57 Benjamin, *Hegemony, Op. cit.*, p. 14, *A Study of Cuba*, chap. 16 and Jenks, *Colony*, pp. 154ff.

58 See: Pease to W. T. White, Jan. 15, 1916, vol. 265, RG 19, NAC.

59 Graham Towers, *Financing Foreign Trade*, Montreal, 1921. See: *Monetary Times*, Jan. 7, 1921, p. 41.

60 "Royal Bank of Canada–Twenty Years of Progress in Cuba–Opening of New Havana Premises," *The Bankers Magazine*, July 1919.

61 *Journals of the House of Commons, Op. cit.*, pp. 536-37.

62 RBC Minute Book, June 30, 1909.

63 See: "Canadians Abroad," plate 57 in *Historical Atlas of Canada: Addressing the Twentieth Century*, Toronto, 1990, J. Schull and J. D. Gibson, *The Scotiabank Story*, Toronto, 1982 and H. van B. Cleveland and T. F. Huertas, *Citibank 1812-1970*, Cambridge, Mass., 1985.

64 See: Stephen Randall, "The Development of Canadian Business in Puerto Rico," *Revista Interamericana*, vol. VII, #1, Spring 1977, pp. 5-20.

65 J. R. Stewart to S. R. Noble, Oct. 9, 1918, RBC 2 16-31.

66 W. M. Botsford, Staff Defalcation Book, RBC 2 25-63.

67 H. J. Meagher to Pease, June 30, 1914, RBC 3 Martinique.

68 H. Thomasset (Point-à-Pitre) to F. C. Harding, Sept. 20, 1934, RBC 3 Guadeloupe.

69 Jan Kippers Black, *The Dominican Republic: Politics and Development in an Unsovereign State*, London, 1986, p. 19.

70 H. H. Gosling to A. Macpherson, June 27, 1916, RBC 3 Dominican Republic.

71 See: M. M. Knight, *The Americans in Santo Domingo*, New York, 1928, and Bruce Calder, *The Impact of Intervention: The Dominican Republic during the U.S. Occupation of 1916-1924*, Austin, 1984.

72 *Cleveland and Huertas, Citibank, Op. cit.*, pp. 77-79.

73 Manager, Aux Cayes to Inspector, Dominican Republic, Nov. 27, 1930, RBC 3 Haiti.

74 C. A. Crosbie to head office, May 11, 1916, RBC 2 16 7 126.

75 J. W. Ross to New York Agency, August 31, 1916, *Ibid.*

76 Borden to George Foster, Minister of Trade and Commerce, Feb. 22, 1914, White Papers, vol. 1, NAC.

77 Neill to Foster, October 31, 1918, and Foster to Neill, Nov. 1, 1918, RBC 2 16-104. See: *Monetary Times*, June 25, 1915, p. 10, Nov. 19, 1915, p. 9, and March 21, 1919, p. 7.

78 Neill to Rea, Nov. 22, 1918, *Ibid.*. Rea was Pease's nephew-in-law, although one can hardly assume nepotism in such an arduous posting.

79 East Reminiscences, RBC 4 Ea 1-2.

80 C. E. Neill to F. T. Walker, Dec. 24, 1918, RBC 2 16 7. See: Dana Wilgress, *Memoirs*, Toronto, 1967, and Roy Maclaren, *Canadians in Russia*, Toronto, 1975.

81 F. T. Walker, "South America," Aug. 22, 1919, RBC 2 16-25.

82 Pineo to Neill, Sept. 22, 1919, RBC 2 16-5:1.

83 Pineo to Neill, Feb. 19, 1921, RBC 5 Nei-12.

84 Pineo to Neill, Feb. 21, 1921, RBC 5 Nei-12.

85 R. W. Watt Reminiscences, RBC 4.

86 *Monetary Times*, January 2, 1920, p. 37.

87 I have relied heavily on H. G. Hesler's interpretation of the Dance of the Millions.

88 Pease to Pineo, Jan. 30, 1922, RBC 5 Nei-12. See: Pease, "Great Opportunities in Brazil and Argentina," *Royal Bank Magazine*, June 1920.

89 Hon. Smeaton White, *Notes by the Way in South America*, Montreal, 1925.

90 C. R. Beattie, "A Story about Chicle," *Royal Bank Magazine*, Sept. 1922.

91 MBH Minute Book, Dec. 10, 1900. The bank paid the premium but made itself the beneficiary, making payment to a dead employee's family a matter of discretion.

92 *Ibid.*, November 1920, p. 1.

93 Charlottetown *Evening Patriot*, July 10, 1928. My thanks to Kevin Macdonald of the Provincial Archives of P.E.I.

# Chapter Six

—◦◦•◦◦—

[1] N. G. Hart Reminiscences, RBC 4.

[2] *Monetary Times*, Jan. 2, 1927, p. 178-80.

[3] C. E. Neill, "Address to the Graduating Class–University of New Brunswick," RBC 5 Nei-2.

[4] W. M. Botsford Reminiscences, RBC 4.

[5] F. T. Walker Reminiscences, RBC 4.

[6] RBC Minute Book, July 3, 1912.

[7] Montreal Trust Company Minute Books, 1907-10. Royal Bank executives dominated the board of the trust company until the 1967 Bank Act obliged banks and trust companies to distance themselves.

[8] *Royal Bank Magazine*, Feb. 1929, p. 3.

[9] *Journals of the House of Commons–Select Standing Committee on Banking and Commerce*, Ottawa, 1924, C. E. Neill testimony, pp. 249-84.

[10] See: Jeremy Adelman, "Prairie Farm Debt and the Financial Crisis of 1914," *Canadian Historical Review*, LXXI, 4, 1990, pp. 491-519.

[11] *Ibid.*, p. 276.

[12] Pease to Senator W. B. Ross, April 28, 1921, file 87-524-41, CBAA.

[13] Pease to T. R. Whitley, Jan. 27, 1913, RBC 5 Pea-5. *Monetary Times*, January 13, 1912, p. 211.

[14] *The Law Reports, House of Lords*, JCPC & *Peerage Cases*, London, 1913, pp. 283-298, and *Monetary Times*, Feb. 8, 1913, p. 329.

[15] F. T. Walker Reminiscences, RBC 4 and Lougheed, Bennett and McLaws legal bills, RBC 1 K-235.

[16] Pease to Whitley, Dec. 12, 1912, RBC 5 Pea-5. See: R. Craig McIvor, *Canadian Monetary Banking and Fiscal Development*, Toronto, 1958, chap. 4.

[17] Pease to Whitley, April 15, 1913, RBC 5 Pea-5.

[18] Whitley to Pease, April 17, 1913, *Ibid.*

[19] See: *Monetary Times*, Sept. 27, 1913, p. 531.

[20] White to Pease, Aug. 25, 1914, Pease to White, Aug. 27, 1914, and Pease to Whitley, Oct. 14, 1914, RBC 5 Pea-4 & 5.

[21] *Canadian Annual Review*, Toronto, 1915, p. 246.

[22] W. T. White, *The Story of Canada's War Finance*, Montreal, 1921, chap. 1. See: C. A. Curtis, "The Canadian Banks and War Finance," in *Contributions to Canadian Economics* III, Toronto, 1931.

[23] White, *War Finance, Op. cit.*, RBC 5 Pea-4 and *Monetary Times*, Aug. 7, p. 12, Aug. 14, p. 9 and Aug. 28, 1914, p. 7.

[24] Holt to White, Sept. 9, 1914, RBC 5 Pea-4.

[25] White to Pease, Sept. 5, 1914, *Ibid.*

[26] Pease to White, Dec. 29, 1915, vol. 264, RG 19, NAC.

[27] Minutes of CBA General Meeting, Nov. 14, 1918, file 87-524-41, CBAA.

[28] White, *War Finance, Op. cit.*, p. 12.

[29] See: *Monetary Times*, January 5, 1917 and McIvor, *Canadian Monetary, Op. cit.*, pp. 105-08.

[30] Minutes, CBA Council meeting with Finance Minister, Nov. 2, 1915, file 87-500-34, CBAA.

[31] McIvor, *Canadian Monetary, Op. cit.*, p. 114.

[32] *The Canadian Annual Review*, published in Toronto, provided an excellent annual synopsis of war finance.

[33] *Journal of the Canadian Bankers' Association*, vol. 25, #2, July 1917, p. 84.

[34] Pease to Whitley, Oct. 22, 1917, RBC 5 Pea-5.

[35] Borden to Holt, Oct. 8, 1914, #105526-7, Borden Papers, NAC and *Monetary Times*, Nov. 26, 1915, p. 8.

[36] White to Pease, Dec. 19, 1917, file 87-500-37, CBAA.

[37] *Ibid.*, file 87-500-34.

[38] CBA Circular #219, June 7, 1918, CBA archives. For a detailed record of bank-government war bond cooperation, see: RG 19, vols. 2673, 4010, & 4011, NAC.

[39] Pease to Borden, July 16, 1917, RBC 5 Pea-9 and Borden to Holt, Dec. 30, 1930, #156691, Borden Papers, NAC.

[40] White to Pease and Pease to White, cables, Nov. 13, 1918, vol. 1, White Papers, NAC.

41 Pease to Whitley, Dec. 6, 1917, RBC 5 Pea-5.

42 *Monetary Times*, Dec. 20, 1918, p. 12, and Jan. 3, 1919, p. 33.

43 *Monetary Times*, Feb. 20, 1903, p. 1133.

44 *Ibid.*, Jan. 1, 1094, p. 849.

45 *Royal Bank Magazine*, March 1946, p. 15.

46 Mrs. E. B. Reesor, "Women in Banking Life," *Monetary Times*, May 4, 1907, pp. 1734-35.

47 G.H. Balfour to G. Burn (CBA president), Nov. 29, 1915, file 87-516-19, CBAA.

48 Balfour to Burn, Jan. 6, 1916, *Ibid.*

49 Miss J. Macdonald Murray, "Woman in the Banking World," *JCBA*, July 1916, p. 317.

50 *Ibid.*, p. 317 and "Beauty in the Bank," *Saturday Night*, July 27, 1918, p. 5.

51 Mrs. E. G. Cowdry, "Women in the Banking World," *JCBA*, vol. 23, July 1916, p. 318. See also: Jean Graham, "The Woman Bank Employee and the Canadian Bank," *Ibid.*, vol. 26, July 1919.

52 Staff Register, RBC 2 25-22. See: "Women in Banks," *Saturday Night*, March 11, 1922, p. 1.

53 *Royal Bank Magazine*, Dec. 1937, pp. 20 and 32.

54 "A Word to the Wives," *Monetary Times*, July 1, 1931, pp. 402-04.

55 Earle McLaughlin interview, 1979, RBC archives tape.

56 G. W. Mackimmie to A. M. Chandler, Dec. 21, 1927, RBC 3 NB

57 See: file 87-516-17, CBAA, and chap. 3.

58 Murray Latimer, *Industrial Pension Systems in the United States and Canada*, New York, 1932, chap. 2. Latimer incorrectly dates the RBC pension plan to 1904.

59 *Monetary Times*, Jan. 2, 1927, pp. 178-80.

60 See, for instance: *JCBA*, Dec. 1910, pp. 55-57 and Marc, 1911, pp. 175-76.

61 *JCBA*, March 1928, pp. 132-39.

62 See: *JCBA*, Oct. 1919, pp. 96-98.

63 See, for advertising: W. F. Dorward (RBC Rexton, NB), "Advertising to Increase Bank Business," *Monetary Times*, July 23, 1920, pp. 5-6.

64 See: Donald Gordon, "Machinery in Banks," *JCBA*, April 1930, pp. 299-303, C. H. Bible, "A New Labour-Saver," *Royal Bank Magazine*, Jan. 1930, and Thomas Craig, "Streamlining Routine and Procedures," RBC 4.

65 H. Ross to Fielding, May 30, 1923, Box 532, Fielding Papers, PANS.

66 Williams-Taylor to J. S. Dennis (CPR), Oct. 14, 1922, file 87-506-01, CBAA.

67 See: *Monetary Times*, Feb. 23, 1923, p. 7.

68 *Journals, Op. cit.*, 1924, p. 250 and 281.

69 See: C. E. Neill, "Canadian Banks and Local Business," RBC 2-1:95.

70 Neill to Mackenzie King, Jan. 5 and 31, 1922, Mackenzie King Papers, NAC.

71 Mackenzie King to Neill, *Ibid.*, Feb. 6, 1922.

72 Gray to Neill, Nov. 20, 1922, RBC 5 Nei-10.

73 Larkin to Mackenzie King, April 28, 1924, #86961-3, King Papers, NAC. Larkin also banked at the Royal Bank in London and later carried £25,000 line of credit.

74 Neill to J. H. Gundy, Nov. 10, 1926, RBC 5 Nei-10.

75 See: Holt to J. J. Carrick, Jan. 13, 1925, #073017, Meighen Papers, NAC and Neill to J. H. Menzies, May 19, 1927, RBC 5 Nei-11.

76 Neill to Robb, Oct. 28, 1927, RBC 5 Nei 4-1.

77 British Legation, Havana, to Sir Austen Chamberlain, April 15, 1926, vol. 817, RG 19, NAC and *Monetary Times*, March 16 (p.13) and 23 (p.7), 1926.

78 *JCBA*, Jan. 1928, p. 203.

79 See: T. D. Regehr, "A Backwoodsman and an Engineer in Canadian Business," CHA Historical Papers, 1977, p. 172.

80 Neill to Sir John Aird, July 9, 1924, RBC 5 Nei-9.

81 For the convoluted history of Holt's adventures in the paper industry, see: Gilles Piedalue, "Les Groupes Financiers et la Guerre du papier au Canada 1920-1930," *Revue Histoire de l'Amérique Française*, vol. 30, #2, septembre, 1976, pp. 223-58 and *Proceedings of the Select Standing Committee of the House of Commons on Banking and Commerce*, Ottawa, 1934, pp. 764-814 and 892-918.

82 Proceedings, *Op. cit.*, p. 894.

83 RBC Minute Book, Dec. 11, 1926.

84 N. Hart Reminiscences, RBC 4.

85 Wilson to George MacLaren Brown, Jan. 14, 1932, RBC 5 Wil-12.

## Chapter Seven

1 Sept. 14, 1933, evidence before *Royal Commission on Banking and Currency*, Ottawa, 1933, p. 3479.

2 See: S. T. Halton, "Waterton Lakes," *Royal Bank Magazine*, Sept. 1929, pp. 9-13.

3 Foregoing based on Lavoy branch records, Halton personnel file, and interviews with Norm Stewart, Mrs. Matthew Halton, and Mrs. Joan Jewell.

4 See: Reg Fife, "Classic Canadiana came from Royal banker's pen," *Interest*, June/July 1983, p. 17.

5 Bennett to J. A. McLeod, June 1, 1933, Bennett Papers, NAC.

6 H. A. Doraty to F. R. MacMillan, Feb. 28, 1933, and Bennett to Wilson, March 9, 1933, *Ibid.*

7 Wilson to Bennett's secretary, Jan. 3, 1933, and Wilson to Bennett, March 11, 1933, *Ibid.*

8 J. H. Thomas to Secretary of State for External Affairs, Sept. 22, 1931, #144039, Bennett Papers, NAC.

9 *Proceedings of the Select Standing Committee of the House of Commons on Banking and Commerce*, Ottawa, 1934, Wilson evidence, p. 593.

10 H. L. Gagnon Reminiscences, RBC 4.

11 J. A. McLeod, "Historical Outline of Banking Legislation in Canada," presented in Ottawa, Aug. 8, 1933, RG 33/17, vol. 7, RG 33/17.

12 Wilson to S. L. Cork (Winnipeg), Nov. 30, 1929, RBC 5 Wil-6.

13 All quotations from president's and general manager's annual meeting speeches, 1928-33.

14 For an excellent encapsulation of the Depression's impact, see: Plates 40 and

41, *Historical Atlas of Canada – Volume III – Addressing the Twentieth Century 1891–1961*, D. Kerr, D. Holdsworth, and S. Laskin, eds., Toronto, 1990.

15 See: RBC 2 16 31, file 164 and Paul Enzig, *World Finance Since 1914*, London, 1935, chap. 27.

16 N. G. Hart to C. C. Pineo, Dec. 4, 1931, RBC 2 16 31.

17 Wilson to Bennett's secretary, Jan. 3, 1933, Bennett Papers, NAC.

18 RBC Minute Book, Jan. 14, 1932, and letter to directors, Jan. 1932, RBC 2 30B 7.

19 Under Section 114 of the Bank Act, shareholder statistics were submitted annually to the finance department. See: RG 19 C3, NAC.

20 *Canadian Forum*, July 1934, p. 390.

21 S. L. Cork to Wilson, June 12, 1931, RBC 5 Wil-9.

22 W. G. Yule to Wilson, Oct. 6, 1931, *Ibid.*

23 Wilson to Yule, Oct. 10, 1931, *Ibid.* and RBC Minute Book, Nov. 11, 1931.

24 Wilson to Macaulay, April 16, 1932, and Macaulay to Wilson, April 20, 1932, RBC 5 Wil-11.

25 All Islemont documentation is located in RBC 30B 2 8 3.

26 ("I have always thought that some of these difficulties should not have arisen, and would not, had the directors been dealing with other than merely the commercial business of the bank.") Bennett to Dobson, Nov. 29, 1946, Bennett Papers, NAC. Bennett returned to the RBC board in the 1940s.

27 Wilson to Walker, March 31, 1932, RBC 5 Wil-3:5.

28 RBC Minute Book, Dec. 27, 1932.

29 Wilson to Holt plus attached memo, Nov. 30, 1934, RBC 30B 2 8 3.

30 Memorandum of Loans, Nov. 30, 1933, RB C 2 30B 7.

31 See: Memorandum of Agreement with Islemont, May 31, 1943, RBC 30B 2 8 3, and RBC Minute Book, Oct. 29, 1946.

32 British Legation, Havana to Sir John Simon, Sept. 5, 1933, Bennett Papers, NAC.

33 *Proceedings, Op. cit.*, p. 594.

34 Bennett to Sir Charles Gordon, Sept. 15, 1933, Bennett Papers, MG26 K, NAC.

35 RBC Minute Book, Dec. 22, 1933.

36 Wilson to F. T. Walker, Dec. 14, 1933, RBC 5 Wil-10.

37 Wilson to S. L. Cork, Dec. 13, 1933, *Ibid.*

38 T. R. Free to C. S. Tompkins, May 5, 1936, RBC 5 Wil 3:9.

39 *Monetary Times*, Dec. 12, 1929, p. 6.

40 Wilson to Walker, *Op. cit.*

41 P. S. Ross and Sons to RBC President, Jan. 5, 1935, RBC 2 30B 7.

42 *Proceedings, Op. cit.*, p. 924.

43 Bennett to Dobson, Mar. 23, 1937, Bennett Papers, NAC.

44 C. F. Martin to Wilson, March 26, 1934, RBC 5 3:7.

45 *Proceedings, Op. cit.*, p. 447.

46 RBC Minute Books, Nov. 30, 1934, and 1934 *Annual Report*. Wilson's salary as president was $50,000.

47 *Monetary Times*, Dec. 12, 1934, p. 6 and *Halifax Herald*, Sept. 16, 1936.

48 Wilson to R. H. Travers, July 21, 1937, RBC 5 Wil 12 and "Morris Wilson," *Canadian Banker*, July 1937, pp. 366-68.

49 See: R. Craig McIvor, *Canadian Monetary Banking and Fiscal Development*, Toronto, 1958, chap. 7.

50 See: A. B. Jamieson, *Chartered Banking in Canada*, Toronto, 1953, chap. 5.

51 Wilson to Bennett, May 19, 1934, Bennett Papers, NAC. See: P.C. 1577, July 11, 1932, and T. D. Regehr, *The Beauharnois Scandal: A Story of Canadian Entrepreneurship and Politics*, Toronto, 1990.

52 P. C. Order 2490, Nov. 29, 1933 and RBC 5 Wil 5.

53 Holt to Beaverbrook, April 13, 1932, RBC 5 Wil 4.

54 See: "Criticism of Banks," JCBA, July 1935, pp. 442-45, and McIvor, *Op. cit.*, pp. 134-37.

55 M. Calvert to W. G. Yule, Aug. 26, 1931, RBC 5 Wil 9.

56 "Sandwell trip, Sept. 1932," CBAA file 87-529-13.

57 Executive Council meeting with minister of finance, Oct. 24, 1931, CBA file 87-503-23.

58 Holt to Wilson, Aug. 23, 1933, RBC 5 Wil 3:6.

59 "The Monetary Experience of Canada During the Depression" in *Lessons on Monetary Experience*, ed. A. D. Gayer, New York, 1937, pp. 9-10 (off-print). Retired Prime Minister Bennett actually edited Noble's piece.

60 William Noble interview, Oct. 7, 1991. See: D. H. Fullerton, *Graham Towers and His Times*, Toronto, 1986.

61 Noble to J. M. Macdonnell, National Trust, May 22, 1934, RBC 2 29a1.

62 Noble to Irving Fisher, March 30, 1938, *Ibid.*

63 RBC *Monthly Letter*, May 1933. It is interesting to note that Prime Minister Bennett retained a copy of this *Letter* in his papers.

64 Robert Gardiner, *Royal Commission* evidence, p. 824.

65 G. C. Coote submission, vol. 5, RG 33/17.

66 Graham Spry submission, *Ibid.*, vol. 2.

67 W. G. Yule evidence, *Royal Commission, Op. cit.*, p. 1614-15.

68 All Wilson statements from RG 33/17, vol. 4.

69 *Report of the Royal Commission on Banking and Currency in Canada*, Ottawa, 1933. Two commissioners, Beaudry Leman and Sir Thomas White, dissented, citing the adequacy of the 1914 Finance Act.

70 Rhodes speech notes, RG 19E vol. 2673.

71 Towers personnel record, *Royal Bank Magazine*, Sept. 1934, p. 16, and Fullerton, *Op. cit.*, pp. 52-57.

72 *Proceedings, Op. cit.*, p. 919.

73 See: Hanson to Wilson, Mar. 27, 1934, RBC 5 Wil-3:7 and "Bank Act" file, box 80, Power Papers, Queen's University Archives.

74 See: J. R. Mallory, *Social Credit and the Federal Power*, Toronto, 1954.

[75] CBA Executive Council minutes, Sept. 23, 19 36, CBA file 87-501-24.

[76] Confidential legal opinion, H. R. Milner, Sept. 28, 1936, RBC 5 Dob-6.

[77] CBA files 87-529-26 and 24. See: Robert MacIntosh, *Different Drummers: Banking and Politics in Canada*, Toronto, 1991, chap. 7.

[78] Knowles to D. C. Brown, Dec. 31, 1947, RBC 5 Muir.

[79] RBC 5 Dob-6.

[80] R. J. Dinning to A. J. Lester, Oct. 24, 1938, RBC 5 Dob-6.

[81] See: Jamieson, *Chartered Banking*, pp. 87-90, and CBAA file 87-558-27.

[82] CBA file 87-545-04-6.

[83] William Noble interview, October 1991 and Noble personnel file. Keynes was involved in aspects of the famous Lend-Lease and Hyde Park negotiations. In Washington, he met with Arthur Purvis, moved from Canada to head the British Purchasing Commission. See: R. F. Harrod, *Life of John Maynard Keynes*, New York, 1963, pp. 505-6.

# Chapter Eight

[1] C. H. Ince, Inspection Report, July 6, 1938, RBC 3 France.

[2] H. C. Santeugini, "Christmas in Barcelona, Spain," RBC 3 Spain.

[3] McInerney to Dobson, Sept. 1, 1939, RBC 2 16-110.

[4] Paris branch correspondence, RBC 2 16-85.

[5] "The Germans Put Their Nose in our Affairs," J. van Ervan, Nov. 27, 1940, RBC 2 16-5:15.

[6] Hayne memoir, RBC 2 16-85.

[7] C. W. B. Fitzgerald to Dobson, May 6, 1940, RBC 2 16-5:18.

[8] Duke of Windsor to Paul Potter, Sept. 20, 1945, RBC 2 46A PO1.

[9] RBC Minute Book, Mar. 23 and June 8, 1948.

[10] RBC Minute Book, July 10, 1951, and RBC 2 16-31.

[11] F. E. Watson to W. L. Thorp, Nov. 20, 1940, RBC 3.

[12] Muir to McInerney, Oct. 2, 1951, RBC 5 McI-2.

[13] *Proceedings of the Commons Committee on Banking and Commerce*, Ottawa, 1944, p. 582. See: E. P. Neufeld, *Bank of Canada Operations, 1935-54*, Toronto, 1955, esp. chap. 5.

[14] R. Craig McIvor, *Canadian Monetary Banking and Fiscal Development*, Toronto, 1958, pp. 178-79, and Royal Bank *Annual Reports*.

[15] For an excellent synopsis of wartime monetary and fiscal policy, see: McIvor, *Op. cit.*, chap. 9.

[16] See, for instance: J. F. Parkinson, "Some Problems of War Finance in Canada," *Canadian Journal of Economics and Political Science*, vol. VI, 1940, and J. J. Deutsch, "War Finance and the Canadian Economy, 1914-1920," *Ibid.*

[17] General managers' meetings with Governor Towers, 1941-44, CBA file 87-503-27 and 28. See: S. G. Dobson, "Canadian Banks in the War," an address to the American Bankers' Association, New York, Sept. 1943.

[18] RBC *Annual Report*, 1943, RBC 2 1-23, PC Order #6497, Aug. 17, 1943, and vol. 3962, RG 19, NAC.

[19] CL #3322 A, Sept. 27, 1939.

[20] CL #3776 A, April 18, 1940.

[21] "After the War – What?" *Royal Bank Magazine*, Sept. 1944, pp. 6-7.

[22] RBC Minute Book, Aug. 26, 1941.

[23] For the career of one such Royal Bank manager in the Depression, see the Edwin Lucas Papers at the Provincial Archives of British Columbia (Add. MSS. 2402). Lucas lost his managership in Coalmont, B.C., when the branch was closed in 1934. He was brought into Vancouver to work as a clerk.

[24] T. W. H. Thompson (Bank of Montreal), "Gentlemen – the Ladies," *Canadian Banker*, Feb. 1947, pp. 126-29.

[25] RBC *Magazine*, July 1943, p. 2.

[26] Thompson, *Op. cit.*, p. 128.

[27] See, for instance: "Girl behind the Wicket," *RBC Magazine*, March 1954, pp. 4-5 and Helen Stephens, "Women in Canadian Banking," *Canadian Banker*, June 1954, pp. 113-23. For an excellent overview, see: Ruth Pierson, *"They're Still Women After All": The Second World War and Canadian Women*, Toronto, 1986, and A. Prentice, et al., *Canadian Women: A History*, Toronto, 1988, chap. 12.

[28] RBC Minute Book, Sept. 25, 1945.

[29] J. W. Pickersgill, ed., *The Mackenzie King Record, Vol. 1: 1939-1944*, Toronto, 1960, pp. 81-82.

[30] Montreal *Standard*, Sept. 13, 1941.

[31] *Financial Post*, Jan. 9, 1941.

[32] William Chace, British Supply Council, Washington to M. W. Wilson, July 28, 1943, RBC 3 Wilson. See: S. G. Dobson, "Morris Wilson," *RBC Magazine*, Winter 1941, pp. 101-6.

[33] See, for instance: Wilson to James, July 8, 1943, Chancellor Wilson Papers, McGill Archives, RG 1, container 25.

[34] William Noble interview, October 7, 1991.

[35] Noble to H. C. Dudley, Aug. 29, 1944, RBC 2 29a 1. See: Doug Owram, *The Government Generation: Canadian Intellectuals and the State, 1900-1945*, Toronto, 1986, chaps. 10-11.

[36] RBC *Annual Report*, 1943.

[37] Muir to A. W. Rogers, CBA secretary, Dec. 28, 1943, CBAA file 87-516-35.

[38] Memorandum by James Muir, April 13, 1944, MISC 2 20:4.

[39] See: A. W. Rogers, "The 1944 Revision of the Bank Act," *Canadian Banker*, 1945, pp. 138-48.

[40] 1944 Bank Act revision press release, RG 19, vol. 2697, NAC.

[41] See: A. B. Jamieson, *Chartered Banking in Canada*, Toronto, 1953, chap. 8 and W. D. Melvin, "Section 88," *Canadian Banker*, Feb. 1954, pp. 22-35.

[42] *Proceedings, Op. cit.*, p. 1259, and A. B. Jamieson, *Op. cit.*, pp. 133-34.

[43] Noble to King Gordon (editor of *The Nation*), Aug. 30, 1945, RBC 2 29a 1.

[44] RBC *Monthly Letter*, Sept. 1945.

[45] *What Our Branch Managers Say About New Business*, Montreal, 1941, and Circular Letter #4317B, Dec. 10, 1940.

[46] See: E. P. Neufeld, *The Financial System of Canada: Its Growth and Development*, Toronto, 1972, pp. 336-53.

[47] A. D. Insley to C. H. Ince, Nov. 10, 1967, RBC 2 23-1.

[48] A. W. Dancey, "Black Gold," *RBC Magazine*, Sept. 1950, and R. W. Mackenzie memoir, 1979, RBC 2 23-1.

[49] See: Gordon Boreham, "The 1954 Amendments to the Bank Act After Almost a Decade," *Canadian Banker*, Autumn 1964, pp. 33-36, and C. H. Munro, "Banking for the Petroleum Industry," *Ibid.*, Spring 1963.

[50] Gordon Owen interview, April 8, 1991.

[51] Bennett to Dobson, Nov. 29, 1946, Bennett Papers, M-1498, NAC.

[52] *RBC Magazine*, Jan. 1948, p. 16.

[53] *The Montrealer*, March 1941.

[54] G. Goodman to *Interest*, Nov. 18, 1990.

## Chapter Nine

[1] William Zeckendorf, *Zeckendorf*, New York, 1970, p. 167.

[2] George Goodman to *Interest*, Nov. 13, 1990.

[3] *Lake Shore News*, April 14, 1960.

[4] *Royal Bank Magazine*, March-April 1961, p. 25.

[5] E. M. G. McPherson, "A Scotsman is Transplanted," *Canadian Banker*, Winter 1948, pp. 106-113.

[6] "Royal Scots," *Royal Bank Magazine*, Jan/Feb. 1954, pp. 16-18. See: S. G. Checkland, *Scottish Banking – A History, 1695-1973*, Glasgow, 1975, pp. 511-14.

[7] Radio interview with Robert Reford, CBC, 1956, RBC 5 Mui 5:7.

[8] RBC *Annual Report*, 1957.

[9] Morris Wilson to W. L. Mackenzie King, Oct. 6, 1942, NAC, MG26 J, #288789.

[10] Muir to Towers, Nov. 22, 1926, RBC 2 16-7-50.

11 Muir, "The Travail of the Trans-Andean Trail," RBC *Magazine*, Oct. 1926, pp. 805-12.

12 RBC *Magazine*, Jan. 1936.

13 Muir, "The Public and the Banks," speech to Advertising Club of Montreal, Oct. 16, 1935.

14 Vernon Knowles, "Report of Public Relations Advisor," Nov. 17, 1937, CBA file 87-501-27.

15 Vernon Knowles to D. C. Brown, Dec. 31, 1947, RBC 5 Mui-6.

16 William Noble interview, October 1991.

17 RBC Minute Book, Oct. 18, 1949.

18 See, for instance: RBC Minutes, Feb. 21 and April 4, 1950.

19 Muir desk book, 1949, RBC 5 Mui-4.

20 Towers's meeting with general managers, May 17, 1951, CBA file 87-503-34. See: E. P. Neufeld, *Bank of Canada Operations 1935-54*, Toronto, 1955, chap. 6.

21 *Ibid.*, meeting of June 23, 1960.

22 See: E. P. Neufeld, *The Financial System of Canada*, Toronto, 1972, pp. 127-39.

23 RBC Minute Book, Dec. 22, 1953.

24 In 1957, a drive-through branch was opened in Ciudad Trujillo in the Dominican Republic. See: RBC *Magazine*, May-June 1957.

25 *Le Soleil*, September 13, 1957.

26 A. W. Rogers, "The Bank Act Revision Proceedings – 1954," *Canadian Banker*, April 1955, pp. 27-28.

27 "Advertising that 'sells,'" RBC *Magazine*, April-May 1956, p. 7, and "How a bank advertisement is created," *Ibid.*, July-Aug. 1959, p. 4.

28 "To pay the butcher, the baker and the candlestick maker," RBC *Magazine*, May-June 1957, p. 14.

29 See: RBC *Magazine*, June 1955, pp. 2-5, and Jan.-Feb. 1957, p. 47.

30 Frank Croft, "What's happened to the Bankers?" *Maclean's*, Feb. 15, 1955, p. 17.

31 *Ibid.*, p. 89.

32 Jack Webster, *Webster! An Autobiography*, Vancouver, 1990, p. 64.

33 J. D. Gibson, "Banking Since the War – A Story of Restricted Adjustment," *Canadian Banker*, Winter 1967, p. 39.

34 Neufeld, *Financial System, Op. cit.*, p. 112.

35 Neufeld, *Op. cit.*, pp. 326-27.

36 See: J. Schull and J. Douglas Gibson, *The Scotiabank Story: A History of the Bank of Nova Scotia*, Toronto, 1982, chap. 10.

37 *Financial Post*, Dec. 4, 1954.

38 See: Neufeld, *Financial System, Op. cit.*, chap. 7.

39 See: O. J. Firestone, *Residential Real Estate in Canada*, Toronto, 1951.

40 *Monetary Times Annual*, 1954.

41 (copy) C. F. Elderkin to A. W. Rogers, Sept. 30, 1953, CBA archives, 1954 NHA mortgage file.

42 Minutes of CBA Executive Council, Oct. 28, 1953, CBAA file 87-534.

43 *Financial Post*, Feb. 20, 1954.

44 McLaughlin desk book, Feb. 18, 1954.

45 McLaughlin interview, June 9, 1989, and W. E. McLaughlin, "Mortgage Lending by Canadian Banks: Its Background and Introduction," *Canadian Banker*, April 1955.

46 CMHC, *Canadian Housing Statistics*, 1963, Table 35.

47 Royal Commission on Canada's Economic Prospects, *Report*, 1958, p. 397.

48 RBC *Annual Report*, 1949.

49 "Outside the Realm of Routine Banking," RBC *Magazine*, June 1953.

50 See: C. D. Howe to Muir, Aug. 4, 1955, RBC 5 Mui-2-3.

51 Muir desk book, May 8, 1953, RBC 5 Mui-4.

52 *Ibid.*, Oct. 1-4, 1952.

53 RBC Minute Book, March 12, 1957.

54 See: Gibson, "Banking Since the War," *Op. cit.*, p. 47. Royal Bank annual reports did not break assets down on a domestic and foreign basis.

55 RBC Minute Book, Sept. 16, 1958.

56 Warren Bull interview, 1991.

57 Toronto *Star*, May 31, 1956.

58 Muir to D. S. Chuvakhin, Dec. 27, 1955, and Jan. 31, 1956, RBC 5 Mui-6. See also: Morris Wilson to A. Yazikoff, State Bank of U.S.S.R., Dec. 11, 1924, W. L. M. King Papers, NAC.

59 Transcript: "Our Special Speaker," CBC, July 29, 1956, RBC 5 Mui.

60 The *Anglican Outlook*, Aug.-Sept. 1956.

61 See, for instance: James Sinclair to Muir, Aug. 2, 1956, and H. R. MacMillan to Muir, July 19, 1956, RBC 5 Mui 2-1:2

62 Muir, "The Challenge of China," in *Around the World in Eighteen Days*, np, 1958, p. 4.

63 Muir to Cyrus Eaton, April 13, 1959, RBC 5 Mui-6.

64 Vancouver Board of Trade speech, Jan. 29, 1959.

65 RBC Minute Book, July 22, 1958.

66 See: Joseph Schull, *The Great Scot*, Montreal, 1979.

67 See: *Zeckendorf, Op. cit.*, p. 167.

68 See, for instance: RBC Minute Book, March 4, 1958.

69 Memo for Mr. Muir, April 3, 1958, RBC 3 Que.

70 Memo of Conversation with Mr. Muir, April 9, 1958, and W. E. McLaughlin, 1979 interview, RBC 5 McL 3:4.

71 RBC Minute Book and Press Release, May 26, 1958.

72 *Zeckendorf, Op. cit.*, p. 167.

73 Interviews with J. H. Cornish (1989), Gordon Owen (1991), and Jack Boyle (1990).

74 McLaughlin 1979 interview, RBC 5 McL 3:4.

75 Reford CBC interview, *Op. cit.*

76 R. A. Utting interview, 1989

77 R. A. Utting interview, 1989.

78 B. J. McGill interview, 1991.

79 RBC *Magazine*, March 1955 and March 1954.

80 Naomi Mallovy, "A Banking Career and Marriage," *Canadian Banker*, July 1958.

81 *Ibid.*, March-April 1958, p. 4.

82 *Le Devoir*, Sept. 8, 1962.

83 *Canadian Business*, June 1960.

84 RBC Minute Book, May 3 and 10, 1960.

## Chapter Ten

1 E. P. Neufeld, *The Financial System of Canada*, Toronto, 1972, p. 134.

2 J. H. Coleman to Secretary, CBA, March 13, 1967, and "1967 Advertising," Feb. 22, 1967, RBC 2 43-132:1.

3 *Marketing*, April 26, 1968.

4 Toronto *Telegram*, Jan. 5, 1961.

5 *Royal Bank Magazine*, May/June 1960, p. 5.

6 E. P. Taylor to Sedgewick, Dec. 21, 1960, RBC 2 30B-1, and R. W. Shannon interviews, 1989-91.

7 Cornish 1979 interview, RBC 5 McL 3:4.

8 E. P. Taylor to Sedgewick, Dec. 21, 1960, RBC 2 30 B-1.

9 Sedgewick to McLaughlin, Dec. 23, 1960, RBC 2 30 B-1.

10 W. C. Riley to McLaughlin, Dec. 29, 1960, RBC 2 30 B-1.

11 J. M. Cornish 1979 interview and Warren Bull 1991 interview.

12 All Bay of Pigs documentation in: RBC 2 76-78, McLaughlin 1979 interview, and Norm Stanley typescript in RBC 2 16-72.

13 McLaughlin 1979 interview, RBC 5 McL 3:4.

14 Warren Bull interview, 1991.

15 Rod McQueen, "The Last Lion Leaves and the Jungle Falls Quiet," *Maclean's*, Oct. 13, 1980.

16 Dean Walker, "Comfortable with Everyone," *Canadian Banker*, Oct. 1980, p. 5.

17 McLaughlin 1979 interview.

18 Ottawa *Citizen*, Sept. 20, 1980.

19 W. H. Ruel, "The Clearing Problem," *Canadian Banker*, Winter 1962, pp. 84-89.

20 See: review of *Electronics in Banking*, in *Canadian Banker*, Summer 1965, pp. 146-48 and W. H. Ruel, "Computers for the Layman," *Ibid.*, pp. 36-41.

21 CL 6935 A, June 4, 1962. In his "Banking Since the War – A Story of Restricted Development" (*Canadian Banker*, Winter 1967, p. 47), J. D. Gibson pointed to the conservatism of bank management in Canada, especially in personnel matters, and suggested that "personnel will be the main restricting influence" in banks' growth.

22 Interviews with Earle McLaughlin, Warren Bull, Hal Wyatt, and Jim Cornish, 1989–1991.

23 P.C. Order 1961-1484, Oct. 18, 1961.

24 Bev McGill interview, 1991.

25 "March 1965 Marketing Study," RBC 2 11-1:1.

26 Hardy to Coleman, Sept. 2, 1966, RBC 2 43 132.

27 1969 *Annual Report*, pp. 21-22.

28 R. I. C. Picard interview, 1991.

29 Memorandum to Mr. Coleman from Departmental Heads on P. S. Ross Reports, nd, RBC 2 11-2:54.

30 W. L. Bull interview, 1991.

31 *Guidelines to Organization*, 1974, RBC 2 11-6 and 11p-31.

32 See, for instance: Booz-Allan and Hamilton, *The Challenge Ahead for Banking*, New York, 1975.

33 RBC 2 11-20:39.

34 *The Global Outlook: Executive Summary*, March 1981, RBC 2 11-10.

35 *Submissions to the Royal Commission on Banking and Finance: W. Earle McLaughlin*, January 1963, supplement to *Canadian Banker*, Spring 1963, pp. 149-53.

36 *Report of the Royal Commission on Banking and Finance*, Ottawa, 1964, pp. 563-64.

37 McLaughlin, "Some Preliminary Thoughts on the Porter Report," June 10, 1964, in *McLaughlin: Collected Speeches*, Montreal, 1979, pp. 87-102.

38 See: John Fayerweather, *The Mercantile Bank Affair*, New York, 1974, and Robert

MacIntosh, *Different Drummers: Banking and Politics in Canada*, Toronto, 1991, chap. 11. In 1971, Citibank "Canadianized" its 100 per cent ownership of the Mercantile Bank to 25 per cent.

39 "Submission to the Rt. Hon. L. B. Pearson…on the Proposed New Bank Act," July 15, 1965, RBC Porter Commission files.

40 See: "Bank Act," in *Canadian Annual Review of Public Affairs*, Toronto, 1964-67 editions.

41 CL 1742 A, May 10, 1968. In 1969, FarmPlan was introduced to Ontario.

42 H. D. McRorie, "Prairie Agricultural Dept. Development Proposal, 1967," RBC 2 3-3.

43 Hal Wyatt and Norm Stewart interviews, 1991 and Oil and Gas documents, RBC 2 22-23.

44 "Memo to A. F. Mayne – Retail Banking: Mountain or Molehill?" Nov. 3, 1966, and Hardy to Coleman, Nov. 3, 1967, RBC 2 43-133.

45 Meeting with T-D Bank officers, May 25, 1967, RBC 2 43-133 and interviews with H. Hardy and R. Fithern, 1991.

46 J. D. Stewart to Personnel Department, nd, RBC 2 5-8. See: R. D. Breth, "How to Make Credit Cards Profitable," *Banker*, Feb. 1968.

47 McCann-Erickson Advertising of Montreal won a $1-million contract to promote Chargex. Montreal *Gazette*, April 30, 1969.

48 H. S. Hardy, "1967 Advertising," RBC 2 43-132:1.

49 Coleman to CBA Secretary, March 13, 1967, and Hardy, "Royal Bank Position Regarding Broadcast Advertising," *Ibid.*

50 Mary files, RBC 2 2-9:1, and Kathleen Flaherty-Fee interview, 1992.

51 W. L. Robinson, "Mary: An Important Positioning Change," Aug. 7, 1973, *Ibid.*

52 "Memo: Mary as Marketing Personality of the Year," May 1974, *Ibid.*

53 Marianne Bossen, "Manpower Utilization in Canadian Chartered Banks," Royal Commission on the Status of Women, Ottawa, 1971.

54 *Globe and Mail*, Jan. 12, 1974.

[55] Notes of Sabia/ McLaughlin meeting, Jan. 11, 1974, RBC 2 25a 16.

[56] McLaughlin, "Women in Business," *Canadian Business Review*, Summer 1975, p. 9.

[57] See: Rosabeth Moss Kanter, *Men and Women of the Corporation*, New York, 1977, pp. 283-85.

[58] RBC 2 25b 1 and Gwyn Gill interview, 1992.

[59] "Women in Management: Present Status and Proposed Goals," RBC Personnel Policy Committee, July 16, 1987. Here management implies Pay Grade 13 and above.

[60] See, for instance: Heather Menzies, *Women and the Chip*, Montreal, 1981, and *Computers on the Job*, Toronto, 1982.

[61] "CBA Submission to the Labour Canada Task Force on Micro-Electronics and Employment," August 1982, CBAA file 89-518.

[62] See: Ed Finn, "Revised Code Gives Bankers the Jitters," Toronto *Star*, March 6, 1978, *Financial Post*, Dec. 3, 1977, and April 22, 1978, CBAA file 89-629, and The Bank Book Collective, *An Account to Settle: The Story of the United Bank Workers*, Vancouver, 1979.

[63] Graham Lowe, *Bank Unionization in Canada: A Preliminary Analysis*, Toronto, 1980, pp. 84-104.

[64] See: CBA Committee on Personnel, "Submission to the Canada Employment and Immigration Advisory Council," Sept. 1980, CBAA.

[65] E. Innes, R. Perry, and J. Lyon, *The Financial Post 100 Best Companies to Work for in Canada*, Toronto, 1986, pp. 206-9. The *Post* survey was based on interviews with rank-and-file employees, not executives.

[66] "Memorandum of Visit with Prime Minister Diefenbaker," Feb. 2, 1961, RBC 5 McL 1.

[67] See: W. E. McLaughlin, *Collected Speeches 1961-1979*, Montreal, 1979.

[68] T. D'Aquino to R. Frazee, Feb. 3, 1978, RBC 2 11-20:54.

[69] "1975 Reorganization Public Relations Department, Head Office," RBC 2 11p-19, and David Grier interview, 1991.

[70] "Why Am I Here?" April 18, 1977, speech to La Chambre de Commerce du District de Montréal.

[71] RBC Submission to the Parliamentary Committee on Education, Cultural Affairs and Communications – Quebec regarding the Charter of the French Language, June 1977, RBC 2 25a 19:9.

[72] See: *La Presse*, April 27, 1977.

[73] 1979 Quebec Marketing Study, RBC 2 13-12:45.

[74] Memo on Law 101 by W. N. Ancuta and D. D. E. Grier, April 13, 1978, and Memo on CBA dinner, J. G. R. Benard, Feb. 12, 1979, RBC 2 25a 19:9.

[75] *Wall Street Journal*, June 2, 1980.

[76] "1980 Reorganization," RBC 2 11-5. See: "A New Image," *The Banker*, July 1980.

# Acknowledgements

IT SEEMS ONLY FITTING IN A BOOK ON BANKING THAT I PAY MY DEBTS. MY creditors throughout this project have been both generous and, I hope, far-sighted. I must first thank the people of Royal Bank. I have argued throughout these pages that the bank has built its success on the strength of its corporate culture. That culture gave birth to this book. The bank's chairman and chief executive officer, Allan Taylor, and its board of directors initiated this project in 1989 with an eye to celebrating the bank's 125th anniversary in 1994. In some hands, this instinct could easily have been converted into an exercise in superficial celebration. Their intention was instead to give *carte blanche* to an independent academic to write a critical history of their institution. They have never wavered in that commitment. Through hundreds of metres of documents, innumerable interviews and days of just plain snooping around, I have had their unobtrusive support. Beginning with John Cleghorn, the bank's president and chief operating officer, and continuing through a journey that brought me into contact with many, many of the bank's nearly 60,000 employees, I have invariably encountered unquestioned and generous cooperation. Thanks to all of you for making this book possible: it is *my* attempt to understand *your* bank, and I could not have done it if you had not taken me into your midst.

Two people above all others have made this book possible. Long before I began this book, I knew the name of Edward Neufeld. Well-worn copies of his fine books on the evolution of Canadian finance sat on my bookshelf. His career – one straddling the worlds of academe, the federal government, and commercial banking – seemed remarkable. When Ed joined Royal Bank in 1980 as its chief economist, one of his first intuitions was that the bank needed an academically solid, yet readable, history. Towards the end of the decade, he brought the idea forward to Allan Taylor, who was immediately enthusiastic and supportive. After the board of directors endorsed the idea, Ed proceeded to frame and launch the project. Yet, once work began, he never interfered. I set my own agenda. Ed was always there for consultations; this book bears the mark of his rich understanding of the Canadian financial system.

Through Ed, I met Gordon Rabchuk, the bank's archivist. Gordon fulfilled the historian's dream of an archivist. He was alive to my every need; his superb collection of documents was put at my fingertips. When I strayed from the documentary path, Gordon immediately set me back on course. In bending to meet my every need, Gordon never forsook his main responsibility of managing a records-management program for a huge, sprawling organization. A good archive is an archive that is alive to the living needs of an organization, not just the "dead" interests of historians. The bank's assistant archivists, Diane Brazeau and Beth Kirkwood, reinforced Gordon's friendly efficiency. Diane was my unerring guide into the bank's magnificent photo collection. Beth helped me become computer-literate and showed me almost daily what a wonderful union there could be between history, archives, and computers.

I was also blessed by the support of two fantastic research assistants. In David Boucher, I had the finest researcher Montreal had to offer. David was dogged in his ability to track down all those bits of evidence that are so necessary to filling the cracks that emerge as any history takes shape. He built a database that spanned seventy years of the *Monetary Times*. Kathy Minorgan painstakingly created a computer database out of the *Royal Bank Magazine*, thereby putting at my fingertips a wonderful window on the bank's corporate culture since the early 1920s. So often, David and Kathy drew my attention to aspects of the bank's history that I had never noticed. For twelve very happy months in Montreal, Gordon, Diane, Beth, Kathy, David, and I formed a productive crew, dedicated to making the documents and photos of the bank's archive come alive again.

So many other Royal Bankers contributed in both large and small ways to our research. Any list of their names must involuntarily be incomplete. It must, however, include: Bob Baguley (who did so much to manage the day-to-day aspects of this project), Susan Knell-Mitchell, John O'Shaughnessy, Mark McCondach, Allan Kunigis, Liz Gallagher, Jane Lawson, Stephanie Wood, Jane Dysart, Judy Rogers, Roy Fithern, Rosemary Collins, Janis Wheatley, Ross Peters, David Grier, Terry Kirkman, John Stewart, Langevin Côte, Karen Lawlor, Denise Bruno, Sandra Allan, Sally Quintal, Maureen Dunne, Barbara MacDonald, and Heidie Lenhart. Allan Taylor, John Cleghorn, Reg MacDonald, Gord Feeney, Emile Bolduc, Bill McCartney, Vince Kelly, Jack Burnett, and Paul Taylor all took time from their busy executive duties to entertain my enquiries.

Ottawa's Towne Centre branch provided me with my own "financial career" for a most enjoyable year. A sincere thank you to Claude Lauzon, Debbie Kardassilaris, John "Go, Jays, Go" Liepa, Vincenza Oliviero, June Walker, Judy Chapesky, Chris Shaw, Odette David, Viviane Baliki, and Sharon Savage.

In addition to those at the bank, so many others facilitated my work. Barry Cahill at the splendidly helpful Public Archives of Nova Scotia and Brian Davidson at the Canadian Bankers' Association opened the door to their marvellous archival collections. Across Canada, I benefited from the opinions, documents, photos, and kindnesses of numerous former Royal Bankers, academics, and journalists. Thank you therefore to: Whit Shannon, Hal Wyatt, John Dobson, Virginia Cockfield, Norm Stewart, Rowland Frazee, Bev McGill, Jock Finlayson, Bob Utting, Warren Bull, Hugh Hardy, Ross Campbell, William Noble, Suzanne Labarge, John Coleman, Bob Picard, Mrs. John J. Stratford, Jan Soetermans, Arthur Smith, Mrs. John W. Bainton, Laird and Sheila Bovaird, Gwyn Gill, Alex Kearney, Joan Jewell, Robert MacIntosh, David Sutherland, Rick Reiber, Carter Elwood, Linda Rotenberg, Michael Bliss, John Evans, Doug McCalla, Susan Wagg, Ted Regehr, William Hesler, Yolaine Toussaint, and Judith Nefsky. It saddens me that Earle McLaughlin, Jim Cornish, Allan Mackenzie, Jack Boyle, and Gordon Owen did not live to see this book published; their kindness has not been forgotten.

I owe sincere thanks to Pat Kennedy at McClelland & Stewart for her wonderful editing of these pages; it was a joy working with her. Maggie MacDonald's copy-editing reinforced Pat's fine work. Thanks also to Doug Gibson and the entire staff at McClelland & Stewart for so competently bringing this book to fruition. Gilles Gamas in Ottawa undertook the arduous task of not just translating this text into French, but of shaping it to the sensibilities of another language. Sogides in Montreal then transformed his work into *Au coeur de l'action*, the French version of this book. Michael Taylor and his staff at Stonehaven Productions in Montreal laboured hard in creating a video interpretation of this book.

Some debts can never be fully repaid. My wife, Sandy Campbell, as always, found time from her own teaching and writing to listen to, edit, and assuage this writer's thoughts. I count her very much in the assets column of my life.

OTTAWA, 1993

# PICTURE CREDITS

THE VAST MAJORITY OF ILLUSTRATIONS IN THIS BOOK ARE DRAWN FROM Royal Bank's photograph collection. This collection has been recently enhanced by donations by: Robert Picard, John Dobson, Joan Jewell, William Hesler, Veronica Noble, Sheila Boivard, Jack Boyle, and Herbert McNally. Exceptions to the above pattern of credit are: the *Globe and Mail*, p. 421; the Montreal *Gazette*, p. 265; the Bank of Montreal archives, p. 262; the Public Archives of Nova Scotia Notman Collection, pp. 13, 15, 17 (Tobin), 19, 22 (Cunard), 23, 26, 31, 35, and 42; and Notman Photographic Archives, McCord Museum of Canadian History, pp. 52, 58, 62, 66, 76, and 82.

# Index

Knowles, Vernon, 282
Knox, Frank, 6

# L

Labarge, Suzanne, **393**, 395
Larkin, Philip, 234
Lash, Zebulon A., 80-81, 155
Latin America, 195-201, 289, 315, 406, 415-17, 420
Lavoy, Alta., 245-8, **247**
*Le Devoir*, 355-56
*Le Soleil*, 328
Leacock, Stephen, 6, 52, 89, 103, 108-09, **109**, 117, 226, 279, 431
Leduc, François-Xavier, 57
Lesage, Jean, **368**
Less Developed Country debt, 415-17, 420
Lightfoot, Gordon, 8
London, 166, 191, 289-90, 410
Lougheed, James, 128, 211
Luther, W. E. J., 256
Lyman Sons & Co., 58

# M

Macaulay Securities, 257, 265
Macaulay, Thomas B., 239, 243, 257
McCloy, John, 348
McConnell, J. W., 239
McCormick, Robert, 61
Macdonald, John A., 15, 17, 18, 28
McDougald, Bud, 339
McFarlane, George, 372
McGibbon, D. Lorne, 138
McGill, Bev, 401
Machado, Geraldo, 237, 249, 262
McInerney, Blake, 286
MacIntosh, Robert, 428
McKeag, Dawn, 393
Mackenzie, Allan Grant, 104, 121
Mackenzie, Charles E., 99, 179
Mackimmie, G. W., 260
McKinley, William, 168-70
McLaughlin, W. Earle, 121, 334-35, 353, 358-62, **361**, 367, 369, **371**, 372, **392**, 397, **403**, 400-05; credit cards, 386-87; modernization, 374-79; penetrate world of European banking, 407-10; Quebec, 398-400; women's role in banking, 392-93
McLaughlin, Col. R. S., **340**
Maclean, A. K., 86
McLean, Ernest, 311
Maclean, George, 24-25, 40, 41, **44**, 45, 46-47
*Maclean's*, 330, 367, 431
McLeod, J. A., 250
McMahon, Frank, 312, 339

Macmillan Commission (1933), 272-73
McRorie, Doug, 384
managers, 117
Mannix, Fred, 309
*Manual of Canadian Banking*, 96
Maritime Bank, 131
marriage, 98, 111-13, 355
Marsh, Donald B., 227, 329
Marsh, Leonard, 301
Marti, José, 168
Martinique, 191-92, 287
Marvin, Donald M., 226, 271
Marwick, Mitchell, Peat & Co., 144
Mayne, Art, 343, 359-62, 366, 375, 376
Mennell, R. K., **364**
Merchants Bank of Canada, 57, 61, 76, 84, 156-57, 166, 231
Merchants' Bank of Halifax, 1, 23-27, 52, 60, 166; agencies, 36-39, 40, 43; Bermuda, 163-64; Confederation, 27-32; Cuba, 169-73; Maritime economy in 1870s and 1880s, 40-42, 45, 48-50; expansion to the West, 68-72; importance of Montreal, 50, 53-60, 71-72; Kenny's strategy, 32-35; Newfoundland, 165-66; relationship with Bank of Montreal, 53-54, 84; staffing, 97-98
Meredith, Charles, 61, 63
Meredith, Vincent, 54, 155-56
mergers, 141, 143-44, 159; Bank of Hamilton, 144-46; Merchants Bank of Canada, 156-57; Northern Crown Bank, 150, 217; Quebec Bank, 148-49, 217; Sovereign Bank, 127-28; Traders Bank of Canada, 135-39; Union Bank of Canada, 157-58, 160; Union Bank of Halifax, 133-35
Merkel, James, **22**, 22, 28
Michell, Michael, 429-30
Milner, H. Ray, 279, 311
Mitchell, Burnham, 316, 358
Mitchell, G. P. & Sons, 49
Mitchell, George, 22
Mitsubishi Bank, 409
Molsons Bank, 57, 158
*Monetary Times*, 6, 16, 41, 48, 57, 61, 65, 81, 102, 111, 113, 123, 127, 131, 141, 203, 264
Monroe Doctrine, 168
Montgomery, Frances, 222
Montreal Cold Storage and Freezing Company, 80-81
*Montreal Gazette*, 147, 201
Montreal Light, Heat and Power, 239, 256, 269
*Montreal Standard*, 299
*Montreal Star*, 57